Statistics for Industry, Technology, and Engineering

The *Statistics for Industry, Technology, and Engineering* series will present up-to-date statistical ideas and methods that are relevant to researchers and accessible to an interdisciplinary audience: carefully organized authoritative presentations, numerous illustrative examples based on current practice, reliable methods, realistic data sets, and discussions of select new emerging methods and their application potential. Publications will appeal to a broad interdisciplinary readership including both researchers and practitioners in applied statistics, data science, industrial statistics, engineering statistics, quality control, manufacturing, applied reliability, and general quality improvement methods.

Principal Topic Areas:

* Quality Monitoring * Engineering Statistics * Data Analytics * Data Science * Time Series with Applications * Systems Analytics and Control * Stochastics and Simulation * Reliability * Risk Analysis * Uncertainty Quantification * Decision Theory * Survival Analysis * Prediction and Tolerance Analysis * Multivariate Statistical Methods * Nondestructive Testing * Accelerated Testing * Signal Processing * Experimental Design * Software Reliability * Neural Networks *

The series will include professional expository monographs, advanced textbooks, handbooks, general references, thematic compilations of applications/case studies, and carefully edited survey books.

Ron S. Kenett • Shelemyahu Zacks • Peter Gedeck

Industrial Statistics

A Computer-Based Approach with Python

Birkhäuser

Ron S. Kenett
KPA Ltd.
Ra'anana, Israel

Shelemyahu Zacks
Binghamton University
Mc Lean, VA, USA

Peter Gedeck
University of Virginia
Falls Church, VA, USA

ISSN 2662-5555 ISSN 2662-5563 (electronic)
Statistics for Industry, Technology, and Engineering

https://doi.org/10.1007/978-3-031-28482-3

This book is published under the imprint Birkhäuser, www.birkhauser-science.com by the registered company Springer Nature Switzerland AG
The registered company address is: Gewerbestrasse 11, 6330 Cham, Switzerland

To my wife Sima, our children and their children: Yonatan, Alma, Tomer, Yadin, Aviv, Gili, Matan, Eden, and Ethan. RSK

To my wife Hanna, our sons Yuval and David, and their families with love. SZ

To Janet with love. PG

Preface

Knowledge and information are critical assets for any industrial enterprise. It enables businesses to differentiate themselves from competitors and compete efficiently and effectively to the best of their abilities. At present, information technology, telecommunications, and manufacturing are merging as the means of production are becoming increasingly autonomous. Advanced manufacturing, or Industry 4.0, is based on three interconnected pillars: (1) Computerized Product Design and Smart Technology; (2) Smart Sensors, Internet of Things, and Data Collectors integrated in Manufacturing Lines; and (3) Analytics, Control Theory, and Data Science. Advanced manufacturing requires analytics and operational capabilities to interface with devices in real time. Software development has become agile in DevOps operations focused on providing continuous delivery, as opposed to the traditional waterfall versioning approach (Kenett et al. 2018a). Moreover, processing and analytic models have evolved in order to provide a high level of flexibility. The emergence of agile processing models enables the same instance of data to support batch analytics, interactive analytics, global messaging, database, and file-based models. The result is an application platform that supports the broadest range of processing and analytic models. The ability to understand data within a context, and assume the right business action, is a source of competitive advantage (Olavsrud 2017; Kenett and Redman 2019; Kang et al. 2021b).

This book is about industrial statistics. It reflects many years of experience of the authors in doing research, teaching and applying statistics in science, healthcare, business, defense, and industry domains. The book invokes over 40 case studies and provides comprehensive Python applications. In 2020, there were 10 million developers in the world who code using Python which is considered the fastest-growing programming language. A special Python package, *mistat*, and additional Python code are available for download at https://gedeck.github.io/mistat-code-solutions/IndustrialStatistics. Everything in the book can be reproduced with *mistat*. We therefore provide, in this book, an integration of needs, methods, and delivery platform for a large audience and a wide range of applications.

Industrial Statistics: A Computer-Based Approach with Python is a companion volume to *Modern Statistics: A Computer-Based Approach with Python*. Both books include mutual cross-references but are considered as stand-alone publications. *Industrial Statistics: A Computer-Based Approach with Python* can be used as textbook in a one-semester or two-semester course on industrial statistics. Every chapter includes exercises, data sets, and Python applications. These can be used in regular classroom setups, flipped classroom setups and on-line or hybrid education programs. This book is focused on industrial statistics with chapters on advanced process monitoring methods, computer experiments, and Bayesian reliability. *Modern Statistics: A Computer-Based Approach with Python* is a foundational text and can be combined with any program requiring data analysis in its curriculum. This, for example, can be courses in data science, industrial statistics, physics, biology, chemistry, economics, psychology, social sciences, or any engineering discipline.

Modern Statistics: A Computer-Based Approach with Python includes eight chapters. Chapter 1 is on analyzing variability with descriptive statistics. Chapter 2 is on probability models and distribution functions. Chapter 3 introduces statistical inference and bootstrapping. Chapter 4 is on variability in several dimensions and regression models. Chapter 5 covers sampling for estimation of finite population quantities, a common situation when one wants to infer on a population from a sample. Chapter 6 is dedicated to time series analysis and prediction. Chapters 7 and 8 are about modern data analytic methods. The Python code used in this book and the solutions to the exercises of this book are available from https://gedeck.github.io/mistat-code-solutions/ModernStatistics/.

Industrial Statistics: A Computer-Based Approach with Python, this volume, contains 11 chapters: **Chap. 1**—Introduction to Industrial Statistics, **Chap. 2**—Basic Tools and Principles of Process Control, **Chap. 3**—Advanced Methods of Statistical Process Control, **Chap. 4**—Multivariate Statistical Process Control, **Chap. 5**—Classical Design and Analysis of Experiments, **Chap. 6**—Quality by Design, **Chap. 7**—Computer Experiments, **Chap. 8**—Cybermanufacturing and Digital Twins, **Chap. 9**—Reliability Analysis, **Chap. 10**—Bayesian Reliability Estimation and Prediction, and **Chap. 11**—Sampling Plans for Batch and Sequential Inspection. The Python code used in these chapters and the solutions to the exercises of this book are available from https://gedeck.github.io/mistat-code-solutions/IndustrialStatistics/. The book covers (i) statistical process monitoring in Chaps. 2–4, (ii) the design of experiments in Chaps. 5–7, (iii) reliability analysis in Chaps. 9–10, and (iv) sampling testing and sequential inspection in Chap. 11. These four topics can be the topic of one trimester courses or covered in a full-year academic course. In addition, they can be used in focused workshops combining theory, applications, and Python implementations. Practitioners and researchers will find the book topics comprehensive and detailed enough to provide a solid source of reference.

Some of the material in these books builds on a book by the first two authors titled *Modern Industrial Statistics with Applications in R, MINITAB and JMP*, 3rd edition, Wiley. *Modern Statistics: A Computer-Based Approach with Python* and *Industrial Statistics: A Computer-Based Approach with Python* include new and updated chapters on modern analytics and are dedicated to Python and refer to a specially developed Python application titled *mistat* that implements many tools and methods described in the books. A solution manual is also available, with Python examples, so that self-learners and instructors can assess the level of knowledge achieved by studying the book. *Industrial Statistics: A Computer-Based Approach with Python*, this volume, introduces several topics such as cybermanufacturing and computation pipelines. We made every possible effort to ensure the calculations are correct. However, should errors have skipped to the printed version, we would appreciate feedback from readers noticing these. In general, any feedback will be much appreciated.

We thank Bill Meeker, Murat Testik, Alessandro di Bucchianico, Bart De Ketelaere, Nam-Ky Nguyen, and Fabrizio Ruggeri for providing insightful comments on an early draft that helped improve the text. Finally, we would like to thank Christopher Tominich and the team at Springer Birkhäuser. They made everything in the publication process look easy and simple.

Ra'anana, Israel — Ron S. Kenett
Mc Lean, VA, USA — Shelemyahu Zacks
Falls Church, VA, USA — Peter Gedeck
January 2023

Contents

Modern Statistics: A Computer-Based Approach with Python (Companion Volume)

List of Abbreviations

AIC	Akaike Information Criteria
ANOVA	Analysis of Variance
ANSI	American National Standard Institute
AOQ	Average Outgoing Quality
AOQL	Average Outgoing Quality Limit
AQL	Acceptable Quality Level
ARIMA	Autoregressive Integrated Moving Average
ARL	Average Run Length
ASN	Average Sample Number
ASQ	American Society for Quality
ATE	Average Treatment Effect
ATI	Average Total Inspection
BECM	Bayes Estimation of the Current Mean
BI	Business Intelligence
BIBD	Balanced Incomplete Block Design
BIC	Bayesian Information Criteria
BLUP	Best Linear Unbiased Prediction
BN	Bayesian Network
BP	Bootstrap Population
CAD	Computer-Aided Design
CADD	Computer-Aided Drawing and Drafting
CAM	Computer-Aided Manufacturing
CART	Classification And Regression Trees
CBD	Complete Block Design
c.d.f.	cumulative distribution function
CED	Conditional Expected Delay
cGMP	Current Good Manufacturing Practices
CHAID	Chi-square Automatic Interaction Detector
CI	Condition Indicator
CIM	Computer-Integrated Manufacturing
CLT	Central Limit Theorem

CMM	Coordinate Measurement Machines
CMMI	Capability Maturity Model Integrated
CNC	Computerized Numerically Controlled
CPA	Circuit Pack Assemblies
CQA	Critical Quality Attribute
CUSUM	Cumulative Sum
DACE	Design and Analysis of Computer Experiments
DAG	Directed Acyclic Graph
DFIT	Difference in Fits distance
DLM	Dynamic Linear Model
DoE	Design of Experiments
DTM	Document Term Matrix
EBD	Empirical Bootstrap Distribution
ETL	Extract-Transform-Load
EWMA	Exponentially Weighted Moving Average
FDA	Food and Drug Administration
FDA	Functional Data Analysis
FPCA	Functional Principal Component Analysis
FPM	Failures Per Million
GFS	Google File System
GRR	Gage Repeatability and Reproducibility
HPD	Highest Posterior Density
HPLC	High-Performance Liquid Chromatography
IDF	Inverse Document Frequency
i.i.d.	independent and identically distributed
InfoQ	Information Quality
IPO	Initial Public Offering
IPS	Inline Process Control
IQR	InterQuartile Range
ISC	Short-Circuit Current of Solar Cells (in Ampere)
KS	Kolmogorov–Smirnov Test
LCL	Lower Control Limit
LLN	Law of Large Numbers
LQL	Limiting Quality Level
LSA	Latent Semantic Analysis
LSL	Lower Specification Limit
LTPD	Lot Tolerance Percent Defective
LWL	Lower Warning Limit
MAE	Mean Absolute Error
m.g.f.	moment generating function
MLE	Maximum Likelihood Estimator
MSD	Mean Squared Deviation
MSE	Mean Squared Error
MTBF	Mean Time Between Failures
MTTF	Mean Time To Failure

NID	Normal Independently Distributed
OAB	One-Armed Bandit
OC	Operating Characteristic
PCA	Principal Component Analysis
p.d.f.	probability density function
PERT	Project Evaluation and Review Technique
PFA	Probability of False Alarm
PL	Product Limit Estimator
PPM	Defects in Parts Per Million
PSE	Practical Statistical Efficiency
QbD	Quality by Design
QMP	Quality Measurement Plan
QQ-Plot	Quantile vs. Quantile Plot
RCBD	Randomized Complete Block Design
Regex	Regularized Expression
RMSE	Root Mean Squared Error
RSWOR	Random Sample Without Replacement
RSWR	Random Sample With Replacement
SE	Standard Error
SL	Skip Lot
SLOC	Source Lines of Code
SLSP	Skip Lot Sampling Plans
SPC	Statistical Process Control
SPRT	Sequential Probability Ratio Test
SR	Shiryaev Roberts
SSE	Sum of Squares of Errors
SSR	Sum of Squares around the Regression Model
SST	Total Sum of Squares
STD	Standard Deviation
SVD	Singular Value Decomposition
TAB	Two-Armed Bandit
TF	Term Frequency
TTC	Time Till Censoring
TTF	Time Till Failure
TTR	Time Till Repair
TTT	Total Time on Test
UCL	Upper Control Limit
USL	Upper Specification Limit
UWL	Upper Warning Limit
WSP	Wave Soldering Process

Chapter 1
The Role of Statistical Methods in Modern Industry

Preview Industrial statistics is a discipline that needs to be adapted and provide enhanced capabilities to modern industrial systems. This chapter presents the evolution of industry and quality in the last 300 years. The transition between the four industrial revolutions is reviewed as well as the evolution of quality from product quality to process, service, management, design, and information quality. To handle the new opportunities and challenges of big data, a current perspective of information quality is presented, including a comprehensive InfoQ framework. The chapter concludes with a presentation of digital twins which are used in industry as a platform for monitoring, diagnostic, prognostic and prescriptive analytics. The Python code used in this and the following chapters is available from https://gedeck.github.io/mistat-code-solutions/IndustrialStatistics.

1.1 Evolution of Industry

In medieval Europe, most families and social groups made their own goods such as cloth, utensils, and other household items. The only saleable cloth was woven by peasants who paid their taxes in kind to their feudal lords. Barons affixed their marks to the fabric, which came to stand for their levels of quality. While some details differ, the textile industry all over Europe and China was similar and was apparently the first industry to analyze data. Simple production figures, including percentages of defective products, were compiled in British cotton mills early in the nineteenth century. Quality control activities generated data that was aggregated in ledgers for accounting and planning purposes (Juran 1995).

The industrial revolution started in England. Richard Arkwright (1732–1792) was an English inventor and a leading entrepreneur who became known as the "father of the modern industrial factory system". He invented the spinning frame and a rotary carding engine that transformed raw cotton into cotton lap. Arkwright's

---

Supplementary Information The online version contains supplementary material available at (https://doi.org/10.1007/978-3-031-28482-3_1).

R. S. Kenett et al., *Industrial Statistics*, Statistics for Industry, Technology, and Engineering, https://doi.org/10.1007/978-3-031-28482-3_1

achievement was to combine power, machinery, semi-skilled labor and a new raw material, cotton, to create mass-produced yarn. In 10 years, he became the richest man in England.

During the early twentieth century, a constellation of technologies and management techniques expanded mass production. The internal combustion engine (and the oil and gas needed to fuel it) and electricity, powered the way. The production line formalized the division of labor, and huge factories were built. The Taylor System, featuring time and motion studies, drove production tasks and productivity quotas. Companies learned how to manage enormous factories (Chandler 1993). This was the second industrial revolution. As an example, Western Electrics' Hawthorne Works, on the outskirts of Chicago, employed up to 45,000 workers and produced unheard of quantities of telephone equipment and a wide variety of consumer products. It was in this environment that Shewhart realized that manufacturing processes can be controlled using control charts (Shewhart 1926). Control charts minimized the need for inspection, saving time and money and delivering higher quality. W. Edwards Deming and Joseph M. Juran, who both worked for Western Electric in the 1920s, were instrumental in bringing this approach to Japan in the 1950s. Deming emphasized the use of statistical methods (Deming 1982), and Juran developed a comprehensive management system featuring the "quality trilogy" (Godfrey and Kenett 2007). From a data analysis perspective, attention shifted from inspection of final products to production process and the need to understand variation in key parameters. Statistical models and probability played a key role in this shift.

In the third industrial revolution, computers changed manufacturing in several ways. First, computers enabled "mass customization" (Davis 1997). Essentially mass customization combines the scale of large, continuous flow production systems, with the flexibility of a job shop. This allows a massive effort, with batches of size one. A call center that employs screening to route calls to specialized support experts is a good example. Second is automation of so-called back-office functions, such as inventory management and product design. As an example, take the development of an automobile suspension system designed using Computer-Aided Design (CAD). The new suspension must meet customer and testing requirements under a range of specific road conditions. After coming up with an initial design concept, design engineers use computer simulation to show the damping effects of the new suspension design under various road conditions. The design is then iteratively improved. Third is integration. Thus, in parallel to the design of the suspension system, purchasing specialists and industrial engineers proceed with specifying and ordering the necessary raw materials, setting up the manufacturing processes, and scheduling production using computer-aided manufacturing tools (CAM). Then, throughout manufacturing, tests provide the necessary production controls. Finally, computer-integrated manufacturing pulls everything together. Ultimately, the objective is to minimize the impact of failures to products delivered to customers. The application of computer simulations, with no experimental error, required new experimental design methods, such as Latin Hypercubes and Kriging models. In addition, modern advances in optimization of statistically designed experiments led to designs that better address constraints and exploit optimality properties. These methods are introduced in Chap. 7.

The current fourth industrial revolution is fueled by data from sensors and IoT devices and powered by flexible manufacturing systems like added manufacturing and 3D printing. Futurists talk of machines that organize themselves, delivery chains that automatically assemble themselves, and applications that feed customer orders directly into production. This evolution in industrial processes is matched by an evolution in quality methods and approaches. We present this in the next section.

1.2 Evolution of Quality

In tracking the evolution of quality, we highlight several milestones over time. A first step, on this journey, can be found in the old testament. On the sixth day, the Creator completed his work and invoked inspection to determine if further action was needed. The thirty first verse of Genesis reads:

> And God saw everything that he had made, and, behold, it was very good (Genesis I, 31).

Inspection was indeed the leading quality model for many centuries. A vivid picture of inspection in action is depicted in Syndics of the Drapers' Guild, a 1662 oil painting by Rembrandt one can admire in the Rijksmuseum in Amsterdam. A second important milestone, where specification of parts got set before final assembly, is attributed to Eli Whitney (1765–1825), an American inventor, mechanical engineer, and manufacturer. Whitney is known in the USA as the inventor of the concept of mass production of interchangeable parts. In 1797, the US government threatened by war with France, solicited 40,000 muskets from private contractors because the two national armories had produced only 1000 muskets in 3 years. Whitney offered to supply 10,000 muskets in 2 years. He designed machine tools enabling unskilled workman to make parts that were checked against specification. The integration of such parts made a musket. Any part would fit in any musket of similar design. The workforce was now split into production and inspection teams. A third milestone, 120 years later, was the introduction of statistical process control charts by Shewhart (1926). Following this third milestone, attention shifted from quality of product, and inspection, to process quality, and statistical process control. Sixty years later, on the basis of experience gained at Western Electric Joseph Juran formulated the Quality Trilogy, as a universal approach for managing quality. This marked the start of quality management and was a precursor to total quality management and six sigma. A key contributor to this movement was W. Edwards Deming who, together with Juran, had huge success in implementing quality management principles in devastated post world War II Japan (Deming 1982, 1991; Juran 1986, 1995). In a further development in the 1960s a Japanese engineer, Genichi Taguchi, introduced to industry methods for designing statistically designed experiments aimed at improving products and processes by achieving design-based robustness properties (Godfrey 1986; Taguchi 1987). These methods were originally suggested by R. A. Fisher, the founder of modern statistics in agriculture and greatly developed in the chemical industry, by his student and son in law, G.E.P Box (Fisher 1935; Box et al. 2005). In 1981 Taguchi came to Bell Laboratories, the research arm of Western Electric, to share his experience in robust design methodologies. His seminars at Holmdel, New Jersey, were attended by only a dozen people. His English was poor and his ideas so new that it took time to understand his methods. At that time, industry was mostly collecting data on finished product quality with only some data on processes. Thirty years later, industry started facing a big data phenomenon. Sensors and modern data analysis systems offered new options for process and product control. This led to considerations of integrated models combining data from different sources (Godfrey and Kenett 2007). With data analytics and manufacturing execution systems (MES), the business of quality started shifting to information quality (Kenett 2008). To handle this, Kenett and Shmueli (2014) introduced a framework labeled "InfoQ". Technically, the definition of InfoQ is the derived utility (U) from an application of a statistical or data analytic model (f), to a dataset (X), given the research goal (g); InfoQ $= U(f(X \mid g))$. On this basis, data scientists can help organizations generate information quality from their data lakes.

To assess the level of InfoQ in a specific study, Kenett and Shmueli (2014) proposed eight dimensions of InfoQ:

1. Data resolution: The measurement scale and level of aggregation of the data relative to the task at hand must be adequate for the study. For example, consider data on daily purchases of over-the-counter medications at a large pharmacy. If the goal of the analysis is to forecast future inventory levels of different medications when re-stocking is done on a weekly basis, then, weekly aggregated data is preferred to daily aggregate data.
2. Data structure: The data can combine structured quantitative data with unstructured, semantic based data. For example, in assessing the reputation of an organization one might combine data derived from the stock exchange with data mined from text such as newspaper archives or press reports. Doing it enhances information quality.
3. Data integration: Data is often spread out across multiple data sources. Hence, properly identifying the different relevant sources, collecting the relevant data, and integrating the data, directly affect information quality.
4. Temporal relevance: A dataset contains information collected during a certain time framework. The degree of relevance of the data in that time framework to the current goal at hand must be assessed. For instance, in learning about current online shopping behaviors, a dataset with last year's records of online purchasing behavior might be irrelevant.
5. Chronology of data and goal: Depending on the nature of the goal, the chronology of the data can support the goal to different degrees. For example, in process control applications of discrete parts, we might collect data from previous processes that is relevant to a specific part. If the goal is to quantify the effect of previous manufacturing steps on the specific part' quality, then the chronology is

fine. However, if the goal is to predict the final quality of a part, then the required information builds on data collected in future manufacturing steps and, hence, the chronology of data and goal is not met.
6. Generalizability: There are two types of generalizability: statistical and scientific generalizability. Statistical generalizability refers to inferring from a sample to a target population. Scientific generalizability refers to applying a model based on a particular target population to other populations. It may imply either generalizing an estimated population pattern/model to other populations or else applying it from one population to predict individual observations in other populations.
7. Operationalization: Observable data are an operationalization of underlying concepts. "Customer Satisfaction" may be measured via a questionnaire or by evaluating the impact of attributes that were assessed via conjoint analysis. Constructs play a key role in causal models and raise the question of what to measure and how. The sensitivity to what is measured versus the construct of interest depends on the study goal. Action operationalization is about deriving concrete actions from the information provided by a study.
8. Communication: If the information does not reach the right person at the right time in a clear and understandable way, the quality of information becomes poor. Data visualization is crucial for good communications and it is therefore directly related to the quality of information. Poor visualization of findings may lead to degradation of the information quality contained in the analysis performed on the data. Dashboards are about Communication.

For more on InfoQ see Kenett and Shmueli (2016). An application of the information quality framework to chemical process engineering is presented in Reis and Kenett (2018).

After 2010s, organizations started hiring data scientists to leverage the potential in their data and data scientists started getting involved in organizational infrastructures and data quality (Kenett and Redman 2019). Systems Engineering in the Fourth Industrial Revolution: Big data, Novel Technologies, and Modern Systems Engineering is discussed in Kenett et al. (2021a). In summary, quality models evolved through the following milestones: (1) Product quality, (2) Process quality, (3) Management quality, (4) Design quality, and (5) Information quality. The chapters in this book cover the tools and methods of industrial analytics supporting this quality evolution.

1.3 Industry 4.0 Characteristics

Industry 4.0, the so-called fourth industrial revolution, relies on three basic elements:

- Sensor technology that can extensively measure products and processes online.

- Flexible manufacturing capabilities—such as 3D printing—that can efficiently produce batches of varying size.
- Analytics that power the industrial engine with the capability to monitor, diagnose, predict, and optimize decisions.

One significant analytic challenge is data integration. Sensors may collect data with different time cycles. Dynamic time warping (DTW) and Bayesian Networks (BN) can fuse the collected data into an integrated picture (Kenett 2019). In analytic work done in industry, data is collected either actively or passively and models are developed with empirical methods, first principles or hybrid models. The industrial cycle provides opportunities to try out new products or new process set-ups and, based on the results, determine follow-up actions. It is, however, important to make sure that analytic work is reviewed properly to avoid deriving misleading conclusions, which could be very costly and/or time-consuming. For example, a lithium battery manufacturer discovered it had uncalibrated test equipment evaluating end-of-the-line products. The company was able to avoid a major recall by using the plant's control charts to precisely identify the problematic batches. To avoid shipping immature products, or defective batches, good diagnostic capabilities are vital for monitoring and identifying the cause of any reported problems.

Analytic challenges in systems engineering and industrial applications include (Kenett et al. 2021b):

- Engineering design
- Manufacturing systems
- Decision-support systems
- Shop-floor control and layout
- Fault detection and quality improvement
- Condition-based maintenance
- Customer and supplier relationship management
- Energy and infrastructure management
- Cybersecurity and security

These challenges require monitoring products and process; designing new products and processes; and improving products and processes. The next section presents an approach designed to attain all these objectives; the digital twin, also known as a surrogate model.

1.4 Digital Twin

The term "digital twin" is defined in different forms including as a high-fidelity simulation, a virtual organization, a virtual reality representation, and an emulation facility. Its uses are in deploying optimization, monitoring, diagnostic, prognostic, and prescriptive capabilities (Kenett et al. 2018b; Kenett and Bortman 2021). The digital twin originated with the concept of a digital factory (Jain and Shao 2014) and is the digital representation of a physical asset or system, across its life-cycle, using operational real-time data and other sources, adopted to drive business outcomes.

The digital twin concept has been implemented by leading manufacturing companies. Ford Motor Company enhanced assembly line performance by evaluating and optimizing the designs using digital twins (IMT 2013). Volvo Group Global (2017) showed how to validate changes using a digital twin. General Electric developed digital twins of aircraft engines. Major commercial software vendors support development of virtual factories via integrated solutions for product, process and system design, simulation, and visualization (Tolio et al. 2013). A standardization of process control technologies is provided by ANSI (2010). On the other hand, Jain and Shao (2014) attempted to implement a multi-resolution digital twin but found it highly challenging due technology limitations and information availability.

Virtual data management, automatic model generation, static and dynamic simulation, and integration and communication are paramount to realizing a digital twin (Choi et al. 2015). However, most software tools are, in general, not supplied with these capabilities making it a challenge to develop a digital twin. There are efforts addressing different aspects of the challenge. To enhance conventional simulations for a digital twin, Bal and Hashemipour (2009) use Product-Resource-Order-Staff Architecture for modeling controls while the Quest simulation tool models the physical elements. To integrate models and enhance communication, Hints et al. (2011) developed a software tool named Design Synthesis Module. Debevec et al. (2014) use a simulative model to test and improve schedules before implementation in factories of small and medium size. For production planning, Terkaj et al. (2015) present an ontology of a virtual factory or digital twin, in order to aid planning decisions.

The recent concept of "Industry 4.0", or the fourth industrial revolution, includes Cyber-Physical Systems (CPS) as a key component. The function of CPS is the monitoring of physical processes and creating a virtual copy of the physical world to support decentralized decision-making (Hermann et al. 2015). In Industry 4.0 applications, one sees a growing role of twinning a physical plant with simulation-based surrogates. By means of sensors, real-time data about physical items are collected and used to duplicate the physical state of the item and assess the impact of ongoing changes (Kenett et al. 2021a). Digital twins include five main components: physical part, virtual part, connection, data, and service. The virtual and physical parts exchange information collected through the connection part. The interaction between the human and the digital twin is provided by the service part. Digital twins are traditionally used to improve the performance of engineering devices, like wind turbines or jet engines. In this context, they also serve to model systems of devices, to collect and analyze information about processes and people, and to help solve complex problems. Such digital twins provide powerful planning and troubleshooting capabilities and statistical methods play a significant role in both the design and analysis of simulations and computer experiments on digital twin platforms. Digital twins provide a platform that enables a life cycle perspective on products and systems. This emphasizes a transition from engineering the design to engineering the performance.

Simulation models of systems and processes are used to shorten time to market, reduce design, operations and maintenance costs while improving quality. An example is the PENSIM simulation software used in modelling penicillin production in a fed-batch fermentor. The model includes variables such as pH, temperature, aeration rate, agitation power, and feed flow rate of the substrate. It is used in monitoring and process trouble shooting activities. Such simulators are used in fault diagnosis of semiconductors, biotechnological, and chemical production processes. They are also used for research and educational purposes (Reis and Kenett 2018).

Digital twins complement or substitute physical experiments with software-based simulation experiments (Santner et al. 2003). They permit building knowledge of a physical system and supporting decision-making in the design and monitoring of such systems (Kenett and Coleman 2021). A physical experiment consists of executing real life experiments where modifications to input variables are taking place. Similarly, a digital twin can be used to run experiments by a number of runs of a simulation code where factors are parametrized as a subset of the code's inputs. An important application of digital twins is condition-based maintenance (CBM). This approach is based on the idea that maintenance operations should be done only when necessary (Gruber et al. 2021). The purpose of CBM is to prevent a reduction in the effectiveness of a system which can evolve to a total failure of the system. It aims to reduce maintenance costs by enabling planning of maintenance operations in advance and indicate necessary replacement of damaged component. In CBM, prediction of the remaining useful life (RUL) of each component is required. Evaluation of the components' RUL requires not only diagnostics of the fault but also the estimation of the fault location and severity.

Predictive analytics and operational Business Intelligence systems identify potential failures and allow for customer churn prevention initiatives. The application of industrial analytics, within such computerized environments, allows practitioners to concentrate on statistical analysis as opposed to repetitive numerical computations.

1.5 Chapter Highlights

The main concepts and definitions introduced in this chapter include:

- The first industrial revolution
- The second industrial revolution
- The third industrial revolution
- The fourth industrial revolution (Industry 4.0)
- Inspection as a management approach
- Process control and improvement
- Quality by design

- Information quality
- Computer simulations
- Digital twins

1.6 Exercises

Exercise 1.1 Describe three work environments where quality is assured by 100% inspection of outputs (as opposed to process control).

Exercise 1.2 Search periodicals, such as Business Week, Fortune, Time and Newsweek and newspapers such as the New York Times and Wall Street Journal for information on quality initiatives in service, healthcare, governmental and industrial organizations. Summarize three such initiatives indicating what was done and what were the concrete outcomes of these initiatives.

Exercise 1.3 Provide examples of the three types of production systems.

(a) Continuous flow production
(b) Discrete mass production
(c) Industry 4 production

Exercise 1.4 What management approach cannot work with continuous flow production?

Exercise 1.5 What management approach characterizes

(a) A school system?
(b) A group of scouts?
(c) A football team?

Exercise 1.6 Provide examples of how you, personally, apply inspection, process control or quality by design approaches.

(a) As a student
(b) In your parents' house
(c) With your friends

Exercise 1.7 Evaluate the information quality of a case study provided by your instructor.

Chapter 2
Basic Tools and Principles of Process Control

Preview Competitive pressures are forcing many management teams to focus on process control and process improvement, as an alternative to screening and inspection. This chapter discusses techniques used effectively in industrial organizations that have adopted such ideas as concepts. Classical control charts, quality control, and quality planning tools are presented along with modern statistical process control procedures including new statistical techniques for constructing confidence intervals of process capability indices and analyzing Pareto charts. Throughout the chapter, a software piston simulator is used to demonstrate how control charts are set up and used in real-life applications.

2.1 Basic Concepts of Statistical Process Control

In this chapter, we present the basics of **statistical process control** (**SPC**). The general approach is prescriptive and descriptive rather than analytical. With SPC, we do not aim at modeling the distribution of data collected from a given process. Our goal is to control the process with the aid of decision rules for signaling significant discrepancies between the observed data and the standards of a process under control. We demonstrate the application of SPC to various processes by referring to the examples of piston cycle time and strength of fibers, which have been discussed in Chapter 1 in *Modern Statistics* (Kenett et al. 2022b). Other examples used include data on power failures in a computer center and office procedures for scheduling appointments of a university dean. The data on the piston cycle time are generated by the piston simulator function *pistonSimulation* available in the `mistat` package. In order to study the causes for variability in the piston cycle time, we present, in

---

Supplementary Information The online version contains supplementary material available at (https://doi.org/10.1007/978-3-031-28482-3_2).

R. S. Kenett et al., *Industrial Statistics*, Statistics for Industry, Technology, and Engineering, https://doi.org/10.1007/978-3-031-28482-3_2

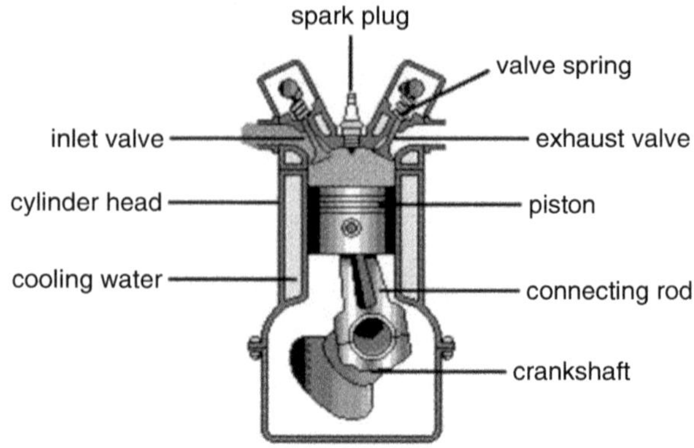

Fig. 2.1 A sketch of the piston

Table 2.1 Operating factors of the piston simulator

Factor	Units	Minimum	Maximum
Piston weight	M [Kg]	30	60
Piston surface area	S [m^2]	0.005	0.020
Initial gas volume	V_0 [m^3]	0.002	0.010
Spring coeff.	K [N/m]	1000	5000
Atmosph. pressure	P_0 [N/m^2]	90,000	110,000
Ambient temperat.	T [°K]	290	296
Filling gas temperat.	T_0 [°K]	340	360

Fig. 2.1, a sketch of a piston and, in Table 2.1, seven factors that can be controlled to change the cycle time of a piston.

Figure 2.2 is a run chart (also called "connected line plot"), and Fig. 2.3 is a histogram, of 50 piston cycle times (seconds) measured under stable operating conditions. Throughout the measurement time frame, the piston operating factors remained fixed at their maximum levels. The data can be found in dataset **OTURB1.csv**.

The average cycle time of the 50 cycles is 0.392 [sec] with a standard deviation of 0.114 [sec].

Even though no changes occurred in the operating conditions of the piston, we observe variability in the cycle times. From Fig. 2.2, we note that cycle times vary between 0.22 and 0.69 s. The histogram in Fig. 2.3 indicates some skewness in the data. The normal probability plot of the 50 cycle times (Fig. 2.4) also leads to the conclusion that the cycle time distribution is skewed.

Another example of variability is provided by the yarn strength data presented in Chapter 1 in *Modern Statistics* (Kenett et al. 2022b). The yarn strength test results indicate that there is variability in the properties of the product. High yarn strength indicates good spinning and weaving performance. Yarn strength is considered a function of the fiber length, fiber fineness, and fiber tensile strength. As a general rule, longer cottons are fine-fibered and shorter cottons coarse-fibered. Very fine fibers, however, tend to reduce the rate of processing, so that the degree of fiber

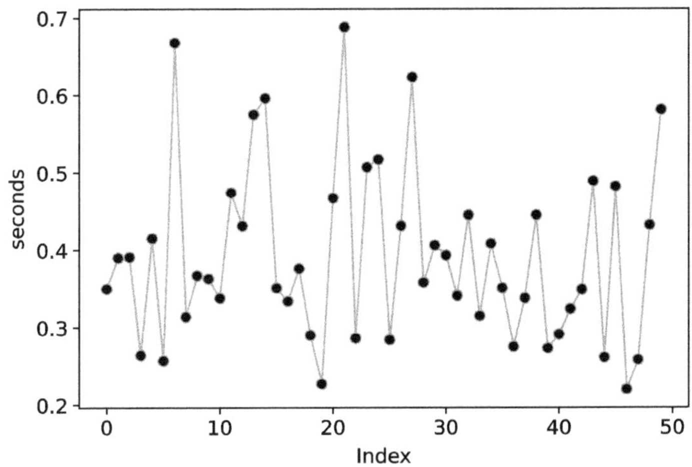

Fig. 2.2 Run chart or connected line plot of 50 piston cycle times [sec]

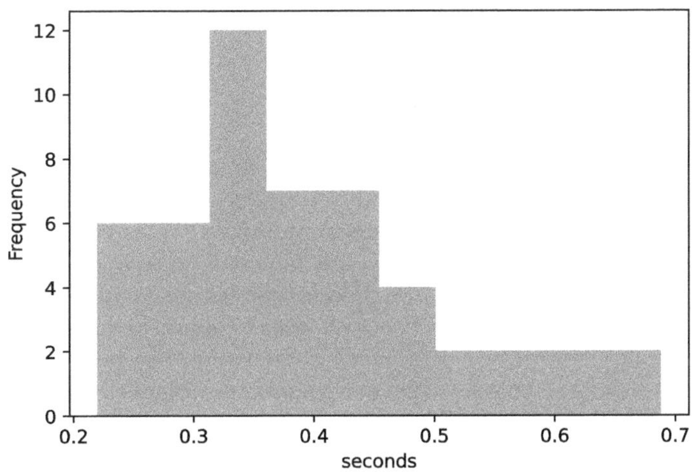

Fig. 2.3 Histogram of 50 piston cycle times

fineness depends upon the specific end product use. Variability in fiber fineness is a major cause of variability in yarn strength and processing time.

In general, a production process has many sources or causes of variation. These can be further subdivided as process inputs and process operational characteristics including equipment, procedures, and environmental conditions. Environmental conditions consist of factors such as temperature and humidity or work tools. Visual guides, for instance, might not allow operators to precisely position parts on fixtures. The complex interactions between material, tools, machine, work methods, operators, and the environment combine to create variability in the process. Factors that are permanent, as a natural part of the process, are causing **chronic problems**

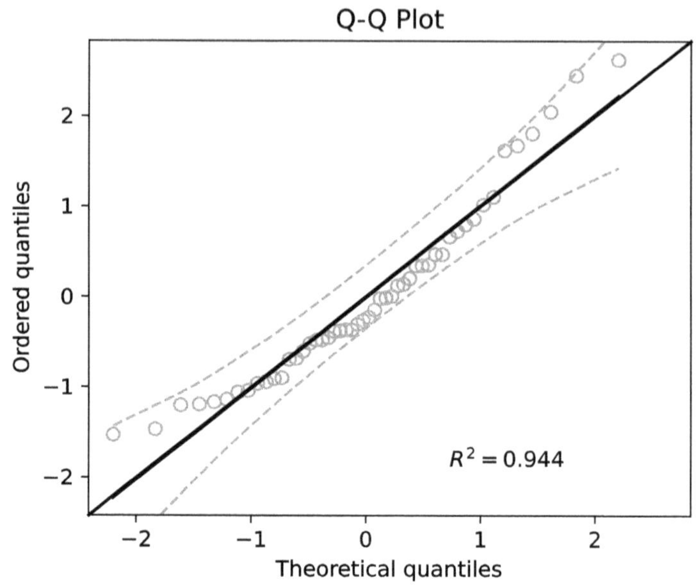

Fig. 2.4 Normal probability plot of 50 piston cycle times

and are called **common causes** of variation. The combined effect of common causes can be described using probability distributions. Such distributions were introduced in Chap. 1 and their theoretical properties presented in Chapter 2 in *Modern Statistics* (Kenett et al. 2022b). It is important to recognize that recurring causes of variability affect every work process and that even under a stable process there are differences in performance over time. Failure to recognize variation leads to wasteful actions and detrimental overcontrol. The only way to reduce the negative effects of chronic, common causes of variability is to modify the process. This modification can occur at the level of the process inputs, the process technology, the process controls, or the process design. Some of these changes are technical (e.g., different process settings), some are strategic (e.g., different product specifications), and some are related to human resources management (e.g., training of operators). **Special causes**, **assignable causes**, or **sporadic spikes** arise from external temporary sources that are not inherent to the process. These terms are used here interchangeably. For example, an increase in temperature can potentially affect the piston's performance. The impact can be in terms of changes in both the average cycle times and the variability in cycle times.

In order to signal the occurrence of special causes, we need a control mechanism. Specifically in the case of the piston, such a mechanism can consist of taking samples or subgroups of 5 consecutive piston cycle times. Within each subgroup, we compute the subgroup average and standard deviation.

Figures 2.5 and 2.6 display charts of the average and standard deviations of 20 samples of 5 cycle time measurements. To generate these charts with Python, we use:

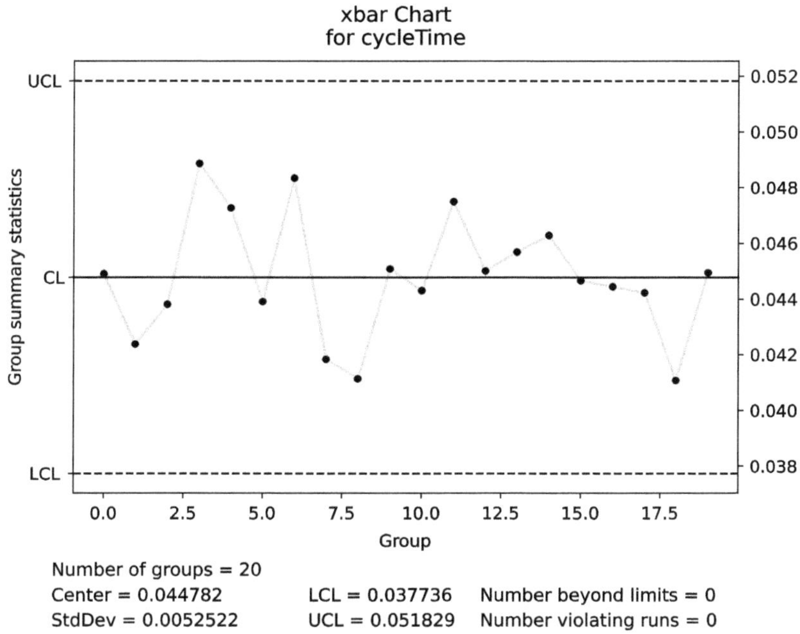

Fig. 2.5 X-bar chart of cycle times under stable operating conditions

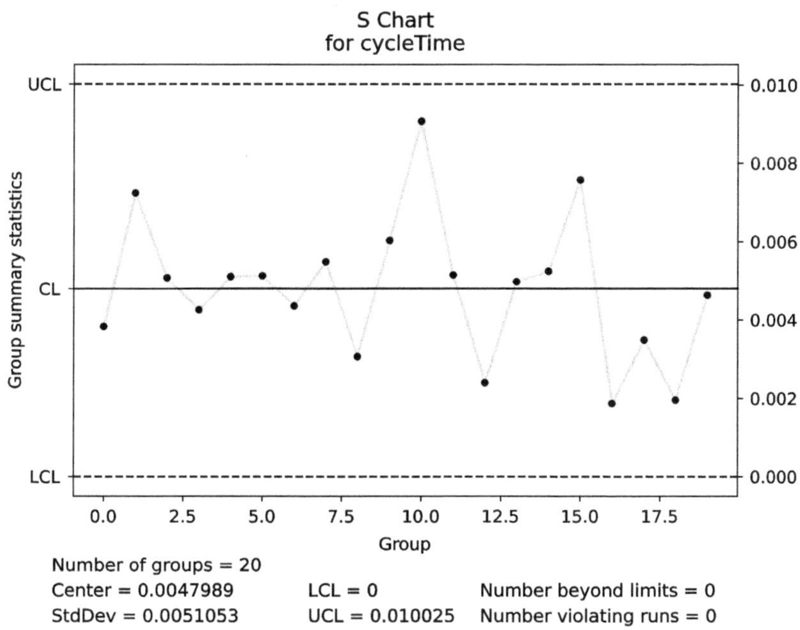

Fig. 2.6 S-chart of cycle times under stable operating conditions

```
simulator = mistat.PistonSimulator(n_simulation=20, n_replicate=5, seed=1)
Ps = simulator.simulate()

Ps['seconds'].groupby(Ps['group']).apply(np.mean)
```

```
group
1     0.044902
2     0.042374
3     0.043812
4     0.048865
5     0.047265
6     0.043910
7     0.048345
8     0.041833
9     0.041135
10    0.045080
11    0.044307
12    0.047490
13    0.045008
14    0.045684
15    0.046281
16    0.044656
17    0.044445
18    0.044227
19    0.041077
20    0.044947
Name: seconds, dtype: float64
```

The chart of averages is called an X-bar chart, and the chart of standard deviations is called an S-chart. All 100 measurements were taken under fixed operating conditions of the piston (all factors set at the maximum levels). We note that the average of cycle time averages is 0.045 s and that the average of the standard deviations of the 20 subgroups is 0.0048 s. All these numbers were generated by the piston computer simulation model that allows us to change the factors affecting the operating conditions of the piston. Again we know that no changes were made to the control factors. The observed variability is due to common causes only such as variability in atmospheric pressure or filling gas temperature.

We now rerun the piston simulator introducing a forced change in the piston ambient temperature. At the beginning of the 8th sample, temperature begins to rise at a rate of 20% per group. Can we flag this special cause? The X-bar chart of these new simulated data is presented in Fig. 2.7. Up to the 7th sample, the chart is identical to that of Fig. 2.5. At the 8th sample, we note a small increase in cycle time. As of the 11th sample, the subgroup averages are consistently above 0.05 s. This run persists until the 21st sample when we stopped the simulation. To have 10 points in a row above the average is unlikely to occur by chance alone. The probability of such an event is $(1/2)^{10} = 0.00098$. The implication of the 10 points run is that common causes are no longer the only causes of variation and that a special factor has begun affecting the piston's performance. In this particular case, we know that it is an increase in ambient temperature. The S-chart of the same data (Fig. 2.8) shows a downward trend with several points falling below the average of 0.004 beginning at the 8th sample. This indication occurs earlier than that in the X-bar chart. The information obtained from both charts indicates that a special cause has been in

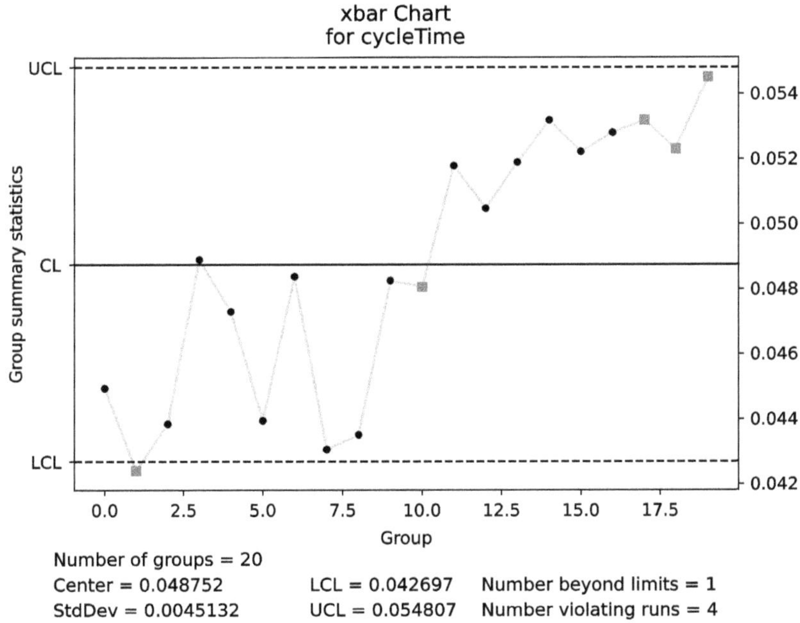

Fig. 2.7 X-bar chart of cycle times with a trend in ambient temperature

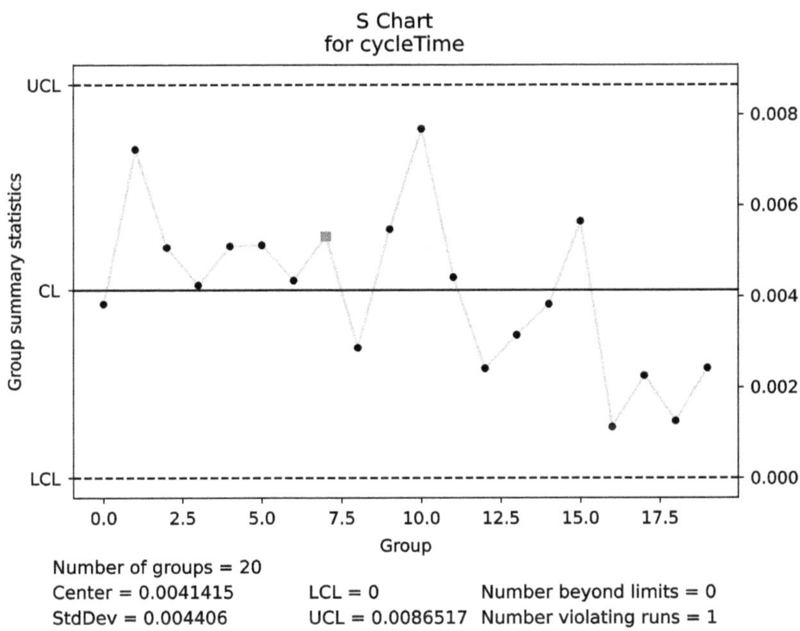

Fig. 2.8 S-chart of cycle times with a trend in ambient temperature

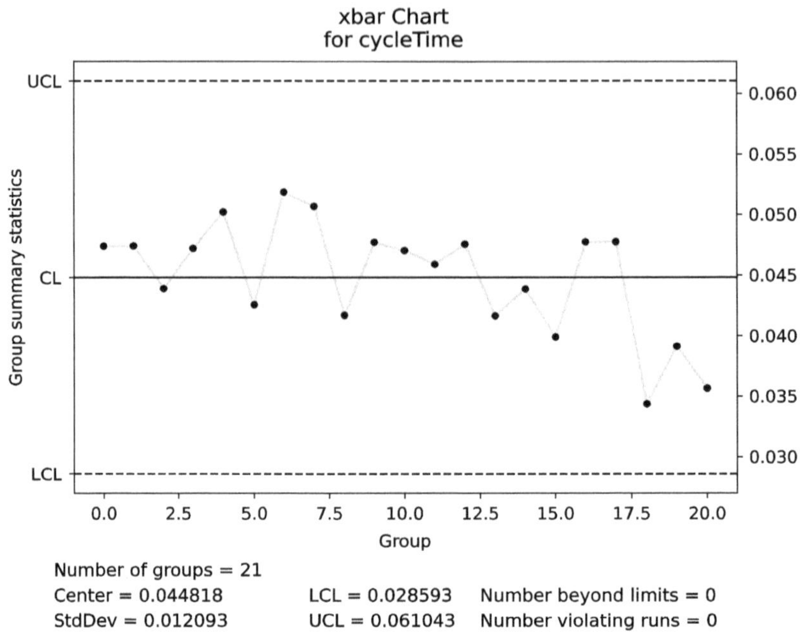

Fig. 2.9 X-bar chart of cycle times with a trend in spring coefficient precision

effect from the 8th sample onward. Its effect has been to increase cycle times and reduce variability. The new average cycle time appears to be around 0.052 s.

The piston simulator allows us to try other types of changes in the operational parameters of the piston. For example, we can change the spring that controls the intake valve in the piston gas chamber. In the next simulation, the standard deviation of the spring coefficient is increasing at a 15% rate past the 8th sample. Figures 2.9 and 2.10 are X-bar and S-charts corresponding to this scenario. Until the 8th sample, these charts are identical to those in Figs. 2.5 and 2.6. After the 8th sample, changes appear in the chart. In particular, we see a large drop in cycle times at the end. We also see changes in the S-chart in Fig. 2.10. We see that after the 13th sample, the standard deviation trends upward.

Control charts have wide applicability throughout an organization. Top managers can use a control chart to study variation in sales and decide on new marketing strategies. Operators can use the same tool to determine if and when to adjust a manufacturing process. An example with universal applicability comes from the scheduling process of daily appointments in a university dean's office. At the end of each working day, the various meetings and appointment coordinated by the office of the Dean were classified as being "on time" or with a problem such as "late beginning," "did not end on time," "was interrupted," etc.... The ratio of problem appointments to the total number of daily appointments was tracked and control limits computed. Figure 2.11 is the Dean's control chart (see Kelly et al. 1991).

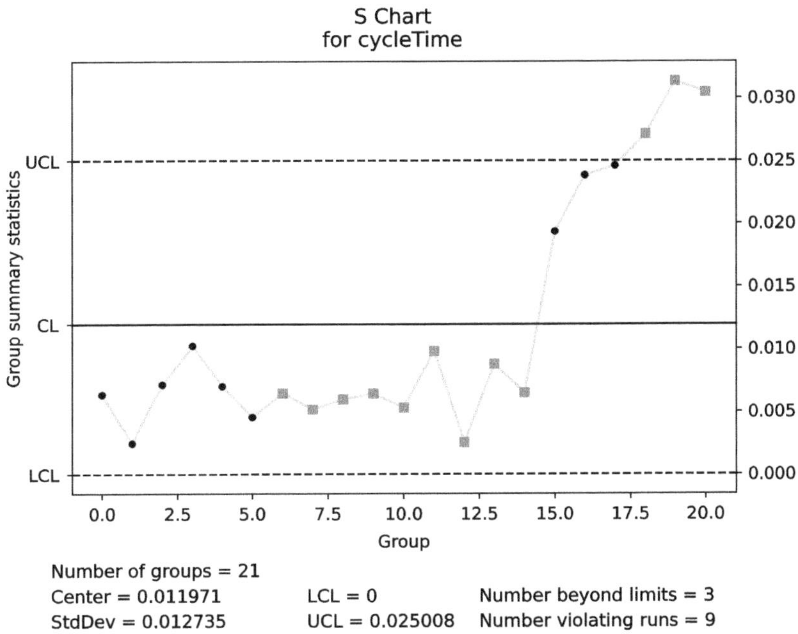

Fig. 2.10 S-chart of cycle times with a trend in spring coefficient precision

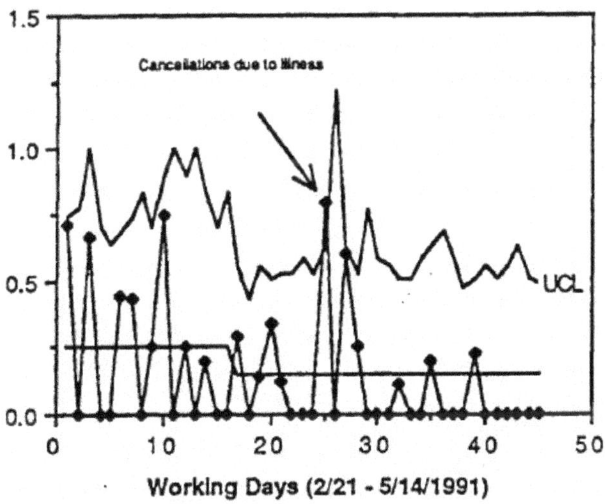

Fig. 2.11 Control chart for proportion of appointments with scheduling problems (based on a chart prepared by Dean of the School of Management at SUNY Binghamton)

Another example of a special cause is the miscalibration of spinning equipment and yarn strength mentioned above. Miscalibration can be identified by ongoing monitoring of yarn strength. Process operators analyzing X-bar and S-charts can stop and adjust the process as trends develop or sporadic spikes appear. Timely indication of a sporadic spike is crucial to the effectiveness of process control mechanisms. **Ongoing chronic problems, however, cannot be resolved by using local operator adjustments**. The statistical approach to process control allows us to distinguish between chronic problems and sporadic spikes. This is crucial since these two different types of problems require different approaches. Process control ensures that a process performs at a level determined "doable" by a process capability study. Section 2.3 discusses how to conduct such studies and how to set control limits.

So far we focused on the analysis of data for process control. Another essential component of process control is the generation and routing of relevant and timely data through proper feedback loops. We distinguish between two types of feedback loops: **External feedback loops** and **internal feedback loops**. An external feedback loop consists of information gathered at a subsequent downstream process or by direct inspection of the process outputs.

To illustrate these concepts and ideas, let us look at the process of driving to work. The time it takes you to get to work is a variable that depends on various factors such as how many other cars are on the road, how you happen to catch the traffic lights, your mood that morning, and so on. These are factors that are part of the process, and you have little or no control over them. Such common causes create variation in the time it takes you to reach work. One day it may take you 15 min and the next day 12 min. If you are particularly unlucky and had to stop at all the red lights, it might take you 18 min. Suppose, however, that on one particular day it took you 45 min to reach work. Such a long trip is outside the normal range of variation and is probably associated with a special cause such as a flat tire, a traffic jam, or road constructions.

External feedback loops rely on measurements of the process outcome. They provide information like looking at a rear view mirror. The previous example consisted of monitoring time after you reached work. In most cases, identifying a special cause at that point in time is too late. Suppose that we had a local radio station that provided its listeners live coverage of the traffic conditions. If we monitor, on a daily basis, the volume of traffic reported by the radio, we can avoid traffic jams, road constructions, and other unexpected delays. Such information will help us eliminate certain special causes of variation. Moreover, if we institute a predictive maintenance program for our car, we can eliminate many types of engine problems, further reducing the impact of special causes. To eliminate the occasional flat tire would involve improvements in road maintenance—a much larger task. The radio station is a source of internal feedback that provides information that can be used to correct your route and thus arrive at work on time almost every day. This is equivalent to driving the process while looking ahead. Most drivers are able to avoid getting off the road, even when obstacles present themselves unexpectedly. We now proceed to describe how control charts are used for "staying on course."

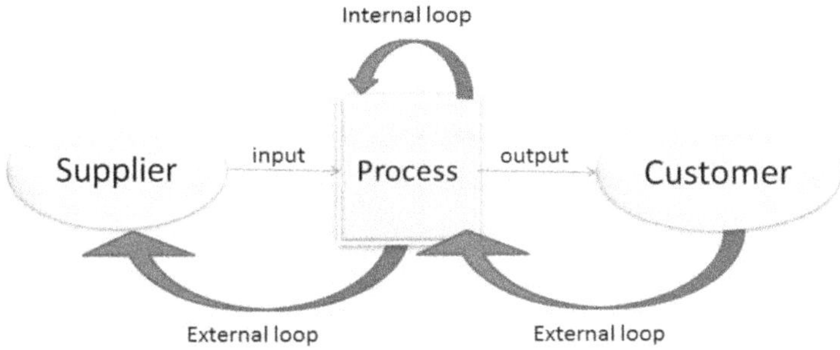

Fig. 2.12 The supplier–process–customer structure and its feedback loops

Manufacturing examples consist of physical dimensions of holes drilled by a numerically controlled CNC machine, piston cycle times, or yarn strength. The finished part leaving a CNC machine can be inspected immediately after the drilling operation or later, when the part is assembled into another part. Piston cycle times can be recorded online or stored for off-line analysis. Another example is the testing of electrical parameters at final assembly of an electronic product. The test data reflect, among other things, the performance of the components' assembly process. Information on defects such as missing components, wrong or misaligned components should be fed back, through an external feedback loop, to the assembly operators. Data collected on process variables, measured internally to the process, are the basis of an internal feedback loop information flow. An example of such data is the air pressure in the hydraulic system of a CNC machine. Air pressure can be measured so that trends or deviations in pressure are detected early enough to allow for corrective action to take place. Another example consists of the tracking of temperature in the surroundings of a piston. Such information will directly point out the trend in temperature that was indirectly observed in Figs. 2.7 and 2.8. Moreover, routine direct measurements of the precision of the spring coefficient will exhibit the trend that went unnoticed in Figs. 2.9 and 2.10. The relationship between a process, its suppliers, and its customers is presented in Fig. 2.12. Internal and external feedback loops depend on a coherent structure of suppliers, processes, and customers. It is in this context that one can achieve effective statistical process control.

We discussed in this section the concepts of feedback loops, chronic problems (common causes), and sporadic spikes (special causes). Data funneled through feedback loops are used to indicate what are the types of forces affecting the measured process. Statistical process control is "a rule of behavior that will strike a balance for the net economic loss from two sources of mistake: (1) looking for special causes too often, or overadjusting; (2) not looking often enough" (excerpt from Deming 1967). In the implementation of statistical process control, one distinguishes between two phases: (1) achieving control and (2) maintaining control. Achieving control consists of a study of the causes of variation followed by an effort to eliminate the special causes and a thorough understanding of the remaining permanent factors affecting the process, the common causes. Tools such as graphic displays (Chaps. 1 and 4 in the *Modern Statistics* companion volume, Kenett et al. 2022b), correlation and regression analysis (Section 4.3, also in *Modern Statistics*), control charts (Chaps. 2–4), and designed experiments (Chaps. 5 and 6) are typically used in a process capability study whose objective is to achieve control. Section 2.3 will discuss the major steps of a process capability study and the determination of control limits on the control charts. Once control is achieved, one has to maintain it. The next section describes how control is maintained with the help of control limits.

2.2 Driving a Process with Control Charts

Control charts allow us to determine when to take action in order to adjust a process that has been affected by a special cause. Control charts also tell us when to leave a process alone and not misinterpret variations due to common causes. Special causes need to be addressed by corrective action. Common causes are the focus of ongoing efforts aimed at improving the process.

We distinguish between **control charts for variable data** and **control charts for attribute data**. Attribute data require an operational definition of what constitutes a problem or defect. When the observation unit is classified into one of the two categories (e.g., "pass" vs. "fail" or conforming vs. nonconforming), we can track the proportion of nonconforming units in the observation sample. Such a chart is called a **p-chart**. If the size of the observation sample is fixed, we can simply track the number of nonconforming units and derive an **np-chart**. When an observation consists of the number of nonconformities per unit of observation, we track either the number of nonconformities (**c-charts**) or rates of nonconformities (**u-charts**). Rates are computed by dividing the number of nonconformities by the number of opportunities for errors or problems. For variable data, we distinguish between processes that can be repeatedly sampled under uniform conditions and processes where measurements are derived one at a time (e.g., monthly sales). In the latter case, we will use control charts for individual data also called moving range charts. When data can be grouped, we can use a variety of charts such as the X-bar chart or the median chart discussed in detail in Chap. 3. We proceed to demonstrate how X-bar control charts actually work using the piston cycle times discussed earlier. An X-bar control chart for the piston's cycle time is constructed by first grouping observations by time period and then summarizing the location and variability statistics in these subgroups. An example of this was provided in Figs. 2.5 and 2.6 where the average and standard deviations of 5 consecutive cycle times were tracked over 20 such subgroups. The three lines that are added to the simple run charts are the **center line**, positioned at the grand average, the **lower control limits** (LCL), and the **upper control limits** (UCL). The UCL and LCL indicate the range of variability we expect to observe around the center line, under stable operating conditions. Figure 2.5 shows averages of 20 subgroups of 5 consecutive cycle times each. The center line and control limits are computed from the average of the 20 subgroup averages and the estimated standard deviation for averages of samples of size 5. The center line is at 0.394 s. When using the classical 3-sigma charts developed by Shewhart, the control limits are positioned at three standard deviations of $\bar{X}$, namely $3\sigma/\sqrt{n}$, away from the center line. In this example, we find that UCL = 0.562 s and LCL = 0.227 s. Under stable operating conditions, with only common causes affecting performance, the chart will typically have all points within the control limits. Specifically with 3-sigma control limits, we expect to have, on the average, only one out of 370 points (1/.0027), outside these limits, a rather rare event. Therefore, when a point falls beyond the control limits, we can safely question the stability of the process. The risk that such an alarm will turn to be false is 0.0027. A false alarm occurs when the sample mean falls outside the control limits, and we suspect an assignable cause, but only common causes are operating. Moreover, stable random variation does not exhibit patterns such as upward or downward trends, or consecutive runs of points above or below the center line. We saw earlier how a control chart was used to detect an increase in ambient temperature of a piston from the cycle times. The X-bar chart (Fig. 2.7) indicates a run of six or more points above the center line. Figure 2.13 shows several patterns that indicate non-randomness. These are:

1. A single point outside the control limits
2. A run of nine or more points in a row above (or below) the center line
3. Six consecutive points increasing (trend up) or decreasing (trend down)
4. Two out of three points in a region between $\mu \pm 2\sigma/\sqrt{n}$ and $\mu \pm 3\sigma/\sqrt{n}$

A comprehensive discussion of detection rules and properties of the classical 3-sigma control charts and of other modern control chart techniques is presented in Chap. 3.

As we saw earlier, there are many types of control charts. Selection of the control chart to use in a particular application primarily depends on the type of data that will flow through the feedback loops. The piston provides us with an example of variable data, and we used an X-bar and S-chart to monitor the piston's performance. Examples of attribute data are blemishes on a given surface, wave solder defects, below standard service level at the bank, and missed shipping dates. Each type of data leads to a different type of control chart. All control charts have a center line and upper and lower control limits (UCL and LCL). In general, the rules for flagging special causes are the same in every type of control chart. Figure 2.14 presents a classification of the various control charts. Properties of the different types of charts, including the more advanced EWMA and CUSUM charts, are presented in Chap. 3.

We discussed earlier several examples of control charts and introduced different types of control charts. The block diagram in Fig. 2.14 organizes control charts by the type of data flowing through feedback loops. External feedback loops typically rely on properties of the process' products and lead to control charts based on counts or classification. If products are classified using "pass" versus "fail" criteria, one will use np-charts or p-charts depending on whether the products are tested in fixed or variable subgroups. The advantage of such charts is that several criteria can be combined to produce a definition of what constitutes a "fail" or defective product.

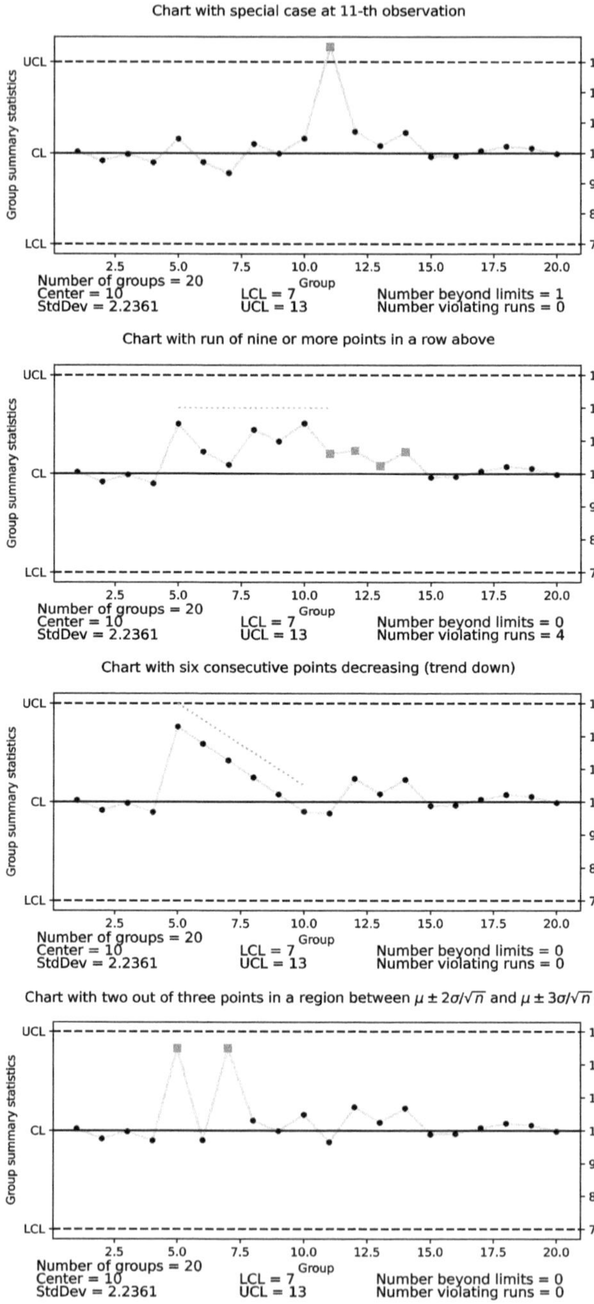

Fig. 2.13 Patterns to detect special causes

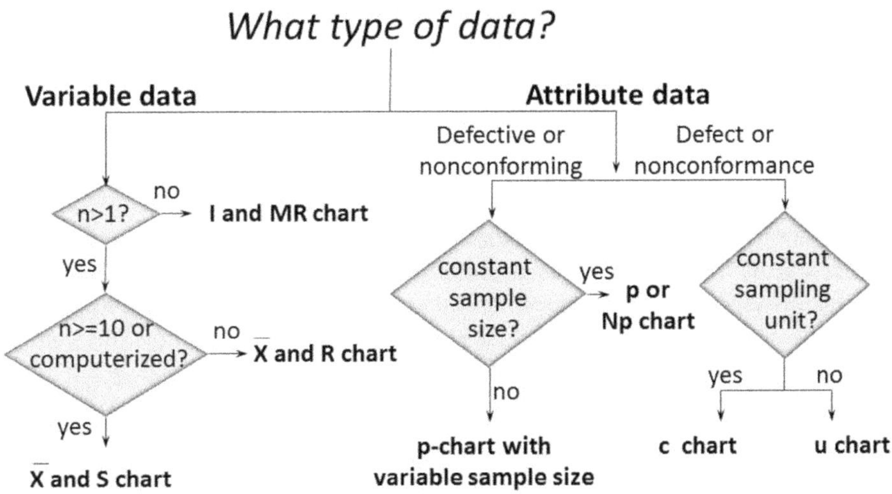

Fig. 2.14 Classification of control charts

When counting nonconformities or incidences of a certain event or phenomenon, one is directed to use c-charts or u-charts. These charts provide more information than p-charts or np-charts since the actual number of nonconformities in a product is accounted for. The drawback is that several criteria cannot be combined without weighing the different types of nonconformities. C-charts assume a fixed likelihood of incidence, and u-charts are used in cases of varying likelihood levels. For large subgroups (subgroup sizes larger than 1000), the number of incidences, incidences per unit, the number of defectives or percent defectives can be considered as individual measurements, and an X -chart for subgroups of size 1 can be used. Internal feedback loops and, in some cases, also external feedback loops rely on variable data derived from measuring product or process characteristics. If measurements are grouped in samples, one can combine X-bar charts with R-charts or S-charts. Such combinations provide a mechanism to control stability of a process with respect to both location and variability. X-bar charts track the sample averages, R-charts track sample ranges (maximum–minimum), and S-charts are based on sample standard deviations. For samples larger than 10, S-charts are recommended over R-charts. For small samples and manual maintenance of control charts, R-charts are preferred. When sample sizes vary, only S-charts should be used to track variability.

2.3 Setting Up a Control Chart: Process Capability Studies

Setting up control limits of a control chart requires a detailed study of process variability and of the causes creating this variability. Control charts are used to detect occurrence of special, sporadic causes while minimizing the risk of misinterpreting special causes as common causes. In order to achieve this objective, one needs to assess the effect of chronic, common causes and then set up control limits that reflect the variability resulting from such common causes. The study of process variability that precedes the setting up of control charts is called a **process capability study**. We distinguish between attribute process capability studies and variable process capability studies.

Attribute process capability studies determine a process capability in terms of fraction of defective or nonconforming output. Such studies begin with data collected over several time periods. A rule of thumb is to use three time periods with 20 to 25 samples of size 50 to 100 units each. For each sample, the control chart statistic is computed and a control chart is drawn. This will lead to a p-, np-, c-, or u-chart and investigation patterns flagging special causes such as those in Fig. 2.13. Special causes are then investigated and possibly removed. This requires changes to the process that justify removal of the measurements corresponding to the time periods when those special causes were active. The new control charts, computed without these points, indicate the capability of the process. Its center line is typically used as a measure of process capability. For example in Fig. 2.11, one can see that the process capability of the scheduling of appointments at the Dean's office improved from 25% of appointments with problems to 15% after introducing a change in the process. The change consisted of acknowledging appointments with a confirmation note spelling out, time, date and topic of appointment, a brief agenda, and a scheduled ending time. On the 25th working day, there was one sporadic spike caused by illness. The Dean had to end early that day and several appointments got canceled. When sample sizes are large (over 1000 units), control charts for attribute data become ineffective because of very narrow control limits and X-charts for individual measurements are used.

Variable process capability studies determine a process capability in terms of the distribution of measurements on product or process characteristics. Setting up of control charts for variable data requires far less data than attribute data control charts. Data are collected in samples, called **rational subgroups**, selected from a time frame so that relatively homogeneous conditions exist within each subgroup. The design strategy of rational subgroups is aimed at measuring variability due to common causes only. Control limits are then determined from measures of location and variability in each rational subgroup. The control limits are set to account for variability due to these common causes. Any deviation from stable patterns relative to the control limits (see Fig. 2.13) indicates a special cause. For example, in the piston case study, a rational subgroup consists of 5 consecutive cycle times. The statistics used are the average and standard deviation of the subgroups. The 3-sigma control limits are computed to be $\mathrm{UCL} = 0.052$ and $\mathrm{LCL} = 0.038$. From an analysis of Fig. 2.5, we conclude that the X-bar chart, based on a connected time plot of 20 consecutive averages, exhibits a pattern that is consistent with a stable process. We can now determine the process capability of the piston movement within the cylinder.

```
         LCL        UCL
0  0.037736  0.051829
Process Capability Analysis

Number of obs = 100          Target = 0.04
       Center = 0.04            LSL = 0.03
       StdDev = 0.005252        USL = 0.05

Capability indices:

         Value     2.5%    97.5%
Cp       0.6347  0.5463  0.7228
Cp_l     0.9382  0.8156  1.0608
Cp_u     0.3312  0.2640  0.3983
Cp_k     0.3312  0.2512  0.4111
Cpm      0.4693  0.3910  0.5474

Exp<LSL   0%    Obs<LSL   0%
Exp>USL  16%    Obs>USL  17%
z_target: -0.910
z_usl: 0.994
p_above_usl: 0.160
```

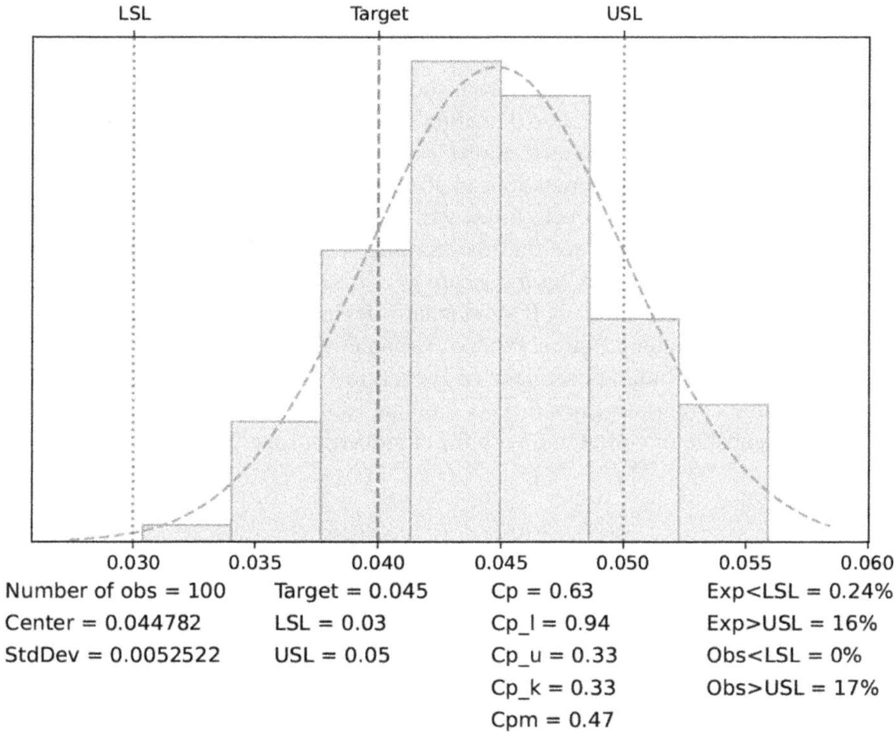

Process capability for variable data is a characteristic that reflects the probability of the individual outcomes of a process to be within the engineering specification limits. Assume that the piston engineering specifications stipulate a nominal value of 0.04 s and maximum and minimum values of 0.05 and 0.03 s, respectively. Table 2.2 shows the output from the process capability analysis included in the `mistat` package.

Table 2.2 Process capability analysis of piston cycle time

```
simulator = mistat.PistonSimulator(n_simulation=20, n_replicate=5, seed=1)
Ps = simulator.simulate()

cycleTime = mistat.qcc_groups(Ps['seconds'], Ps['group'])
qcc = mistat.QualityControlChart(cycleTime)
print(qcc.limits)

pc = mistat.ProcessCapability(qcc, spec_limits = [0.03, 0.05])

pc.plot()
plt.show()
pc.summary()
z_target = (0.04 - 0.04478) / 0.0052521
z_usl = (0.05 - 0.04478) / 0.0052521
p_above_usl = 1-stats.norm.cdf((0.05 - 0.04478) / 0.0052521)
print(f'z_target: {z_target:.3f}')
print(f'z_usl: {z_usl:.3f}')
print(f'p_above_usl: {p_above_usl:.3f}')
```

The 50 measurements that were produced under stable conditions have a mean (average) of 0.045 s and a standard deviation of 0.005 s. The predicted proportion of cycle times beyond the specification limits is computed using the normal distribution as an approximation. The computations yield that, under stable operating conditions, an estimated 16% of future cycle times will be above 0.05 s, and that 0.24% will be below 0.03 s. We clearly see that the nominal value of 0.04 s is slightly lower than the process average, having a Z-score of −0.91, and that the upper limit, or maximum specification limit, is 0.99 standard deviations above the average. The probability that a standard normal random variable is larger than 0.99 is 0.16. This is an estimate of the future percentage of cycle times above the upper limit of 0.5 s, provided stable conditions prevail. It is obvious from this analysis that the piston process is incapable of complying with the engineering specifications.

2.4 Process Capability Indices

In assessing the process capability for variable data, two indices are used: C_p and C_{pk}. The first index is an indicator of the potential of a process to meet two-sided specifications with as few defects as possible. For symmetric specification limits, the full potential is actually achieved when the process is centered at the mid-point between the specification limits. In order to compute C_p, one simply divides the process tolerance by six standard deviations, i.e.,

$$C_p = \frac{\text{Upper Specification Limit} - \text{Lower Specification Limit}}{6 \times \text{Standard Deviation}}. \tag{2.4.1}$$

The numerator indicates how wide the specifications are, the denominator measures the width of the process. Under normal assumptions, the denominator is a range of values that accounts for 99.73% of the observations from a centered process, operating under stable conditions with variability only due to common causes. When $C_p = 1$, we expect 0.27% of the observations to fall outside the specification limits. A target for many modern industries is to reach, on every process, a level of $C_p = 2$, which practically guarantees that under stable conditions, and for processes kept under control around the process nominal values, there will be no defective products ("zero defects"). With $C_p = 2$, the theoretical estimate under normal assumptions, allowing for a possible shift in the location of the process mean by as much as 1.5 standard deviations, is 3.4 cases per million observations outside specification limits.

Another measure of process capability is

$$C_{pk} = \text{minimum}(C_{pu}, C_{pl}), \tag{2.4.2}$$

where

$$C_{pu} = \frac{\text{Upper Specification Limit} - \text{Process Mean}}{3 \times \text{Standard Deviation}} \tag{2.4.3}$$

and

$$C_{pl} = \frac{\text{Process Mean} - \text{Lower Specification Limit}}{3 \times \text{Standard Deviation}}.$$

When the process mean is not centered midway between the specification limits, C_{pk} is different from C_p. Non-centered processes have their potential capability measured by C_p, and their actual capability measured by C_{pk}. As shown in Table 2.2, for the piston data, estimates of C_p and C_{pk} are $\hat{C}_p = 0.63$ and $\hat{C}_{pk} = 0.33$. This indicates that something could be gained by centering the piston cycle times around 0.04 s. Even if this is possible to achieve, there will still be observations outside the upper and lower limits, since the standard deviation is too large.

The validity of the C_p and C_{pk} indices is questionable in cases where the measurements on X are not normally distributed but have skewed distributions. The proper form of a capability index under non-normal conditions can be treated with bootstrapping (Chapter 3, *Modern Statistics*, Kenett et al. 2022b). Some authors offered partial analytic solutions (Kotz and Johnson 1993).

It is common practice to estimate C_p or C_{pk}, by substituting the sample mean, $\bar{X}$, and the sample standard deviation S, for the process mean, μ, and the process standard deviation σ, i.e.,

$$\hat{C}_{pu} = \frac{\xi_U - \bar{X}}{3S}, \qquad \hat{C}_{pl} = \frac{\bar{X} - \xi_L}{3S} \tag{2.4.4}$$

and $\hat{C}_{pk} = \min(\hat{C}_{pu}, \hat{C}_{pl})$, where ξ_L and ξ_U are the lower and upper specification limits. The question is how close is $\hat{C}_{pk}$ to the true process capability value? We develop below confidence intervals for C_{pk}, which have confidence levels close to the nominal $(1-\alpha)$ in large samples. The derivation of these intervals depends on the following results that invoke mathematical derivations and can be skipped without loss of continuity:

1. In a large size random sample from a normal distribution, the sampling distribution of S is approximately normal, with mean σ and variance $\sigma^2/2n$.
2. In a random sample from a normal distribution, the sample mean, $\bar{X}$, and the sample standard deviation S are independent.
3. If A and B are events such that $\Pr\{A\} = 1 - \alpha/2$ and $\Pr\{B\} = 1 - \alpha/2$, then $\Pr\{A \cap B\} \geq 1 - \alpha$. (This inequality is called the **Bonferroni inequality**.)

In order to simplify notation, let

$$\rho_1 = C_{pl}, \quad \rho_2 = C_{pu} \quad \text{and} \quad \omega = C_{pk}.$$

Notice that since $\bar{X}$ is distributed like $N\left(\mu, \frac{\sigma^2}{n}\right)$, $\bar{X} - \xi_L$ is distributed like $N\left(\mu - \xi_L, \frac{\sigma^2}{n}\right)$. Furthermore, by the above results 1 and 2, the distribution of $\bar{X} - \xi_L - 3S\rho_1$ in large samples is like that of

$$N\left(0, \frac{\sigma^2}{n}\left(1 + \frac{9}{2}\rho_1^2\right)\right).$$

It follows that, in large samples,

$$\frac{(\bar{X} - \xi_L - 3S\rho_1)^2}{\frac{S^2}{n}\left(1 + \frac{9}{2}\rho_1^2\right)}$$

is distributed like $F[1, n-1]$. Or,

$$\Pr\left\{\frac{(\bar{X} - \xi_L - 3S\rho_1)^2}{\frac{S^2}{n}\left(1 + \frac{9}{2}\rho_1^2\right)} \leq F_{1-\alpha/2}[1, n-1]\right\} = 1 - \alpha/2. \tag{2.4.5}$$

Thus, let $\rho_{1,\alpha}^{(L)}$ and $\rho_{1,\alpha}^{(U)}$ be the two real roots (if they exist) of the quadratic equation in ρ_1

$$(\bar{X} - \xi_L)^2 - 6S\rho_1(\bar{X} - \xi_L) + 9S^2\rho_1^2 = F_{1-\alpha/2}[1, n-1]\frac{S^2}{n}\left(1 + \frac{9}{2}\rho_1^2\right). \tag{2.4.6}$$

Equivalently, $\rho_{1,\alpha}^{(L)}$ and $\rho_{1,\alpha}^{(U)}$ are the two real roots ($\rho_{1,\alpha}^{(L)} \leq \rho_{1,\alpha}^{(U)}$) of the quadratic equation

$$9S^2\left(1-\frac{F_{1-\alpha/2}[1,n-1]}{2n}\right)\rho_1^2 - 6S(\bar{X}-\xi_L)\rho_1 + \left((\bar{X}-\xi_L)^2 - \frac{F_{1-\alpha/2}[1,n-1]}{S^2 n}\right) = 0. \quad (2.4.7)$$

Substituting in this equation $(\bar{X}-\xi_L) = 3S\hat{C}_{pl}$, we obtain the equation

$$\left(1-\frac{F_{1-\alpha/2}[1,n-1]}{2n}\right)\rho_1^2 - 2\hat{C}_{pl}\rho_1 + \left(\hat{C}_{pl}^2 - \frac{F_{1-\alpha/2}[1,n-1]}{9n}\right) = 0. \quad (2.4.8)$$

We assume that n satisfies $n > \frac{F_{1-\alpha}[1,n-1]}{2}$. Under this condition,

$$1-\frac{F_{1-\alpha/2}[1,n-1]}{2n} > 0,$$

and the two real roots of the quadratic equation are

$$\rho_{1,\alpha}^{(U,L)} = \frac{\hat{C}_{pl} \pm \sqrt{\frac{F_{1-\alpha/2}[1,n-1]}{n}}\left(\frac{\hat{C}_{pl}^2}{2} + \frac{1}{9}\left(1-\frac{F_{1-\alpha/2}[1,n-1]}{2n}\right)\right)^{1/2}}{1-\frac{F_{1-\alpha/2}[1,n-1]}{2n}}. \quad (2.4.9)$$

From the above inequalities, it follows that $(\rho_{1,\alpha}^{(L)}, \rho_{1,\alpha}^{(U)})$ is a confidence interval for ρ_1 at confidence level $1-\alpha/2$.

Similarly, $(\rho_{2,\alpha}^{(L)}, \rho_{2,\alpha}^{(U)})$ is a confidence interval for ρ_2, at confidence level $1-\alpha/2$, where $\rho_{2,\alpha}^{(U,L)}$ are obtained by replacing $\hat{C}_{pl}$ by $\hat{C}_{pu}$ in the above formula of $\rho_{1,\alpha}^{(U,L)}$. Finally, from the Bonferroni inequality and the fact that $C_{pk} = \min\{C_{pl}, C_{pu}\}$, we obtain that confidence limits for C_{pk}, at level of confidence $(1-\alpha)$, are given by

$$C_{pk}^{(L)} = \min\left(\rho_{1,\alpha}^{(L)}, \rho_{2,\alpha}^{(L)}\right)$$

$$C_{pk}^{(U)} = \min\left(\rho_{1,\alpha}^{(U)}, \rho_{2,\alpha}^{(U)}\right).$$

Example 2.1 In the present example, we illustrate the computation of the confidence interval for C_{pk}. Suppose that the specification limits are $\xi_L = -1$ and $\xi_U = 1$. Suppose that $\mu = 0$ and $\sigma = 1/3$. In this case, $C_{pk} = 1$. We simulate now, using Python, a sample of size $n = 20$, from a normal distribution with mean $\mu = 0$ and standard deviation $\sigma = 1/3$.

```
np.random.seed(seed=1) # fix random seed for reproducibility
X = stats.norm.rvs(size=20, scale=1/3)
Xbar = np.mean(X)
S = np.std(X)
```

We obtain a random sample with $\bar{X} = -0.04445$ and standard deviation $S = 0.3666$.

```
Cpl = (Xbar - (-1)) / (3 * S)
Cpu = (1 - Xbar) / (3 * S)
Cpk = min(Cpu, Cpl)
F = stats.f.ppf(0.975, 1, 19)
```

For this sample, $\hat{C}_{pl} = 0.8688$ and $\hat{C}_{pu} = 0.9497$. Thus, the estimate of C_{pk} is $\hat{C}_{pk} = 0.9497$. For $\alpha = 0.05$, $F_{0.975}[1, 19] = 5.9216$. Obviously, $n = 20 > \frac{F_{0.975}[1,19]}{2} = 2.9608$. According to the formula,

$$\rho_{1,0.05}^{(U,L)} = \frac{0.8688 \pm \sqrt{\frac{5.9216}{20}} \left(\frac{(0.8688)^2}{2} + \frac{1-\frac{5.9216}{40}}{9} \right)^{1/2}}{1 - \frac{5.9216}{40}}.$$

```
b = 1 - F/40
a = np.sqrt(F/20) * np.sqrt( Cpl**2/2 + b/9)
rho_1U = (Cpl + a) / b
rho_1L = (Cpl - a) / b
a = np.sqrt(F/20) * np.sqrt( Cpu**2/2 + b/9)
rho_2U = (Cpu + a) / b
rho_2L = (Cpu - a) / b
```

Thus, $\rho_{1,0.05}^{(L)} = 0.581$ and $\rho_{1,0.05}^{(U)} = 1.4586$. Similarly, $\rho_{2,0.05}^{(L)} = 0.6429$ and $\rho_{2,0.05}^{(U)} = 1.5865$. Therefore, the confidence interval, at level 0.95, for C_{pk} is (0.581, 1.4586) (0.5859, 1.4687). ■

2.5 Seven Tools for Process Control and Process Improvement

In this section, we review seven tools that have proven extremely effective in helping organizations control processes and implement process improvement projects. Some of these tools were already presented. For completeness, all the tools are briefly reviewed here.

The preface to the English edition of the famous text by Ishikawa (1986) on Quality Control states: "the book was written to introduce quality control practices in Japan which contributed tremendously to the country's economic and industrial

<table>
<tr><th rowspan="2">DEFECT</th><th colspan="4">Period 7</th><th colspan="4">Period 8</th><th rowspan="2">Total</th></tr>
<tr><th>Wk 1</th><th>Wk 2</th><th>Wk 3</th><th>Wk 4</th><th>Wk 1</th><th>Wk 2</th><th>Wk 3</th><th>Wk 4</th></tr>
<tr><td>Contamination</td><td>||</td><td></td><td>||||</td><td>||</td><td>||</td><td>|||</td><td>|</td><td>|||</td><td>17</td></tr>
<tr><td>Mixed Product</td><td></td><td></td><td>|</td><td>||</td><td>|||</td><td></td><td>|</td><td></td><td>7</td></tr>
<tr><td>Wrong Product</td><td>|||</td><td></td><td></td><td>|</td><td>||</td><td></td><td>||</td><td>||||</td><td>12</td></tr>
<tr><td>Electrical</td><td>|</td><td>||||</td><td>|</td><td>卌</td><td>||</td><td>||</td><td>卌</td><td>||</td><td>22</td></tr>
<tr><td>Bent Leads</td><td>||</td><td></td><td>|</td><td></td><td></td><td>|</td><td>||</td><td></td><td>6</td></tr>
<tr><td>Chips</td><td></td><td>||</td><td></td><td></td><td></td><td></td><td></td><td></td><td>2</td></tr>
<tr><td>Permanency</td><td>|</td><td></td><td>||</td><td></td><td></td><td>|</td><td></td><td></td><td>4</td></tr>
<tr><td>Total</td><td>9</td><td>6</td><td>9</td><td>10</td><td>9</td><td>7</td><td>11</td><td>9</td><td>70</td></tr>
</table>

Fig. 2.15 A typical check sheet

development." The Japanese work force did indeed master an elementary set of tools that helped them improve processes. Seven of the tools were nicknamed the "magnificent seven," and they are: The flow chart, the check sheet, the run chart, the histogram, the Pareto chart, the scatterplot, and the cause and effect diagram.

Flow Charts Flow charts are used to describe a process being studied or to describe a desired sequence of a new, improved process. Often this is the first step taken by a team looking for ways to improve a process. The differences between how a process could work and how it actually does work expose redundancies, misunderstandings, and general inefficiencies.

Check Sheets Check sheets are basic manual data collection mechanisms. They consist of forms designed to tally the total number of occurrences of certain events by category. They are usually the starting point of data collection efforts. In setting up a check sheet, one needs to agree on the categories definitions, the data collection time frame, and the actual data collection method. An example of a check sheet is provided in Fig. 2.15.

Run Charts Run charts are employed to visually represent data collected over time. They are also called connected time plots. Trends and consistent patterns are easily identified on run charts. Example of a run chart is given in Fig. 2.2.

Histograms The histogram was presented in Section 1.4 of *Modern Statistics* (Kenett et al. 2022b) as a graphical display of the distribution of measurements collected as a sample. It shows the frequency or number of observations of a particular value or within a specified group. Histograms are used extensively in process capability studies to provide clues about the characteristics of the process generating the data. However, as we saw in Sect. 2.3, they ignore information on the order by which the data were collected.

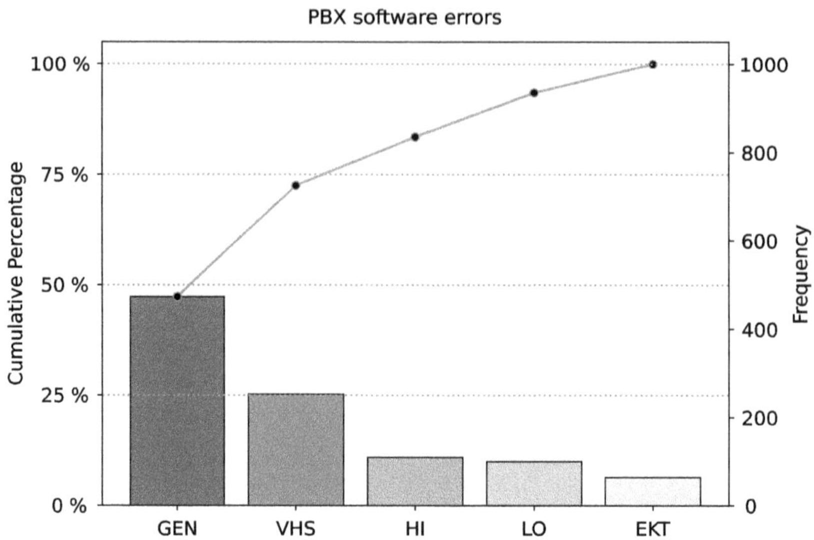

Fig. 2.16 Pareto chart of software errors

Pareto Charts Pareto charts are used extensively in modern organizations. These charts help to focus on the important few causes for trouble. When observations are collected and classified into different categories using valid and clear criteria, one can construct a Pareto chart. The Pareto chart is a display, using bar graphs sorted in descending order, of the relative importance of events such as errors, by category. The importance can be determined by the frequency of occurrence or weighted, for example, by considering the product of occurrence and cost. Superimposed on the bars is a cumulative curve that helps point out the important few categories that contain most of cases. Pareto charts are used to choose the starting point for problem solving, monitor changes, or identify the basic cause of a problem. Their usefulness stems from the Pareto principle that states that in any group of factors contributing to a common effect, a relative few (20%) account for most of the effect (80%). A Pareto chart of software errors found in testing a PBX electronic switch is presented in Fig. 2.16. Errors are labeled according to the software unit where they occurred. For example, the "EKT" (Electronic Key Telephone) category makes up 6.5% of the errors. What can we learn from this about the software development process? The "GEN," "VHS," and "HI" categories account for over 80% of the errors. These are the causes of problems on which major improvement efforts should initially concentrate. Section 2.6 discusses a statistical test for comparing Pareto charts. Such tests are necessary if one wants to distinguish between differences that can be attributed to random noise and significant differences that should be investigated for identifying an assignable cause.

Scatterplots Scatterplots are used to exhibit what happens to one variable, when another variable changes. Such information is needed in order to test a theory

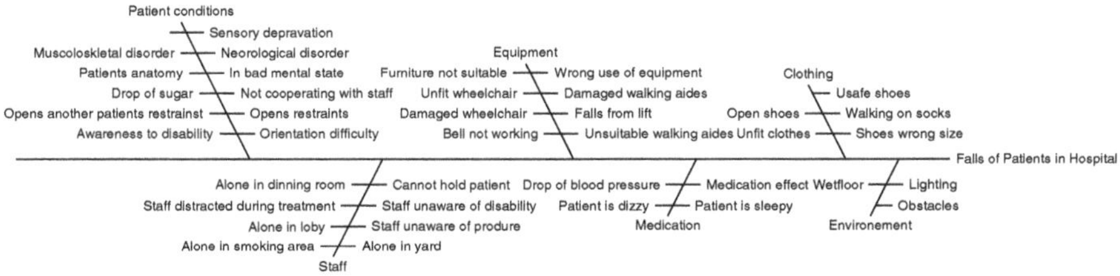

Fig. 2.17 A cause and effect diagram of patient falls during hospitalization

or make forecasts. For example, one might want to verify the theory that the relative number of errors found in engineering drawings declines with increasing drawing sizes.

Cause and Effect Diagrams Cause and effect diagrams (also called **fishbone charts** or **Ishikawa diagrams**) are used to identify, explore, and display all the possible causes of a problem or event. The diagram is usually completed in a meeting of individuals who have firsthand knowledge of the problem investigated. Figure 2.17 shows a cause and effect diagram listing causes for falls of hospitalized patients. A typical group to convene for completing such a diagram consists of nurses, physicians, administrative staff, housekeeping personnel, and physiotherapists. It is standard practice to weight the causes by impact on the problem investigated and then initiate projects to reduce the harmful effects of the main causes. Cause and effect diagrams can be derived after data were collected and presented, for example, using a Pareto chart or be entirely based on collective experience without supporting data.

The successful efforts of previous improvement are data-driven. In attempting to reduce levels of defects, or output variability, a team will typically begin by collecting data and charting the process. Flow charts and check sheets are used in these early stages. Run charts, histograms, and Pareto charts can then be prepared from the data collected on check sheets or otherwise. Diagnosing the current process is carried out, using in addition scatterplots and cause and effect diagrams. Once solutions for improvement are implemented, their impact can be assessed using run charts, histograms, and Pareto charts. A statistical test for comparing Pareto charts is presented next.

2.6 Statistical Analysis of Pareto Charts

Pareto charts are often compared over time or across processes. In such comparisons, one needs to know whether differences between two Pareto charts should be attributed to random variation or to special significant causes. In this section, we present a statistical test that is used to flag statistically significant differences between two Pareto charts (Kenett 1991). Once the classification of observations into different categories is completed, we have the actual number of observations, per category. The reference Pareto chart is a Pareto chart constructed in an earlier time period or on a different, but comparable, process. Other terms for the reference Pareto chart are the benchmark or standard Pareto chart. The proportion of observations in each category of the reference Pareto chart is the expected proportion. We expect to find these proportions in Pareto charts of data collected under the conditions of the reference Pareto chart. The expected number of observations in the different categories of the Pareto chart is computed by multiplying the total number of observations in a Pareto chart by the corresponding expected proportion. The standardized residuals are assessing the significance of the deviations between the new Pareto chart and the reference Pareto chart. The statistical test relies on computation of standardized residuals:

$$Z_i = \frac{n_i - Np_i}{[Np_i(1 - p_i)]^{1/2}}, \quad i = 1, \cdots, K, \tag{2.6.1}$$

where:

N = the total number of observations in Pareto chart
p_i = the proportion of observations in category i, in reference Pareto chart
Np_i = the expected number of observations in category i, given a total of N observations
n_i = the actual number of observations in category i

In performing the statistical test, one assumes that observations are independently classified into distinct categories. The actual classification into categories might depend on the data gathering protocol. Typically, the classification relies on the first error cause encountered. A different test procedure could therefore produce different data. The statistical test presented here is more powerful than the standard chi-squared test. It will therefore recognize differences between a reference Pareto chart and a current Pareto chart that will not be determined as significant by the chi-squared test.

In order to perform the statistical analysis, we first list the error categories in a fixed order. A natural order to use is the alphabetic order of the categories' names. This organization of the data is necessary in order to permit meaningful comparisons. The test itself consists of seven steps. The last step is being an interpretation of the results. To demonstrate these steps, we use data on timecard errors presented in Table 2.3.

Example 2.2 The data come from a monitoring system of timecard entries in a medium size company with 15 departments. During a management meeting, the human resources manager of the company was asked to initiate an improvement project aimed at reducing timecard errors. The manager asked to see a reference Pareto chart of last months' timecard errors by department. Departments # 6, 7, 8, and 12 were responsible for 46% of the timecard errors. The manager appointed a special improvement team to learn the causes for these errors. The team

Table 2.3 Timecard errors data in 15 departments

Department #	Reference Pareto	Current Pareto
1	23	14
2	42	7
3	37	85
4	36	19
5	17	23
6	50	13
7	60	48
8	74	59
9	30	2
10	25	0
11	10	12
12	54	14
13	23	30
14	24	20
15	11	0

recommended to change the input format of the time card. The new format was implemented throughout the company. Three weeks later, a new Pareto chart was prepared from 346 newly reported timecard errors. A statistical analysis of the new Pareto chart was performed in order to determine what department had a significant change in its relative contribution of timecard errors.

The steps in applying the statistical test are:

1. Compute for each department its proportion of observations in the reference Pareto chart:

$$p_1 = 23/516 = 0.04457$$

$$\vdots$$

$$p_{15} = 11/516 = 0.0213.$$

2. Compute the total number of observations in the new Pareto chart:

$$N = 14 + 7 + 85 + \cdots + 20 = 346.$$

3. Compute the expected number of observations in department # i, $E_i = Np_i$, $i = 1, \cdots, 15$.

$$E_1 = 346 \times 0.04457 = 15.42$$

$$\vdots$$

$$E_{15} = 346 \times 0.0213 = 7.38.$$

Table 2.4 Critical values for standardized residuals

	Significance level		
K	10%	5%	1%
4	1.95	2.24	2.81
5	2.05	2.32	2.88
6	2.12	2.39	2.93
7	2.18	2.44	2.99
8	2.23	2.49	3.04
9	2.28	2.53	3.07
10	2.32	2.57	3.10
20	2.67	2.81	3.30
30	2.71	2.94	3.46

Table 2.5 Table of standardized residuals for the timecards error

Department #	Pareto	Ei	Zi	
1	14	15	−0.26	
2	7	28	−4.13	*
3	85	25	12.50	*
4	19	24	−1.06	
5	23	11	3.61	*
6	13	34	−3.82	*
7	48	40	1.34	
8	59	50	1.38	
9	2	20	−4.14	*
10	0	17	−4.26	*
11	12	7	1.95	
12	14	36	−3.86	*
13	30	15	3.91	*
14	20	16	1.02	
15	0	7	−2.61	

4. Compute the standardized residuals: $Z_i = (N_i - Np_i)/(Np_i(1 - p_i))^{1/2}$, $i = 1, \ldots, 15$.

$$Z_1 = (14 - 15.42)/[15.42(1 - 0.04457)]^{1/2} = -0.37$$

$$\vdots$$

$$Z_{15} = (0 - 7.38)/[7.38(1 - 0.0213)]^{1/2} = -2.75.$$

5. Look up Table 2.4 for $K = 15$. Interpolate between $K = 10$ and $K = 20$. For $\alpha = 0.01$ significance level, the critical value is approximately $(3.10+3.30)/2 = 3.20$.
6. Identify categories with standardized residuals larger, in absolute value, than 3.20. Table 2.5 indicates with a star the departments where the proportion of errors was significantly different from that in the reference Pareto.

7. Departments # 2, 3, 5, 6, 9, 10, 12, and 13 are flagged with a $*$ that indicates significant changes between the new Pareto data from the reference Pareto chart. In category 3, we expected 25 occurrences, a much smaller number than the actual 85.

■

The statistical test enables us to systematically compare two Pareto charts with the same categories. Focusing on the differences between Pareto charts complements the analysis of trends and changes in overall process error levels. Increases or decreases in such error levels may result from changes across all error categories. On the other hand, there may be no changes in error levels but significant changes in the mix of errors across categories. The statistical analysis reveals such changes. Another advantage of the statistical procedure is that it can apply to different time frames. For example, the reference Pareto can cover a period of one year, and the current Pareto can span a period of three weeks.

The critical values are computed on the basis of the **Bonferroni Inequality** approximation. This inequality states that, since we are examining simultaneously K standardized residuals, the overall significance level is not more than K times the significance level of an individual comparison. Dividing the overall significance level of choice by K, and using the normal approximation, produces the critical values in Table 2.4. For more details on this procedure, see Kenett (1991).

2.7 The Shewhart Control Charts

The Shewhart control charts is a detection procedure in which every h units of time a sample of size n is drawn from the process. Let θ denote a parameter of the distribution of the observed random sample $x_1, \cdots, x_n$. Let $\hat{\theta}_n$ denote an appropriate estimate of θ. If θ_0 is a desired operation level for the process, we construct around θ_0 two limits UCL and LCL. As long as $\text{LCL} \le \hat{\theta}_n \le \text{UCL}$, we say that the process is under statistical control.

More specifically, suppose that $x_1, x_2, \cdots$ are normally distributed and independent. Every h hours (time units) a sample of n observations is taken.

Suppose that when the process is under control $x_i \sim N(\theta_0, \sigma^2)$ and that σ^2 is known. We set $\hat{\theta}_n \equiv \bar{x}_n = \frac{1}{n}\sum_{j=1}^{n} x_j$. The control limits are

$$\begin{aligned} \text{UCL} &= \theta_0 + 3\frac{\sigma}{\sqrt{n}} \\ \text{LCL} &= \theta_0 - 3\frac{\sigma}{\sqrt{n}}. \end{aligned} \qquad (2.7.1)$$

The warning limits are set at

$$\text{UWL} = \theta_0 + 2\frac{\sigma}{\sqrt{n}}$$
$$\text{LWL} = \theta_0 - 2\frac{\sigma}{\sqrt{n}}. \tag{2.7.2}$$

Notice that:

(i) The samples are independent.
(ii) All $\bar{x}_n$ are distributed as $N\left(\theta_0, \frac{\sigma^2}{n}\right)$ as long as the process is under control.
(iii) If α is the probability of observing $\bar{x}_n$ outside the control limits, when $\theta = \theta_0$, then $\alpha = 0.0027$. We expect one every $N = 370$ samples to yield a value of $\bar{x}_n$ outside the control limits.
(iv) We expect about 5% of the $\bar{x}_n$ points to lie outside the warning limits, when the process is under control. Thus, testing the null hypothesis $H_0 : \theta = \theta_0$ against $H_1 : \theta \neq \theta_0$, we may choose a level of significance $\alpha = 0.05$ and use the limits UWL, LWL as rejection limits. In the control case, the situation is equivalent to that of simultaneously (or repeatedly) testing many hypotheses. For this reason, we consider a much smaller α, like $\alpha = 0.0027$, derived from the use of the 3-sigma limits.
(v) In many applications of the Shewhart 3-sigma control charts, the samples taken are of small size, $n = 4$ or $n = 5$, and the frequency of samples is high (h small). Shewhart recommended such small samples in order to reduce the possibility that a shift in θ will happen during sampling. On the other hand, if the samples are picked very frequently, there is a higher chance to detect a shift early. The question of how frequently to sample and what should be the sample size is related to the idea of rational subgroups discussed earlier in Sect. 2.3. An economic approach to the determination of rational subgroups will be presented in Sect. 3.3.1.

Figure 2.18 shows a Shewhart control chart of a process where all samples are falling inside the control limits. We provide now formulae for the control limits of various Shewhart type control charts.

2.7.1 Control Charts for Attributes

We consider here control charts when the control statistic is the sample fraction defectives $\hat{p}_i = \frac{x_i}{n_i}$ $i = 1, \cdots, N$. Here n_i is the size of the ith sample, and x_i is the number of defective items in the ith sample.

Given N samples, we estimate the common parameter θ by $\hat{\theta} = \frac{\sum_{i=1}^{N} x_i}{\sum_{i=1}^{N} n_i}$. The upper and lower control limits are

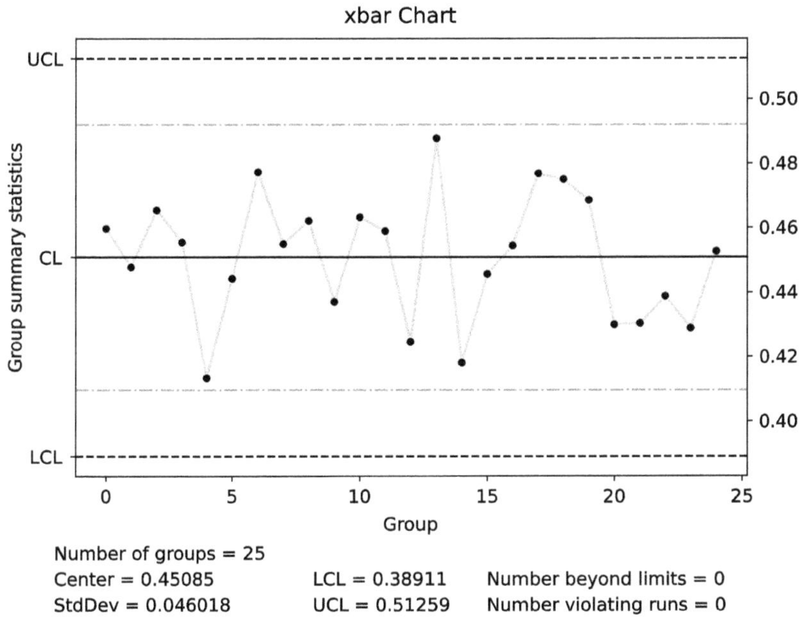

Fig. 2.18 Shewhart control chart

$$
\begin{aligned}
\mathrm{LCL} &= \hat{\theta} - 3\sqrt{\frac{\hat{\theta}(1-\hat{\theta})}{n}} \\
\mathrm{UCL} &= \hat{\theta} + 3\sqrt{\frac{\hat{\theta}(1-\hat{\theta})}{n}}.
\end{aligned}
\tag{2.7.3}
$$

In Table 2.6, we present, for example, the number of defective items found in random samples of size $n = 100$, drawn daily from a production line.

In Fig. 2.19, we present the control chart for the data of Table 2.6. We see that there is indication that the fraction defectives in two days were significantly high, but the process on the whole remained under control during the month. Deleting these two days, we can revise the control chart, by computing a modified estimate of θ. We obtain a new value of $\hat{\theta} = 139/2900 = 0.048$. This new estimator yields a revised upper control limit

$$
\mathrm{UCL}' = 0.112.
$$

Table 2.6 The number of defects in daily samples (sample size is $n = 100$)

Sample/day	# of Defects	Sample/day	# of Defects
i	x_i	i	x_i
1	6	16	6
2	8	17	4
3	8	18	6
4	13	19	8
5	6	20	2
6	6	21	7
7	9	22	4
8	7	23	4
9	1	24	2
10	8	25	1
11	5	26	5
12	2	27	15
13	4	28	1
14	5	29	4
15	4	30	1
		31	5

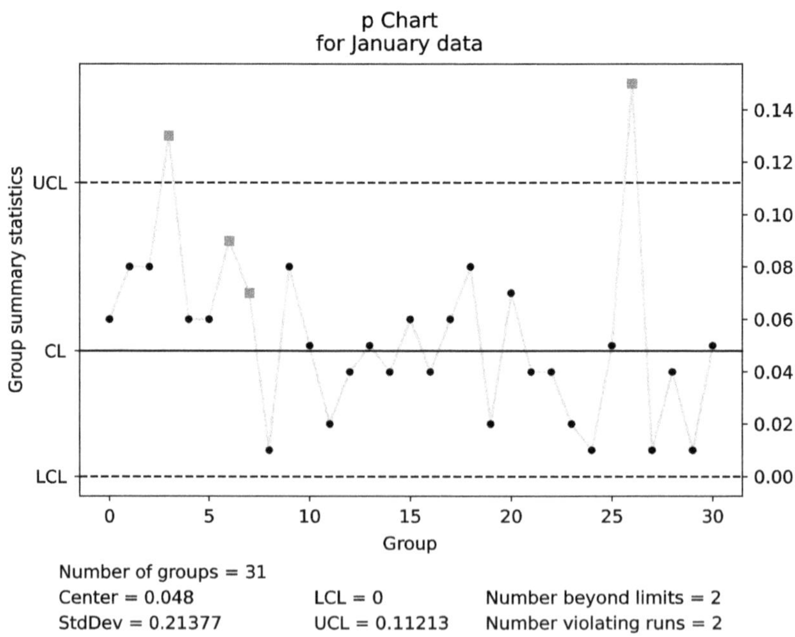

Fig. 2.19 p-chart for January data

2.7.2 *Control Charts for Variables*

2.7.2.1 $\bar{X}$-Charts

After the process has been observed for k sampling periods, we can compute estimates of the process mean and standard deviation. The estimate of the process mean is

$$\bar{\bar{X}} = \frac{1}{k}\sum_{i=1}^{k} \bar{X}_i .$$

This will be the center line for the control chart. The process standard deviation can be estimated using either the average sample standard deviation

$$\hat{\sigma} = \bar{S}/c(n), \tag{2.7.4}$$

where

$$\bar{S} = \frac{1}{k}\sum_{i=1}^{k} S_i ,$$

or the average sample range

$$\hat{\hat{\sigma}} = \bar{R}/d(n), \tag{2.7.5}$$

where

$$\bar{R} = \frac{1}{k}\sum_{i=1}^{k} R_i .$$

The factors $c(n)$ and $d(n)$ guarantee that we obtain unbiased estimates of σ. We can show, for example, that $E(\bar{S}) = \sigma c(n)$, where

$$c(n) = \left[\Gamma(n/2)/\Gamma\left(\frac{n-1}{2}\right)\right]\sqrt{2/(n-1)}. \tag{2.7.6}$$

Moreover, $E\{R_n\} = \sigma d(n)$, where from the theory of order statistics (see Section 2.7 in *Modern Statistics*, Kenett et al. 2022b), we obtain that

$$d(n) = \frac{n(n-1)}{2\pi}\int_0^{\infty} y \int_{-\infty}^{\infty} \exp\left\{-\frac{x^2+(y+x)^2}{2}\right\}[\Phi(x+y)-\Phi(x)]^{n-2}\,\mathrm{d}x\,\mathrm{d}y. \tag{2.7.7}$$

Table 2.7 Factors $c(n)$ and $d(n)$ for estimating σ

n	$c(n)$	$d(n)$
2	0.7979	1.2838
3	0.8862	1.6926
4	0.9213	2.0587
5	0.9400	2.3259
6	0.9515	2.5343
7	0.9594	2.7044
8	0.9650	2.8471
9	0.9693	2.9699
10	0.9727	3.0774

In Table 2.7, we present the factors $c(n)$ and $d(n)$ for $n = 2, 3, \cdots, 10$.

The control limits are now computed as

$$\text{UCL} = \bar{\bar{X}} + 3\hat{\sigma}/\sqrt{n} \tag{2.7.8}$$

and

$$\text{LCL} = \bar{\bar{X}} - 3\hat{\sigma}/\sqrt{n}.$$

Despite the wide use of the sample ranges for estimating the process standard deviation, this method is neither very efficient nor robust. It is popular only because the sample range is easier to compute than the sample standard deviation. However, since many hand calculators now have built-in programs for computing the sample standard deviation, the computational advantage of the range should not be considered. In any case, the sample ranges should not be used when the sample size is greater than 10.

Example 2.3 We illustrate the construction of an $\bar{X}$-chart for the data in Table 2.8.

These measurements represent the length (in cm) of the electrical contacts of relays in samples of size five, taken hourly from the running process. Both the sample standard deviation and the sample range are computed for each sample, for the purposes of illustration. The center line for the control chart is $\bar{\bar{X}} = 2.005$. From Table 2.7, we find for $n = 5$, $c(5) = 0.9400$. Let

$$A_1 = 3/(c(5)\sqrt{n}) = 1.427.$$

The control limits are given by

$$\text{UCL} = \bar{\bar{X}} + A_1\bar{S} = 2.186$$

Table 2.8 20 samples of 5 electric contact lengths

Hour								
i	x_1	x_2	x_3	x_4	x_5	$\bar{X}$	S	R
1	1.9890	2.1080	2.0590	2.0110	2.0070	2.0348	0.04843	0.11900
2	1.8410	1.8900	2.0590	1.9160	1.9800	1.9372	0.08456	0.21800
3	2.0070	2.0970	2.0440	2.0810	2.0510	2.0560	0.03491	0.09000
4	2.0940	2.2690	2.0910	2.0970	1.9670	2.1036	0.10760	0.30200
5	1.9970	1.8140	1.9780	1.9960	1.9830	1.9536	0.07847	0.18300
6	2.0540	1.9700	2.1780	2.1010	1.9150	2.0436	0.10419	0.26300
7	2.0920	2.0300	1.8560	1.9060	1.9750	1.9718	0.09432	0.23600
8	2.0330	1.8500	2.1680	2.0850	2.0230	2.0318	0.11674	0.31800
9	2.0960	2.0960	1.8840	1.7800	2.0050	1.9722	0.13825	0.31600
10	2.0510	2.0380	1.7390	1.9530	1.9170	1.9396	0.12552	0.31200
11	1.9520	1.7930	1.8780	2.2310	1.9850	1.9678	0.16465	0.43800
12	2.0060	2.1410	1.9000	1.9430	1.8410	1.9662	0.11482	0.30000
13	2.1480	2.0130	2.0660	2.0050	2.0100	2.0484	0.06091	0.14300
14	1.8910	2.0890	2.0920	2.0230	1.9750	2.0140	0.08432	0.20100
15	2.0930	1.9230	1.9750	2.0140	2.0020	2.0014	0.06203	0.17000
16	2.2300	2.0580	2.0660	2.1990	2.1720	2.1450	0.07855	0.17200
17	1.8620	2.1710	1.9210	1.9800	1.7900	1.9448	0.14473	0.38100
18	2.0560	2.1250	1.9210	1.9200	1.9340	1.9912	0.09404	0.20500
19	1.8980	2.0000	2.0890	1.9020	2.0820	1.9942	0.09285	0.19100
20	2.0490	1.8790	2.0540	1.9260	2.0080	1.9832	0.07760	0.17500
					Average	2.0050	0.09537	0.23665
						$\bar{\bar{X}}$	$\bar{S}$	$\bar{R}$

and

$$\text{LCL} = \bar{\bar{X}} - A_1\bar{S} = 1.824.$$

The resulting control chart is shown in Fig. 2.20. If we use the **sample ranges** to determine the control limits, we first find that $d(5) = 2.326$ and

$$A_2 = 3/(d(5)\sqrt{n}) = 0.577.$$

This gives us control limits of

$$\text{UCL}' = \bar{\bar{X}} + A_2\bar{R} = 2.142$$

$$\text{LCL}' = \bar{\bar{X}} - A_2\bar{R} = 1.868.$$

■

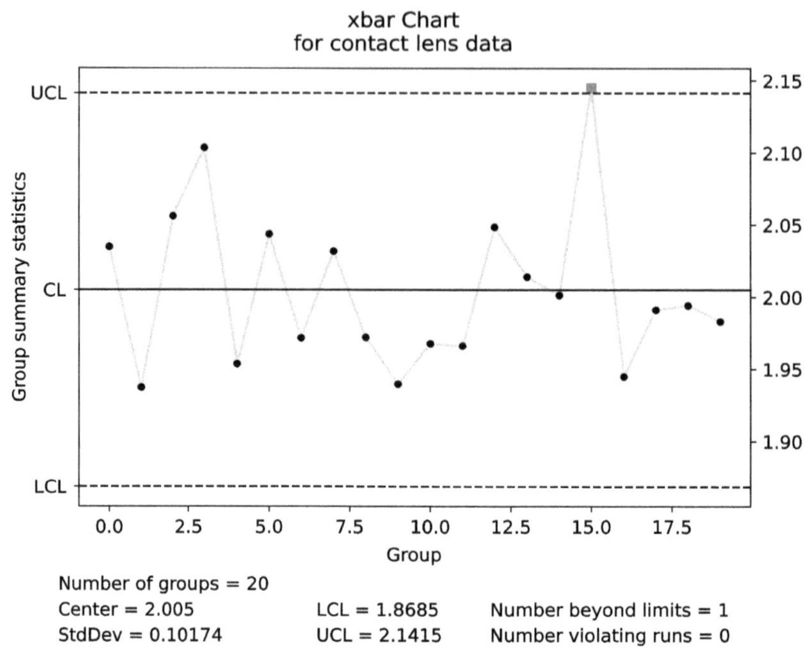

Fig. 2.20 $\bar{X}$-control chart for contact data

2.7.2.2 *S*-Charts and *R*-Charts

As discussed earlier, control of the process variability can be as important as control of the process mean. Two types of control charts are commonly used for this purpose: an R-chart, based on sample ranges, and an S-chart, based on sample standard deviations. Since ranges are easier to compute than standard deviations, R-charts are probably more common in practice. The R-chart is not very efficient. In fact, its efficiency declines rapidly as the sample size increases, and the sample range should not be used for a sample size greater than 5. However, we shall discuss both types of charts.

To construct control limits for the S-chart, we will use a normal approximation to the sampling distribution of the sample standard deviation, S. This means that we will use control limits

$$\mathrm{LCL} = \bar{S} - 3\hat{\sigma}_s \tag{2.7.9}$$

and

$$\mathrm{UCL} = \bar{S} + 3\hat{\sigma}_s,$$

where $\hat{\sigma}_s$ represents an estimate of the standard deviation of S. This standard deviation is

$$\sigma_s = \sigma/\sqrt{2(n-1)}. \tag{2.7.10}$$

Using the unbiased estimate $\hat{\sigma} = \bar{S}/c(n)$, we obtain

$$\hat{\sigma}_s = \bar{S}/(c(n)\sqrt{2(n-1)}), \tag{2.7.11}$$

and hence, the control limits

$$\text{LCL} = \bar{S} - 3\bar{S}/(c(n)\sqrt{2(n-1)}) = B_3\bar{S}$$

and

$$\text{UCL} = \bar{S} + 3\bar{S}/(c(n)\sqrt{2(n-1)}) = B_4\bar{S}. \tag{2.7.12}$$

The factors B_3 and B_4 can be determined from Table 2.7.

Example 2.4 Using the electrical contact data in Table 2.8, we find

$$\text{centerline} = \bar{S} = 0.095,$$

$$\text{LCL} = B_3\bar{S} = 0,$$

and

$$\text{UCL} = B_4\bar{S} = 2.089(0.095) = 0.199.$$

The S-chart is given in Fig. 2.21.

An R-chart is constructed using similar techniques, with a center line $= \bar{R}$, and control limits:

$$\text{LCL} = D_3\bar{R},$$

and

$$\text{UCL} = D_4\bar{R}, \tag{2.7.13}$$

where

$$D_3 = \left(1 - \frac{3}{d(n)\sqrt{2(n-1)}}\right)^+ \quad \text{and} \quad D_4 = \left(1 + \frac{3}{d(n)\sqrt{2(n-1)}}\right). \tag{2.7.14}$$

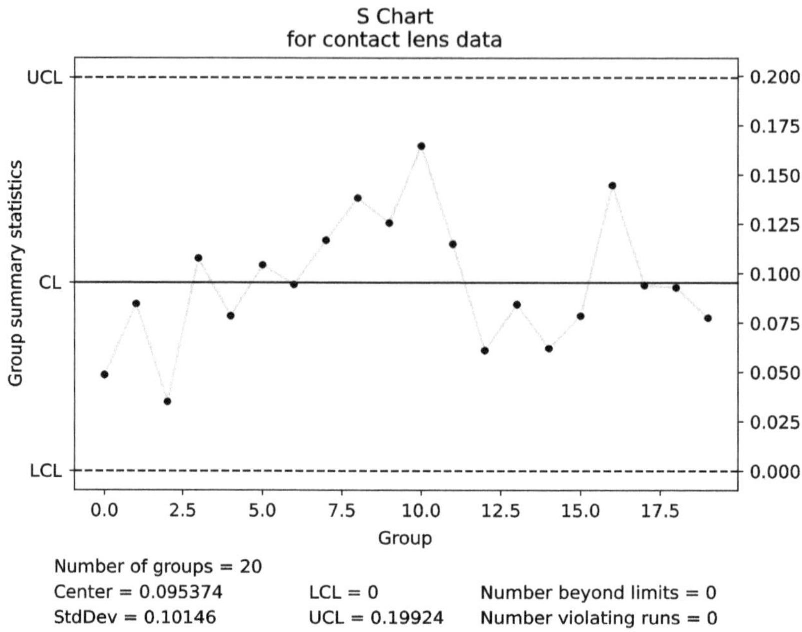

Fig. 2.21 *S*-chart for contact data

Using the data of Table 2.8, we find

$$\text{centerline} = \bar{R} = 0.237,$$

$$\text{LCL} = D_3\bar{R} = 0,$$

and

$$\text{UCL} = D_4\bar{R} = (2.114)(0.237) = 0.501.$$

The *R*-chart is shown in Fig. 2.22. ■

The decision of whether to use an *R*-chart or *S*-chart to control variability ultimately depends on which method works best in a given situation. Both methods are based on several approximations. There is, however, one additional point that should be considered. The average value of the range of n variables depends to a great extent on the sample size n. As n increases, the range increases. The *R*-chart based on 5 observations per sample will look quite different from an *R*-chart based on 10 observations. For this reason, it is difficult to visualize the variability characteristics of the process directly from the data. On the other hand, the sample standard deviation, S, used in the *S*-chart is a good estimate of the process standard deviation σ. As the sample size increases, S will tend to be even closer to the true

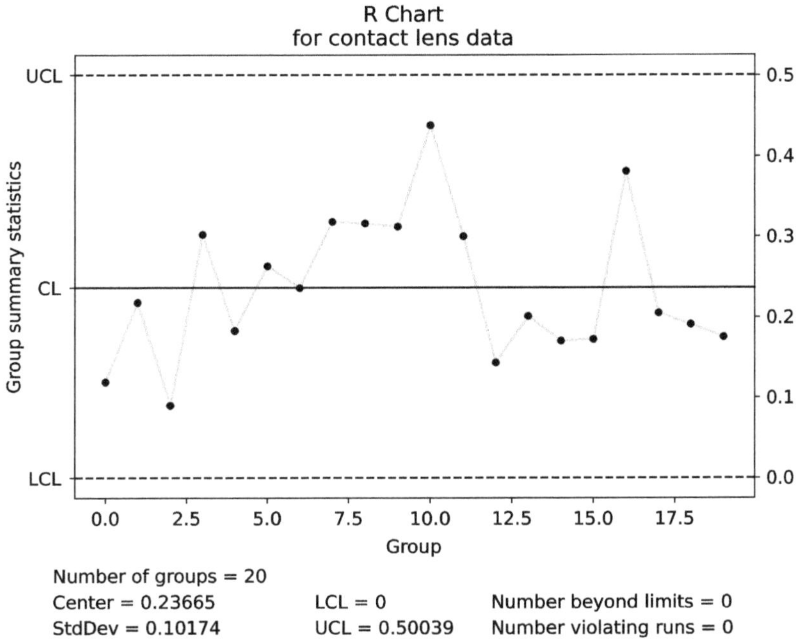

Fig. 2.22 *R*-chart for contact data

value of σ. The process standard deviation is the key to understanding the variability of the process. An alternative approach, originally proposed by Fuchs and Kenett (1987), is to determine control limits on the basis of tolerance intervals derived either analytically (Section 3.5, *Modern Statistics*, Kenett et al. 2022b) or through nonparametric bootstrapping (Section 3.10, *Modern Statistics*, Kenett et al. 2022b). We discuss this approach, in the multivariate case, in Sect. 4.5.

2.8 Process Analysis with Data Segments

In previous sections, we introduced the basic elements of statistical process control. Section 2.2 is about using a control chart for running a process under statistical control, and Sect. 2.3 is about process capability analysis that is conducted retrospectively on data to characterize a process under control and set up the control limits of a control chart. In this section, we expand on the process capability analysis by considering time-related patterns. Specifically, we focus on data segments that can show up in the data collected during process capability analysis. If such segments are detected, and investigations reveal the causes for such segments, the analyst might decide to focus on a data segment representing a steady state stable process, as opposed to the full data collected for process capability analysis. In this

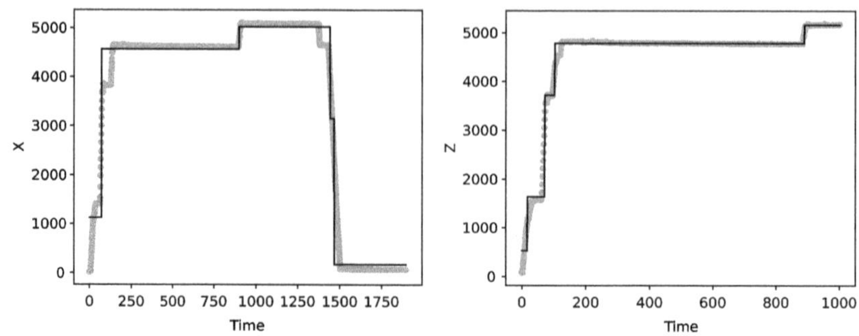

Fig. 2.23 Run charts of sensors X and Z over time

context, one will aim at identifying transient periods and not include them in the computation of control limits.

We provide here two methods for identifying such segments. One method is based on decision trees introduced in Section 7.6 of *Modern Statistics* (Kenett et al. 2022b). The second method is applying functional data analysis introduced in Section 8.1 of *Modern Statistics*. Additional options include fitting step functions to time series data using least squares, see Chapter 6 in *Modern Statistics*.

2.8.1 Data Segments Based on Decision Trees

In Fig. 2.23, we show run charts of sensors X and Z over time. The sensors are tracking a tank filling process with an impeller operating at variable speed. The process is operating at various time segments. To identify the time segments, we apply a decision tree with 4 splits with the time index as covariate. For an introduction to decision trees, see Section 7.6 of *Modern Statistics* (Kenett et al. 2022b). The decision tree identifies the time instances for the various optimal splits corresponding to a maximized difference in average level and minimum variance. We want to identify the starting and ending points of the central data segment.

```
data = mistat.load_data('PROCESS_SEGMENT')

# Load and prepare data for analysis
def sensorData(data, label):
    series = data[label]
    return pd.DataFrame({
        'Time': np.arange(len(series)),
        'values': series,
    })
sensorX = sensorData(data, 'X')
sensorZ = sensorData(data, 'Z')

# Build decision trees for segment analysis
def addSegmentAnalysis(sensor, max_leaf_nodes):
  model = tree.DecisionTreeRegressor(max_leaf_nodes=max_leaf_nodes)
  model.fit(sensor[['Time']], sensor['values'])
```

	Range	Count	Mean	SEM	[0.025	0.975]
Level 1	Time < 72	72	1125.0	33.2	1059.9	1190.0
Level 2	72 ≤ Time < 899	827	4566.8	9.8	4547.6	4586.0
Level 3	899 ≤ Time < 1443	544	5027.0	12.1	5003.3	5050.6
Level 4	1443 ≤ Time < 1467	24	3147.5	57.4	3034.8	3260.2
Level 5	1467 ≤ Time	430	170.0	13.6	143.4	196.6

```
  sensor['predicted'] = model.predict(sensor[['Time']])
  return sensor, model
sensorX, modelX = addSegmentAnalysis(sensorX, 5)
sensorZ, modelZ = addSegmentAnalysis(sensorZ, 5)

# Plot data
def plotSegmentAnalysis(sensor, label, ax):
  sensor.plot.scatter(x='Time', y='values', ax=ax, color='grey')
  ax.plot(sensor['Time'], sensor['predicted'], color='black')
  ax.set_xlabel('Time')
  ax.set_ylabel(label)

data = mistat.load_data('PROCESS_SEGMENT')
fig, axes = plt.subplots(ncols=2, figsize=(10, 4))
plotSegmentAnalysis(sensorX, 'X', axes[0])
plotSegmentAnalysis(sensorZ, 'Z', axes[1])
plt.tight_layout()
```

Figure 2.24 presents the decision trees for X and Z. The first split for the X series is at $t = 72$. The first split for the Z series is at $t = 17$.

The identified levels for sensor X are:
and the levels identified for sensor Z are:

	Range	Count	Mean	SEM	[0.025	0.975]
Level 1	Time < 17	17	527.8	28.5	471.9	583.6
Level 2	17 ≤ Time < 71	54	1641.5	16.0	1610.1	1672.8
Level 3	71 ≤ Time < 102	31	3715.7	21.1	3674.3	3757.1
Level 4	102 ≤ Time < 891	789	4784.5	4.2	4776.3	4792.7
Level 5	891 ≤ Time	111	5163.8	11.1	5141.9	5185.6

In considering the variability of sensors X and Z, we can distinguish transient states, at the beginning and end of the series, from steady states, at the central part of the series. We can then set up control limits based on mean levels and variability in steady states. For sensor X, the steady state is achieved at Level 2 ($72 \leq \text{Time} < 899$). For sensor Z, it corresponds to Level 4 ($102 \leq \text{Time} < 891$).

As shown, the decision tree provides an easy and interpretable approach to data segmentation. One should note, however, that the splits in a decision tree are done using a greedy algorithm that considers one split at a time, without accounting for follow-up steps. In that sense, decision trees reach local solutions and do not offer globally optimized solutions. This technical nuance has, at worst, little impact on data segmentation applications.

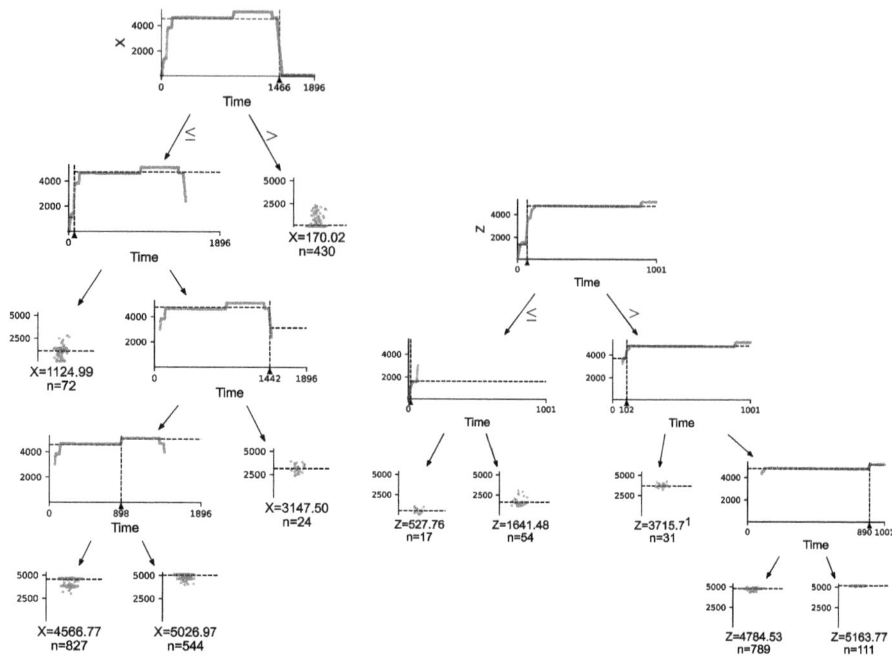

Fig. 2.24 Decision trees for sensors X (left) and Z (right) by time index

2.8.2 Data Segments Based on Functional Data Analysis

A second approach for identifying data segments is to fit functional models to the data. Specifically, we fit step functions at knots whose location was determined to minimize the residual sum of squares (SSR) using the Python package `pwlf`.

For sensor X, we fit a step function using 8 knots (9 segments). For sensor Z, we get a reasonable fit using only 5 knots (6 segments).

```
def fitPiecewiseLinearFit(sensor, segments):
  model = pwlf.PiecewiseLinFit(sensor['Time'], sensor['values'], degree=0)
  model.fit(segments)
  return model

modelX = fitPiecewiseLinearFit(sensorX, 9)
modelX = fitPiecewiseLinearFit(sensorZ, 6)
```

In Fig. 2.25, we show fits of step functions for X and Z using 8 and 5 knots, respectively. For sensor X, the step function is:

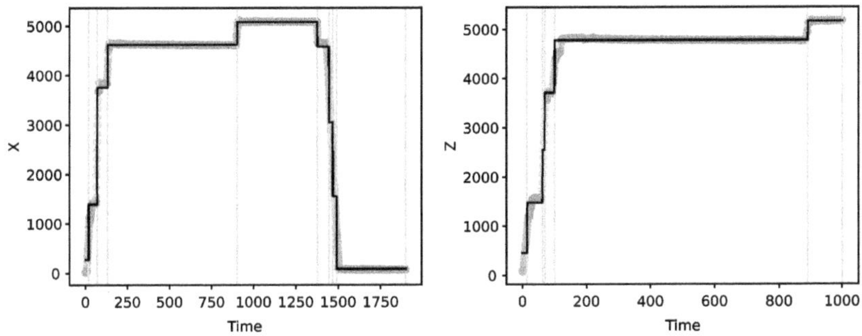

Fig. 2.25 Step function fits for sensors X (left) and Z (right) by time index. The gray vertical lines indicate the position of the knots

	Range	Prediction
Level 1	Time < 69.4	275.0
Level 2	69.4 ≤ Time < 131.6	1400.1
Level 3	131.6 ≤ Time < 902.2	3751.9
Level 4	902.2 ≤ Time < 1377.3	4628.8
Level 5	1377.3 ≤ Time < 1444.8	5086.7
Level 6	1444.8 ≤ Time < 1467.8	4580.9
Level 7	1467.8 ≤ Time < 1490.2	3049.1
Level 8	1490.2 ≤ Time < 1896.0	1556.1
Level 9	1896.0 ≤ Time	86.0

For sensor Z, we get the following result:

	Range	Prediction
Level 1	Time < 63.5	460.2
Level 2	63.5 ≤ Time < 70.6	1486.1
Level 3	70.6 ≤ Time < 101.1	2554.4
Level 4	101.1 ≤ Time < 890.1	3715.5
Level 5	890.1 ≤ Time < 1001.0	4784.3
Level 6	1001.0 ≤ Time	5163.5

The segments that can be used to characterize a process under control are $131.6 \leq \text{Time} < 902$ for X and $101.1 \leq \text{Time} < 890.1$. These segments are shorter for sensor X than the segments identified by a decision tree (Sect. 2.8.1). Functional data analysis provides, however, more degrees of freedom in terms of the functional model being used and the number of knots applied in a specific fit.

2.9 Chapter Highlights

The main concepts and definitions introduced in this chapter include:

- Statistical process control
- Chronic problems
- Common causes
- Special causes
- Assignable causes
- Sporadic spikes
- External feedback loops
- Internal feedback loops
- Control charts
- Lower control limit (LCL)
- Upper control limit (UCL)
- Upper warning limit (UWL)
- Lower warning limit (LWL)
- Process capability study
- Rational subgroups
- Process capability indexes
- Flow charts
- Check sheets
- Run charts
- Histograms
- Pareto charts
- Scatterplots
- Cause and effect diagrams
- Control charts for attributes
- Control charts for variables
- Data segments
- Decision trees
- Functional data analysis

2.10 Exercises

Exercise 2.1 Use Python and dataset **OELECT.csv** to chart the individual electrical outputs of the 99 circuits. Do you observe any trend or non-random pattern in the data? Create a $\bar{X}$-chart with Python.

Exercise 2.2 Chart the individual variability of the length of steel rods, in dataset **STEELROD.csv**. Is there any perceived assignable cause of non-randomness?

Exercise 2.3 Examine the chart of the previous exercise for possible patterns of non-randomness.

Exercise 2.4 Test the data in dataset **OTURB2.csv** for lack of randomness. In this dataset, we have three columns. In the first, we have the sample size. In the second and third, we have the sample means and standard deviation. Chart the individual means. For the historical mean, use the mean of column `xbar`. For historical standard deviation, use $(\hat{\sigma}^2/5)^{1/2}$, where $\hat{\sigma}^2$ is the pooled sample **variance**.

Exercise 2.5 A sudden change in a process lowers the process mean by one standard deviation. It has been determined that the quality characteristic being measured is approximately normally distributed and that the change had no effect on the process variance:

(a) What percentage of points are expected to fall outside the control limits on the $\bar{X}$-chart if the subgroup size is 4?
(b) Answer the same question for subgroups of size 6.
(c) Answer the same question for subgroups of size 9.

Exercise 2.6 Make capability analysis of the electric output (volts) of 99 circuits in dataset **OELECT.csv**, with target value of $\mu_0 = 220$ and $LSL = 210$, $USL = 230$.

Exercise 2.7 Estimate the capability index C_{pk} for the output of the electronic circuits, based on dataset **OELECT.csv** when $LSL = 210$ and $USL = 230$. Determine the point estimate as well as its confidence interval, with confidence level 0.95.

Exercise 2.8 Estimate the capability index for the steel rods, given in dataset **STEELROD.csv**, when the length specifications are $\xi_L = 19$ and $\xi_U = 21$ [cm] and the level of confidence is $1 - \alpha = 0.95$.

Exercise 2.9 The specification limits of the piston cycle times are 0.05 ± 0.01 s. Generate 20 cycle times at the lower level of the 7 control parameters:

(a) Compute C_p and C_{pk}.
(b) Compute a 95% confidence interval for C_{pk}.

Generate 20 cycle times at the upper level of the 7 control factors:

(c) Recompute C_p and C_{pk}.
(d) Recompute a 95% confidence interval for C_{pk}.
(e) Is there a significant difference in process capability between lower and upper operating levels in the piston simulator?

Exercise 2.10 A fiber manufacturer has a large contract that stipulates that its fiber, among other properties, has tensile strength greater than 1.800 [grams/fiber] in 95% of the fibers used. The manufacturer states the standard deviation of the process is 0.015 grams.

(a) Assuming a process under statistical control, what is the smallest nominal value of the mean that will assure compliance with the contract?

(b) Given the nominal value in part a), what are the control limits of $\bar{X}$ and S-charts for subgroups of size 6?
(c) What is the process capability, if the process mean is $\mu = 1.82$?

Exercise 2.11 The output voltage of a power supply is specified as 350 ± 5 volts DC. Subgroups of four units are drawn from every batch and submitted to special quality control tests. The data from 30 subgroups on output voltage produced $\sum_{i=1}^{30} \bar{X} = 10,950.00$ and $\sum_{i=1}^{30} R_i = 77.32$:

(a) Compute the control limits for $\bar{X}$ and R.
(b) Assuming statistical control and a normal distribution of output voltage, what properties of defective product are being made?
(c) If the power supplies are set to a nominal value of 350 volts, what is now the proportion of defective products?
(d) Compute the new control limits for $\bar{X}$ and R.
(e) If these new control limits are used, but the adjustment to 350 volts is not carried out, what is the probability that this fact will not be detected on the first subgroup?
(f) What is the process capability before and after the adjustment of the nominal value to 350 volts? Compute both C_p and C_{pk}.

Exercise 2.12 The following data were collected in a circuit pack production plant during October:

	Number of nonconformities
Missing component	293
Wrong component	431
Too much solder	120
Insufficient solder	132
Failed component	183

An improvement team recommended several changes that were implemented in the first week of November. The following data were collected in the second week of November.

	Number of nonconformities
Missing component	34
Wrong component	52
Too much solder	25
Insufficient solder	34
Failed component	18

(a) Construct Pareto charts of the nonconformities in October and the second week of November.
(b) Has the improvement team produced significant differences in the type of nonconformities?

Exercise 2.13 Control charts for $\bar{X}$ and R are maintained on total soluble solids produced at 20 °C in parts per million (ppm). Samples are drawn from production containers every hour and tested in a special test device. The test results are organized into subgroups of $n = 5$ measurements, corresponding to 5 h of production. After 125 h of production, we find that $\sum_{i=1}^{25} \bar{X}_i = 390.8$ and $\sum_{i=1}^{25} R_i = 84$. The specification on the process states that containers with more than 18 ppm of total soluble solids should be reprocessed.

(a) Compute an appropriate capability index.
(b) Assuming a normal distribution and statistical control, what proportion of the sample measurements are expected to be out of spec?
(c) Compute the control limits for $\bar{X}$ and R.

Exercise 2.14 Part I: Run the piston simulator at the lower levels of the 7 piston parameters and generate 100 cycle times. Add 0.02 to the last 50 cycle times.

(a) Compute control limits of $\bar{X}$ and R by constructing subgroups of size 5, and analyze the control charts.

Part II: Randomly shuffle the cycle times using the Python function *random.sample*.

(b) Recompute the control limits of $\bar{X}$ and R and reanalyze the control charts.
(c) Explain the differences between (a) and (b).

Exercise 2.15 Part I: Run the piston simulator by specifying the 7 piston parameters within their acceptable range. Record the 7 operating levels you used and generate 20 subgroups of size 5.

1. Compute the control limits for $\bar{X}$ and S.

Part II: Rerun the piston simulator at the same operating conditions and generate 20 subgroups of size 10.

2. Recompute the control limits for $\bar{X}$ and S.
3. Explain the differences between (a) and (b).

Exercise 2.16 Repeat the data segment analysis from Sect. 2.8.2 with a piecewise linear regression fit. This can be done using *pwlf.PiecewiseLinFit* initialized with the keyword argument `degree=1`.

(a) Prepare models with a variety of knots.
(b) Compare the results to the step function fits.
(c) When would you use a piecewise linear fit compared to a step function fit?

Chapter 3
Advanced Methods of Statistical Process Control

Preview Following Chap. 2, we present in this chapter more advanced methods of statistical process control. We start with testing whether data collected over time are randomly distributed around a mean level, or whether there is a trend or a shift in the data. The tests which we consider are nonparametric **run tests**. These tests are required as a first step in checking the statistical stability of a process. This is followed with a section on modified Shewhart type control charts for the mean. Modifications of Shewhart charts were introduced as SPC tools, in order to increase the power of sequential procedures to detect change. Section 3.3 is devoted to the problem of determining the size and frequency of samples for proper statistical control of processes by Shewhart control charts. In Sect. 3.4, we introduce an alternative control tool, based on cumulative sums we develop and study the famous **CUSUM** procedures based on Page's control schemes. Special computer programs are given in Sect. 3.4 for the estimation of the probability of false alarm, conditional expected delay, and expected run length; an example is *cusumPfaCed*. The chapter concludes with sections on modern topics introducing the readers to non-standard techniques and applications. In Sect. 3.5, Bayesian detection procedures are presented. Section 3.6 is devoted to procedures of process control that track the process level. The last section introduces tools from engineering control theory, which are useful in automatically controlled processes. These include dynamic linear models (DLMs), stochastic control, proportional rules, and dynamic programming.

3.1 Tests of Randomness

In performing process capability analysis (see Chap. 2) or analyzing retroactively data for constructing a control chart, the first thing we would like to test is whether these data are randomly distributed around their mean. This means that the process

---

Supplementary Information The online version contains supplementary material available at (https://doi.org/10.1007/978-3-031-28482-3_3).

R. S. Kenett et al., *Industrial Statistics*, Statistics for Industry, Technology, and Engineering, https://doi.org/10.1007/978-3-031-28482-3_3

is statistically stable and only common causes affect the variability. In this section, we discuss such tests of randomness.

Consider a sample $x_1, x_2, \cdots, x_n$, where the index of the values of x indicates some kind of ordering. For example, x_1 is the first observed value of X, x_2 is the second observed value, etc., while x_n is the value observed last. If the sample is indeed random, there should be no significant relationship between the values of X and their position in the sample. Thus, tests of randomness usually test the hypothesis that all possible configurations of the x's are equally probable, against the alternative hypothesis that some significant clustering of members takes place. For example, suppose that we have a sequence of 5 0's and 5 1's. The ordering $0, 1, 1, 0, 0, 0, 1, 1, 0, 1$ seems to be random, while the ordering $0, 0, 0, 0, 0, 1, 1, 1, 1, 1$ seems, conspicuously, not to be random.

3.1.1 *Testing the Number of Runs*

In a sequence of m_1 0's and m_2 1's, we distinguish between **runs** of 0's, i.e., an uninterrupted string of 0's, and **runs** of 1's. Accordingly, in the sequence 0 1 1 1 0 0 1 0 1 1, there are 4 0's and 6 1's, and there are 3 runs of 0's and 3 runs of 1's, i.e., a total of 6 runs. We denote the total number of runs by R. The probability distribution of the total number of runs, R, is determined under the model of randomness. It can be shown that if there are m_1 0's and m_2 1's, then

$$\Pr\{R = 2k\} = \frac{2\binom{m_1-1}{k-1}\binom{m_2-1}{k-1}}{\binom{n}{m_2}} \tag{3.1.1}$$

and

$$\Pr\{R = 2k+1\} = \frac{\binom{m_1-1}{k-1}\binom{m_2-1}{k} + \binom{m_1-1}{k}\binom{m_2-1}{k-1}}{\binom{n}{m_2}}. \tag{3.1.2}$$

Here, n is the sample size, $m_1 + m_2 = n$.

One alternative to the hypothesis of randomness is that there is a tendency for **clustering** of the 0's (or 1's). In such a case, we expect to observe longer runs of 0's (or 1's) and, consequently, a smaller number of total runs. In this case, the hypothesis of randomness is rejected if the total number of runs, R, is too small. On the other hand, there could be an alternative to randomness that is the reverse of clustering. This alternative is called "**mixing**." For example, the following sequence of 10 0's and 10 1's is completely mixed and is obviously not random:

$$0,\ 1,\ 0,\ 1,\ 0,\ 1,\ 0,\ 1,\ 0,\ 1,\ 0,\ 1,\ 0,\ 1,\ 0,\ 1,\ 0,\ 1,\ 0,\ 1.$$

The total number of runs here is $R = 20$. Thus, if there are too many runs, one should also reject the hypothesis of randomness. Consequently, if we consider the null hypothesis H_0 of randomness against the alternative H_1 of clustering, the lower (left) tail of the distribution should be used for the rejection region. If the alternative, H_1, is the hypothesis of mixing, then the upper (right) tail of the distribution should be used. If the alternative is either clustering or mixing, the test should be two-sided.

We test the hypothesis of randomness by using the test statistic R, which is the total number of runs. The critical region for the one-sided alternative that there is clustering is of the form:

$$R \le R_\alpha,$$

where R_p is the pth quantile of the null distribution of R. For the one-sided alternative of mixing, we reject H_0 if $R \ge R_{1-\alpha}$. In cases of large samples, we can use the normal approximations

$$R_\alpha = \mu_R - z_{1-\alpha}\sigma_R$$

and

$$R_{1-\alpha} = \mu_R + z_{1-\alpha}\sigma_R,$$

where

$$\mu_R = 1 + 2m_1m_2/n \tag{3.1.3}$$

and

$$\sigma_R = \left[\frac{2m_1m_2(2m_1m_2 - n)}{n^2(n-1)}\right]^{1/2}, \tag{3.1.4}$$

are the mean and standard deviation, respectively, of R under the hypothesis of randomness. We can also use the normal distribution to approximate the P-value of the test. For one-sided tests, we have

$$\alpha_L = \Pr\{R \le r\} \cong \Phi((r - \mu_R)/\sigma_R) \tag{3.1.5}$$

and

$$\alpha_U = \Pr\{R \ge r\} \cong 1 - \Phi((r - \mu_R)/\sigma_R), \tag{3.1.6}$$

where r is the observed number of runs. For the two-sided alternative, the P-value of the test is approximated by

$$\alpha' = \begin{cases} 2\alpha_L, & \text{if } R < \mu_R \\ 2\alpha_U, & \text{if } R > \mu_R. \end{cases} \tag{3.1.7}$$

3.1.2 Runs Above and Below a Specified Level

The runs test for the randomness of a sequence of 0's and 1's can be applied to test whether the values in a sequence, which are continuous in nature, are randomly distributed. We can consider whether the values are above or below the sample average or the sample median. In such a case, every value above the specified level will be assigned the value 1, while all the others will be assigned the value 0. Once this is done, the previous runs test can be applied.

For example, suppose that we are given a sequence of $n = 30$ observations, and we wish to test for randomness using the number of runs, R, above and below the median, M_e. There are 15 observations below and 15 above the median. In this case, we take $m_1 = 15$, $m_2 = 15$, and $n = 30$. In Table 3.1, we present the p.d.f. and c.d.f. of the number of runs, R, below and above the median, of a random sample of size $n = 30$.

For a level of significance of $\alpha = 0.05$ if $R \leq 10$ or $R \geq 21$, the two-sided test rejects the hypothesis of randomness. Critical values for a two-sided runs test, above and below the median, can be obtained also by the large sample approximation

$$\begin{aligned} R_{\alpha/2} &= \mu_R - z_{1-\alpha/2}\sigma_R \\ R_{1-\alpha/2} &= \mu_R + z_{1-\alpha/2}\sigma_R. \end{aligned} \tag{3.1.8}$$

Substituting $m = m_1 = m_2 = 15$ and $\alpha = 0.05$, we have $\mu_R = 16$, $\sigma_R = 2.69$, $z_{0.975} = 1.96$. Hence, $R_{\alpha/2} = 10.7$ and $R_{1-\alpha/2} = 21.3$. Thus, according to the large sample approximation, if $R \leq 10$ or $R \geq 22$, the hypothesis of randomness is rejected.

This test of the total number of runs, R, above and below a given level (e.g., the mean or the median of a sequence) can be performed by using Python.

Example 3.1 In the present example, we have used Python to perform a run test on a simulated random sample of size $n = 28$ from the normal distribution $N(10, 1)$. The test is of runs above and below the distribution mean 10. We obtain a total of $R = 14$ with $m_1 = 13$ values below and $m_2 = 15$ values above the mean. In Fig. 3.1, we present this random sequence.

In Python, we use the *runsTest* command provided in the `mistat` package.

```
rnorm10 = mistat.load_data('RNORM10')

x = [0 if xi <= 10 else 1 for xi in rnorm10]
_ = mistat.runsTest(x, alternative='less', verbose=True)
```

```
Runs Test

Standard Normal = -0.3596, p-value = 0.3596
alternative hypothesis: less
```

■

Table 3.1 Distribution of R, in a random sample of size $n = 30$, $m_1 = 15$

R	p.d.f.	c.d.f.
2	0.00000	0.00000
3	0.00000	0.00000
4	0.00000	0.00000
5	0.00002	0.00002
6	0.00011	0.00013
7	0.00043	0.00055
8	0.00171	0.00226
9	0.00470	0.00696
10	0.01292	0.01988
11	0.02584	0.04572
12	0.05168	0.09739
13	0.07752	0.17491
14	0.11627	0.29118
15	0.13288	0.42407
16	0.15187	0.57593
17	0.13288	0.70882
18	0.11627	0.82509
19	0.07752	0.90261
20	0.05168	0.95428
21	0.02584	0.98012
22	0.01292	0.99304
23	0.00470	0.99774
24	0.00171	0.99945
25	0.00043	0.99987
26	0.00011	0.99998
27	0.00002	1.00000
28	0.00000	1.00000
29	0.00000	1.00000
30	0.00000	1.00000

3.1.3 Runs Up and Down

Tests of the total number of runs above or below a specified level may not be sufficient in cases where the alternative hypothesis to randomness is cyclical fluctuations in the level of the process. For example, a sequence may show consistent fluctuations up and down, as in the following example:

$$-1, -0.75, -0.50, -0.25, 0, 0.5, 1, 0.5, 0.25, -0.75, \cdots.$$

Here we see a steady increase from -1 to 1 and then a steady decrease. This sequence is obviously not random, and even the previous test of the total number of runs above and below 0 will reject the hypothesis of randomness. If the development

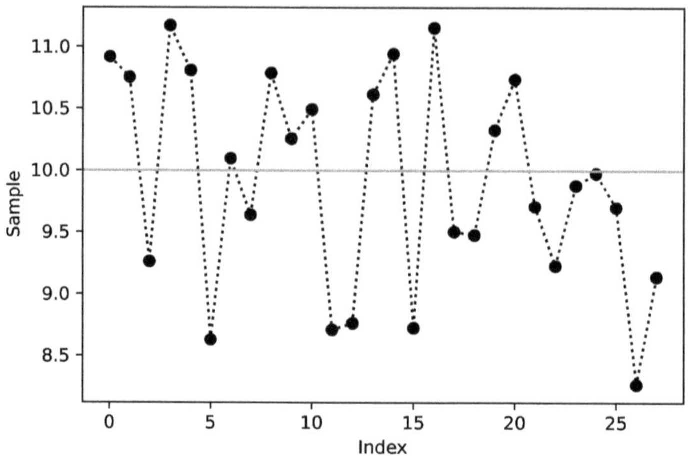

Fig. 3.1 Random normal sequence and the runs above and below the level 10

of the sequence is not as conspicuous as that above, as, for example, in the sequence

$$-1,\ -0.75,\ -0.50,\ 1,\ 0.5,\ -0.25,\ 0,\ 0.25,\ -0.25,\ 1,\ 0.5,\ 0.25,\ -0.75,\ \cdots,$$

the runs test above and below 0 may not reject the hypothesis of randomness. Indeed, in the present case, if we replace every negative number by 0 and every non-negative number by +1, we find that $m_1 = 6$, $m_2 = 7$, and $R = 7$. In this case, the exact value of α_L is 0.5, and the hypothesis of randomness is not rejected.

To test for possible cyclical effects, we use a test of **runs up and down**. Let $x_1, x_2, \cdots, x_n$ be a given sequence, and let us define

$$y_i = \begin{cases} +1, & \text{if } x_i < x_{i+1} \\ -1, & \text{if } x_i \geq x_{i+1} \end{cases}$$

for $i = 1, \cdots, n-1$. We count, then, the total number of runs, R, up and down. A run up is a string of +1's, while a run down is a string of −1's. In the previous sequence, we have the following values of x_i and y_i:

x_i	−1.00	−0.75	−0.50	1.00	0.050	−0.25	0.00	0.25	−0.25	1.00	0.50	0.25	−0.75
y_i		1	1	1	−1	−1	1	1	−1	1	−1	−1	−1

We thus have a total of $R^* = 6$ runs, 3 up and 3 down, with $n = 13$.

To test the hypothesis of randomness based on the number of runs up and down, we need the null distribution of R^*.

When the sample size is sufficiently large, we can use the normal approximation

$$R^*_\alpha = \mu_{R^*} - z_{1-\alpha}\sigma_{R^*}$$

and

$$R^*_{1-\alpha} = \mu_{R^*} + z_{1-\alpha}\sigma_{R^*},$$

where

$$\mu_{R^*} = (2n - 1)/3 \tag{3.1.9}$$

and

$$\sigma_{R^*} = [(16n - 29)/90]^{1/2}. \tag{3.1.10}$$

The attained significance levels are approximated by

$$\alpha^*_L = \Phi((r^* - \mu_{R^*})/\sigma_{R^*}) \tag{3.1.11}$$

and

$$\alpha^*_U = 1 - \Phi((r^* - \mu_{R^*})/\sigma_{R^*}). \tag{3.1.12}$$

Example 3.2 The sample in dataset **YARNSTRG.csv** contains 100 values of log-yarn strength. In this sample, there are $R^* = 64$ runs up or down, 32 runs up and 32 runs down. The expected value of R^* is

$$\mu_{R^*} = \frac{199}{3} = 66.33,$$

and its standard deviation is

$$\sigma_{R^*} = \left(\frac{1600 - 29}{90}\right)^{1/2} = 4.178.$$

The attained level of significance is

$$\alpha_L = \Phi\left(\frac{64 - 66.33}{4.178}\right) = 0.289.$$

The hypothesis of randomness is not rejected. ■

Table 3.2 Expected values of R_k as a function of n

k	$E\{R_k\}$
1	$(2n-1)/3$
2	$(3n-5)/12$
3	$(4n-11)/60$
4	$(5n-19)/360$
5	$(6n-29)/2520$
6	$(7n-41)/20160$
7	$(8n-55)/181440$

3.1.4 Testing the Length of Runs Up and Down

In the previous sections, we have considered tests of randomness based on the total number of runs. If the number of runs is small relative to the size of the sequence, n, we obviously expect some of the runs to be rather long. We shall now consider the question of just how long the runs can be under a state of randomness.

Consider runs up and down, and let R_k $(k = 1, 2, \cdots)$ be the total number of runs, up or down, of length greater than or equal to k. Thus, $R_1 = R^*$, R_2 is the total number of runs, up or down, of length 2 or more, etc. The following are formulas for the expected values of each R_k, i.e., $E\{R_k\}$, under the assumption of randomness. Each expected value is expressed as a function of the size n of the sequence (Table 3.2).

In general, we have

$$E\{R_k\} = \frac{2[n(k+1) - k^2 - k + 1]}{(k+2)!}, \quad 1 \leq k \leq n-1. \tag{3.1.13}$$

If $k \geq 5$, we have $E\{R_k\} \doteq V\{R_k\}$, and the Poisson approximation to the probability distribution of R_k is considered good, provided $n > 20$. Thus, if $k \geq 5$, according to the Poisson approximation, we find

$$\Pr\{R_k \geq 1\} \doteq 1 - \exp(-E\{R_k\}). \tag{3.1.14}$$

For example, if $n = 50$, we present $E\{R_k\}$ and $\Pr\{R_k \geq 1\}$ in the following table.

k	$E\{R_k\}$	$\Pr\{R_k \geq 1\}$
5	0.1075	0.1020
6	0.0153	0.0152
7	0.0019	0.0019

We see in the above table that the probability to observe even 1 run, up or down, of length 6 or more is quite small. This is the reason for the rule of thumb, to **reject the hypothesis of randomness if a run is of length 6 or more**. This and other rules of thumb were presented in Chap. 2 for ongoing process control.

3.2 Modified Shewhart Control Charts for $\bar{X}$

The modified Shewhart control chart for $\bar{X}$, to detect possible shifts in the means of the parent distributions, gives a signal to stop, whenever the sample means $\bar{X}$ fall outside the control limits $\theta_0 \pm a\frac{\sigma}{\sqrt{n}}$, or whenever a **run** of r sample means falls outside the warning limits (all on the same side) $\theta_0 \pm w\frac{\sigma}{\sqrt{n}}$.

We denote the modified scheme by (a, w, r). For example, 3-σ control charts, with warning lines at 2-σ and a run of $r = 4$ is denoted by $(3, 2, 4)$. If $r = \infty$, the scheme $(3, 0, \infty)$ is reduced to the common Shewhart 3-σ procedure. Similarly, the scheme $(a, 3, 1)$ for $a > 3$ is equivalent to the Shewhart 3-σ control charts. A control chart for a $(3, 1.5, 2)$ procedure is shown in Fig. 3.2. The means are of samples of size 5. There is no run of length 2 or more between the warning and action limits.

The **run length**, of a control chart, is the number of samples taken until an "out of control" alarm is given. The **average run length**, ARL, of an (a, w, r) plan is smaller than that of the simple Shewhart a-σ procedure. We denote the average run length of an (a, w, r) procedure by ARL (a, w, r). Obviously, if w and r are small, we will tend to stop too soon, even when the process is under control. For example, if $r = 1$, $w = 2$, then any procedure $(a, 2, 1)$ is equivalent to Shewhart 2-σ procedure, which stops on the average every 20 samples, when the process is under control.

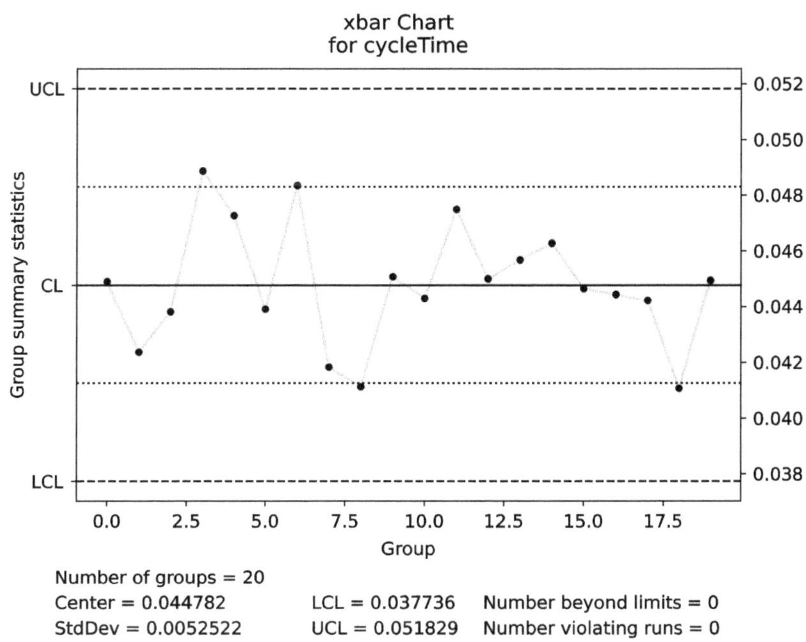

Fig. 3.2 A modified Shewhart $\bar{X}$-chart

Weindling (1967) and Page (1962) derived the formula for the average run length ARL(a, w, r). Page used the theory of runs, while Weindling used another theory (Markov chains theory). An excellent expository paper discussing the results was published by Weindling et al. (1970).

The basic formula for the determination of the average run length is

$$\text{ARL}_\theta(a, w, r) =$$

$$\left[P_\theta(a) + H_\theta^r(a, w)\frac{1 - H_\theta(a, w)}{1 - H_\theta^r(a, w)} + L_\theta^r(a, w)\frac{1 - L_\theta(a, w)}{1 - L_\theta^r(a, w)}\right]^{-1}, \tag{3.2.1}$$

where

$$\begin{aligned} P_\theta(a) &= P_\theta\left\{\bar{X} \le \theta_0 - a\frac{\sigma}{\sqrt{n}}\right\} + P_\theta\left\{\bar{X} \ge \theta_0 + a\frac{\sigma}{\sqrt{n}}\right\} \\ H_\theta(a, w) &= P_\theta\left\{\theta_0 + w\frac{\sigma}{\sqrt{n}} \le \bar{X} \le \theta_0 + a\frac{\sigma}{\sqrt{n}}\right\} \\ L_\theta(a, w) &= P_\theta\left\{\theta_0 - a\frac{\sigma}{\sqrt{n}} \le \bar{X} \le \theta_0 - w\frac{\sigma}{\sqrt{n}}\right\}. \end{aligned} \tag{3.2.2}$$

In Table 3.3, we present some values of ARL(a, w, r) for $a = 3$, $w = 1(.5)2.5$, $r = 2(1)7$, when the samples are of size $n = 5$ from a normal distribution, and the shift in the mean is of size $\theta - \theta_0 = \delta\sigma$. We see in the table that the procedures (3, 1, 7), (3, 1.5, 5), (3, 2, 3) and (3, 2.5, 2) yield similar ARL functions. However, these modified procedures are more efficient than the Shewhart 3-σ procedure. They all have close ARL values when $\delta = 0$, but when $\delta > 0$ their ARL values are considerably smaller than the Shewhart's procedure.

3.3 The Size and Frequency of Sampling for Shewhart Control Charts

In the present section, we discuss the importance of designing the sampling procedure for Shewhart control charts. We start with the problem of the economic design of sampling for $\bar{X}$-charts.

3.3.1 The Economic Design for $\bar{X}$-charts

Duncan (1956, 1971, 1978) studied the question of optimally designing the $\bar{X}$ control charts. We show here, in a somewhat simpler fashion, how this problem can

Table 3.3 Values of ARL(a, w, r), $a = 3.00$ against $\delta = (\mu_1 - \mu_0)/\sigma$, $n = 5$

w	δ	r = 2	3	4	5	6	7
1.00	0.00	22.0	107.7	267.9	349.4	366.9	369.8
	0.25	11.2	32.1	67.1	101.3	120.9	129.0
	0.50	4.8	9.3	14.9	20.6	25.4	28.8
	0.75	2.8	4.4	5.8	7.1	8.1	8.9
	1.00	2.0	2.7	3.3	3.7	3.9	4.1
	1.25	1.6	2.0	2.2	2.3	2.3	2.4
	1.50	1.4	1.5	1.5	1.6	1.6	1.6
	1.75	1.2	1.2	1.2	1.2	1.2	1.2
	2.00	1.1	1.1	1.1	1.1	1.1	1.1
	2.25	1.0	1.0	1.0	1.0	1.0	1.0
1.50	0.00	93.1	310.2	365.7	370.1	370.4	370.4
	0.25	31.7	88.1	122.8	131.3	132.9	133.1
	0.50	9.3	18.8	26.8	31.0	32.6	33.1
	0.75	4.0	6.4	8.2	9.4	10.1	10.4
	1.00	2.4	3.2	3.7	4.1	4.3	4.4
	1.25	1.7	2.1	2.2	2.3	2.4	2.4
	1.50	1.4	1.5	1.5	1.6	1.6	1.6
	1.75	1.2	1.2	1.2	1.2	1.2	1.2
	2.00	1.1	1.1	1.1	1.1	1.1	1.1
	2.25	1.0	1.0	1.0	1.0	1.0	1.0
2.00	0.00	278.0	367.8	370.3	370.4	370.4	370.4
	0.25	84.7	128.3	132.8	133.1	133.2	133.2
	0.50	19.3	30.0	32.8	33.3	33.4	33.4
	0.75	6.5	9.2	10.3	10.6	10.7	10.7
	1.00	3.1	3.9	4.3	4.4	4.5	4.5
	1.25	1.9	2.2	2.3	2.4	2.4	2.4
	1.50	1.4	1.5	1.6	1.6	1.6	1.6
	1.75	1.2	1.2	1.2	1.2	1.2	1.2
	2.00	1.1	1.1	1.1	1.1	1.1	1.1
	2.25	1.0	1.0	1.0	1.0	1.0	1.0
2.50	0.00	364.1	370.4	370.4	370.4	370.4	370.4
	0.25	127.3	133.0	133.2	133.2	133.2	133.2
	0.50	30.6	33.2	33.4	33.4	33.4	33.4
	0.75	9.6	10.6	10.7	10.8	10.8	10.8
	1.00	4.0	4.4	4.5	4.5	4.5	4.5
	1.25	2.2	2.4	2.4	2.4	2.4	2.4
	1.50	1.5	1.6	1.6	1.6	1.6	1.6
	1.75	1.2	1.2	1.2	1.2	1.2	1.2
	2.00	1.1	1.1	1.1	1.1	1.1	1.1
	2.25	1.0	1.0	1.0	1.0	1.0	1.0

be approached. More specifically, assume that we sample from a normal population and that σ^2 is known. A shift of size $\delta = (\theta_1 - \theta_0)/\sigma$ or larger should be detected with high probability.

Let c [\$/hour] be the hourly cost of a shift in the mean of size δ. Let d[\$] be the cost of sampling (and testing the items). Assuming that the time of shift from θ_0 to $\theta_1 = \theta_0 + \delta\sigma$ is exponentially distributed with mean $1/\lambda$ [hr] and that a penalty of 1[\$] is incurred for every unneeded inspection, the total expected cost is

$$K(h, n) \doteq \frac{ch + dn}{1 - \Phi(3 - \delta\sqrt{n})} + \frac{1 + dn}{\lambda h}. \tag{3.3.1}$$

This function can be minimized with respect to h and n, to determine the optimal sample size and frequency of sampling. Differentiating partially with respect to h and equating to zero, we obtain the formula of the optimal h, for a given n, namely

$$h^0 = \left(\frac{1 + d \cdot n}{c\lambda}\right)^{1/2} (1 - \Phi(3 - \delta\sqrt{n}))^{1/2}. \tag{3.3.2}$$

However, the function $K(h, n)$ is increasing with n, due to the contribution of the second term on the RHS. Thus, for this expected cost function, we take every h^0 hours a sample of size $n = 4$. Some values of h^0 are:

δ	d	c	λ	h^0
2	0.5	3.0	0.0027	17.6
1	0.1	30.0	0.0027	1.7

For additional reading on this subject, see Gibra (1971).

3.3.2 *Increasing the Sensitivity of p-charts*

The **operating characteristic function** for a Shewhart p-chart is the probability, as a function of p, that the statistic $\hat{p}_n$ falls between the lower and upper control limits. Thus, the operating characteristic of a p-chart, with control limits $p_0 \pm 3\sqrt{\frac{p_0(1-p_0)}{n}}$, is

$$OC(p) = \Pr_\theta\left\{p_0 - 3\sqrt{\frac{p_0(1 - p_0)}{n}} < \hat{p}_n < p_0 + 3\sqrt{\frac{p_0(1 - p_0)}{n}}\right\}, \tag{3.3.3}$$

where $\hat{p}_n$ is the proportion of defective items in the sample. $n \times \hat{p}_n$ has the binomial distribution, with c.d.f. $B(j; n, p)$. Accordingly,

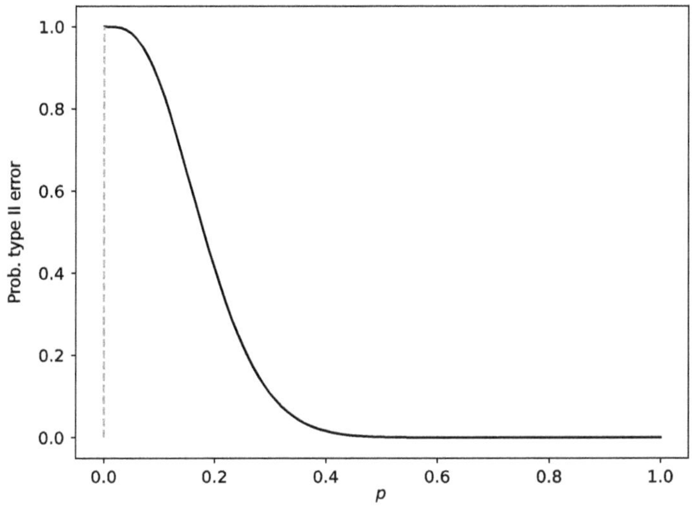

Fig. 3.3 Typical OC curve for a p-chart

$$\begin{aligned} OC(p) &= B\left(np_0 + 3\sqrt{np_0(1-p_0)};\ n, p\right) \\ &\quad - B\left(np_0 - 3\sqrt{np_0(1-p_0)};\ n, p\right). \end{aligned} \tag{3.3.4}$$

For large samples, we can use the normal approximation to $B(j; n, p)$ and obtain

$$\mathrm{OC}(p) \cong \Phi\left(\frac{(\mathrm{UCL}-p)\sqrt{n}}{\sqrt{p(1-p)}}\right) - \Phi\left(\frac{(\mathrm{LCL}-p)\sqrt{n}}{\sqrt{p(1-p)}}\right). \tag{3.3.5}$$

The value of the $\mathrm{OC}(p)$ at $p = p_0$ is $2\Phi(3) - 1 = 0.997$. The values of $\mathrm{OC}(p)$ for $p \neq p_0$ are smaller. A typical $\mathrm{OC}(p)$ function looks as in Fig. 3.3.

When the process is in control with process fraction defective p_0, we have $\mathrm{OC}(p_0) = 0.997$; otherwise, $\mathrm{OC}(p) < 0.997$. The probability that we will detect a change in quality to level p_1, with a **single** point outside the control limits, is $1 - \mathrm{OC}(p_1)$. As an example, suppose we have estimated p_0 as $\bar{p} = 0.15$ from past data. With a sample of size $n = 100$, our control limits are

$$\mathrm{UCL} = 0.15 + 3((0.15)(0.85)/100)^{1/2} = 0.257$$

and

$$\mathrm{LCL} = 0.15 - 3((0.15)(0.85)/100)^{1/2} = 0.043.$$

In Table 3.4, we see that it is almost certain that a single point will fall outside the control limits when $p = 0.40$, but it is unlikely that it will fall there when

Table 3.4 Operating characteristic values for p-chart with $\bar{p} = 0.15$ and $n = 100$

p	OC(p)	1 − OC(p)	1 − [OC(p)]^5
0.05	0.6255	0.3745	0.9043
0.10	0.9713	0.0287	0.1355
0.15	0.9974	0.0026	0.0130
0.20	0.9236	0.0764	0.3280
0.25	0.5636	0.4364	0.9432
0.30	0.1736	0.8264	0.9998
0.40	0.0018	0.9982	1.0000

$p = 0.20$. However, if the process fraction defective remains at the $p = 0.20$ level for several measurement periods, the probability of detecting the shift increases. The probability that at least one point falls outside the control limits when $p = 0.20$ for 5 consecutive periods is

$$1 - [\mathrm{OC}(0.20)]^5 = 0.3279.$$

The probability of detecting shifts in the fraction defective is even greater than 0.33 if we apply run tests on the data.

The OC curve can also be useful for determining the required sample size for detecting, with high probability, a change in the process fraction defective in a single measurement period. To see this, suppose that the system is in control at level p_0, and we wish to detect a shift to level p_t with specified probability, $1 - \beta$. For example, to be 90% confident that the sample proportion will be outside the control limits immediately after the process fraction defective changes to p_t, we require that

$$1 - \mathrm{OC}(p_t) = 0.90.$$

We can solve this equation to find that the required sample size is

$$n \doteq \frac{(3\sqrt{p_0(1-p_0)} + z_{1-\beta}\sqrt{p_t(1-p_t)})^2}{(p_t - p_0)^2}. \tag{3.3.6}$$

If we wish that with probability $(1 - \beta)$ the sample proportion will be outside the limits at least once within k sampling periods, when the precise fraction defective is p_t, the required sample size is

$$n \doteq \frac{(3\sqrt{p_0(1-p_0)} + z_{1-b}\sqrt{(p_t(1-p_t)})^2}{(p_t - p_0)^2}, \tag{3.3.7}$$

where $b = \beta^{1/k}$.

These results are illustrated in Table 3.5 for a process with $p_0 = 0.15$.

It is practical to take at each period a small sample of $n = 5$. We see in Table 3.5 that in this case, a change from 0.15 to 0.40 would be detected within 5 periods with a probability of 0.9. To detect smaller changes requires larger samples.

Table 3.5 Sample size required for probability 0.9 of detecting a shift to level p_t from level $p_0 = 0.15$ (in one period and within five periods)

p_t	One period	5 periods
0.05	183	69
0.10	847	217
0.20	1003	156
0.25	265	35
0.30	122	14
0.40	46	5

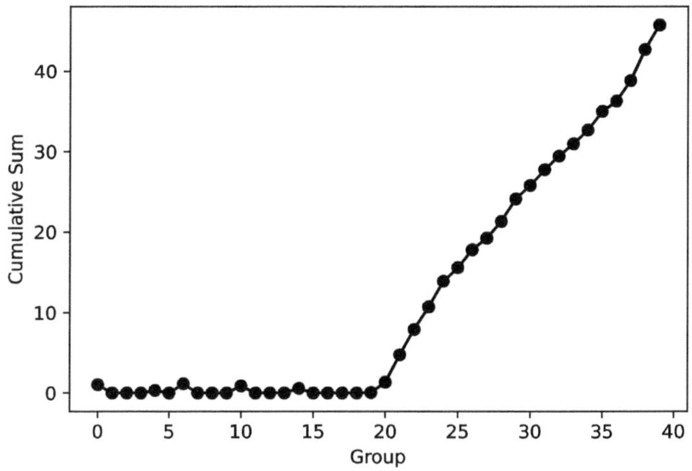

Fig. 3.4 A plot of cumulative sums with drift after $t = 20$

3.4 Cumulative Sum Control Charts

3.4.1 Upper Page's Scheme

When the process level changes from a past or specified level, we expect that a control procedure will trigger an "alarm." Depending on the size of the change and the size of the sample, it may take several sampling periods before the alarm occurs. A method that has a smaller ARL than the standard Shewhart control charts, for detecting certain types of changes, is the **cumulative sum** (or CUSUM) control chart that was introduced by Barnard (1959) and Page (1954).

CUSUM charts differ from the common Shewhart control chart in several respects. The main difference is that instead of plotting the individual value of the statistic of interest, such as X, $\bar{X}$, S, R, p, or c, a statistic based on the cumulative sums is computed and tracked. By summing deviations of the individual statistic from a target value, T, we get a consistent increase, or decrease, of the cumulative sum when the process is above, or below, the target. In Fig. 3.4, we show the behavior of the cumulative sums

$$S_t = \sum_{i=1}^{t}(X_i - 10) \tag{3.4.1}$$

Table 3.6 The number of monthly computer crashes due to power failures

t	X_t	t	X_t	t	X_t
1	0	11	0	21	0
2	2	12	0	22	1
3	0	13	0	23	3
4	0	14	0	24	2
5	3	15	0	25	1
6	3	16	2	26	1
7	0	17	2	27	3
8	0	18	1	28	5
9	2	19	0		
10	1	20	0		

of data simulated from a normal distribution with mean

$$\mu_t = \begin{cases} 10, & \text{if } t \leq 20 \\ 13, & \text{if } t > 20 \end{cases}$$

and $\sigma_t = 1$ for all t.

We see that as soon as the shift in the mean of the data occurred, a pronounced drift in S_t started. Page (1954) suggested to detect an upward shift in the mean by considering the sequence

$$S_t^+ = \max\{S_{t-1}^+ + (X_k - K^+), 0\}, \quad t = 1, 2, \cdots, \tag{3.4.2}$$

where $S_0^+ \equiv 0$, and decide that a shift has occurred, as soon as $S_t^+ > h^+$. The statistics X_t, $t = 1, 2, \cdots$, upon which the (truncated) cumulative sums are constructed, could be means of samples of n observations, standard deviations, sample proportions, or individual observations. In the following section, we will see how the parameters K^+ and h^+ are determined. We will see that if X_t are means of samples of size n, with process variance σ^2, and if the desired process mean is θ_0, while the maximal tolerated process mean is θ_1, $\theta_1 - \theta_0 > 0$, then

$$K^+ = \frac{\theta_0 + \theta_1}{2} \quad \text{and} \quad h^+ = -\frac{\sigma^2 \log \alpha}{n(\theta_1 - \theta_0)}. \tag{3.4.3}$$

$0 < \alpha < 1$.

Example 3.3 The above procedure of Page is now illustrated. The data in Table 3.6 represent the number of computer crashes per month, due to power failures experienced at a computer center, over a period of 28 months. After a crash, the computers are made operational with an "Initial Program Load." We refer to the data as the IPL dataset.

Power failures are potentially very harmful. A computer center might be able to tolerate such failures when they are far enough apart. If they become too frequent,

Table 3.7 The S_t^+ statistics for the IPL data

t	X_t	$X_t - 1.07$	S_t^+
1	0	−1.07	0
2	2	0.93	0.93
3	0	−1.07	0
4	0	−1.07	0
5	3	1.93	1.93
6	3	1.93	3.86
7	0	−1.07	2.79
8	0	−1.07	1.72
9	2	0.93	2.65
10	1	−0.07	2.58
11	0	−1.07	1.51
12	0	−1.07	0.44
13	0	−1.07	0
14	0	−1.07	0
15	0	−1.07	0
16	2	0.93	0.93
17	2	0.93	1.86
18	1	−0.07	1.79
19	0	−1.07	0.72
20	0	−1.07	0
21	0	−1.07	0
22	1	−0.07	0
23	3	1.93	1.93
24	2	0.93	2.86
25	1	−0.07	2.79
26	1	−0.07	2.72
27	3	1.93	4.65
28	5	3.93	8.58

one might decide to invest in an uninterruptable power supply. It seems intuitively clear from Table 3.6 that computer crashes due to power failures become more frequent. Is the variability in failure rates due to chance alone (common causes) or can it be attributed to special causes that should be investigated? Suppose that the computer center can tolerate, at the most, an average of one power failure in 3 weeks (21 days) or 30/21 = 1.43 crashes per month. It is desirable that there will be less than 1 failure per 6 weeks, or 0.71 per month. In Table 3.7, we show the computation of Page's statistics S_t^+, with $K^+ = \frac{1}{2}(0.71 + 1.43) = 1.07$.

For $\alpha = 0.05$, $\sigma = 1$, $n = 1$, we obtain the critical level $h^+ = 4.16$. Thus we see that the first time an alarm is triggered is after the 27th month. In Fig. 3.5, we present the graph of S_t^+ versus t. This graph is called a **CUSUM Chart**.

We see in Fig. 3.5 that although S_6^+ is close to 4, the graph falls back toward zero, and there is no alarm triggered until the 27th month. ■

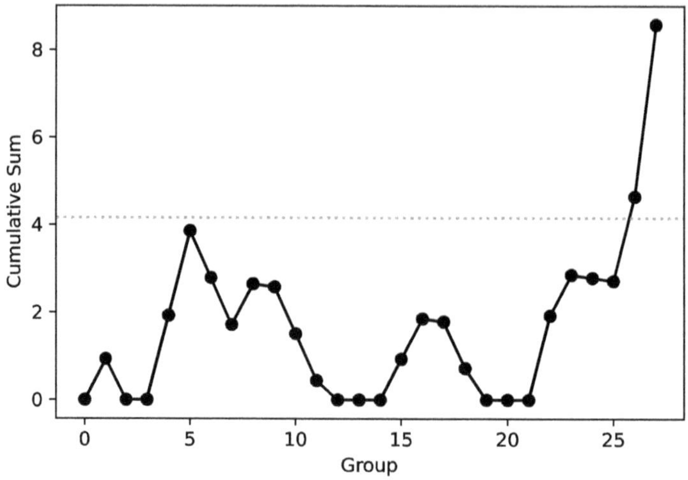

Fig. 3.5 Page's CUSUM chart of IPL data

3.4.2 Some Theoretical Background

Generally, if $X_1, X_2, \cdots$ is a sequence of i.i.d. random variables (continuous or discrete), having a p.d.f. $f(x; \theta)$, and we wish to test two simple hypotheses: $H_0 : \theta = \theta_0$ versus $H_1 : \theta = \theta_1$, with Types I and II error probabilities α and β, respectively, the Wald Sequential Probability Ratio Test (SPRT) is a sequential procedure that, after t observations, $t \geq 1$, considers the likelihood ratio

$$\Lambda(X_1, \cdots, X_t) = \prod_{i=1}^{t} \frac{f(X_i; \theta_1)}{f(X_i; \theta_0)}. \tag{3.4.4}$$

If $\frac{\beta}{1-\alpha} < \Lambda(X_1, \cdots, X_t) < \frac{1-\beta}{\alpha}$, then another observation is taken; otherwise, sampling terminates. If $\Lambda(X_1, \cdots, X_t) < \frac{\beta}{1-\alpha}$, then H_0 is accepted. H_0 is rejected, if $\Lambda(X_1, \cdots, X_t) > \frac{1-\beta}{\alpha}$.

In an upper control scheme, we can consider only the upper boundary, by setting $\beta = 0$. Thus, we can decide that the true hypothesis is H_1, as soon as

$$\sum_{i=1}^{t} \log \frac{f(X_i; \theta_1)}{f(X_i; \theta_0)} \geq -\log \alpha.$$

We will examine now the structure of this testing rule in a few special cases.

A. Normal Distribution

We consider X_i to be normally distributed with **known** variance σ^2 and mean θ_0 or θ_1. In this case,

$$\begin{aligned}\log \frac{f(X_i;\theta_1)}{f(X_i;\theta_0)} &= -\frac{1}{2\sigma^2}\{(X_i-\theta_1)^2-(X_i-\theta_0)^2\}\\ &= \frac{\theta_1-\theta_0}{\sigma^2}\left(X_i-\frac{\theta_0+\theta_1}{2}\right).\end{aligned} \tag{3.4.5}$$

Thus, the criterion

$$\sum_{i=1}^{t} \log \frac{f(X_i;\theta_1)}{f(X_i;\theta_0)} \geq -\log\alpha$$

is equivalent to

$$\sum_{i=1}^{t}\left(X_i-\frac{\theta_0+\theta_1}{2}\right) \geq -\frac{\sigma^2\log\alpha}{\theta_1-\theta_0}.$$

For this reason, we use in the upper Page control scheme

$$K^+ = \frac{\theta_0+\theta_1}{2}, \quad \text{and} \quad h^+ = -\frac{\sigma^2\log\alpha}{\theta_1-\theta_0}.$$

If X_t is an average of n independent observations, then we replace σ^2 by σ^2/n.

B. Binomial Distributions

Suppose that X_t has a binomial distribution $B(n,\theta)$. If $\theta \leq \theta_0$, the process level is under control. If $\theta \geq \theta_1$, the process level is out of control ($\theta_1 > \theta_0$). Since

$$f(x;\theta) = \binom{n}{x}\left(\frac{\theta}{1-\theta}\right)^x (1-\theta)^n,$$

$$\sum_{i=1}^{t} \log \frac{f(X_i;\theta_1)}{f(X_i;\theta_0)} \geq -\log\alpha \ \text{ if,}$$

$$\sum_{i=1}^{t}\left(X_i - \frac{n\log\left(\frac{1-\theta_0}{1-\theta_1}\right)}{\log\left(\frac{\theta_1}{1-\theta_1}\cdot\frac{1-\theta_0}{\theta_0}\right)}\right) \geq -\frac{\log\alpha}{\log\left(\frac{\theta_1}{1-\theta_1}\cdot\frac{1-\theta_0}{\theta_0}\right)}. \tag{3.4.6}$$

Accordingly, in an upper Page's control scheme, with binomial data, we use

$$K^{+} = \frac{n \log\left(\frac{1-\theta_0}{1-\theta_1}\right)}{\log\left(\frac{\theta_1}{1-\theta_1} \cdot \frac{1-\theta_0}{\theta_0}\right)} \tag{3.4.7}$$

and

$$h^{+} = -\frac{\log \alpha}{\log\left(\frac{\theta_1}{1-\theta_1} \cdot \frac{1-\theta_0}{\theta_0}\right)}. \tag{3.4.8}$$

C. Poisson Distributions

When the statistics X_t have Poisson distribution with mean λ, then for specified levels λ_0 and λ_1, $0 < \lambda_0 < \lambda_1 < \infty$,

$$\sum_{i=1}^{t} \log \frac{f(X_i; \lambda_1)}{f(X_i; \lambda_0)} = \log\left(\frac{\lambda_1}{\lambda_0}\right) \sum_{i=1}^{t} X_i - t(\lambda_1 - \lambda_0). \tag{3.4.9}$$

It follows that the control parameters are

$$K^{+} = \frac{\lambda_1 - \lambda_0}{\log(\lambda_1/\lambda_0)} \tag{3.4.10}$$

and

$$h^{+} = -\frac{\log \alpha}{\log(\lambda_1/\lambda_0)}. \tag{3.4.11}$$

3.4.3 *Lower and Two-Sided Page's Scheme*

In order to test whether a significant drop occurred in the process level (mean), we can use a lower page scheme. According to this scheme, we set $S_0^{-} \equiv 0$ and

$$S_t^{-} = \min\{S_{t-1}^{-} + (X_t - K^{-}), 0\}, \quad t = 1, 2, \cdots. \tag{3.4.12}$$

Here the CUSUM values S_t^{-} are either zero or negative. We decide that a shift down in the process level, from θ_0 to θ_1, $\theta_1 < \theta_0$, occurred as soon as $S_t^{-} < h^{-}$. The control parameters K^{-} and h^{-} are determined by the formula of the previous section by setting $\theta_1 < \theta_0$.

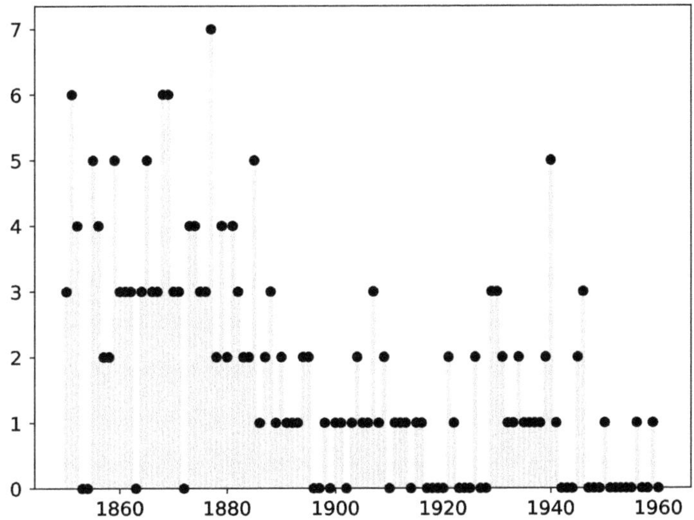

Fig. 3.6 The number of yearly coal mine disasters in England

Example 3.4 In dataset **COAL.csv**, one can find data on the number of coal mine disasters (explosions) in England, per year, for the period 1850 to 1961. These data are plotted in Fig. 3.6. It seems that the average number of disasters per year dropped after 40 years from 3 to 2 and later settled around an average of one per year. We apply here the lower Page's scheme to see when do we detect this change for the first time. It is plausible to assume that the number of disasters per year, X_t, is a random variable having a Poisson distribution. We therefore set $\lambda_0 = 3$ and $\lambda_1 = 1$. The formulae of the previous section, with K^+ and h^+ replaced by K^- and h^-, yield, for $\alpha = 0.01$,

$$K^- = \frac{\lambda_1 - \lambda_0}{\log(\lambda_1/\lambda_0)} = 1.82 \quad \text{and} \quad h^- = -\frac{\log(0.01)}{\log(1/3)} = -4.19.$$

In Table 3.8, we find the values of X_t $X_t - K^-$ and S_t^- for $t = 1, \cdots, 50$. We see that $S_t^- < h^-$ for the first time at $t = 47$. The graph of S_t^- versus t is plotted in Fig. 3.7.

■

If we wish to control simultaneously against changes in the process level in either upward or downward directions, we use an upper and lower Page's schemes together and trigger an alarm as soon as either $S_t^+ > h^+$ or $S_t^- < h^-$. Such a two-sided scheme is denoted by the four control parameters (K^+, h^+, K^-, h^-).

Example 3.5 Yashchin (1991) illustrates the use of a two-sided Page's control scheme on data, which are the difference between the thickness of the grown silicon layer and its target value. He applied the control scheme $(K^+ = 3, h^+ = 9,$

Table 3.8 Page's lower control scheme for the coal mine disasters data

t	X_t	$X_t - K^-$	S_t^-
1	3	1.179	0
2	6	4.179	0
3	4	2.179	0
4	0	−1.820	−1.820
5	0	−1.820	−3.640
6	5	3.179	−0.461
7	4	2.179	0
8	2	0.179	0
9	2	0.179	0
10	5	3.179	0
11	3	1.179	0
12	3	1.179	0
13	3	1.179	0
14	0	−1.820	−1.820
15	3	1.179	−0.640
16	5	3.179	0
17	3	1.179	0
18	3	1.179	0
19	6	4.179	0
20	6	4.179	0
21	3	1.179	0
22	3	1.179	0
23	0	−1.820	−1.820
24	4	2.179	0
25	4	2.179	0
26	3	1.179	0
27	3	1.179	0
28	7	5.179	0
29	2	0.179	0
30	4	2.179	0
31	2	0.179	0
32	4	2.179	0
33	3	1.179	0
34	2	0.179	0
35	2	0.179	0
36	5	3.179	0
37	1	−0.820	−0.820
38	2	0.179	−0.640
39	3	1.179	0
40	1	−0.820	−0.820

(continued)

Table 3.8 (continued)

t	X_t	$X_t - K^-$	S_t^-
41	2	0.179	−0.640
42	1	−0.820	−1.461
43	1	−0.820	−2.281
44	1	−0.820	−3.102
45	2	0.179	−2.922
46	2	0.179	−2.743
47	0	−1.820	−4.563
48	0	−1.820	−6.384
49	1	−0.820	−7.204
50	0	−1.820	−9.025

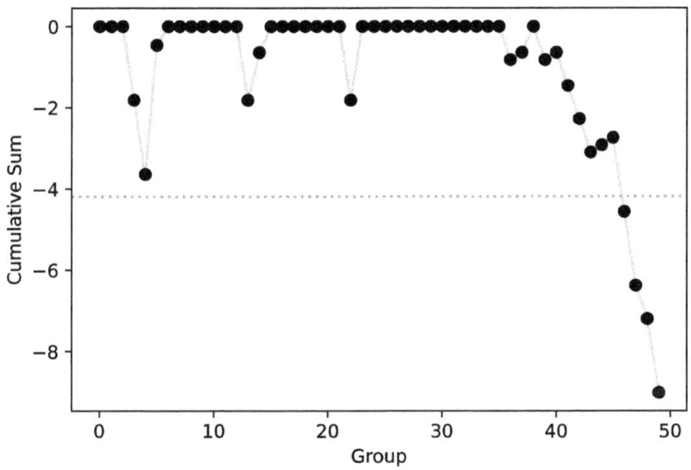

Fig. 3.7 Page's lower CUSUM control chart

$K^- = -2$, $h^- = -5$). We present the values of X_t, S_t^+, and S_t^- in Table 3.9. We see in this table that $S_t^+ > h^+$ for the first time at $t = 40$. There is an indication that a significant drift upward in the level of thickness occurred.

In Fig. 3.8, we present the two-sided control chart for the data of Table 3.9. ■

The two-sided Page's control scheme can be boosted by changing the values of S_0^+ and S_0^- to non-zero. These are called **headstart values**. The introduction of non-zero headstarts was suggested by Lucas and Crosier (1982) in order to bring the history of the process into consideration and accelerate the initial response of the scheme. Lucas (1982) suggested also to combine the CUSUM scheme with the Shewhart Control Chart. If any X_t value exceeds an upper limit UCL, or falls below a lower limit LCL, an alarm should be triggered.

Table 3.9 Computation of (S_t^+, S_t^-) in a two-sided control scheme

t	X_t	$X_t - K^+$	$X_t - K^-$	S_t^+	S_t^-
1	−4	−7	−2	0	−2
2	−1	−4	1	0	−1
3	3	0	5	0	0
4	−2	−5	0	0	0
5	−2.5	−5.5	−0.5	0	−0.5
6	−0.5	−3.5	1.5	0	0
7	1.5	−1.5	3.5	0	0
8	−3	−6	−1	0	−1
9	4	1	6	1	0
10	3.5	0.5	5.5	1.5	0
11	−2.5	−5.5	−0.5	0	−0.5
12	−3	−6	−1	0	−1.5
13	−3	−6	−1	0	−2.5
14	−0.5	−3.5	1.5	0	−1
15	−2.5	−5.5	−0.5	0	−1.5
16	1	−2	3	0	0
17	−1	−4	1	0	0
18	−3	−6	−1	0	−1
19	1	−2	3	0	0
20	4.5	−2	6.5	1.5	0
21	−3.5	−6.5	−1.5	0	−1.5
22	−3	−6	−1	0	−2.5
23	−1	−4	1	0	−1.5
24	4	1	6	1	0
25	−0.5	−3.5	1.5	0	0
26	−2.5	−5.5	−0.5	0	−0.5
27	4	1	6	1	0
28	−2	−5	0	0	0
29	−3	−6	−1	0	−1
30	−1.5	−4.5	0.5	0	−0.5
31	4	1	6	1	0
32	2.5	−0.5	4.5	0.5	0
33	−0.5	−3.5	1.5	0	0
34	7	4	9	4	0
35	5	2	7	6	0
36	4	1	6	7	0
37	4.5	1.5	6.5	8.5	0
38	2.5	−0.5	4.5	8	0
39	2.5	−0.5	4.5	7.5	0
40	5	2	3	9.5	0

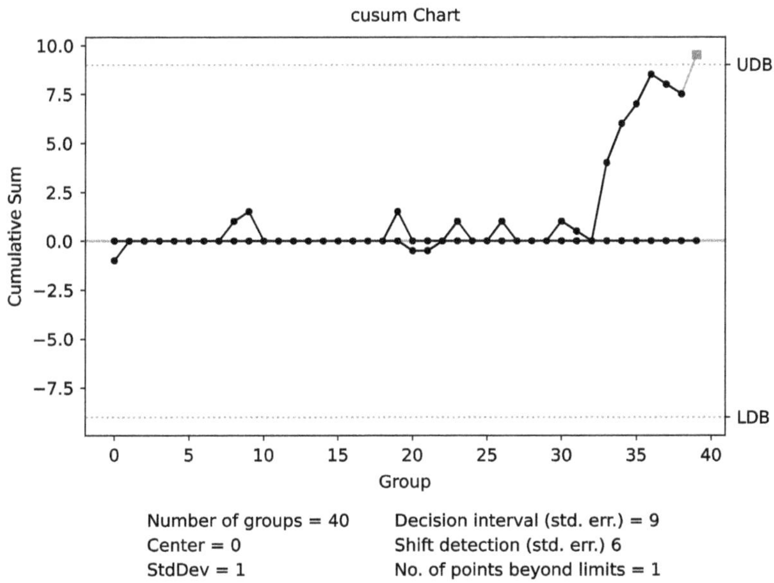

Fig. 3.8 CUSUM two-sided control chart for thickness difference, control parameters ($K^+ = 3$, $h^+ = 9$, $K^- = -2$, $h^- = -5$)

3.4.4 Average Run Length, Probability of False Alarm, and Conditional Expected Delay

The **run length** (RL) is defined as the number of time units until either $S_t^+ > h_t^+$ or $S_t^- < h^-$, for the first time. We have seen already that the **average run length** (ARL) is an important characteristic of a control procedure, when there is either no change in the mean level (ARL(0)), or the mean level has shifted to $\mu_1 = \mu_0 + \delta\sigma$, before the control procedure started (ARL(δ)). When the shift from μ_0 to μ_1 occurs at some change-point τ, $\tau > 0$, then we would like to know what is the probability of false alarm, i.e., that the run length is smaller than τ, and the conditional expected run length, given that RL $> \tau$. It is difficult to compute these characteristics of the Page control scheme analytically. The theory required for such an analysis is quite complicated (see Yashchin 1985). We provide Python methods in the `mistat` package that approximate these characteristics numerically by simulation.

The method *cusumArl* computes the average run length, ARL, and *cusumPfaCed* returns the probability of false alarm, FPA, and conditional expected delay, CED, for a given distribution, e.g., normal, binomial, or Poisson.

In Table 3.10, we present estimates of the ARL(δ) for the normal distribution, with NR = 100 runs. S.E. = standard deviation(RL)/$\sqrt{\text{NR}}$.

Table 3.10 ARL(δ) estimates for the normal distribution, $\mu = \delta, \sigma = 1$ NR = 100, ($K^+ = 1, h^+ = 3$, $K^- = -1, h^- = -3$)

δ	ARL	2*S.E.
0	1225.0	230.875
0.5	108.0	22.460
1.0	18.7	3.393
1.5	7.1	0.748

```
results = []
for loc in (0, 0.5, 1.0, 1.5):
    arl = mistat.cusumArl(randFunc=stats.norm(loc=loc), N=100,
                          limit=10_000, seed=100, verbose=False)
    results.append({
        'theta': loc,
        'ARL': arl['statistic']['ARL'],
        '2 S.E.': 2 * arl['statistic']['Std. Error'],
    })
print(pd.DataFrame(results))
```

```
   theta     ARL      2 S.E.
0    0.0  978.71  294.600536
1    0.5  126.66   36.962435
2    1.0   16.54    4.265489
3    1.5    5.86    1.386506
```

Program **cusumArl** can also be used to determine the values of the control parameters h^+ and h^- so that a certain ARL(0) is attained. For example, if we use the Shewhart 3-sigma control charts for the sample means in the normal case, the probability that, under no shift in the process level, a point will fall outside the control limits is 0.0026, and ARL(0) = 385. Suppose we wish to devise a two-sided CUSUM control scheme, when $\mu_0 = 10$, $\sigma = 5$, $\mu_1^+ = 14$, and $\mu_1^- = 6$. We obtain $K^+ = 12$ and $K^- = 8$. If we take $\alpha = 0.01$, we obtain $h^+ = \frac{-25\times\log(0.01)}{4} = 28.78$. Program **cusumArl** yields, for the parameters $\mu = 10$, $\sigma = 5$, $K^+ = 12$, $h^+ = 29$, $K^- = 8$, $h^- = -29$, the estimate ARL(0) = 411 $\pm$ 33.6. If we use $\alpha = 0.05$, we obtain $h^+ = 18.72$. Under the control parameters (12, 18.7, 8, -18.7), we obtain ARL(0) = 70.7 $\pm$ 5.5. We can now run the program for several $h^+ = -h^-$ values to obtain an ARL(0) estimate close to 385. The value in Fig. 3.9 ARL is 411.4 with an SE of 33.6.

```
for h in (18.7, 28, 28.5, 28.6, 28.7, 29, 30):
  arl = mistat.cusumArl(randFunc=stats.norm(loc=10, scale=5),
            N=300, limit=7000, seed=1, kp=12, km=8, hp=h, hm=-h,
            verbose=False)
  print(f"h {h:5.1f}: ARL(0) {arl['statistic']['ARL']:5.1f} ",
        f"+/- {arl['statistic']['Std. Error']:4.1f}")
```

```
h  18.7: ARL(0)  70.7  +/-  5.5
h  28.0: ARL(0) 363.2  +/- 30.0
h  28.5: ARL(0) 387.7  +/- 31.5
h  28.6: ARL(0) 394.7  +/- 32.4
h  28.7: ARL(0) 397.3  +/- 32.5
h  29.0: ARL(0) 411.4  +/- 33.6
h  30.0: ARL(0) 484.0  +/- 42.0
```

Thus, $h^+ = 29$ would yield a control scheme having an ARL(0) close to that of a Shewhart 3σ scheme.

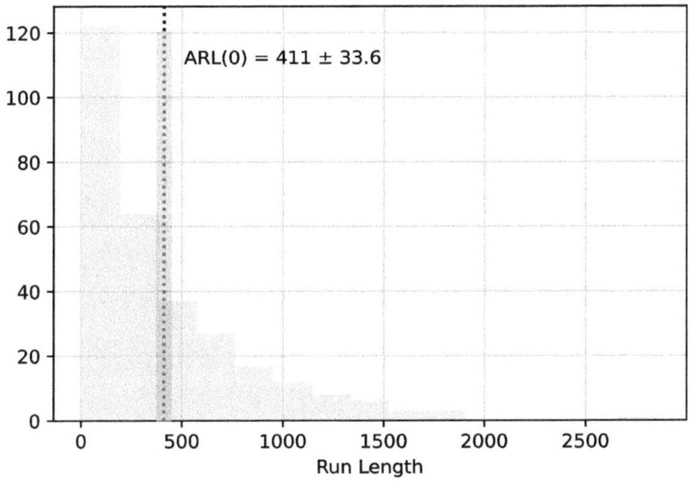

Fig. 3.9 Histogram of RL for $\mu = 10$, $\sigma = 5$, $K^+ = 12$, $h^+ = 29$, $K^- = 8$, $h^- = -29$

The function **cusumArl** can also compute the estimates of the ARL(δ) for the binomial distribution. To illustrate, consider the case of the binomial distribution $B(n, \theta)$ with $n = 100$, $\theta = 0.05$. A two-sided Page's control scheme, protecting against a shift above $\theta_1^+ = 0.07$ or below $\theta_1^- = 0.03$, can use the control parameters $K^+ = 5.95$, $h^+ = 12.87$, $K^- = 3.92$, and $h^- = -8.66$.

```
results = []
for p in (0.05, 0.06, 0.07):
    arl = mistat.cusumArl(randFunc=stats.binom(n=100, p=p), N=100, limit=2000,
                          seed=1, kp=5.95, km=3.92, hp=12.87, hm=-8.66)
    results.append({
        'p': p,
        'delta': p/0.05,
        'ARL': arl['statistic']['ARL'],
        '2 S.E.': 2 * arl['statistic']['Std. Error'],
    })
print(pd.DataFrame(results))
```

```
      p  delta     ARL     2 S.E.
0  0.05    1.0  291.71  78.261710
1  0.06    1.2   41.00  10.528704
2  0.07    1.4   11.78   2.636513
```

The program **cusumArl** yields, for NR = 100 runs, the estimate ARL(0) = 291.7 ± 39.13. Furthermore, for $\delta = \theta_1/\theta_0$, we obtain for the same control scheme

$$\text{ARL}\left(\frac{6}{5}\right) = 41.0 \pm 10.53, \qquad \text{ARL}\left(\frac{7}{5}\right) = 11.8 \pm 2.64.$$

Similarly, program **cusumArl** can be used to estimate the ARL(δ) in the Poisson case. For example, suppose that X_t has a Poisson distribution with mean $\lambda_0 = 10$. We wish to control the process against shifts in λ greater than $\lambda_1^+ = 15$ or smaller

Table 3.11 Estimates of PFA and CED, normal distribution $\mu_0 = 0$, $\sigma = 1$, control parameters $(K^+ = 1, h^+ = 3, K^- = -1, h^- = -3)$, $\tau = 100$, NR = 500

δ	PFA	CED
0.5	0.08	109.2 ± 21.7
1	0.08	15.66 ± 12.0
1.5	0.08	4.87 ± 10.9

than $\lambda_1^- = 7$. We use the control parameters $K^+ = 12.33$, $h^+ = 11.36$, $K^- = 8.41$, and $h^- = -12.91$.

```
arl = mistat.cusumArl(randFunc=stats.poisson(mu=10), N=100, limit=2000, seed=1,
                      kp=12.33, km=8.41, hp=11.36, hm=-12.91)
arl['statistic']
```

```
{'ARL': 289.6363636363636, 'Std. Error': 43.223677106723144}
```

The obtained estimate is ARL(0) = 289.6 ± 43.224.

We can use now program **cusumPfaCed** to estimate the probability of false alarm, PFA, and the conditional expected delay if a change in the mean of magnitude $\delta\sigma$ occurs at time τ. In Table 3.11, we present some estimates obtained from this method.

```
results = []
for loc in (0.5, 1.0, 1.5):
    pfaced = mistat.cusumPfaCed(randFunc1=stats.norm(),
                                randFunc2=stats.norm(loc=loc),
                                tau=100, N=100, limit=1_000, seed=1,
                                verbose=False)
    results.append({
        'theta': loc,
        'PFA': pfaced['statistic']['PFA'],
        'CED': pfaced['statistic']['CED'],
        'S.E.': pfaced['statistic']['Std. Error'],
    })
```

3.5 Bayesian Detection

The Bayesian approach to the problem of detecting changes in distributions can be described in the following terms. Suppose that we decide to monitor the stability of a process with a statistic T, having a distribution with p.d.f. $f_T(t; \boldsymbol{\theta})$, where $\boldsymbol{\theta}$ designates the parameters on which the distribution depends (process mean, variance, etc.). The statistic T could be the mean, $\bar{X}$, of a random sample of size n, the sample standard deviation, S, or the proportion defectives in the sample. A sample of size n is drawn from the process at predetermined epochs. Let T_i $(i = 1, 2, \cdots)$ denote the monitoring statistic at the ith epoch. Suppose that m such samples were drawn and that the statistics $T_1, T_2, \cdots, T_m$ are independent. Let

$\tau = 0, 1, 2, \cdots$ denote the location of the point of change in the process parameter $\boldsymbol{\theta}_0$, to $\boldsymbol{\theta}_1 = \boldsymbol{\theta}_0 + \boldsymbol{\Delta}$. τ is called the **change-point** of $\boldsymbol{\theta}_0$. The event $\{\tau = 0\}$ signifies that all the n samples have been drawn after the change-point. The event $\{\tau = i\}$, for $i = 1, \cdots, m-1$, signifies that the change-point occurred between the ith and $(i+1)$st sampling epoch. Finally, the event $\{\tau = m^+\}$ signifies that the change-point has not occurred before the first m sampling epochs.

Given $T_1, \cdots, T_m$, the **likelihood function** of τ, for specified values of $\boldsymbol{\theta}_0$ and $\boldsymbol{\theta}_1$, is defined as

$$L_m(\tau; T_1, \cdots, T_m) = \begin{cases} \prod_{i=1}^{m} f(T_i; \boldsymbol{\theta}_1), & \text{if } \tau = 0 \\ \prod_{i=1}^{\tau} f(T_i, \boldsymbol{\theta}_0) \prod_{j=\tau+1}^{m} f(T_j; \boldsymbol{\theta}_1), & \text{if } 1 \le \tau \le m-1, \\ \prod_{i=1}^{m} f(T_i; \boldsymbol{\theta}_0), & \text{if } \tau = m^+. \end{cases} \tag{3.5.1}$$

A **maximum likelihood** estimator of τ, given $T_1, \cdots, T_m$, is the argument maximizing $L_m(\tau; T_1, \cdots, T_m)$.

In the Bayesian framework, the statistician gives the various possible values of τ non-negative weights, which reflect his belief where the change-point could occur. High weight expresses higher confidence. In order to standardize the approach, we will assume that the sum of all weights is one, and we call these weights, the **prior probabilities** of τ. Let $\pi(\tau)$, $\tau = 0, 1, 2, \cdots$, denote the prior probabilities of τ. If the occurrence of the change-point is a realization of some random process, the following modified-geometric prior distribution could be used

$$\pi_m(\tau) = \begin{cases} \pi, & \text{if } \tau = 0 \\ (1-\pi)p(1-p)^{i-1}, & \text{if } 1 \le \tau \le m-1 \\ (1-\pi)(1-p)^{m-1}, & \text{if } \tau = m^+, \end{cases} \tag{3.5.2}$$

where $0 < \pi < 1$, $0 < p < 1$ are prior parameters. Applying Bayes formula, we convert the prior probabilities $\pi(t)$ after observing $T_1, \cdots, T_m$ into **posterior probabilities**. Let π_m denote the posterior probability of the event $\{\tau \le m\}$, given $T_1, \cdots, T_m$. Using the above modified-geometric prior distribution, and employing Bayes theorem, we obtain the formula

$$\pi_m = \frac{\frac{\pi}{(1-\pi)(1-p)^{m-1}} \prod_{j=1}^{m} R_j + \frac{p}{(1-p)^{m-1}} \sum_{i=1}^{m-1} (1-p)^{i-1} \prod_{j=i+1}^{m} R_j}{\frac{\pi}{(1-\pi)(1-p)^{m-1}} \prod_{j=1}^{m} R_j + \frac{p}{(1-p)^{m-1}} \sum_{i=1}^{m-1} (1-p)^{i-1} \prod_{j=i+1}^{m} R_j + 1}, \tag{3.5.3}$$

where

$$R_j = \frac{f(T_j; \boldsymbol{\theta}_1)}{f(T_j; \boldsymbol{\theta}_0)}, \quad j = 1, 2, \cdots \tag{3.5.4}$$

A Bayesian detection of a change-point is a procedure that detects a change as soon as $\pi_m \geq \pi^*$, where π^* is a value in (0, 1), close to 1.

The above procedure can be simplified, if we believe that the monitoring starts when $\boldsymbol{\theta} = \boldsymbol{\theta}_0$ (i.e., $\pi = 0$) and p is very small, we can represent π_m then, approximately, by

$$\tilde{\pi}_m = \frac{\sum_{i=1}^{m-1} \prod_{j=i+1}^{m} R_j}{\sum_{i=1}^{m-1} \prod_{j=i+1}^{m} R_j + 1}. \tag{3.5.5}$$

The statistic

$$W_m = \sum_{i=1}^{m-1} \prod_{j=i+1}^{m} R_j \tag{3.5.6}$$

is called the **Shiryaev–Roberts** (S.R.) statistic. Notice that $\tilde{\pi}_m \geq \pi^*$ if $W_m \geq \frac{\pi^*}{1-\pi^*}$. $\frac{\pi^*}{1-\pi^*}$ is called the **stopping threshold**. Thus, for example, if the Bayes procedure is to "flag" a change as soon as $\tilde{\pi}_m \geq 0.95$, the procedure that "flags" as soon as $W_m \geq 19$ is equivalent.

We illustrate now the use of the S.R. statistic in the special case of monitoring the mean θ_0 of a process. The statistic T is the sample mean, $\bar{X}_n$, based on a sample of n observations. We will assume that $\bar{X}_n$ has a normal distribution $N\left(\theta_0, \frac{\sigma}{\sqrt{n}}\right)$, and at the change-point, θ_0 shifts to $\theta_1 = \theta_0 + \delta\sigma$. It is straightforward to verify that the likelihood ratio is

$$R_j = \exp\left\{-\frac{n\delta^2}{2\sigma^2} + \frac{n\delta}{\sigma^2}(\bar{X}_j - \theta_0)\right\}, \quad j = 1, 2, \cdots. \tag{3.5.7}$$

Accordingly, the S.R. statistic is

$$W_m = \sum_{i=1}^{m-1} \exp\left\{\frac{n\delta}{\sigma^2} \sum_{j=i+1}^{m} (\bar{X}_j - \theta_0) - \frac{n\delta^2(m-i)}{2\sigma^2}\right\}. \tag{3.5.8}$$

Example 3.6 We illustrate the procedure numerically. Suppose that $\theta_0 = 10$, $n = 5$, $\delta = 2$, $\pi^* = 0.95$, and $\sigma = 3$. The stopping threshold is 19. Suppose that $\tau = 10$. The values of $\bar{X}_j$ have the normal distribution $N\left(10, \frac{3}{\sqrt{5}}\right)$ for $j = 1, \cdots, 10$ and $N\left(10 + \delta\sigma, \frac{3}{\sqrt{5}}\right)$ for $j = 11, 12, \cdots$. In Table 3.12, we present the values of W_m.

We see that the S.R. statistic detects the change-point quickly if δ is large. ■

Table 3.12 Values of W_m for $\delta = 0.5(0.5)2.0$, $n = 5$, $\tau = 10$, $\sigma = 3$, $\pi^* = 0.95$

m	$\delta = 0.5$	$\delta = 1.0$	$\delta = 1.5$	$\delta = 2.0$
2	0.3649	0.0773	0.0361	0.0112
3	3.1106	0.1311	0.0006	0.0002
4	3.2748	0.0144	0.0562	0.0000
5	1.1788	0.0069	0.0020	0.0000
6	10.1346	0.2046	0.0000	0.0291
7	14.4176	0.0021	0.0527	0.0000
8	2.5980	0.0021	0.0015	0.0000
9	0.5953	0.6909	0.0167	0.0000
10	0.4752	0.0616	0.0007	0.0001
11	1.7219	5.6838	848.6259	1538.0943
12	2.2177	73.8345		
13	16.3432			
14	74.9618			

Table 3.13 Estimates of PFA and CED for $\mu_0 = 10$, $\sigma = 3$, $n = 5$, $\tau = 10$, and stopping threshold = 99

	$\delta = 0.5$	$\delta = 1.0$	$\delta = 1.5$	$\delta = 2.0$
PFA	0.00	0.01	0.01	0.01
CED	7.17	2.50	1.61	1.09

The larger is the critical level $w^* = \pi^*/(1 - \pi^*)$, the smaller will be the frequency of detecting the change-point before it happens (false alarm). Two characteristics of the procedure are of interest:

(i) The **probability of false alarm** (PFA)
(ii) The **conditional expected delay** (CED), given that the alarm is given after the change-point

The functions **shroArlPfaCedNorm** and **shroArlPfaCedPois** estimate the ARL(0) of the procedure for the normal and Poisson cases. Functions **shroArlPfaCedNorm** and **shroArlPfaCedPois** estimate the PFA and CED of these procedures. In Table 3.13, we present simulation estimates of the PFA and CED for several values of δ. The estimates are based on 100 simulation runs.

```
common = {'mean0': 10, 'sd': 3, 'n': 5, 'tau': 10, 'w': 99, 'seed': 1,
          'verbose': False}
pd.DataFrame([
    mistat.shroArlPfaCedNorm(delta=0.5, **common)['statistic'],
    mistat.shroArlPfaCedNorm(delta=1.0, **common)['statistic'],
    mistat.shroArlPfaCedNorm(delta=1.5, **common)['statistic'],
    mistat.shroArlPfaCedNorm(delta=2.0, **common)['statistic'],
], index=[0.5, 1.0, 1.5, 2.0])
```

```
       ARL  Std. Error   PFA       CED  CED-Std. Error
0.5  17.17    0.250621  0.00  7.170000        1.580130
1.0  12.45    0.106184  0.01  2.505051        1.234753
1.5  11.55    0.080467  0.01  1.606061        1.156715
2.0  11.04    0.059867  0.01  1.090909        1.109741
```

Table 3.14 Average run length of Shiryaev–Roberts procedure, $\mu_0 = 10$, $\delta = 2$, $\sigma = 3$, $n = 5$

Stopping Threshold	ARL(0)
19	48.81 ± 4.41
50	106.32 ± 10.87
99	186.49 ± 18.29

We see that if the amount of shift δ is large ($\delta > 1$), then the conditional expected delay (CED) is small. The estimates of PFA are small due to the large threshold value. Another question of interest is, what is the average run length (ARL) when there is no change in the mean. We estimated the ARL(0), for the same example of normally distributed sample means using function *shroArlPfaCedNorm*. 100 independent simulation runs were performed. In Table 3.14, we present the estimated values of ARL(0), as a function of the stopping threshold.

```
common = {'mean0': 10, 'sd': 3, 'n': 5, 'delta': 2.0, 'seed': 1,
          'verbose': False}
pd.DataFrame([
    mistat.shroArlPfaCedNorm(w=19, **common)['statistic'],
    mistat.shroArlPfaCedNorm(w=50, **common)['statistic'],
    mistat.shroArlPfaCedNorm(w=99, **common)['statistic'],
], index=[19, 50, 99])
```

```
       ARL  Std. Error
19   48.81    4.411115
50  106.32   10.868872
99  186.49   18.288885
```

Thus, the procedure based on the Shiryaev–Roberts detection is sensitive to changes, while in a stable situation (no changes), it is expected to run long till an alarm is given. Figure 3.10 shows a box plot of the run length with stopping threshold of 99, when there is no change. For more details on data analytic aspects of the Shiryaev–Roberts procedure, see Kenett and Pollak (1996).

3.6 Process Tracking

Process **tracking** is a procedure that repeatedly estimates certain characteristics of the process that is being monitored. The CUSUM detection procedure, as well as that of Shiryaev–Roberts, is designed to provide warning quickly after changes occur. However, at times of stopping, these procedures do not provide direct information on the current location of the process mean (or the process variance). In the Shewhart $\bar{X}$-bar control chart, each point provides an estimate of the process mean at that specific time. The precision of these estimates is generally low, since they are based on small samples. One may suggest that, as long as there is no evidence that a change in the process mean has occurred, an average of all previous sample means can serve as an estimator of the current value of the process mean. Indeed, if after observing m samples, each of size n, the grand average

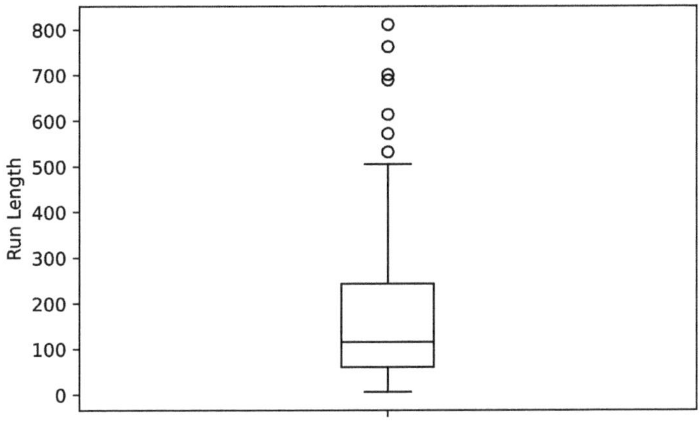

Fig. 3.10 Box and whisker plots of 100 run lengths of the Shiryaev–Roberts procedure, normal distribution $\mu_0 = 10$, $\delta = 2$, $\sigma = 3$, $n = 5$, stopping threshold 99

$\bar{\bar{X}}_m = \frac{1}{m}(\bar{X}_1 + \cdots + \bar{X}_m)$ has the standard error $\sigma/\sqrt{nm}$, while the standard error of the last mean, $\bar{X}_m$, is only $\sigma/\sqrt{n}$. It is well -established by statistical estimation theory that, as long as the process mean μ_0 does not change, $\bar{\bar{X}}_m$ is the best (minimum variance) unbiased estimator of $\mu_m = \mu_0$. On the other hand, if μ_0 has changed to $\mu_1 = \mu_0 + \delta\sigma$, between the τth and the $(\tau + 1)$st sample, where $\tau < m$, the grand mean $\bar{\bar{X}}_m$ is a biased estimator of μ_1 (the current mean). The expected value of $\bar{\bar{X}}_m$ is

$$\frac{1}{m}(\tau\mu_0 + (m - \tau)\mu_1) = \mu_1 - \frac{\tau}{m}\delta\sigma.$$

Thus, if the change-point, τ, is close to m, the bias of $\bar{\bar{X}}$ can be considerable. The bias of the estimator of the current mean, when $1 < \tau < m$, can be reduced by considering different types of estimators. In the present chapter, we focus attention on four procedures for tracking and monitoring the process mean: the exponentially weighted moving average procedure (EWMA), the Bayes estimation of the current mean (BECM), the Kalman filter, and the quality measurement plan (QMP).

3.6.1 The EWMA Procedure

The **exponentially weighted moving average (EWMA) chart** is a control chart for the process mean that at time t $(t = 1, 2, \cdots)$ plots the statistic

$$\hat{\mu}_t = (1 - \lambda)\hat{\mu}_{t-1} + \lambda\bar{X}_t, \tag{3.6.1}$$

where $0 < \lambda < 1$, and $\hat{\mu}_0 = \mu_0$ is the initial process mean. The Shewhart $\bar{X}$-chart is the limiting case of $\lambda = 1$. Small values of λ give high weight to the past data. It is customary to use the values of $\lambda = 0.2$ or $\lambda = 0.3$.

By repeated application of the recursive formula, we obtain

$$\begin{aligned}\hat{\mu}_t &= (1-\lambda)^2\hat{\mu}_{t-2} + \lambda(1-\lambda)\bar{X}_{t-1} + \lambda\bar{X}_t \\ &= \cdots \\ &= (1-\lambda)^t\mu_0 + \lambda\sum_{i=1}^{t}(1-\lambda)^{t-i}\bar{X}_i.\end{aligned} \tag{3.6.2}$$

We see in this formula that $\hat{\mu}_t$ is a weighted average of the first t means $\bar{X}_1, \cdots, \bar{X}_t$ and μ_0, with weights that decrease geometrically, as $t - i$ grows.

Let τ denote the epoch of change from μ_0 to $\mu_1 = \mu_0 + \delta\sigma$. As in the previous section, $\{\tau = i\}$ implies that

$$E\{\bar{X}_j\} = \begin{cases}\mu_0, & \text{for } j = 1, \cdots, i \\ \mu_1, & \text{for } j = i+1, i+2, \cdots\end{cases} \tag{3.6.3}$$

Accordingly, the expected value of the statistic $\hat{\mu}_t$ (an estimator of the current mean μ_t) is

$$E\{\hat{\mu}_t\} = \begin{cases}\mu_0, & \text{if } t \le \tau \\ \mu_1 - \delta\sigma(1-\lambda)^{t-\tau}, & \text{if } t > \tau.\end{cases} \tag{3.6.4}$$

We see that the bias of $\hat{\mu}_t$, $-\delta\sigma(1-\lambda)^{t-\tau}$, decreases to zero geometrically fast as t grows above τ. This is a faster decrease in bias than that of the grand mean, $\bar{\bar{X}}_t$, which was discussed earlier.

The variance of $\hat{\mu}_t$ can be easily determined, since $\bar{X}_1, \bar{X}_2, \cdots, \bar{X}_t$ are independent and $\text{Var}\{\bar{X}_j\} = \frac{\sigma^2}{n}$, $j = 1, 2, \cdots$. Hence,

$$\begin{aligned}\text{Var}\{\hat{\mu}_t\} &= \frac{\sigma^2}{n}\lambda^2\sum_{i=1}^{t}(1-\lambda)^{2(t-i)} \\ &= \frac{\sigma^2}{n}\lambda^2\frac{1-(1-\lambda)^{2t}}{1-(1-\lambda)^2}.\end{aligned} \tag{3.6.5}$$

This variance converges to

$$\text{Avar}\{\hat{\mu}_t\} = \frac{\sigma^2}{n}\frac{\lambda}{2-\lambda}, \tag{3.6.6}$$

as $t \to \infty$. An **EWMA control chart** for monitoring shifts in the mean is constructed in the following manner. Starting at $\hat{\mu}_0 = \mu_0$, the points $(t, \hat{\mu}_t)$, $t = 1, 2, \cdots$, are plotted. As soon as these points cross either one of the control limits

$$\text{CL} = \mu_0 \pm L\frac{\sigma}{\sqrt{n}}\sqrt{\frac{\lambda}{2-\lambda}}, \tag{3.6.7}$$

an alarm is given that the process mean has shifted.

In Fig. 3.11, we present an EWMA chart with $\mu_0 = 10$, $\sigma = 3$, $n = 5$, $\lambda = 0.2$, and $L = 2$. The values of $\hat{\mu}_t$ indicate that a shift in the mean took place after the eleventh sampling epoch. An alarm for change is given after the fourteenth sample.

As in the previous sections, we have to characterize the efficacy of the EWMA chart in terms of PFA and CED when a shift occurs, and the ARL when there is no shift. In Table 3.15, we present estimates of PFA and CED based on 1000 simulation runs. The simulations were from normal distributions, with $\mu_0 = 10$, $\sigma = 3$, and

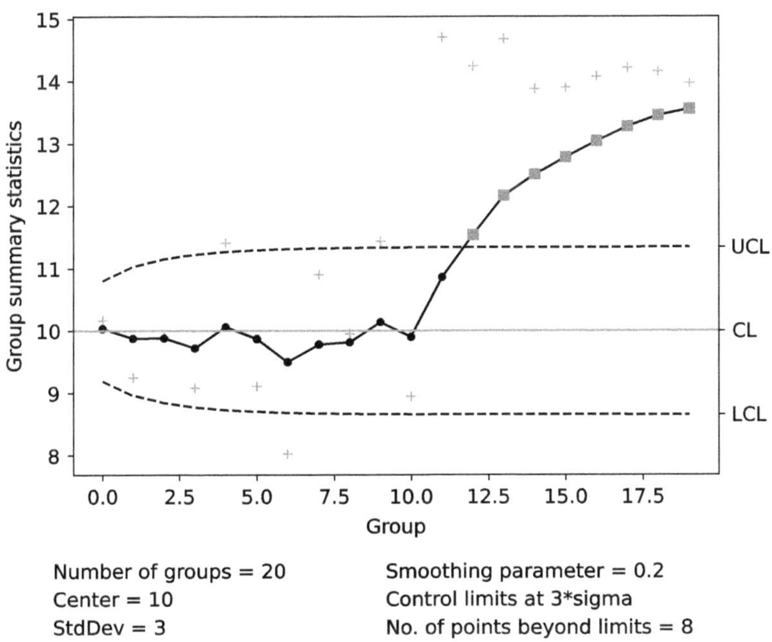

Fig. 3.11 EWMA chart, $\mu_0 = 10$, $\sigma = 3$, $\delta = 0$, $n = 5$, $\lambda = 0.2$ (smooth), and $L = 2$

Table 3.15 Simulation estimates of PFA and CED of an EWMA chart

		CED			
L	PFA	$\delta = 0.5$	$\delta = 1.0$	$\delta = 1.5$	$\delta = 2.0$
2	0.168	3.93	2.21	1.20	1.00
2.5	0.043	4.35	2.67	1.41	1.03
3	0.002	4.13	3.36	1.63	1.06

$n = 5$. The change-point was at $\tau = 10$. The shift was from μ_0 to $\mu_1 = \mu_0 + \delta\sigma$. The estimates $\hat{\mu}_t$ were determined with $\lambda = 0.2$. We see in this table that if we construct the control limits with the value of $L = 3$, then the PFA is very small, and the CED is not large.

The estimated ARL values for this example are

L	2	2.5	3.0
ARL	48.7	151.36	660.9

3.6.2 *The BECM Procedure*

In this section, we present a Bayesian procedure for estimating the current mean μ_t $(t = 1, 2, \cdots)$. Let $\bar{X}_1, \bar{X}_2, \cdots, \bar{X}_t$, $t = 1, 2, \cdots$, be means of samples of size n. The distribution of $\bar{X}_i$ is $N\left(\mu_i, \frac{\sigma}{\sqrt{n}}\right)$, where σ is the process standard deviation. We will assume here that σ is known and fixed throughout all sampling epochs. This assumption is made in order to simplify the exposition. In actual cases, one has to monitor also whether σ changes with time.

If the process mean stays stable throughout the sampling periods, then

$$\mu_1 = \mu_2 = \cdots = \mu_t = \mu_0.$$

Let us consider this case first and present the Bayes estimator of μ_0. In the Bayesian approach, the model assumes that μ_0 itself is random, with some prior distribution. If we assume that the prior distribution of μ_0 is normal, say $N(\mu^*, \tau)$, then using Bayes theorem one can show that the posterior distribution of μ_0, given the t sample means, is normal with mean

$$\hat{\mu}_{B,t} = \left(1 - \frac{nt\tau^2}{\sigma^2 + nt\tau^2}\right)\mu^* + \frac{nt\tau^2}{\sigma^2 + nt\tau^2} = \bar{X}_t = \frac{1}{t}\sum_{i=1}^{t} \bar{X}_i \tag{3.6.8}$$

and variance

$$w_t^2 = \tau^2 \left(1 - \frac{nt\tau^2}{\sigma^2 + nt\tau^2}\right). \quad (3.6.9)$$

The mean $\hat{\mu}_{B,t}$ of the posterior distribution is commonly taken as the Bayes estimator of μ_0 (see Chapter 3, *Modern Statistics*, Kenett et al. 2022b).

It is interesting to notice that $\hat{\mu}_{B,t}$, $t = 1, 2, \cdots$, can be determined recursively by the formula

$$\hat{\mu}_{B,t} = \left(1 - \frac{nw_{t-1}^2}{\sigma^2 + nw_{t-1}^2}\right)\hat{\mu}_{B,t-1} + \frac{nw_{t-1}^2}{\sigma^2 + nw_{t-1}^2}\bar{X}_t, \quad (3.6.10)$$

where $\hat{\mu}_{B,0} = \mu^*$, $w_0^2 = \tau^2$, and

$$w_t^2 = \frac{\sigma^2 w_{t-1}^2}{\sigma^2 + nw_{t-1}^2}. \quad (3.6.11)$$

This recursive formula resembles that of the EWMA estimator. The difference here is that the weight λ is a function of time, i.e.,

$$\lambda_t = \frac{nw_{t-1}^2}{\sigma^2 + nw_{t-1}^2}. \quad (3.6.12)$$

From the above recursive formula for w_t^2, we obtain that $w_t^2 = \lambda_t \frac{\sigma^2}{n}$, or $\lambda_t = \lambda_{t-1}/(1+\lambda_{t-1})$, $t = 2, 3, \cdots$ where $\lambda_1 = n\tau^2/(\sigma^2+n\tau^2)$. The procedures become more complicated if change-points are introduced. We discuss in the following section a dynamic model of change.

3.6.3 *The Kalman Filter*

In the present section, we present a model of dynamic changes in the observed sequence of random variables and a Bayesian estimator of the current mean, called the **Kalman filter**.

At time t, let Y_t denote an observable random variable, having mean μ_t. We assume that μ_t may change at random from one time epoch to another, according to the model

$$\mu_t = \mu_{t-1} + \Delta_t, \quad t = 1, 2, \cdots$$

where Δ_t, $t = 1, 2, \cdots$, is a sequence of i.i.d. random variables having a normal distribution $N(\delta, \sigma_2)$. Furthermore, we assume that $\mu_0 \sim N(\mu_0^*, w_0)$, and the observation equation is

$$Y_t = \mu_t + \epsilon_t, \quad t = 1, 2, \cdots,$$

where ϵ_t are i.i.d. $N(0, \sigma_\epsilon)$. According to this dynamic model, the mean at time t (the current mean) is normally distributed with mean

$$\hat{\mu}_t = B_t(\hat{\mu}_{t-1} + \delta) + (1 - B_t)Y_t, \tag{3.6.13}$$

where

$$B_t = \frac{\sigma_\epsilon^2}{\sigma_\epsilon^2 + \sigma_2^2 + w_{t-1}^2}, \tag{3.6.14}$$

$$w_t^2 = B_t(\sigma_2^2 + w_{t-1}^2). \tag{3.6.15}$$

The posterior variance of μ_t is w_t^2. $\hat{\mu}_t$ is the Kalman filter.

If the prior parameters σ_ϵ^2, σ_2^2, and δ are unknown, we could use a small portion of the data to estimate these parameters.

According to the dynamic model, we can write

$$y_t = \mu_0 + \delta t + \epsilon_t^*, \quad t = 1, 2, \cdots,$$

where $\epsilon_t^* = \sum_{i=1}^t [(\Delta_i - \delta) + \epsilon_i]$. Notice that $E\{\epsilon_t^*\} = 0$ for all t and $V\{\epsilon_t^*\} = t(\sigma_2^2 + \sigma_\epsilon^2)$. Let $U_t = y_t/\sqrt{t}, t = 1, 2, \cdots$; then we can write the regression model

$$U_t = \mu_0 x_{1t} + \delta x_{2t} + \eta_t, \quad t = 1, 2, \cdots,$$

where $x_{1t} = 1/\sqrt{t}$ and $x_{2t} = \sqrt{t}$ and η_t, $t = 1, 2 \cdots$, are independent random variables, with $E\{\eta_t\} = 0$ and $V\{\eta_t\} = (\sigma_2^2 + \sigma_e^2)$.

Using the first m points of (t, y_t) and fitting, by the method of least squares (see Chapter 3, *Modern Statistics*, Kenett et al. 2022b), the regression equation of U_t against (x_{1t}, x_{2t}), we obtain estimates of μ_0, δ and of $(\sigma_2^2 + \sigma_\epsilon^2)$. Estimate of σ_e^2 can be obtained, if y_t are group means, by estimating within groups variance; otherwise, we assume a value for σ_ϵ^2, smaller than the least squares estimate of $\sigma_2^2 + \sigma_\epsilon^2$. We illustrate this now by example.

Example 3.7 In Fig. 3.12, we present the Dow–Jones financial index for the 300 business days of 1935 (dataset **DOJO1935.csv**). The Kalman filter estimates of the current means are plotted in this figure too. These estimates were determined by the formula

$$\hat{\mu}_t = B_t(\hat{\mu}_{t-1} + \delta) + (1 - B_t)y_t, \tag{3.6.16}$$

where the prior parameters were computed as suggested above, on the basis of the first $m = 20$ data points.

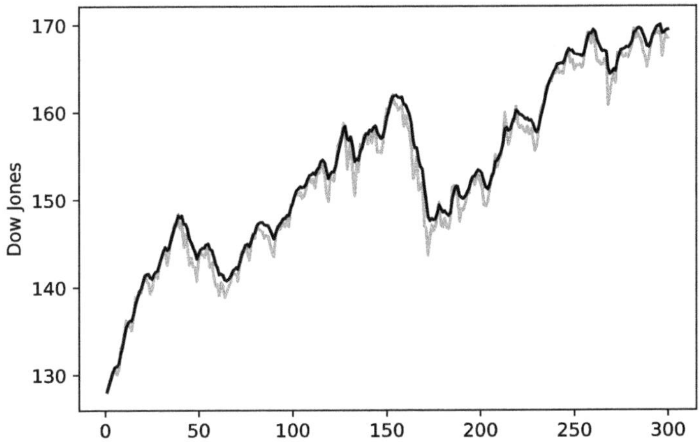

Fig. 3.12 The daily Dow–Jones financial index for 1935

```
dojo1935 = mistat.load_data('DOJO1935')

# solve the regression equation
m = 20
sqrt_t = np.sqrt(range(1, m + 1))
df = pd.DataFrame({
    'Ut': dojo1935[:m]/sqrt_t,
    'x1t': 1 / sqrt_t,
    'x2t': sqrt_t,
})
model = smf.ols(formula='Ut ~ x1t + x2t - 1', data=df).fit()
mu0, delta = model.params
var_eta = np.var(model.resid, ddof=2)
pd.Series({'mu0': mu0, 'delta': delta, 'Var(eta)': var_eta})
```

```
mu0          127.484294
delta          0.655591
Var(eta)       0.073094
dtype: float64
```

The least squares estimates of μ_0, δ, and $\sigma_2^2+\sigma_\epsilon^2$ are, respectively, $\hat{\mu}_0 = 127.484$, $\hat{\delta} = 0.656$, and $\hat{\sigma}_2^2+\hat{\sigma}_\epsilon^2 = 0.0731$. For $\hat{\sigma}_\epsilon^2$, we have chosen the value 0.0597, and for w_0^2, the value 0.0015. Using these starting values, we can apply the Kalman filter.

```
# choose sig2e and w20
sig2e = 0.0597
w20 = 0.0015

# apply the filter
results = []
mu_tm1 = mu0
w2_tm1 = w20
y_tm1 = mu0
for i in range(0, len(dojo1935)):
    y_t = dojo1935[i]
    B_t = sig2e / (var_eta + w2_tm1)
    mu_t = B_t * (mu_tm1 + delta) + (1 - B_t) * y_t
    results.append({
```

```
        't': i + 1, # adjust for Python indexing starting at 0
        'y_t': y_t,
        'mu_t': mu_t,
    })
    w2_tm1 = B_t * (var_eta - sig2e + w2_tm1)
    mu_tm1 = mu_t
    y_tm1 = y_t
results = pd.DataFrame(results)
```

The first 50 values of the data, y_t, and the estimate $\hat{\mu}_t$, are given in Table 3.16. ■

3.6.4 The QMP Tracking Method

Hoadley (1981) introduced at Bell Laboratories a **quality measurement plan** (QMP), which employs Bayesian methods of estimating the current mean of a

Table 3.16 The Dow–Jones index for the first 50 days of 1935, and the Kalman filter estimates

t	y_t	μ_t	t	y_t	μ_t
1	128.06	128.12	26	141.31	141.54
2	129.05	128.86	27	141.20	141.82
3	129.76	129.60	28	141.07	141.95
4	130.35	130.29	29	142.90	142.72
5	130.77	130.88	30	143.40	143.38
6	130.06	130.99	31	144.25	144.12
7	130.59	131.25	32	144.36	144.62
8	132.99	132.31	33	142.56	144.26
9	133.56	133.19	34	143.59	144.42
10	135.03	134.29	35	145.59	145.27
11	136.26	135.44	36	146.32	146.07
12	135.68	135.94	37	147.31	146.95
13	135.57	136.21	38	147.06	147.40
14	135.13	136.22	39	148.44	148.20
15	137.09	136.95	40	146.65	148.03
16	138.96	138.11	41	147.37	148.19
17	138.77	138.77	42	144.61	147.26
18	139.58	139.48	43	146.12	147.24
19	139.42	139.87	44	144.72	146.71
20	140.68	140.58	45	142.59	145.58
21	141.47	141.33	46	143.38	145.16
22	140.78	141.53	47	142.34	144.52
23	140.49	141.55	48	142.35	144.11
24	139.35	141.14	49	140.72	143.25
25	139.74	141.02	50	143.58	143.79

process. This QMP provides reporting capabilities of large datasets and, in a certain sense, is an improvement over the Shewhart 3-sigma control. These plans were implemented throughout Western Electric Co. in the late 1980s. The main idea is that the process mean does not remain at a constant level but changes at random every time period according to some distribution. This framework is similar to that of the Kalman filter but was developed for observations X_t having Poisson distributions with means λ_t $(t = 1, 2, \cdots)$, and where $\lambda_1, \lambda_2, \cdots$ are independent random variables having a common gamma distribution $G(\nu, \Lambda)$. The parameters ν and Λ are **unknown** and are estimated from the data. At the end of each period, a box plot is put on a chart. The center line of the box plot represents the posterior mean of λ_t, given past observations. The lower and upper sides of the box represent the 0.05th and 0.95th quantiles of the posterior distribution of λ_t. The lower whisker starts at the 0.01th quantile of the posterior distribution, and the upper whisker ends at the 0.99th quantile of that distribution. These box plots are compared to a desired quality level.

QMP is a mixed model with random effects, in contrast with fixed effects. It is a best linear unbiased prediction (BLUP). BLUP estimates of realized values of a random variable are linear in the sense that they are linear functions of the data. They are unbiased in the sense that the average value of the estimate is equal to the average value of the quantity being estimated and best in the sense that they have minimum sum of squared errors within the class of linear unbiased estimators. Estimators of random effects are called predictors, to distinguish them from estimators of fixed effects called estimators. BLUP estimates are solutions to mixed model equations and are usually different from generalized linear regression estimates used for fixed effects.

It is interesting to consider random versus fixed effects in the context of the analytic studies versus enumerative studies dichotomy introduced by Deming (1982). Enumerative studies are focused on estimation used to explain existing conditions. Acceptance sampling covered in Chap. 11 is enumerative. Analytic studies focus on predictions of performance in new circumstances. The QMP model is analytic in that it predicts the impact of data measured over time. The design of experiments covered in Chaps. 5–7 can be considered as both enumerative, when focused on explaining the effects of a list of factors on responses, or analytic, in predictive future responses. This distinction is reflected by optimality criteria discussed in Sect. 5.10. We proceed with an analysis of the QMP model.

We show in Sect. 3.8.3 of *Modern Statistics* (Kenett et al. 2022b) that if X_t has a Poisson distribution $P(\lambda_t)$, and λ_t has a gamma distribution $G(\nu, \Lambda)$, then the posterior distribution of λ_t, given X_t, is the gamma distribution $G\left(\nu + X_t, \frac{\Lambda}{1+\Lambda}\right)$. Thus, the Bayes estimate of λ_t, for a squared error loss, is the posterior expectation

$$\hat{\lambda}_t = (\nu + X_t)\frac{\Lambda}{1+\Lambda}. \tag{3.6.17}$$

Similarly, the pth quantile of the posterior distribution is

$$\lambda_{t,p} = \frac{\Lambda}{1+\Lambda} G_p(\nu + X_t, 1), \quad (3.6.18)$$

where $G_p(\nu + X_t, 1)$ is the pth quantile of the standard gamma distribution $G(\nu + X_t, 1)$. We remark that if ν is an integer, then

$$G_p(\nu + X_t, 1) = \frac{1}{2}\chi_p^2[2(\nu + X_t)]. \quad (3.6.19)$$

We assumed that $\lambda_1, \lambda_2, \cdots$ are independent and identically distributed. This implies that $X_1, X_2, \cdots$ are independent, having the same **negative binomial** predictive distribution, with predictive expectation

$$E\{X_t\} = \nu\Lambda \quad (3.6.20)$$

and predictive variance

$$V\{X_t\} = \nu\Lambda(1 + \Lambda). \quad (3.6.21)$$

We therefore can estimate the prior parameters ν and Λ by the consistent estimators

$$\hat{\Lambda}_T = \left(\frac{S_T^2}{\bar{X}_T} - 1\right)^+ \quad (3.6.22)$$

and

$$\hat{\nu}_T = \frac{\bar{X}_T}{\hat{\Lambda}_T}, \quad (3.6.23)$$

where $\bar{X}_T$ and S_T^2 are the sample mean and sample variance of $X_1, X_2, \cdots, X_T$. For determining $\hat{\lambda}_t$ and $\lambda_{t,p}$, we can substitute $\hat{\Lambda}_T$ and $\hat{\nu}_T$ in the above equations, with $T = t - 1$. We illustrate this estimation method, called **parametric empirical Bayes** method, in the following example.

Example 3.8 In dataset **SOLDEF.csv**, we present results of testing batches of circuit boards for defects in solder points, after wave soldering. The batches include boards of similar design. There were close to 1000 solder points on each board. The results X_t are the number of defects per 10^6 points (**PPM**). The quality standard is $\lambda^0 = 100$ (PPM). λ_t values below λ^0 represent high-quality soldering. In this dataset, there are $N = 380$ test results. Only 78 batches had an X_t value greater than $\lambda^0 = 100$. If we take UCL $= \lambda^0 + 3\sqrt{\lambda^0} = 130$, we see that only 56 batches had X_t values greater than the UCL. All runs of consecutive X_t values greater than 130 are of length not greater than 3. We conclude therefore that the occurrence of low-quality batches is sporadic, caused by common causes. These batches are excluded from the analysis.

```
soldef = mistat.load_data('SOLDEF')

print('Batches above quality standard: ', sum(soldef > 100))
print('Batches above UCL: ', sum(soldef > 130))

xbar = np.cumsum(soldef) / np.arange(1, len(soldef)+1)
results = []
for i in range(2, len(soldef)):
    xbar_tm1 = np.mean(xbar[i-1])
    S2_tm1 = np.var(soldef[:i])
    gamma_tm1 = S2_tm1/xbar_tm1 - 1
    nu_tm1 = xbar_tm1 / gamma_tm1
    result = {
        't': i + 1,
        'Xt': soldef[i],
        'xbar_tm1': xbar_tm1,
        'S2_tm1': S2_tm1,
        'Gamma_tm1': gamma_tm1,
        'nu_tm1': nu_tm1,
    }
    f = gamma_tm1 / (gamma_tm1 + 1)
    shape = nu_tm1 + soldef[i]
    result['lambda_t'] = f * shape
    result.update(((f'lambda({p})', f * stats.gamma.ppf(p, a=shape, scale=1))
                   for p in (0.01, 0.05, 0.95, 0.99)))
    results.append(result)
results = pd.DataFrame(results)
```

```
Batches above quality standard:  78
Batches above UCL:  56
```

In Table 3.17, we present the X_t values and the associated values of $\bar{X}_{t-1}$, S^2_{t-1}, $\hat{\Lambda}_{t-1}$, and $\hat{\nu}_{t-1}$, associated with $t = 10, \cdots, 20$. The statistics $\bar{X}_{t-1}$, etc., are functions of $X_1, \cdots, X_{t-1}$. In Table 3.18, we present the values of $\hat{\lambda}_t$ and the quantiles $\lambda_{t,p}$ for $p = 0.01, 0.05, 0.95$, and 0.99. ■

Table 3.17 The number of defects (PPM) and associated statistics for the SOLDEF data

t	X_t	$\bar{X}_{t-1}$	S^2_{t-1}	$\hat{\Lambda}_{t-1}$	$\hat{\nu}_{t-1}$
10	29	23.67	75.56	2.19	10.79
11	16	24.20	70.56	1.92	12.63
12	31	23.45	69.70	1.97	11.89
13	19	24.08	68.24	1.83	13.13
14	18	23.69	64.83	1.74	13.65
15	20	23.29	62.35	1.68	13.88
16	103	23.07	58.86	1.55	14.86
17	31	28.06	429.56	14.31	1.96
18	33	28.24	404.77	13.34	2.12
19	12	28.50	383.47	12.46	2.29
20	46	27.63	376.86	12.64	2.19

Table 3.18 Empirical Bayes estimates of λ_t and $\lambda_{t,p}$, $p = 0.01, 0.05, 0.95, 0.99$

t	λ_t	$\lambda_{t,0.01}$	$\lambda_{t,0.05}$	$\lambda_{t,0.95}$	$\lambda_{t,0.99}$
10	27.33	18.27	20.61	34.82	38.40
11	18.81	11.61	13.43	24.94	27.94
12	28.46	19.34	21.71	35.97	39.53
13	20.79	13.22	15.15	27.17	30.26
14	20.08	12.72	14.59	26.29	29.30
15	21.23	13.67	15.61	27.56	30.62
16	71.68	57.22	61.17	82.87	87.92
17	30.81	19.71	22.54	40.13	44.65
18	32.67	21.22	24.16	42.23	46.84
19	13.23	6.46	8.04	19.46	22.69
20	44.65	31.06	34.62	55.73	60.96

3.7 Automatic Process Control

Certain production lines are fully automated, like in chemical industries, paper industries, automobile industry, etc. In such production lines, it is often possible to build in feedback and control mechanism, so that if there is indication that the process mean or standard deviation changes significantly, then a correction is made automatically via the control mechanism. If μ_t denotes the level of the process mean at time t, and u_t denotes the control level at time t, the **dynamic linear model** (DLM) of the process mean is

$$\mu_t = \mu_{t-1} + \Delta_t + bu_{t-1}, \quad t = 1, 2, \cdots, \tag{3.7.1}$$

the observations equation is as before

$$Y_t = \mu_t + \epsilon_t, \quad t = 1, 2, \cdots, \tag{3.7.2}$$

and Δ_t is a random disturbance in the process evolution. The recursive equation of the DLM is linear, in the sense that the effect on μ_t of u_{t-1} is proportional to u_{t-1}. The control could be on a vector of several variables, whose level at time t is given by a vector $\mathbf{u}_t$. The question is how to determine the levels of the control variables? This question of optimal control of systems, when the true level μ_t of the process mean is not known exactly, but only estimated from the observed values of Y_t, is a subject of studies in the field of **stochastic control**. We refer the reader to the book of Aoki (1989). The reader is referred also to the paper by Box and Kramer (1992).

It is common practice, in many industries, to use the **proportional rule** for control. That is, if the process level (mean) is targeted at μ_0, and the estimated level at time t is $\hat{\mu}_t$, then

$$u_t = -p(\hat{\mu}_t - \mu_0), \tag{3.7.3}$$

where p is some factor, which is determined by the DLM, by cost factors, etc. This rule is not necessarily optimal. It depends on the objectives of the optimization. For example, suppose that the DLM with control is

$$\mu_t = \mu_{t-1} + bu_{t-1} + \Delta_t, \quad t = 1, 2, \cdots, \tag{3.7.4}$$

where the process mean is set at μ_0 at time $t = 0$. Δ_T is a random disturbance, having a normal distribution $N(\delta, \sigma)$. The process level μ_t is estimated by the Kalman filter, which was described in the previous section. We have the option to adjust the mean, at each time period, at a cost of $c_A u^2$ [$]. On the other hand, at the end of T periods, we pay a penalty of $ $c_d(\mu_T - \mu_0)^2$, for the deviation of μ_T from the target level. In this example, the optimal levels of u_t, for $t = 0, \cdots, T-1$, are given by

$$u_t^0 = -\frac{bq_{t+1}}{c_A + q_{t+1}b^2}(\hat{\mu}_t - \mu_0), \tag{3.7.5}$$

where

$$q_T = c_d$$

and, for $t = 0, \cdots, T-1$,

$$q_t = \frac{c_A q_{t+1}}{c_A + q_{t+1}b^2}. \tag{3.7.6}$$

These formulae are obtained as special cases from general result given in Aoki (1989, pp. 128). Thus, we see that the values that u_t obtains, under the optimal scheme, are proportional to $-(\hat{\mu}_t - \mu_0)$, but with varying factor of proportionality,

$$p_t = bq_{t+1}/(c_A + q_{t+1}b^2). \tag{3.7.7}$$

In Table 3.19, we present the optimal values of p_t for the case of $c_A = 100$, $c_d = 1000$, $b = 1$, and $T = 15$.

```
c_A = 100
c_d = 1000
b = 1
q_tp1 = c_d
data = []
for t in range(14, 0, -1):
    q_t = c_A * q_tp1 / (c_A + q_tp1 * b**2)
    p_t = b * q_tp1 / (c_A + q_tp1 * b**2)
    data.append({'t': t, 'q_t': q_t, 'p_t': p_t})
    q_tp1 = q_t
result = pd.DataFrame(data)
```

If the penalty for deviation from the target is cumulative, we wish to minimize the total expected penalty function, namely

Table 3.19 Factors of proportionality in optimal control

t	q_t	p_t
15	–	–
14	90.909	0.909
13	47.619	0.476
12	32.258	0.323
11	24.390	0.244
10	19.608	0.196
9	16.393	0.164
8	14.085	0.141
7	12.346	0.123
6	10.989	0.110
5	9.901	0.099
4	9.009	0.090
3	8.264	0.083
2	7.634	0.076
1	7.092	0.071

$$J_t = c_d \sum_{t=1}^{T} E\{(\mu_t - \mu_0)^2\} + c_A \sum_{t=0}^{T-1} u_t^2. \tag{3.7.8}$$

The optimal solution in this case is somewhat more complicated than the above rule, and it is also not one with fixed factor of proportionality p. The method of obtaining this solution is called **dynamic programming**. We do not present here this optimization procedure. The interested reader is referred to Aoki (1989). We just mention that the optimal solution using this method yields for example that the last control is at the level (when $b = 1$) of

$$u_{T-1}^0 = -\frac{cd}{c_A + c_d}(\hat{\mu}_{T-1} - \mu_0). \tag{3.7.9}$$

The optimal control at $t = T - 2$ is

$$u_{T-2}^0 = -\frac{cd}{c_A + 2c_d}(\hat{\mu}_{T-2} - \mu_0), \tag{3.7.10}$$

and so on.

We conclude this section mentioning that a simple but reasonable method of automatic process control is to use the EWMA chart, and whenever the trend estimates, $\hat{\mu}_t$, are above or below the upper or lower control limits, then a control is applied of size

$$u = -(\hat{\mu}_t - \mu_0). \tag{3.7.11}$$

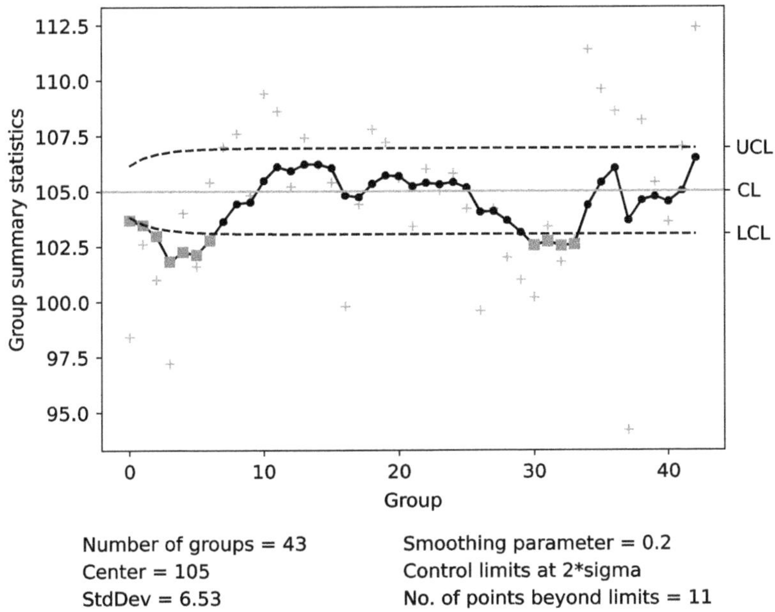

Fig. 3.13 EWMA chart for average film speed in subgroups of $n = 5$ film rolls, $\mu_0 = 105$, $\sigma = 6.53$, $\lambda = 0.2$

In Fig. 3.13, we present the results of such a control procedure on the film speed (dataset **FILMSP.csv**) in a production process of coating film rolls. This EWMA chart was constructed with $\mu_0 = 105$, $\sigma = 6.53$, $\lambda = 0.2$, $L = 2$, and $n = 5$. Notice that at the beginning the process was out of control. After a remedial action, the process returned to a state of control. At time 30, it drifted downward but was corrected again.

3.8 Chapter Highlights

The main concepts and definitions introduced in this chapter include:

- Run tests
- Average run length
- Operating characteristic functions
- Multivariate control charts
- Cumulative sum control charts
- Bayesian detection
- Shiryaev–Roberts statistic
- Probability of false alarm
- Conditional expected delay

- Process tracking
- Exponentially weighted moving average (EWMA)
- Kalman filter
- Quality measurement plan
- Automatic process control
- Dynamic programming

3.9 Exercises

Exercise 3.1 Generate the distribution of the number of runs in a sample of size $n = 25$, if the number of elements above the sample mean is $m_2 = 10$:

(i) What are Q_1, Me, and Q_3 of this distribution?
(ii) Compute the expected value, μ_R, and the standard deviation σ_R.
(iii) What is $\Pr\{10 \le R \le 16\}$?
(iv) Determine the normal approximation to $\Pr\{10 \le R \le 16\}$.

Exercise 3.2 Use Python to perform a run test on the simulated cycle times from the pistons, which are in dataset **CYCLT.csv**. Is the number of runs above the mean cycle time significantly different than its expected value?

Exercise 3.3

(i) What is the expected number of runs up or down, in a sample of size 50?
(ii) Compute the number of runs up or down in the cycle time data (**CYCLT.csv**).
(iii) Is this number significantly different than expected?
(iv) What is the probability that a random sample of size 50 will have at least one run of size greater or equal to 5?

Exercise 3.4 Analyze the observations in **YARNSTRG.csv** for runs.

Exercise 3.5 Run the piston simulator at the upper level of the seven control parameters and generate 50 samples of size 5. Analyze the output for runs in both $\bar{X}$- and S-charts.

Exercise 3.6

(i) Run the piston simulator at the upper level of the seven control parameters, and generate 50 samples of size 5 (both $\bar{X}$- and S-charts)
(ii) Repeat the exercise allowing T to change over time (provide a list of T which specify the changing ambient temperatur over time)
(iii) Compare the results in (i) and (ii). with those of Exercise 3.3

Exercise 3.7 Construct a p-chart for the fraction of defective substrates received at a particular point in the production line. One thousand ($n = 1000$) substrates are sampled each week. Remove data for any week for which the process is not in control. Be sure to check for runs as well as points outside the control limits.

Table 3.20 Dataset for Exercise 3.7

Week	No. Def.	Week	No. Def.
1	18	16	38
2	14	17	29
3	9	18	35
4	25	19	24
5	27	20	20
6	18	21	23
7	21	22	17
8	16	23	20
9	18	24	19
10	24	25	17
11	20	26	16
12	19	27	10
13	22	28	8
14	22	29	10
15	20	30	9

Construct the revised p-chart and be sure to check for runs again. The data are in Table 3.20.

Exercise 3.8 Substrates were inspected for defects on a weekly basis, on two different production lines. The weekly sample sizes and the number of defectives are indicated below in the dataset in Table 3.21. Plot the data and indicate which of the lines is not in a state of statistical control. On what basis do you make your decision? Use Python to construct control charts for the two production lines.

Note When the sample size is not the same for each sampling period, we use **variable** control limits. If $X(i)$ and $n(i)$ represent the number of defects and sample size, respectively, for sampling period i, then the upper and lower control limits for the ith period are

$$UCL_i = \bar{p} + 3(\bar{p}(1-\bar{p})/n_i)^{1/2}$$

and

$$LCL_i = \bar{p} - 3(\bar{p}(1-\bar{p})/n_i)^{1/2},$$

where

$$\bar{p} = \sum X(i) / \sum n(i)$$

is the center line for the control chart.

Table 3.21 Dataset for Exercise 3.8

	Line 1		Line 2	
Week	X_i	n_i	X_i	n_i
1	45	7920	135	2640
2	72	6660	142	2160
3	25	6480	16	240
4	25	4500	5	120
5	33	5840	150	2760
6	35	7020	156	2640
7	42	6840	140	2760
8	35	8460	160	2980
9	50	7020	195	2880
10	55	9900	132	2160
11	26	9180	76	1560
12	22	7200	85	1680

Exercise 3.9 In designing a control chart for the fraction defectives p, a random sample of size n is drawn from the productions of each day (very large lot). How large should n be so that the probability of detecting a shift from $p_0 = 0.01$ to $p_t = 0.05$, within a 5-day period, will not be smaller than 0.8?

Exercise 3.10 The data in Table 3.22 represent dock-to-stock cycle times for a certain type of shipment (class D). Incoming shipments are classified according to their "type," which is determined by the size of the item and the shipment, the type of handling required, and the destination of the shipment. Samples of five shipments per day are tracked from their initial arrival to their final destination, and the time it takes for this cycle to be complete is noted. The samples are selected as follows: at five preselected times during the day, the next class D shipment to arrive is tagged, and the arrival time and identity of the shipment are recorded. When the shipment reaches its final destination, the time is again recorded. The difference between these times is the cycle time. The cycle time is always recorded for the day of arrival:

(i) Construct $\bar{X}$ and S-charts from the data. Are any points out of control? Are there any trends in the data? If there are points beyond the control limits, assume that we can determine special causes for the points, and recalculate the control limits, excluding those points that are outside the control limits.
(ii) Use a t-test to decide whether the mean cycle time for days 21 and 22 was significantly greater than 45.
(iii) Make some conjectures about possible causes of unusually long cycle times. Can you think of other appropriate data that might have been collected, such as the times at which the shipments reached intermediate points in the cycle? Why would such data be useful?

Table 3.22 Dock-to-stock cycle times

Day	Times				
1	27	43	49	32	36
2	34	29	34	31	41
3	36	32	48	35	33
4	31	41	51	51	34
5	43	35	30	32	31
6	28	42	35	40	37
7	38	37	41	34	44
8	28	44	44	34	50
9	44	36	38	44	35
10	30	43	37	29	32
11	36	40	50	37	43
12	35	36	44	34	32
13	48	49	44	27	32
14	45	46	40	35	33
15	38	36	43	38	34
16	42	37	40	42	42
17	44	31	36	42	39
18	32	28	42	39	27
19	41	41	35	41	44
20	44	34	39	30	37
21	51	43	36	50	54
22	52	50	50	44	49
23	52	34	38	41	37
24	40	41	40	23	30
25	34	38	39	35	33

Exercise 3.11 Consider the modified Shewhart control chart for sample means, with $a = 3$, $w = 2$, and $r = 4$. What is the ARL of this procedure when $\delta = 0$, 1, 2, and the sample size is $n = 10$?

Exercise 3.12 Repeat the previous exercise for $a = 3$, $w = 1$, $r = 15$, when $n = 5$ and $\delta = 0.5$.

Exercise 3.13 Write a Python application to simulate ARL and compare the results from the simulation to Exercises 3.11 and 3.12.

Exercise 3.14 Suppose that a shift in the mean is occurring at random, according to an exponential distribution with mean of 1 h. The hourly cost is \$100 per shift of size $\delta = \frac{\mu_1 - \mu_0}{\sigma}$. The cost of sampling and testing is $d = \$10$ per item. How often should samples of size $n = 5$ be taken, when shifts of size $\delta \geq 1.5$ should be detected?

Exercise 3.15 Compute the $OC(p)$ function, for a Shewhart 3-sigma control chart for p, based on samples of size $n = 20$, when $p_0 = 0.10$. (Use the formula for exact computations.)

Exercise 3.16 How large should the sample size n be, for a 3-sigma control chart for p, if we wish that the probability of detecting a shift from $p_0 = 0.01$ to $p_t = 0.05$ be $1 - \beta = 0.90$?

Exercise 3.17 Suppose that a measurement X, of hardness of brackets after heat treatment, has a normal distribution. Every hour a sample of n units is drawn and a $\bar{X}$-chart with control limits $\mu_0 \pm 3\sigma/\sqrt{n}$ is used. Here, μ_0 and σ are the assumed process mean and standard deviation. The OC function is

$$OC(\delta) = \Phi(3 - \delta\sqrt{n}) + \Phi(3 + \delta\sqrt{n}) - 1,$$

where $\delta = (\mu - \mu_0)/\sigma$ is the standardized deviation of the true process mean from the assumed one:

(i) How many hours, on the average, would it take to detect a shift in the process mean of size $\delta = 1$, when $n = 5$?
(ii) What should be the smallest sample size, n, so that a shift in the mean of size $\delta = 1$ would be on the average detected in less than 3 h?
(iii) One has two options: to sample $n_1 = 5$ elements every hour or to sample $n_2 = 10$ elements every 2 h. Which one would you choose? State your criterion for choosing between the two options and make the necessary computations.

Exercise 3.18 Electric circuits are designed to have an output of 220 (volts, DC). If the mean output is above 222 (volts DC), you wish to detect such a shift as soon as possible. Examine the sample of dataset **OELECT.csv** for such a shift. For this purpose, construct a CUSUM upward scheme with K^+ and h^+ properly designed (consider for h^+ the value $\alpha = 0.001$). Each observation is of sample of size $n = 1$. Is there an indication of a shift in the mean?

Exercise 3.19 Estimate the probability of false alarm and the conditional expected delay in the Poisson case, with a CUSUM scheme. The parameters are $\lambda_0 = 15$, $\lambda_1^+ = 25$ and $\lambda_1^- = 7$. Use $\alpha = 0.001$, $\tau = 30$.

Exercise 3.20 A CUSUM control scheme is based on sample means:

(i) Determine the control parameters K^+, h^+, K^-, h^-, when $\mu_0 = 100$, $\mu_1^+ = 110$, $\mu_1^- = 90$, $\sigma = 20$, $n = 5$, $\alpha = 0.001$.
(ii) Estimate the PFA and CED, when the change-point is at $\tau = 10, 20, 30$.
(iii) How would the properties of the CUSUM change if each sample size is increased from 5 to 20.

Exercise 3.21 Show that the Shiryaev–Roberts statistic W_n, for detecting a shift in a Poisson distribution from a mean λ_0 to a mean $\lambda_1 = \lambda_0 + \delta$, is

$$W_m = (1 + W_{m-1})R_m,$$

where $W_0 \equiv 0$, $R_m = \exp\{-\delta + x_m \log(\rho)\}$, and $\rho = \lambda_1/\lambda_0$.

Exercise 3.22 Analyze the data in data **OELECT**, with an EWMA control chart with $\lambda = 0.2$.

Exercise 3.23 Analyze the variable diameters in the dataset **ALMPIN** with an EWMA control chart with $\lambda = 0.2$. Explain how you would apply the automatic process control technique described at the end of Sect. 3.7.

Exercise 3.24 Construct the Kalman filter for the Dow–Jones daily index, which is given in the dataset **DOW1941**.

Chapter 4
Multivariate Statistical Process Control

Preview As was discussed in Chap. 4 in *Modern Statistics* (Kenett et al. (Modern statistics: a computer-based approach with Python, 1st edn. Springer, Birkhäuser, 2022)), multivariate observations require special techniques for visualization and analysis. This chapter presents techniques for multivariate statistical process control (MSPC) based on the Mahalanobis T^2 chart. Like in previous chapters, examples of MSPC using Python are provided. Section 4.3 introduces the reader to multivariate extensions of process capability indices. These are expansions of the capability indices presented in Chap. 2. A special role is played in this context by the concept of multivariate tolerance regions (TR). Section 4.4 considers four scenarios for setting up and running MSPC: (1) internally derived targets, (2) using an external reference sample, (3) externally assigned targets and (4) measurements units considered as batches. These four cases cover most practical applications of MSPC. Two subsections cover the special cases of measurement units considered as batches and a variable decomposition of indices used for process monitoring. Section 4.5 is a special application of MSPC to the monitoring of bioequivalence of drug product dissolution profiles. In this application tablets manufactured by a generic drug company are compared to the original product at several dissolution times. The Food and Drug Administration allows for a gap of at most 15%, a requirement that define multivariate specification limits. We show how TR are used in such cases. More on multivariate applications in pharmaceuticals will be discussed in Chap. 6 on Quality by Design.

4.1 Introduction

Univariate control charts track observations on one dimension. Multivariate data is much more informative than a collection of one dimensional variables. Simultaneously accounting for variation in several variables requires both an overall measure

Supplementary Information The online version contains supplementary material available at (https://doi.org/10.1007/978-3-031-28482-3_4).

R. S. Kenett et al., *Industrial Statistics*, Statistics for Industry, Technology, and Engineering, https://doi.org/10.1007/978-3-031-28482-3_4

of departure of the observation from the targets as well as an assessment of the data covariance structure. Multivariate control charts were developed for that purpose. We present here the construction of multivariate control charts with the multivariate data on aluminum pins, which were introduced in Chapter 4 of *Modern Statistics* (Kenett et al. 2022b), dataset **ALMPIN.csv**.

The following is the methodology for constructing a multivariate control chart. We use the first 30 cases of the dataset as a base sample. The other 40 observations will be used as observations from a production process which we wish to control.

The observations in the base sample provide estimates of the means, variance and covariances of the six variables being measured. Let $\bar{X}_i$ denote the mean of variable X_i $(i = 1, \cdots, p)$ in the base sample.

Let S_{ij} denote the covariance between X_i and X_j $(i, j = 1, \cdots, p)$, namely

$$S_{ij} = \frac{1}{n-1} \sum_{l=1}^{n} (X_{il} - \bar{X}_{i.})(X_{jl} - \bar{X}_{j.}). \tag{4.1.1}$$

Notice that S_{ii} is the sample variance of X_i $(i = 1, \cdots, p)$. Let $\mathbf{S}$ denote the $p \times p$ covariance matrix, i.e.,

$$\mathbf{S} = \begin{bmatrix} S_{11} & S_{12} & \cdots & S_{1p} \\ S_{21} & S_{22} & \cdots & S_{2p} \\ \vdots & \vdots & & \vdots \\ S_{p1} & S_{p2} & \cdots & S_{pp} \end{bmatrix}. \tag{4.1.2}$$

Notice that $S_{ij} = S_{ji}$ for every i, j. Thus, $\mathbf{S}$ is a **symmetric** and **positive definite** matrix.

Let $\mathbf{M}$ denote the $(p \times 1)$ vector of sample means, whose transpose is

$$\mathbf{M}' = (\bar{X}_{1.}, \cdots, \bar{X}_{p.}).$$

Finally, we compute the inverse of $\mathbf{S}$, namely $\mathbf{S}^{-1}$. This inverse exists, unless one (or some) of the variable(s) is (are) linear combinations of the others. Such variables should be excluded.

Suppose now that every time unit we draw a sample of size m $(m \geq 1)$ from the production process, and observe on each element the p variables of interest. In order to distinguish between the sample means from the production process to those of the base sample, we will denote by $\bar{Y}_{i.}(t)$, $t = 1, 2, \cdots$ the sample mean of variable X_i from the sample at time t. Let $\mathbf{Y}(t)$ be the vector of these p means, i.e., $\mathbf{Y}'(t) = (\bar{Y}_{1.}(t), \cdots, \bar{Y}_{p.}(t))$. We construct now a control chart, called the $\mathbf{T^2}$**-Chart**. The objective is to monitor the means $\mathbf{Y}(t)$, of the samples from the production process, to detect when a significant change from $\mathbf{M}$ occurs. We assume that the covariances do not change in the production process. Thus, for every time period t, $t = 1, 2, \cdots$ we compute the T^2 statistics

$$\mathbf{T}_t^2 = (\mathbf{Y}(t) - \mathbf{M})'\mathbf{S}^{-1}(\mathbf{Y}(t) - \mathbf{M}). \tag{4.1.3}$$

It can be shown that as long as the process mean and covariance matrix are the same as those of the base sample,

$$T^2 \sim \frac{(n-1)p}{n-p} F[p, n-p]. \tag{4.1.4}$$

Accordingly, we set up the (upper) control limit for T^2 at

$$\text{UCL} = \frac{(n-1)p}{n-p} F_{0.997}[p, n-p]. \tag{4.1.5}$$

If a point $T(t)$ falls above this control limit, there is an indication of a significant change in the mean vector in the baseline data and, after investigations, we might decide to remove such points.

After establishing the baseline control limits, the UCL used in follow up monitoring is computed so as to account for the number of observations in the baseline phase. The UCL for monitoring is:

$$\text{UCL} = \frac{(n-1)(n+1)p}{n(n-p)} F_{0.997}[p, n-p]. \tag{4.1.6}$$

Example 4.1 The base sample consists of the first 30 rows of dataset **ALMPIN.csv**. The mean vector of the base sample is

$$\mathbf{M}' = (9.99, 9.98, 9.97, 14.98, 49.91, 60.05).$$

The covariance matrix of the base sample is $\mathbf{S}$, where $10^3\mathbf{S}$ is

$$\begin{bmatrix} 0.1826 & 0.1708 & 0.1820 & 0.1826 & -0.0756 & -0.0054 \\ & 0.1844 & 0.1853 & 0.1846 & -0.1002 & -0.0377 \\ & & 0.2116 & 0.1957 & -0.0846 & 0.0001 \\ & & & 0.2309 & -0.0687 & -0.0054 \\ & & & & 1.3179 & 1.0039 \\ & & & & & 1.4047 \end{bmatrix}$$

(Since $\mathbf{S}$ is symmetric we show only the upper matrix). The inverse of $\mathbf{S}$ is

$$\mathbf{S}^{-1} = \begin{bmatrix} 53191.3 & -22791.0 & -17079.7 & -9343.4 & 145.0 & -545.3 \\ & 66324.2 & -28342.7 & -10877.9 & 182.0 & 1522.8 \\ & & 50553.9 & -6467.9 & 853.1 & -1465.1 \\ & & & 25745.6 & -527.5 & 148.6 \\ & & & & 1622.3 & -1156.1 \\ & & & & & 1577.6 \end{bmatrix}.$$

We compute now for the last 40 rows of this dataset the T_t^2 values. We consider as though each one of these rows is a vector of a sample of size one taken every 10 min. In Table 4.1, we present these 40 vectors and their corresponding T^2 values. ■

For example, T_1^2 of the table is computed according to the formula

$$\mathbf{T}_1^2 = (\mathbf{Y}(1) - \mathbf{M})'\mathbf{S}^{-1}(\mathbf{Y}(1) - \mathbf{M}) = 3.523.$$

The 40 values of T_t^2 of Table 4.1 are plotted in Fig. 4.1. The UCL in this chart is UCL $= 34.56$.

We remark here that the computations can be performed by the following Python program. Note that *MultivariateQualityControlChart* labels the control limit for the base (the first 30 observations), UCL, and for the ongoing monitoring (the following 40 observations), UPL.

```
almpin = mistat.load_data('ALMPIN')

base = almpin.iloc[:30,]
newdata = almpin.iloc[30:,]

mqcc = mistat.MultivariateQualityControlChart(base, qcc_type='T2single',
           confidence_level=0.997, newdata=newdata)
mqcc.plot()
plt.show()
```

4.2 A Review Multivariate Data Analysis

Chapters 2 and 3 present applications of statistical process control (SPC) to measurements in one dimension. To extend the approach to measurements consisting of several dimensions lead us to multivariate statistical process control (MSPC), as introduced in Sect. 4.1. MSPC requires applications of methods and tools of multivariate data analysis presented in Chapter 4 of *Modern Statistics* (Kenett et al. 2022b). In this section we expand on the material presented so far and use the components placement data of Examples 4.1 and 4.2. The case study consists of displacement co-ordinates of 16 components placed by a robot on a printed circuit board. Overall, there are 26 printed circuit boards and therefore a total of 416 placed components (see **PLACE.csv**). The components' co-ordinates are measured in three dimensions, representing deviations with respect to the target in the horizontal, vertical and angular dimensions. The measured variables are labeled xDev, yDev, and tDev. The placement of components on the 26 boards was part of a validation test designed to fine tune the placement software in order to minimize the placement deviations.

Figure 4.2 presents a scatterplot matrix of xDev, yDev, and tDev with nonparametric densities providing a visual display of the two dimensional distribution densities. On the yDev xDev scatterplot there are clearly three groups of boards. In

Table 4.1 Dimensions of aluminum pins in a production process and their T^2 value

X_1	X_2	X_3	X_4	X_5	X_6	T^2
10.00	9.99	9.99	14.99	49.92	60.03	3.523
10.00	9.99	9.99	15.00	49.93	60.03	6.983
10.00	10.00	9.99	14.99	49.91	60.02	6.411
10.00	9.99	9.99	14.99	49.92	60.02	4.754
10.00	9.99	9.99	14.99	49.92	60.00	8.161
10.00	10.00	9.99	15.00	49.94	60.05	7.605
10.00	9.99	9.99	15.00	49.89	59.98	10.299
10.00	10.00	9.99	14.99	49.93	60.01	10.465
10.00	10.00	9.99	14.99	49.94	60.02	10.771
10.00	10.00	9.99	15.00	49.86	59.96	10.119
10.00	9.99	9.99	14.99	49.90	59.97	11.465
10.00	10.00	10.00	14.99	49.92	60.00	14.317
10.00	10.00	9.99	14.98	49.91	60.00	13.675
10.00	10.00	10.00	15.00	49.93	59.98	20.168
10.00	9.99	9.98	14.98	49.90	59.98	8.985
9.99	9.99	9.99	14.99	49.88	59.98	9.901
10.01	10.01	10.01	15.01	49.87	59.97	14.420
10.00	10.00	9.99	14.99	49.81	59.91	15.998
10.01	10.00	10.00	15.01	50.07	60.13	30.204
10.01	10.00	10.00	15.00	49.93	60.00	12.648
10.00	10.00	10.00	14.99	49.90	59.96	19.822
10.01	10.01	10.01	15.00	49.85	59.93	21.884
10.00	9.99	9.99	15.00	49.83	59.98	9.535
10.01	10.01	10.00	14.99	49.90	59.98	18.901
10.01	10.01	10.00	15.00	49.87	59.96	13.342
10.00	9.99	9.99	15.00	49.87	60.02	5.413
9.99	9.99	9.99	14.98	49.92	60.03	8.047
9.99	9.98	9.98	14.99	49.93	60.03	5.969
9.99	9.99	9.98	14.99	49.89	60.01	4.645
10.00	10.00	9.99	14.99	49.89	60.01	5.674
9.99	9.99	9.99	15.00	50.04	60.15	23.639
10.00	10.00	10.00	14.99	49.84	60.03	10.253
10.00	10.00	9.99	14.99	49.89	60.01	5.674
10.00	9.99	9.99	15.00	49.88	60.01	5.694
10.00	10.00	9.99	14.99	49.90	60.04	4.995
9.90	9.89	9.91	14.88	49.99	60.14	82.628
10.00	9.99	9.99	15.00	49.91	60.04	4.493
9.99	9.99	9.99	14.98	49.92	60.04	7.211
10.01	10.01	10.00	15.00	49.88	60.00	8.737
10.00	9.99	9.99	14.99	49.95	60.10	3.421

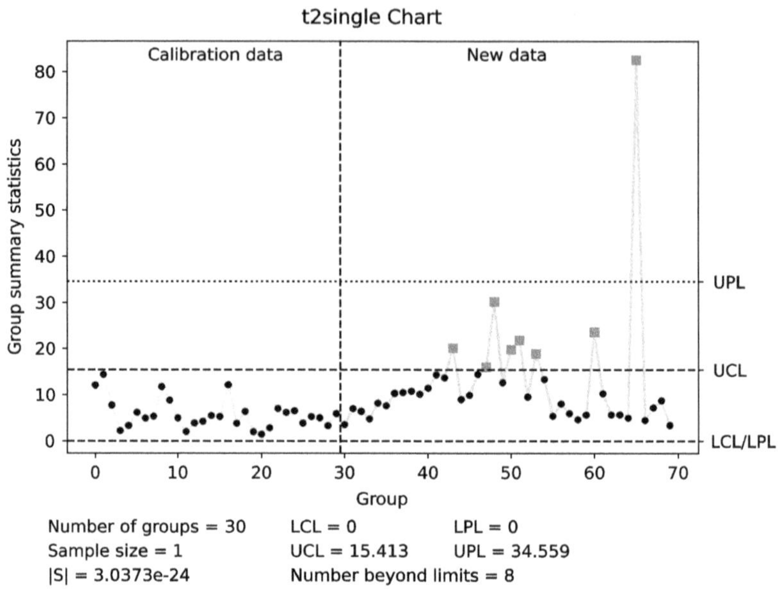

Fig. 4.1 T^2-chart for aluminum pins

Section 4.1.2 of *Modern Statistics* (Kenett et al. 2022b) we identified them with box plots and confirmed the classification with coding and redrawing the scatterplot.

Figure 4.3 presents the histograms of xDev, yDev and tDev with the low values of xDev highlighted. Through dynamic linking, the figure highlights, the corresponding values for yDev and tDev. We can see that components position on the left of the target tend to be also placed below the target, with some components in this group being positioned on target in the vertical direction (the group of yDev between −0.001 and 0.002).

To further characterize the components placed on the left of the target (negative xDev) we draw a plot of xDev and yDev versus the board number (Fig. 4.4). On each board we get 16 measurements of xDev (circle) and yDev (cross). The highlighted points correspond to the highlighted values in Fig. 4.3. One can see from Fig. 4.4 that up to board number 9 we have components placed to the right and below the target. In boards 10, 11 and 12 there has been a correction in component placement which resulted in components being placed above the target in the vertical direction and on target in the horizontal direction. These are the components in the histogram of yDev in Fig. 4.3 with the high trailing values between −0.001 and 0.002 mentioned above. For these first 12 circuit boards we do not notice any specific pattern in tDev. We will use the placement data example again in Sect. 4.4 to demonstrate the application of a multivariate control chart.

Software such as Python or R provide visualization and exploration technologies that complement the application of MSPC. Specialized packages like `plotly` or `Dash` allow the development of dashboards for interactive data analysis.

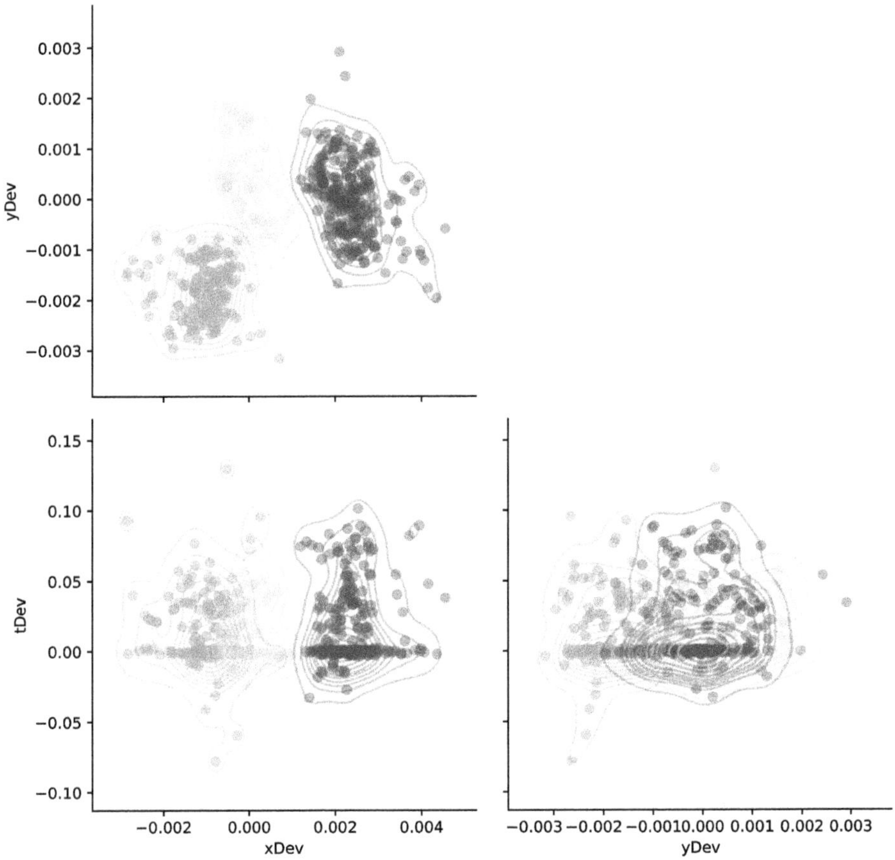

Fig. 4.2 Scatterplot matrix of placement data with nonparametric densities

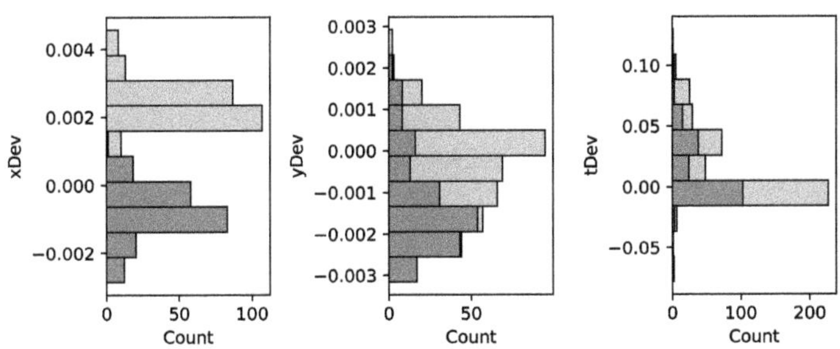

Fig. 4.3 Histograms of xDev, yDev and tDev, with conditional linking

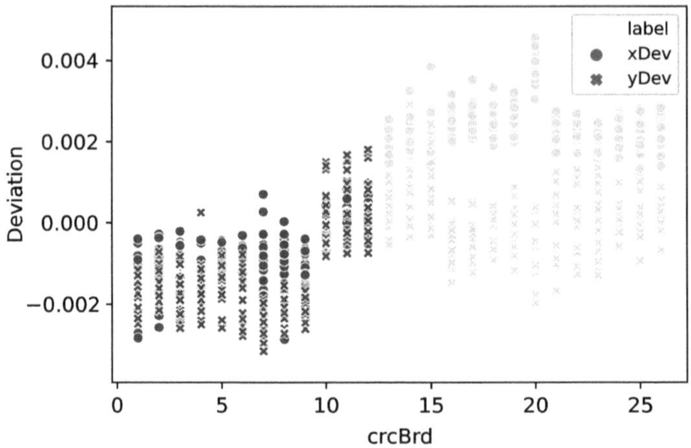

Fig. 4.4 Plot of xDev and yDev versus circuit board number

4.3 Multivariate Process Capability Indices

Chapter 4.4 introduced process capability studies that are a prerequisite to the setup of control limits in control charts. Section 2.4 presented several univariate process capability indices such as C_p and C_{pk} that are used to characterize the performance of a process by comparing the quality attributes specifications to the process variability. These indices map processes in terms of their ability to deliver high critical quality parameters. In this section we focus on multivariate data and develop several multivariate process capability indices.

As in the univariate case, the multivariate capability indices are based on the multivariate normal distribution. Chapter 2 of *Modern Statistics* (Kenett et al. 2022b) introduces the bivariate normal distribution. We introduce here the m-variate normal distribution as a joint distribution of a vector $\mathbf{X}' = (X_1, \ldots, X_m)$ of m random variable. The expected value of such a vector is the vector $\boldsymbol{\mu}' = (E\{X_1\}, \ldots, E\{X_m\})$. The covariance matrix of this vector is an $m \times m$, symmetric, positive definite matrix $\boldsymbol{\Sigma} = \left(\sigma_{ij}; i, j = 1, \ldots, m\right)$, where $\sigma_{ij} = \text{cov}(X_i, X_j)$. The multivariate normal vector is denoted by $N(\boldsymbol{\mu}, \boldsymbol{\Sigma})$. The joint p.d.f. of $\mathbf{X}$ is

$$f(\mathbf{x}; \boldsymbol{\mu}, \boldsymbol{\Sigma}) = \frac{1}{(2\pi)^{m/2}|\boldsymbol{\Sigma}|^{1/2}} \exp\left\{-\frac{1}{2}(\mathbf{x} - \boldsymbol{\mu})'\boldsymbol{\Sigma}^{-1}(\mathbf{x} - \boldsymbol{\mu})\right\}. \tag{4.3.1}$$

In the multivariate normal distribution, the marginal distribution of X_i is normal $N(\mu_i, \sigma_i^2)$, $i = 1, \ldots, m$.

We describe now some of the multivariate capability indices. The reader is referred to papers of Chen (1994), Haridy et al. (2011) and Jalili et al. (2012).

A **tolerance region**, TR,

is a region around a **target** point, **T**. We will consider here two possible regions: (i) a hyper-rectangular, RTR, and (ii) a sphere, CTR. In case (i) the region is specified by parameters $(\delta_1, \ldots, \delta_m)$ and is the set

$$\text{RTR} = \{\mathbf{x} : |x_i - T_i| \leq \delta_i, i = 1, \ldots, m\}. \tag{4.3.2}$$

In case (ii) the tolerance region is

$$\text{CTR} = \{\mathbf{x} : |\mathbf{X} - \mathbf{T}| \leq r\}, \tag{4.3.3}$$

where r is the radius of a sphere centered at **T**.

In the paper of Jalili et al. (2012) a tolerance region, which is the largest ellipsoidal region in the RTR (4.3.2), is considered. In the present section we will confine attention to (4.3.2) and (4.3.3). Chen (1994) suggested the following multivariate capability index (MC_p). Suppose that the TR is CTR, with a specified radius r. Let r_α be the value of r, for which $P\{|\mathbf{X} - T| \leq r_\alpha\} = 1 - \alpha$, with $\alpha = 0.0027$. Then the MC_p index is

$$\text{MC}_p = \frac{r}{r_\alpha}. \tag{4.3.4}$$

In the case of a RTR, Chen suggested the index

$$\text{MC}_p = \frac{\delta_s}{\delta_\alpha}, \tag{4.3.5}$$

where δ_α is the value for which

$$P\left\{\max\left\{\frac{|X_i - T_i|}{\delta_i}, i = 1, \ldots, m\right\} \leq \delta_\alpha\right\} = 1 - \alpha.$$

$\delta_s = \max\{\delta_i, i = 1, \ldots, m\}$. We will show later how to compute these indices in the case of $m = 2$. In the special case where $\mathbf{X} \sim N(\mathbf{T}, \sigma^2 I)$, i.e., all the m components of $\mathbf{X}$ are independent with $\mu_i = T_i$ and $\sigma_i^2 = \sigma^2$ we have a simple solution. If $\delta_i = \delta$ for all i, then

$$\max\left\{\frac{|X_i - T_i|}{\delta}, i = 1, \ldots, m\right\} \sim \left(\frac{\sigma}{\delta}\right)|Z|_{(m)},$$

where $|Z|_{(m)} = \max\{|Z_i|, i = 1, \ldots, m\}$ and $Z \sim N(0, 1)$. Thus

$$\begin{aligned} P\left\{\frac{\sigma}{\delta}|Z|_{(m)} \leq y\right\} &= P\{|Z| \leq y\delta/\sigma\}^m \\ &= \left(2\Phi\left(\frac{y\delta}{\sigma}\right) - 1\right)^m. \end{aligned}$$

Hence, δ_α is a solution of $\left(2\Phi\left(\frac{\delta_\alpha\delta}{\sigma}\right)-1\right)^m = 1-\alpha$, or

$$\delta_\alpha = \frac{\sigma}{\delta}\Phi^{-1}\left(\frac{1}{2}+\frac{1}{2}(1-\alpha)^{1/m}\right). \tag{4.3.6}$$

Haridy et al. (2011) suggested a different type of index, based on the principal components of $\boldsymbol{\Sigma}$.

Let H' be an orthogonal matrix, whose column vectors are the orthogonal eigenvectors of $\boldsymbol{\Sigma}$. Let $\lambda_1 \geq \lambda_2 \geq \cdots \geq \lambda_m > 0$ be the corresponding eigenvalues. Recall that

$$H\boldsymbol{\Sigma}H' = \begin{pmatrix} \lambda_1 & & 0 \\ & \ddots & \\ 0 & & \lambda_m \end{pmatrix}. \tag{4.3.7}$$

The transformed vector

$$\mathbf{Y} = H(\mathbf{X}-\boldsymbol{\mu}) \tag{4.3.8}$$

is called the **principal component vector**.

The distribution of $\mathbf{Y}$ is that of $N(\mathbf{0}, \Lambda)$, where $\Lambda = \text{diag}\{\lambda_i, i = 1, \ldots, m\}$. Here λ_i is the variance of Y_i. Also, $Y_1, \ldots, Y_m$ are independent.

The vector of upper specification limits in the RTR is $\mathbf{U} = \mathbf{T}+\boldsymbol{\delta}$. The corresponding vector of lower specification limits is $\mathbf{L} = \mathbf{T}-\boldsymbol{\delta}$. These vectors are transformed into $\mathbf{U}^* = H\boldsymbol{\delta}$ and $\mathbf{L}^* = -H\boldsymbol{\delta}$.

Suppose that $\mathbf{X}_1, \ldots, \mathbf{X}_n$ is a random sample from the process. These n vectors are independent and identically distributed. The maximum likelihood estimator of $\boldsymbol{\mu}$ is $\mathbf{M} = \frac{1}{n}\sum_{i=1}^n \mathbf{X}_i$. An estimator of $\boldsymbol{\Sigma}$ is the sample covariance matrix S (see (4.1.1)). Let $\hat{H}'$ and $\hat{\Lambda}$ be the corresponding matrices of eigenvectors and eigenvalues of S. The estimated vectors of the principal components are

$$\hat{\mathbf{Y}}_i = \hat{H}(\mathbf{X}_i - \mathbf{M}), \quad i = 1, \ldots, n. \tag{4.3.9}$$

Let $\{\hat{Y}_{1j}, \cdots, \hat{Y}_{n,j}\}$ be the sample of the j-th ($j = 1, \ldots, m$) principal components. Let

$$C_{p,pc_j} = \frac{U^*-L^*}{6\hat{\sigma}_{y_j}}, \quad j = 1, \ldots, m, \tag{4.3.10}$$

where $\hat{\sigma}^2_{y_j} = \frac{1}{n-1}\sum_{i=1}^n (\hat{Y}_{ij} - \bar{Y}_j)^2$. The MCP index, based on the principal components is

$$\text{MCP} = \left(\prod_{j=1}^m C_{p,pc_j}\right)^{1/m}. \tag{4.3.11}$$

We derive now explicit formula for a RTR, when $m = 2$ (bivariate normal distribution). The distribution of $\mathbf{X}$ is

$$N\left(\begin{bmatrix}\xi\\ \eta\end{bmatrix}, \begin{bmatrix}\sigma_1^2 & \rho\sigma_1\sigma_2\\ \bullet & \sigma_2^2\end{bmatrix}\right).$$

The conditional distribution of X_2, given X_1, is $N\left(\eta + \rho\frac{\sigma_2}{\sigma_1}(X_1 - \xi), \sigma_2^2(1-\rho^2)\right)$. Accordingly, the probability that $\mathbf{X}$ belongs to the rectangular tolerance region, RTR, with specified $\boldsymbol{\delta} = (\delta_1, \delta_2)'$, is

$$\begin{aligned} &P\{\mathbf{X} \in \mathrm{RTR}(\boldsymbol{\delta})\}\\ &= \int_{T_1-\delta_1-\xi_1/\sigma_1}^{(T_1+\delta_1-\xi_1)/\sigma_1} \phi(z)\left[\Phi\left(\frac{T_2+\delta_2-(\eta+\rho\frac{\sigma_2}{\sigma_1}(z-(\xi-T_1)))}{\sigma_2(1-\rho^2)^{1/2}}\right)\right.\\ &\left.-\Phi\left(\frac{T_2-\delta_2-(\eta+\rho\frac{\sigma_2}{\sigma_1}(z-(\xi-T_1))}{\sigma_2(1-\rho^2)^{1/2}}\right)\right] \mathrm{d}z. \end{aligned} \tag{4.3.12}$$

In particular, if $T_1 = \xi$ and $T_2 = \eta$ then

$$\begin{aligned} P\{\mathbf{X} \in \mathrm{RTR}(\boldsymbol{\delta})\} = \int_{-\frac{\delta_1}{\sigma_1}}^{\frac{\delta_1}{\sigma_1}} \phi(z)\left[\Phi\left(\frac{\sigma_1\delta_2 - \rho\sigma_2 z}{\sigma_1\sigma_2(1-\rho^2)^{1/2}}\right)\right.\\ \left.-\Phi\left(\frac{-\sigma_1\delta_2 - \rho\sigma_2 z}{\sigma_1\sigma_2(1-\rho^2)^{1/2}}\right)\right] \mathrm{d}z. \end{aligned} \tag{4.3.13}$$

$\phi(z) = \frac{1}{\sqrt{2\pi}}\exp(-\frac{1}{2}z^2)$ is the standard normal density.

If the tolerance region is circular, CRC(r), with radius r, $(\xi, \eta) = (T_1, T_2) = \mathbf{0}$, then

$$P\{\mathbf{X} \in \mathrm{CRC}(r)\} = P\{\lambda_1^{-1}Y_1^2 + \lambda_2^{-1}Y_2^2 \le r\}, \tag{4.3.14}$$

where λ_1 and λ_2 are the eigenvalues of $\boldsymbol{\Sigma} = \begin{pmatrix}\sigma_1^2 & \rho\sigma_1\sigma_2\\ \bullet & \sigma_2^2\end{pmatrix}$, and Y_1^2, Y_2^2 are independent, having a $\chi^2[1]$ distribution. Thus,

$$P\{\mathbf{X} \in \mathrm{CRC}(r)\} = \frac{1}{\sqrt{2\pi}}\int_0^{\sqrt{\lambda r}} x^{-1/2}e^{-x/2} \cdot [2\Phi((\lambda_1, \lambda_2 r^2 - \lambda_2 x)^{1/2}) - 1]\,\mathrm{d}x. \tag{4.3.15}$$

Example 4.2 We compute now the capability index MC_p according to (4.3.5), for the **ALMPIN.csv** dataset. We restrict attention to the last two variables in the dataset, i.e., `LengthNocp` and `LengthWcp`. The sample consists of the first

30 data vectors, described in Sect. 4.1. We use Eq. (4.3.13) with the $r = 0.7377$, $\sigma_1^2 = 1.3179$, $\sigma_2^2 = 1.4047$. We assume that $T_1 = \xi = 49.91$ and $T_2 = \eta = 60.05$. From Eq. (4.3.13) we find that for $\boldsymbol{\delta} = (3.5, 3.5)'$ $P\{\mathbf{X} \in \text{RTR}(\boldsymbol{\delta})\} = 0.9964$. If the tolerance region is specified by $\boldsymbol{\delta}_s = (1.5, 1.5)'$ then we get index $MC_p = \frac{1.5}{3.5} = 0.4286$.

If the tolerance region is circular, we get according to (4.3.15) $r_\alpha = 4.5$. Thus, $MC_p = \frac{1.5}{4.5} = 0.333$. We compute now the MC_P index (4.3.11), for the 6-dimensional vector of the **ALMPIN.csv** dataset. We base the estimation on the last 37 vectors of the dataset. Notice that the expected value of the principal components **Y** is zero. Hence, we consider the upper tolerance limit for Y to be $USL = 0.015$ and the lower tolerance limit to be $LSL = -0.015$. For these specifications we get $MC_P = 0.4078$. If we increase the tolerance limits to ± 0.03 we obtain $MC_P = 0.8137$. ■

4.4 Advanced Applications of Multivariate Control Charts

4.4.1 Multivariate Control Charts Scenarios

The Hotelling T^2 chart introduced in Sect. 4.2 plots the T^2 statistic, which is the squared standardized distance of a vector from a target point (see Eq. (4.1.3)). Values of T^2 represent equidistant vectors along a multidimensional ellipse centered at the target vector point. The chart has an upper control limit (UCL) determined by the F distribution (see Eq. (4.1.5)). Points exceeding UCL are regarded as an out-of-control signal. The charted T^2 statistic is a function that reduces multivariate observations into a single value while accounting for the covariance matrix. Out-of-control signals on the T^2 chart trigger an investigation to uncover the causes for the signal.

The setup of an MSPC chart is performed by a process capability study. The process capability study period is sometimes referred to as **phase I**. The ongoing control using control limits determined in phase I is then called **phase II**. The distinction between these two phases is important.

In setting MSPC charts, one meets several alternative scenarios derived from the characteristics of the reference sample and the appropriate control procedure. These include:

1. Internally derived target
2. Using an external reference sample
3. Externally assigned target
4. Measurements units considered as batches

We proceed to discuss these four scenarios.

4.4.2 Internally Derived Target

Internally derived targets are a typical scenario for process capability studies. The parameters to be estimated include the vector of process means, the process covariance matrix, and the control limit for the control chart. Consider a process capability study with a base sample of size n of p-dimensional observations, $X_1, X_2, \ldots, X_n$. When the data are grouped and k subgroups of observations of size m are being monitored, $n = km$, the covariance matrix estimator, S_p can be calculated as the pooled covariances of the subgroups. In that case, for the j-th subgroup, the Hotelling T^2 statistic is then given by:

$$T^2 = \mathbf{m}(\bar{X}_j - \bar{\bar{X}})' S_p^{-1} (\bar{X}_j - \bar{\bar{X}}), \tag{4.4.1}$$

where $\bar{X}_j$ is the mean of the j-th subgroup, $\bar{\bar{X}}$ is the overall mean, and S_p^{-1} is the inverse of the pooled estimated covariance matrix. The UCL for this case is

$$UCL = \frac{p(k-1)(m-1)}{k(m-1)-p+1} F_{1-\alpha}[p, k(m-1)-p+1]. \tag{4.4.2}$$

When the data is ungrouped, and individual observations are analyzed, the estimation of the proper covariance matrix and control limits requires further consideration. Typically in this case, the covariance matrix is estimated from the pooled individual observations as $S = \frac{1}{n-1}\sum_{i=1}^{n}(X_i - \bar{X})(X_i - \bar{X})'$, where $\bar{X}$ is the mean of the n observations. The corresponding T^2 statistic for the i-th observation, $i = 1, \ldots, n$ is given by $T^2 = (X_i - \bar{X})' S^{-1} (X_i - \bar{X})$. In this case, $(X_i - \bar{X})$ and S are not independently distributed and the appropriate upper control for T^2 is based on the Beta distribution with

$$UCL = \frac{(n-1)^2}{n} B_{1-\alpha/2}\left(\frac{p}{2}, \frac{n-p-1}{2}\right) \tag{4.4.3}$$

and

$$LCL = \frac{(n-1)^2}{n} B_{\alpha/2}\left(\frac{p}{2}, \frac{n-p-1}{2}\right), \tag{4.4.4}$$

where $B_\alpha(\nu_1, \nu_2)$ is the $(1-\alpha)$-th quantile of the Beta distribution with ν_1 and ν_2 as parameters. While theoretically the lower control limit (LCL) can be calculated as above, in most circumstances LCL is set to zero.

Example 4.3 Figure 4.5 presents the T^2 Hotelling Control Chart for the placement data used in Fig. 4.2.

In Fig. 4.5, phase I was conducted over the first 9 printed circuit boards. The implication is that the first 144 observations are used to derive estimates of the means and covariances of xDev, yDev, and tDev and, with these estimates, the Upper Control Limit is determined.

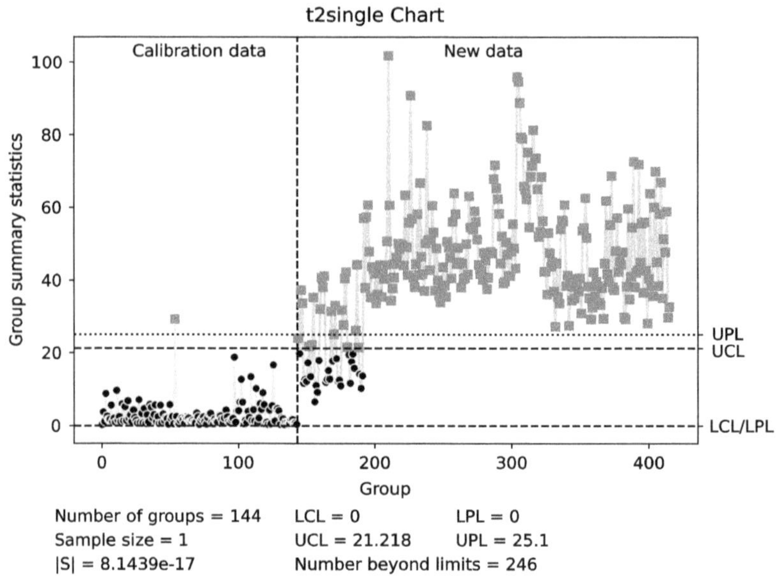

Fig. 4.5 T^2 control chart of xDev, yDev and tDev with control limits and correlation structure set up with data from first 9 printed circuit boards

```
place = mistat.load_data('PLACE')

columns = ['xDev', 'yDev', 'tDev']
calibration = place[place.crcBrd <= 9][columns]
newdata = place[place.crcBrd > 9][columns]

mqcc = mistat.MultivariateQualityControlChart(calibration,
        qcc_type='T2single', newdata=newdata,
        confidence_level=(1-0.0000152837)**3)
mqcc.plot()
plt.show()
```

The chart in Fig. 4.5 indicates an out-of-control point at observations 55 from board 4 due to very low horizontal and vertical deviations (xDev = −0.0005200, yDev = 0.0002500) and an extreme deviation in angular placement, t (tDev = 0.129810). In the components inserted on the first 9 boards, the average and standard deviations (in bracket) of xDev, yDev and tDev are, respectively: −0.001062 (0.000602), −0.001816 (0.000573), +0.01392 (0.02665).

Referring again to Fig. 4.5, we see a deviation in performance after board 9 with a significant jump after board 12. We already studied what happened on boards 10-12 and know that the shift is due to a correction in the vertical direction, increasing the values of yDev to be around zero (see Sect. 4.2). ■

4.4.3 External Reference Sample

Consider again a process yielding independent observations $X_1, X_2, \ldots$ of a p-dimensional random variable $\mathbf{X}$, such as the quality characteristics of a manufactured item or process measurements. Initially, when the process is "in control," the observations follow a distribution F, with density f. We now assume that we have a "reference" sample $X_1, \ldots, X_n$ of F from an in-control period. To control the quality of the produced items, multivariate data is monitored for potential change in the distribution of $\mathbf{X}$, by sequentially collecting and analyzing the observations X_i. At some time $t = n + k$, k time units after n, the process may run out of control and the distribution of the X_i's changes to G. Our aim is to detect, in phase II, the change in the distribution of subsequent observations X_{n+k}, $k \geq 1$, as quickly as possible, subject to a bound $\alpha \in (0, 1)$ on the probability of raising a false alarm at each time point $t = n + k$ (that is, the probability of erroneously deciding that the distribution of X_{n+k} is not F). The reference sample $X_1, \ldots, X_n$ does not incorporate the observations X_{n+k} taken after the "reference" stage, even if no alarm is raised, so that the rule is conditional only on the reference sample.

When the data in phase II is grouped, and the reference sample from historical data includes k subgroups of observations of size m, $n = km$, with the covariance matrix estimator S_p calculated as the pooled covariances of the subgroups, the T^2 for a new subgroup of size m with mean $\bar{Y}$ is given by

$$T^2 = \mathbf{m}(\bar{Y} - \bar{\bar{X}})' S_p^{-1} (\bar{Y} - \bar{\bar{X}}),$$

and the UCL is given by

$$UCL = \frac{p(k+1)(m-1)}{k(m-1) - p + 1} F_{1-\alpha}[p, k(m-1) - p + 1].$$

Furthermore, if in phase I, l subgroups were outside the control limits and assignable causes were determined, those subgroups are omitted from the computation of $\bar{\bar{X}}$ and S_p^{-1}, and the control limits for this case are

$$UCL = \frac{p(k-l+1)(m-1)}{(k-l)m-1) - p + 1} F_{1-\alpha}[p, (k-l/(m-1) - p + 1].$$

The T^2 Control Charts constructed in phase I, and used both in phase I and in phase II, are the multivariate equivalent of the Shewhart Control Chart. Those charts, as well as some more advanced ones, simplify the calculations down to single-number criteria and produce a desired Type I error or in-control run length.

While we focused on the reference sample provided by phase I of the multivariate process control, other possibilities can occur as well. In principle, the reference in-control sample can also originate from historical data. In this case, the statistical analysis will be the same but this situation has to be treated with precaution since both the control limits and the possible correlations between observations may shift.

4.4.4 Externally Assigned Target

If all parameters of the underlying multivariate distribution are known and externally assigned, the T^2 value for a single multivariate observation of dimension p is computed as

$$T^2 = (\mathbf{Y} - \boldsymbol{\mu})'\Sigma^{-1}(\mathbf{Y} - \boldsymbol{\mu}), \tag{4.4.5}$$

where $\boldsymbol{\mu}$ and $\boldsymbol{\Sigma}$ are the expected value and covariance matrix, respectively.

The probability distribution of the T^2 statistic is a χ^2 distribution with p degrees of freedom. Accordingly, the 0.95 UCL for T^2 is $UCL = \chi^2_{\nu,0.95}$. When the data are grouped in subgroups of size m, and both $\boldsymbol{\mu}$ and $\boldsymbol{\Sigma}$ are known, the T^2 value of the mean vector $\bar{Y}$ is $T^2 = m(\bar{Y} - \boldsymbol{\mu})'\boldsymbol{\Sigma}^{-1}(\bar{Y} - \boldsymbol{\mu})$ with the same UCL as above.

If only the expected value of the underlying multivariate distribution, $\boldsymbol{\mu}$, is known and externally assigned, the covariance matrix has to be estimated from the tested sample. The T^2 value for a single multivariate observation of dimension p is computed as $T^2 = (\mathbf{Y} - \boldsymbol{\mu})'S^{-1}(\mathbf{Y} - \boldsymbol{\mu})$, where $\boldsymbol{\mu}$ is the expected value and S is the estimate of the covariance matrix $\boldsymbol{\Sigma}$, estimated either as the pooled contribution of the individual observations, i.e., $S = \frac{1}{n-1}\sum_{i=1}^{n}(X_i - \bar{X})(X_i - \bar{X})'$, or by a method which accounts for possible lack of independence between observations.

In this case, the 0.95 UCL for T^2 is

$$UCL = \frac{p(n-1)}{n(n-p)} F_{0.95}[p, n-p].$$

When the tested observations are grouped, the mean vector of a subgroup with m observations (a rational sample) will have the same expected value as the individual observations, $\boldsymbol{\mu}$, and a covariance matrix $\boldsymbol{\Sigma}/m$. The covariance matrix $\boldsymbol{\Sigma}$ can be estimated by S or as S_p obtained by pooling the covariances of the k subgroups.

When $\boldsymbol{\Sigma}$ is estimated by S, the T^2 value of the mean vector $\bar{Y}$ of m tested observations is $T^2 = m(\bar{Y} - \boldsymbol{\mu})'S^{-1}(\bar{Y} - \boldsymbol{\mu})$ and the 0.95 UCL is

$$UCL = \frac{p(m-1)}{m-p} F_{0.95}[p, m-p]. \tag{4.4.6}$$

When $\boldsymbol{\Sigma}$ is estimated by S_p, the 0.95 UCL of $T^2 = m(\bar{Y} - \boldsymbol{\mu})'S_p^{-1}(\bar{Y} - \boldsymbol{\mu})$ is

$$UCL = \frac{pk(m-1)}{k(m-1)-p+1} F_{0.95}[p, k(m-1)-p+1]. \tag{4.4.7}$$

4.4.5 Measurement Units Considered as Batches

In the semiconductor industry, production is typically organized in batches or production lots. In such cases, the quality control process can be performed either at the completion of the batch or sequentially, in a curtailed inspection, aiming at reaching a decision as soon as possible. When the quality control method used is reaching a decision at the completion of the process, the possible outcomes are (a) determine the production process to be in statistical control and accept the batch or (b) stop the production flow because of a signal that the process is out of control. On the other hand, in a curtailed inspection, based on a statistical stopping rule, the results from the first few items tested may suffice to stop the process prior to the batch completion.

Consider a batch of size n, with the tested items $\mathbf{Y}_1, \ldots, \mathbf{Y}_n$. The curtailed inspection tests the items sequentially. Assume that the targets are specified, either externally assigned or from a reference sample or batch. With respect to those targets, let $V_i = 1$ if the T^2 of the ordered i-th observation exceeds the critical value κ and $V_i = 0$, otherwise. For the i-th observation, the process is considered to be in control if for a prespecified P, say $P = 0.95$, $Pr(V_i = 0) \geq P$. Obviously, the inspection will be curtailed only at an observation i for which $V_i = 1$ (not necessarily the first).

Let $N(g) = \sum_{i=1}^{g} V_i$ be the number of rejections up to the g-th tested item. For each number of individual rejections U (out of n), $R(U)$ denotes the minimal number of observations allowed up to the U-th rejection, without rejecting the overall null hypothesis. Thus, for each U, $R(U)$ is the minimal integer value such that under the null hypothesis, $Pr\left(\sum_{i=1}^{R(U)} V_i \leq U\right) \geq \alpha$. For fixed U, the random variable $\sum_{i=1}^{U} V_i$ has a negative binomial distribution, and we can compute $R(N(g))$ from the inverse of the negative binomial distribution. For example, when $n = 13$, $P = 0.95$, and $\alpha = 0.01$, the null hypothesis is rejected if the second rejection occurred at or before the third observation, or if the third rejection occurred at or before the ninth observation, and so on.

4.4.6 Variable Decomposition and Monitoring Indices

Data in batches is naturally grouped, but even if quality control is performed on individual items, grouping the data into rational consequent subgroups may yield relevant information on within subgroups variability, in addition to deviations from targets. In the j-th subgroup (or batch) of size n_j, the individual T_{ij}^2 values, $i = 1, \ldots, n_j$ are given by $T_{ij}^2 = (\mathbf{Y}_{ij} - \boldsymbol{\theta})' G^{-1} (\mathbf{Y}_{ij} - \boldsymbol{\theta})$. When the targets are externally assigned then $\boldsymbol{\theta} = \boldsymbol{\mu}$. If the covariance matrix is also externally assigned then $G = \Sigma$, otherwise G is the covariance matrix estimated either from the tested or from the reference sample. In the case of targets derived from an external reference sample

$\boldsymbol{\theta} = \mathbf{m}$ and $G = S$, where $\mathbf{m}$ and S are the mean and the covariance matrix of a reference sample of size n. Within the j-th subgroup, let us denote the mean of the subgroup observations by $\bar{Y}_j$ and the mean of the target values in the j-th subgroup by $\boldsymbol{\theta}_j$.

The sum of the individual T^2_{ij} values, $T^2_{0j} = \sum_{i=1}^{n} T^2_{ij}$ can be decomposed into two measurements of variability, one representing the deviation of the subgroup mean from the multivariate target denoted by T^2_{Mj}, and the other measuring the internal variability within the subgroup, denoted by T^2_{Dj}. The deviation of the subgroup mean from the multivariate target is estimated by $T^2_{Mj} = (\bar{Y}_j - \boldsymbol{\theta}_j)' G^{-1} (\bar{Y}_j - \boldsymbol{\theta}_j)$, while the internal variability within the subgroup is estimated by

$$T^2_{Dj} = (\mathbf{Y}_{ij} - \bar{Y}_j)' G^{-1} (\mathbf{Y}_{ij} - \bar{Y}_j), \quad \text{with} \quad T^2_{0j} = (n-1) T^2_{Mj} + T^2_{Dj}. \qquad (4.4.8)$$

Since asymptotically, T^2_{Mj} and T^2_{Dj} have a χ^2 distribution with p and $(n-1)p$ degrees of freedom, respectively, one can further compute two indices, I_1 and I_2, to determine whether the overall variability is mainly due to the distances between the means of the tested subgroup from targets or to the within subgroup variability. The indices are relative ratios of the normalized versions of the two components of T^2_{0j}, i.e., $I_1 = I_1^*/(I_1^* + I_2^*)$, and $I_2 = I_2^*/(I_1^* + I_2^*)$, where $I_1^* = T^2_{Mj/p}$ and $I_2^* = T^2_{Dj}/[(n-1)p]$. We can express the indices in terms of the original T^2 statistics as, $I_1 = (n-1)T^2_{Mj}/[(n-1)T^2_{Mj} + T^2_{Dj}]$ and $I_2 = T^2_{Dj}/[(n-1)T^2_{Mj} + T^2_{Dj}]$. Tracking these indices provides powerful monitoring capabilities.

4.5 Multivariate Tolerance Specifications

Multivariate tolerance regions are based on estimates of quantiles from a multivariate distribution with parameters either known or estimated from the data (John 1963). Setting up a process control scheme, on the basis of tolerance regions, involves estimating the level set $\{f \geq c\}$ of the density f which generates the data, with a prespecified probability content $1 - \boldsymbol{\alpha}$. With this approach, originally proposed in Fuchs and Kenett (1987), the rejecting region is $X_{n+1} \in \{f \geq c\}$. This method provides an exact false alarm probability of $\boldsymbol{\alpha}$. Since f is usually unknown, the population tolerance region $\{f \geq c\}$ needs to be estimated by an estimator of f. A similar approach was adopted by the Food and Drug Administration to determine equivalence of a drug product tablet before and after a change in manufacturing processes such as introduction of new equipment, a transfer of operations to another site or the scaling up of production to larger vessels. The equivalence is evaluated by comparing tablet dissolution profiles of a batch under test with dissolution profiles of tablets from a reference batch and allowing for at most a 15% difference. We expand on this example using the procedure proposed by Tsong et al. (1996).

When comparing the dissolution data of a new product and a reference approved product, the goal is to assess the similarity between the mean dissolution values at several observed sample time points. The decision of accepting or rejecting the hypothesis that the two batches have similar dissolution profiles, i.e., are bioequivalent, is based on determining if the difference in mean dissolution values between the test and reference products is no larger than the maximum expected difference between any two batches of the approval product. When dissolution value is measured at a single time point, the confidence interval of the true difference between the two batches is compared with prespecified similarity limits. When dissolution values are measured at several time points, the Mahalanobis D^2_M defined below can be used to compare the overall dissolution profiles.

The important property of the Mahalanobis D^2, is that differences at points with low variability are given a higher weight than differences at points with higher variability. This ensures that the experimental noise is properly addressed.

Let $X_1 = (x_{11}x_{12}, \ldots, x_{1p})$ and $X_2 = (x_{21}, x_{22}, \ldots, x_{2p})$ represent the mean dissolution values at p time instances of the reference and the batch under test, respectively. These means can correspond to a different number of replicates, say n and m.

The Mahalanobis distance between any two vectors $\mathbf{X}_1$ and $\mathbf{X}_2$, having the same dispersion matrix $\boldsymbol{\Sigma}$, is

$$D_M(\mathbf{X}_1, \mathbf{X}_2) = \left((\mathbf{X}_1 - \mathbf{X}_2)'\boldsymbol{\Sigma}^{-1}(\mathbf{X}_1 - \mathbf{X}_2)\right)^{1/2}. \tag{4.5.1}$$

If we estimate $\boldsymbol{\Sigma}$ by covariance matrices S_1 and S_2, we substitute for $\boldsymbol{\Sigma}$ in (4.5.1) the pooled estimator, S_{pooled}. A confidence region for the difference $\boldsymbol{\Delta} = \boldsymbol{\mu}_1 - \boldsymbol{\mu}_2$, between the expected value of the batch and the reference populations, at confidence level $1 - \alpha$, is

$$CR = \left\{\mathbf{Y} : (\mathbf{Y} - (\mathbf{X}_1 - \mathbf{X}_2))' S^{-1}_{\text{pooled}}(\mathbf{Y} - (\mathbf{X}_1 - \mathbf{X}_2)') \le K F_{1-\alpha}[p, 2n - p - 1], \right\} \tag{4.5.2}$$

where p is the dimension of the vectors, and

$$K = \frac{4(n-1)p}{n(2n - p - 1)}. \tag{4.5.3}$$

Example 4.4 To demonstrate the procedure we use an example where Y is the percent dissolution of a tablet, measured at two time instances, 15 min and 90 min (see Table 4.2 and dataset **DISS.csv**). Calculations with Python are implemented in the *MahalanobisT2* function of the `mistat` package.

Table 4.2 Dissolution data of reference and batch under test

	Batch	Tablet	15	90
1	REF	1	65.58	93.14
2	REF	2	67.17	88.01
3	REF	3	65.56	86.83
4	REF	4	66.51	88.00
5	REF	5	69.06	89.70
6	REF	6	69.77	88.88
7	TEST	1	47.77	92.39
8	TEST	2	49.46	89.93
9	TEST	3	47.76	90.19
10	TEST	4	49.72	94.12
11	TEST	5	52.68	93.80
12	TEST	6	51.01	94.45

```
diss = mistat.load_data('DISS')
columns = ['batch', 'min15', 'min90']

mahalanobisT2 = mistat.MahalanobisT2(diss[columns], 'batch',
    compare_to=[15,15], conf_level=0.95)
mahalanobisT2.summary()
```

```
Coordinates
            min15     min90
LCR     14.558418 -2.810708
Center  17.541667 -3.386667
UCR     20.524915 -3.962625

Mahalanobis
LCR        8.664879
Center    10.440449
UCR       12.216019
dtype: float64

  comparison: 9.6308
```

A scatterplot of the data shows the difference between test and reference. At 15 min dissolution is lower in the tested batch than the reference, at 90 min this is reversed (see Fig. 4.6). Our tested material therefore starts dissolving slower than the reference but then things change and it reaches high dissolution levels faster than the reference.

```
def to_coord_rep(coord):
    return f'({coord[0]:.2f}, {coord[1]:.2f})'
center_s = to_coord_rep(mahalanobisT2.coord.loc['Center', :])
lcr_s = to_coord_rep(mahalanobisT2.coord.loc['LCR', :])
ucr_s = to_coord_rep(mahalanobisT2.coord.loc['UCR', :])
```

For this data, $n = 6$, $p = 2$, $K = 1.35$, $F_{2,19,0.95} = 4.26$, $(X_2 - X_1) = (17.54, -3.39)$ and $D_M = 10.44$. A contour plot with the limits of CR set at 4.26 is presented in Fig. 4.7.

The center of the ellipsoid is set at $(17.54, -3.39)$ and, as mentioned above, at that point, $D_M = 10.44$. The line from the origin connecting to this point is

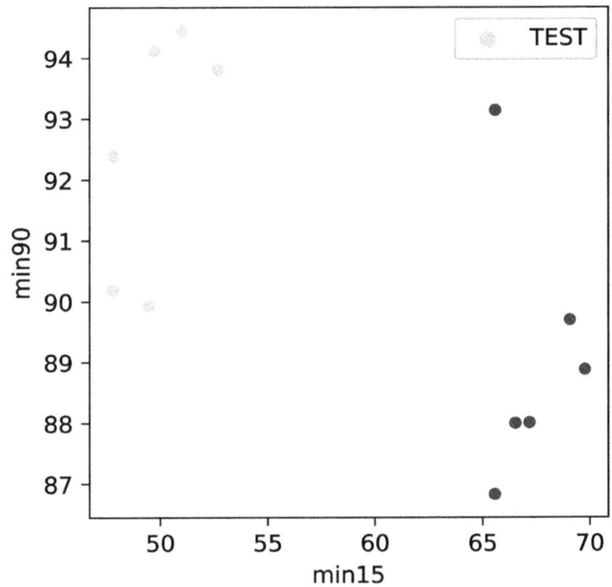

Fig. 4.6 Scatterplot of reference and batch under test

$Y = -0.193X$. It crosses the ellipse first at (14.56, −2.81) labeled as "1" on Fig. 4.7 and then at (20.52, −3.96) labeled as "2" with D_M values of $D_M^l = 8.66$ and $D_M^u = 12.22$, respectively.

To determine equivalence, with a 15% buffer, we consider the contour corresponding to results within this buffer. The D_M value for these point $RD = Sqrt[(15, 15)' S_{\text{pooled}}^{-1} (15, 15)] = 9.63$.

Since $D_M^u > RD$ we have a confidence region for the true difference in mean dissolution that exceeds the 15% buffer. We therefore declare the batch under test not to be equivalent to the reference.

An index that can be used to assess process capability in terms of equivalence between reference and batch under test is $Ceq = RD/D_M^u$. To determine the batch under test equivalent to the reference we need to show that $Ceq > 1$. ■

4.6 Tracking Structural Changes

In many industrial processes, consecutive measurements are auto and cross-correlated. This is due to inertial elements such as raw materials, storage tanks, reactors, refluxes, environmental conditions, etc. with dynamics larger than the sampling frequency. Classical linear regression models typically assume that the relationships between the inputs and the outputs in a system are instantaneous. However, as mentioned, dynamic processes often show inertias and delayed

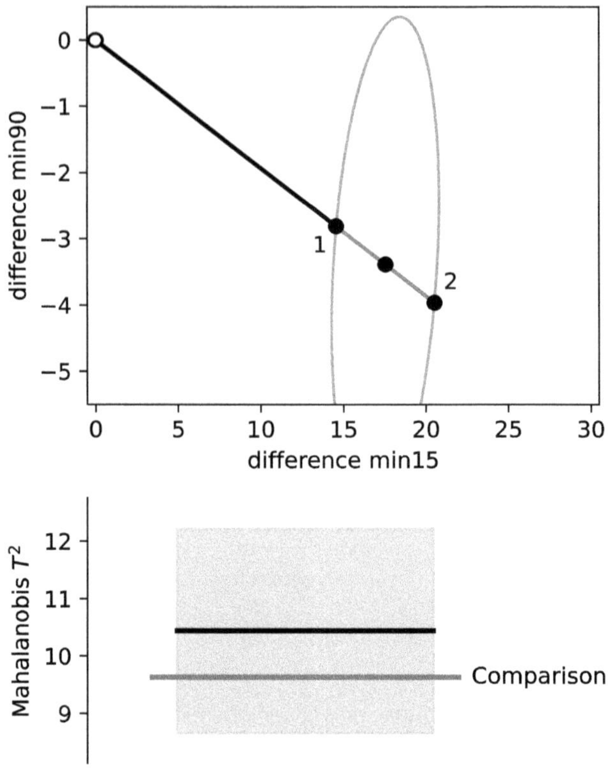

Fig. 4.7 Difference between dissolution of batch under test and reference at 15 and 90 min

responses. In this section we focus on tracking structural changes over time. It expands on Chapter 6 of *Modern Statistics* (Kenett et al. 2022b) ("Time Series Analysis and Prediction"). A comprehensive treatment of univariate time series models is available in Box et al. (2015).

4.6.1 The Synthetic Control Method

Comparative case studies are often applied to the evaluation of interventions or the impact of events such as occurrence of faults or other interventions. The synthetic control method (SCM) is based on the idea that a combination of affected and unaffected time units provides a comparison that can establish causality. It formalizes the weighting of the comparison time units using a data driven procedure, see Abadie et al. (2015) and Ben-Michael et al. (2021a), Ben-Michael et al. (2021b).

Suppose we obtain data (y, X) from $m + 1$ systems at n time intervals: $t = t_1, t_2, \ldots, t_n$. The $n \times 1$ vector y from a system where at time t_0 an intervention,

Table 4.3 Data structure for synthetic control method (SCM)

					Treatment		
Time t	1	2	...	t_0	$t_0 + 1$	...	t_n
Treated y	y_1	y_2	...	y_{t_0}	y_{t_0+1}	...	y_{t_n}
Untreated X healthy	$X_{1,1}$	$X_{2,1}$	...	$X_{t_0,1}$	$X_{t_0+1,1}$	...	$X_{t_n,1}$
	$\vdots$	$\vdots$		$\vdots$	$\vdots$		$\vdots$
	$X_{1,m}$	$X_{2,m}$	...	$X_{t_0,m}$	$X_{t_0+1,m}$	...	$X_{t_n,m}$
Additional covariates C	$C_{1,1}$	$C_{2,1}$	...	$C_{t_0,k}$	$C_{t_0+1,1}$	...	$C_{t_n,1}$
	$\vdots$	$\vdots$		$\vdots$	$\vdots$		$\vdots$
	$C_{1,k}$	$C_{2,k}$	...	$C_{t_0,k}$	$C_{t_0+1,k}$	...	$C_{t_n,k}$

such as a fault or a change, occurred. This intervention affects the time interval $(t_0 + 1, t_n)$. The $n \times m$ matrix X are similar data from untreated, healthy systems. The data structure is shown in Table 4.3. This table also includes optional covariates C $(n \times k)$ that if available can be combined with the matrix X. In the following, we will not explicitly include the covariates in the description of the method.

We first split the dataset into pre-intervention data (X^P, y^P) and post-intervention, treatment data (X^T, y^T).

$$
\begin{aligned}
y^P &= (y_i)' & i &= 1, \ldots, t_0 \\
X^P &= (X_{i,j}) & i &= 1, \ldots, t_0 \text{ and } j = 1, \ldots, m \\
y^T &= (y_i)' & i &= t_0 + 1, \ldots, n \\
X^T &= (X_{i,j}) & i &= t_0 + 1, \ldots, n \text{ and } j = 1, \ldots, m.
\end{aligned}
$$

The idea of the synthetic control method is to estimate y using a model f based on the pre-intervention data using the following model.

$$
\hat{y}_i^P = f(Y^P) = \sum_{j=1}^{m} w_j Y_{i,j}.
$$

The matrix of weights is found by choosing to minimize W^* to minimize $||y^N - WX^N||$. In the original publication, Abadie et al. (2015) estimated the weights using W
$ggt0$ and $\sum_1^m w_j = 1$ as an additional constraint. This means, the weights form a convex combination of the untreated data. In our example, we use a different form or regularization by adding the L_1 penalty, i.e., adding $\lambda \sum_{j=1}^m |w_j|$. This is also known as Lasso regression.

Once we have a model, we can construct an estimated synthetic control for all time periods. In particular, we can estimate the treatment effect using

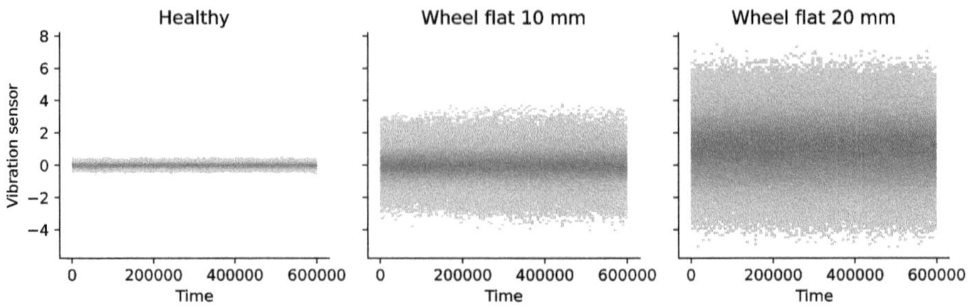

Fig. 4.8 Amplitude of accelerometer sensor of railway vehicle suspension over time with healthy and faulty system data shown as a two-dimensional density plot

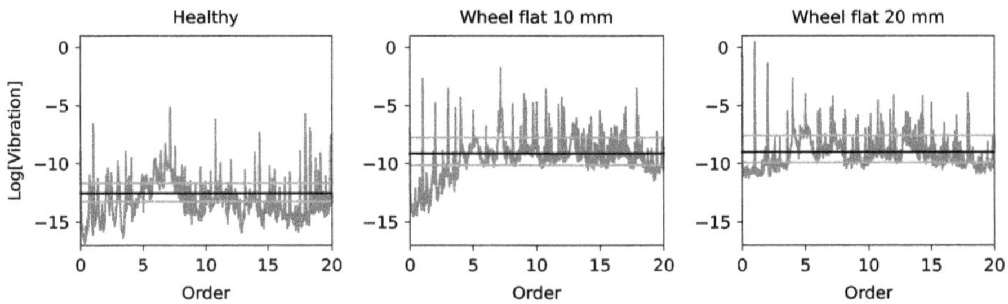

Fig. 4.9 Amplitude of accelerometer data after angular transformation

$$\hat{\tau}_t = y_t^T - \hat{Y}_t^T.$$

Because the synthetic control is constructed from untreated units, when the intervention occurs at time t_0, the difference between the synthetic control and the treated unit is the estimated treatment effect.

Example 4.5 Davidyan et al. (2021) provide an example of time series tracking engine vibrations of railway vehicle suspension systems. These suspensions are affected by several potential fault including wheel flats. Such faults can have significant impact on system performance and safety. Figure 4.8 presents vibration sensor data amplitude over time, in a healthy system and with wheel flats of 10 and 20 mm. With increasing asymmetry of the wheel, the vibration sensor detects increased vibrations.

Figure 4.9 presents the same data after angular transformation.

The dataset **SCM_WHEELS.csv** contains vibrational amplitude data for 40 wheels. For each wheel, we have a time series of 100 steps. The first wheel is damaged at step 60. We use SCM to identify this event.

We load and preprocess the data for further analysis.

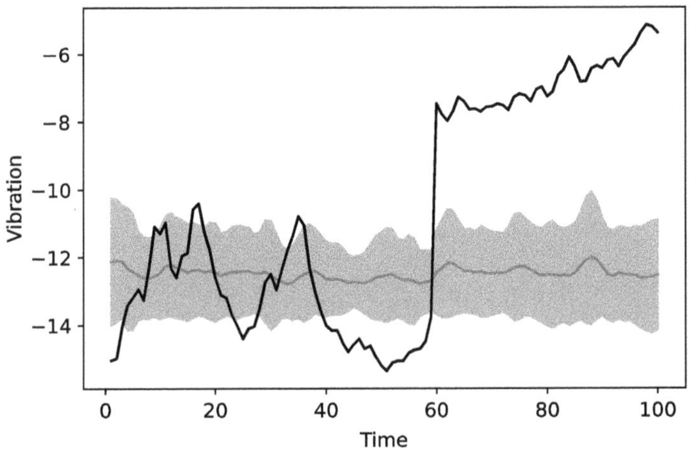

Fig. 4.10 Change in vibration amplitude over 100 time steps for flat wheel. The shaded area shows the mean and +/− one standard deviation of all 40 wheels

```
data = mistat.load_data('SCM_WHEELS.csv')
nr_wheels = 40
scm_data = defaultdict(list)
n = len(data)
for i in range(1, nr_wheels+1):
    scm_data['wheel'].extend([i] * n)
    scm_data['time'].extend(range(1, n+1))
    scm_data['vibrations'].extend(data[f'Wheel-{i}'])
    scm_data['status'].extend([True if i == 1 else False] * n)
    scm_data['after_event'].extend([False] * 59)
    scm_data['after_event'].extend([True] * 41)

scm_data = pd.DataFrame(scm_data).sort_values(by=['time', 'wheel'])
```

Figure 4.10 shows the change of vibration amplitude over time. The effect of the wheel damage at time point 60 is clearly visible.

The method *train_predict_SCM_model* implements the SCM method. It is defined as a function that takes the data, the number of a selected wheel, and the event date. The SCM model requires the data in a matrix where the wheels are in columns and the vibration and sensor data in rows. The model is then trained to learn the sensor data of the selected wheel using information from the other wheels. We use *Lasso*, a L1-regularized linear regression model, from the `scikit-learn` package. The function returns a data frame that contains the actual and synthetic data and their residual.

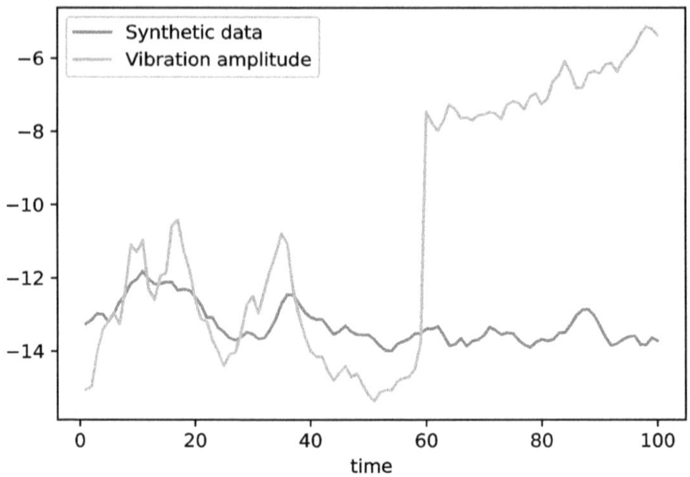

Fig. 4.11 SCM estimated effect of flat wheel on the vibration sensor data. Actual (orange) and predicted (blue)

```
def train_predict_SCM_model(scm_data, wheel, event):
    # convert data into a table with vibration and sensor data in rows and
    # wheels in columns
    features = ['vibrations']
    full_data = scm_data.pivot(index='wheel', columns='time')[features].T

    # filter pre-damage event period (make a slice on the multi-index)
    pre_event = full_data.loc[('vibrations', 1):('vibrations', event)]

    # train regularized regression model
    X = pre_event.drop(columns=wheel).values  # other wheels
    y = pre_event[wheel].values # selected wheel
    model = Lasso(fit_intercept=False, max_iter=10_000, alpha=2,
                  selection='random', random_state=1)
    model.fit(X, y)

    vibrations = full_data.loc['vibrations']
    pred_y = model.predict(vibrations.drop(columns=wheel))
    return pd.DataFrame({
        'time': scm_data.query(f'wheel == {wheel}')['time'],
        'vibrations': scm_data.query(f'wheel == {wheel}')['vibrations'],
        'synthetic': pred_y,
        'residual': scm_data.query(f'wheel == {wheel}')['vibrations'] - pred_y,
    })
```

The function can be used to predict the expected vibration amplitude for the damaged wheel. Figure 4.11 contains the resulting graph.

```
scm_faulty = train_predict_SCM_model(scm_data, 1, 60)
ax = scm_faulty.plot(x='time', y='synthetic', label='Synthetic data')
scm_faulty.plot(x='time', y='vibrations', label='Vibration amplitude', ax=ax)
plt.show()
```

We can repeat this model building and prediction for each of the 40 wheels. Figure 4.12 summarizes the results graphically. Unsurprisingly, the residuals before

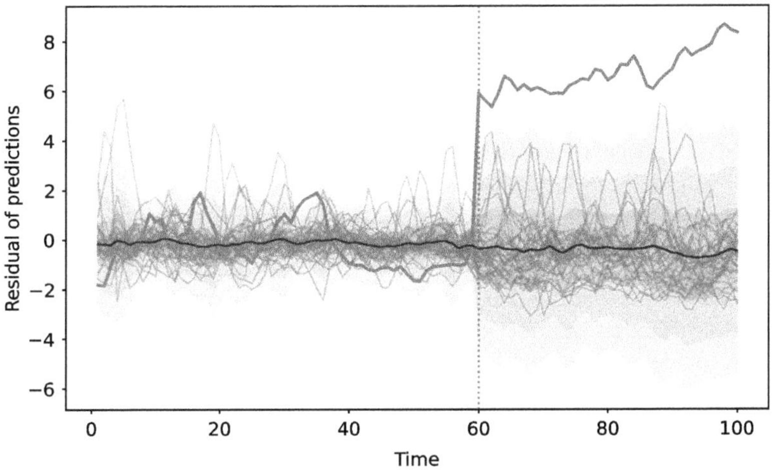

Fig. 4.12 Comparison of the residual of the SCM estimated effect for healthy (brown) and flat (blue) wheel on the vibration sensor data. The shaded area shows mean and +/− one, two, and three standard deviations of all residuals

the damage occurred fluctuate less compared to the residuals after. Only the data between 1 and 60 time steps are used in the model training. We can also see that the damaged wheel has residuals that are more than three standard deviations away from the mean. The SCM method reveals that the change is unexpected. ■

4.7 Chapter Highlights

The main concepts and tools introduced in this chapter include:

- Mean vector
- Covariance matrix
- Mahalanobis T2
- Multivariate statistical process control
- Multivariate process capability indices
- Multivariate tolerance region
- Hyper-rectangular tolerance regions
- Circular tolerance regions
- Principal components
- Internal targets
- Reference sample
- External targets
- Multivariable control of data in samples
- Synthetic control method (SCM)

4.8 Exercises

Exercise 4.1 In dataset **TSQ** we find 368 T^2 values corresponding to the vectors (x, y, θ) in the **PLACE** dataset. The first $n = 48$ vectors in **PLACE** dataset were used as a base sample, to compute the vector of means **m** and the covariance matrix S. The T^2 values are for the other individual vectors $(m = 1)$. Plot the T^2 values in the dataset **TSQ.csv**. Compute the UCL and describe from the plot what might have happened in the placement process generating the (x, y, θ) values.

Exercise 4.2 Prove that if **X** has a multivariate normal distribution, $N_v(\boldsymbol{\mu}, \boldsymbol{\sigma})$, then $(\mathbf{X} - \boldsymbol{\mu})'\boldsymbol{\Sigma}^{-1}(\mathbf{X} - \boldsymbol{\mu})$ has a χ^2 distribution with v degrees of freedom where $R = \chi^2_{1-p}[v]$ is the corresponding $(1 - p)$ quantile of the χ^2 distribution with v degrees of freedom.

Exercise 4.3 Sort the dataset **CAR** by variable `cyl`, indicating the number of cylinders in a car, and run a T^2 chart with internally derived targets for the variables `turn`, `hp`, `mpg`, with separate computations for cars with 4, 6 and 8 cylinders. How is the number of cylinders affecting the overall performance of the cars?

Exercise 4.4 Sort the dataset **CAR.csv** by variable `origin`, indicating the country of origin, and run a T^2 chart with internally derived targets for the variables `turn`, `hp`, `mpg`, with separate computations for cars from 1 = US; 2 = Europe; 3 = Asia. How is the country of origin affecting the overall performance of the cars?

Exercise 4.5 Load the dataset **GASOL.csv** and compute a T^2 chart for $x1$, $x2$, `astm`, `endPt`, `yield`. Design the chart with an external assigned target based on observations 12–24. Compare the charts. Explain the differences.

Exercise 4.6 Repeat Exercise 4.5, but this time design the chart with an externally assigned target based on observations 25–32. Explain the computational difficulty.

Exercise 4.7 Calculate control limits for grouped data with 20 subgroups of size 5 and 6 dimensions, with internally derived targets (Eq. (4.4.2)). How will the control limits change if you start monitoring a process with similar data?

Exercise 4.8 Let $X_1 = (x_{11}, x_{12}, \ldots, x_{1p})$ and $X_2 = (x_{21}, x_{22}, \ldots, x_{2p})$ represent the mean dissolution values of tablets at p time instances of a reference product and a batch under test, respectively. The Mahalanobis distance T^2, between X_1 and X_2, is defined here as $D_M = \sqrt{(X_2 - X_1)' S^{-1}_{\text{pooled}}(X_2 - X_1)}$, where $S_{\text{pooled}} = (S_{\text{reference}} + S_{\text{test}})/2$, is the pooled covariance matrix of the reference and test samples. The confidence region, CR, of the difference between batch and reference consists of all vectors Y satisfying: $[(Y - (X_2 - X_1)' S^{-1}_{\text{pooled}}(Y - (X_2 - X_1)] \leq K F_{0.90}[p, 2n - p - 1]$ where $F_{0.90}[p, 2n - p - 1]$ is the 90th quantile of the F-distribution with degrees of freedom p and $(2n-p-1)$. Prove that for measurements conducted at one time instance $(p = 1)$ these formulae correspond to the confidence intervals presented in Chapter 3 of *Modern Statistics* (Kenett et al. 2022b).

Chapter 5
Classical Design and Analysis of Experiments

Preview Experiments are used in industry to improve productivity, reduce variability, enhance quality and obtain robust products and manufacturing processes. In this chapter we study how to design and analyze experiments which are aimed at testing scientific or technological hypotheses. These hypotheses are concerned with the effects of procedures or treatments on quality and productivity; or the general relationship between variables. Designed experiments help determine the conditions under which a production process yields maximum output or other optimum results, etc. The chapter presents the classical methods of design of experiments. It starts with an introductory section with examples and discusses guiding principles in designing experiments. The chapter covers the range of classical experimental designs including complete block designs, Latin squares, full and fractional factorial designs with factors at two and three levels. The basic approach to the analysis is through modeling the response variable and computing ANOVA tables. Particular attention is given to the generation of designs using Python.

5.1 Basic Steps and Guiding Principles

The following are guiding principles for statistically designed experiments. They ensure high information quality (InfoQ) of a study, as introduced in Chap. 1.

1. The **objectives** of a study should be well stated, and criteria established to test whether these objectives have been met.
2. The **response variable(s)** should be clearly defined so that the study objectives are properly translated to measurable variables. At this stage measurement uncertainty should be established.
3. All factors which might affect the response variable(s) should be listed and specified. We call these the **controllable factors**. This requires interactive brainstorming with content experts.

Supplementary Information The online version contains supplementary material available at (https://doi.org/10.1007/978-3-031-28482-3_5).

R. S. Kenett et al., *Industrial Statistics*, Statistics for Industry, Technology, and Engineering, https://doi.org/10.1007/978-3-031-28482-3_5

4. The type of **measurements** or observations on all variables should be specified.
5. The **levels** of the controllable factors to be tested should be determined.
6. A statistical **model** should be formulated concerning the relationship between the pertinent variables, and their error distributions. This can rely on prior knowledge or literature search.
7. An **experimental layout** or **experimental array** should be designed so that the inference from the gathered data will be:

   a. **valid**
   b. **precise**
   c. **generalizable**
   d. **easy to obtain**

8. The trials should be performed, if possible, in a **random order**, to avoid bias by factors which are not taken into consideration.
9. A **protocol** of execution should be prepared, including the method of analysis. The method of analysis and data collection depends on the design.
10. The execution of the experiment should carefully follow the protocol with proper documentation.
11. The results of the experiments should be carefully analyzed and reported ensuring proper documentation and traceability. Modern technology can ensure that data, analysis and conclusions are fully integrated and reproducible.
12. Confirmatory experiments should be conducted, to validate the inference (conclusions) of the experiments.

We illustrate the above principles with two examples.

Example 5.1 The first example deals with a problem of determining with experiments the weights of four objects. It illustrates what is an experimental layout (design) and why an optimal one should be chosen.

Step 1: Formulation of Objectives
The **objective** is to devise a measurement plan that will yield weight estimates of chemicals with maximal precision with four weighing operations.

Step 2: Description of Response
The weight measurement device is a chemical balance, with right and left pans. One or more objects can be put on either pan. The **response** variable Y, is the measurement read on the scale of the chemical balance. This is equal to the total weight of objects on the right pan (+) minus the total weight of objects on the left pan (−), plus a measurement error.

Step 3: Controllable Variables
We have four objects O_1, O_2, O_3, O_4, with unknown weights w_1, w_2, w_3, w_4. The controllable (influencing) variables are

$$X_{ij} = \begin{cases} 1, & \text{if } j\text{-th object is put on } + \text{ pan} \\ & \text{in the } i\text{-th measurement} \\ \\ -1, & \text{if } j\text{-th object is put on } - \text{ pan} \\ & \text{in the } i\text{-th measurement.} \end{cases}$$

$i, j = 1, 2, 3, 4.$

Step 4: Type of Measurements
The response Y is measured on a continuous scale in an interval (y^*, y^{**}). The observations are a realization of continuous random variables.

Step 5: Levels of Controllable Variables
$X_{ij} = \pm 1$, as above.

Step 6: A Statistical Model
The measurement model is linear, i.e.,

$$Y_i = w_1 X_{i1} + w_2 X_{i2} + w_3 X_{i3} + w_4 X_{i4} + e_i$$

$i = 1, \cdots, 4$, where e_1, e_2, e_3, e_4 are independent random variables, with $E\{e_i\} = 0$ and $V\{e_i\} = \sigma^2$, $i = 1, 2, \cdots, 4$.

Step 7: Experimental Layout
An experimental layout is represented by a 4×4 matrix

$$(X) = (X_{ij}; i, j = 1, \cdots, 4).$$

Such a matrix is called a **design matrix**.

Given a design matrix (X), and a vector of measurements $\mathbf{Y} = (Y_1, \cdots, Y_4)'$, we estimate $\mathbf{w} = (w_1, \cdots, w_4)'$ by

$$\hat{\mathbf{W}} = (L)\mathbf{Y},$$

where (L) is a 4×4 matrix. We say that the design is **valid**, if there exists a matrix L such that $E\{\hat{\mathbf{W}}\} = \mathbf{w}$. Any **non-singular** design matrix (X) represents a valid design with $(L) = (X)^{-1}$.

Indeed, $E\{\mathbf{Y}\} = (X)\mathbf{w}$. Hence

$$E\{\hat{\mathbf{W}}\} = (X)^{-1} E\{\mathbf{Y}\} = \mathbf{w}.$$

The **precision** of the design matrix (X) is measured by $\left(\sum_{i=1}^{4} V\{\hat{W}_i\}\right)^{-1}$. The problem is to find a design matrix $(X)^0$ which **maximizes the precision**.

It can be shown that an optimal design is given by the **orthogonal array**

$$(X)^0 = \begin{bmatrix} 1 & -1 & -1 & 1 \\ 1 & 1 & -1 & -1 \\ 1 & -1 & 1 & -1 \\ 1 & 1 & 1 & 1 \end{bmatrix}$$

or any row (or column) permutation of this matrix. Notice that in this design, in each one of the first three weighing operation (row) two objects are put on the left pan (−) and two on the right. Also, each object, excluding the first, is put twice on (−) and twice on (+). The weight estimates under this design as

$$\hat{\mathbf{W}} = \frac{1}{4} \begin{bmatrix} 1 & 1 & 1 & 1 \\ -1 & 1 & -1 & 1 \\ -1 & -1 & 1 & 1 \\ 1 & -1 & -1 & 1 \end{bmatrix} \begin{bmatrix} Y_1 \\ Y_2 \\ Y_3 \\ Y_4 \end{bmatrix}.$$

Moreover,

$$\sum_{i=1}^{4} V\{\hat{W}_i\} = \sigma^2.$$

The order of measurements is **random**. ■

Example 5.2 The second example illustrates a complex process, with a large number of factors which may affect yield variables.

Wave soldering of circuit pack assemblies (CPA) is an automated process of soldering which, if done in an optimal fashion, can raise quality and productivity. The process, however, involves three phases and many variables. We analyze the various steps required for designing an experiment to learn the effects of the various factors on the process. We follow the process description of Lin and Kacker (2012).

If the soldering process yields good results, the CPA's can proceed directly to automatic testing. This is a big savings in direct labor cost and increase in productivity. The wave soldering process (WSP) is in three phases. In Phase I, called **fluxing**, the solder joint surfaces are cleaned by the soldering flux, which also protects it against reoxidation. The fluxing lowers the surface tension for better solder wetting and solder joint formation.

Phase II of the WSP is the **soldering assembly**. This is performed in a cascade of wave soldering machine. After preheating the solution, the non-component side of the assembly is immersed in a solder wave for 1–2 s. All solder points are completed when the CPA exits the wave. Preheating must be gradual. The correct heating is essential to effective soldering. Also important is the conveyor speed and the conveyor's angle. The last phase, Phase III, of the process is that of **detergent cleaning**. The assembly is first washed in detergent solution, then rinsed in water and finally dried with hot air. The temperature of the detergent solution is raised to achieve effective cleaning and prevent excessive foaming. The rinse water is heated to obtain effective rinsing.

We list now the design steps:

1. **Objectives**. To find the effects of the various factors on the quality of wave soldering and optimize the process.
2. **Response Variables**. There are four yield variables

    a. Insulation resistance
    b. Cleaning characterization
    c. Soldering efficiency
    d. Solder mask cracking

3. **Controllable Variables**. There are 17 variables (factors) associated with the three phases of the process.

    I. **Flux formulation**
    A. Type of activator
    B. Amount of activator
    C. Type of surfactant
    D. Amount of surfactant
    E. Amount of antioxidant
    F. Type of solvent
    G. Amount of solvent

    II. **Wave Soldering**
    H. Amount of Flux
    I. Preheat time
    J. Solder temperature
    K. Conveyor speed
    L. Conveyor angle
    M. Wave height setting

    III. **Detergent cleaning**
    N. Detergent concentration
    O. Detergent temperature
    P. Cleaning conveyor speed
    Q. Rinse water temperature

4. **Measurements**

    a. Insulation resistance test at 30 min, 1 and 4 days after soldering at

        - −35C, 90% RN, no bias voltage
        - −65C, 90% RH, no bias voltage
        - (continuous variable).

    b. Cleaning characterization: The amounts of residues on the board (continuous variable).
    c. Soldering efficiency: Visual inspection of no solder, insufficient solder, good solder, excess solder and other defects (discrete variables).
    d. Solder mask cracking: Visual inspection of cracked spots on the solder mask (discrete variables).

5. **Levels of Controllable Factors**

Factor	# levels	Factor	# levels	Factor	# levels
A	2	H	3	N	2
B	3	I	3	O	2
C	2	J	3	P	3
D	3	K	3	Q	2
E	3	L	3		
F	2	M	2		
G	3				

6. **The Statistical Model**. The response variables are related to the controllable variables by linear models having "main effects" and "interaction" parameters, as will be explained in Sect. 5.3.
7. **The Experiment Layout**. A fractional factorial experiment, as explained in Sect. 5.8, is designed. Such a design is needed, because a full factorial design contains $3^{10}2^7 = 7{,}558{,}272$ possible combinations of factor levels. A fractional replication design chooses a manageable fraction of the full factorial in a manner that allows valid inference, and precise estimates of the parameters of interest.
8. **Protocol of Execution**. Suppose that it is decided to perform a fraction of $3^3 2^2 = 108$ trials at certain levels of the 17 factors. However, the set-up of the factors takes time and one cannot perform more than 4 trials a day. The experiment will last 27 days. It is important to construct the design so that the important effects, to be estimated, will not be confounded with possible differences between days (blocks). The order of the trials within each day is randomized as well as, the trials which are assigned to different days. **Randomization** is an important component of the design, which comes to enhance its validity. The execution protocol should clearly specify the order of execution of the trials.

■

5.2 Blocking and Randomization

Blocking and randomization are used in planning of experiments, in order to increase the precision of the outcome and ensure the validity of the inference. Blocking is used to reduce errors. A block is a portion of the experimental material that is expected to be more homogeneous than the whole aggregate. For example, if the experiment is designed to test the effect of polyester coating of electronic circuits on their current output, the variability between circuits could be considerably bigger than the effect of the coating on the current output. In order to reduce this component of variance, one can block by circuit. Each circuit will be tested under two treatments: no-coating and coating. We first test the current output of a circuit without coating. Later we coat the circuit, and test again. Such a comparison of before and after a treatment, of the same units, is called **paired comparison**.

Another example of blocking is the boy's shoes examples of Box et al. (2005). Two kinds of shoe soles' materials are to be tested by fixing the soles on n pairs of boys' shoes, and measuring the amount of wear of the soles after a period of actively wearing the shoes. Since there is high variability between activity of boys, if m pairs will be with soles of one type and the rest of the other, it will not be clear whether any difference that might be observed in the degree of wearout is due to differences between the characteristics of the sole material or to the differences between the boys. By blocking by pair of shoes, we can reduce much of the variability. Each pair of shoes is assigned the two types of soles. The comparison within each block is free of the variability between boys. Furthermore, since boys use their right or left foot differently, one should assign the type of soles to the left or right shoes at random. Thus, the treatments (two types of soles) are assigned within each block at random.

Other examples of blocks could be machines, shifts of production, days of the week, operators, etc.

Generally, if there are t treatments to compare, and b blocks, and if all t treatments can be performed within a single block, we assign all the t treatments to each block. The order of applying the treatments within each block should be **randomized**. Such a design is called a **randomized complete block design**. We will see later how a proper analysis of the yield can validly test for the effects of the treatments.

If not all treatments can be applied within each block it is desirable to assign treatments to blocks in some balanced fashion. Such designs, to be discussed later, are called **balanced incomplete block designs** (BIBD).

Randomization within each block is important also to validate the assumption that the error components in the statistical model are independent. This assumption may not be valid if treatments are not assigned at random to the experimental units within each block.

5.3 Additive and Non-additive Linear Models

Seventeen factors which might influence the outcome in WSP are listed in Example 5.2. Some of these factors, like type of activator (A), or type of surfactant (C) are categorical variables. The number of levels listed for these factors was 2. That is, the study compares the effects of two types of activators and two types of surfactants.

If the variables are continuous, like amount of activator (B), we can use a regression linear model to represent the effects of the factors on the yield variables. Such models will be discussed later (Sect. 5.7). In the present section linear models which are valid for both categorical or continuous variables are presented.

For the sake of explanation, let us start first with a simple case, in which the response depends on one factor only. Thus, let A designate some factor, which is applied at different levels, $A_1, \cdots, A_a$. These could be a categories. The levels of A are also called "**treatments**."

Suppose that at each level of A we make n independent repetitions (replicas) of the experiment. Let Y_{ij}, $i = 1, \cdots, a$ and $j = 1, \cdots, n$ denote the observed yield at the j-th replication of level A_i. We model the random variables Y_{ij} as

$$Y_{ij} = \mu + \tau_i^A + e_{ij}, \quad i = 1, \cdots, a, \quad j = 1, \cdots, n, \tag{5.3.1}$$

where μ and $\tau_1^A, \cdots, \tau_a^A$ are unknown parameters, satisfying

$$\sum_{i=1}^{a} \tau_i^A = 0. \tag{5.3.2}$$

$e_{ij}, i = 1, \cdots, a, j = 1, \cdots, n$, are independent random variables such that,

$$E\{e_{ij}\} = 0 \text{ and } V\{e_{ij}\} = \sigma^2, \tag{5.3.3}$$

for all $i = 1, \cdots, a; j = 1, \cdots, n$.

Let

$$\bar{Y}_i = \frac{1}{n}\sum_{j=1}^{n} Y_{ij}, \quad i = 1, \cdots, a.$$

The expected values of these means are

$$E\{\bar{Y}_i\} = \mu + \tau_i^A, \quad i = 1, \cdots, k. \tag{5.3.4}$$

Let

$$\bar{\bar{Y}} = \frac{1}{k}\sum_{i=1}^{k}, \bar{Y}_i. \tag{5.3.5}$$

This is the mean of all $N = k \times n$ observations (the grand mean), since $\sum_{i=1}^{a} \tau_i^A = 0$, we obtain that

$$E\{\bar{\bar{Y}}\} = \mu. \tag{5.3.6}$$

The parameter τ_i^A is called the **main effect** of A at level i.

If there are two factors, A and B, at a and b levels respectively, there are $a \times b$ **treatment combinations** (A_i, B_j), $i = 1, \cdots, a$, $j = 1, \cdots, b$. Suppose also that n independent replicas are made at each one of the treatment combinations. The yield at the k-th replication of treatment combination (A_i, B_j) is given by

$$Y_{ijk} = \mu + \tau_i^A + \tau_j^B + \tau_{ij}^{AB} + e_{ijk}. \tag{5.3.7}$$

The error terms e_{ijk} are independent random variables satisfying

$$E\{e_{ijl}\} = 0, \quad V\{e_{ijl}\} = \sigma^2, \tag{5.3.8}$$

for all $i = 1, \cdots, a$, $j = 1, \cdots, b$, $k = 1, \cdots, n$.

We further assume that

$$\sum_{j=1}^{b} \tau_{ij}^{AB} = 0, \quad i = 1, \cdots, a$$

$$\sum_{i=1}^{a} \tau_{ij}^{AB} = 0, \quad j = 1, \cdots, b.$$

$$\sum_{i=1}^{a} \tau_i^A = 0, \tag{5.3.9}$$

$$\sum_{j=1}^{b} \tau_j^B = 0.$$

τ_i^A is the **main effect** of A at level i, τ_j^B is the **main effect** of B at level j, and τ_{ij}^{AB} is the **interaction effect** at (A_i, B_j).

If all the interaction effects are zero then the model reduces to

$$Y_{ijk} = \mu + \tau_i^A + \tau_j^B + e_{ijk}. \tag{5.3.10}$$

Such a model is called **additive**. If not all the interaction components are zero then the model is called **non-additive**.

This model is generalized in a straightforward manner to include a larger number of factors. Thus, for three factors, there are three types of main effect terms, τ_i^A, τ_j^B and τ_k^C; three types of interaction terms τ_{ij}^{AB}, τ_{ik}^{AC} and τ_{jk}^{BC}; and one type of interaction τ_{ijk}^{ABC}.

Generally, if there are p factors, there are 2^p types of parameters,

$$\mu, \tau_i^A, \tau_j^B, \cdots, \tau_{ij}^{AB}, \tau_{ik}^{AC}, \cdots, \tau_{ijk}^{ABC}, \cdots$$

etc. Interaction parameters between two factors are called 1st order interactions. Interaction parameters between three factors are called 2-nd order interactions, and so on. In particular modelling it is often assumed that all interaction parameters of higher than 1st order are zero.

5.4 The Analysis of Randomized Complete Block Designs

5.4.1 Several Blocks, Two Treatments per Block: Paired Comparison

As in the shoe soles example, or the example of the effect of polyester coating on circuits output, there are two treatments applied in each one of n blocks. The linear model can be written as

$$Y_{ij} = \mu + \tau_i + \beta_j + e_{ij}, \quad i = 1, 2; \ j = 1, \cdots, n, \tag{5.4.1}$$

where τ_i is the effect of the i-th treatment and β_j is the effect of the j-th block. e_{ij} is an independent random variable, representing the experimental random error or deviation. It is assumed that $E\{e_{ij}\} = 0$ and $V\{e_{ij}\} = \sigma_e^2$. Since we are interested in testing whether the two treatments have different effects, the analysis is based on the within block differences

$$D_j = Y_{2j} - Y_{1j} = \tau_2 - \tau_1 + e_j^*, \quad j = 1, \cdots, n. \tag{5.4.2}$$

The error terms e_j^* are independent random variables with $E\{e_j^*\} = 0$ and $V\{e_j^*\} = \sigma_d^2$, $j = 1, \cdots, n$ where $\sigma_d^2 = 2\sigma_e^2$.

An unbiased estimator of σ_d^2 is

$$S_d^2 = \frac{1}{n-1} \sum_{j=1}^{n} (D_j - \bar{D}_n)^2, \tag{5.4.3}$$

where $\bar{D}_n = \frac{1}{n} \sum_{j=1}^{n} D_j$. The hypotheses to be tested are:

$$H_0 : \delta = \tau_2 - \tau_1 = 0$$

against

$$H_1 : \delta \neq 0.$$

5.4.1.1 The t-Test

Most commonly used is the t-test, in which H_0 is tested by computing the test statistic

$$t = \frac{\sqrt{n}\, \bar{D}_n}{S_d}. \tag{5.4.4}$$

If $e_1^*, \cdots, e_n^*$ are i.i.d., normally distributed then, under the null hypothesis, t has a t-distribution with $(n-1)$ degrees of freedom. In this case, H_0 is rejected if

$$|t| > t_{1-\alpha/2}[n-1],$$

where α is the selected level of significance.

Table 5.1 Sign assignments and values of $\bar{Y}$

Signs				D
−1	−1	−1	−1	−0.55
1	−1	−1	−1	0
−1	1	−1	−1	−0.4
1	1	−1	−1	0.15
−1	−1	1	−1	−0.20
1	−1	1	−1	0.35
−1	1	1	−1	−0.05
1	1	1	−1	0.50
−1	−1	−1	1	−0.50
1	−1	−1	1	0.05
−1	1	−1	1	−0.35
1	1	−1	1	0.2
−1	−1	1	1	−0.15
1	−1	1	1	0.40
−1	1	1	1	0
1	1	1	1	0.55

5.4.1.2 Randomization Tests

A randomization test for paired comparison, constructs a **reference distribution** of all possible averages of the differences that can be obtained by randomly assigning the sign $+$ or $-$ to the value of D_i. It computes then an average difference $\bar{D}$ for each one of the 2^n sign assignments.

The P-value of the test, for the two-sided alternative, is determined according to this reference distribution, by

$$P = \Pr\{\bar{Y} \geq \text{Observed } \bar{D}\}.$$

For example, suppose we have four differences, with values 1.1, 0.3, −0.7, −0.1. The mean is $\bar{D}_4 = 0.15$. There are $2^4 = 16$ possible ways of assigning a sign to $|D_i|$. Let $X_i = \pm 1$ and $\bar{Y} = \frac{1}{4}\sum_{i=1}^{4} X|D_i|$. The possible combinations are listed in Table 5.1

Under the reference distribution, all these possible means are equally probable. The P-value associated with the observed $\bar{D} = 0.15$ is $P = \frac{7}{15} = 0.47$. If the number of pairs (blocks) n is large the procedure becomes cumbersome, since we have to determine all the 2^n sign assignments. If $n = 20$ there are $2^{20} = 1{,}048{,}576$ such assignments. We can, however, estimate the P-value by taking a RSWR from this reference distribution. In Python this is performed with the following commands:

Fig. 5.1 Stem-and-leaf plot of 200 random difference averages

1	-4	3
2	-3	7
7	-3	55333
16	-3	097766555
25	-2	444433111
38	-2	0999998776666
62	-1	555444433333333333222211
82	0	99999999888887776655
(34)	0	5444333332222111110000112333333444
84	0	5666666666777779999999999
59	1	011133333333555
44	1	555555666666799999
26	2	01112222333
15	2	5677888
8	3	0002
4	3	99
2	4	1
1	4	5

```
random.seed(1)
X = [1.1, 0.3, -0.7, -0.1]
m = 20000

Di = pd.DataFrame([random.choices((-1, 1), k=len(X)) for _ in range(m)])
DiX = (Di * X)

np.mean(DiX.mean(axis=1) > np.mean(X))
```

```
0.31425
```

Example 5.3 We analyze here the results of the shoe soles experiment, as reported in Box et al. (2005). The observed differences in the wear of the soles, between type B and type A, for $n = 10$ children, are:

$$0.8,\ 0.6,\ 0.3,\ -0.1,\ 1.1,\ -0.2,\ 0.3,\ 0.5,\ 0.5,\ 0.3.$$

The average difference is $\bar{D}_{10} = 0.41$.

A t-test of H_0, using the observed differences, is obtained using *ttest_1samp* from the `scipy` package.

```
X = [0.8, 0.6, 0.3, -0.1, 1.1, -0.2, 0.3, 0.5, 0.5, 0.3]
statistic, pvalue = stats.ttest_1samp(X, 0.0)
print(f't {statistic:.2f}')
print(f'pvalue {pvalue:.4f}')
```

```
t 3.35
pvalue 0.0085
```

The randomization test is also straightforward in Python. A stem-and-leaf plot of the 200 random difference averages is shown in Fig. 5.1.

```
random.seed(1)
X = [0.8, 0.6, 0.3, -0.1, 1.1, -0.2, 0.3, 0.5, 0.5, 0.3]
m = 200

Di = pd.DataFrame([random.choices((-1, 1), k=len(X)) for _ in range(m)])
DiX = (Di * X)

means = DiX.mean(axis=1)
Pestimate = np.mean(DiX.mean(axis=1) > np.mean(X))
print(f'P_estimate: {Pestimate}')
```

```
P_estimate: 0.01
```

According to this, the P-value is estimated as

$$\hat{P} = 0.01.$$

This estimate is almost the same as the P-value of the t-test. ■

5.4.2 Several Blocks, t Treatments per Block

As mentioned earlier, the **Randomized Complete Block Designs** (RCBD) are those in which each block contains all the t treatments. The treatments are assigned to the experimental units in each block at random. Let b denote the number of blocks. The linear model for these designs is

$$Y_{ij} = \mu + \tau_i + \beta_j + e_{ij}, \quad i = 1, \cdots, t \;\; j = 1, \cdots, b, \tag{5.4.5}$$

where Y_{ij} is the yield of the i-th treatment in the j-th block. The main effect of the i-th treatment is τ_i, and the main effect of the j-th block is β_j. It is assumed that the effects are additive (no interaction). Under this assumption, each treatment is tried only once in each block. The different blocks serve the role of replicas. However, since the blocks may have additive effects, β_j, we have to adjust for the effects of blocks in estimating σ^2. This is done as shown in the ANOVA table below.

Further assume that, e_{ij} are the error random variables with $E\{e_{ij}\} = 0$ and $V\{e_{ij}\} = \sigma^2$ for all (i, j). The ANOVA for this model is presented in Table 5.2. In this table,

Table 5.2 ANOVA table for RCBD

Source of variation	DF	SS	MS	$E\{MS\}$
Treatments	$t-1$	$SSTR$	$MSTR$	$\sigma^2 + \frac{b}{t-1}\sum_{i=1}^{t}\tau_i^2$
Blocks	$b-1$	$SSBL$	$MSBL$	$\sigma^2 + \frac{t}{b-1}\sum_{j=1}^{b}\beta_j^2$
Error	$(t-1)(b-1)$	SSE	MSE	σ^2
Total	$tb-1$	SST	–	

$$SST = \sum_{i=1}^{t}\sum_{j=1}^{b}(Y_{ij} - \bar{\bar{Y}})^2, \tag{5.4.6}$$

$$SSTR = b\sum_{i=1}^{t}(\bar{Y}_{i.} - \bar{\bar{Y}})^2, \tag{5.4.7}$$

$$SSBL = t\sum_{j=1}^{b}(\bar{Y}_{.j} - \bar{\bar{Y}})^2, \tag{5.4.8}$$

and

$$SSE = SST - SSTR - SSBL.$$

$$\bar{Y}_{i.} = \frac{1}{b}\sum_{j=1}^{b} Y_{ij}, \qquad \bar{Y}_{.j} = \frac{1}{t}\sum_{i=1}^{t} Y_{ij} \tag{5.4.9}$$

and $\bar{\bar{Y}}$ is the grand mean.

The significance of the treatment effects is tested by the F-statistic

$$F_t = \frac{MSTR}{MSE}. \tag{5.4.10}$$

The significance of the block effects is tested by

$$F_b = \frac{MSBL}{MSE}. \tag{5.4.11}$$

These statistics are compared with the corresponding $(1 - \alpha)$-th quantile of the F-distribution. Under the assumption that $\sum_{i=1}^{t} \tau_i = 0$, the main effects of the treatments are estimated by

$$\hat{\tau}_i = \bar{Y}_{i.} - \bar{\bar{Y}}, \quad i = 1, \cdots, t. \tag{5.4.12}$$

These are least squares estimates. Each such estimation is a linear contrast

$$\hat{\tau}_i = \sum_{i'=1}^{t} c_{ii'}\bar{Y}_{i'.}, \tag{5.4.13}$$

where

$$c_{ii'} = \begin{cases} 1 - \frac{1}{t}, & \text{if } i = i' \\ -\frac{1}{t}, & \text{if } i \neq i'. \end{cases} \tag{5.4.14}$$

Hence,

$$
\begin{aligned}
V\{\hat{\tau}_i\} &= \frac{\sigma^2}{b}\sum_{i'=1}^{t} c_{ii'}^2 \\
&= \frac{\sigma^2}{b}\left(1-\frac{1}{t}\right), \quad i = 1, \cdots, t.
\end{aligned}
\tag{5.4.15}
$$

An unbiased estimator of σ^2 is given by MSE. Thus, simultaneous confidence intervals for τ_i $(i = 1, \cdots, t)$, according to the Scheffé method, are

$$
\hat{\tau}_i \pm S_\alpha\left(\frac{MSE}{b}\left(1-\frac{1}{t}\right)\right)^{1/2}, \quad i = 1, \cdots, t, \tag{5.4.16}
$$

where

$$
S_\alpha = ((t-1)F_{1-\alpha}[t-1, (t-1)(b-1)])^{1/2}.
$$

Example 5.4 In Example 4.2 we estimated the effects of hybrids on the resistance in cards. We have $t = 6$ hybrids (treatments) on a card, and 32 cards. We can test now whether there are significant differences between the cards, by considering the cards as blocks, and using the ANOVA for RCBD. In this case, $b = 32$. Using two-way Anova in `statsmodels` and dataset **HADPAS.csv**.

```
hadpas = mistat.load_data('HADPAS')

model = smf.ols('res3 ~ C(diska) + C(hyb)', data=hadpas).fit()
print(anova.anova_lm(model))
```

```
              df        sum_sq        mean_sq           F        PR(>F)
C(diska)    31.0  2.804823e+06   90478.160618   26.863283  1.169678e-47
C(hyb)       5.0  1.780741e+06  356148.170833  105.741638  4.017015e-48
Residual   155.0  5.220551e+05    3368.097715         NaN           NaN
```

The ANOVA table is shown in Table 5.3. Since $F_{0.99}[5, 155] = 2.2725$ and $F_{0.99}[31, 155] = 1.5255$, both the treatment effects and the card effects are significant.

The estimator of σ, $\hat{\sigma}_p = (MSE)^{1/2}$, according to the above ANOVA, is $\hat{\sigma}_p = 58.03$. Notice that this estimator is considerably smaller than the pooled estimator of σ of 133.74 (see Example 4.16, *Modern Statistics*, Kenett et al. 2022b). This is due to the variance reduction effect of the blocking.

Table 5.3 ANOVA for hybrid data

Source	DF	SS	MS	F
Hybrids	5	1,780,741	356,148	105.7
Cards	31	2,804,823	90,478	26.9
Error	155	522,055	3368	–
Total	191	5,107,619	–	–

The simultaneous confidence intervals, at level of confidence 0.95, for the treatment effects (the average hybrid measurements minus the grand average of 1965.2) are:

$$
\begin{aligned}
&\text{Hybrid 1}: && 178.21 \pm 28.66;\\
&\text{Hybrid 2}: && -62.39 \pm 28.66;\\
&\text{Hybrid 3}: && -114.86 \pm 28.66.\\
&\text{Hybrid 4}: && -64.79 \pm 28.66;\\
&\text{Hybrid 5}: && 15.36 \pm 28.66;\\
&\text{Hybrid 6}: && 48.71 \pm 28.66;
\end{aligned}
$$

Accordingly, the effects of Hybrid 2 and Hybrid 4 are not significantly different, and that of Hybrid 5 is not significantly different from zero. In Python, we get the confidence intervals from the model:

```
model.conf_int().tail(5)
```

```
                       0           1
C(hyb)[T.2] -269.254303 -211.933197
C(hyb)[T.3] -321.723053 -264.401947
C(hyb)[T.4] -271.660553 -214.339447
C(hyb)[T.5] -191.504303 -134.183197
C(hyb)[T.6] -158.160553 -100.839447
```

```
ci = model.conf_int().tail(5)
hyb_mean = hadpas.groupby(by='hyb').mean()['res3'] - hadpas['res3'].mean()
print(hyb_mean.round(2))
(ci.iloc[:,1] - ci.iloc[:,0]) / 2
```

```
hyb
1    178.17
2    -62.43
3   -114.90
4    -64.83
5     15.32
6     48.67
Name: res3, dtype: float64
```

```
C(hyb)[T.2]    28.660553
C(hyb)[T.3]    28.660553
C(hyb)[T.4]    28.660553
C(hyb)[T.5]    28.660553
C(hyb)[T.6]    28.660553
dtype: float64
```

■

5.5 Balanced Incomplete Block Designs

As mentioned before, it is often the case that the blocks are not sufficiently large to accommodate all the t treatments. For example, in testing the wearout of fabric one uses a special machine (Martindale wear tester) which can accommodate only four pieces of clothes simultaneously. Here the block size is fixed at $k = 4$, while the number of treatments t, is the number of types of cloths to be compared. **Balanced Incomplete Block Designs** (BIBD) are designs which assign t treatment to b blocks of size k $(k < t)$ in the following manner.

1. Each treatment is assigned only once to any one block.
2. Each treatment appears in r blocks. r is the number of replicas.
3. Every pair of two different treatments appears in λ blocks.
4. The order of treatments within each block is randomized.
5. The order of blocks is randomized.

According to these requirements there are, altogether, $N = tr = bk$ trials. Moreover, the following equality should hold

$$\lambda(t-1) = r(k-1). \tag{5.5.1}$$

The question is how to design a BIBD, for a given t and k. One can obtain a BIBD by the complete combinatorial listing of the $\binom{t}{k}$ selections without replacements of k out of t letters. In this case, the number of blocks is

$$b = \binom{t}{k}. \tag{5.5.2}$$

The number of replicas is $r = \binom{t-1}{k-1}$, and $\lambda = \binom{t-2}{k-2}$. The total number trials is

$$\begin{aligned} N = tr = t\binom{t-1}{k-1} &= \frac{t!}{(k-1)!(t-k)!} = k\binom{t}{k} \\ &= kb. \end{aligned} \tag{5.5.3}$$

Such designs of BIBD are called **combinatoric designs**. They might be, however, too big. For example, if $t = 8$ and $k = 4$ we are required to have $\binom{8}{4} = 70$ blocks. Thus, the total number of trials is $N = 70 \times 4 = 280$ and $r = \binom{7}{3} = 35$. Here $\lambda = \binom{6}{2} = 15$.

There are advanced algebraic methods which can yield smaller designs for $t = 8$ and $k = 4$. Box et al. (2005) list a BIBD of $t = 8$, $k = 4$ in $b = 14$ blocks. Here $N = 14 \times 4 = 56$, $r = 7$, and $\lambda = 3$.

It is not always possible to have a BIBD smaller in size than a complete combinatoric design. Such a case is $t = 8$ and $k = 5$. Here the smallest number of blocks possible is $\binom{8}{5} = 56$, and $N = 56 \times 5 = 280$.

Table 5.4 ANOVA for a BIBD

Source of variation	DF	SS	MS	$E\{MS\}$
Blocks	$b-1$	$SSBL$	$MSBL$	$\sigma^2 + \frac{t}{b-1}\sum_{i=1}^{b}\beta_i^2$
Treatments adjusted	$t-1$	$SSTR$	$MSTR$	$\sigma^2 + \frac{b}{t-1}\sum_{j=1}^{t}\tau_j^2$
Error	$N-t-b+1$	SSE	MSE	σ^2
Total	$N-1$	SST	–	–

The reader is referred to Box et al. (2005) for a list of some useful BIBD's for $k = 2, \cdots, 6$, $t = k, \cdots, 10$. Let B_i denote the set of treatments in the i-th block. For example, if block 1 contains the treatments 1, 2, 3, 4 then $B_1 = \{1, 2, 3, 4\}$. Let Y_{ij} be the yield of treatment $j \in B_i$. The effects model is

$$Y_{ij} = \mu + \beta_i + \tau_j + e_{ij}, \quad i = 1, \cdots, b \;\; j \in B_i \tag{5.5.4}$$

$\{e_{ij}\}$ are random experimental errors, with $E\{e_{ij}\} = 0$ and $V\{e_{ij}\} = \sigma^2$ all (i, j). The block and treatment effects, $\beta_1, \cdots, \beta_b$ and $\tau_1, \cdots, \tau_t$ satisfy the constraints $\sum_{j=1}^{t} \tau_j = 0$ and $\sum_{i=1}^{b} \beta_i = 0$.

Let T_j be the set of all indices of blocks containing the j-th treatment. The least squares estimates of the treatment effects are obtained in the following manner.

Let $W_j = \sum_{i \in T_j} Y_{ij}$ be the sum of all Y values under the j-th treatment. Let W_j^* be the sum of the values in all the r blocks which contain the j-th treatment, i.e., $W_j^* = \sum_{i \in T_j} \sum_{l \in B_i} Y_{il}$. Compute

$$Q_j = kW_j - W_j^*, \quad j = 1, \cdots, t. \tag{5.5.5}$$

The least squares error (LSE) of τ_j is

$$\hat{\tau}_j = \frac{Q_j}{t\lambda}, \quad j = 1, \cdots, t. \tag{5.5.6}$$

Notice that $\sum_{j=1}^{t} Q_j = 0$. Thus, $\sum_{j=1}^{t} \hat{\tau}_j = 0$. Let $\bar{\bar{Y}} = \frac{1}{N} \sum_{i=1}^{b} \sum_{l \in B_i} Y_{il}$. The **adjusted treatment average** is defined as $\bar{Y}_j^* = \bar{\bar{Y}} + \hat{\tau}_j$, $j = 1, \cdots, t$. The ANOVA for a BIBD is given in Table 5.4. Here,

$$SST = \sum_{i=1}^{b} \sum_{l \in B_i} Y_{il}^2 - \left(\sum_{i=1}^{b} \sum_{l \in B_i} Y_{il} \right)^2 / N; \tag{5.5.7}$$

$$SSBL = \frac{1}{k} \sum_{i=1}^{b} \left(\sum_{l \in B_i} Y_{il} \right)^2 - N\bar{\bar{Y}}^2; \tag{5.5.8}$$

$$SSTR = \frac{1}{\lambda k t} \sum_{j=1}^{t} Q_j^2 \tag{5.5.9}$$

Table 5.5 Block sets

i	B_i	i	B_i	i	B_i
1	1, 2, 3, 4	6	1, 2, 5, 6	11	2, 3, 4, 5
2	1, 2, 3, 5	7	1, 3, 4, 5	12	2, 3, 4, 6
3	1, 2, 3, 6	8	1, 3, 4, 6	13	2, 3, 5, 6
4	1, 2, 4, 5	9	1, 3, 5, 6	14	2, 4, 5, 6
5	1, 2, 4, 6	10	1, 4, 5, 6	15	3, 4, 5, 6

Table 5.6 Values of Y_{il}, $l \in B_i$

i	Y_{il}	i	Y_{il}	i	Y_{il}
1	24.7, 20.8, 29.4, 24.9	6	21.4, 20.1, 30.1, 34.1	11	21.4, 29.6, 24.8, 31.2
2	24.1, 20.4, 29.8, 30.3	7	23.2, 28.7, 24.9, 31.0	12	21.3, 28.9, 25.3, 35.1
3	23.4, 20.6, 29.2, 34.4	8	23.1, 29.3, 27.1, 34.4	13	21.6, 29.5, 30.4, 33.6
4	23.2, 20.7, 26.0, 30.8	9	22.0, 29.8, 31.9, 36.1	14	20.1, 25.1, 32.9, 33.9
5	21.5, 22.1, 25.3, 35.4	10	22.8, 22.6, 33.2, 34.8	15	30.1, 24.0, 30.8, 36.5

Table 5.7 The set T_j and the statistics W_j, W_j^*, Q_j

j	T_j	W_j	W_j^*	Q_j
1	1, 2, 3, 4, 5, 6, 7, 8, 9, 10	229.536	1077.7	−159.56
2	1, 2, 3, 4, 5, 6, 11, 12, 13, 14	209.023	1067.4	−231.31
3	1, 2, 3, 7, 8, 9, 11, 12, 13, 15	294.125	1107.6	68.90
4	1, 4, 5, 7, 8, 10, 11, 12, 14, 15	249.999	1090.9	−90.90
5	2, 4, 6, 7, 9, 10, 11, 13, 14, 15	312.492	1107.5	142.47
6	3, 5, 6, 8, 9, 10, 12, 13, 14, 15	348.176	1123.8	268.90

and

$$SSE = SST - SSBL - SSTR. \tag{5.5.10}$$

The significance of the treatments effects is tested by the statistic

$$F = \frac{MSTR}{MSE}. \tag{5.5.11}$$

Example 5.5 Six different adhesives ($t = 6$) are tested for the bond strength in a lamination process, under curing pressure of 200 [psi]. Lamination can be done in blocks of size $k = 4$.

A combinatoric design will have $\binom{6}{4} = 15$ blocks, with $r = \binom{5}{3} = 10$, $\lambda = \binom{4}{2} = 6$ and $N = 60$. The treatment indices of the 15 blocks are listed in Table 5.5. The observed bond strength in these trials are listed in Table 5.6. The grand mean of the bond strength is $\bar{\bar{Y}} = 27.389$. The sets T_j and the sums W_j, W_j^* are summarized in Table 5.7. The resulting ANOVA table is Table 5.8. The adjusted mean effects of the adhesives are in Table 5.9

Table 5.8 ANOVA for BIBD

Source	DF	SS	MS	F
Blocks	14	161.78	11.556	23.99
Treat. adj.	5	1282.76	256.552	532.54
Error	40	19.27	0.48175	–
Total	59	1463.81		

Table 5.9 Mean effects and their S.E.

Treatment	$\bar{Y}_i^*$	S.E.$\{\bar{Y}_i^*\}$
1	22.96	1.7445
2	20.96	1.7445
3	29.33	1.7445
4	24.86	1.7445
5	31.35	1.7445
6	34.86	1.7445

The variance of each adjusted mean effect is

$$V\{\bar{Y}_j^*\} = \frac{k\sigma^2}{t\lambda}, \quad j = 1, \cdots, t. \tag{5.5.12}$$

Thus, the S.E. of $\bar{Y}_i^*$ is

$$\text{S.E.}\{\bar{Y}_j^*\} = \left(\frac{k\,MSE}{t\lambda}\right)^{1/2}, \quad j = 1, \cdots, t. \tag{5.5.13}$$

It seems that there are two homogeneous groups of treatments $\{1, 2, 4\}$ and $\{3, 5, 6\}$. ■

5.6 Latin Square Design

Latin Square designs are such that we can block for two error inducing factors in a balanced fashion, and yet save considerable amount of trials.

Suppose that we have t treatments to test, and we wish to block for two factors. We assign the blocking factors t levels (the number of treatments) in order to obtain squared designs. For example, suppose that we wish to study the effects of 4 new designs of keyboards for desktop computers. The design of the keyboard might have effect on the speed of typing or on the number of typing errors. Noisy factors are typist or type of job. Thus we can block by typist and by job. We should pick at random 4 typists and 4 different jobs. We construct a square with 4 rows and 4 columns for the blocking factors (see Table 5.10).

Let A, B, C, D denote the 4 keyboard designs. We assign the letters to the cells of the above square so that

Table 5.10 A 4 × 4 Latin square

	Job 1	Job 2	Job 3	Job 4
Typist 1	*A*	*B*	*C*	*D*
Typist 2	*B*	*A*	*D*	*C*
Typist 3	*C*	*D*	*A*	*B*
Typist 4	*D*	*C*	*B*	*A*

1. Each letter appears exactly once in a row.
2. Each letter appears exactly once in a column.

Finally, the order of performing these trials is random. Notice that a design which contains all the combinations of typist, job and keyboard spans over $4 \times 4 \times 4 = 64$ combinations. Thus, the Latin square design saves many trials. However, it is based on the assumption of no interactions between the treatments and the blocking factors. That is, in order to obtain valid analysis, the model relating the response to the factor effects should be **additive**, i.e.,

$$Y_{ijk} = \mu + \beta_i + \gamma_j + \tau_k + e_{ijk}, \quad i, j, k = 1, \cdots, t, \tag{5.6.1}$$

where μ is the grand mean, β_i are the row effects, γ_j are the column effects and τ_k are the treatment effects. The experimental error variables are $\{e_{ijk}\}$, with $E\{e_{ijk}\} = 0$ and $V\{e_{ijk}\} = \sigma^2$ for all (i, j). Furthermore,

$$\sum_{i=1}^{t} \beta_i = \sum_{j=1}^{t} \gamma_j = \sum_{k=1}^{t} \tau_k = 0. \tag{5.6.2}$$

The Latin square presented in Table 5.10 is not unique. There are other 4 × 4 Latin squares. For example,

$$\begin{array}{cccc} A & B & C & D \\ D & C & B & A \\ B & A & D & C \\ C & D & A & B \end{array} \qquad \begin{array}{cccc} A & B & C & D \\ C & D & A & B \\ D & C & B & A \\ B & A & D & C \end{array}.$$

A few Latin square designs, for $t = 3, \cdots, 9$ are given in Box et al. (2005).

If we perform only 1 replication of the Latin square, the ANOVA for testing the main effects is shown in Table 5.11

Formulae for the various SS terms will be given below. At this time we wish to emphasize that if t is small, say $t = 3$, then the number of DF for SSE is only 2. This is too small. The number of DF for the error SS can be increased by performing replicas. One possibility is to perform the same Latin square r times independently, and as similarly as possible. However, significant differences between replicas may emerge. The ANOVA, for r identical replicas is as in Table 5.12.

Table 5.11 ANOVA for a Latin square, one replication

Source	DF	SS	MS	F
Treatments	$t-1$	$SSTR$	$MSTR$	$MSTR/MSE$
Rows	$t-1$	SSR	MSR	MSR/MSE
Columns	$t-1$	SSC	MSC	MSC/MSE
Error	$(t-1)(t-2)$	SSE	MSE	–
Total	t^2-1	SST	–	–

Table 5.12 ANOVA for replicated Latin square

Source	D.F.	SS	MS	F
Treatments	$t-1$	$SSTR$	$MSTR$	$MSTR/MSE$
Rows	$t-1$	SSR	MSR	–
Columns	$t-1$	SSC	MSC	–
Replicas	$r-1$	$SSREP$	$MSREP$	–
Error	$(t-1)[r(t+1)-3]$	SSE	MSE	–
Total	$r(t^2-1)$	SST	–	–

Notice that now we have rt^2 observations. Let $T_{....}$ and $Q_{....}$ be the sum and sum of squares of all observations. Then,

$$SST = Q_{....} - T_{....}^2/rt^2. \tag{5.6.3}$$

Let $T_{i...}$ denote the sum of rt observations in the i-th row of all r replications. Then

$$SSR = \frac{1}{tr}\sum_{i=1}^{t} T_{i...}^2 - \frac{T_{....}^2}{rt^2}. \tag{5.6.4}$$

Similarly, let $T_{.j..}$ and $T_{..k.}$ be the sums of all rt observations in column j of all replicas, and treatment k of all r replicas, then

$$SSC = \frac{1}{rt}\sum_{j=1}^{t} T_{.j..}^2 - \frac{T_{....}^2}{rt^2} \tag{5.6.5}$$

and

$$SSTR = \frac{1}{rt}\sum_{k=1}^{t} T_{..k.}^2 - \frac{T_{....}^2}{rt^2}. \tag{5.6.6}$$

Finally, let $T_{...l}$ $(l = 1, \cdots, r)$ denote the sum of all t^2 observations in the l-th replication. Then,

Table 5.13 Latin square design, $t = 5$

	Job				
Typist	1	2	3	4	5
1	A	B	C	D	E
2	B	C	D	E	A
3	C	D	E	A	B
4	D	E	A	B	C
5	E	A	B	C	D

$$SSREP = \frac{1}{t^2} \sum_{l=1}^{r} t_{...l}^2 - \frac{T_{....}^2}{rt^2}. \tag{5.6.7}$$

The pooled sum of squares for error is obtained by

$$SSE = SSD - SSR - SSC - SSTR - SSREP. \tag{5.6.8}$$

Notice that if $t = 3$ and $r = 3$, the number of DF for SSE increases from 2 (when $r = 1$) to 18 (when $r = 3$).

The most important hypothesis is that connected with the main effects of the treatments. This we test with the statistic

$$F = MSTR/MSE. \tag{5.6.9}$$

Example 5.6 Five models of keyboards (treatments) were tested in a Latin square design in which the blocking factors are typist and job. Five typists were randomly selected from a pool of typists of similar capabilities. Five typing jobs were selected. Each typing job had 4000 characters. The yield, Y_{ijk}, is the number of typing errors found at the i-th typist, j-th job under the k-th keyboard. The Latin square design used is presented in Table 5.13.

The five keyboards are denoted by the letters A, B, C, D, E. The experiment spanned over 5 days. In each day a typist was assigned a job at random (from those not yet tried). The keyboard used is the one associated with the job. Only one job was tried in a given day. The observed number of typing errors (per 4000 characters) are summarized in Table 5.14.

Figure 5.2 present box plots of the error rates for the three different factors. The only influencing factor is the typist effect.

The total sum of squares is

$$Q = 30636.$$

Thus,

$$SST = 30636 - \frac{798^2}{25} = 5163.84.$$

Table 5.14 Number of typing errors

Typist	Job 1	2	3	4	5	Row sums
1	*A*	*B*	*C*	*D*	*E*	100
	20	18	25	17	20	
2	*B*	*C*	*D*	*E*	*A*	277
	65	40	55	58	59	
3	*C*	*D*	*E*	*A*	*B*	140
	30	27	35	21	27	
4	*D*	*E*	*A*	*B*	*C*	94
	21	15	24	16	18	
5	*E*	*A*	*B*	*C*	*D*	187
	42	38	40	35	32	
Column sum	178	138	179	147	156	798

Sums	*A*	*B*	*C*	*D*	*E*
Keyboard	162	166	148	152	170

Similarly,

$$
\begin{aligned}
SSR &= \frac{1}{5}(100^2 + 277^2 + \cdots + 187^2) - \frac{798^2}{25} \\
&= 4554.64 \\
SSC &= \frac{1}{5}(178^2 + 138^2 + \cdots + 156^2) - \frac{798^2}{25} \\
&= 270.641
\end{aligned}
$$

and

$$
\begin{aligned}
SSTR &= \frac{1}{5}(162^2 + 166^2 + \cdots + 170^2) - \frac{798^2}{25} \\
&= 69.4395.
\end{aligned}
$$

The analysis of variance, following Table 5.12, is summarized in Table 5.15. In Python, we can perform the analysis of variance as follows:

```
keyboards = mistat.load_data('KEYBOARDS.csv')
model = smf.ols('errors ~ C(keyboard) + C(job) + C(typist)', data=keyboards).fit()
print(anova.anova_lm(model))
```

```
               df   sum_sq      mean_sq          F        PR(>F)
C(keyboard)   4.0    69.44    17.360000   0.774078  5.627148e-01
C(job)        4.0   270.64    67.660000   3.016944  6.158117e-02
C(typist)     4.0  4554.64  1138.660000  50.772592  2.009919e-07
Residual     12.0   269.12    22.426667        NaN           NaN
```

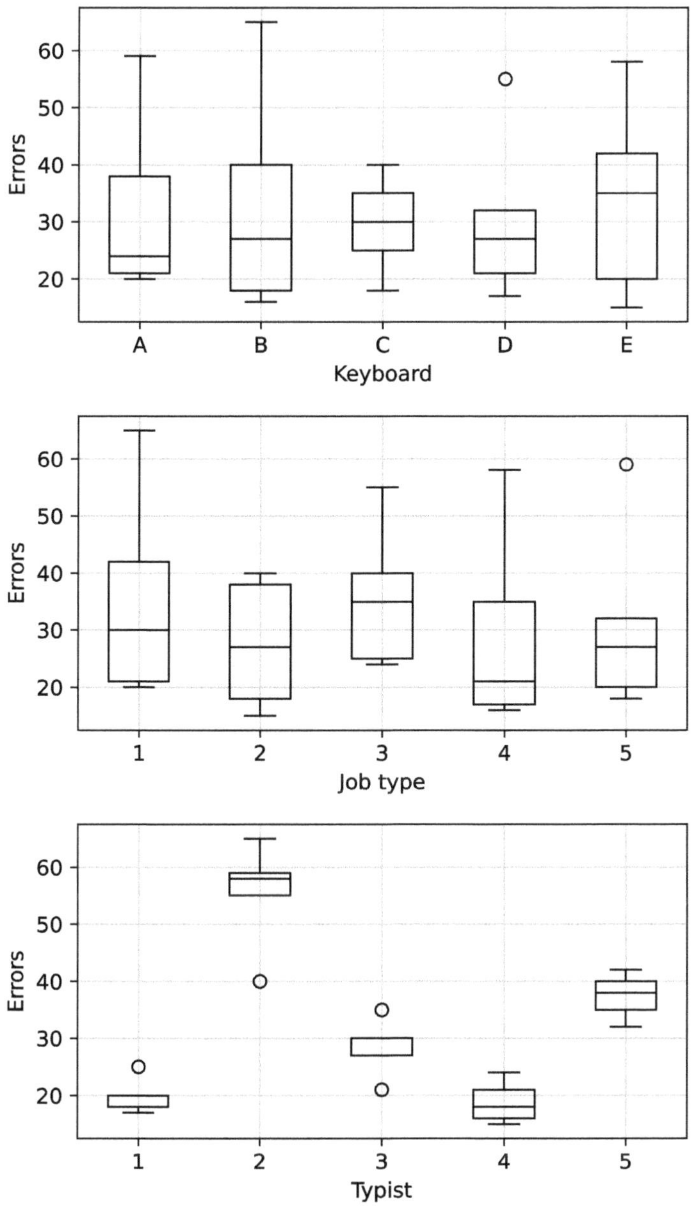

Fig. 5.2 Effect of factors on error rate

The null hypothesis that the main effects of the keyboards are zero cannot be rejected. The largest source of variability in this experiment were the typists. The different jobs contributed also to the variability. The P-value for the F test of Jobs is 0.062. ■

Table 5.15 ANOVA for keyboard Latin square experiment

Source	DF	SS	MS	F
Typist	4	4554.640	1138.66	50.772
Job	4	270.641	67.66	3.017
Keyboard	4	69.439	17.3598	0.774
Error	12	269.120	22.4267	–
Total	24	5163.840	–	–

5.7 Full Factorial Experiments

5.7.1 *The Structure of Factorial Experiments*

Full factorial experiments are those in which complete trials are performed of all the combinations of the various factors at all their levels. For example, if there are five factors, each one tested at three levels, there are altogether $3^5 = 243$ treatment combinations. All these 243 treatment combinations are tested. The full factorial experiment may also be replicated several times. The order of performing the trials is random.

In full factorial experiments, the number of levels of different factors do not have to be the same. Some factors might be tested at two levels and others at three or four levels. Full factorial, or certain fractional factorials which will be discussed later, are necessary, if the statistical model is not additive. In order to estimate or test the **effects** of **interactions**, one needs to perform factorial experiments, full or fractional. In a full factorial experiment, all the main effects and interactions can be tested or estimated. Recall that if there are p factors $A, B, C, \cdots$ there are p types of main effects, $\binom{p}{2}$ types of pairwise interactions $AB, AC, BC, \cdots$, $\binom{p}{3}$ interactions between three factors, $ABC, ABD, \cdots$ and so on. On the whole there are, together with the grand mean μ, 2^p types of parameters.

In the following section we discuss the structure of the ANOVA for testing the significance of main effects and interaction. This is followed by a section on the estimation problem. In Sects. 5.7.4 and 5.7.5 we discuss the structure of full factorial experiments with 2 and 3 levels per factor, respectively.

5.7.2 *The ANOVA for Full Factorial Designs*

The analysis of variance for full factorial designs is done for testing the hypotheses that main effects or interaction parameters are equal to zero. We present the ANOVA for a two factor situation, factor A at a levels and factor B at b levels. The method can be generalized to any number of factors.

The structure of the experiment is such that all $a \times b$ treatment combinations are tested. Each treatment combination is repeated n times. The model is

$$Y_{ijk} = \mu + \tau_i^A + \tau_j^B + \tau_{ij}^{AB} + e_{ijk}, \tag{5.7.1}$$

$i = 1, \cdots, a$; $j = 1, \cdots, b$; $k = 1, \cdots, n$. e_{ijk} are independent random variables $E\{e_{ijh}\} = 0$ and $V\{e_{ijk}\} = \sigma^2$ for all i, j, k. Let

$$\bar{Y}_{ij} = \frac{1}{n}\sum_{k=1}^{n} Y_{ijk} \tag{5.7.2}$$

$$\bar{Y}_{i.} = \frac{1}{b}\sum_{j=1}^{b} \bar{Y}_{ij}, \quad i = 1, \cdots, a \tag{5.7.3}$$

$$\bar{Y}_{.j} = \frac{1}{a}\sum_{i=1}^{a} Y_{ij}, \quad j = 1, \cdots, b \tag{5.7.4}$$

and

$$\bar{\bar{Y}} = \frac{1}{ab}\sum_{i=1}^{a}\sum_{j=1}^{b} \bar{Y}_{ij}. \tag{5.7.5}$$

The ANOVA partitions first the total sum of squares of deviations from $\bar{\bar{Y}}$, i.e.,

$$SST = \sum_{i=1}^{a}\sum_{j=1}^{b}\sum_{k=1}^{n}(Y_{ijk} - \bar{\bar{Y}})^2 \tag{5.7.6}$$

to two components

$$SSW = \sum_{i=1}^{a}\sum_{j=1}^{b}\sum_{k=1}^{n}(Y_{ijk} - \bar{Y}_{ij})^2 \tag{5.7.7}$$

and

$$SSB = n\sum_{i=1}^{a}\sum_{j=1}^{b}(\bar{Y}_{ij} - \bar{\bar{Y}})^2. \tag{5.7.8}$$

It is straightforward to show that

$$SST = SSW + SSB. \tag{5.7.9}$$

In the second stage, the sum of squares of deviations SSB is partitioned to three components SSI, $SSMA$, $SSMB$, where

Table 5.16 Table of ANOVA for a 2-factor factorial experiment

Source of variation	DF	SS	MS	F
A	$a-1$	$SSMA$	MSA	F_A
B	$b-1$	$SSMB$	MSB	F_B
AB	$(a-1)(b-1)$	SSI	$MSAB$	F_{AB}
Between	$ab-1$	SSB	–	–
Within	$ab(n-1)$	SSW	MSW	–
Total	$N-1$	SST	–	–

$$SSI = n\sum_{i=1}^{a}\sum_{j=1}^{b}\left(\bar{Y}_{ij} - \bar{Y}_{i.} - \bar{Y}_{.j} + \bar{\bar{Y}}\right)^2, \tag{5.7.10}$$

$$SSMA = nb\sum_{i=1}^{a}(\bar{Y}_{i.} - \bar{\bar{Y}})^2 \tag{5.7.11}$$

and

$$SSMB = na\sum_{j=1}^{b}(\bar{Y}_{.j} - \bar{\bar{Y}})^2, \tag{5.7.12}$$

i.e.,

$$SSB = SSI + SSMA + SSMB. \tag{5.7.13}$$

All these terms are collected in a table of ANOVA (see Table 5.16).

Thus,

$$MSA = \frac{SSMA}{a-1}, \tag{5.7.14}$$

$$MSB = \frac{SSMB}{b-1}, \tag{5.7.15}$$

and

$$MSAB = \frac{SSI}{(a-1)(b-1)}, \tag{5.7.16}$$

$$MSW = \frac{SSW}{ab(n-1)}. \tag{5.7.17}$$

Finally, we compute the F-statistics

$$F_A = \frac{MSA}{MSW}, \tag{5.7.18}$$

$$F_B = \frac{MSB}{MSW} \tag{5.7.19}$$

and

$$F_{AB} = \frac{MSAB}{MSW}. \tag{5.7.20}$$

F_A, F_B, and F_{AB} are test statistics to test, respectively, the significance of the main effects of A, the main effects of B and the interactions AB.

If $F_A < F_{1-\alpha}[a-1, ab(n-1)]$ the null hypothesis

$$H_0^A : \tau_1^A = \cdots = \tau_a^A = 0$$

cannot be rejected.

If $F_B < F_{1-\alpha}[b-1, ab(n-1)]$ the null hypothesis

$$H_0^B : \tau_1^B = \cdots = \tau_b^B = 0$$

cannot be rejected.

Also, if

$$F_{AB} < F_{1-\alpha}[(a-1)(b-1), ab(n-1)],$$

we cannot reject the null hypothesis

$$H_0^{AB} : \tau_{11}^{AB} = \cdots = \tau_{ab}^{AB} = 0.$$

The ANOVA for two factors can be performed using Python. We illustrate this estimation and testing in the following example.

Example 5.7 In Chap. 2 we introduced the piston example. Seven prediction factors for the piston cycle time were listed. These are

A: Piston weight m, 30–60 [Kg]
B: Piston surface area s, 0.005–0.020 [m^2]
C: Spring coefficient k, 1000–5000 [N/m]
D: Ambient temperature t, 290–296 [°K]
E: Atmospheric pressure $p0$, 90,000–110,000 [N/m^2]
F: Initial gas volume $v0$, 0.002–0.010 [m^3]
G: Filling gas temperature $t0$, 340–360[°K]

We are interested to test the effects of the piston surface area s and the spring coefficient k on the cycle times (seconds). For this purpose we designed a factorial experiment at three levels of s, and three levels of k. The levels are

$$s_1 = 0.005\ [\mathrm{m}^2], \quad s_2 = 0.0125\ [\mathrm{m}^2] \quad \text{and} \quad s_3 = 0.02\ [\mathrm{m}^2].$$

The levels of factor k (spring coefficient) are

$$k_1 = 1500\,[\mathrm{N/m}], \quad k_2 = 3000\,[\mathrm{N/m}] \quad \text{and} \quad k_3 = 4500\,[\mathrm{N/m}].$$

Five replicas were performed at each treatment combination ($n = 5$).

The data can be obtained by using the piston simulator from the `mistat` package. The five factors which were not under study were kept at the levels $m = 30$ [Kg], $t = 293$ [°K], $p0 = 0.005$ [m^3], $v0 = 95{,}000$ [N/m^2], and $t0 = 350$ [°K].

```
from mistat.design import doe
np.random.seed(2)

# Build design from factors
FacDesign = doe.full_fact({
    'k': [1500, 3000, 4500],
    's': [0.005, 0.0125, 0.02],
})

# Randomize design
FacDesign = FacDesign.sample(frac=1).reset_index(drop=True)

# Setup and run simulator with five replicates
# for each combination of factors
simulator = mistat.PistonSimulator(n_replicate=5, **FacDesign,
                                   m=30, v0=0.005, p0=95_000, t=293, t0=350)
result = simulator.simulate()

model = smf.ols('seconds ~ C(k) * C(s)', data=result).fit()
print(anova.anova_lm(model).round(4))
```

```
             df  sum_sq  mean_sq        F  PR(>F)
C(k)        2.0  0.0037   0.0019   2.0451  0.1441
C(s)        2.0  0.0997   0.0499  54.5429  0.0000
C(k):C(s)   4.0  0.0057   0.0014   1.5600  0.2060
Residual   36.0  0.0329   0.0009      NaN     NaN
```

Figure 5.3 shows the effect of the factors spring coefficient k and piston surface area s on cycle time. A spring coefficient at 1500 [N/m] decreases the variability of mean cycle time. For the piston surface area, we see a strong effect on the cycle time. Increasing the surface area, leads to a decrease of cycle time and at the same time to a decrease in variability. Figure 5.4 is an **interaction plot** showing the effect of combinations of the two factors on the mean cycle time.

```
anova_result = anova.anova_lm(model)
not_signif = ['C(k)', 'C(k):C(s)', 'Residual']
SS = anova_result['sum_sq'].loc[not_signif].sum()
DF = anova_result['df'].loc[not_signif].sum()
sigma2 = SS / DF
print(SS, DF, sigma2)
```

```
0.04234590915737198 5 42.0 0.0010082359323183806
```

The P-values are computed with the appropriate F-distributions. We see in the ANOVA table that only the main effects of the piston surface area (s) are significant.

Since the effects of the spring coefficient (k) and that of the interaction are not significant, we can estimate σ^2 by a pooled estimator, which is

$$\hat{\sigma}^2 = \frac{SSW + SSI + SSMA}{36 + 4 + 2} = \frac{0.0423}{42.0}$$
$$= 0.00101.$$

```
Ymean = result.groupby('s').mean()['seconds']
print('Ymean', Ymean)
print('Grand', Ymean.sum() / 3)
print('Main effects', Ymean - Ymean.sum() / 3)
```

```
Ymean s
0.0050     0.126664
0.0125     0.035420
0.0200     0.019997
Name: seconds, dtype: float64
Grand 0.06069373963767 4736
Main effects s
0.0050     0.065970
0.0125    -0.025274
0.0200    -0.040696
Name: seconds, dtype: float64
```

To estimate the main effects of s we pool all data from samples having the same level of s together. We obtain pooled samples of size $n_p = 15$. The means of the cycle time for these samples are

The standard error of these main effects is S.E.$\{\hat{\tau}_j^s\} = \sqrt{0.00101/(2 \times 15)} = 0.0058$.

Since we estimate on the basis of the pooled samples, and the main effects $\hat{\tau}_j^s$ $(j = 1, 2, 3)$ are contrasts of 3 means, the coefficient S_α for the simultaneous

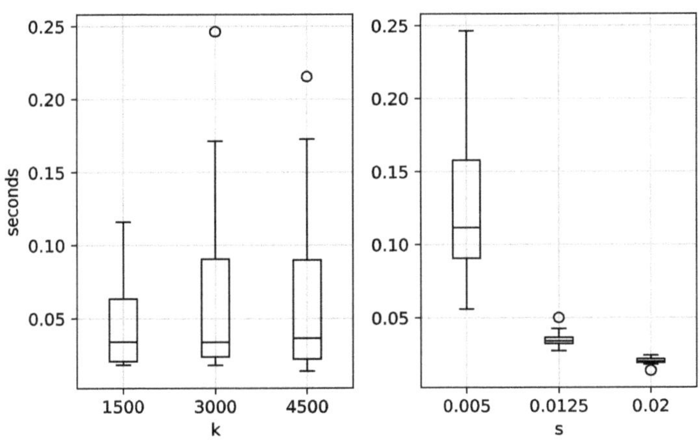

Fig. 5.3 Effect of spring coefficient k and piston surface area s on cycle time

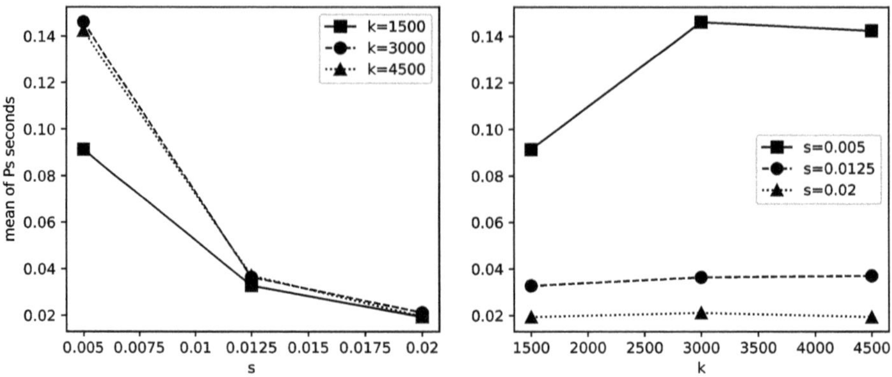

Fig. 5.4 Interaction plot of piston weight spring coefficient

	s_1	s_2	s_3	Grand
$\bar{Y}$	0.127	0.035	0.02	0.0607
Main effects	0.066	−0.025	−0.041	–

confidence intervals has the formula

$$S_\alpha = (2F_{0.95}[2, 42])^{1/2}$$
$$= \sqrt{2 \times 3.22} = 2.538.$$

```
Salpha = np.sqrt(2 * stats.f.ppf(0.95, 2, 42))
```

The simultaneous confidence intervals for τ_j^s, at $\alpha = 0.05$, are calculated using

$$\hat{\tau}_j^s \pm S_\alpha \cdot \text{S.E.}\{\hat{\tau}_j^s\}$$

	Lower Limit	Upper Limit
τ_1^s :	0.0513	0.0807
τ_2^s :	−0.0400	− 0.0106
τ_3^s :	−0.0554	− 0.0260

We see that none of the confidence intervals for τ_i^s covers zero. Thus, all main effects are significant.

■

5.7.3 Estimating Main Effects and Interactions

In this section we discuss the estimation of the main effects and interaction parameters. Our presentation is confined to the case of two factors A and B, which are at a and b levels, respectively. The number of replicas of each treatment combinations is n. We further assume that the errors $\{e_{ijk}\}$ are i.i.d., having a normal distribution $N(0, \sigma^2)$.

Let

$$\bar{Y}_{ij} = \frac{1}{n} \sum_{l=1}^{n} Y_{ijl} \tag{5.7.21}$$

and

$$Q_{ij} = \sum_{l=1}^{n} (Y_{ijl} - \bar{Y}_{ij})^2, \tag{5.7.22}$$

$i = 1, \cdots, a$; $j = 1, \cdots, b$. It can be shown that the **least squares** estimators of τ_i^A, τ_j^B and τ_{ij}^{AB} are, respectively,

$$\begin{aligned} \hat{\tau}_{i.}^A &= \bar{Y}_{i.} - \bar{\bar{Y}}, \quad i = 1, \cdots, a \\ \hat{\tau}_{.j}^B &= \bar{Y}_{.j} - \bar{\bar{Y}}, \quad j = 1, \cdots, b \end{aligned} \tag{5.7.23}$$

and

$$\hat{\tau}_{ij}^{AB} = \bar{Y}_{ij} - \bar{Y}_{i.} - \bar{Y}_{.j} + \bar{\bar{Y}}, \tag{5.7.24}$$

where

$$\bar{Y}_{i.} = \frac{1}{m} \sum_{j=1}^{m} \bar{Y}_{ij}, \tag{5.7.25}$$

and

$$\bar{Y}_{.j} = \frac{1}{k} \sum_{i=1}^{k} \bar{Y}_{ij}. \tag{5.7.26}$$

Furthermore, an unbiased estimator of σ^2 is

$$\hat{\sigma}^2 = \frac{\sum_{i=1}^{a} \sum_{j=1}^{b} Q_{ij}}{ab(n-1)}. \tag{5.7.27}$$

The standard errors of the estimators of the interactions are

$$\text{S.E.}\{\hat{\tau}_{ij}^{AB}\} = \frac{\hat{\sigma}}{\sqrt{n}}\left(\left(1-\frac{1}{a}\right)\left(1-\frac{1}{b}\right)\right)^{1/2}, \tag{5.7.28}$$

for $i = 1, \cdots, a$; $j = 1, \cdots, b$. The standard errors of the estimators of the main effects are

$$\text{S.E.}\{\hat{\tau}_i^A\} = \frac{\hat{\sigma}}{\sqrt{nb}}\left(1-\frac{1}{a}\right)^{1/2}, \quad i = 1, \cdots, a \tag{5.7.29}$$

and

$$\text{S.E.}\{\hat{\tau}_j^B\} = \frac{\hat{\sigma}}{\sqrt{na}}\left(1-\frac{1}{b}\right)^{1/2}, \quad j = 1, \cdots, b. \tag{5.7.30}$$

Confidence limits at level $(1-\alpha)$ for such a parameter are obtained by

$$\begin{aligned} &\hat{\tau}_i^A \pm S_\alpha \cdot \text{S.E.}\{\hat{\tau}_i^A\} \\ &\hat{\tau}_j^B \pm S_\alpha \cdot \text{S.E.}\{\hat{\tau}_j^B\} \end{aligned} \tag{5.7.31}$$

and

$$\hat{\tau}_{ij}^{AB} \pm S_\alpha \; \text{S.E.}\{\hat{\tau}_{ij}^{AB}\} \tag{5.7.32}$$

where

$$S_\alpha = ((ab-1)F_{1-\alpha}[ab-1, ab(n-1)])^{1/2}.$$

Multiplying the S_α guarantees that all the confidence intervals are simultaneously covering the true parameters with probability $(1-\alpha)$. Any confidence interval which covers the value zero implies that the corresponding parameter is not significantly different than zero.

5.7.4 2^m Factorial Designs

2^m factorial designs are full factorials of m factors, each one at two levels. The levels of the factors are labelled as "Low" and "High" or 1 and 2. If the factors are categorical then the labelling of the levels is arbitrary and the values of the main effects and interaction parameters depend on this arbitrary labeling. We will discuss here experiments in which the levels of the factors are measured on a continuous scale, like in the case of the factors effecting the piston cycle time. The levels of the i-th factor ($i = 1, \cdots, m$) are fixed at x_{i1} and x_{i2}, where $x_{i1} < x_{i2}$.

By simple transformation all factor levels can be reduced to

$$c_i = \begin{cases} +1, & \text{if } x = x_{i2} \\ & \text{to 1truein}, i = 1, \cdots, m. \\ -1, & \text{if } x = x_{i1} \end{cases}$$

In such a factorial experiment there are 2^m possible treatment combinations. Let $(i_1, \cdots, i_m)$ denote a treatment combination, where $i_1, \cdots, i_m$ are indices, such that

$$i_j = \begin{cases} 0, & \text{if } c_i = -1 \\ 1, & \text{if } c_i = 1. \end{cases}$$

Thus, if there are $m = 3$ factors, the number of possible treatment combinations is $2^3 = 8$. These are given in Table 5.17

The index ν of the standard order, is given by the formula

$$\nu = \sum_{j=1}^{m} i_j 2^{j-1}. \tag{5.7.33}$$

Notice that ν ranges from 0 to $2^m - 1$. This produces tables of the treatment combinations for a 2^m factorial design, arranged in a standard order which can be useful to compare different design (see Table 5.18). The implementation in the `mistat` package does not generate the rows in standard order. However, as we mentioned in Sect. 5.2, it is advisable to randomize the designs prior to use, so the initial order is in practice lost anyway.

A full factorial experiment is a combination of fractional factorial designs. In Python we obtain a fraction of a full factorial design with the `mistat` package.

Table 5.17 Treatment combinations of a 2^3 experiment

ν	i_1	i_2	i_3
0	0	0	0
1	1	0	0
2	0	1	0
3	1	1	0
4	0	0	1
5	1	0	1
6	0	1	1
7	1	1	1

Table 5.18 The labels in standard order for a 2^5 factorial design

ν	l_1	l_2	l_3	l_4	l_5	ν	l_1	l_2	l_3	l_4	l_5
0	1	1	1	1	1	16	1	1	1	1	2
1	2	1	1	1	1	17	2	1	1	1	2
2	1	2	1	1	1	18	1	2	1	1	2
3	2	2	1	1	1	19	2	2	1	1	2
4	1	1	2	1	1	20	1	1	2	1	2
5	2	1	2	1	1	21	2	1	2	1	2
6	1	2	2	1	1	22	1	2	2	1	2
7	2	2	2	1	1	23	2	2	2	1	2
8	1	1	1	2	1	24	1	1	1	2	2
9	2	1	1	2	1	25	2	1	1	2	2
10	1	2	1	2	1	26	1	2	1	2	2
11	2	2	1	2	1	27	2	2	1	2	2
12	1	1	2	2	1	28	1	1	2	2	2
13	2	1	2	2	1	29	2	1	2	2	2
14	1	2	2	2	1	30	1	2	2	2	2
15	2	2	2	2	1	31	2	2	2	2	2

```
d1 = {
    'A': [-1, 1],
    'B': [-1, 1],
    'C': [-1, 1],
    'D': [-1, 1],
    'E': [-1, 1],
}
mistat.addTreatments(doe.frac_fact_res(d1, 4), mainEffects=['A', 'B', 'C', 'D',
 'E'])
```

	Treatments	A	B	C	D	E
0	(1)	-1	-1	-1	-1	-1
1	AE	1	-1	-1	-1	1
2	BE	-1	1	-1	-1	1
3	AB	1	1	-1	-1	-1
4	CE	-1	-1	1	-1	1
5	AC	1	-1	1	-1	-1
6	BC	-1	1	1	-1	-1
7	ABCE	1	1	1	-1	1
8	D	-1	-1	-1	1	-1
9	ADE	1	-1	-1	1	1
10	BDE	-1	1	-1	1	1
11	ABD	1	1	-1	1	-1
12	CDE	-1	-1	1	1	1
13	ACD	1	-1	1	1	-1
14	BCD	-1	1	1	1	-1
15	ABCDE	1	1	1	1	1

This is a half-fractional replications of a 2^5 designs as will be explained in Sect. 5.8. In Table 5.18 we present the design of a 2^5 full factorial experiment derived using Python.

```
d1 = {
    'A': [1, 2],
    'B': [1, 2],
    'C': [1, 2],
    'D': [1, 2],
```

Table 5.19 Treatment means in a 2^2 design

	Factor A		
Factor B	1	2	Row means
1	$\bar{Y}_0$	$\bar{Y}_1$	$\bar{Y}_{1.}$
2	$\bar{Y}_2$	$\bar{Y}_3$	$\bar{Y}_{2.}$
Column means	$\bar{Y}_{0.1}$	$\bar{Y}_{0.2}$	$\bar{\bar{Y}}$

```
    'E': [1, 2],
}
Design = doe.full_fact(d1)
Design = mistat.addTreatments(Design, mainEffects=['A', 'B', 'C', 'D', 'E'])
print(Design.head(3).round(0))
print(Design.tail(3).round(0))
```

```
  Treatments  A  B  C  D  E
0        (1)  1  1  1  1  1
1          A  2  1  1  1  1
2          B  1  2  1  1  1
   Treatments  A  B  C  D  E
29       ACDE  2  1  2  2  2
30       BCDE  1  2  2  2  2
31      ABCDE  2  2  2  2  2
```

Let Y_ν, $\nu = 0, 1, \cdots, 2^m - 1$, denote the yield of the ν-th treatment combination. We discuss now the estimation of the main effects and interaction parameters. Starting with the simple case of 2 factors, the variables are presented schematically, in the Table 5.19

According to our previous definition there are four main effects τ_1^A, τ_2^A, τ_1^B, τ_2^B and four interaction effects τ_{11}^{AB}, τ_{12}^{AB}, τ_{21}^{AB}, τ_{22}^{AB}. But since $\tau_1^A + \tau_2^A = \tau_1^B + \tau_2^B = 0$, it is sufficient to represent the main effects of A and B by τ_2^A and τ_2^B. Similarly, since $\tau_{11}^{AB} + \tau_{12}^{AB} = 0 = \tau_{11}^{AB} + \tau_{21}^{AB}$ and $\tau_{12}^{AB} + \tau_{22}^{AB} = 0 = \tau_{21}^{AB} + \tau_{22}^{AB}$, it is sufficient to represent the interaction effects by τ_{22}^{AB}.

The main effect τ_2^A is estimated by

$$\begin{aligned}\hat{\tau}_2^A &= \bar{Y}_{0.2} - \bar{\bar{Y}} = \\ &= \frac{1}{2}(\bar{Y}_1 + \bar{Y}_3) - \frac{1}{4}(\bar{Y}_0 + \bar{Y}_1 + \bar{Y}_2 + \bar{Y}_3) \\ &= \frac{1}{4}(-\bar{Y}_0 + \bar{Y}_1 - \bar{Y}_2 + \bar{Y}_3).\end{aligned}$$

The estimator of τ_2^B is

$$\begin{aligned}\hat{\tau}_2^B &= \bar{Y}_{2.} - \bar{\bar{Y}} \\ &= \frac{1}{2}(\bar{Y}_2 + \bar{Y}_3) - \frac{1}{4}(\bar{Y}_0 + \bar{Y}_1 + \bar{Y}_2 + \bar{Y}_3) \\ &= \frac{1}{4}(-\bar{Y}_0 - \bar{Y}_1 + \bar{Y}_2 + \bar{Y}_3).\end{aligned}$$

Finally, the estimator of τ_{22}^{AB} is

$$\begin{aligned}\hat{\tau}_{22}^{AB} &= \bar{Y}_3 - \bar{Y}_{2.0} - \bar{Y}_{0.2} + \bar{\bar{Y}} \\ &= \bar{Y}_3 - \frac{1}{2}(\bar{Y}_2 + \bar{Y}_3) - \frac{1}{2}(\bar{Y}_1 + \bar{Y}_3) \\ &\quad + \frac{1}{4}(\bar{Y}_0 + \bar{Y}_1 + \bar{Y}_2 + \bar{Y}_3) \\ &= \frac{1}{4}(\bar{Y}_0 - \bar{Y}_1 - \bar{Y}_2 + \bar{Y}_3).\end{aligned}$$

The parameter μ is estimated by the grand mean $\bar{\bar{Y}} = \frac{1}{4}(\bar{Y}_0 + \bar{Y}_1 + \bar{Y}_2 + \bar{Y}_3)$. All these estimators can be presented in a matrix form as

$$\begin{bmatrix} \hat{\mu} \\ \hat{\tau}_2^A \\ \hat{\tau}_2^B \\ \hat{\tau}_{22}^{AB} \end{bmatrix} = \frac{1}{4}\begin{bmatrix} 1 & 1 & 1 & 1 \\ -1 & 1 & -1 & 1 \\ -1 & -1 & 1 & 1 \\ 1 & -1 & -1 & 1 \end{bmatrix} \cdot \begin{bmatrix} \bar{Y}_0 \\ \bar{Y}_1 \\ \bar{Y}_2 \\ \bar{Y}_3 \end{bmatrix}.$$

The indices in a 2^2 design are given in the following 4×2 matrix

$$D_{2^2} = \begin{bmatrix} 1 & 1 \\ 2 & 1 \\ 1 & 2 \\ 2 & 2 \end{bmatrix}.$$

The corresponding C coefficients are the 2nd and 3rd columns in the matrix

$$C_{2^2} = \begin{bmatrix} 1 & -1 & -1 & 1 \\ 1 & 1 & -1 & -1 \\ 1 & -1 & 1 & -1 \\ 1 & 1 & 1 & 1 \end{bmatrix}.$$

The fourth column of this matrix is the product of the elements in the second and third columns. Notice also that the linear model for the yield vector is

$$\begin{bmatrix} Y_0 \\ Y_1 \\ Y_2 \\ Y_3 \end{bmatrix} = \begin{bmatrix} 1 & -1 & -1 & 1 \\ 1 & 1 & -1 & -1 \\ 1 & -1 & 1 & -1 \\ 1 & 1 & 1 & 1 \end{bmatrix} \begin{bmatrix} \mu \\ \tau_2^A \\ \tau_2^B \\ \tau_{22}^{AB} \end{bmatrix} + \begin{bmatrix} e_1 \\ e_2 \\ e_3 \\ e_4 \end{bmatrix},$$

where e_1, e_2, e_3 and e_4 are independent random variables, with $E\{e_i\} = 0$ and $V\{e_i\} = \sigma^2$, $i = 1, 2, \cdots, 4$.

Let $\mathbf{Y}^{(4)} = (Y_0, Y_1, Y_2, Y_3)'$, $\boldsymbol{\theta}^{(4)} = (\mu, \tau_2^A, \tau_2^B, \tau_{22}^{AB})'$ and $\mathbf{e}^{(4)} = (e_1, e_2, e_3, e_4)'$ then the model is

$$\mathbf{Y}^{(4)} = C_{2^2}\boldsymbol{\theta}^{(4)} + \mathbf{e}^{(4)}.$$

This is the usual linear model for multiple regression. The least squares estimator of $\boldsymbol{\theta}^{(4)}$ is

$$\hat{\boldsymbol{\theta}}^{(4)} = [C'_{2^2}C_{2^2}]^{-1}C'_{2^2}\mathbf{Y}^{(4)}.$$

The matrix C_{2^2} has orthogonal column (row) vectors and

$$C'_{2^2}C_{2^2} = 4I_4,$$

where I_4 is the identity matrix of rank 4. Therefore,

$$\hat{\boldsymbol{\theta}}^{(4)} = \frac{1}{4}C'_{2^2}\mathbf{Y}^{(4)} = \frac{1}{4}\begin{bmatrix} 1 & 1 & 1 & 1 \\ -1 & 1 & -1 & 1 \\ -1 & -1 & 1 & 1 \\ 1 & -1 & -1 & 1 \end{bmatrix}\begin{bmatrix} \bar{Y}_0 \\ \bar{Y}_1 \\ \bar{Y}_2 \\ \bar{Y}_3 \end{bmatrix}.$$

This is identical with the solution obtained earlier.

The estimators of the main effects and interactions are the least squares estimators, as has been mentioned before.

This can now be generalized to the case of m factors. For a model with m factors there are 2^m parameters. The mean μ, m main effects $\tau^1, \cdots, \tau^m$, $\binom{m}{2}$ first order interactions τ^{ij}, $i \neq j = 1, \cdots, m$, $\binom{m}{3}$ second order interactions τ^{ijk}, $i \neq j \neq k$, etc. We can now order the parameters in a standard manner in the following manner. Each one of the 2^m parameters can be represented by a binary vector $(j_1, \cdots, j_m)$, where $j_i = 0, 1$ $(i = 1, \cdots, m)$. The vector $(0, 0, \cdots, 0)$ represents the grand mean μ. A vector $(0, 0, \cdots, 1, 0, \cdots, 0)$ where the 1 is the i-th component, represents the main effect of the i-th factor $(i = 1, \cdots, m)$. A vector with two ones, at the i-th and j-th component $(i = 1, \cdots, m-1;\ j = i+1, \cdots, m)$ represent the first order interaction between factor i and factor j. A vector with three ones, at i, j, k components, represents the second order interaction between factors i, j, k, etc.

Let $\omega = \sum_{i=1}^{m} j_i 2^{i-1}$ and β_ω be the parameter represented by the vector with index ω. For example, β_3 corresponds to $(1, 1, 0, \cdots, 0)$, which represents the first order interaction between factors 1 and 2.

Let $\mathbf{Y}^{(2^m)}$ be the yield vector, whose components are arranged in the standard order, with index $\nu = 0, 1, 2, \cdots, 2^m - 1$. Let C_{2^m} be the matrix of coefficients, that is obtained recursively by the equations

$$C_2 = \begin{bmatrix} 1 & -1 \\ 1 & 1 \end{bmatrix}, \tag{5.7.34}$$

and

$$C_{2^l} = \begin{bmatrix} C_{2^{l-1}} & -C_{2^{l-1}} \\ C_{2^{l-1}} & C_{2^{l-1}} \end{bmatrix}, \tag{5.7.35}$$

$l = 2, 3, \cdots, m$. Then, the linear model relating $\mathbf{Y}^{(2m)}$ to $\boldsymbol{\beta}^{(2m)}$ is

$$\mathbf{Y}^{(2^m)} = C_{2^m} \cdot \boldsymbol{\beta}^{(2^m)} + \mathbf{e}^{(2^m)}, \tag{5.7.36}$$

where

$$\boldsymbol{\beta}^{(2^m)} = (\beta_0, \beta_1, \cdots, \beta_{2^m-1})'.$$

Since the column vectors of C_{2^m} are orthogonal, $(C_{2^m})'C_{2^m} = 2^m I_{2^m}$, the least squares estimator (LSE) of $\boldsymbol{\beta}^{(2^m)}$ is

$$\hat{\boldsymbol{\beta}}^{(2^m)} = \frac{1}{2^m}(C_{2^m})'\mathbf{Y}^{(2^m)}. \tag{5.7.37}$$

Accordingly, the LSE of β_ω is

$$\hat{\beta}_\omega = \frac{1}{2^m} \sum_{\nu=0}^{2^m-1} c^{(2^m)}_{(\nu+1),(\omega+1)} \mathbf{Y}_\nu, \tag{5.7.38}$$

where $c^{(2^m)}_{ij}$ is the i-th row and j-th column element of C_{2^m}, i.e., multiply the components of $\mathbf{Y}^{(2^m)}$ by those of the column of C_{2^m}, corresponding to the parameter β_ω, and divide the sum of products by 2^m.

We do not have to estimate all the 2^m parameters, but can restrict attention only to parameters of interest, as will be shown in the following example.

Since $c^{(2^m)}_{ij} = \pm 1$, the variance of $\hat{\beta}_\omega$ is

$$V\{\hat{\beta}_\omega\} = \frac{\sigma^2}{2^m}, \quad \text{for all } \omega = 0, \cdots, 2^m - 1. \tag{5.7.39}$$

Finally, if every treatment combination is repeated n times, the estimation of the parameters is based on the means $\bar{Y}_\nu$ of the n replications. The variance of $\hat{\beta}_\omega$ becomes

$$V\{\hat{\beta}_\omega\} = \frac{\sigma^2}{n2^m}. \tag{5.7.40}$$

The variance σ^2 can be estimated by the pooled variance estimator, obtained from the between replication variance within each treatment combinations. That is, if $Y_{\nu j}$, $j = 1, \cdots, n$, are the observed values at the ν-th treatment combination then

$$\hat{\sigma}^2 = \frac{1}{(n-1)2^m} \sum_{\nu=1}^{2^m} \sum_{j=1}^{n} (Y_{\nu j} - \bar{Y}_\nu)^2. \tag{5.7.41}$$

Example 5.8 In Example 5.7 we studied the effects of two factors on the cycle time of a piston in a gas turbine, keeping all the other five factors fixed. In the present example we perform a 2^5 experiment with the piston varying factors m, s, $v0$, k, and t at two levels, keeping the atmospheric pressure (factor E) fixed at 90,000 [N/m^2] and the filling gas temperature (factor G) at 340 [°K]. The two levels of each factor are those specified, in Example 5.7, as the limits of the experimental range. Thus, for example, the low level of piston weight (factor A) is 30 [Kg] and its high level is 60 [Kg]. The treatment combinations are listed in Table 5.20. The table also lists the average response $\bar{Y}_\nu$.

```
np.random.seed(3)
factors = {
  'm': [30, 60],
  's': [0.005, 0.02],
  'v0': [0.002, 0.01],
  'k': [1000, 5000],
  't': [290, 296],
}
Design = doe.full_fact(factors)

# Randomize design
Design = Design.sample(frac=1).reset_index(drop=True)

# Run the simulation with 5 replications for each setting
simulator = mistat.PistonSimulator(**{k:list(Design[k]) for k in Design},
                                   p0=90_000, t0=340, n_replicate=5)
result = simulator.simulate()
```

```
# Pooled standard deviation 13.7.41
byFactors = result.groupby(list(factors.keys()))
groupedStd = byFactors.std()['seconds']
pooledVar = np.mean(groupedStd**2)
Vparam = pooledVar  / (5 * len(byFactors))
SE = np.sqrt(Vparam)
```

The number of replications is $n = 5$. Denote the means $\bar{Y}_\nu$ and the standard deviations, S_ν, of the five observations in each treatment combination. We obtain the value $\hat{\sigma}^2 = 0.00079$ and the estimated variance of all LSE of the parameters is

$$\hat{V}\{\hat{\beta}_\omega\} = \frac{\hat{\sigma}^2}{5 \times 32} = 4.9e-06,$$

or standard error of $\text{S.E.}\{\hat{\beta}_\omega\} = 0.00222$. For example, as an estimate of the main effect of m we obtain the value $\hat{\beta}_1 = 0.001852$. In the following tables derived using

Table 5.20 Labels of treatment combinations and average response

m	s	v0	k	t	$\bar{Y}_\nu$	S_ν
30	0.005	0.002	1000	290	0.027	0.016
30	0.005	0.002	1000	296	0.035	0.019
30	0.005	0.002	5000	290	0.045	0.017
30	0.005	0.002	5000	296	0.040	0.023
30	0.005	0.010	1000	290	0.164	0.047
30	0.005	0.010	1000	296	0.188	0.013
30	0.005	0.010	5000	290	0.200	0.034
30	0.005	0.010	5000	296	0.207	0.036
30	0.020	0.002	1000	290	0.008	0.002
30	0.020	0.002	1000	296	0.009	0.001
30	0.020	0.002	5000	290	0.009	0.002
30	0.020	0.002	5000	296	0.006	0.002
30	0.020	0.010	1000	290	0.042	0.002
30	0.020	0.010	1000	296	0.042	0.003
30	0.020	0.010	5000	290	0.050	0.003
30	0.020	0.010	5000	296	0.050	0.005
60	0.005	0.002	1000	290	0.022	0.007
60	0.005	0.002	1000	296	0.021	0.009
60	0.005	0.002	5000	290	0.049	0.008
60	0.005	0.002	5000	296	0.037	0.019
60	0.005	0.010	1000	290	0.213	0.079
60	0.005	0.010	1000	296	0.224	0.072
60	0.005	0.010	5000	290	0.238	0.050
60	0.005	0.010	5000	296	0.294	0.065
60	0.020	0.002	1000	290	0.008	0.001
60	0.020	0.002	1000	296	0.010	0.003
60	0.020	0.002	5000	290	0.009	0.002
60	0.020	0.002	5000	296	0.011	0.003
60	0.020	0.010	1000	290	0.049	0.003
60	0.020	0.010	1000	296	0.050	0.004
60	0.020	0.010	5000	290	0.059	0.006
60	0.020	0.010	5000	296	0.061	0.006

Python we present the LSE's of all the 5 main effects and 10 first order interactions. The S.E. values in the table are the standard errors of the estimates and the t values are $t = \frac{\text{LSE}}{\text{SE}}$.

```
# Perform analysis of variance
Design['response'] = result['seconds']
model = smf.ols('seconds ~ (m + s + v0 + k + t) ** 2', data=result).fit()
# print(anova.anova_lm(model))
print(f'r2={model.rsquared}')
```

```
r2=0.9064681668404627
```

Table 5.21 LSE of main effects and interactions

	LSE	S.E.	t	
m	−0.0054	0.00222	−2.44	
s	37.9277	0.00222	17097.52	**
v0	−61.9511	0.00222	−27927.08	**
k	−0.0000	0.00222	−0.00	
t	−0.0001	0.00222	−0.07	
m:s	−0.0413	0.00222	−18.62	**
m:v0	0.1332	0.00222	60.03	**
m:k	0.0000	0.00222	0.00	
m:t	0.0000	0.00222	0.01	
s:v0	−1165.8813	0.00222	−525569.93	**
s:k	−0.0004	0.00222	−0.17	
s:t	−0.1173	0.00222	−52.86	**
v0:k	0.0005	0.00222	0.21	
v0:t	0.2834	0.00222	127.76	**
k:t	0.0000	0.00222	0.00	

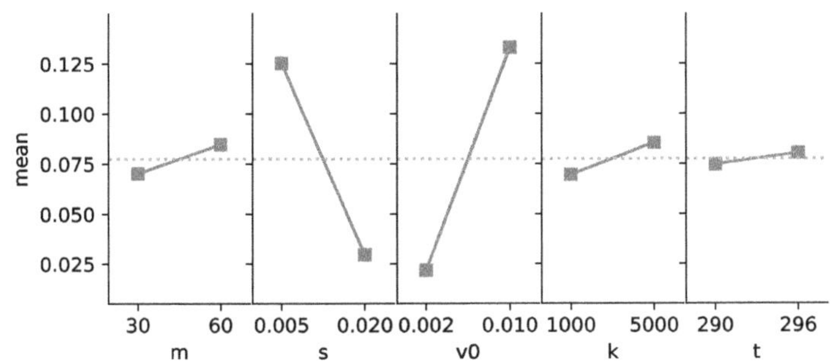

Fig. 5.5 Main effects plot

```
print(np.var(model.predict(result)))
```

```
0.0068959316771731935
```

Values of t which are greater in magnitude than 2.6 are significant at $\alpha = 0.02$. If we wish, however, that all 15 tests have simultaneously a level of significance of $\alpha = 0.05$ we should use as critical value the Scheffé coefficient $\sqrt{32 \times F_{0.95}[32, 128]} = 7.01$, since all the LSE are contrasts of 32 means. In Table 5.21 we marked with one * the t values greater in magnitude than 2.6, and with ** those greater than 7. When we execute this regression, we obtain $R^2 = 0.906$. The variance around the regression surface is $s_y^2 = 0.00761$. This is significantly greater than $\hat{\sigma}^2/5 = 0.00016$. This means that there might be significant high order interactions, which have not been estimated.

Figure 5.5 is a graphical display of the main effects of factors m, s, $v0$, k and t. The left limit of a line shows the average response at a low level and the right limit

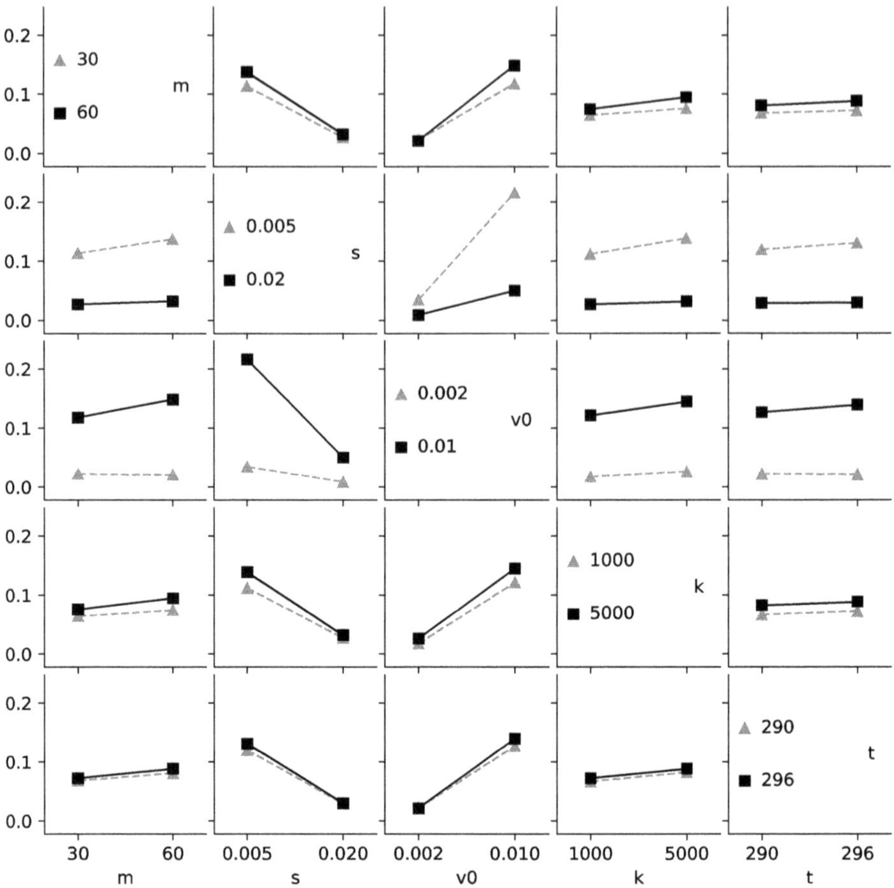

Fig. 5.6 Two-way interaction plots

that at a high level. Factors s and $v0$ seem to have the highest effect, as is shown by the t-values in Table 5.21. Figure 5.6 shows the two-way interactions of the various factors. Interaction (s $*$ v0) is the most pronounced.

From Fig. 5.5 we see that s has a big impact on cycle time. In Fig. 5.6 we realize that the effect of s at its lowest level ($s = 0.005$) is observed at the high level of $v0$ ($v0 = 0.01$). If we only look at the main effect plots (Fig. 5.5) we can be mislead that the effect of s does not depend on $v0$.

In general, main effects and interactions need to be considered simultaneously. We should stress that interactions are not to be considered as secondary to main effects. To emphasize this point, Kenett and Vogel (1991) suggested graphing main effects and interactions on the same plot. To achieve this, main effects are drawn vertically next to interaction plots. Figure 5.7 shows such a plot for the same data. ■

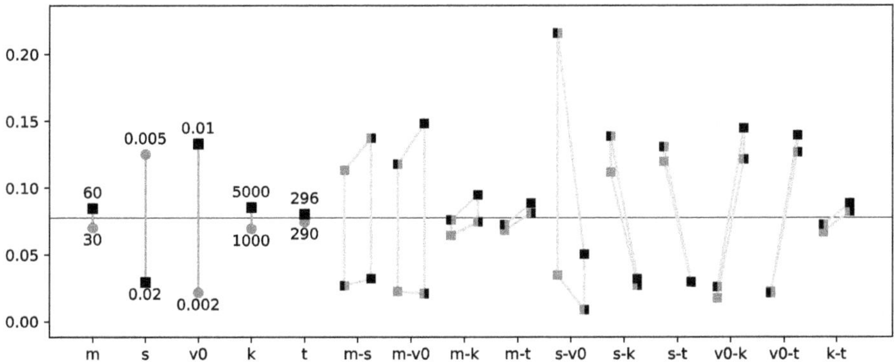

Fig. 5.7 Combined main effects (left) and interaction plots (right). For the main effects, the lower factor levels are identified as red circles, and the higher factor level as a black square. For the interaction part, lower factor levels are identified as red and higher factor levels as black half squares

5.7.5 3^m Factorial Designs

We discuss here the estimation and testing of model parameters, when the design is full factorial, of m factors each one at $p = 3$ levels. We assume that the levels are measured on a continuous scale, and are labelled Low, Medium and High. We introduce the indices i_j ($j = 1, \cdots, m$), with values 0, 1, 2 for the Low, Medium and High levels, correspondingly, of each factor. Thus, we have 3^m treatment combinations, represented by vectors of indices $(i_1, i_2, \cdots, i_m)$. The index ν of the **standard order** of treatment combination is

$$\nu = \sum_{j=1}^{m} i_j 3^{j-1}. \tag{5.7.42}$$

This index ranges from 0 to $3^m - 1$. Let $\bar{Y}_\nu$ denote the yield of n replicas of the ν-th treatment combination, $n \geq 1$.

Since we obtain the yield at three levels of each factor we can, in addition to the linear effects estimate also the quadratic effects of each factor. For example, if we have $m = 2$ factors, we can use a multiple regression method to fit the model

$$\begin{aligned} Y = \beta_0 + \beta_1 x_1 + \beta_2 x_1^2 + \beta_3 x_2 + \beta_4 x_1 x_2 + \\ \beta_5 x_1^2 x_2 + \beta_6 x_2^2 + \beta_7 x_1 x_2^2 + \beta_8 x_1^2 x_2^2 + e. \end{aligned} \tag{5.7.43}$$

This is a quadratic model in two variables. β_1 and β_3 represent the linear effects of x_1 and x_2. β_2 and β_6 represent the quadratic effects of x_1 and x_2. The other coefficients represent interaction effects. β_4 represents the linear $\times$ linear interaction, β_5

represents the quadratic × linear interaction, etc. We have two main effects for each factor (linear and quadratic) and 4 interaction effects.

Generally, if there are m factors we have, in addition to β_0, $2m$ parameters for main effects (linear and quadratic) $2^2\binom{m}{2}$ parameters for interactions between 2 factors, $2^3\binom{m}{3}$ interactions between 3 factors, etc. Generally, we have 3^m parameters, where

$$3^m = \sum_{j=0}^{m} 2^j \binom{m}{j}.$$

As in the case of 2^m models, each parameter in a 3^m model is represented by a vector of m indices $(\lambda_1, \lambda_2, \cdots, \lambda_m)$ where $\lambda_j = 0, 1, 2$. Thus, for example, the vector $(0, 0, \cdots, 0)$ represent the grand mean $\mu = \gamma_0$. A vector $(0, \cdots, 0, 1, 0, \cdots, 0)$ with 1 at the i-th component represents the linear effect of the i-th factor. Similarly, $(0, 0, \cdots, 0, 2, 0, \cdots, 0)$ represents the quadratic effect of the i-th factor. Two indices equal to 1 and all the rest zero, represent the linear × linear interaction of the i-th and j-th factor, etc. The standard order of the parameters is

$$\omega = \sum_{j=1}^{m} \lambda_j 3^{j-1}, \quad \omega = 0, \cdots, 3^m - 1.$$

If m is not too large, it is customary to label the factors by the letters $A, B, C, \cdots$ and the parameters by $A^{\lambda_1} B^{\lambda_2} C^{\lambda_3} \cdots$. In this notation a letter to the zero power is omitted. In Table 5.22 we list the parameters of a 3^3 system.

Table 5.22 The main effects and interactions of a 3^3 factorial

ω	Parameter	Indices	ω	Parameter	Indices
0	Mean	(0,0,0)	15	B^2C	(0,2,1)
1	A	(1,0,0)	16	AB^2C	(1,2,1)
2	A^2	(2,0,0)	17	A^2B^2C	(2,2,1)
3	B	(0,1,0)	18	C^2	(0,0,2)
4	AB	(1,1,0)	19	AC^2	(1,0,2)
5	A^2B	(2,1,0)	20	A^2C^2	(2,0,2)
6	B^2	(0,2,0)	21	BC^2	(0,1,2)
7	AB^2	(1,2,0)	22	ABC^2	(1,1,2)
8	A^2B^2	(2,2,0)	23	A^2BC^2	(2,1,2)
9	C	(0,0,1)	24	B^2C^2	(0,2,2)
10	AC	(1,0,1)	25	AB^2C^2	(1,2,2)
11	A^2C	(2,0,1)	26	$A^2B^2C^2$	(2,2,2)
12	BC	(0,1,1)			
13	ABC	(1,1,1)			
14	A^2BC	(2,1,1)			

It is simple to transform the x-values of each factor to

$$X_j = \begin{cases} -1, & \text{if } i_j = 0 \\ 0, & \text{if } i_j = 1 \\ 1, & \text{if } i_j = 2. \end{cases}$$

However, the matrix of coefficients X that is obtained, when we have quadratic and interaction parameters, is not orthogonal. This requires then the use of the computer to obtain the least squares estimators, with the usual multiple regression program. Another approach is to redefine the effects so that the statistical model will be linear with a matrix having coefficients obtained by the method of orthogonal polynomials (see Draper and Smith 1998). Thus, consider the model

$$\mathbf{Y}^{(3^m)} = \Psi_{(3^m)}\boldsymbol{\gamma}^{(3^m)} + \mathbf{e}^{(3^m)}, \tag{5.7.44}$$

where

$$\mathbf{Y}^{(3^m)} = (\bar{Y}_0, \cdots, \bar{Y}_{3^m-1})',$$

and $\mathbf{e}^{(3^m)} = (e_0, \cdots, e_{3^m-1})'$ is a vector of random variables with

$$E\{e_\nu\} = 0, \qquad V\{e_\nu\} = \sigma^2 \qquad \text{all } \nu = 0, \cdots, 3^m - 1.$$

Moreover for $m = 1$

$$\Psi_{(3)} = \begin{bmatrix} 1 & -1 & 1 \\ 1 & 0 & -2 \\ 1 & 1 & 1 \end{bmatrix}. \tag{5.7.45}$$

For $m \geq 2$ it can be calculated iteratively using the Kronecker product of $\Psi_{(3)}$ and $\Psi_{(3^{m-1})}$,

$$\Psi_{(3^m)} = \Psi_{(3)} \otimes \Psi_{(3^{m-1})} = \begin{bmatrix} \Psi_{(3^{m-1})} & -\Psi_{(3^{m-1})} & \Psi_{(3^{m-1})} \\ \Psi_{(3^{m-1})} & 0 & -2\Psi_{(3^{m-1})} \\ \Psi_{(3^{m-1})} & \Psi_{(3^{m-1})} & \Psi_{(3^{m-1})} \end{bmatrix}. \tag{5.7.46}$$

The matrices $\Psi_{(3^m)}$ have orthogonal column vectors and

$$(\Psi_{(3^m)})'(\Psi_{(3^m)}) = \Delta_{(3^m)}, \tag{5.7.47}$$

where $\Delta_{(3^m)}$ is a diagonal matrix whose diagonal elements are equal to the sum of squares of the elements in the corresponding column of $\Psi_{(3^m)}$. For example, for $m = 1$,

$$\Delta_{(3)} = \begin{pmatrix} 3 & 0 & 0 \\ 0 & 2 & 0 \\ 0 & 0 & 6 \end{pmatrix}.$$

For $m = 2$ we obtain

$$\Psi_{(9)} = \begin{bmatrix} 1 & -1 & 1 & -1 & 1 & -1 & 1 & -1 & 1 \\ 1 & 0 & -2 & -1 & 0 & 2 & 1 & 0 & -2 \\ 1 & 1 & 1 & -1 & -1 & -1 & 1 & 1 & 1 \\ 1 & -1 & 1 & 0 & 0 & 0 & -2 & 2 & -2 \\ 1 & 0 & -2 & 0 & 0 & 0 & -2 & 0 & 4 \\ 1 & 1 & 1 & 0 & 0 & 0 & -2 & -2 & -2 \\ 1 & -1 & 1 & 1 & -1 & 1 & 1 & -1 & 1 \\ 1 & 0 & -2 & 1 & 0 & -2 & 1 & 0 & -2 \\ 1 & 1 & 1 & 1 & 1 & 1 & 1 & 1 & 1 \end{bmatrix}$$

and

$$\Delta_{(9)} = \begin{bmatrix} 9 & & & & & & & & \\ & 6 & & & & & & & \\ & & 18 & & & 0 & & & \\ & & & 6 & & & & & \\ & & & & 4 & & & & \\ & & & & & 12 & & & \\ & & 0 & & & & 18 & & \\ & & & & & & & 12 & \\ & & & & & & & & 36 \end{bmatrix}.$$

Thus, the LSE of $\boldsymbol{\gamma}^{(3^m)}$ is

$$\hat{\boldsymbol{\gamma}}^{(3^m)} = \Delta^{-1}_{(3^m)}(\Psi_{(3^m)})'\mathbf{Y}^{(3^m)}. \tag{5.7.48}$$

These LSE are best linear unbiased estimators and

$$V\{\hat{\gamma}_\omega\} = \frac{\sigma^2}{n\sum_{i=1}^{3^m}(\Psi^{(3^m)}_{i,\omega+1})^2}. \tag{5.7.49}$$

If the number of replicas, n, is greater than 1 then σ^2 can be estimated by

$$\hat{\sigma}^2 = \frac{1}{3^m(n-1)} \sum_{\nu=0}^{3^m-1} \sum_{l=1}^{n} (Y_{\nu l} - \bar{Y}_\nu)^2. \tag{5.7.50}$$

If $n = 1$ we can estimate σ^2 if it is known a priori that some parameters γ_ω are zero. Let Λ_0 be the set of all parameters which can be assumed to be negligible. Let K_0 be the number of elements of Λ_0. If $\omega \in \Lambda_0$ then $\hat{\gamma}_\omega^2 \left(\sum_{j=1}^{3^m} (\Psi_{i,\omega+1}^{(3^m)})^2\right)$ is distributed like $\sigma^2\chi^2[1]$. Therefore, an unbiased estimator of σ^2 is

$$\hat{\hat{\sigma}}^2 = \frac{1}{k_0} \sum_{\omega \in \Lambda_0} \hat{\gamma}_\omega^2 \left(\sum_{j=1}^{3^m} (\Psi_{j,\omega+1}^{(3^m)})^2 \right). \tag{5.7.51}$$

Example 5.9 Oikawa and Oka (1987) reported the results of a 3^3 experiment to investigate the effects of three factors A, B, C on the stress levels of a membrane Y. The data is given in dataset **STRESS.csv**. The first three columns of the dataset provide the levels of the three factors, and column 4 presents the stress values.

In order to use the methodology derived in this section, we first define a few utility functions. The function *getStandardOrder* determines the position of a combination of levels in the standard order as shown in Table 5.22.

```
def getStandardOrder(levels, labels):
    parameter = ''
    omega = 0
    for i, (level, label) in enumerate(zip(levels, labels), 1):
        omega += level * 3**(i-1)
        if level == 1:
            parameter = f'{parameter}{label}'
        elif level == 2:
            parameter = f'{parameter}{label}2'
    if parameter == '':
        parameter = 'Mean'
    return {'omega': omega, 'Parameter': parameter}
```

This function can be used to sort the dataset **STRESS.csv** in standard order.

```
stress = mistat.load_data('STRESS')
standardOrder = pd.DataFrame(getStandardOrder(row[['A','B','C']], 'ABC')
                             for _, row in stress.iterrows())

# add information to dataframe stress and sort in standard order
stress.index = standardOrder['omega']
stress['Parameter'] = standardOrder['Parameter']
stress = stress.sort_index()
```

The function *get_psi3m* calculates the matrix $\Psi^{(3^m)}$ recursively. Here, we use the function *np.kron* to calculate the Kronecker product.

```
def get_psi3m(m):
    psi31 = np.array([[1, -1, 1], [1, 0, -2], [1, 1, 1]] )
    if m == 1:
        return psi31
```

```
    psi3m1 = get_psi3m(m-1)
    return np.kron(psi31, psi3m1)
```

This allows us to calculate the LSE estimates $\hat{\boldsymbol{\gamma}}^{(3^m)}$.

```
Y_3m = stress['stress']

psi3m = get_psi3m(3)
delta3m = np.matmul(psi3m.transpose(), psi3m)
inv_delta3m = np.diag(1/np.diag(delta3m))
gamma_3m = np.matmul(inv_delta3m, np.matmul(psi3m.transpose(), Y_3m))

estimate = pd.DataFrame({
    'Parameter': stress['Parameter'],
    'LSE': gamma_3m,
})
```

Suppose that from technological considerations we decide that all interaction parameters involving quadratic components are negligible (zero). In this case we can estimate σ^2 by $\hat{\hat{\sigma}}^2$. In the present example the set Λ_0 contains 16 parameters, i.e.,

$$\Lambda_0 = \{A^2B, AB^2, A^2B^2, A^2C, A^2BC, B^2C, AB^2C, A^2B^2C, AC^2, \\ A^2C^2, BC^2, ABC^2, A^2BC, B^2C^2, AB^2C^2, A^2B^2C^2\}.$$

Thus $K_0 = 16$ and the estimator $\hat{\hat{\sigma}}^2$ has 16 degrees of freedom. The estimate of σ^2 is $\hat{\hat{\sigma}}^2 = 95.95$. It is calculated in Python as follows.

```
# determine Lambda0 set as interactions that include quadratic terms
lambda0 = [term for term in stress['Parameter'] if '2' in term and len(term) > 2]
print(f'lambda0 : {lambda0}')
estimate['Significance'] = ['n.s.' if p in lambda0 else ''
                            for p in estimate['Parameter']]

# estimate sigma2 using non-significant terms in lambda0
sigma2 = 0
for idx, row in estimate.iterrows():
    p = row['Parameter']
    if p not in lambda0:
        continue
    idx = int(idx)
    sigma2 += row['LSE']**2 * np.sum(psi3m[:, idx]**2)
K0 = len(lambda0)
sigma2 = sigma2 / K0
print(f'K0 = {K0}')
print(f'sigma2 = {sigma2.round(2)}')
```

```
lambda0 : ['A2B', 'AB2', 'A2B2', 'A2C', 'A2BC', 'B2C', 'AB2C',
'A2B2C', 'AC2', 'A2C2', 'BC2', 'ABC2', 'A2BC2', 'B2C2', 'AB2C2',
'A2B2C2']
K0 = 16
sigma2 = 95.95
```

Using the estimate $\hat{\hat{\sigma}}^2$ we can now derive standard errors for our parameter estimates. The sum $\sum_{j=1}^{3^m}(\Psi_{j,\omega+1}^{(3^m)})^2$ is the sum of column ω of `psi3m**2`. Using

Table 5.23 The LSE of the parameters of the 3^3 system

Parameter	LSE	Significance
Mean	223.781	
A	44.917	
A^2	−1.843	
B	−42.494	
AB	−16.558	
A^2B	−1.897	n.s.
B^2	6.557	
AB^2	1.942	n.s.
A^2B^2	−0.171	n.s.
C	26.817	
AC	22.617	
A^2C	0.067	n.s.
BC	−3.908	
ABC	2.012	
A^2BC	1.121	n.s.
B^2C	−0.708	n.s.
AB^2C	0.246	n.s.
A^2B^2C	0.287	n.s.
C^2	−9.165	
AC^2	−4.833	n.s.
A^2C^2	0.209	n.s.
BC^2	2.803	n.s.
ABC^2	−0.879	n.s.
A^2BC^2	0.851	n.s.
B^2C^2	−0.216	n.s.
AB^2C^2	0.288	n.s.
$A^2B^2C^2$	0.059	n.s.

np.sum with `axis=0` to calculate this sum, we get the variance and standard error as follows.

```
n = len(psi3m)
variance = sigma2 / (n * np.sum(psi3m**2, axis=0))
estimate['S.E.'] = np.sqrt(n * variance)
```

The estimates of the standard errors (S.E.) in Table 5.23 use this estimate. If other parameters are assumed negligible, the standard error estimates will change. ■

Example 5.10 If not all possible interactions need to be studied, we can also use ordinary linear least squares to analyze the data from Example 5.9.

The main effects and interaction plots in Fig. 5.8 as well as the combined main effects and interaction plot from Fig. 5.9 give an indication of the importance of quadratic terms and interactions.

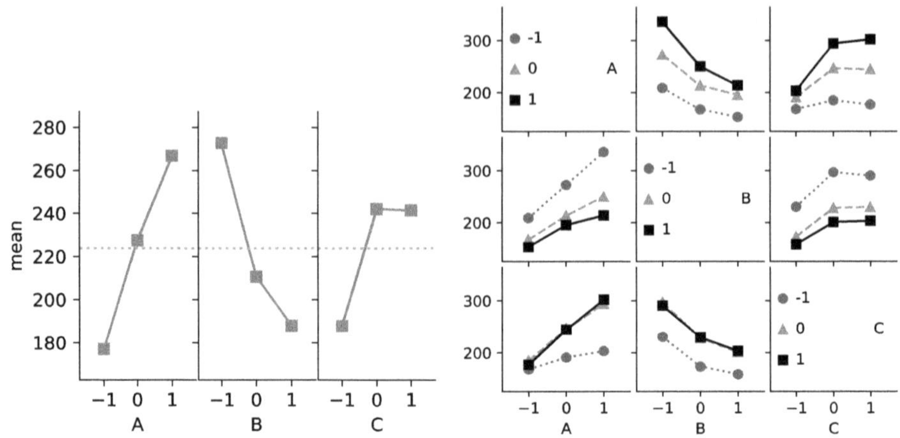

Fig. 5.8 Main effects and interaction plot for 3^3 design

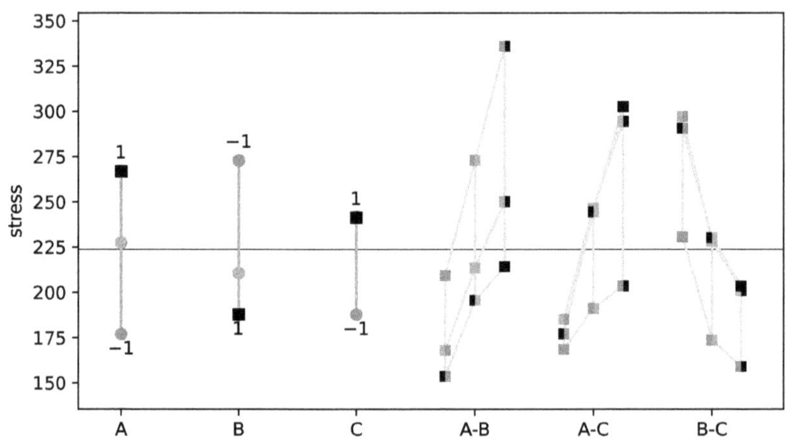

Fig. 5.9 Combined main effect and interaction plot for 3^3 design. The grey circle relate to results at intermediate factor levels

The main effects plot shows for A only a small deviation from linearity which means that the quadratic term A^2 has only little importance. This is also reflected in the combined main effects plot. Here the grey circle for A is almost centered between the red circle and black square. If the position of the grey circle is off center like for B and even more so for C, quadratic components may be important.

For the interaction plots, we analyze the parallelity of the lines. The interactions AB and AC demonstrate deviations from it while for BC, the lines deviation from parallelity is very small. From this, we expect that the interaction BC will be of less importance than AB and AC.

Table 5.24 Parameter estimates for **STRESS.csv** using a reduced model

Coef.	Std.Err.	t	P>|t|	[0.025	0.975]
232.681	4.988	46.652	0.000	222.108	243.255
44.917	2.309	19.454	0.000	40.022	49.811
−42.494	2.309	−18.405	0.000	−47.389	−37.600
26.817	2.309	11.615	0.000	21.922	31.711
−16.558	2.828	−5.856	0.000	−22.553	−10.564
22.617	2.828	7.998	0.000	16.622	28.611
−3.908	2.828	−1.382	0.186	−9.903	2.086
2.012	3.463	0.581	0.569	−5.329	9.354
−5.528	3.999	−1.382	0.186	−14.005	2.950
19.672	3.999	4.919	0.000	11.195	28.150
−27.494	3.999	−6.875	0.000	−35.972	−19.017

To analyze this data quantitatively with Python we apply:

```
stress = mistat.load_data('STRESS')

# convert factor levels from (0,1,2) to (-1,0,1)
stress['A'] = stress['A'] - 1
stress['B'] = stress['B'] - 1
stress['C'] = stress['C'] - 1

# train a model including interactions and quadratic terms
formula = ('stress ~ A + B + C + A:B + A:C + B:C + A:B:C + ' +
           'I(A**2) + I(B**2) + I(C**2)')
model = smf.ols(formula, data=stress).fit()
model.summary2()
```

As can be seen in Table 5.24, most components in the model are highly significant. The interactions BC and ABC, as well as the quadratic component A^2 are not significant.

■

5.8 Blocking and Fractional Replications of 2^m Factorial Designs

Full factorial experiments with large number of factors might be impractical. For example, if there are $m = 12$ factors, even at $p = 2$ levels, the total number of treatment combinations is $2^{12} = 4096$. This size of an experiment is generally not necessary, because most of the high order interactions might be negligible and there is no need to estimate 4096 parameters. If only main effects and first order interactions are considered, a priori of importance, while all the rest are believed to be negligible, we have to estimate and test only $1 + 12 + \binom{12}{2} = 79$ parameters. A fraction of the experiment, of size $2^7 = 128$ would be sufficient. Such a fraction can be even replicated several times. The question is, how do we choose the fraction of the full factorial in such a way that desirable properties of orthogonality, equal variances of estimators, etc. will be kept, and the parameters of interest will be estimable unbiasedly.

The problem of fractioning the full factorial experiment arises also when the full factorial cannot be performed in one block, but several blocks are required to accommodate all the treatment conditions. For example, a 2^5 experiment is designed, but only $8 = 2^3$ treatment combinations can be performed in any given block (day, machine, etc.). We have to design the fractions that will be assigned to each block in such a way that, if there are significant differences between the blocks, the block effects will not confound or obscure parameters of interest. We start with a simple illustration of the fractionization procedure, and the properties of the ensuing estimators.

Consider 3 factors A, B, C at 2 levels. We wish to partition the $2^3 = 8$ treatment combinations to two fractions of size $2^2 = 4$. Let $\lambda_i = 0, 1$ $(i = 1, 2, 3)$ and let $A^{\lambda_1} B^{\lambda_2} C^{\lambda_3}$ represent the 8 parameters. One way of representing the treatment combinations, when the number of factors is not large, is by using low case letters $a, b, c, \cdots$. The letter a indicates that factor A is at the High level $(i_1 = 1)$, similarly about other factors. The absence of a letter indicates that the corresponding factor is at Low level. The symbol (1) indicates that all levels are Low. Thus, the treatment combinations and the associated coefficients $c_{ij}^{(2^3)}$ are shown in Table 5.25.

Suppose now that the treatment combinations should be partitioned to two fractional replications (blocks) of size 4. We have to choose a parameter, called a **defining parameter**, according to which the partition will be done. This defining parameter is in a sense sacrificed. Since its effects will be either confounded with the block effects or inestimable if only one block of trials is performed. Thus, let us choose the parameter ABC, as a defining parameter. Partition the treatment combinations to two blocks, according to the signs of the coefficients corresponding to ABC. These are the products of the coefficients in the A, B, and C columns. Thus, two blocks are obtained

$$B_- = \{(1), ab, ac, bc\},$$

$$B_+ = \{a, b, c, abc\}.$$

Table 5.25 A 2^2 factorial

	Main effects			Defining parameter
Treatments	A	B	C	ABC
(1)	−1	−1	−1	−1
A	1	−1	−1	1
B	−1	1	−1	1
AB	1	1	−1	−1
C	−1	−1	1	1
AC	1	−1	1	−1
BC	−1	1	1	−1
ABC	1	1	1	1

In Python, we can use the method *fracfact* from the pyDOE2 package.

```
from pyDOE2 import fracfact
# define the generator
generator = 'A B C ABC'
design = pd.DataFrame(fracfact(generator), columns=generator.split())
block_n = design[design['ABC'] == -1]
block_p = design[design['ABC'] == 1]
```

The two blocks are:

	Main effects			Defining parameter
Treatments	A	B	C	ABC
(1)	−1	−1	−1	−1
AB	1	1	−1	−1
AC	1	−1	1	−1
BC	−1	1	1	−1

	Main effects			Defining parameter
Treatments	A	B	C	ABC
A	1	−1	−1	1
B	−1	1	−1	1
C	−1	−1	1	1
ABC	1	1	1	1

If 2^m treatment combinations are partitioned to $2^k = 2$ blocks, we say that the **degree of fractionation** is $k = 1$, the fractional replication is of size 2^{m-k}, and the design is $1/2^k$ fraction of a full factorial. If, for example, $m = 5$ factors and we wish to partition to 4 blocks of 8, the degree of fractionization is $k = 2$. Select $k = 2$ parameters to serve as defining parameters, e.g., ACE and BDE, and partition the treatment combinations according to the signs ± 1 of the coefficients in the ACE and BDE columns. This becomes very cumbersome if m and k are large. Function *fac.design* performs this partitioning and prints into a file the block which is requested. We will return to this later. It is interesting to check now what are the properties of estimators in the 2^{3-1} fractional replication, if only the block B_- was performed. The defining parameter was ABC.

Let $Y(1)$ be the response of treatment combination (1), this is Y_0 in the standard order notation, let $Y(a)$ be the response of 'a', etc. The results of performing B_-, with the associated coefficients of parameters of interest can be presented as in Table 5.26.

We see that the six columns of coefficients are orthogonal to each other, and each column has 2 -1's and 2 $+1$'s. The LSE of the above parameters are orthogonal contrasts, given by

Table 5.26 Coefficients and response for several treatment combinations (t.c.)

t.c.	A	B	C	AB	AC	BC	Y
(1)	−1	−1	−1	1	1	1	$Y(1)$
ab	1	1	−1	1	−1	−1	$Y(ab)$
ac	1	−1	1	−1	1	−1	$Y(ac)$
bc	−1	1	1	−1	−1	1	$Y(bc)$

$$\hat{A} = \frac{1}{4}(-Y(1) + Y(ab) + Y(ac) - Y(bc)),$$

$$\hat{B} = \frac{1}{4}(-Y(1) + Y(ab) - Y(ac) + Y(bc)),$$

etc. The variances of all these estimators, when $n = 1$, are equal to $\frac{\sigma^2}{4}$. However, the estimators might be **biased**. The expected value of the first estimator is

$$E\{\hat{A}\} = \frac{1}{4}(-E\{Y(1)\} + E\{Y(ab)\} + E\{Y(ac)\} - E\{Y(bc)\}).$$

Now,

$$E\{Y(1)\} = \mu - A - B - C + AB + AC + BC - ABC,$$

$$E\{Y(ab)\} = \mu + A + B - C + AB - AC - BC - ABC,$$

$$E\{Y(ac)\} = \mu + A - B + C - AB + AC - BC - ABC,$$

and

$$E\{Y(bc)\} = \mu - A + B + C - AB - AC + BC - ABC.$$

Collecting all these terms, the result is

$$E\{\hat{A}\} = A - BC.$$

Similarly, one can show that

$$E\{\hat{B}\} = B - AC,$$

$$E\{\hat{C}\} = C - AB,$$

$$E\{\hat{AB}\} = AB - C,$$

etc. The LSE of all the parameters are biased, unless $AB = AC = BC = 0$. The bias terms are called **aliases**. The aliases are obtained by multiplying the parameter of interest by the defining parameter, when any letter raised to the power 2 is eliminated, e.g.,

$$A \otimes ABC = A^2BC = BC.$$

The sign of the alias is the sign of the block. Since we have used the block B_-, all the aliases appear above with a negative sign. The general rules for finding the aliases in 2^{m-k} designs is as follows.

To obtain a 2^{m-k} fractional replication one needs k defining parameters. The multiplication operation of parameters was illustrated above. The k defining parameters should be **independent**, in the sense that none can be obtained as a product of the other ones. Such independent defining parameters are called **generators**. For example, to choose 4 defining parameters, when the factors are A, B, C, D, E, F, G, H, choose first two parameters, like $ABCH$ and $ABEFG$. The product of these two is $CEFGH$. In the next step choose, for the third defining parameter, any one which is different than $\{ABCH, ABEFG, CEFGH\}$. Suppose one chooses $BDEFH$. The three independent parameters $ABCH$, $ABEFG$, and $BDEFH$ generate a subgroup of eight parameters, including the mean μ. These are:

$$\begin{array}{cc} \mu & BDEFH \\ ABCH & ACDEF \\ ABEFG & ADGH \\ CEFGH & BCDG \end{array}$$

The utility function *mistat.subgroupOfDefining* can be used to enumerate the subgroup based on the defining parameters.

```
mistat.subgroupOfDefining(['ABCH', 'ABEFG', 'BDEFH'])
```

```
['', 'ABCH', 'ABEFG', 'ACDEF', 'ADGH', 'BCDG', 'BDEFH', 'CEFGH']
```

Finally, to choose a fourth independent defining parameter, one can choose any parameter which is not among the eight listed above. Suppose that the parameter $BCEFH$ is chosen. Now we obtain a subgroup of $2^4 = 16$ defining parameter, by adding to the eight listed above their products with $BCEFH$. Thus, this subgroup is

$$\begin{array}{cc} \mu & BCEFH \\ ABCH & AEF \\ ABEFG & ACGH \\ CEFGH & BG \\ BDEFH & CD \\ ACDEF & ABDH \\ ADGH & ABCDEFG \\ BCDG & DEFGH \end{array}$$

Notice that this subgroup includes, excluding the mean, two first order interactions CD and BG. This shows that the choice of defining parameters was not a good one.

Table 5.27 The aliases to the main effects in a 2^{8-4} design, the generators are $ABCH$, $ABEFG$, $BDEFH$, and $BCEFH$

Main effects	Aliases
A	$ABCDG$, $ABCEFH$, $ABDEFH$, ABG, ACD, $ACEFGH$, $ADEFGH$, $BCDEFG$, BCH, BDH, $BEFG$, $CDEF$, CGH, DGH, **EF**
B	$ABCDEF$, $ABCGH$, $ABDGH$, $ABEF$, $ACDEFG$, ACH, ADH, $AEFG$, BCD, $BCEFGH$, $BDEFGH$, CDG, $CEFH$, $DEFH$, **G**
C	$ABCDH$, $ABCEFG$, $ABDEFG$, ABH, $ACDGH$, $ACEF$, $ADEF$, AGH, $BCDEFH$, BCG, BDG, $BEFH$, $CDEFGH$, **D**, $EFGH$
D	$ABCDH$, $ABCEFG$, $ABDEFG$, ABH, $ACDGH$, $ACEF$, $ADEF$, AGH, $BCDEFH$, BCG, BDG, $BEFH$, $CDEFGH$, **C**, $EFGH$
E	$ABCDFG$, $ABCEH$, $ABDEH$, $ABFG$, $ACDF$, $ACEGH$, $ADEGH$, **AF**, $BCDEG$, $BCFH$, $BDFH$, BEG, CDE, $CFGH$, $DFGH$
F	$ABCDEG$, $ABCFH$, $ABDFH$, $ABEG$, $ACDE$, $ACFGH$, $ADFGH$, **AE**, $BCDFG$, $BCEH$, $BDEH$, BFG, CDF, $CEGH$, $DEGH$
G	$ABCDEF$, $ABCGH$, $ABDGH$, $ABEF$, $ACDEFG$, ACH, ADH, $AEFG$, **B**, BCD, $BCEFGH$, $BDEFGH$, CDG, $CEFH$, $DEFH$
H	ABC, $ABCDEFGH$, ABD, $ABEFGH$, $ACDEFH$, ACG, ADG, $AEFH$, $BCDGH$, $BCEF$, $BDEF$, BGH, CDH, $CEFG$, $DEFG$

Since the aliases which will be created by these defining parameters will include main effects and other low order interactions.

Given a subgroup of defining parameters, the aliases of a given parameter are obtained by **multiplying** the parameter by the defining parameters. In Table 5.27 we list the aliases of the eight main effects, with respect to the above subgroup of 2^4 defining parameters.

We see in this table that most of the aliases to the main effects are high order interactions (that are generally negligible). However, among the aliases to A there is EF. Among the aliases to B there is the main effect G. Among the aliases to C there is D, etc. This design is not good since it may yield strongly biased estimators. The **resolution of a 2^{m-k} design is the length of the smallest word (excluding μ) in the subgroup of defining parameters**. For example, if in a 2^{8-4} design we use the following four generators $BCDE$, $ACDF$, $ABCG$, and $ABDH$, we obtain the 16 defining parameters

$$\{\mu,\ BCDE,\ ACDF,\ ABEF,\ ABCG,\ ADEG,\ BDFG,\ CEFG,\ ABDH,\ ACEH,\ BDFH,\ DEFH,\ CDGH,\ BEGH,\ AFGH,\ ABCDEFGH\}.$$

The length of the smallest word, excluding μ, among these defining parameters is four. Thus the present 2^{8-4} design is a **resolution IV** design. In this design, all aliases of main effects are second order interactions or higher (words of length greater or equal to three). Aliases to first order interactions are interactions of first order or higher. The present design is obviously better, in terms of resolution, than the previous one (which is of resolution II). We should always try to get resolution IV or higher. If the degree of fractionation is too high there may not exist resolution IV designs. For example, in 2^{6-3} and 2^{7-4}, 2^{9-5}, 2^{10-6} and 2^{11-7} we have only resolution III designs. One way to reduce the bias is to choose several fractions at random. For example, in a 2^{11-7} we have $2^7 = 128$ blocks of size $2^4 = 16$. If we execute only one block, the best we can have is resolution III. In this case some main effects are biased (confounded) with some first order interactions. If one chooses n blocks at **random** (RSWOR) out of the 128 possible ones, and compute the average estimate of the effects, the bias is reduced to zero, but the variance of the estimators is increased.

To illustrate this, suppose that we have a 2^{6-2} design with generators $ABCE$ and $BCDF$. This will yield a resolution IV design. There are 4 blocks and the corresponding bias terms of the LSE of A are

block	
0	$-BCE - ABCDF + DEF$
1	$BCE - ABCDF - DEF$
2	$-BCE + ABCDF - DEF$
3	$BCE + ABCDF + DEF$

If we choose one block at random, the expected bias is the average of the four terms above, which is zero. The total variance of $\hat{A}$ is $\frac{\sigma^2}{16}$ + Variance of conditional bias $= \frac{\sigma^2}{16} + [(BCE)^2 + (ABCDF)^2 + (DEF)^2]/4$.

Example 5.11 In the present example we illustrate the construction of fractional replications. The case that is illustrated is a 2^{8-4} design. Here we can construct 16 fractions, each one of size 16. As discussed before, four generating parameters should be specified. Let these be $BCDE$, $ACDF$, $ABCG$, $ABDH$. These parameters generate resolution 4 design where the degree of fractionation, k=4. The blocks can be indexed $0, 1, \cdots, 15$. Each index is determined by the signs of the four generators, which determine the block. Thus, the signs $(-1, -1, 1, 1)$ correspond to $(0, 0, 1, 1)$ which yields the index $\sum_{j=1}^{4} i_j 2^{j-1} = 12$.

The index of generator 1 ($BCDE = A^0B^1C^1D^1E^1F^0G^0H^0$) is 0, 1, 1, 1, 1, 0, 0, 0, for generator 2: 1, 0, 1, 1, 0, 1, 0, 0; for generator 3: 1, 1, 1, 0, 0, 0, 1, 0 and for generator 4: 1, 1, 0, 1, 0, 0, 0, 1.

We can generate the first block in Python as follows:

```
mainEffects = ['A', 'B', 'C', 'D', 'E', 'F', 'G', 'H']
defining = ['ABCH', 'ABEFG', 'BDEFH', 'BCEFH']
design = pd.DataFrame(fracfact(' '.join(mainEffects)), columns=mainEffects)
design = mistat.addTreatments(design, mainEffects)
subgroup = mistat.subgroupOfDefining(defining, noTreatment='(1)')
block1 = design[design['Treatments'].isin(subgroup)]
block1
```

```
   Treatments    A    B    C    D    E    F    G    H
0         (1) -1.0 -1.0 -1.0 -1.0 -1.0 -1.0 -1.0 -1.0
12         CD -1.0 -1.0  1.0  1.0 -1.0 -1.0 -1.0 -1.0
```

```
49         AEF  1.0 -1.0 -1.0 -1.0  1.0  1.0 -1.0 -1.0
61       ACDEF  1.0 -1.0  1.0  1.0  1.0  1.0 -1.0 -1.0
66          BG -1.0  1.0 -1.0 -1.0 -1.0 -1.0  1.0 -1.0
78        BCDG -1.0  1.0  1.0  1.0 -1.0 -1.0  1.0 -1.0
115      ABEFG  1.0  1.0 -1.0 -1.0  1.0  1.0  1.0 -1.0
127    ABCDEFG  1.0  1.0  1.0  1.0  1.0  1.0  1.0 -1.0
135       ABCH  1.0  1.0  1.0 -1.0 -1.0 -1.0 -1.0  1.0
139       ABDH  1.0  1.0 -1.0  1.0 -1.0 -1.0 -1.0  1.0
182      BCEFH -1.0  1.0  1.0 -1.0  1.0  1.0 -1.0  1.0
186      BDEFH -1.0  1.0 -1.0  1.0  1.0  1.0 -1.0  1.0
197       ACGH  1.0 -1.0  1.0 -1.0 -1.0 -1.0  1.0  1.0
201       ADGH  1.0 -1.0 -1.0  1.0 -1.0 -1.0  1.0  1.0
244      CEFGH -1.0 -1.0  1.0 -1.0  1.0  1.0  1.0  1.0
248      DEFGH -1.0 -1.0 -1.0  1.0  1.0  1.0  1.0  1.0
```

In Table 5.28 two blocks derived with Python are printed. Use the command `fold(block1[mainEffects], columns=[1, 2, 3])` to generate Block 1.

■

In Box et al. (2005) there are recommended generators for 2^{m-k} designs. Some of these generators are given in Table 5.29.

The LSE of the parameters is performed by writing first the columns of coefficients $c_{i,j} = \pm 1$ corresponding to the design, multiplying the coefficients by the Y values, and dividing by 2^{m-k}.

Table 5.28 Blocks of 2^{8-4} designs

Block 0								Block 1							
1	1	1	1	1	1	1	1	1	2	2	2	1	1	1	1
1	2	2	2	2	1	1	1	1	1	1	1	2	1	1	1
2	1	2	2	1	2	1	1	2	2	1	1	1	2	1	1
2	2	1	1	2	2	1	1	2	1	2	2	2	2	1	1
2	2	2	1	1	1	2	1	2	1	1	2	1	1	2	1
2	1	1	2	2	1	2	1	2	2	2	1	2	1	2	1
1	2	1	2	1	2	2	1	1	1	2	1	1	2	2	1
1	1	2	1	2	2	2	1	1	2	1	2	2	2	2	1
2	2	1	2	1	1	1	2	2	1	2	1	1	1	1	2
2	1	2	1	2	1	1	2	2	2	1	2	2	1	1	2
1	2	2	1	1	2	1	2	1	1	1	2	1	2	1	2
1	1	1	2	2	2	1	2	1	2	2	1	2	2	1	2
1	1	2	2	1	1	2	2	1	2	1	1	1	1	2	2
1	2	1	1	2	1	2	2	1	1	2	2	2	1	2	2
2	1	1	1	1	2	2	2	2	2	2	2	1	2	2	2
2	2	2	2	2	2	2	2	2	1	1	1	2	2	2	2

Table 5.29 Some generators for 2^{m-k} designs

	m			
k	5	6	7	8
1	$ABCDE$	$ABCDEF$	$ABCDEFG$	$ABCDEFGH$
2	ABD	$ABCE$	$ABCDF$	$ABCDG$
	ACE	$BCDF$	$ABDEG$	$ABEFH$
3		ABD	$ABCE$	$ABCF$
		ACD	$BCDF$	$ABDG$
		BCF	$ACDG$	$BCDEH$
4			ABD	$BCDE$
			ACE	$ACDF$
			BCF	$ABCG$
			$ABCG$	$ABDH$

5.9 Exploration of Response Surfaces

The functional relationship between the yield variable Y and the experimental variables $(x_1, \cdots, x_k)$ is modeled as

$$Y = f(x_1, \cdots, x_k) + e,$$

where e is a random variable with zero mean and a finite variance, σ^2. The set of points $\{f(x_1, \cdots, x_k),\ x_i \in D_i,\ i = 1, \cdots, k\}$, where $(D_1, \cdots, D_k)$ is the experimental domain of the x-variables, is called a **response surface**. Two types of response surfaces were discussed before, the **linear**

$$f(x_1, \cdots, x_k) = \beta_0 + \sum_{i=1}^{k} \beta_i x_i \tag{5.9.1}$$

and the **quadratic**

$$f(x_1, \cdots, x_k) = \beta_0 + \sum_{i=1}^{k} \beta_i x_i + \sum_{i=1}^{k} \beta_{ii} x_i^2 + \sum\sum_{i \neq j} \beta_{ij} x_i x_j. \tag{5.9.2}$$

Response surfaces may be of complicated functional form. We assume here that in local domains of interest, they can be approximated by linear or quadratic models.

Researchers are interested in studying, or exploring, the nature of response surfaces, in certain domains of interest, for the purpose of predicting future yield, and in particular for optimizing a process, by choosing the x-values to maximize (or minimize) the expected yield (or the expected loss). In the present section we present special designs for the exploration of quadratic surfaces, and for the determination of optimal domains (conditions). Designs for quadratic models are called **second**

order designs. We start with the theory of second order designs, and conclude with the optimization process.

5.9.1 Second Order Designs

Second order designs are constructed in order to estimate the parameters of the quadratic response function

$$E\{Y\} = \beta_0 + \sum_{i=1}^{k} \beta_i x_i + \sum_{i=1}^{k} \beta_{ii} x_i^2 + \sum_{i=1}^{k-1} \sum_{j=i+1}^{k} \beta_{ij} x_i x_j. \tag{5.9.3}$$

In this case the number of regression coefficients is $p = 1 + 2k + \binom{k}{2}$. We will arrange the vector $\boldsymbol{\beta}$ in the form

$$\boldsymbol{\beta}' = (\beta_0, \beta_{11}, \cdots, \beta_{kk}, \beta_1, \cdots, \beta_k, \beta_{12}, \cdots, \beta_{1k}, \beta_{23}, \cdots, \beta_{2k}, \cdots, \beta_{n-1,k}).$$

Let N be the number of x-points. The design matrix takes the form

$$(X) = \begin{bmatrix} 1 & x_{11}^2 & \cdots & x_{1k}^2 & x_{11} & \cdots & x_{1k} & x_{11}x_{12} & \cdots & x_{1,k-1}x_{1,k} \\ 1 & x_{21}^2 & \cdots & x_{2k}^2 & x_{21} & \cdots & x_{2k} & x_{21}x_{22} & \cdots & x_{2,k-1}x_{2,k} \\ 1 & x_{31}^2 & \cdots & x_{3k}^2 & x_{31} & \cdots & x_{3k} & x_{31}x_{32} & \cdots & x_{3,k-1}x_{3,k} \\ \vdots & \vdots & & \vdots & \vdots & & \vdots & \vdots & & \vdots \\ 1 & x_{N1}^2 & \cdots & x_{Nk}^2 & x_{N1} & \cdots & x_{Nk} & x_{N1}x_{N2} & \cdots & x_{N,k-1}x_{N,k} \end{bmatrix}$$

Impose on the x-values the conditions:

(i) $\sum_{j=1}^{N} x_{ji} = 0,\ i = 1, \cdots, k$
(ii) $\sum_{j=1}^{N} x_{ji}^3 = 0,\ i = 1, \cdots, k$
(iii) $\sum_{j=1}^{N} x_{ji}^2 x_{jl} = 0,\ i \neq l$
(iv) $\sum_{j=1}^{N} x_{ji}^2 = b,\ i = 1, \cdots, k$ (5.9.4)
(v) $\sum_{j=1}^{N} x_{ji}^2 x_{jl}^2 = c,\ i \neq l$
(vi) $\sum_{j=1}^{N} x_{ji}^4 = c + d.$

The matrix $(S) = (X)'(X)$ can be written in the form

$$(S) = \begin{bmatrix} (U) & 0 \\ 0 & (B) \end{bmatrix}, \tag{5.9.5}$$

where (U) is the $(k+1) \times (k+1)$ matrix

$$(U) = \begin{bmatrix} N & b\mathbf{1}'_k \\ \mathbf{b1}_k & d\mathbf{I}_k + c\mathbf{J}_k \end{bmatrix} \tag{5.9.6}$$

and (B) is a diagonal matrix of order $\frac{k(k+1)}{2}$

$$(B) = \begin{bmatrix} b & & & & & \\ & \ddots & & & 0 & \\ & & b & & & \\ & & & c & & \\ & 0 & & & \ddots & \\ & & & & & c \end{bmatrix}. \tag{5.9.7}$$

One can verify that

$$(U)^{-1} = \begin{bmatrix} p & q\mathbf{1}'_k \\ q\mathbf{1}_k & tI_k + sJ_k \end{bmatrix}, \tag{5.9.8}$$

where

$$\begin{aligned} p &= \frac{d + kc}{N(d + kc) - b^2k}, \\ q &= -\frac{b}{N(d + kc) - b^2k}, \\ t &= \frac{1}{d} \\ s &= \frac{b^2 - Nc}{d[N(d + kc) - b^2k]}. \end{aligned} \tag{5.9.9}$$

Notice that U is singular if $N(d + kc) = b^2k$. We therefore say that **the design is non-singular** if

$$N \neq \frac{b^2k}{d + kc}.$$

Furthermore, if $N = b^2/c$ then $s = 0$. In this case the design is called **orthogonal**.

Let $\mathbf{x}^{\mathbf{0}'} = (x_1^0, \cdots, x_k^0)$ be a point in the experimental domain, and

$$\boldsymbol{\xi}^{\mathbf{0}\prime} = (1, (x_1^0)^2, \cdots, (x_k^0)^2, x_1^0, \cdots, x_k^0, x_1^0x_2^0, x_1^0x_3^0, \cdots, x_{k-1}^0x_k^0).$$

The variance of the predicted response at $\mathbf{x}^0$ is

$$V\{\hat{Y}(\mathbf{x}^0)\} = \sigma^2 \boldsymbol{\xi}^{\mathbf{0}\prime} \left[\begin{array}{c|cccccc} (U)^{-1} & & & \mathbf{0} & & & \\ \hline & b^{-1} & & & & & \\ & & \ddots & & 0 & & \\ \mathbf{0} & & & b^{-1} & & & \\ & & & & c^{-1} & & \\ & & 0 & & & \ddots & \\ & & & & & & c^{-1} \end{array}\right] \boldsymbol{\xi}^0. \tag{5.9.10}$$

This can be expanded as follows.

$$\begin{aligned} V\{\hat{Y}(\mathbf{x}^0)\} = \sigma^2 \Bigg[& p + \frac{1}{b}\sum_{i=1}^{k}(x_i^0)^2 + (t+s)\sum_{i=1}^{k}(x_i^0)^4 \\ & + \frac{1}{c}\sum\sum_{h<j}(x_h^0)^2(x_j^0)^2 + 2b\sum_{i=1}^{k}(x_i^0)^2 \\ & + 2s\sum\sum_{h<j}(x_h^0)^2(x_j^0)^2\Bigg] \qquad (5.9.11) \\ = \sigma^2 \Bigg[& p + \rho^2\left(2b + \frac{1}{b}\right) + (t+s)\sum_{i=1}^{k}(x_i^0)^4 \\ & + 2\left(s + \frac{1}{2c}\right)\sum\sum_{h<j}(x_n^0)^2(x_j^0)^2\Bigg], \end{aligned}$$

where $\rho^2 = \sum_{i=1}^{k}(x_i^0)^2$. Notice that

$$\rho^4 = \left(\sum_{i=1}^{k}(x_i^0)^2\right)^2 = \sum_{i=1}^{k}(x_i^0)^4 + 2\sum\sum_{h<j}(x_h^0)^2(x_j^0)^2.$$

Thus, if $d = 2c$ then $t + s = s + \frac{1}{2c}$ and

$$V\{\hat{Y}(\mathbf{x}^0)\} = \sigma^2\left[p + \rho^2\left(2b + \frac{1}{b}\right) + (t+s)\rho^4\right]. \tag{5.9.12}$$

Such a design ($d = 2c$) is called **rotatable**, since $V\{\hat{Y}(\mathbf{x}^0)\}$ is constant for all points $\mathbf{x}^0$ on the circumference of a circle of radius ρ, centered at the origin.

5.9.2 *Some Specific Second Order Designs*

5.9.2.1 3^k-Designs

Consider a factorial design of k factors, each one at three levels $-1, 0, 1$. In this case the number of points is $N = 3^k$. Obviously $\sum_{j=1}^{3^k} x_{ji} = 0$ for all $i = 1, \cdots, k$. Also $\sum_{j=1}^{3} x_{ji}^3 = 0$ and $\sum_{j=1}^{3^k} x_{ji}^2 x_{jk} = 0$, $i \neq k$.

$$\begin{aligned} b &= \sum_{j=1}^{3^k} x_{ji}^2 = \frac{2}{3} 3^k = 2 \cdot 3^{k-1}. \\ c &= \sum_{j=1}^{3^k} x_{ji}^2 x_{jl}^2 = \frac{2}{3} b = 4 \cdot 3^{k-2}. \\ c + d &= b. \end{aligned} \tag{5.9.13}$$

Hence

$$d = 2 \cdot 3^{k-1} - 4 \cdot 3^{k-2} = 2 \cdot 3^{k-2}. \tag{5.9.14}$$

$b^2 = 4 \cdot 3^{2k-2}$ and $N \cdot c = 3^k \cdot 4 \cdot 3^{k-2} = 4 \cdot 3^{2k-2}$. Thus, $Nc = b^2$. The design is orthogonal. However, $d \neq 2 \cdot c$. Thus, the design is not rotatable.

5.9.2.2 Central Composite Designs

A Central Composite Design is one in which we start with $n_c = 2^k$ points of a factorial design, in which each factor is at levels -1 and $+1$. To these points we add $n_a = 2k$ axial points which are at a fixed distance α from the origin. These are the points

$$(\pm\alpha, 0, \cdots, 0), (0, \pm\alpha, 0, \cdots, 0), \cdots, (0, 0, \cdots, 0, \pm\alpha).$$

Finally, put n_0 points at the origin. These n_0 observations yield an estimate of the variance σ^2. Thus, the total number of points is $N = 2^k + 2k + n_0$. In such a design,

$$\begin{aligned} b &= 2^k + 2\alpha^2, \\ c &= 2^k, \\ c + d &= 2^k + 2\alpha^4, \quad \text{or} \\ d &= 2\alpha^4. \end{aligned} \tag{5.9.15}$$

The rotatability condition is $d = 2c$. Thus, the design is rotatable if

$$\alpha^4 = 2^k \quad \text{or} \quad \alpha = 2^{k/4}. \tag{5.9.16}$$

For this reason, in central composite designs, with $k = 2$ factors we use $\alpha = \sqrt{2} = 1.414$. For $k = 3$ factors we use $\alpha = 2^{3/4} = 1.6818$. For rotatability and orthogonality, the following should be satisfied

$$n_0 + 2^k = \frac{4\alpha^2(2^k + \alpha^2)}{2^k}, \tag{5.9.17}$$

and since $\alpha^2 = 2^{k/2}$ (for rotatability)

$$n_0 = 4(2^{k/2} + 1) - 2^k. \tag{5.9.18}$$

Thus, if $k = 2$, the number of points at the origin is $n_0 = 8$. For $k = 4$ we need $n_0 = 4$ points at the origin. For $k = 3$ there is no rotatability, since $4(2^{3/2}+1)-8 = 7.313$.

Example 5.12 In Example 5.7 the piston simulation experiment was considered. We tested there, via a 3^2 experiment, the effects of piston surface area (factor s) and the spring coefficient (factor k). It was found that the effects of the piston surface area were significant, while the spring coefficient had no significant effect on the cycle time. We will conduct now a Central Composite Design of four factors, in order to explore the response surface. The factors chosen are: Piston surface area (factor s); Initial gas volume (factor $v0$); spring coefficient (factor k) and filling gas temperature (factor $t0$).

The experiment is performed with the piston simulator designed to attain both orthogonality and rotatability. Since $k = 4$, we have $\alpha = 2$ and $n_0 = 4$. The number of replications is $n_r = 50$. We can create the design using the function *central_composite* from the `mistat` package (Table 5.30).

```
factors = {
  's': [0.01, 0.015],
  'v0': [0.00625, 0.00875],
  'k': [2000, 4000],
  't0': [345, 355],
}
Design = doe.central_composite(factors, alpha='r', center=[4, 4])
```

Table 5.30 Factors and level in piston simulator experiment

Factor	Code	Levels				
Piston surface area s	x_1	0.0075	0.01	0.0125	0.015	0.0175
Initial gas volume v_0	x_2	0.0050	0.00625	0.0075	0.00875	0.0100
Spring coefficient k	x_3	1000	2000	3000	4000	5000
Filling gas temperature t_0	x_4	340	345	350	355	360
	Code	−2	−1	0	1	2

Using the Design, run the piston simulation and aggregate the results by group.

```
simulator = mistat.PistonSimulator(**Design, m=60, p0=110_000, t=296,
                                   n_replicate=50, seed=2)
result = simulator.simulate()

# calculate mean and std of response by group
result = result.groupby(by='group')
result = result.agg({'s': 'mean', 'v0': 'mean', 'k': 'mean',
                     't0': 'mean', 'seconds':['mean','std']})
result.columns = ['s', 'v0', 'k', 't0', 'Ymean', 'Ystd']
```

We also define a number of variables that will help transforming between factor and code co-ordinates.

```
# transformation between factors and code levels
factor2x = {factor: f'x{i}' for i, factor in enumerate(factors, 1)}
x2factor = {f'x{i}': factor for i, factor in enumerate(factors, 1)}
center = {factor: 0.5 * (max(values) + min(values))
          for factor, values in factors.items()}
unit = {factor: 0.5 * (max(values) - min(values))
        for factor, values in factors.items()}

# define helper function to convert code co-ordinates to factor co-ordinates
def toFactor(code, codeValue):
    ''' convert code to factor co-ordinates '''
    factor = x2factor[code]
    return center[factor] + codeValue * unit[factor]

# add code levels to table
for c in factors:
    result[factor2x[c]] = (result[c] - center[c]) / unit[c]
```

The experimental design and response outcomes are presented in Table 5.31. Figure 5.10 presents the main effects plot for the above four factors. The piston surface area ($x1$) and the initial gas volume ($x2$) have similar main effects. The cycle time average is monotonically changing with increasing levels of these two factors. It decreases for the piston surface area and changes in the opposite direction for the initial gas volume.

In the following table we present the results of regression analysis of the mean cycle time $\bar{Y}$ on 14 predictors x_1^2, x_2^2, x_3^2, x_4^2, x_1, x_2, x_3, x_4, x_1x_2, x_1x_3, x_1x_4, x_2x_3, x_2x_4, x_3x_4, where x_1 corresponds to factor s, x_2 to factor v_0, x_3 to factor k and x_4 to factor t_0. The result of the regression analysis is summarized in Table 5.32. The contour lines for the mean cycle time, corresponding to $x_2 = x_4 = 0$, are shown in Fig. 5.11.

We see in Table 5.32 that only factor s (x_1, piston surface area) has a significant quadratic effect. Factor s (x_1), v_0 (x_2), and k (x_3) have significant linear effects. The interaction effect of s with k ($x_1 : x_3$) will also be added. Thus, the response surface can be approximated with a reduced model based on x_1, x_2, x_3, x_1x_2, x_1x_3 and x_1^2. regression analysis of the reduced model is shown in Table 5.32. ■

Table 5.31 The central composite design and the mean and standard deviations of cycle time

Group	x1	x2	x3	x4	Ymean	Ystd
1	−1	−1	−1	−1	0.056	0.0078
2	0	−1	−1	−1	0.037	0.0045
3	−1	1	−1	−1	0.083	0.0108
4	0	1	−1	−1	0.054	0.0052
5	−1	−1	1	−1	0.066	0.0099
6	0	−1	1	−1	0.041	0.0043
7	−1	1	1	−1	0.103	0.0162
8	0	1	1	−1	0.062	0.0060
9	−1	−1	−1	1	0.052	0.0059
10	0	−1	−1	1	0.037	0.0044
11	−1	1	−1	1	0.084	0.0102
12	0	1	−1	1	0.055	0.0057
13	−1	−1	1	1	0.067	0.0116
14	0	−1	1	1	0.043	0.0050
15	−1	1	1	1	0.103	0.0141
16	0	1	1	1	0.064	0.0076
17	0	0	0	0	0.060	0.0079
18	0	0	0	0	0.061	0.0078
19	0	0	0	0	0.060	0.0066
20	0	0	0	0	0.059	0.0064
21	−2	0	0	0	0.107	0.0189
22	1	0	0	0	0.043	0.0030
23	0	−2	0	0	0.036	0.0052
24	0	2	0	0	0.083	0.0107
25	0	0	−2	0	0.050	0.0045
26	0	0	2	0	0.068	0.0081
27	0	0	0	−2	0.060	0.0080
28	0	0	0	2	0.061	0.0077
29	0	0	0	0	0.059	0.0074
30	0	0	0	0	0.059	0.0079
31	0	0	0	0	0.060	0.0081
32	0	0	0	0	0.061	0.0079

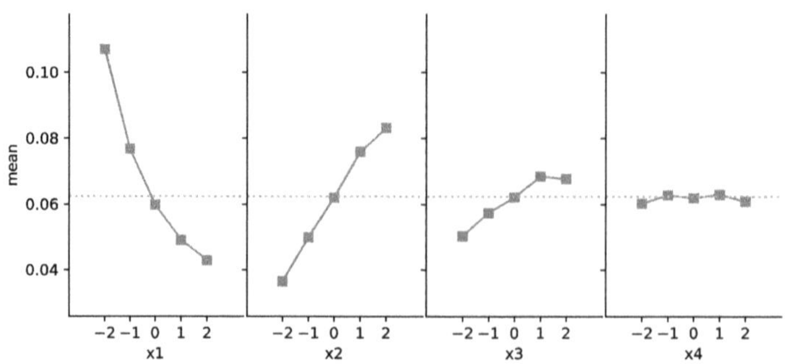

Fig. 5.10 Main effects plot

Table 5.32 Python regression analysis of the full and reduced model

```
formula = ('Ymean ~ (x1+x2+x3+x4)**2 + ' +
           'I(x1**2) + I(x2**2) + I(x3**2) + I(x4**2)')
model = smf.ols(formula, data=result).fit()
print(model.summary2())
```

```
                Results: Ordinary least squares
==================================================================
Model:              OLS              Adj. R-squared:     0.989
Dependent Variable: Ymean            AIC:                -301.2069
Date:               2022-12-02 21:28 BIC:                -279.2208
No. Observations:   32               Log-Likelihood:     165.60
Df Model:           14               F-statistic:        208.0
Df Residuals:       17               Prob (F-statistic): 3.71e-16
R-squared:          0.994            Scale:              3.5252e-06
-------------------------------------------------------------------
              Coef.   Std.Err.    t       P>|t|    [0.025   0.975]
-------------------------------------------------------------------
Intercept     0.0599   0.0007   90.2640  0.0000   0.0585   0.0613
x1           -0.0146   0.0004  -38.1172  0.0000  -0.0154  -0.0138
x2            0.0126   0.0004   32.8412  0.0000   0.0118   0.0134
x3            0.0052   0.0004   13.4893  0.0000   0.0044   0.0060
x4            0.0001   0.0004    0.3034  0.7653  -0.0007   0.0009
x1:x2        -0.0033   0.0005   -7.0326  0.0000  -0.0043  -0.0023
x1:x3        -0.0023   0.0005   -4.8492  0.0002  -0.0033  -0.0013
x1:x4         0.0003   0.0005    0.6054  0.5529  -0.0007   0.0013
x2:x3         0.0013   0.0005    2.6971  0.0153   0.0003   0.0023
x2:x4         0.0003   0.0005    0.6170  0.5454  -0.0007   0.0013
x3:x4         0.0004   0.0005    0.8523  0.4059  -0.0006   0.0014
I(x1 ** 2)    0.0037   0.0003   10.5681  0.0000   0.0029   0.0044
I(x2 ** 2)   -0.0001   0.0003   -0.3867  0.7038  -0.0009   0.0006
I(x3 ** 2)   -0.0003   0.0003   -0.9792  0.3412  -0.0011   0.0004
I(x4 ** 2)    0.0001   0.0003    0.1551  0.8785  -0.0007   0.0008
------------------------------------------------------------------
Omnibus:               0.162        Durbin-Watson:          3.015
Prob(Omnibus):         0.922        Jarque-Bera (JB):       0.093
Skew:                  0.108        Prob(JB):               0.954
Kurtosis:              2.849        Condition No.:          4
==================================================================
```

```
formula = ('Ymean ~ x1 + x2 + x3 + x1:x3 + x1:x2 + I(x1**2)')
reduced_model = smf.ols(formula, data=result).fit()
print(reduced_model.summary2())
```

```
                Results: Ordinary least squares
==================================================================
Model:              OLS              Adj. R-squared:     0.989
Dependent Variable: Ymean            AIC:                -302.4490
Date:               2022-12-02 21:28 BIC:                -292.1888
No. Observations:   32               Log-Likelihood:     158.22
Df Model:           6                F-statistic:        448.4
Df Residuals:       25               Prob (F-statistic): 3.42e-24
R-squared:          0.991            Scale:              3.8018e-06
-------------------------------------------------------------------
              Coef.   Std.Err.    t       P>|t|    [0.025   0.975]
-------------------------------------------------------------------
Intercept     0.0596   0.0004  136.6637  0.0000   0.0587   0.0605
x1           -0.0146   0.0004  -36.7047  0.0000  -0.0154  -0.0138
x2            0.0126   0.0004   31.6243  0.0000   0.0118   0.0134
x3            0.0052   0.0004   12.9895  0.0000   0.0044   0.0060
x1:x3        -0.0023   0.0005   -4.6695  0.0001  -0.0033  -0.0013
x1:x2        -0.0033   0.0005   -6.7720  0.0000  -0.0043  -0.0023
I(x1 ** 2)    0.0037   0.0004   10.3340  0.0000   0.0029   0.0044
------------------------------------------------------------------
Omnibus:              0.768         Durbin-Watson:          2.210
Prob(Omnibus):        0.681         Jarque-Bera (JB):       0.817
Skew:                 -0.229        Prob(JB):               0.665
Kurtosis:             2.365         Condition No.:          2
==================================================================
```

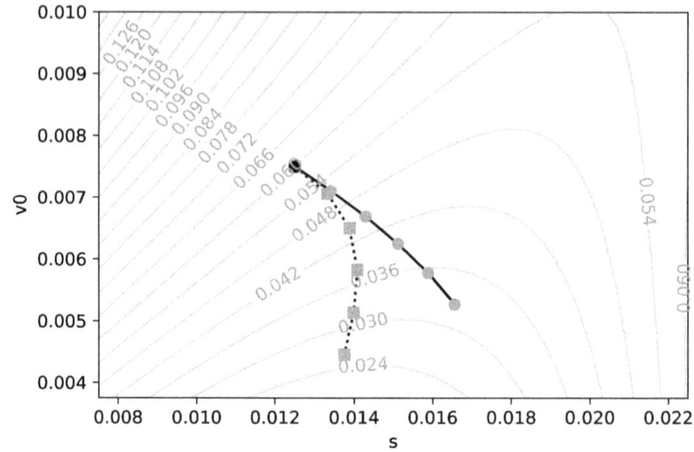

Fig. 5.11 Contour lines of the response surface setting $x_2 = x_4 = 0$. Paths show minimization of the function using steepest descent (circles) and constrained optimization (squares)

5.9.3 Approaching the Region of the Optimal Yield

Very often, the purpose for fitting a response surface is to locate the levels of the factors, which yield optimal results.

Initially one might be far from the optimal regions. A series of small experiments may be performed, in order to move toward the optimal region. Thus, we start with simple first order experiments, like 2^k factorial, and fit to the results a linear model of the form

$$\hat{Y} = b_0 + b_1 x_1 + \cdots + b_k x_k.$$

We wish to determine now a new point, $\boldsymbol{\xi}^*$ say, whose distance from the center of the 1st stage experiment (say 0) is R, and with maximal (or minimal) predicted yield. The predicted yield at $\boldsymbol{\xi}^*$ is

$$\hat{y}^* = b_0 + \sum_{i=1}^{k} b_i \xi_i^*.$$

To find $\boldsymbol{\xi}^*$ we differentiate the Lagrangian

$$L = b_0 + \sum_{i=1}^{k} b_i \xi_i^* + \lambda \left(R^2 - \sum_{i=1}^{k} (\xi_i^*)^2 \right)$$

with respect to ξ_i^* $(i = 1, \cdots, k)$ and λ. The solution is

$$\xi_i^* = R\frac{b_i}{\sqrt{\sum_{i=1}^k b_i^2}}, \qquad i = 1, \cdots, k.$$

The direction of the **steepest accent** (descent) is in the direction of the normal (perpendicular) to the contours of equal response.

At the second stage we perform experiments at a few points along the direction of the steepest ascent (at $R_1, R_2, \cdots$) until there is no further increase in the mean yield. We then enter the third stage, at which we perform a second order design, centered at a new region, where the optimal conditions seem to prevail.

Example 5.13 Continuing with the full model of the previous example, we iteratively minimize the cycle time using steepest descent. At each iteration, we determining the gradient at the current position and making a step along its direction to get a new position. The `mistat` package provides the class *ResponseSurfaceMethod* that calculates the gradient using the information from a second order model.

```
# calculate gradient and create steps along gradient to descend
codes = ['x1', 'x2', 'x3', 'x4']
rsm = mistat.ResponseSurfaceMethod(model, codes)
distance = np.arange(0, 2.6, 0.5)
direction = {code: np.zeros(len(distance)) for code in codes}
x = pd.Series(np.zeros(4), index=codes)
for step in range(len(distance)):
    for code in codes:
        direction[code][step] = x[code]
    gradient = rsm.gradient(x)
    x = x - 0.5 * gradient
```

Alternatively, we can use the *constrainedOptimization* method which in addition to steepest descent, makes adjustments at each step to further optimize the function at the specified distance.

```
path = rsm.constrainedOptimization((0, 0, 0, 0), distances=(0.5, 1, 1.5, 2, 2.5),
                                   maximize=False)
steps = pd.DataFrame({x2factor[code]: toFactor(code, path[code])
                      for code in rsm.codes})
```

Table 5.33 gives the steps for steepest descent in factor co-ordinates and the predicted cycle time ($yhat$). The paths for steepest descent and constrained optimization are shown in Fig. 5.11. The additional optimization at each step with constrained optimization leads to faster minimization. ■

5.9.4 Canonical Representation

The quadratic response function

Table 5.33 Path of steepest descent

Distance	x1	x2	x3	x4	s	v0	k	t0	yhat
0.0	0.00	0.00	0.00	0.00	0.0125	0.0075	3000	350	0.060
0.5	0.37	−0.32	−0.13	−0.00	0.0134	0.0071	2870	349	0.051
1.0	0.72	−0.65	−0.26	−0.01	0.0143	0.0067	2742	349	0.044
1.5	1.05	−1.00	−0.38	−0.01	0.0151	0.0062	2616	349	0.039
2.0	1.35	−1.38	−0.50	−0.01	0.0159	0.0058	2495	349	0.035
2.5	1.62	−1.78	−0.62	−0.01	0.0166	0.0053	2379	349	0.033

$$\hat{Y} = b_0 + \sum_{i=1}^{k} b_i x_i + \sum_{i=1}^{k} b_{ii} x_i^2 + 2 \sum\sum_{i<j} b_{ij} x_i x_j \tag{5.9.19}$$

can be written in the matrix form

$$\hat{Y} = b_0 + \mathbf{b}'\mathbf{x} + \mathbf{x}'\mathbf{B}\mathbf{x}, \tag{5.9.20}$$

where $\mathbf{x}' = (x_1, \cdots, x_k)$, $\mathbf{b}' = (b_1, \cdots, b_k)$ and

$$\mathbf{B} = \begin{bmatrix} b_{11} & b_{12} & \cdots & b_{1k} \\ b_{12} & \ddots & & \vdots \\ \vdots & & \ddots & \vdots \\ b_{1k} & \cdots & \cdots & b_{kk} \end{bmatrix}.$$

Let $\nabla\hat{Y}$ be the gradient of $\hat{Y}$, i.e.,

$$\nabla\hat{Y} = \frac{\partial}{\partial \mathbf{x}}\hat{Y} = \mathbf{b} + 2B\mathbf{x}.$$

Let $\mathbf{x}^0$ be a point at which the gradient is zero, namely

$$\mathbf{x}^0 = -\frac{1}{2}\mathbf{B}^{-1}\mathbf{b}, \tag{5.9.21}$$

assuming that the matrix $\mathbf{B}$ is non-singular. Making the transformation (change of origin to $\mathbf{x}^0$) $\mathbf{z} = \mathbf{x} - \mathbf{x}^0$, we obtain

$$\begin{aligned} \hat{Y} &= b_0 + (\mathbf{x}^0 + \mathbf{z})'\mathbf{b} + (\mathbf{x}^0 + \mathbf{z})'\mathbf{B}(\mathbf{x} + \mathbf{z}) \\ &= \hat{Y}_0 + \mathbf{z}'\mathbf{B}\mathbf{z}, \end{aligned} \tag{5.9.22}$$

where $\hat{Y}_0 = b_0 + \mathbf{b}'\mathbf{x}^0$.

The matrix B is real symmetric. Thus, there exists an orthogonal matrix $\mathbf{H}$, which consists of the normalized eigenvectors of B, such that

$$\mathbf{HBH}' = \begin{pmatrix} \lambda_1 & & \\ 0 & \ddots & 0 \\ & & \lambda_k \end{pmatrix},$$

where λ_i $(i = 1, \cdots, k)$ are the eigenvalues of B. We make now a new transformation (rotation), namely

$$\mathbf{w} = \mathbf{HZ}.$$

Since H is orthogonal, $\mathbf{z} = \mathbf{H}'\mathbf{w}$ and

$$\begin{aligned} \mathbf{z}'\mathbf{Bz} &= \mathbf{w}'\mathbf{HBH}'\mathbf{w} \\ &= \sum_{i=1}^{k} \lambda_i w_i^2. \end{aligned}$$

In these new co-ordinates,

$$\hat{Y} = \hat{Y}_0 + \sum_{i=1}^{k} \lambda_i w_i^2. \tag{5.9.23}$$

This representation of the quadratic surface is called the **canonical form**. We see immediately that if $\lambda_i > 0$ for all $i = 1, \cdots, k$, then $\hat{Y}_0$ is a point of **minimum**. If $\lambda_i < 0$ for all $i = 1, \cdots, k$ then $\hat{Y}_0$ is a **maximum**. If some eigenvalues are positive and some are negative, then $\hat{Y}_0$ is a **saddle point**.

The following examples of second order equations are taken from Box et al. (2005). They are visualized in Fig. 5.12 using contour lines.

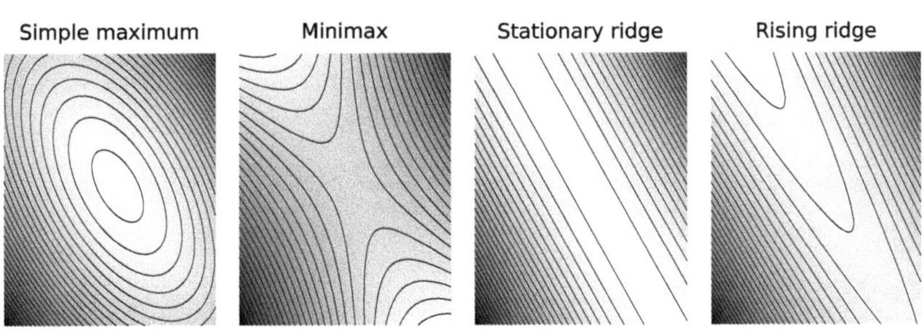

Fig. 5.12 Contour lines of different response surfaces

1. Simple maximum:

$$\hat{Y} = 83.57 + 9.39x_1 + 7.12x_2 - 7.44x_1^2 - 3.71x_2^2 - 5.80x_1x_2$$
$$= 87.69 - 902w_1^2 - 2.13w_2^2.$$

2. Minimax:

$$\hat{Y} = 84.29 + 11.06x_1 + 4.05x_2 - 6.46x_1^2 - 0.43x_2^2 - 9.38x_1x_2$$
$$= 87.69 - 9.02w_1^2 + 2.13w_2^2.$$

3. Stationary ridge:

$$\hat{Y} = 83.93 + 10.23x_1 + 5.59x_2 - 6.95x_1^2 - 2.07x_2^2 - 7.59x_1x_2$$
$$= 87.69 - 9.02w_1^2 + 0.00w_2^2.$$

4. Rising ridge:

$$\hat{Y} = 82.71 + 8.80x_1 + 8.19x_2 - 6.95x_1^2 - 2.07x_2^2 - 7.59x_1x_2$$
$$= 87.69 - 9.02w_1^2 + 2.97w_2.$$

Example 5.14 Continuing with the model from Example 5.13, we identify the stationary point using the *ResponseSurfaceMethod*.

```
codes = ['x1', 'x2', 'x3', 'x4']
rsm = mistat.ResponseSurfaceMethod(model, codes)
stationary = rsm.stationary_point()

factor_stationary = pd.Series({x2factor[code]: toFactor(code, d)
                               for code, d in stationary.items()})
factor_stationary
```

```
s           0.018796
v0          0.009571
k        1451.172868
t0        317.713341
dtype: float64
```

Next, starting from the stationary point, we minimize the function in steps using constraint optimization. The path can be seen in Fig. 5.13.

```
path = rsm.constrainedOptimization(rsm.stationary_point(), maximize=False,
                                   reverse=True)
steps = pd.DataFrame({x2factor[code]: toFactor(code, path[code])
                      for code in rsm.codes})
steps.head()
```

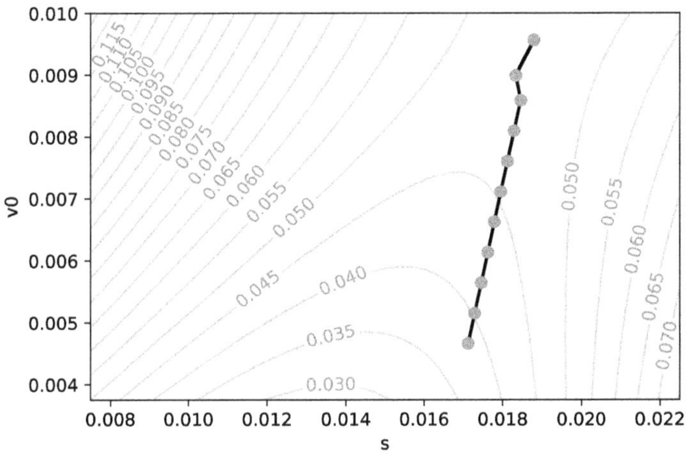

Fig. 5.13 Minimizing the function starting from the stationary point

	s	v0	k	t0
0	0.018796	0.009571	1451.172868	317.713341
1	0.018337	0.008990	1441.344186	317.749174
2	0.018461	0.008589	2055.556297	317.775331
3	0.018293	0.008099	2357.674709	317.806241
4	0.018126	0.007608	2659.852584	317.837251

■

5.10 Evaluating Designed Experiments

The classic approach to the design of experiments (DoE) introduced in this chapter includes orthogonal arrays with mixed level designs including full, fractional and central composite designs (see also Box et al. 2005; Nguyen and Pham 2016). With the availability of enhanced computational power, industrial statistics has seen major improvements in experimental design methodology including computer based experiments presented in Chap. 7. These developments permit to design optimal designs that account for constraints in the design space, for blocking and split plots to accommodate hard to change factors and for designing experiments with various optimality properties. The pioneers of optimal design include Kiefer (1959) who solved an approximate optimal design problem that consists in determining a probability measure over the design space, Wynn (1972) proposed to compute optimal designs with an exchange-based method and Zacks (1973) introduced optimal sequential designs.

Optimal designs are constructed using several approaches. Their optimality is determined by different criteria that lead to different solutions. The **D-optimality** criterion minimizes the determinant of the covariance matrix of the model coefficient estimates, the information matrix $X'X$ of the design. D-optimality aims at deriving precise estimates of effects, i.e., main effects, quadratic effects and interactions. This assumes a known prespecified model and is fully determined by the experimental design before the experiment is conducted. D-optimal designs are used in experiments conducted to test for significance of effects in order to best interpret the fitted model. Their main application is in designs aimed at distinguishing active from inert factors. A design is **A-optimal** if it minimizes the sum of the variances of the regression coefficients, the trace of the inverse of the information matrix. This is another approach to obtain precise estimates of the effects. **I-optimal** designs minimize the average variance of prediction over the design space. If the primary experimental goal is to predict a response or determine regions in the design space where the response falls within an acceptable range, the I-optimality criterion is more appropriate than the D-optimality criterion. In these cases, precise prediction of the response takes precedence over precise estimation of the parameters. A related approach is **G-optimal** designs, which minimize the maximum prediction variance over the design region. The maximum entry in the diagonal of the hat matrix $X^{-1}(X'X)^{-1}X$. These designs are calculated using Monte Carlo experiments of the design space. The minimum G-aberration criterion is useful when selecting good, regular two-level fractional factorial designs and is used to discriminate among regular fractional factorial designs with the same resolution. Minimum aberration compares the frequency of aliases of regular designs at different levels. Regular designs with the smallest frequency of worst aliases are considered the best. The minimum G-aberration criterion can also handle irregular design spaces (Tang and Deng 1999; Goos 2011).

When considering what method to use to generate an experimental design, we are reminded that experiments are conducted to produce information. This requires a managed transition from problem elicitation to data collection, data analysis, derivation and communication of findings. Eventually, this roadmap produces information (Kenett and Shmueli 2016). Experimental designs are used to generate the dataset used in a study used to derive information. Information quality (InfoQ) is different from data quality and analysis quality. A key requirement for determining InfoQ is the understanding the study goal and whether it is explanatory, predictive, or descriptive. An explanatory goal can be based on causal hypotheses or can seek causal answers. A predictive goal predicts future or new individual observations. A descriptive goal quantifies an observed effect using a statistical or other approximation. In designing an experiment, the study goal should be accounted for.

The definition of InfoQ consists of the utility (U) from the application of a statistical or data analytic model (f) to a dataset (X) given the research goal (g). The assessment of InfoQ is performed by considering eight dimensions:

1. Data resolution
2. Data structure
3. Data integration
4. Temporal relevance
5. Chronology of data and goal

6. Generalizability
7. Operationalization
8. Communication

These eight dimensions, introduced in Chap. 1, should be considered when designing an experiment. As an example, consider the piston simulator introduced in Chap. 2. The performance of the piston is measured by the cycle time of a full revolution, in seconds. The seven factors that potentially affect cycle time are:

X1 : Piston weight m (30–60 Kg)
X2 : Piston surface area s (0.005–0.2 m^2)
X3 : Initial gas volume $v0$ (0.002–0.01 m^3)
X4 : Spring coefficient k (1000–5000 N/m)
X5 : Atmospheric pressure $p0$ (90,000–110,000 N/m^2)
X6 : Ambient temperature t (290–296 °K)
X7 : Gas temperature $t0$ (340–360 °K)

The levels of these factors (shown in parentheses) represent extremes on the operating range that cannot be exceeded. In designing experiments to learn the performance of the piston, we have a wide range of options as presented in this chapter and in Chaps. 6 and 7. To compare these experimental set ups we can invoke a set of tools including:

- Cost (size of the experiment)
- Correlations between estimates of main effects and interactions
- Prediction precision throughout design space (fraction of design space plot)
- Ability to assess curvature from quadratic terms
- Prediction variance
- Power

These criteria provide a broad perspective of experimental design capabilities. The levels of these factors (shown in parentheses) represent extremes on the operating range that cannot be exceeded without affecting the smooth operation of the engine. When designing experiments to investigate the performance of the piston, one can consider various questions to help set up a goal. For example:

- Do you want to accurately estimate the effect of the seven factors to derive engineering insights on the system's design?
- Do you want a good predictive model of piston performance to design an optimal control system?
- Do you want to compare different models of the piston to assess the effect of engineering modifications?
- What can you achieve with an experimental budget of 14 experimental runs? What about 16 runs? Is there a difference?

Specifically, we compare here three designs of experiments with the piston simulator. These include experimental arrays with 35, 80, and 169 experimental runs.

These designs are available as **CUSTOMDESIGN_35**, **CUSTOMDESIGN_80**, and **CUSTOMDESIGN_169**.

```
design35 = mistat.load_data('CUSTOMDESIGN_35')
design80 = mistat.load_data('CUSTOMDESIGN_80')
design169 = mistat.load_data('CUSTOMDESIGN_169')
```

The first design with 35 runs was designed using a coordinate exchange algorithm with seven factors at two levels each. The second and third designs are central composite designs with 80 and 169 runs and seven factors at three levels and five levels, respectively. Table 5.34 shows the first design.

The correlations between estimates of main effects and interactions are determined by the experimental design. Figure 5.14 shows the correlation plots of the three designs with the seven factors listed in Table 5.34. The correlation plots show correlations between estimates of main effects and interactions. A correlation of one indicates full aliasing so that these paired estimates are indistinguishable. Independence of estimates is indicated by a correlation of zero. For the two level design with 35 runs we see that the main effects are estimated without confounding. The 80 runs central composite designs has confounded quadratic effects, the 169 run experiments has no confounding and all main effects, two-way interactions and quadratic effects are estimable.

The fraction of design space (FDS) plot shows the proportion of the design space for which the scaled prediction variance (SPV) falls below a specific value. FDS plots are constructed by sampling n values from throughout the design space and obtaining all corresponding SPVs, which are then ordered and plotted against the quantiles (Zahran et al. 2003). The idea is the closer the FDS for an SPV is to the minimum, the better the design. In this example, a high FDS produces a low prediction variance from models created after collecting data. Moreover, the flatter the line, the more stable the SPV distribution for that design. In the example in Fig. 5.15, the increase of experimental runs from 35 to 80 and to 169 clearly reduces the SPV.

The SPV is significantly smaller for the 169 runs design which has no confounding effects. The 80 runs design can estimate, without confounding main effects, all two-way interactions and some quadratic terms. For screening main effects, the 35 runs design suffices. Experimental design evaluation is based on different criteria, including experimental size, correlation plots and Fraction of Design Space plots. In this section we presented these criteria with examples.

5.11 Chapter Highlights

The main concepts and definitions introduced in this chapter include:

- Response variable
- Controllable factor

Table 5.34 The experimental arrays with 35 runs for the piston simulator

m	s	v0	k	p0	t0	t
30	0.020	0.010	1000	0.0009	360	296
60	0.020	0.002	1000	0.0011	340	296
30	0.020	0.010	5000	0.0011	360	290
30	0.020	0.010	5000	0.0009	360	296
30	0.005	0.002	1000	0.0009	340	290
60	0.005	0.010	5000	0.0009	340	296
30	0.005	0.002	1000	0.0009	360	296
60	0.020	0.002	1000	0.0011	360	290
30	0.020	0.010	1000	0.0009	360	296
60	0.005	0.010	5000	0.0009	360	290
30	0.005	0.010	1000	0.0011	340	296
60	0.005	0.010	1000	0.0011	340	296
60	0.005	0.010	5000	0.0009	360	290
60	0.020	0.002	1000	0.0009	360	290
30	0.005	0.002	5000	0.0011	340	290
60	0.020	0.002	1000	0.0011	340	296
30	0.005	0.002	5000	0.0011	340	290
30	0.020	0.010	1000	0.0009	340	290
30	0.005	0.002	5000	0.0011	360	296
30	0.005	0.002	1000	0.0009	360	296
60	0.005	0.002	5000	0.0009	360	290
30	0.020	0.010	1000	0.0009	340	290
60	0.005	0.010	1000	0.0011	360	290
60	0.005	0.010	1000	0.0011	360	290
30	0.005	0.002	1000	0.0009	340	290
60	0.020	0.002	5000	0.0009	340	290
30	0.020	0.002	5000	0.0011	360	296
60	0.005	0.010	1000	0.0011	340	296
60	0.020	0.002	5000	0.0009	340	296
60	0.020	0.002	1000	0.0011	360	290
30	0.005	0.002	5000	0.0011	360	296
60	0.005	0.010	5000	0.0009	340	296
60	0.020	0.010	5000	0.0011	360	296
30	0.020	0.010	5000	0.0011	340	290
30	0.020	0.010	5000	0.0011	340	290

- Factor level
- Statistical model
- Experimental array
- Blocking
- Randomization
- Block designs
- Main effects

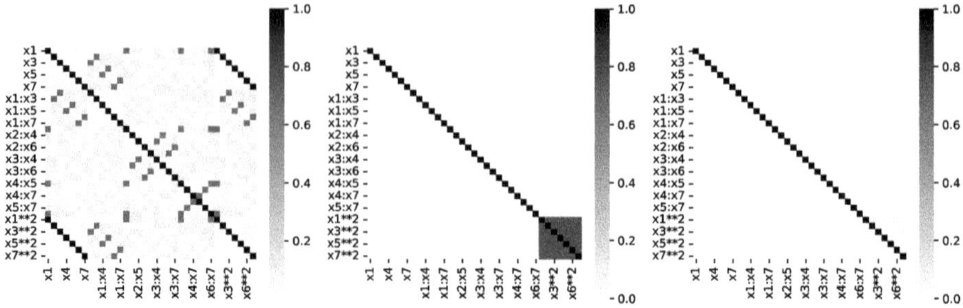

Fig. 5.14 Correlation plots of experimental arrays with 35, 80, and 169 experimental runs

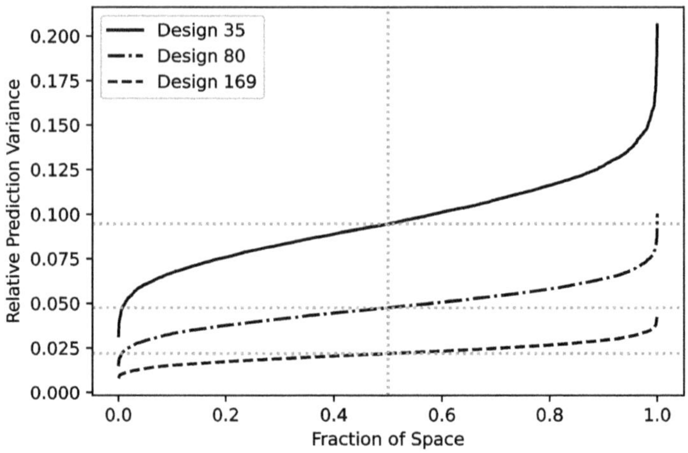

Fig. 5.15 Fraction of design space plot for the three designs

- Interactions
- Analysis of variance
- Latin squares
- Factorial designs
- Fractional factorial designs
- Experimental design evaluation
- Experimental design optimality
- Fraction of design space
- Response surfaces
- D optimality
- I optimality
- Path of steepest ascent

5.12 Exercises

Exercise 5.1 Describe a production process familiar to you, like baking of cakes, or manufacturing concrete. List the pertinent variables. What is (are) the response variable(s)? Classify the variables which affect the response to noise variables and control variables. How many levels would you consider for each variable?

Exercise 5.2 Different types of adhesives are used in a lamination process, in manufacturing a computer card. The card is tested for bond strength. In addition to the type of adhesive, a factor which might influence the bond strength is the curing pressure (currently at 200 psi). Follow the basic steps of experimental design to set a possible experiment for testing the effects of adhesives and curing pressure on the bond strength.

Exercise 5.3 Provide an example where blocking can reduce the variability of a product.

Exercise 5.4 Three factors A, B, C are tested in a given experiment, designed to assess their effects on the response variable. Each factor is tested at 3 levels. List all the main effects and interactions.

Exercise 5.5 Let x_1, x_2 be two quantitative factors and Y a response variable. A regression model $Y = \beta_0 + \beta_1 x_1 + \beta_2 x_2 + \beta_{12} x_1 x_2 + e$ is fitted to the data. Explain why β_{12} can be used as an interaction parameter.

Exercise 5.6 Consider the ISC values for times t_1, t_2 and t_3 in dataset **SOCELL.csv**. Make a paired comparison for testing whether the mean ISC in time t_2 is different from that in time t_1, by using a t-test.

Exercise 5.7 Use *permutation_test* from `scipy` to perform a randomization test for the differences in the ISC values of the solar cells in times t_2 and t_3 (dataset **SOCELL.csv**).

Exercise 5.8 Box et al. (2005) give the results of four treatments A, B, C, D in penicillin manufacturing in five different blends (blocks) shown in Table 5.35.

Perform an ANOVA to test whether there are significant differences between the treatments or between the blends.

Table 5.35 Result of four treatments in penicillin manufacturing

	Treatments			
Blends	A	B	C	D
1	89	88	97	94
2	84	77	92	79
3	81	87	87	85
4	87	92	89	84
5	79	81	80	88

Table 5.36 Results of treatments $A, B, C, \cdots, H$ for different treatments

Block	Treatments				Block	Treatments			
1	*A*	38	*B*	30	15	*D*	11	*G*	24
2	*C*	50	*D*	27	16	*F*	37	*H*	39
3	*E*	33	*F*	28	17	*A*	23	*F*	40
4	*G*	62	*H*	30	18	*B*	20	*D*	14
5	*A*	37	*C*	25	19	*C*	18	*H*	10
6	*B*	38	*H*	52	20	*E*	22	*G*	52
7	*D*	89	*E*	89	21	*A*	66	*G*	67
8	*F*	27	*G*	75	22	*B*	23	*F*	46
9	*A*	17	*D*	25	23	*C*	22	*E*	28
10	*B*	47	*G*	63	24	*D*	20	*H*	40
11	*C*	32	*F*	39	25	*A*	27	*H*	32
12	*E*	20	*H*	18	26	*B*	10	*E*	40
13	*A*	5	*E*	15	27	*C*	32	*G*	33
14	*B*	45	*C*	38	28	*D*	18	*F*	23

Table 5.37 Compressive strengths of cement for different treatments

	Batches			
Days	1	2	3	4
1	*A*	*B*	*C*	*D*
	312	299	315	290
2	*C*	*A*	*D*	*B*
	295	317	313	300
3	*B*	*D*	*A*	*C*
	295	298	312	315
4	*D*	*C*	*B*	*A*
	313	314	299	300

Exercise 5.9 Eight treatments $A, B, C, \cdots, H$ were tested in a BIBD of 28 blocks, $k = 2$ treatments per block, $r = 7$ and $\lambda = 1$. The results of the experiments are shown in Table 5.36

Make an ANOVA to test the significance of the block effects, treatment effects, If the treatment effects are significant, make multiple comparisons of the treatments.

Exercise 5.10 Four different methods of preparing concrete mixtures A, B, C, D were tested, these methods consisted of two different mixture ratios of cement to water and two blending duration). The four methods (treatments) were blocks in four batches and 4 days, according to a Latin square design. The concrete was poured to cubes and tested for compressive strength [Kg/cm^2] after 7 days of storage in special rooms with 20 °C temperature and 50% relative humidity. The results are in Table 5.37

Are the differences between the strength values of different treatments significant? [Perform the ANOVA.]

Table 5.38 Results of 3^2 factorial experiment with $n = 3$ observations

	A_1	A_2	A_3
B_1	18.3	17.9	19.1
	17.9	17.6	19.0
	18.5	16.2	18.9
B_2	20.5	18.2	22.1
	21.1	19.5	23.5
	20.7	18.9	22.9
B_3	21.5	20.1	22.3
	21.7	19.5	23.5
	21.9	18.9	23.3

Exercise 5.11 Repeat the experiments described in Example 5.7 at the low levels of factors m, v_0, p_0, t, and t_0. Perform the ANOVA for the main effects and interaction of spring coefficient k and piston weight m on the cycle time. Use a marginal interaction plot to visualize both main effects and interaction. Are your results different from those obtained in the example?

Exercise 5.12 For the data from Exercise 5.11 compute the least squares estimates of the main effects on the means and on the standard deviations.

Exercise 5.13 A 2^4 factorial experiment gave the following response values, arranged in standard order: 72, 60, 90, 80, 65, 60, 85, 80, 60, 50, 88, 82, 58, 50, 84, 75.

(i) Estimate all possible main effects.
(ii) Estimate σ^2 under the assumption that all the interaction parameters are zero.
(iii) Determine a confidence interval for σ^2 at level of confidence 0.99.

Exercise 5.14 A 3^2 factorial experiment, with $n = 3$ replications, gave the observations in Table 5.38.

Perform an ANOVA to test the main effects and interactions. Break the between treatments sum of squares to one degree of freedom components. Use the Scheffé S_α coefficient to determine which effects are significant.

Exercise 5.15 Construct a 2^{8-2} fractional replication, using the generators $ABCDG$ and $ABEFH$. What is the resolution of this design? Write the aliases to the main effects, and to the first order interactions with the factor A.

Exercise 5.16 Consider a full factorial experiment of $2^6 = 64$ runs. It is required to partition the runs to 8 blocks of 8. The parameters in the group of defining parameters are confounded with the effects of blocks and are not estimable. Show which parameters are not estimable if the blocks are generated by ACE, $ABEF$, and $ABCD$.

Exercise 5.17 A 2^2 factorial design is expanded by using 4 observations at 0. The design matrix and the response are in Table 5.39.

Table 5.39 Design matrix and response of 2^2 factorial design

X_1	X_2	Y
−1	−1	55.8
−1	−1	54.4
1	−1	60.3
1	−1	60.9
−1	1	63.9
−1	1	64.4
1	1	67.9
1	1	68.5
0	0	61.5
0	0	62.0
0	0	61.9
0	0	62.4

Table 5.40 Design matrix and the response for a control composite design of Exercise 5.18

X_1	X_2	Y
1.0	0.000	95.6
0.5	0.866	77.9
−0.5	0.866	76.2
−1.0	0	54.5
−0.5	−0.866	63.9
0.5	−0.866	79.1
0	0	96.8
0	0	94.8
0	0	94.4

(i) Fit a response function of the form: $Y = \beta_0 + \beta_1 X_1 + \beta_2 X_2 + \beta_{12} X_1 X_2 + e$, and plot its contour lines.
(ii) Estimate the variance σ^2 and test the goodness of fit of this model.

Exercise 5.18 Table 5.40 represents a design matrix and the response for a control composite design.

(i) Estimate the response function and its stationary point.
(ii) Plot contours of equal response, in two dimensions.
(iii) Conduct an ANOVA.

Chapter 6
Quality by Design

Preview Quality is largely determined by decisions made in the early planning phases of products and processes. A particularly powerful technique for making optimal design decisions is the statistically designed experiment introduced in Chap. 5. This chapter covers the basics of experimental designs in the context of engineering and economic optimization problems. Taguchi's loss function, signal-to-noise ratios, factorial models, and orthogonal arrays are discussed using case studies and simple examples. A special section is dedicated to the application of quality by design (QbD) in the pharmaceutical industry. QbD is supported internationally by the International Conference on Harmonization of Technical Requirements for Registration of Pharmaceuticals for Human Use (ICH) and by the Food and Drug Administration (FDA).

Factorial designs discussed in the previous chapter were developed in the 1930s by R.A. Fisher and F. Yates in Rothamsted agricultural station in Britain. Fractional replications were developed in the 1940s by D. Finney, also in Rothamsted. After World War II, these experimental design methods were applied to industrial problems in the Imperial Chemical Laboratories (ICL) in Britain. The objective of agronomists is to find treatment combinations that lead to maximal yield in agricultural product growth. The chemical engineer wishes to find the right combinations of pressure, temperature, and other factors, which lead to a maximal amount of the product coming out of a reactor. The objective in manufacturing engineering is, on the other hand, to design the process so that the products will be as close as possible to some specified target, without much fluctuations over time.

Flaws in engineering design can cause severe problems over time, and here is an example. A small British electronics company called Encrypta designed an ingenious electronic seal for lorries and store rooms. Industrial versions of D-size batteries were used to drive the circuit and numeric display. Encrypta started to receive defective seals returned by customers. A failure mode analysis

Supplementary Information The online version contains supplementary material available at (https://doi.org/10.1007/978-3-031-28482-3_6).

R. S. Kenett et al., *Industrial Statistics*, Statistics for Industry, Technology, and Engineering, https://doi.org/10.1007/978-3-031-28482-3_6

revealed that, when dropped on a hard surface, the batteries would heat up and cause a short circuit. Encrypta won 30,000 pounds in compensations from the batteries manufacturer and switched to Vidor batteries made by Fuji who passed the test. Encrypta found that the D-batteries failed on dropping because a cloth-like separation inside ruptures. This produced an active chemicals mix that discharged the battery. Fuji uses a tough, rolled separator that eliminates the problem Fox (1988).

In this chapter, we discuss methods and tools compatible with advanced quality and industrial standards mentioned in Chap. 3. It applies to organizations that adopted a quality by design approach that requires high organizational maturity. An example of quality by design is the comprehensive quality engineering approach developed by the Japanese engineer Genichi Taguchi. Taguchi labeled his methodology **off-line quality control**. The basic ideas of off-line quality control originated, while Taguchi was working at the Electrical Communications Laboratory (ECL) of the Nippon Telephone and Telegraph Company (NTT). Taguchi's task was to help Japanese engineers develop high-quality products with raw materials of poor quality, outdated manufacturing equipment, and an acute shortage of skilled engineers. Central to his approach is the application of statistically designed experiments. Taguchi's impact on Japan has expanded to a wide range of industries. He won the 1960 Deming prize for application of quality as well as three Deming prizes for publications on quality in 1951, 1953, and 1984. In 1959, the Japanese company NEC followed Taguchi's methods and ran 402 such experiments. In 1976, Nippon Denso, which was a 20,000-employee company producing electrical parts for automobiles, reported to have run 2,700 experiments using the Taguchi off-line quality control method. Off-line quality control was first applied in the West to integrated circuit manufacturing (see Phadke et al. 1983). Applications of off-line quality control range now from the design of automobiles, copiers, and electronic systems to cash-flow optimization in banking, improvements in computer response times, and runway utilization in an airport. Another industry that has adopted quality by design, to ensure high quality and reduced inefficiencies, is the pharmaceutical industry. The chapter will cover both the Taguchi methods and the application of quality by design in pharmaceutical companies. Chapter 8 is about cybermanufacturing and digital twins, methods deployed in Industry 4.0 manufacturing. The next chapter, Chap. 7, is an introduction to computer experiments, in general.

6.1 Off-Line Quality Control, Parameter Design, and the Taguchi Method

Kackar (1985), Dehnad (1989), Phadke (1989), John (1990), Box et al. (1988), and others explain the Taguchi methodology for off-line experimentation. We provide here a concise summary of this approach.

The performance of products or processes is typically quantified by performance measures. Examples include measures such as piston cycle time, yield of a production process, output voltage of an electronic circuit, noise level of a compressor, or response times of a computer system. These performance measures might be affected by several factors that have to be set at specific levels to get desired results. For example, the piston simulator introduced in previous chapters has seven factors that can be used to control the piston cycle time. The aim of off-line quality control is to determine the factor-level combination that gives the least variability to the appropriate performance measure, while keeping the mean value of the measure on target. The goal is to control **both** accuracy and variability. In the next section, we discuss an optimization strategy that solves this problem by minimizing various loss functions.

6.1.1 Product and Process Optimization Using Loss Functions

Optimization problems of products or processes can take many forms that depend on the objectives to be reached. These objectives are typically derived from customer requirements. Performance parameters such as dimensions, pressure, or velocity usually have a target or nominal value. The objective is to reach the target within a range bounded by upper and lower specification limits. We call such cases "**nominal is best**." Noise levels, shrinkage factors, and amount of wear and deterioration are usually required to be as low as possible. We call such cases "**the smaller the better**." When we measure strength, efficiency, yields, or time to failure, our goal is, in most cases, to reach the maximum possible levels. Such cases are called "**the larger the better**." These three types of cases require different objective (target) functions to optimize. Taguchi introduced the concept of **loss function** to help determine the appropriate optimization procedure.

When "nominal is best," specification limits are typically two-sided with an upper specification limit (USL) and a lower specification limit (LSL). These limits are used to differentiate between conforming and nonconforming products. Nonconforming products are usually fixed, retested, and sometimes downgraded or simply scrapped. In all cases, defective products carry a loss to the manufacturer. Taguchi argues that only products on target should carry no loss. Any deviation carries a loss that is not always immediately perceived by the customer or production personnel. Taguchi proposes a quadratic function as a simple approximation to a graduated loss function that measures loss on a continuous scale. A quadratic loss function has the form

$$L(y, M) = K(y - M)^2, \tag{6.1.1}$$

where y is the value of the performance characteristic of a product, M is the target value of this characteristic, and K is a positive constant, which yields monetary or other utility value to the loss. For example, suppose that $(M - \Delta, M + \Delta)$ is the **customer's tolerance interval** around the target. When y falls out of this interval, the product has to be repaired or replaced at a cost of \$$A$. Then, for this product,

$$A = K\Delta^2 \tag{6.1.2}$$

or

$$K = A/\Delta^2. \tag{6.1.3}$$

The **manufacturer's tolerance interval** is generally tighter than that of the customer, namely $(M - \delta, M + \delta)$, where $\delta < \Delta$. One can obtain the value of δ in the following manner. Suppose the cost to the manufacturer to repair a product that exceeds the customer's tolerance, before shipping the product, is $\$B$, $B < A$. Then

$$B = \left(\frac{A}{\Delta^2}\right)(Y - M)^2,$$

or

$$Y = M \pm \Delta\left(\frac{B}{A}\right)^{1/2}. \tag{6.1.4}$$

Thus,

$$\delta = \Delta\left(\frac{B}{A}\right)^{1/2}. \tag{6.1.5}$$

The manufacturer should reduce the variability in the product performance characteristic so that process capability C_{pk} for the tolerance interval $(M - \delta, M + \delta)$ should be high. See Fig. 6.1 for a schematic presentation of these relationships.

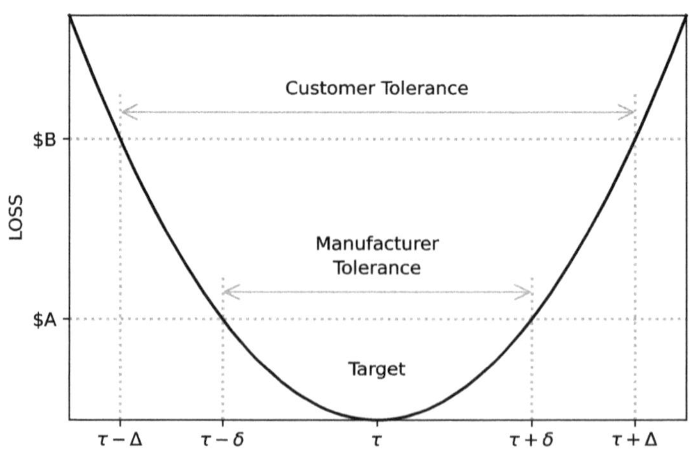

Fig. 6.1 Quadratic loss and tolerance intervals

Notice that the expected loss is

$$E\{L(Y, M)\} = K(\text{Bias}^2 + \text{Variance}), \tag{6.1.6}$$

where Bias $= \mu - M$, $\mu = E\{Y\}$ and Variance $= E\{(Y - \mu)^2\}$. Thus, the objective is to have a manufacturing process with μ as close as possible to the target M and variance, σ^2, as small as possible ($\sigma < \frac{\delta}{3}$ so that $C_{pk} > 1$). Recall that Variance + Bias^2 is the mean squared error, MSE. Thus, when "normal is best," the objective should be to minimize the MSE.

Objective functions for cases of "the bigger the better" or "the smaller the better" depend on the case under consideration. In cases where the performance measure is the life length of a product, the objective might be to design the product to maximize the expected life length. In the literature, we may find the objective of minimizing $\frac{1}{n}\sum \frac{1}{y^j}$, which is an estimator of $E\left\{\frac{1}{Y}\right\}$. This parameter, however, may not always exist (e.g., when Y has an exponential distribution), and this objective function might be senseless.

6.1.2 Major Stages in Product and Process Design

A major challenge of industry is to reduce variability in products and processes. The previous section dealt with measuring the impact of such variability. In this section, we discuss methods for actually reducing variability. Design of products or processes involves two main steps: designing the system and setting tolerances. System design is the stage where engineering skills, innovation, and technology are pooled together to create a basic design. Once the design is ready to go into production, one has to specify tolerances of parts and subassemblies so that the product or process meets its requirements. Loose tolerances are typically less expensive than tight tolerances. Taguchi proposed to change the classical approach to the design of products and processes and add an intermediate stage of **parameter design**. Thus, the three major stages in designing a product or a process are:

I. **System Design**—This is when the product architecture and technology are determined.
II. **Parameter Design**—At this stage, a planned optimization program is carried out in order to minimize variability and costs.
III. **Tolerance Design**—Once the optimum performance is determined, tolerances should be specified, so that the product or process stays within specifications. The setting of optimum values of the tolerance factors is called tolerance design.

Table 6.1 (adapted from Phadke (1989)) shows the relationships between the type of problems experienced in industrial products and processes and the various design phases.

Table 6.1 Noise factors and design phases

Activity	Design phase	Leverage on noise factors: External	Manufacturing imperf	Natural deterioration	Comments
Product design	(a) System design	High	High	High	Involves innovation to reduce sensitivity to all noise factors
	(b) Parameter design	High	High	High	Most important step for reducing sensitivity to all noise factors
	(c) Tolerance design	High	High	High	Method for selecting most economical grades of materials, components, and manufacturing equipment, and operating environment for the product
Manufacturing process design	(a) Concept design	Low	High	Low	Involves innovation to reduce the effect of manufacturing imperfections
	(b) Parameter design	Low	High	Low	Important for reducing sensitivity of unit-to-unit variation to manufacturing variations
	(c) Tolerance design	Low	High	Low	Method for determining tolerance on manufacturing process parameters
Manufacturing	(a) Concept design	Low	High	Low	Method of detecting problems when they occur and correcting them
	(b) Parameter design	Low	High	Low	Method of compensating for known problems
	(c) Tolerance design	Low	High	Low	Last alternative, useful when process capability is poor
Customer usage	Warranty and repair	Low	Low	Low	

6.1.3 Design Parameters and Noise Factors

Taguchi classifies the variables that affect the performance characteristics into two categories: **design parameters** and **source of noise**. All factors that cause variability are included in the source of noise. Sources of noise are classified into two categories: **external sources** and **internal sources**. External sources are those external to the product, like environmental conditions (temperature, humidity, dust, etc.), human variations in operating the product, and other similar factors. Internal sources of variability are those connected with manufacturing imperfections and product degradation or natural deterioration.

The design parameters, on the other hand, are controllable factors that can be set at predetermined values (level). The product designer has to specify the values of the design parameters to achieve the objectives. This is done by running an experiment that is called **parameter design**. In manufacturing conditions, the values of these parameters may slightly vary from values determined in the parameter design stage (the nominal ones). In **tolerance designs**, we test the effects of such variability and determine tolerances that yield the desired results at lower cost.

Example 6.1 An RL circuit is an electrical circuit of alternating current that obtains an input of voltage 100 [V] AC and frequency 55 [Hz]. The output current of the circuit is aimed at 10 [A], with tolerances of $\Delta = \pm 4$ [A]. There are four factors that influence the output y:

V: Input voltage [V].
f: Input frequency [Hz].
R: Resistance [Ohm].
L: Self-Inductance [H].

R and L are controllable factors, while V and f are noise factors. Assume that V has a distribution between 90 and 110 [V] and f has a distribution between 55 and 65 [Hz]. R and L are design parameters. What should be values of R [Ω] and L [H] to obtain an output y distributed around the target of $M = 10$ [A], with minimal mean squared error and lowest cost? In the next section, we study how one can take advantage of the non-linear relationship between the above factors to attain lower variability and high accuracy. ■

6.1.4 *Parameter Design Experiments*

In a parameter design experiment, we test the effects of the controllable factors and the noise factors on the performance characteristics of the product, in order to:

(a) Make the product robust (insensitive) to environmental conditions.
(b) Make the product insensitive to components variation.
(c) Minimize the mean squared error about a target value.

We distinguish between two types of experiments, **physical experiments** and **computer based** simulation experiments. In Chap. 7, we discuss this type of computer based simulation experiments. Let $\boldsymbol{\theta} = (\theta_1, \cdots, \theta_k)$ be the vector of design parameters. The vector of noise variables is denoted by $\mathbf{x} = (x_1, \cdots, x_m)$.

The response function $y \in f(\boldsymbol{\theta}, \mathbf{x})$ involves in many situations the factors $\boldsymbol{\theta}$ and $\mathbf{x}$ in a non-linear fashion. The RL circuit described in Example 6.1 involves the four factors V, f, R, L and the output y according to the non-linear response function

$$y = \frac{V}{(R^2 + (2\pi f L)^2)^{1/2}}.$$

If the noise factors V and f had no variability, one could determine the values of R and L to always obtain a target value $y_0 = M$. The variability of V and f around their nominal values turns y to be a random variable, Y, with expected value μ and variance σ^2, which depend on the setting of the design parameters R and L and on the variances of V and f. The effects of the non-linearity on the distribution of Y will be studied in Sect. 6.2. The objective of parameter design experiments is to take advantage of the effects of the non-linear relationship. The strategy is to perform a factorial experiment to investigate the effects of the design parameters (controllable factors). If we learn from the experiments that certain design parameters affect the mean of Y but not its variance and, on the other hand, other design factors affect the variance but not the mean, we can use the latter group to reduce the variance of Y as much as possible and then adjust the levels of the parameters in the first group to set μ close to the target M. We illustrate this approach in the following example.

Example 6.2 The data for the present example are taken from (John 1990, p. 335). Three factors A, B, C (controllable) affect the output, Y, of a system. In order to estimate the main effects of A, B, C, a 2^3 factorial experiment was conducted. Each treatment combination was repeated 4 times, at the “low” and “high” levels of two noise factors. The results and the mean, $\bar{Y}$, and standard deviation, S, of Y at the 8 treatment combinations are given in Table 6.2.

```
response = pd.DataFrame([
  [-1, -1, -1, 60.5, 61.7, 60.5, 60.8],
  [ 1, -1, -1, 47.0, 46.3, 46.7, 47.2],
  [-1,  1, -1, 92.1, 91.0, 92.0, 91.6],
  [ 1,  1, -1, 71.0, 71.7, 71.1, 70.0],
  [-1, -1,  1, 65.2, 66.8, 64.3, 65.2],
  [ 1, -1,  1, 49.5, 50.6, 49.5, 50.5],
  [-1,  1,  1, 91.2, 90.5, 91.5, 88.7],
  [ 1,  1,  1, 76.0, 76.0, 78.3, 76.4],
], columns=['A', 'B', 'C', 'y1', 'y2', 'y3', 'y4'])
response['Ymean'] = response[['y1', 'y2', 'y3', 'y4']].mean(axis=1)
response['S'] = response[['y1', 'y2', 'y3', 'y4']].std(ddof=0, axis=1)
```

```
model = smf.ols('Ymean ~ A + B + C', data=response).fit()
print(f'rsquared: {model.rsquared:.3f}')
model_S = smf.ols('S ~ A + B + C', data=response).fit()
print(f'rsquared: {model_S.rsquared:.3f}')
```

```
rsquared: 0.991
rsquared: 0.816
```

Table 6.2 Response and mean, $\bar{Y}$, and standard deviation, S, at a 2^3 factorial experiment

A	B	C	y_1	y_2	y_3	y_4	$\bar{Y}$	S
−1	−1	−1	60.5	61.7	60.5	60.8	60.875	0.4918
1	−1	−1	47.0	46.3	46.7	47.2	46.800	0.3391
−1	1	−1	92.1	91.0	92.0	91.6	91.675	0.4323
1	1	−1	71.0	71.7	71.1	70.0	70.950	0.6103
−1	−1	1	65.2	66.8	64.3	65.2	65.375	0.9010
1	−1	1	49.5	50.6	49.5	50.5	50.025	0.5262
−1	1	1	91.2	90.5	91.5	88.7	90.475	1.0871
1	1	1	76.0	76.0	78.3	76.4	76.675	0.9523

Regressing the column $\bar{Y}$ on the 3 orthogonal columns under A, B, C in Table 6.2, we obtain

$$\text{Mean} = 69.1 - 7.99A + 13.3B + 1.53C$$

with $R^2 = 0.991$. Moreover, the coefficient 1.53 of C is not significant (a P value of 0.103). Thus, the significant main effects on the mean yield are the factors A and B only. Regressing the column of S on A, B, C, we obtain the equation

$$\text{STD} = 0.668 - 0.060A + 0.103B + 0.199C,$$

with $R^2 = 0.816$. Only the main effect of C is significant. Factors A and B have no effects on the standard deviation. The strategy is therefore to set the value of C at -1 (as small as possible) and the values of A and B to adjust the mean response to be equal to the target value M. If $M = 85$, we find A and B that solve the equation

$$85 = 69.1 - 7.99A + 13.3B - 1.53$$

$$A = \frac{-17.43 + 13.3B}{7.99}.$$

Letting $B = 0.75$, then $A = -0.933$. The optimal setting of the design parameters A, B, C is at $A = -0.742$, $B = 0.75$, and $C = -1$. ■

6.1.5 Performance Statistics

As we have seen in the previous example, the performance characteristic y at various combinations of the design parameters is represented by the mean, $\bar{Y}$, and standard deviation, S, of the y values observed at various combinations of the noise factors. We performed the analysis first on $\bar{Y}$ and then on S to detect which design parameters influence $\bar{Y}$ but not S, and which influences S but not $\bar{Y}$. Let $\eta(\boldsymbol{\theta})$ denote the expected value of Y, as a function of the design parameters $\theta_1, \cdots, \theta_k$. Let $\sigma^2(\boldsymbol{\theta})$ denote the variance of Y as a function of $\boldsymbol{\theta}$. The situation described above corresponds to the case that $\eta(\boldsymbol{\theta})$ and $\sigma^2(\boldsymbol{\theta})$ are independent. The **objective** in setting the values of $\theta_1, \cdots, \theta_k$ is to minimize the mean squared error

$$MSE(\boldsymbol{\theta}) = B^2(\boldsymbol{\theta}) + \sigma^2(\boldsymbol{\theta}), \tag{6.1.7}$$

where $B(\boldsymbol{\theta}) = \eta(\boldsymbol{\theta}) - M$. The **performance statistic** is an estimator of MSE($\boldsymbol{\theta}$), namely,

$$\widehat{MSE}(\boldsymbol{\theta}) = (\bar{Y}(\boldsymbol{\theta}) - M)^2 + S^2(\boldsymbol{\theta}). \tag{6.1.8}$$

If $\bar{Y}(\boldsymbol{\theta})$ and $S^2(\boldsymbol{\theta})$ depend on different design parameters, we perform the minimization in two steps. First we minimize $S^2(\boldsymbol{\theta})$ and then $\hat{B}^2(\boldsymbol{\theta}) = (\bar{Y}(\theta) - M)^2$. If $\eta(\boldsymbol{\theta})$ and $\sigma^2(\boldsymbol{\theta})$ are **not** independent, the problem is more complicated.

Taguchi recommends devising a function of $\eta(\boldsymbol{\theta})$ and $\sigma(\boldsymbol{\theta})$, which is called a **signal-to-noise ratio** (SN), and maximizing an estimator of this SN function. Taguchi devised a large number of such performance statistics. In particular, Taguchi recommended to maximize the performance statistic

$$\eta = 10 \log \left(\frac{\bar{Y}^2}{S^2} - \frac{1}{n} \right), \tag{6.1.9}$$

which is being used in many studies. As can be shown by the method of the next section, the variance of $\log(\bar{Y})$ in large samples is approximately

$$V\{\log(\bar{Y})\} \cong \frac{\sigma^2}{n\mu^2}. \tag{6.1.10}$$

Thus,

$$-\log V\{\log(\bar{Y})\} = \log \left(\frac{\mu^2}{\sigma^2} \right) + \log n.$$

In the case of a normal distribution of Y, $\frac{\bar{Y}^2}{S^2} - \frac{1}{n}$ is an **unbiased** estimator of $\frac{\mu^2}{\sigma^2}$. Thus,

$$10 \log \left(\frac{\bar{Y}^2}{S^2} - \frac{1}{n} \right) \tag{6.1.11}$$

is an estimator of $-10 \log(nV\{\log(\bar{Y})\})$, although not an unbiased one. It is difficult to give any other justification to the performance statistic η(SN ratio). One has to be careful, since maximizing this SN might achieve bad results if $\eta(\boldsymbol{\theta})$ is far from the target M. Thus, if the objective is to set the design parameters to obtain means close to M and small standard deviations, one should minimize the mean squared error and not necessarily maximize the above SN ratio.

6.2 The Effects of Non-linearity

As mentioned in the previous section, the response function $f(\boldsymbol{\theta}, \mathbf{x})$ might be non-linear in $\boldsymbol{\theta}$ and $\mathbf{x}$, and an example was given for the case of output current of an RL circuit, namely

$$Y = \frac{V}{(R^2 + (2\pi f L)^2)^{1/2}}.$$

This is a non-linear function of the design parameters R and L and the noise factor f. We have assumed that V and f are random variables and R and L are constant parameters. The output current is the random variable Y. What is the expected value and variance of Y? Generally, one can estimate the expected value of Y and its variance by simulation, using the function $f(\boldsymbol{\theta}, \mathbf{X})$, and the assumed joint distribution of $\mathbf{X}$. An approximation to the expected value and the variance of Y can be obtained by the following method.

Let the random variables $X_1, \cdots, X_k$ have expected values $\xi_1, \cdots, \xi_k$ and variance–covariance matrix

$$V = \begin{bmatrix} \sigma_1^2 & \sigma_{12} & \cdots & \sigma_{1k} \\ \sigma_{21} & \sigma_2^2 & & \sigma_{2k} \\ \vdots & & \ddots & \vdots \\ \sigma_{k1} & \sigma_{k2} & \cdots & \sigma_k^2 \end{bmatrix}.$$

Assuming that $f(\boldsymbol{\theta}, \mathbf{X})$ can be expanded into a Taylor series around the means $\boldsymbol{\xi}_1 = (\xi_1, \cdots, \xi_k)$, we obtain the approximation

$$f(\boldsymbol{\theta}, \mathbf{X}) \cong f(\boldsymbol{\theta}, \boldsymbol{\xi}) + \sum_{i=1}^{k} (x_i - \xi_i) \frac{\partial}{\partial x_i} f(\boldsymbol{\theta}, \boldsymbol{\xi}) + \frac{1}{2} (\mathbf{X} - \boldsymbol{\xi})' H(\boldsymbol{\theta}, \boldsymbol{\xi})(\mathbf{X} - \boldsymbol{\xi}), \tag{6.2.1}$$

where $H(\boldsymbol{\theta}, \boldsymbol{\xi})$ is a $k \times k$ matrix of second order partial derivatives, evaluated at $\boldsymbol{\xi}_i$ with (i, j)th element equal to

$$H_{ij}(\boldsymbol{\theta}, \boldsymbol{\xi}) = \frac{\partial^2}{\partial x_i \partial x_j} f(\boldsymbol{\theta}, \boldsymbol{\xi}), \quad i, j = 1, \cdots, k. \tag{6.2.2}$$

Thus, the expected value of $f(\boldsymbol{\theta}, \mathbf{X})$ is approximated by

$$E\{f(\boldsymbol{\theta}, \mathbf{X})\} \cong f(\boldsymbol{\theta}, \boldsymbol{\xi}) + \frac{1}{2} \sum_{i=1}^{k} \sum_{j=1}^{i} \sigma_{ij} H_{ij}(\boldsymbol{\theta}, \boldsymbol{\xi}), \tag{6.2.3}$$

and the variance of $f(\boldsymbol{\theta}, \mathbf{X})$ is approximated by

$$V\{f(\boldsymbol{\theta}, \mathbf{X})\} \cong \sum_{i=1}^{k} \sum_{j=1}^{k} \sigma_{ij} \frac{\partial}{\partial x_i} f(\boldsymbol{\theta}, \boldsymbol{\xi}) \frac{\partial}{\partial x_j} f(\boldsymbol{\theta}, \boldsymbol{\xi}). \tag{6.2.4}$$

As seen in these approximations, if the response variable Y is a non-linear function of the random variables $X_1, \cdots, X_m$, its expected value depends also on the variances and covariances of the X's. This is not the case if Y is a linear function of the x's. Moreover, in the linear case, the formula for $V\{Y\}$ is exact.

Example 6.3 Consider the function

$$Y = \frac{V}{(R^2 + (2\pi f L)^2)^{1/2}},$$

where $R = 5.0$ [Ω] and $L = 0.02$ [H]. V and f are independent random variables having normal distributions:

$$V \sim N(100, 9)$$
$$f \sim N(55, 25/9).$$

Notice that

$$\frac{\partial y}{\partial v} = \frac{1}{(R^2 + (2\pi f L)^2)^{1/2}}$$

$$\frac{\partial y}{\partial f} = -4V(R^2 + (2\pi f L)^2)^{-3/2} \pi^2 L^2 f$$

$$\frac{\partial^2 y}{\partial v^2} = 0$$

$$\frac{\partial^2 y}{\partial v \partial f} = -4(R^2 + (2\pi f L)^2)^{-3/2} \pi^2 L^2 f.$$

Also,

$$\frac{\partial^2 y}{\partial f^2} = -4V \left(R^2 + (2\pi f L)^2\right)^{-3/2} \pi^2 L^2 + 48V \left(R^2 + (2\pi f L)^2\right)^{-5/2} \pi^4 L^4 f^2.$$

Substituting in these derivatives the values of R and L and the expected values of V and f, we obtain

$$\begin{aligned}
\frac{\partial y}{\partial v} &= \frac{1}{8.5304681} = 0.11723 \\
\frac{\partial y}{\partial f} &= -0.13991 \\
\frac{\partial^2 y}{\partial v^2} &= 0 \\
\frac{\partial^2 y}{\partial v \partial f} &= -0.0013991 \\
\frac{\partial^2 y}{\partial f^2} &= -0.0025438 + 0.0050098 \\
&= 0.002466.
\end{aligned}$$

Accordingly, an approximation for $E\{Y\}$ is given by

$$E\{Y\} \cong 11.722686 + \frac{1}{2}(9 \times 0 + 2.7778 \times 0.002466) = 11.7261.$$

The variance of Y is approximated by

$$V\{Y\} \cong 9 \times (0.11723)^2 + \frac{25}{9} \times (-0.13991)^2 = 0.17806.$$

To check the goodness of these approximations, we do the following simulation using Python.

We simulate $N = 500$ normal random variables having mean 100 and standard deviation 3 (V). Similarly, 500 normal random variables having mean 55 and standard deviation 1.67 are simulated and stored in variable `f`. We then calculate the values of `Y` and calculate mean and variance.

```
np.random.seed(seed=1)

def Y(R, L, V, f):
  d = R**2 + (2*np.pi*f*L)**2
  return V / np.sqrt(d)
R = 5
L = 0.02
V = stats.norm.rvs(loc=100, scale=np.sqrt(9), size=500)
f = stats.norm.rvs(loc=55, scale=np.sqrt(25/9), size=500)
Ysimulated = Y(R, L, V, f)
Ymean = np.mean(Ysimulated)
Yvar = np.var(Ysimulated)
delta = 2 * np.sqrt(Yvar / 500)
CI = (Ymean - delta, Ymean + delta)
```

The results obtained are $\bar{Y}_{500} = 11.739$ and $S^2_{500} = 0.16942$. The analytical approximations are very close to the simulation estimates. Actually, a .95 confidence interval for $E\{Y\}$ is given by $\bar{Y}_{500} \pm 2\frac{S_{500}}{\sqrt{500}}$, which is (11.702, 11.776). The result of the analytical approximation, 11.7261, is within the confidence limits. The approximation is quite good.

It is interesting to estimate the effects of the design parameters R and L on $E\{Y\}$ and $V\{Y\}$. We conduct a small experiment on the computer for estimating $E\{Y\}$ and $V\{Y\}$ by a 3^2 factorial experiment. The levels of R and L as recommended by G. Taguchi, in his review paper (see Ghosh 1990, pp. 1–34), are:

	0	1	2
R	0.05	5.00	9.50
L	0.01	0.02	0.03

In each treatment combination, we simulate 500 y-values. The results are given in Table 6.3.

```
from mistat.design import doe
np.random.seed(1)

# Build design from factors
FacDesign = doe.full_fact({
    'R': [0.05, 5, 9.5],
    'L': [0.01, 0.02, 0.03],
})
results = []
for _, (R, L) in FacDesign.iterrows():
  V = stats.norm.rvs(loc=100, scale=np.sqrt(9), size=500)
  f = stats.norm.rvs(loc=55, scale=np.sqrt(25/9), size=500)

  Ysimulated = Y(R, L, V, f)
  Ymean = np.mean(Ysimulated)
  Yvar = np.var(Ysimulated)

  target = 10
  MSE = (Ymean - target) **2 + Yvar
  results.append({
    'R': R,
    'L': L,
    'Ymean': Ymean,
    'Yvar': Yvar,
    'MSE': MSE,
  })
results = pd.DataFrame(results)
```

The objective is to find the combinations of R and L that yield minimum MSE $= (E\{Y\} - M)^2 + V\{Y\}$, where M is the target of 10 [Ω]. It seems that the best setting of the design parameters is $R = 9.5$ [Ω] and $L = 0.01$ [H]. The combination $R = 0.05$ [Ω] and $L = 0.03$ [H] also yields very small MSE. One should choose the least expensive setting. ■

Table 6.3 The means, variances, and MSE of Y in a 3^2 experiment

R	L	$\bar{Y}_{500}$	S^2_{500}	MSE
0.050	0.01	28.984	1.446	361.84
5.000	0.01	16.495	0.275	42.45
9.500	0.01	9.889	0.089	0.10
0.050	0.02	14.510	0.396	20.74
5.000	0.02	11.721	0.182	3.14
9.500	0.02	8.515	0.072	2.28
0.050	0.03	9.668	0.170	0.28
5.000	0.03	8.676	0.126	1.88
9.500	0.03	7.109	0.062	8.42

6.3 Taguchi's Designs

In order to simulate the effect of noise factors, Taguchi advocates the combination of two experimental arrays, an **inner array** and an **outer array**. The inner array is used to determine factor-level combinations of factors that can be controlled by the designer of the product or process. The outer array is used to generate the variability due to noise factors that is experienced by the product or process under optimization, in its day-to-day operation.

The experimental arrays used by Taguchi are **orthogonal array** designs. An example of a design with 15 factors at two levels each, using 16 experiments, is given in Table 6.4. The levels are indicated by 1 and 2, and the first row consists of all factors at level 1. This experimental array was introduced in Chap. 5 as a 2^{15-11} fractional factorial design that is a fully saturated design with 15 factors and 16 experimental runs. The corresponding full factorial design consists of $2^{15} = 32768$ experiments. Taguchi labeled several experimental arrays using a convenient notation and reproduced them in tables that were widely distributed among engineers (see Taguchi and Konishi 1987). The availability of these tables made it convenient for practitioners to design and run such experiments.

One can note from Table 6.4 that if we run the experiment using the order of the experiment array, we will find it convenient to assign to column 1 a factor that is difficult to change from level 1 to level 2. For example, if changing the temperature of a solder bath requires 5 h, the assignment of temperature to column 1 would require one change only. Column 15, on the other hand, has 9 changes between levels. Taguchi recommends that in some cases randomization be abandoned for the benefit of simplicity and cost. If we choose to run the experiment in the order of the experimental array, we can reduce the practical difficulties in running the experiment by proper assignment of factors to columns. An easily changed factor can get assigned to column 15 with low penalty. However, assigning a factor that is difficult to change to column 15 might make the whole experiment impractical.

In order to simulate the noise factors, we can design a second experiment using an external array. In some cases, noise cannot be directly simulated, and the external array consists of replicating the internal array experiments over a specified length

Table 6.4 Factor-level combinations of 15 factors at two levels each in an $L_{16}(2^{15})$ orthogonal array

	Columns														
Trial	1	2	3	4	5	6	7	8	9	10	11	12	13	14	15
1	1	1	1	1	1	1	1	1	1	1	1	1	1	1	1
2	1	1	1	1	1	1	1	2	2	2	2	2	2	2	2
3	1	1	1	2	2	2	2	1	1	1	1	2	2	2	2
4	1	1	1	2	2	2	2	2	2	2	2	1	1	1	1
5	1	2	2	1	1	2	2	1	1	2	2	1	1	2	2
6	1	2	2	1	1	2	2	2	2	1	1	2	2	1	1
7	1	2	2	2	2	1	1	1	1	2	2	2	2	1	1
8	1	2	2	2	2	1	1	2	2	1	1	1	1	2	2
9	2	1	2	1	2	1	2	1	2	1	2	1	2	1	2
10	2	1	2	1	2	1	2	2	1	2	1	2	1	2	1
11	2	1	2	2	1	2	1	1	2	1	2	2	1	2	1
12	2	1	2	2	1	2	1	2	1	2	1	1	2	1	2
13	2	2	1	1	2	2	1	1	2	2	1	1	2	2	1
14	2	2	1	1	2	2	1	2	1	1	2	2	1	1	2
15	2	2	1	2	1	1	2	1	2	2	1	2	1	1	2
16	2	2	1	2	1	1	2	2	1	1	2	1	2	2	1

of time or amount of material. In Sect. 6.6, we describe two such experiments. The first experiment deals with a speedometer cable where the percentage of shrinkage is measured on several pieces of cable taken from various parts of a spool and running a heat test. The external array simply consists of the sampled parts of the spool. The second experiment deals with optimizing the response time of a computer system. Here the inner array experiment was carried out on an operational system so that the variabilities induced by various users were not specifically simulated. A retrospective study verified that there was no bias in user methods.

The design given in Table 6.4 can be used for up to 15 factors. It allows us to compute estimates of main effects, provided there are **no interactions** of any order between them. If, on the other hand, **all** first order interactions can be potentially significant, this design cannot be used with more than 5 factors. (The resolution of the above design is III.) In order to assist the engineer with the correct choice of columns from the table of orthogonal arrays, Taguchi devised a graphical method of presenting the columns of an orthogonal array table that are confounded with first order interactions of some factors. These graphs are called **linear graphs**.

In Fig. 6.2, we present two linear graphs associated with Table 6.4. Linear graph LG_1 corresponds to the case where **all** interactions might be significant. The graph has five vertices and 10 lines connecting the vertices. The factors A, B, C, D, E are assigned to the columns with numbers at the vertices. Thus, the assignment of the factors to columns is, according to this linear graph:

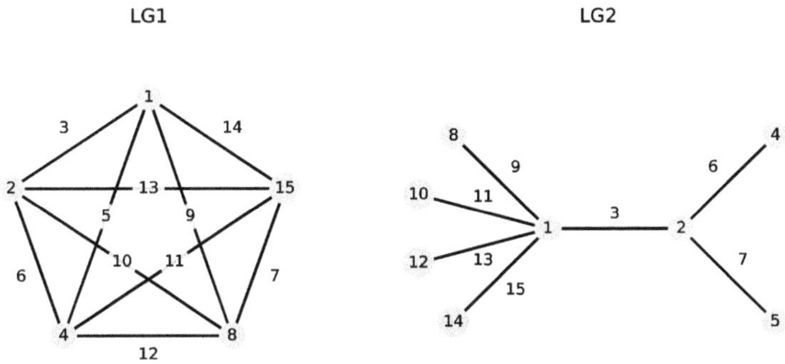

Fig. 6.2 Two linear graphs for $L_{16}(2^{15})$

Factor	A	B	C	D	E
Column	1	2	4	8	15

We also see that column 3 can be used to estimate the interaction AB, column 6 for the interaction BC, column 5 for the interaction AC, etc.

The second linear graph, LG_2, represents the case where only some interactions are significant. These are: AB, AC, AD, AE, FG, and FH. In this case, we can perform the 16 trials experiment with 8 factors and assign them to columns:

Factor	A	B	C	D	E	F	G	H
Column	1	8	10	12	14	2	4	5

The columns that can be used to estimate the interactions are 3, 6, 7, 9, 11, 13, 15.

Although the emphasis in Taguchi's methodology is on estimating main effects, one should not forget that interactions might exist. It is better to be cautious and not to over-saturate a small design with too many factors. Recall that when fractional replications are used, the estimates of main effects might be confounded. We wish to choose a design with sufficient resolution (see Chap. 5), and this may require sufficiently large fractions. The table that we presented (Table 6.4) is a fraction of a 2^{15} factorial experiment. Taguchi also prepared tables of orthogonal arrays for 3^n factorial experiments, and for mixtures of factors with 2 and 3 levels ($2^m \times 3^k$ factorials). The reader is referred to the tables of Taguchi and Konishi (1987) and also Appendix C of Phadke (1989).

6.4 Quality by Design in the Pharmaceutical Industry

6.4.1 Introduction to Quality by Design

A product or process in the pharmaceutical industry is well understood when all critical sources of variability are identified and explained, variability is proactively managed, and product quality attributes can be accurately and reliably predicted. Drug manufacturing processes must meet current good manufacturing practices (cGMP) to ensure that drug products meet safety and efficacy requirements. Traditionally, the pharmaceutical industry has performed process validation studies on three batches. This approach, however, does not represent routine manufacturing and therefore is unlikely to cover all potential sources of variability (e.g., raw materials, operators, shifts, reactor vessels). The Office of New Drug Quality Assessment at the Food and Drug Administration has identified this issue as a challenge to the regulatory process and launched a quality by design initiative with a focus on product and process understanding (Nasr 2007).

Quality by design (QbD) in the pharmaceutical industry is a systematic approach to development of drug products and drug manufacturing processes that begins with predefined objectives, emphasizes product, and process understanding and sets up process control based on sound science and quality risk management. In the traditional approach, product quality and performance are achieved predominantly by restricting flexibility in the manufacturing process and by end product testing. Under the QbD paradigm, pharmaceutical quality is assured by understanding and controlling manufacturing and formulation variables. End product testing is used to confirm the quality of the product and is not part of the ongoing consistency assurance and/or process control. The Food and Drug Administration (FDA) and the International Conference on Harmonization of Technical Requirements for Registration of Pharmaceuticals for Human Use (ICH) are promoting QbD in an attempt to curb rising development costs and regulatory barriers to innovation and creativity (Kenett and Kenett 2008). ICH guidelines published several guidelines that define QbD for both the pharmaceutical and biopharmaceutical industry (ICH Q8-Q11). The implementation of QbD involves the application of statistical design of experiments (DoE) described in Chap. 5 in the development of products, processes, analytical methods and pharmaceutical formulations (Rathore and Mhatre 2009; Faltin et al. 2012). This section introduces QbD with a focus on the application of statistically designed experiments in this context.

Under QbD, statistically designed experiments are used for efficiently and effectively investigating potential main effects and interactions among process and product factors. The mathematical models derived from such designed experiments are then used together with the acceptable boundaries of critical quality attributes to define a design space for a given process step. The normal operating range that is embedded within the design space yields quality attribute measurements that fall within the lower and upper control limits (LCL and UCL) representing the process performance (see Chaps. 2–4). When the LCL and UCL fall well within the lower and upper specification limits (LSL and USL), the process step is predicted to be highly capable of delivering product that meets the requirements of subsequent steps in the process. Excursions outside the normal operating range are expected to deliver product with quality attributes that are acceptable for further processing, as long as the operating parameters are held to limits defined by the design space. When operations are affected by several quality attributes, the design space for the unit operation is obtained from overlays of the design spaces derived from analyses of multiple attributes, or from a multivariate analysis of the system.

The ICH Q10 guideline for Quality Systems indicates that controls for a product consist not only of process controls and final specifications for drug substance and drug product but also controls associated with the raw materials, excipients, container and closure, manufacturing equipment, and facility. It is a state of control in which all of the "planned controls" work together to ensure that the product delivered to the patient meets the patient's needs. Design space boundaries, as described above, are an integral part of a comprehensive control strategy. The control strategy for a product is expected to evolve through the product lifecycle. The purpose of a control strategy for a product is to ensure that sufficient controls are in place to maintain the risks associated with the product at a tolerable level. Risk management and control strategy principles are described in ICH Q9 (for a comprehensive treatment of operational risks, see Kenett and Raanan (2010)). A well-designed control strategy that results from appropriate leveraging of QbD principles, then, leads to reliable product quality and patient safety profiles. The steps to develop a QbD drug application consist of: (1) Determine the quality target product profile, (2) Define the critical quality attributes (CQAs), (3) Conduct a risk assessment to identify potential critical process parameters, (4) Conduct statistically designed experiments (DoE) to identify actual critical process parameters, (5) Determine an appropriate control strategy, and (6) Revise the risk assessment. In the next section, we present a QbD case study focusing on the setting up of a design space.

6.4.2 A Quality by Design Case Study: The Full Factorial Design

The case study is a steroid lotion formulation of a generic product designed to match the properties of an existing brand using in vitro tests. In vitro release is one of several standard methods that can be used to characterize performance characteristics of a finished topical dosage form. Important changes in the characteristics of a drug product formula or the chemical and physical properties of the drug it contains should show up as a difference in drug release. Release is theoretically proportional to the square root of time when the formulation in question is in control of the release process because the release is from a receding boundary. In vitro release method for topical dosage forms described in SUPAC (1997) is based on an open chamber diffusion cell system such as a Franz cell system, fitted usually with a synthetic

Table 6.5 Risk assessment of manufacturing process variables

CQA	Manufacturing process variables				
	Temperature of reaction	Blending time	Cooling temperature	Cooling time	Order of ingredient addition
Appearance	High	High	Low	Low	High
Viscosity	High	High	Low	High	High
Assay	Low	Low	Low	Low	Low
In vitro permeability	High	High	Low	High	High

membrane. The test product is placed on the upper side of the membrane in the open donor chamber of the diffusion cell, and a sampling fluid is placed on the other side of the membrane in a receptor cell. Diffusion of drug from the topical product to and across the membrane is monitored by assay of sequentially collected samples of the receptor fluid. A plot of the amount of drug released per unit area (mcg/cm2) against the square root of time yields a straight line, the slope of which represents the release rate. This release rate measure is formulation-specific and can be used to monitor product quality. The typical in vitro release testing apparatus has six cells where the tested and brand products are being compared. A 90% confidence interval for the ratio of the median in vitro release rate in the tested and brand products is computed and expressed in percentage terms. If the interval falls within the limits of 75% to 133.33%, the tested and brand products are considered equivalent.

An initial risk assessment mapped risks in meeting specifications of critical quality attributes (CQAs). Table 6.5 presents expert opinions on the impact of manufacturing process variables on various CQAs. Cooling temperature was considered to have low impact, and the order of ingredient addition was determined using risk contamination considerations. Later, both these factors were not studied in setting up the process design space.

The responses that will be considered in setting up the process design space include 8 quality attributes: (1) Assay of active ingredient, (2) In vitro permeability lower confidence interval, (3) In vitro permeability upper confidence interval, (4) 90th percentile of particle size, (5) Assay of material A, (6) Assay of material B, (7) Viscosity, and (8) pH values. Three process factors are considered: (A) Temperature of reaction, (B) Blending time, and (C) Cooling time.

In order to elicit the effect of the three factors on the eight responses, we will use a full factorial experiment with two center points (see Table 6.6 that presents the experimental array in standard order).

We can compare different designs by comparing the relative prediction variance in the design space. The relative prediction variance at any point x in the design space is defined as

$$x'(X'X)^{-1}x,$$

Table 6.6 Full factorial design with two center points

Pattern	Temperature	Blending time	Cooling time
− − −	60	2	30
+ − −	75	2	30
− + −	60	5	30
+ + −	75	5	30
0 0 0	67.5	3.5	105
0 0 0	67.5	3.5	105
− − +	60	2	180
+ − +	75	2	180
− + +	60	5	180
+ + +	75	5	180

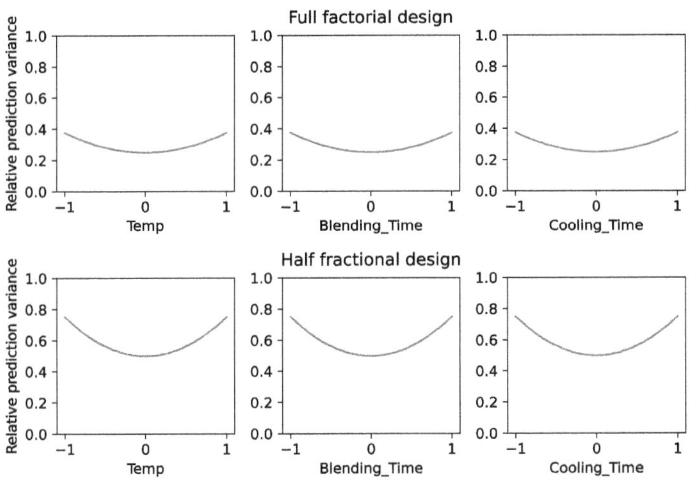

Fig. 6.3 Relative prediction variance profiles for the full factorial design of Table 6.6 and the related half-fraction design along the edge of the design space cube

where X is the design matrix. For our full factorial design, the relative prediction variance is minimized at the center of the design and largest at the corners of the design space. Figure 6.3 shows the profile of the relative prediction variance along one of the edges of the design space. If we choose a half-fraction replication with only four experimental runs on the corners of the cube, instead of the 9 points full factorial, our variance will double.

The data with the experimental arrays are available in the dataset **QBD.csv**. After loading, we convert the data into factors and build a model to predict viscosity based on temperature, blending time, and cooling time with included interaction terms. The required Python code is shown in Table 6.7.

The model coefficients are summarized in Table 6.8. The predicted viscosity values are shown in the cube display in Fig. 6.4. Both results show that increasing temperature clearly increases viscosity. The two center points in the experimental

Table 6.7 Preprocessing and model building for the QBD dataset

```
# data loading and preprocessing
df = mistat.load_data('QBD')
df.columns = [s.replace(' ', '_').replace('-', '_') for s in df.columns]
predictors = ['Temp', 'Blending_Time', 'Cooling_Time']
outcome = 'Viscosity'
data = df[predictors + [outcome]]

# convert data to factors
FFdesign = data.copy()
for predictor in predictors:
    values = FFdesign[predictor]
    toFactor = {min(values): -1, max(values): 1, np.mean(values): 0}
    values = [toFactor[v] for v in values]
    FFdesign[predictor] = values
FFdesign = FFdesign.sort_values(by=['Cooling_Time', 'Blending_Time', 'Temp'])
FFdesign = FFdesign.reset_index(drop=True)

formula = 'Viscosity ~ (Temp + Blending_Time + Cooling_Time)**2'
ff_model = smf.ols(formula=formula, data=FFdesign).fit()
FFdesign['predicted'] = ff_model.predict(FFdesign)
```

Table 6.8 Coefficients of the model based on the full factorial design

	Coef.	Std. Err.	t	$P > \|t\|$	[0.025	0.975]
Intercept	4708.4	173.6	27.127	0.000	4156.0	5260.8
Temp	236.9	194.1	1.221	0.309	−380.7	854.4
Blending_Time	32.9	194.1	0.169	0.876	−584.7	650.4
Cooling_Time	−180.9	194.1	−0.932	0.420	−798.4	436.7
Temp:Blending_Time	126.6	194.1	0.653	0.561	−490.9	744.2
Temp:Cooling_Time	−105.6	194.1	−0.544	0.624	−723.2	511.9
Blending_Time:Cooling_Time	−162.1	194.1	−0.835	0.465	−779.7	455.4

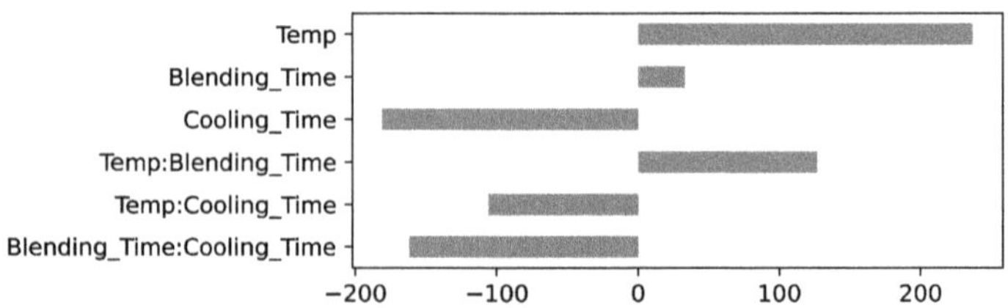

array allow us to test for non-linearity in the response surface by comparing the average responses at the center points, e.g., for viscosity (4135.5) with the average of the responses on the corners of the cube (4851.6). The difference between the averages of 716.1, in an analysis considering third order interactions as noise, is not found significant at the 1% level of significance (Table 6.9). None of the other effects was found significant at that level. The analysis shows that no significant non-linearity is observed.

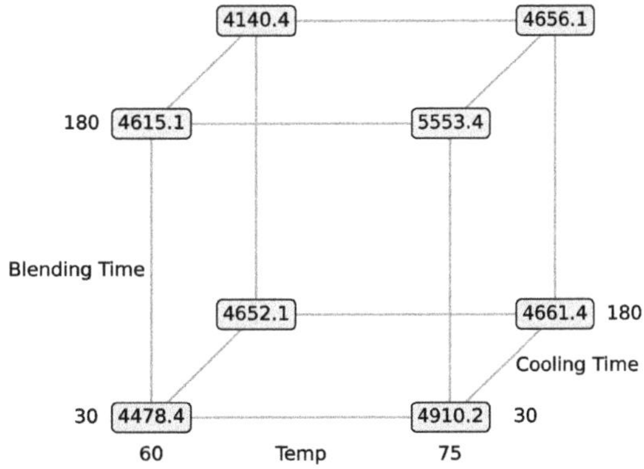

Fig. 6.4 Cube display of predicted viscosity response

Table 6.9 Analysis considering third order interactions as noise to test for non-linearity

```
# add additional feature that identifies the center point
FFdesign['center'] = [1 if t == 0 else 0 for t in FFdesign['Temp']]
# and include it in the model
formula = 'Viscosity ~ (Temp + Blending_Time + Cooling_Time)**2 + center'
ff_model_center = smf.ols(formula=formula, data=FFdesign).fit()
```

	Coef.	Std. Err.	t	$P > \|t\|$	[0.025	0.975]
Intercept	4851.6	72.1	67.266	0.000	4541.3	5162.0
Temp	236.9	72.1	3.284	0.082	−73.5	547.2
Blending_Time	32.9	72.1	0.456	0.693	−277.5	343.2
Cooling_Time	−180.9	72.1	−2.508	0.129	−491.2	129.5
Temp:Blending_Time	126.6	72.1	1.756	0.221	−183.7	437.0
Temp:Cooling_Time	−105.6	72.1	−1.464	0.281	−416.0	204.7
Blending_Time:Cooling_Time	−162.1	72.1	−2.248	0.154	−472.5	148.2
Center	−716.1	161.3	−4.440	0.047	−1410.0	−22.2

6.4.3 A Quality by Design Case Study: The Desirability Function

The design space we are seeking is simultaneously addressing requirements on 8 responses named: (1) Active assay, (2) In vitro lower (3) In vitro upper (4) D90 (5) A assay (6) B assay (7) Viscosity, and (8) pH. Our goal is to identify operating ranges of temperature, blending time, and cooling time that guarantee that all 8 responses are within specification limits. To achieve this objective, we apply a popular solution called the desirability function (Derringer and Suich 1980). Other techniques exist such as principal components analysis and non-linear principal components (Figini et al. 2010).

In order to combine the 8 responses simultaneously, we first compute a desirability function using the characteristics of each response $Y_i(x), i = 1, \ldots, 8$. For each response, $Y_i(x)$, the univariate desirability function $d_i(Y_i)$ assigns numbers between 0 and 1 to the possible values of Y_i, with $d_i(Y_i) = 0$ representing a completely

Table 6.10 Definition of calculation of desirability functions for the 8 responses

```
# define functions that generate a variety of profiles
# note that the function returns a function profile(x)
def rampProfile(lower, upper, reverse=False):
    def wrapped(x):
        condlist = [x < lower, x >= lower, x > upper]
        funclist = [0, lambda x: (x-lower)/(upper-lower), 1]
        if reverse:
            funclist = [1, lambda x: (upper-x)/(upper-lower), 0]
        return np.piecewise(x, condlist, funclist)
    return wrapped

def triangleProfile(lower, middle, upper):
    def wrapped(x):
        condlist = [x < lower, x >= lower, x >= middle, x >= upper]
        funclist = [0, lambda x: (x-lower)/(middle-lower),
                    lambda x: (upper-x) / (upper-middle), 0]
        return np.piecewise(x, condlist, funclist)
    return wrapped

desirabilityProfiles = {
    'Active_Assay': rampProfile(95, 105),
    'In_Vitro_Lower': rampProfile(80, 125),
    'In_Vitro_Upper': rampProfile(110, 135, reverse=True),
    'D90': triangleProfile(1, 1.5, 2),
    'A_Assay': rampProfile(95, 105),
    'B_Assay': rampProfile(95, 105),
    'Viscosity': triangleProfile(4000, 5000, 5750),
    'pH': triangleProfile(4.7, 5.2, 5.6),
}
```

undesirable value of Y_i and $d_i(Y_i) = 1$ representing a completely desirable or ideal response value. The desirability functions for the 8 responses are defined and shown graphically in Table 6.10. For active assay, we want to be above 95% and up to 105%. Assay values below 95% yield desirability of zero, and assay above 105% yield desirability of 1. We describe the desirability using a function that is zero below 95, then linearly increases until 105 to one, and remains a constant one above 105. For in vitro upper, we do not want to be above 135% and therefore describe it using a reverse ramp function. In vitro lower and the two Assay A and B responses are defined using similar desirability functions. Our target for D90 is 1.5 with results above 2 and below 1 having zero desirability. We describe this desirability profile using a triangle function. Similar profiles are defined for viscosity and pH.

The desirability functions scale the various responses to a value between 0 and 1. We can assess the design space by an overall desirability index using the geometric mean of the individual desirabilities:

$$\text{Desirability Index} = [d_1(Y_1) * d_2(Y_2) * \ldots d_k(Y_k)]^{\frac{1}{k}}$$

Table 6.11 Calculation of individual and overall desirability for a given target setting

```
def overallDesirability(x):
    x = np.array(list(x))
    if any(xi == 0 for xi in x): # handle 0-desirability case
        return 0
    return stats.gmean(x)

def calculateDesirability(target, models, desirabilityProfiles):
    targetPredictions = {response: model.predict(target).values[0]
                         for response, model in models.items()}

    # determine overall desirability for targetPredictions
    targetDesirabilities = {response: float(desirabilityProfiles[response]
                            (value)) for response, value in targetPredictions.
                            items()}

    targetDesirabilities['overall'] = overallDesirability(targetDesirabilities.
                                      values())

    return {
      'individual': pd.DataFrame({'predictions': targetPredictions,
                                  'desirability': targetDesirabilities}),
      'overall': overallDesirability(targetDesirabilities.values()),
    }

models = {}
for response in desirabilityProfiles:
    formula = f'{response} ~ (Temp + Blending_Time + Cooling_Time)**2'
    models[response] = smf.ols(formula=formula, data=df).fit()

target = pd.DataFrame(
    {'Temp': 65, 'Blending_Time': 2.5, 'Cooling_Time': 150},
    index=['target'])

targetDesirabilities = calculateDesirability(target, models,
                                desirabilityProfiles)
targetDesirabilities['overall']
```

```
0.33976276040548653
```

with k denoting the number of measures (in our case, $k = 8$). Notice that if any response Yi is completely undesirable ($d_i(Y_i) = 0$), then the overall desirability is zero.

Example 6.4 After training individual models for all the responses using the data from Sect. 6.4.2, we can determine individual and overall desirability indices for a setting of Temp = 65, Blending Time = 2.5, and Cooling Time = 150. In Table 6.11, we can see that setting gives us an overall desirability index = 0.34.

We can also determine the effect of variability in the factor levels, similar to what is implemented in the piston simulator. We describe the variability of each factor level using normal distributions.

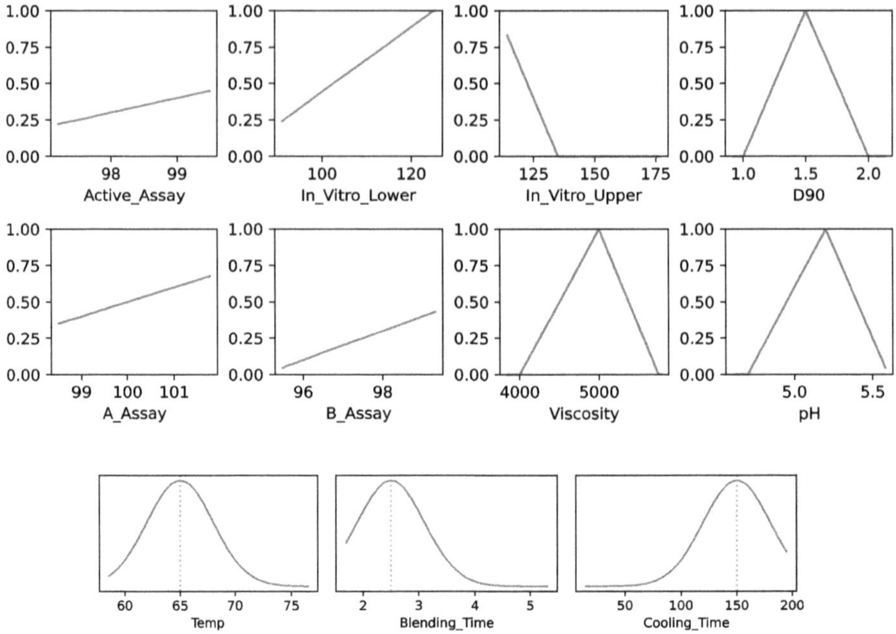

Fig. 6.5 Variability of the factor levels around target settings

```
variability = {
    'Temp': stats.norm(loc=65, scale=3),
    'Blending_Time': stats.norm(loc=2.5, scale=0.6),
    'Cooling_Time': stats.norm(loc=150, scale=30),
}
```

Figure 6.5 shows the three normal distributions for the settings of Temp, Blending Time, and Cooling Time. This variability is then transferred to the 8 responses and to the overall desirability index.

```
# simulate data with variability around the target settings
np.random.seed(1)
random_df = pd.DataFrame({
    factor: variability[factor].rvs(5000)
    for factor in target
})

predictions = {response: model.predict(random_df)
               for response, model in models.items()}

variableDesirabilities = pd.DataFrame({
    response: desirability(predictions[response].values)
    for response, desirability in desirabilityProfiles.items()
})

variableDesirabilities['overall'] = \
       variableDesirabilities.apply(overallDesirability, axis=1)
```

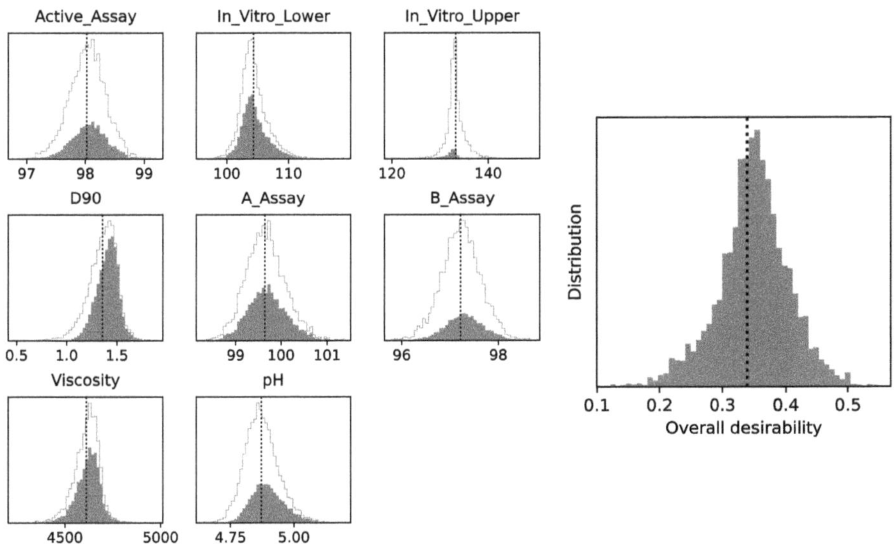

Fig. 6.6 Distribution of individual and overall desirabilities due to variability in factor levels: Temp = 65, Blending time = 2.5, and Cooling time = 150

Figure 6.6 shows the distribution of the individual and overall desirabilities due to variability in factor levels. The graphs for individual responses show two distributions. The outline shows the distributions of the predicted response; the overlayed filled histogram is the distribution weighted by desirability. Viscosity and both in vitro responses show the smallest variability relative to the experimental range. As many of the simulated in vitro upper predictions are close to the undesirable 135% threshold, we see that the distribution of this response is strongly affected by desirability. In fact, about 14% of the simulated responses have an overall desirability of zero. ■

6.4.4 A Quality by Design Case Study: The Design Space

To conclude the analysis, we study the design space using the models fitted to the experimental data with main effects and two-way interactions. Figure 6.7 shows contours of the models. The previous analysis showed that of all quality attributes, *in vitro upper* leads to the lowest undesirability. The dark shaded areas identify the region where the undesirability is zero (greater 135); in the light shaded area, its value is between 133 and 135. We can see that our initial target settings of temperature at 65, blending time of 2.5, and cooling time of 150 are in the light shaded area. If we increase the temperature slightly to 67, our process moves into a

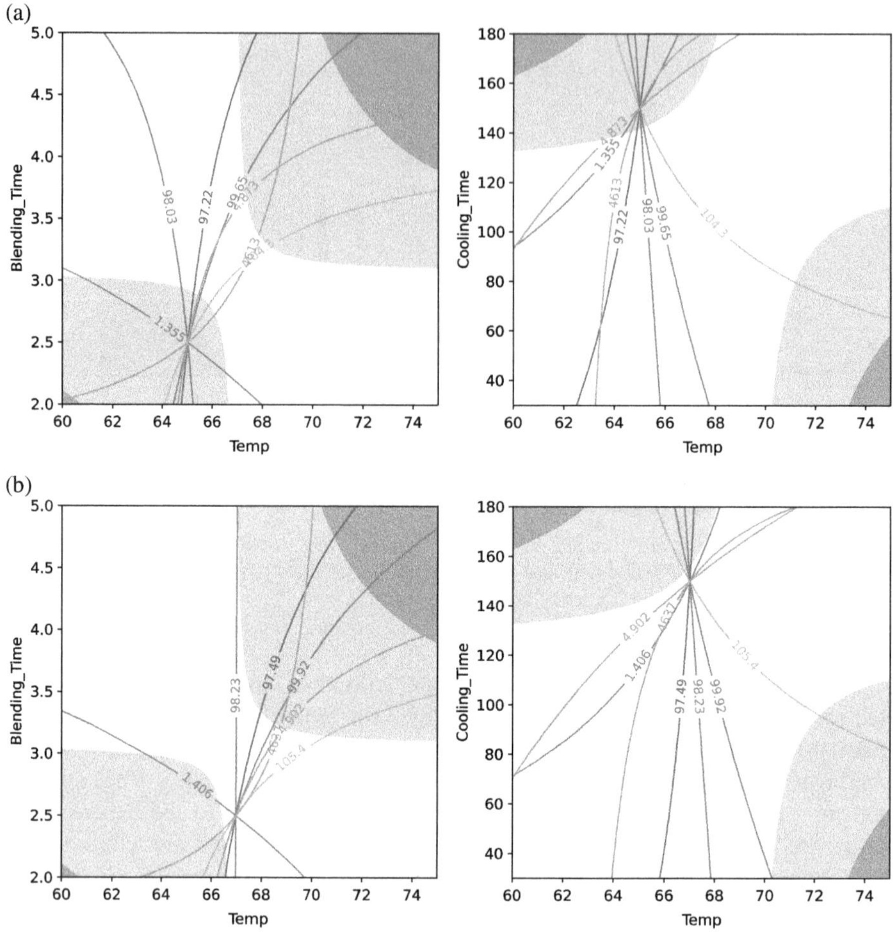

Fig. 6.7 Contour plots with overlay of eight responses for the initial (**a**) and changed (**b**) target settings. The shaded areas identify the areas with very low desirability of *in vitro upper*

more desirable region with respect to in vitro upper. Indeed, our overall desirability increases from 0.34 to 0.38.

Using these visualizations of the design space, we can identify operating regions with higher desirability. Once approved by the regulator, these areas of operations are defined as the normal range of operation. Under QbD, any changes within these regions do not require pre-approval, only post change notification. This change in regulatory strategy is considered a breakthrough in traditional inspection doctrines and provides a significant regulatory relief.

An essential component of QbD submissions to the FDA is the design of a control strategy. Control is established by determining expected results and tracking actual results in the context of expected results. The expected results are used to set up upper and control limits. The use of simulations, as presented in Fig. 6.7, can be used for this purpose. A final step in a QbD submission is to revise the risk assessment analysis. At this stage, the experts agreed that with the defined design space and an effective control strategy accounting for the variability presented in Fig. 6.6, all risks in Table 6.5 have been reset as low.

In this section, we covered the essential steps in preparing a QbD submission. We focused on the application of statistically designed experiments and show how they can be used to achieve robust and optimized process design standard operating procedures.

6.5 Tolerance Designs

Usually, parts installed in systems, such as resistors, capacitors, transistors, and other parts of mechanical nature, have some deviations in their characteristics from the nominal ones. For example, a resistor with a nominal resistance of 8200 [Ohm] will have an actual resistance value that is a random deviate around the nominal value. Parts are classified according to their tolerances. Grade A could be with a tolerance interval $\pm 1\%$ of the nominal value. Grade B of $\pm 5\%$, grade C of $\pm 10\%$, etc. Parts with high-grade tolerances are more expensive than low-grade ones. Due to the non-linear dependence of the system output (performance characteristic) on the input values of its components, not all component variances contribute equally to the variance of the output. We have also seen that the variances of the components affect the means of the output characteristics. It is therefore important to perform experiments to determine which tolerance grade should be assigned to each component. We illustrate such a problem in the following example.

Example 6.5 Taguchi (1987, Vol. 1, pp. 379) describes a tolerance design for a circuit that converts alternating current of 100 [V] AC into a direct current of 220 [V] DC. This example is based on an experiment performed in 1974 at the Shin Nippon Denki Company.

The output of the system, Y, depends in a complicated manner on 17 factors. The simulator *PowerCircuitSimulation* (`mistat` package) was designed to experiment with this system.

In this example, we use *PowerCircuitSimulation* to execute a fractional replication of 2^{13-8} to investigate the effects of two tolerance grades of 13 components, 10 resistors, and 3 transistors, on the output of the system. The two design levels for each factor are the two tolerance grades. For example, if we specify for a given factor a tolerance of 10%, then the experiment at level 1 will use at level 1 a tolerance of 5% and at level 2 a tolerance of 10%. The value of a given factor is simulated according to a normal distribution with mean at the nominal value of that factor. The standard deviation is 1/6 of the length of the tolerance interval. For example, if the nominal value for factor A is 8200 [Ohm], and the tolerance level is 10%, the standard deviation for level 1 is 136.67 [Ohm] and for level 2 is 273.33 [Ohm].

Table 6.12 Factor levels for the 2^{13-8} design

	A	B	C	D	E	F	G	H	I	J	K	L	M
1	1	1	1	1	1	1	1	1	1	1	1	1	1
2	2	1	1	1	1	2	2	2	2	2	2	1	1
3	1	2	1	1	1	2	2	2	1	1	1	2	2
4	2	2	1	1	1	1	1	1	2	2	2	2	2
5	1	1	2	1	1	2	1	1	2	2	1	2	2
6	2	1	2	1	1	1	2	2	1	1	2	2	2
7	1	2	2	1	1	1	2	2	2	2	1	1	1
8	2	2	2	1	1	2	1	1	1	1	2	1	1
9	1	1	1	2	1	1	2	1	2	1	2	2	1
10	2	1	1	2	1	2	1	2	1	2	1	2	1
11	1	2	1	2	1	2	1	2	2	1	2	1	2
12	2	2	1	2	1	1	2	1	1	2	1	1	2
13	1	1	2	2	1	2	2	1	1	2	2	1	2
14	2	1	2	2	1	1	1	2	2	1	1	1	2
15	1	2	2	2	1	1	1	2	1	2	2	2	1
16	2	2	2	2	1	2	2	1	2	1	1	2	1
17	1	1	1	1	2	1	1	2	1	2	2	1	2
18	2	1	1	1	2	2	2	1	2	1	1	1	2
19	1	2	1	1	2	2	2	1	1	2	2	2	1
20	2	2	1	1	2	1	1	2	2	1	1	2	1
21	1	1	2	1	2	2	1	2	2	1	2	2	1
22	2	1	2	1	2	1	2	1	1	2	1	2	1
23	1	2	2	1	2	1	2	1	2	1	2	1	2
24	2	2	2	1	2	2	1	2	1	2	1	1	2
25	1	1	1	2	2	1	2	2	2	2	1	2	2
26	2	1	1	2	2	2	1	1	1	1	2	2	2
27	1	2	1	2	2	2	1	1	2	2	1	1	1
28	2	2	1	2	2	1	2	2	1	1	2	1	1
29	1	1	2	2	2	2	2	2	1	1	1	1	1
30	2	1	2	2	2	1	1	1	2	2	2	1	1
31	1	2	2	2	2	1	1	1	1	1	1	2	2
32	2	2	2	2	2	2	2	2	2	2	2	2	2

As mentioned earlier, the control factors are 10 resistors labeled A-J and 3 transistors labeled K-M. The nominal levels of these factors are:

$$A = 8200, \quad B = 220000, \quad C = 1000, \quad D = 33000, \quad E = 56000, \quad F = 5600,$$

$$G = 3300, \quad H = 58.5, \quad I = 1000, \quad J = 120, \quad K = 130, \quad L = 100, \quad M = 130^{\cdot}$$

The levels of the 13 factors in the 2^{13-8} fractional replicate are given in Table 6.12.

We perform this experiment on the computer, using *PowerCircuitSimulation*. We wish to find a treatment combination (run) that yields a small MSE at low cost per circuit. We will assume that grade B parts (5% tolerance) cost \$1 and grade C parts (10% tolerance) cost \$0.5. In order to obtain sufficiently precise estimates of the MSE, we perform at each run a simulated sample of size $n = 100$. The results of this experiment are given in Table 6.13.

```
np.random.seed(1)

# Prepare design
tolerances = [f'tl{c}' for c in 'ABCDEFGHIJKLM']
factors = {tl: [5, 10] for tl in tolerances}
Design = doe.frac_fact_res(factors, 4)

# Randomize and create replicates
nrepeat = 100
Design = Design.sample(frac=1).reset_index(drop=True)
Design = Design.loc[Design.index.repeat(nrepeat)].reset_index(drop=True)

# Run simulation
simulator = mistat.PowerCircuitSimulation(**{k: list(Design[k]) for k in Design})
result = simulator.simulate()
result = mistat.simulationGroup(result, nrepeat)

Design['response'] = result['volts']
Design['group'] = result['group']

# calculate mean, standard deviation, and total cost for each group
def groupAggregation(g):
    # calculate cost of design (tolerance 10 = 0.5, tolerance 5 = 1)
    groupTolerances = g.iloc[0,:][tolerances]
    tc = 0.5 * sum(groupTolerances == 10) + 1 * sum(groupTolerances == 5)
    return {
        'mean': g['response'].mean(),
        'STD': g['response'].std(),
        'MSE': g['response'].var(ddof=0),
        'TC': tc,
        **groupTolerances,
    }
results = pd.DataFrame(list(Design.groupby('group').apply(groupAggregation)))
```

We see that the runs having small mean squared errors (MSE) are 1, 12, 13, and 31. Among these, the run with the smallest total cost (TC) is 13. We could, however, accept the slightly higher cost of run 31 to get the lower MSE. ■

6.6 Case Studies

6.6.1 The Quinlan Experiment

This experiment was carried out at Flex Products in Midvale Ohio (Quinlan 1985). Flex Products is a subcontractor of General Motors, manufacturing mechanical speedometer cables. The basic cable design has not changed for fifteen years, and General Motors had experienced many disappointing attempts at reducing the speedometer noise level. Flex Products decided to apply the off-line quality control

Table 6.13 Performance characteristics of tolerance design experiment

	Mean	STD	MSE	TC		Mean	STD	MSE	TC
24	230.32	3.5976	12.8130	13	25	230.24	5.7056	32.2279	9
27	229.43	4.3597	18.8173	10	22	229.73	5.7172	32.3599	9
29	229.80	4.4109	19.2617	10	1	229.50	5.7244	32.4413	9
31	230.99	4.6552	21.4542	10	17	230.44	5.7973	33.2726	9
15	230.85	4.7367	22.2119	10	8	230.88	5.8922	34.3706	10
30	230.91	4.7774	22.5954	9	20	230.46	5.9800	35.4024	10
7	229.93	4.8452	23.2415	10	19	230.27	6.0310	36.0092	10
3	230.03	4.8563	23.3477	9	6	230.46	6.1385	37.3047	10
21	229.73	4.9575	24.3307	9	11	230.35	6.2171	38.2664	9
4	229.60	5.1094	25.8444	9	16	229.50	6.2814	39.0608	10
10	229.93	5.2639	27.4314	9	18	230.19	6.2949	39.2299	10
23	231.29	5.3464	28.2980	10	12	229.77	6.5423	42.3742	9
14	230.08	5.4595	29.5084	10	28	229.52	6.6241	43.4396	10
13	230.70	5.5159	30.1212	9	5	230.01	6.8145	45.9726	9
32	229.79	5.5959	31.0005	9	9	230.50	7.1933	51.2260	10
2	230.59	5.5979	31.0229	9	26	230.26	7.2022	51.3528	6

and involve in the project customers, production personnel, and engineers with experience in the product and manufacturing process. A large experiment involving 15 factors was designed and completed. The data showed that much improvement could be gained by few simple changes. The results were dramatic, and the loss per unit was reduced from \$2.12 to \$0.13 by changing the braid type, the linear material, and the braiding tension.

We proceed to describe the experiment using an eight points template:

1. **Problem Definition**. The product under investigation is an extruded thermoplastic speedometer casing used to cover the mechanical speedometer cable on automobiles. Excessive shrinkage of the casing is causing noise in the mechanical speedometer cable assembly.
2. **Response variable**. The performance characteristic in this problem is the post-extrusion shrinkage of the casing. The percent shrinkage is obtained by measuring approximately 600 mm of casing that has been properly conditioned (A), placing that casing in a two-hour heat soak in an air circulating oven, reconditioning the sample, and measuring the length (B). Shrinkage is computed as: Shrinkage $= 100 \times (A - B)/A$.
3. **Control factors**:
4. **Factor Levels**. Existing (1)—Changed (2).
5. **Experimental Array**. $L_{16}(2^{15})$ orthogonal array.
6. **The Number of Replications**. Four random samples of 600mm from the 3000 feet manufactured at each experimental run.

Liner Process:	A: Liner O.D.
	B: Liner die
	C: Liner material
	D: Liner line speed
Wire braiding:	E: Wire braid type
	F: Braiding tension
	G: Wire diameter
	H: Liner tension
	I: Liner temperature
Coating process:	J: Coating material
	K: Coating dye type
	L: Melt temperature
	M: Screen pack
	N: Cooling method
	O: Line speed

7. **Data Analysis**. Signal-to-noise ratios (SN) are computed for each experimental run and analyzed using main effect plots and an ANOVA. Savings are derived from loss function computations.
   The signal-to-noise formula used by Quinlan is

$$\eta = -10 \log_{10} \left(\frac{1}{n} \sum_{i=1}^{n} y_i^2 \right).$$

   For example, experimental run number 1 produced shrinkage factors of: 0.49, 0.54, 0.46, 0.45. The SN is 6.26. The objective is to maximize the SN by proper setup of the 15 controllable factors.
   Table 6.14 shows the factor levels and the SN values, for all 16 experimental runs.
   Notice that Quinlan, by using the orthogonal array $L_{16}(2^{15})$ for all the fifteen factors, assumes that there are no significant interactions. If this assumption is correct, then the main effects of the fifteen factors are:
   Figure 6.8 presents the main effects plot for this experiment. Factors E and G seem to be most influential. These main effects, as defined in Ch. 3, are the regression coefficients of SN on the design coefficients ± 1. As mentioned in Chap. 5, these are sometimes called "half effects." Only the effects of factors E and G are significant. If the assumption of no interaction is wrong, and all the first order interactions are significant, then, as shown in the linear graph LG_1 in Fig. 6.2, only the effects of factors A, B, D, H and O are not confounded. The effects of the other factors are confounded with first order interactions. The main effect of factor E is confounded with the interaction AD, and that of G is confounded with HO. In order to confirm the first hypothesis that all interactions are negligible, an additional experiment should be performed, in which factors E and G will be assigned columns that do not represent possible interactions (like

Table 6.14 Factor levels and *SN* values

	A	B	C	D	E	F	G	H	I	J	K	L	M	N	O	SN
1	1	1	1	1	1	1	1	1	1	1	1	1	1	1	1	6.26
2	1	1	1	1	1	1	1	2	2	2	2	2	2	2	2	4.80
3	1	1	1	2	2	2	2	1	1	1	1	2	2	2	2	21.04
4	1	1	1	2	2	2	2	2	2	2	2	1	1	1	1	15.11
5	1	2	2	1	1	2	2	1	1	2	2	1	1	2	2	14.03
6	1	2	2	1	1	2	2	2	2	1	1	2	2	1	1	16.69
7	1	2	2	2	2	1	1	1	1	2	2	2	2	1	1	12.91
8	1	2	2	2	2	1	1	2	2	1	1	1	1	2	2	15.05
9	2	1	2	1	2	1	2	1	2	1	2	1	2	1	2	17.67
10	2	1	2	1	2	1	2	2	1	2	1	2	1	2	1	17.27
11	2	1	2	2	1	2	1	1	2	1	2	2	1	2	1	6.82
12	2	1	2	2	1	2	1	2	1	2	1	1	2	1	2	5.43
13	2	2	1	1	2	2	1	1	2	2	1	1	2	2	1	15.27
14	2	2	1	1	2	2	1	2	1	1	2	2	1	1	2	11.20
15	2	2	1	2	1	1	2	1	2	2	1	2	1	1	2	9.24
16	2	2	1	2	1	1	2	2	1	1	2	1	2	2	1	4.68

Factor	*A*	*B*	*C*	*D*	*E*	*F*	*G*	*H*
Main effect	−1.145	0.29	1.14	−0.86	3.60	1.11	2.37	−0.82

Factor	*I*	*J*	*K*	*L*	*M*	*N*	*O*
Main effect	0.49	−0.34	−1.19	0.41	0.22	0.28	0.22

columns 1 and 2 of Table 6.4). The results of the additional experiment should reconfirm the conclusions of the original experiment.

8. **Results**. As a result of Quinlan's analysis, factors *E* and *G* were changed. This reduced the average shrinkage index from 26% to 5%. The shrinkage standard deviation was also reduced, from 0.05 to 0.025. This was considered a substantial success in quality improvement.

6.6.2 Computer Response Time Optimization

The experiment described in Pao et al. (1985) was part of an extensive effort to optimize a UNIX operating system running on a VAX 11-780 machine. The machine had 48 user terminal ports, two remote job entry links, four megabytes of memory, and five disk drives. The typical number of users logged on at a given time was between 20 to 30:

1. **Problem Definition**. Users complained that the system performance was very poor, especially in the afternoon. The objective of the improvement effort was to both minimize response time and reduce variability in response.

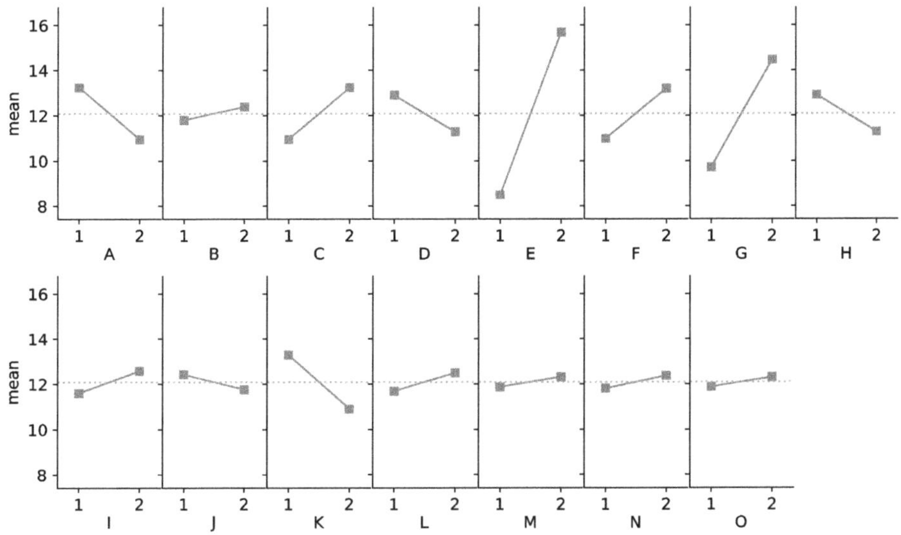

Fig. 6.8 Main effects plot for Quinlan experiment

2. **Response variable**. In order to get an objective measurement of the response time, two specific representative commands called **standard** and **trivial** were used. The **standard** command consisted of creating, editing, and removing a file. The **trivial** command was the UNIX system "date" command. Response times were measured by submitting these commands every 10 m and clocking the time taken for the system to complete their execution.
3. **Control factors**:

A: Disk drives

B: File distribution

C: Memory size

D: System buffers

E: Sticky bits

F: KMCs used

G: INODE table entries

H: Other system tables

4. **Factor Levels**.

Factor	Levels		
A: RM05 & RP06	4 & 1	4 & 2	4 & 3
B: File distribution	a	b	c
C: Memory size (MB)	4	3	3.5
D: System buffers	1/5	1/4	1/3
E: Sticky bits	0	3	8
F: KMCs used	2		0
G: INODE table entries	400	500	600
H: Other system tables	a	b	c

5. **Experimental Array**. The design was an orthogonal array $L_{18}(3^8)$. This and the mean response are given in the following table.
   Each mean response in Table 6.15 is over $n = 96$ measurements.
6. **Data Analysis**. The measure of performance characteristic used was the S/N ratio

$$\eta = -10 \log_{10} \left(\frac{1}{n} \sum_{i=1}^{n} y_i^2 \right),$$

   where y_i is the ith response time.
   Figure 6.9 is the main effects plot of these eight factors.
   We see that factors having substantial effects are A, C, D, E, and H. As a result, the number of disk drives was changed to 4 and 2. The system buffers were changed from 1/3 to 1/4. The number of sticky bits was changed from 0 to 8. After introducing these changes, the average response time dropped from 6.15 (s) to 2.37 (s) with a substantial reduction in response times variability.

Factor	Linear	Quadratic
A	0.97	—
B	0.19	−0.15
C	−1.24	−1.32
D	−0.37	−1.23
E	1.72	1.86
F	0.44	—
G	0.17	−0.63
H	0.05	1.29

Table 6.15 Factor levels and mean response[a]

	F	B	C	D	E	A	G	H	Mean	SN
1	1	1	1	1	1	1	1	1	4.65	−14.66
2	1	1	2	2	2	2	2	2	5.28	−16.37
3	1	1	3	3	3	3	3	3	3.06	−10.49
4	1	2	1	1	2	2	3	3	4.53	−14.85
5	1	2	2	2	3	3	1	1	3.26	−10.94
6	1	2	3	3	1	1	2	2	4.55	−14.96
7	1	3	1	2	1	3	2	3	3.37	−11.77
8	1	3	2	3	2	1	3	1	5.62	−16.72
9	1	3	3	1	3	2	1	2	4.87	−14.67
10	2	1	1	3	3	2	2	1	4.13	−13.52
11	2	1	2	1	1	3	3	2	4.08	−13.79
12	2	1	3	2	2	1	1	3	4.45	−14.19
13	2	2	1	2	3	1	3	2	3.81	−12.89
14	2	2	2	3	1	2	1	3	5.87	−16.75
15	2	2	3	1	2	3	2	1	3.42	−11.65
16	2	3	1	3	2	3	1	2	3.66	−12.23
17	2	3	2	1	3	1	2	3	3.92	−12.81
18	2	3	3	2	1	2	3	1	4.42	−13.71

[a] Factor A had only 2 levels. All levels 3 in the table were changed to level 2

Fig. 6.9 Main effects plot

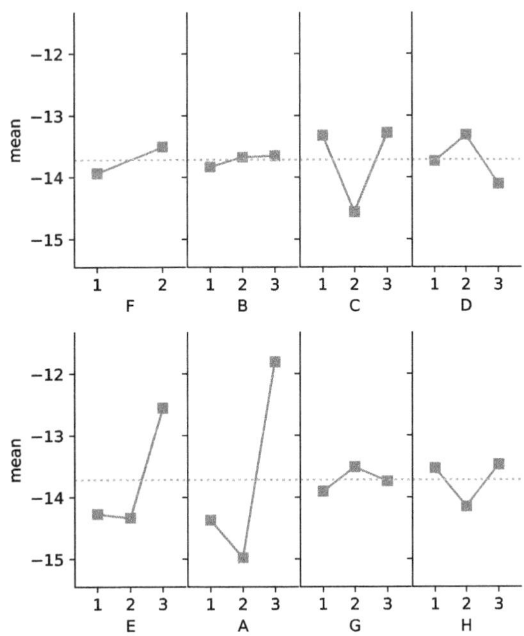

6.7 Chapter Highlights

The main concepts and definitions introduced in this chapter include:

- Design of experiments
- Robust design
- Quality planning
- Quality engineering
- Off-line quality control
- Loss functions
- Parameter design
- Tolerance design
- Response surfaces
- Mixture designs
- Inner array
- Outer array
- Linear graph
- Signal-to-noise
- Performance measures
- Quality by design (QbD)
- Design space
- Control strategy
- Risk management
- Critical quality attributes (CQAs)
- ICH Guidelines Q8-Q11
- Desirability function
- Current good manufacturing practices (cGMPs)
- Desirability function

6.8 Exercises

Exercise 6.1 The objective is to find the levels of the factors of the piston, which yield an average cycle time of 0.02 (sec). Execute a *PistonSimulation*, with sample size $n = 100$:

(i) Determine which treatment combination yields the smallest

$$MSE = (\bar{Y} - 0.45)^2 + S^2.$$

(ii) Determine which treatment combination yields the largest SN ratio,

$$\eta = 10 \log_{10}\left(\frac{Y^2}{S^2} - \frac{1}{100}\right).$$

What is the MSE at this treatment combination?

The five factors that are varied are: piston weight, piston surface area, initial gas volume, spring coefficient, and ambient temperature. The factors atmospheric pressure and filling gas temperature are kept constant at the midrange level.

Exercise 6.2 Run a *PistonSimulation* with sample size of $n = 100$ and generate the sample means and standard deviation of the $2^7 = 128$ treatment combinations of a full factorial experiment, for the effects on the piston cycle time. Perform regression analysis to find which factors have significant effects on the signal-to-noise ratio $SN = \log((\bar{X}/S)^2)$.

Exercise 6.3 Let (X_1, X_2) have joint distribution with means (ξ_1, ξ_2) and covariance matrix

$$V = \begin{pmatrix} \sigma_1^2 & \sigma_{12} \\ \sigma_{12} & \sigma_2^2 \end{pmatrix}.$$

Find approximations to the expected values and variances of:

(i) $Y = X_1/X_2$.
(ii) $Y = \log(X_1^2/X_2^2)$.
(iii) $Y = (X_1^2 + X_2^2)^{1/2}$.

Exercise 6.4 The relationship between the absorption ratio Y of a solid image in a copied paper and the light intensity X is given by the function

$$Y = 0.0782 + \frac{0.90258}{1 + 0.6969X^{-1.4258}}.$$

Assuming that X has the gamma distribution $G(1, 1.5)$, approximate the expected value and variance of Y.

Exercise 6.5 Let $\bar{X}_n$ and S_n^2 be the mean and variance of a random sample of size n from a normal distribution $N(\mu, \sigma)$. We know that $\bar{X}_n$ and S_n^2 are independent, $\bar{X}_n \sim N\left(\mu, \frac{\sigma}{\sqrt{n}}\right)$ and $S_n^2 \sim \frac{\sigma^2}{n-1}\chi^2[n-1]$. Find an approximation to the expected value and variance of $Y = \log\left(\frac{\bar{X}_n^2}{S_n^2}\right)$.

Exercise 6.6 An experiment based on an L_{18} orthogonal array involving eight factors gave the results listed in Table 6.16 (see Phadke et al. 1983). Each run had $n = 5$ replications.

Analyze the effects of the factors of the SN ratio $\eta = \log(\bar{X}/S)$.

Exercise 6.7 Using *PistonSimulation*, perform a full factorial (2^7), a $1/8$ (2^{7-3}), $1/4$ (2^{7-2}), and $1/2$ (2^{7-1}) fractional replications of the cycle time experiment. Estimate the main effects of the seven factors with respect to $SN = \log(\bar{X}/S)$ and compare the results obtained from these experiments. Use $n = 5$ replicates for each combination of factors.

Table 6.16 Results of experiment based on L_{18} orthogonal array

Run	Factors									
	1	2	3	4	5	6	7	8	$\bar{X}$	S
1	1	1	1	1	1	1	1	1	2.500	0.0827
2	1	1	2	2	2	2	2	2	2.684	0.1196
3	1	1	3	3	3	3	3	3	2.660	0.1722
4	1	2	1	1	2	2	3	3	1.962	0.1696
5	1	2	2	2	3	3	1	1	1.870	0.1168
6	1	2	3	3	1	1	2	2	2.584	0.1106
7	1	3	1	2	1	3	2	3	2.032	0.0718
8	1	3	2	3	2	1	3	1	3.267	0.2101
9	1	3	3	1	3	2	1	2	2.829	0.1516
10	2	1	1	3	3	2	2	1	2.660	0.1912
11	2	1	2	1	1	3	3	2	3.166	0.0674
12	2	1	3	2	2	1	1	3	3.323	0.1274
13	2	2	1	2	3	1	3	2	2.576	0.0850
14	2	2	2	3	1	2	1	3	2.308	0.0964
15	2	2	3	1	2	3	2	1	2.464	0.0385
16	2	3	1	3	2	3	1	2	2.667	0.0706
17	2	3	2	1	3	1	2	3	3.156	0.1569
18	2	3	3	2	1	2	3	1	3.494	0.0473

Exercise 6.8 To see the effect of the variances of the random variables on the expected response, in non-linear cases, execute *PistonSimulation*, with $n = 20$ replicates, and compare the output means to the values in Exercise 6.7.

Exercise 6.9 Run *PowerCircuitSimulation* with 1% and 2% tolerances, and compare the results to those of Table 6.13.

Chapter 7
Computer Experiments

Preview Computer experiments are integrated in modern product and service development activities. Technology is providing advanced digital platforms for studying various properties of suggested designs, without the need to physically concretize them. This chapter is about computer experiments and the special techniques required for designing such experiments and analyzing their outcomes. A specific example of such experiments is the piston simulator used throughout the book to demonstrate statistical concepts and tools. In this simulator, random noise is induced on the control variables themselves, a non-standard approach in modeling physical phenomena. The experiments covered include space filling designs and Latin hypercubes. The analysis of the experimental outputs is based on Kriging or design and analysis of computer experiments (DACE) models. The chapter discusses the concept of a stochastic emulator where a model derived from the simulation outputs is used to optimize the design in a robust way. A special section is discussing several approaches to integrate the analysis of computer and physical experiments.

7.1 Introduction to Computer Experiments

Experimentation via computer modeling has become very common in many areas of science and technology. In computer experiments, physical processes are simulated by running a computer code that generates output data for given input values. In physical experiments, data are generated directly from a physical process. In both physical and computer experiments, a study is designed to answer specific research questions, and appropriate statistical methods are needed to design the experiment and to analyze the resulting data. Chapters 5 and 6 present such methods and many examples. In this chapter, we focus on computer experiments and specific design and analysis methods relevant to such experiments.

Supplementary Information The online version contains supplementary material available at (https://doi.org/10.1007/978-3-031-28482-3_7).

R. S. Kenett et al., *Industrial Statistics*, Statistics for Industry, Technology, and Engineering, https://doi.org/10.1007/978-3-031-28482-3_7

Because of experimental error, a physical experiment will produce a different output for different runs at the same input settings. Computer experiments are deterministic, and the same inputs will always result in the same output. Thus, none of the traditional principles of blocking, randomization, and replication can be used in the design and analysis of computer experiments data. On the other hand, computer experiments use extensively random number generators, and these are described in Sect. 7.6.

Computer experiments consist of a number of runs of a simulation code, and factor-level combinations correspond to a subset of code inputs. By considering computer runs as a realization of a stochastic process, a statistical framework is available both to design the experimental points and to analyze the responses. A major difference between computer numerical experiments and physical experiments is the logical difficulty in specifying a source of randomness for computer experiments.

The complexity of the mathematical models implemented in the computer programs can, by themselves, build equivalent sources of random noise. In complex code, a number of parameters and model choices give the user many degrees of freedom that provide potential variability to the outputs of the simulation. Examples include different solution algorithms (i.e., implicit or explicit methods for solving differential systems), approach to discretization intervals, and convergence thresholds for iterative techniques. In this very sense, an experimental error can be considered in the statistical analysis of computer experiments. The nature of the experimental error in both physical and simulated experiments is our ignorance about the phenomena and the intrinsic error of the measurements. Real-world phenomena are too complex for the experimenter to keep under control by specifying all the factors affecting the response of the experiment. Even if it were possible, the physical measuring instruments, being not ideal, introduce problems of accuracy and precision. Perfect knowledge would be achieved in physical experiments only if all experimental factors can be controlled and measured without any error. Similar phenomena occur in computer experiments. A complex code has several degrees of freedom in its implementation that are not controllable.

A specific case where randomness is introduced to computer experiments consists of the popular finite element method (FEM) programs. These models are applied in a variety of technical sectors such as electromagnetics, fluid dynamics, mechanical design, and civil design. The FEM mathematical models are based on a system of partial differential equations defined on a time–space domain for handling linear or non-linear, steady state, or dynamic problems. FEM software can deal with very complex shapes as well as with a variety of material properties, boundary conditions, and loads. Applications of FEM simulations require subdivision of the space domain into a finite number of subdomains, named finite elements, and solving the partial differential system within each subdomain, letting the field function to be continuous on its border.

Experienced FEM practitioners are aware that results of complex simulations (complex shapes, non-linear constitutive equations, dynamic problems, contacts among different bodies, etc.) can be sensitive to the choice of manifold model parameters. Reliability of FEM results is a critical issue for the single simulation and even more for a series of computer experiments. The model parameters used in the discretization of the geometry are likely to be the most critical. Discretization of the model geometry consists in a set of points (nodes of the mesh) and a set of elements (two-dimensional patches or three-dimensional volumes) defined through a connectivity matrix whose rows list the nodes enclosing the elements. Many degrees of freedom are available to the analyst when defining a mesh on a given model. Changing the location and the number of nodes, the shape, and the number of elements, an infinity of meshes are obtained. Any of them will produce different results. How can we model the effects of different meshes on the experimental response? In principle, the finer the discretization, the better the approximation of numerical solution, even if numerical instabilities may occur using very refined meshes. Within a reasonable approximation, a systematical effect can be assigned to mesh density; it would be a fixed-effect factor if it is included in the experiment. A number of topological features (node locations, element shape), which the analyst has no meaningful effect to assign to, are generators of random variability. One can assume that they are randomized along the experiment or random-effect factors with nuisance variance components if they are included as experimental factors.

Mesh selection also has a direct economical impact as computational complexity grows with the power of the number of the elements. In the case of computer experiments, the problem of balancing reliability and cost of the experiment needs to be carefully addressed. In principle, for any output of a numerical code, the following deterministic model holds:

$$y = f(\mathbf{x}) + g(\mathbf{x}; \mathbf{u}), \tag{7.1.1}$$

where the function f represents the dependence of the output y on the vector x of experimental factors, and g describes the contribution of parameters, u, which are necessary for the setup of the computer model. Since the function g may have interactions with engineering parameters, x is also an argument of function g. Generally, an engineer is interested in the estimation of function f, while he considers g as a disturbance. In general, two options are available for analyzing computer experiments: (1) considering the model parameters as additional experimental factors or (2) fixing them along the whole experiment. The first option allows the estimation of the deterministic model written in (7.1.1). This is a good choice since the influence of both engineering and model parameters on the experimental response can be evaluated. This requires, however, an experimental effort that cannot be often affordable. Keeping every model parameter at a fixed value in the experiment, only the first term f of model (7.1.1) can be estimated. This results in a less expensive experiment but has two dangerous drawbacks: (1) the presence of effects of model parameters on the function g in (7.1.1) can cause a bias in the response and (2) the estimates of the effects of engineering parameters are distorted by the interactions between model and engineering parameters according to the function g. A different approach is to randomize along the experiment those

Table 7.1 Different models for computer experiments

Option	Model	Model nature	Advantages	Disadvantages
Fixed model factors	$y = f(\mathbf{x})$	Deterministic	Inexpensive	Possible bias and distortion of effects of engineering parameters
Model of factor effects is included in the experiment	$y = f(\mathbf{x}) + g(\mathbf{x}; \mathbf{u})$	Deterministic	More accurate. Systematic effect of **u** can be discovered	More programming is required
Randomizing model parameters with random effects	$y = f(\mathbf{x}) + g^*(\mathbf{x}; \mathbf{u}) + \epsilon$	Stochastic	Possibility of calibrating experimental error.	Even more programming is required.

model parameters whose effects can reasonably be assumed to be normal random variables with zero average. In this case, the underlying model becomes a stochastic one:

$$y = f(\mathbf{x}) + g^*(\mathbf{x}; \mathbf{u}) + \epsilon, \tag{7.1.2}$$

where g^* in (7.1.2) is a function that represents the mixed contribution between engineering and fixed-effects model parameters, after random-effects model parameters have been accounted for in building the experimental error. Any model parameter that is suspected to have a substantial interaction with some engineering parameters should be included as experimental factor so that the systematic deviation of effects of such engineering parameters is prevented. Randomization of model parameters yields two simultaneous benefits. On the one hand, the model has acquired a random component equivalent to the experimental error of physical experiments; and in this way, the rationale of replications is again justified so that a natural measurement scale for effects is introduced and usual statistical significance tests can be adopted. On the other hand, without any increase of experimental effort, possible interactions between randomized model parameters and engineering parameters do not give rise to distortion of effects of engineering parameters or experimental factors. Moreover, it becomes possible to tune the experimental error of the computer experiment to that of the experimental error of a related physical experiment. In the case where several u parameters are present, it is likely that the normality assumption for random errors is reasonable. Table 7.1, adapted from Romano and Vicario (2002), summarizes a variety of approaches to computer experiments that are presented below in some detail.

One of the modeling methods applied to computer experiments data is Kriging also called Gaussian process models. Section 7.3 is dedicated to Kriging methods for data analysis. Throughout this chapter, we refer to the piston simulator that we already used in the previous chapters. A Python version of this simulator,

PistonSimulation, is included in the `mistat` package. We describe next the mathematical foundation of the piston simulator.

Example 7.1 The piston cycle time data are generated by software simulating a piston moving within a cylinder. The piston's linear motion is transformed into circular motion by connecting a linear rod to a disk. The faster the piston moves inside the cylinder, the quicker the disk rotation and therefore the faster the engine will run. The piston's performance is measured by the time it takes to complete one cycle, in seconds. The purpose of the simulator is to study the causes of variability in piston cycle time. The following factors (listed below with their units and ranges) affect the piston's performance:

M	Piston weight (Kg), 30–60
S	Piston surface area (m^2), 0.005–0.020
V_0	Initial gas volume (m^3), 0.002–0.010
k	Spring coefficient (N/m), 1000–5000
P_0	Atmospheric pressure (N/m^2), 90,000$-$110,000
T	Ambient temperature ($^\circ K$), 290–296
T_0	Filling gas temperature ($^\circ K$), 340–360

These factors affect the cycle time via a chain of non-linear equations:

$$\text{Cycle Time} = 2\pi \sqrt{\frac{M}{k + S^2 \frac{P_0 V_0}{T_0} \frac{T}{V^2}}}, \tag{7.1.3}$$

where

$$V = \frac{S}{2k}\left(\sqrt{A^2 + 4k\frac{P_0 V_0}{T_0}T} - A\right) \quad \text{and} \quad A = P_0 S + 19.62M - \frac{kV_0}{S}. \tag{7.1.4}$$

Randomness in cycle time is induced by generating observations for factors set up around design points with noise added to the nominal values.

We can run the simulator by fixing a specific factor-level combination or by using statistically designed experimental arrays. In this chapter, the arrays we will refer to are called, in general, space filling experiments. The simulator was used in the context of statistical process control (Sect. 2.1). We use it here in the context of statistically designed computer experiments. The next section deals with designing computer experiments. We will discuss there space filling designs that are specific to computer experiments where the factor-level combinations can be set freely, without physical constraints at specific levels. The section after that, Sect. 7.3, deals with models used in the analysis of computer experiments. These models are called Kriging, Dace, or Gaussian process models. They will be introduced at a general level designed to provide basic understanding of their properties, without getting into their theoretical development. ■

7.2 Designing Computer Experiments

Experimentation via computer modeling has become very common. We introduce here two popular designs for such experiments: the uniform design and the Latin hypercube design.

Suppose that the experimenter wants to estimate μ, the overall mean of the response y on the experimental domain X. The best design for this purpose is one whose empirical distribution approximates the uniform distribution. This idea arose first in numerical integration methods for high-dimensional problems, called quasi-Monte Carlo methods that were proposed in the early 1960s.

The discrepancy function, $D(\cdot)$, or measure of uniformity, quantifies the difference between the uniform distribution and the empirical distribution of the design. Designs with minimum discrepancy are called uniform designs. There are different possible forms of discrepancy functions, depending on the norm used to measure the difference between the uniform distribution and the empirical distribution of the design.

In general, the discrepancy function is a Kolmogorov–Smirnov type goodness-of-fit statistic. For estimating μ in the overall mean model, the uniform design has optimal average mean squared error assuming random h and optimal maximum mean square error assuming deterministic h. This implies that the uniform design is a type of robust design.

Latin hypercube designs are easy to generate. They achieve maximum uniformity in each of the univariate margins of the design region, thus allowing the experimenter to use models that are capable of capturing the complex dependence of the response variable on the input variables. Another reason that contributes to the popularity of Latin hypercube designs is that they have no repeated runs.

In computer experiments, repeated runs do not provide additional information since running a deterministic computer code twice yields the identical output. Latin hypercube designs are a very large class of designs that, however, do not necessarily perform well in terms of criteria such as orthogonality or space filling.

An $n \times m$ matrix $D = (d_{ij})$ is called a Latin hypercube design of n runs for m factors if each column of D is a permutation of $1, \ldots, n$. What makes Latin hypercube designs distinctly different from other designs is that every factor in a Latin hypercube design has the same number of levels as the run size.

Let $y = f(x_1, \ldots, x_m)$ be a real-valued function with m variables defined on the region given by $0 \leq x_j \leq 1$ for $j = 1, \ldots, m$. The function represents the deterministic computer model in the case of computer experiments or the integrand in the case of numerical integration. There are two natural ways of generating design points based on a given Latin hypercube. The first is through

$$x_{ij} = (d_{ij} - 0.5)/n,$$

with the n points given by $(x_{i1}, \ldots, x_{im})$ with $i = 1, \ldots, n$. The other is through

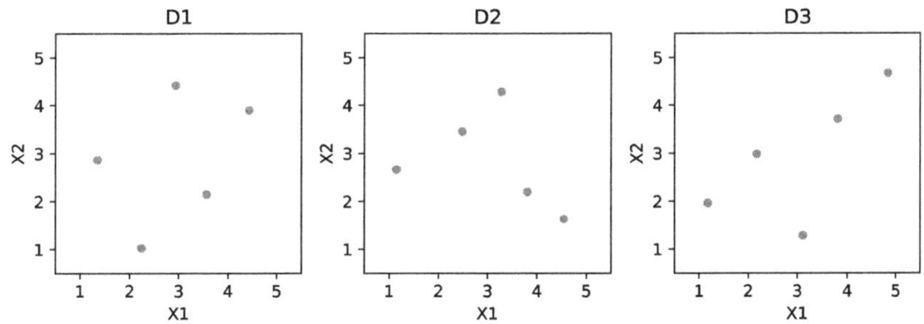

Fig. 7.1 Three Latin hypercube designs with 5 runs and 2 factors

$$x_{ij} = (d_{ij} - u_{ij})/n,$$

with the n points given by $(x_{i1}, \ldots, x_{im})$ with $i = 1, \ldots, n$, where u_{ij} are independent random variables with a common uniform distribution on $(0, 1]$. The difference between the two methods can be seen as follows. When projected onto each of the m variables, both methods have the property that one and only one of the n design points falls within each of the n small intervals defined by $[0, 1/n), [1/n, 2/n), \ldots, [(n-1)/n, 1]$. The first method gives the mid-points of these intervals, while the second gives the points that uniformly distributed in their corresponding intervals. Figure 7.1 presents three Latin hypercube designs of $n = 5$ runs for $m = 2$ factors.

Although they are all Latin hypercube designs, design D1 provides a higher coverage of the design region than design D2 or D3. This raises the need of developing specific methods for selecting better Latin hypercube designs. Basic Latin hypercube designs are very easy to generate. By simply combining several permutations of $1, \ldots, n$, one obtains a Latin hypercube design. There is no restriction whatsoever on the run size n and the number m of factors. Since a Latin hypercube design has n distinct levels in each of its factors, it achieves the maximum uniformity in each univariate margin. Two useful properties follow from this simple fact: (1) the maximum number of levels, a Latin hypercube design presents the experimenter with the opportunity of modeling the complex dependence of the response variable on each of the input variables and (2) there is no repeated levels in each factor. Since running computer code twice at the same setting of input variables produces the same output, using repeated runs in computer experiments is necessarily a waste of resources.

By definition, a Latin hypercube does not guarantee any property in two- or higher-dimensional margins. It is therefore up to the user to find the "right permutations" so that the resulting design has certain desirable properties in two or higher dimensions. One simple strategy is to use a random Latin hypercube design in which the permutations are selected randomly. This helps eliminate the possible systematic patterns in the resulting design, but there is no guarantee that the design will perform well in terms of other useful design criteria. A Latin hypercube design will provide a good coverage of the design region if all the points are farther apart, i.e., no two points are too close to each other. This idea can be formally developed using the maximin distance criterion, according to which designs should be selected by maximizing $\min_{i=j} d(p_i, p_j)$, where $d(p_i, p_j)$ denotes the distance between design points p_i and p_j. Euclidean distance is commonly used, but other distance measures are also useful.

Example 7.2 To design a space filling experiment, we can use various functions from the `mistat` package. The following Python code uses the *space_filling_lhs* to create a design and uses it with the piston simulator.

```
from mistat.design import doe
np.random.seed(1)
Factors = {
    'm': [30, 60],
    's': [0.005, 0.02],
    'v0': [0.002, 0.01],
    'k': [1_000, 5_000],
    'p0': [90_000, 110_000],
    't': [290, 296],
    't0': [340, 360],
}
Design = doe.lhs(Factors, num_samples=14)

# Randomize and create replicates
nrepeat = 50
Design = Design.sample(frac=1).reset_index(drop=True)
Design = Design.loc[Design.index.repeat(nrepeat)].reset_index(drop=True)

kwargs = {c: list(Design[c]) for c in Design.columns}
simulator = mistat.PistonSimulator(**kwargs)
result = simulator.simulate()
result = mistat.simulationGroup(result, nrepeat)

mean_result = result.groupby('group').mean()
```

The design and average response time are shown in Table 7.2 and Fig. 7.2. The graphs show that the design covers the space well. ■

The next section is focused on models used for analyzing computer experiments.

7.3 Analyzing Computer Experiments[1]

As already mentioned in Sect. 7.1, Kriging was developed for modeling spatial data in geostatistics.

Matheron (1963) named this method after D. G. Krige, a South African mining engineer who in the 1950s developed empirical methods for estimating true ore grade distributions based on sample ore grades. At the same time, the same ideas were developed in meteorology under Gandin (1963) in the Soviet Union. Gandin

[1] This section includes mathematical derivations and can be skipped without loss of continuity.

Table 7.2 Mean response from piston simulator using a Latin hypercube design

Group	m	s	v0	k	p0	t	t0	Seconds
1	43.5	0.0137	0.00691	4831	92,407	291.32	346.7	0.054
2	45.3	0.0065	0.00338	1731	108,910	292.57	344.0	0.037
3	53.4	0.0058	0.00910	1405	95,564	294.36	352.4	0.165
4	38.5	0.0123	0.00639	2842	99,869	293.21	353.7	0.048
5	59.9	0.0176	0.00288	2263	108,091	291.94	350.1	0.015
6	30.9	0.0111	0.00745	3060	93,058	290.04	359.4	0.066
7	50.2	0.0188	0.00411	1086	97,083	295.04	356.2	0.020
8	41.4	0.0102	0.00976	3486	90,210	290.94	357.3	0.110
9	48.4	0.0079	0.00533	4088	101,575	292.70	340.3	0.073
10	38.9	0.0125	0.00549	4704	98,214	293.61	342.7	0.044
11	56.3	0.0086	0.00870	2108	104,854	295.96	349.0	0.108
12	54.3	0.0194	0.00200	2434	100,379	290.52	355.6	0.009
13	34.3	0.0147	0.00779	3761	103,593	294.26	348.2	0.051
14	32.9	0.0159	0.00434	4395	106,605	295.41	344.3	0.023

named the method optimal interpolation. The central feature of Kriging models is that spatial trends can be modeled using spatial correlation structures, similar to time series models, in which observations are assumed to be dependent. Spatial models, however, need to be more flexible than time series models, as there is dependence in a multitude of directions. In general, the approach is a method of optimal spatial linear prediction based on minimum mean squared error. The use of Kriging for modeling data from computer experiments was originally labeled DACE (Design and Analysis of Computer Experiments) by Sacks et al. (1989). Kriging models are also known as Gaussian process models. Computer experiments may have many input variables, whereas spatial models have just 2 or 3. The DACE algorithm uses a model that treats the deterministic output of a computer code as the realization of a stochastic process. This nonparametric model simultaneously identifies important variables and builds a predictor that adapts to non-linear and interaction effects in the data.

Assume there is a single scalar output $y(x)$, which is a function of a d-dimensional vector of inputs, x. The deterministic response $y(x)$ is treated as a realization of a random function

$$Y(x) = \beta + Z(x). \tag{7.3.1}$$

The random process $Z(x)$ is assumed to have mean 0 and covariance function

$$\mathrm{Cov}(Z(x_i), Z(x_j)) = \sigma^2 R(x_i, x_j) \tag{7.3.2}$$

between $Z(x_i)$ and $Z(x_j)$ at two vector-valued inputs x_i and x_j, where σ^2 is the process variance and $R(x_i, x_j)$ is the correlation.

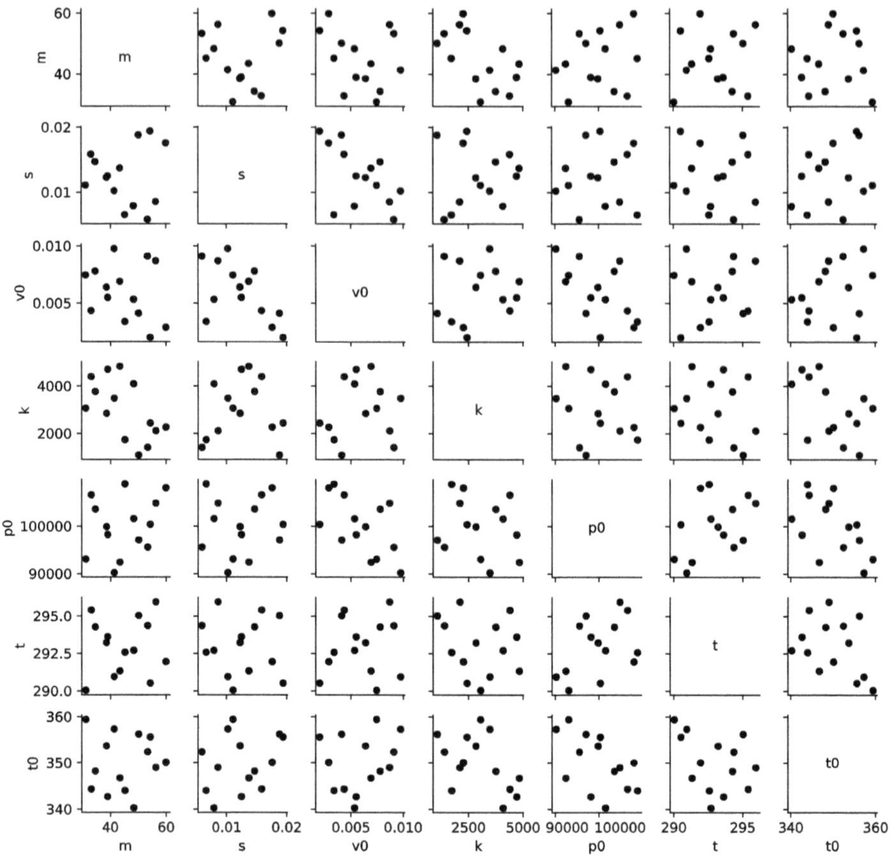

Fig. 7.2 Latin hypercube design for piston simulator

DACE is using the correlation function:

$$R(x_i, x_j) = \prod_{k=1}^{d} \exp(-\theta_k \mid x_{ik} - x_{jk}|^{p_k}), \tag{7.3.3}$$

where $\theta_k \geq 0$ and $0 \leq p_k \leq 2$.

The basic idea behind this covariance is that values of Y for points "near" each other in the design space should be more highly correlated than for points "far" from each other. Thus, we should be able to estimate the value of $Y(x)$ at a new site by taking advantage of observed values at sites that have a high correlation with the new site. The parameters in the correlation function determine which of the input variables are important in measuring the distance between two points. For example, a large value of θ_k means that only a small neighborhood of values on this variable is considered to be "close" to a given input site and will typically correspond to an input with a strong effect.

All the unknown parameters are estimated using maximum likelihood estimation (MLE). Since the global maximization is very problematic from a computational perspective, a pseudo-maximization algorithm is applied using a "stepwise" approach, where at each step the parameters for one input factor are "free" and all the rest are equal.

Given the correlation parameters θ and p, the MLE of β is

$$\hat{\boldsymbol{\beta}} = (\mathbf{J}^T \mathbf{R}_D^{-1} \mathbf{J})^{-1} (\mathbf{J}^T \mathbf{R}_D^{-1} y), \tag{7.3.4}$$

where J is a vector of ones and R_D is the $n \times n$ matrix of correlations $R(x_i, x_j)$.

The generalized least squares estimator, and the MLE, of $\boldsymbol{\sigma}^2$ is

$$\hat{\boldsymbol{\sigma}}^2 = \frac{(y - \mathbf{J}\hat{\beta})^T \mathbf{R}_D^{-1} (y - \mathbf{J}\hat{\beta})}{n}. \tag{7.3.5}$$

The best linear unbiased predictor (BLUP) at an untried x is

$$\hat{y}(x) = \hat{\beta} + \mathbf{r}^T(x) \hat{\mathbf{R}}_D^{-1} (y - \underline{J}\hat{\beta}), \tag{7.3.6}$$

where $r(x) = [R(x_1, x), \ldots, R(x_n, x)]^T$ is the vector of correlations between Z's at the design points and at the new point x. The BLUP interpolates the observed output at sites x that are in the training data.

Example 7.3 We can continue with the result from Example 7.2. We used a Latin hypercube design to define 14 settings for the piston simulator. The result of the simulation is given in Table 7.2.

The Python package `pyKriging` implements kriging models for a larger number of predictors.

```
from pyKriging.krige import kriging
random.seed(1)

outcome = 'seconds'
predictors = ['m', 's', 'v0', 'k', 'p0', 't', 't0']

model = kriging(mean_result[predictors].values, mean_result[outcome].values)
model.train()
```

We can assess the goodness of fit of the kriging model using leave-one-out cross-validation. Leave-one-out cross-validation removes an observation from the dataset, builds a model with the remaining data, and predicts the left out data point. This is repeated for all observations. The following Python code determines the leave-one-out predictions for each data point.

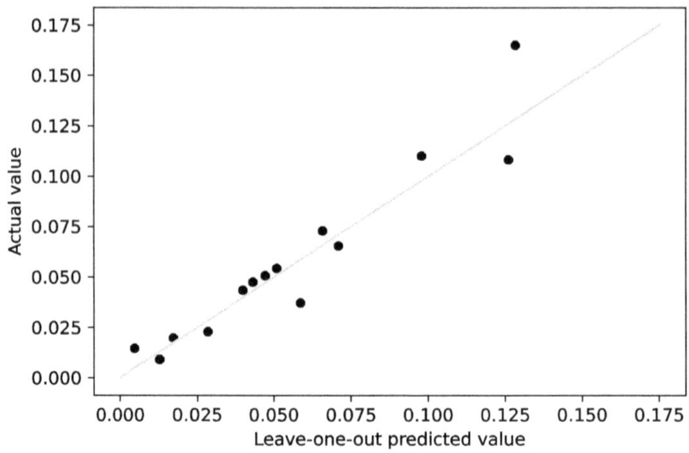

Fig. 7.3 Leave-one-out cross-validation of kriging model

```
def looValidation(data, seed=123):
    random.seed(seed)
    jackknife  = []
    for i, row in data.iterrows():
        subset = data.drop(i)
        model = kriging(subset[predictors].values, subset[outcome].values)
        model.train()
        jackknife.append({
            'actual': row[outcome],
            'predicted': model.predict(row[predictors].values),
        })
    return pd.DataFrame(jackknife)
validation = looValidation(mean_result)
```

Using the calculated predicted and actual values, we get the following leave-one-out performance metrics.

```
from sklearn import metrics
MAE = metrics.mean_absolute_error(validation['actual'], validation['predicted'])
R2 = metrics.r2_score(validation['actual'], validation['predicted'])
print(f'MAE = {MAE:.4f}')
print(f'r2 {R2:.3f}', )
```

```
MAE = 0.0098
r2 0.897
```

Both metrics show that the model performs well. In Fig. 7.3, we compare the observed value with the value predicted from the leave-one-out models. Points lying close to the line of equality indicate a good fit of the model since the observed data points are well predicted by the model.

We can derive marginal effect of factors on cycle time using the kriging model. The result of this analysis is shown in Fig. 7.4. It confirms again that only *v0* and

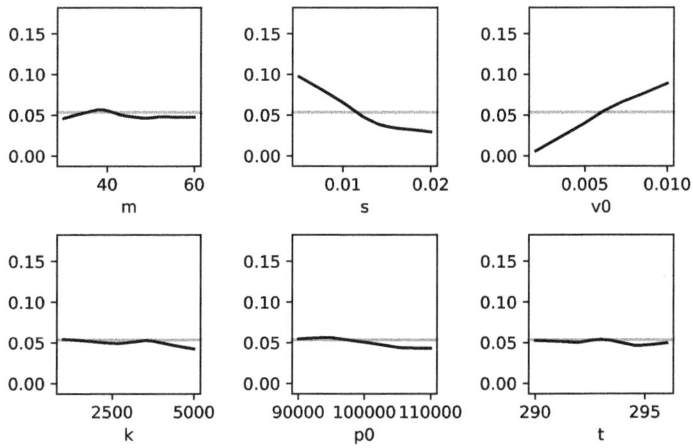

Fig. 7.4 Marginal effect of factors on cycle time derived from the kriging model

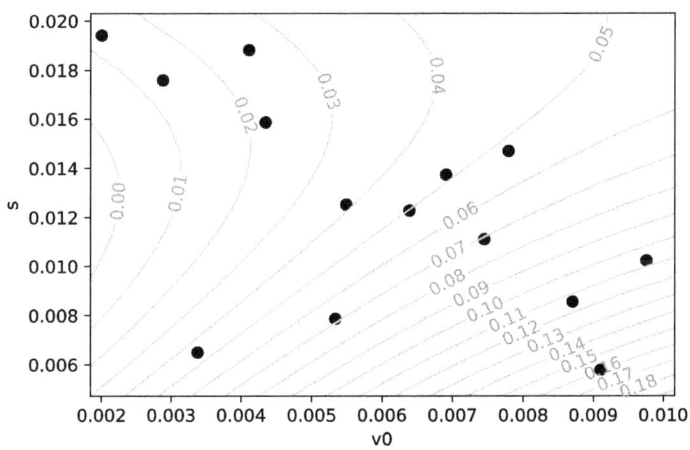

Fig. 7.5 Latin hypercube design for piston simulator

s have a strong effect on the average cycle time; all other factors have only little effect on cycle time. Figure 7.5 shows the dependence of the cycle time across the full range of *v0* and *s*. ■

7.4 Stochastic Emulators

Traditional engineering practice augments deterministic design system predictions with factors of safety or design margins to provide some assurance of meeting requirements in the presence of uncertainty and variability in modeling assumptions, boundary conditions, manufacturing, materials, and customer usage. Modern engineering practice is implementing quality by design methods to account for probability distributions of component or system performance characteristics. Chapter 4 provided several such examples, including the robust design approach developed by Genichi Taguchi in Japan. At Pratt and Whitney, in the USA, Grant Reinman and his team developed a methodology labeled design for variation (DFV) that incorporates the same principles (Reinman et al. 2012). In this chapter, we focus on an essential element of modern quality by design engineering and computer experiments.

The new experimental framework of computer simulators has stimulated the development of new types of experimental designs and methods of analysis that are tailored to these studies. The guiding idea in computer simulation experimental design has been to achieve nearly uniform coverage of the experimental region. The most commonly used design has been the so-called Latin hypercube presented in Sect. 7.2. In Latin hypercube designs, each factor is given a large number of levels, an option that is virtually impossible in physical experiments but very easy when experimenting on a simulator.

In using computer experiments for robust design problems, outcome variation is induced via uncertainty in the inputs. The most direct way to assess such variation is to generate simulator output for a moderate to large sample of input settings (see Sect. 7.1). However, if the simulator is slow and/or expensive, such a scheme may not be practical. The stochastic emulator paradigm, also called metamodel, provides a simple solution by replacing the simulator with an emulator for the bulk of the computations. It was introduced in Bates et al. (2006). The key steps of the stochastic emulator approach are as follows:

1. Begin with a Latin hypercube (or other space filling) design of moderate size.
2. Use the simulator to generate data at points in the design.
3. Model the simulator data to create an emulator, called the stochastic emulator.
4. Use cross-validation to verify that the emulator accurately represents the simulator.
5. Generate a new space filling design. Each configuration in this design is a potential nominal setting at which we will assess properties of the output distribution.
6. At each configuration in the new design, sample a large number of points from the noise factors and compute output data from the stochastic emulator.
7. Construct statistical models that relate features of the output distribution to the design factor settings. These models might themselves be emulators.

This approach can dramatically reduce the overall computational burden by using the stochastic emulator, rather than the simulator, to compute the results in step 6. Stochastic emulators are a primary quality by design tool in organizations that have successfully incorporated simulation experiments in the design of drug products, analytical methods, and scale-up processes.

7.5 Integrating Physical and Computer Experiments[2]

Information from expert opinion, computer experiments, and physical experiments can be combined in a simple regression model of the form:

$$\mathbf{Y} = f(\mathbf{X}, \boldsymbol{\beta}) + \boldsymbol{\epsilon}. \tag{7.5.1}$$

In this model, $\mathbf{X}$ represents the design space corresponding, the vector $\boldsymbol{\beta}$ represents the values of the model coefficients, and $\mathbf{Y}$ represents the k observations, for example, of method resolution. This is achieved by modeling physical experimental data as

$$\mathbf{Y}_p \sim N(\mathbf{X}_p\boldsymbol{\beta}, \boldsymbol{\sigma}^2\mathbf{I}), \tag{7.5.2}$$

where $\boldsymbol{\sigma}^2$ is the experimental variance representing the uncertainty of responses due to experimental conditions and measurement system.

Instead of relying solely on the physical experiments to establish the distribution of the response in the design space, we start by first eliciting estimates from expert opinion and, later, add results from computer experiments. Results from physical experiments are then superimposed on these two sources of information. Suppose there are e expert opinions. Expert opinions on the values of $\boldsymbol{\beta}$ can be described as quantiles of

$$\mathbf{Y}_0 \sim N(\mathbf{X}_0\boldsymbol{\beta} + \boldsymbol{\delta}_0, \boldsymbol{\sigma}^2\boldsymbol{\Sigma}_0), \tag{7.5.3}$$

where $\boldsymbol{\delta}_0$ is the expert-specific location bias.

Assuming the following prior distributions for the unknown parameters $\boldsymbol{\beta}$ and σ^2:

$$\boldsymbol{\beta} \mid \boldsymbol{\sigma}^2 \sim N(\boldsymbol{\mu}_0, \boldsymbol{\sigma}^2\mathbf{C}_0) \tag{7.5.4}$$

$$\boldsymbol{\sigma}^2 \sim IG(\alpha_0, \gamma_0), \tag{7.5.5}$$

where $N(\boldsymbol{\mu}, \boldsymbol{\sigma}^2)$ stands for a normal distribution and $IG(\boldsymbol{\alpha}, \boldsymbol{\gamma})$ is the inverse gamma distribution that we will meet again in Sect. 10.1. Using Bayes' theorem, the resulting posterior distribution of $\boldsymbol{\beta}$ becomes

$$\pi(\boldsymbol{\beta} \mid \boldsymbol{\sigma}^2, \boldsymbol{\eta}, \mathbf{y}_0) \sim N\left(\left(\mathbf{X}_0'\boldsymbol{\Sigma}_0^{-1}\mathbf{X}_0 + \mathbf{C}_0^{-1}\right)^{-1}\mathbf{z},\ \boldsymbol{\sigma}^2\left(\mathbf{X}_0'\boldsymbol{\Sigma}_0^{-1}\mathbf{X}_0 + \mathbf{C}_0^{-1}\right)^{-1}\right) \tag{7.5.6}$$

with

$$\mathbf{z} = \mathbf{X}_0'\boldsymbol{\Sigma}_0'(\mathbf{y}_0 - \boldsymbol{\delta}_0) + \mathbf{C}_0^{-1}\boldsymbol{\mu}. \tag{7.5.7}$$

[2] This and the following section include mathematical derivations and can be skipped without loss of continuity.

The computer experimental data can be described as

$$\mathbf{Y}_c \sim N(\mathbf{X}_c\boldsymbol{\beta} + \boldsymbol{\delta}_c,\ \sigma^2\boldsymbol{\sigma}_c). \tag{7.5.8}$$

Combining these results with the expert opinion posteriors, we derive a second posterior distribution, and then adding estimates from physical experiments through Markov Chain Monte Carlo, we calculate the final distribution for $\boldsymbol{\beta}$.

$$\text{Stage 1 } (\mathbf{Y}_0) \rightarrow \text{Stage 2 } (\mathbf{Y}_0 + \mathbf{Y}_c) \rightarrow \text{Stage 3 } (\mathbf{Y}_0 + \mathbf{Y}_c + \mathbf{Y}_p). \tag{7.5.9}$$

A related approach called "variable fidelity experiments" has been proposed in Huang and Allen (2005) to combine results from experiments conducted at various levels of sophistication.

Consider, for example, combining simple calculations in Excel, to results from a mixing simulation software and actual physical mixing experiments.

The combined model is

$$Y(\mathbf{x}, l) = \mathbf{f}_1(\mathbf{x})'\boldsymbol{\beta}_1 + \mathbf{f}_1(\mathbf{x})'\boldsymbol{\beta}_2 + Z_{\mathrm{sys}}(\mathbf{x}, l) + \epsilon_{\mathrm{means}}(l), \tag{7.5.10}$$

where $l = 1, \ldots, m$ is the fidelity level of the experimental system, $Z_{\mathrm{sys}}(\mathbf{x}, l)$ is the systematic error, and $\epsilon_{\mathrm{means}}(l)$ is the random error ($l = 1$ corresponds to the real system). There are also primary terms and potential terms, and only the primary terms, $\mathbf{f}_1(\mathbf{x})$, are included in the regression model.

Assuming that the covariance matrix $\mathbf{V}$ is known and $\mathbf{Y}$ is a vector that contains data from n experiments, the GLS estimator of β_1 is

$$\hat{\beta}_1 = (\mathbf{X}_1'\mathbf{V}^{-1}\mathbf{X}_1)^{-1}\mathbf{X}_1'\mathbf{V}^{-1}\mathbf{Y}. \tag{7.5.11}$$

Both the integrated model, combining expert opinion with simulation, and physical experiments and the variable fidelity level experiments have proven useful in practical applications where experiments are conducted in different conditions and prior experience has been accumulated.

7.6 Simulation of Random Variables

7.6.1 Basic Procedures

Simulation is an artificial technique of generating on the computer a sequence of random numbers, from a given distribution, in order to explore the properties of a random phenomenon. Observation of random phenomena often takes long time of data collection, until we have sufficient information for analysis. For example, consider patients arriving at random times to a hospital, to obtain a certain treatment in clinical trials. It may take several months until we have a large enough sample for analysis. Suppose that we assume that the epochs of arrival of the patients follow a Poisson process. If we can generate on the computer a sequence of random times, which follow a Poisson process, we might be able to predict how long the trial will continue. Physically, we can create random numbers by flipping a "balanced" coin many times, throwing dice, or shuffling cards. One can use a Geiger counter to count how many particles are emitted from a decaying radio-active process. All these methods are slow and cannot be used universally. The question is, how can we generate random numbers on the computer, which follow a given distribution.

The key for random numbers generation is the well-known result that, if a random variable X has a continuous distribution F, then $F(X)$ is uniformly distributed on the interval (0, 1). Accordingly, if one can generate at random a variable $U \sim R(0, 1)$, then the random variable $X = F^{-1}(U)$ is distributed according to F. In order to generate a uniformly distributed random variable, computer programs such as Python and others generally apply an algorithm that yields, after a while (asymptotically), uniformly distributed results. In Python, we can calculate a uniform random variable R(α, β) using `uniform(α,β)` from the `random` standard library package. While this is sufficient for many use cases, it is better to use the *stats* module in the `scipy` package. It provides a large number of continuous and discrete distributions. With `stats.uniform.rvs(loc=α, scale=β − α, size=n)`, we can generate an array of n random variables. The default values for α and β are 0 and 1. The standard uniform on (0,1) can therefore be obtained with *stats.uniform.rvs(size=n)*. Note that we need to specify the number of random variables using the `size` keyword.

We provide below a few examples of random numbers generation:

1. The exponential distribution with mean $1/\lambda$ is $F(x) = 1 - \exp\{-\lambda x\}$, for $0 \leq x \leq \infty$. Thus, if U has a uniform distribution on (0,1), then $X = -(1/\lambda)\ln(1 - U)$ has an exponential distribution with mean $1/\lambda$. In Python, we can generate an exponential (λ) with the function `stats.expon.rvs(scale=1/λ, size=n)`. Note that we use the inverse of λ here.
2. If X is distributed according to exponential with $\lambda = 1$, then $X^{1/\alpha}$ is distributed like Weibull with shape parameter α and scale parameter 1. The `scipy` function *stats.weibull_min.rvs(*α*)* generates such a random variable. If there is also a scale parameter β, we can use *stats.weibull_min(*α*, scale=*β*)*.
3. A standard normal random variable can be generated by the Uth quantiles $\Phi^{-1}(U)$. In Python, these random variables are generated by *stats.norm.rvs()*. To generate the distribution $N(\mu, \sigma)$, use *stats.norm.rvs(loc=*μ*, scale=*σ*, size=n)*.
4. Random numbers following a discrete distribution can be similarly generated. For example, generating a random number from the binomial(20, 0.6) can be done by the Python function *stats.binom.rvs(20, 0.6)*. If we wish to generate a random sample of n realizations, we add the keyword argument `size`. For example, *stats.binom.rvs(20, 0.6, size=10)*.

7.6.2 Generating Random Vectors

Generating random vectors following a given multivariate distribution is done in stages. Suppose we are given a k-dimensional vector having a multivariate distribution, with density $p(x_1, x_2, \ldots, x_k)$. If the variables are mutually independent, we can generate independently k variables according to their marginal densities. This is the simplest case. On the other hand, if the variables are dependent but exchangeable (all permutations of the components yield the same joint density function), we generate the first variable according to its marginal density. Given a realization of X_1, say x_1, we generate a value of X_2 according to the conditional density $p(x_2|x_1)$, then the value of X_3 according to the conditional density $p(x_3|x_1, x_2)$, and so on. We illustrate this process on the bivariate normal distribution. This distribution has five parameters $\mu = E\{X\}$, $\sigma_1^2 = V\{X\}$, $\eta = E\{Y\}$, $\sigma_2^2 = V\{Y\}$, and $\rho = Corr(X, Y)$. In step 1, we generate

$$X \sim N(\mu, \sigma_1^2).$$

In step 2, we generate

$$Y \sim N\left(\eta + (\sigma_1\rho/\sigma_2)(X - \mu), \sigma_2^2(1 - \rho^2)\right).$$

In Fig. 7.6, we present the generation of 1000 standard bivariate normal vectors ($\mu = \eta = 0$, $\sigma_1 = \sigma_2 = 1$, $\rho = 0.8$), using the following Python code.

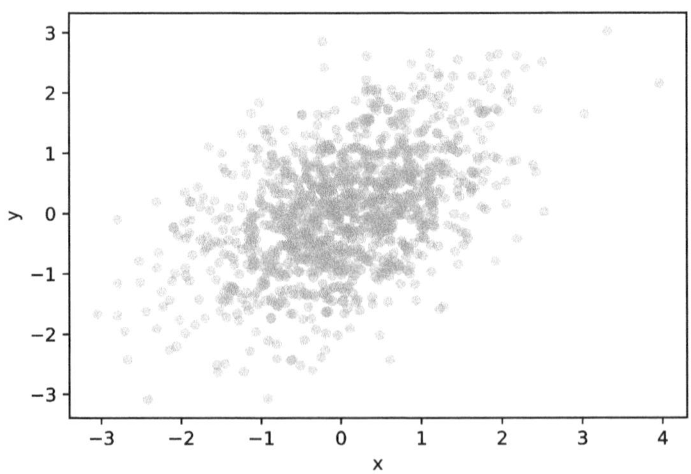

Fig. 7.6 Standard bivariate normal distributed random vector

```
np.random.seed(1)

def standardBivariateNorm(rho, Ns):
  X = stats.norm.rvs(size=Ns)
  Y = rho*X + np.sqrt(1-rho**2)*stats.norm.rvs(size=Ns)
  return pd.DataFrame({'x': X, 'y': Y})

standardBivariateNorm(0.5, 1000).plot.scatter('x', 'y', alpha=0.5, color='gray')
plt.show()
```

The package `scipy` also provides a number of multivariate distributions, e.g., *stats.multivariate_normal*. We can create a sample of random 1000 standard bivariate normal vectors with this method as follows.

```
rv = stats.multivariate_normal.rvs(mean=(0, 0), cov=[[1, 0.5], [0.5, 1]],
                                   size=1000)
pd.DataFrame(rv, columns=('x', 'y')).plot.scatter('x', 'y')
plt.show()
```

7.6.3 Approximating Integrals

Let $g(X, Y)$ be a function of a random vector (X, Y) having a bivariate distribution, with a joint p.d.f. $p(x, y)$. The expected value of $g(X, Y)$, if $E\{|g(X, Y)|\} < \infty$, is

$$E\{g(X, Y)\} = \int_{-\infty}^{\infty}\int_{-\infty}^{\infty} g(x, y)p(x, y)\,\mathrm{d}x\,\mathrm{d}y.$$

According to the strong law of large numbers, under the above condition of absolute integrability,

$$E\{g(X, Y)\} = \lim_{n\to\infty} \frac{1}{n}\sum_{j=1}^{n} g(X_j, Y_j), \qquad \text{a.s.}$$

Accordingly, the mean of $g(X, Y)$ in very large samples approximates its expected value. The following is an example.

Example 7.4 Let $g(X, Y) = \exp(X + Y)$, where $\{(X_j, Y_j), j = 1, \ldots, n\}$ is a sample from the bivariate standard normal distribution. Using moment generating functions of the normal distribution, we obtain that

$$E\{e^{\theta(X+Y)}\} = E\{e^{\theta X} E\{e^{\theta Y}|X\}\} = \exp\{(1 + \rho)\theta^2\}.$$

Thus, for $\theta = 1$ and $\rho = 0.8$, we obtain the exact result that $E\{e^{X+Y}\} = 6.049647$.

On the other hand, for a sample of size 100, we obtain

$$\text{mean}(\exp\{X + Y\}, n = 100) = 7.590243.$$

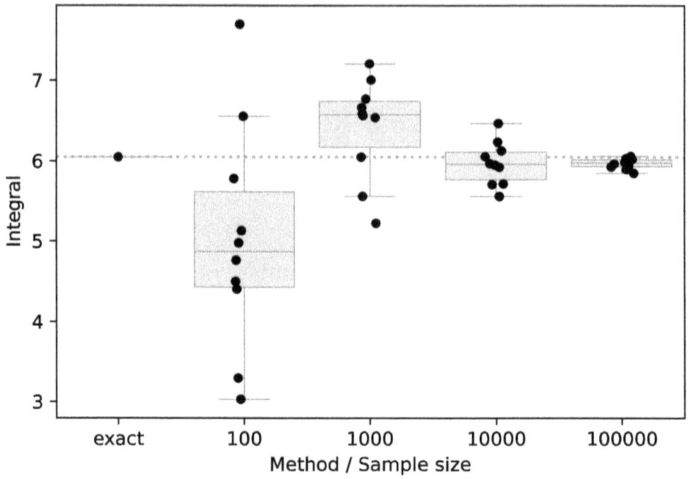

Fig. 7.7 Integral approximations for different sample sizes (10 repeats)

This sample size is not sufficiently large. For $n = 1000$, we obtain

$$\text{mean}(\exp\{X + Y\}, n = 1000) = 5.961779.$$

This result is already quite close to the exact value. These are just two possible approximations for the integral. Figure 7.7 shows the distribution of calculated approximations for sample sizes of 100, 1000, and 10,000. The distribution of approximations for size 100 is very large. It improves for 1000, and at a sample size of 10,000, the approximations are very close to the exact value.

■

7.7 Chapter Highlights

The main concepts and tools introduced in this chapter include:

- Simulation
- Space filling designs
- Latin hypercubes
- Kriging
- Metamodel
- Emulator
- Stochastic emulator
- Physical experiments
- Bayesian hierarchical model
- Fidelity level

- Integrating physical and computer experiments
- Random number generator

7.8 Exercises

Exercise 7.1 The birthday problem states that if there are more than 22 people at a birthday party, the probability that at least two people have the same birthday is greater than 0.5. Write a Python program to simulate this problem. Show that if there are more than 22 people in the party, the probability is greater than 1/2 that at least 2 will have birthdays on the same day.

Exercise 7.2 The Deming funnel experiment was designed to show that an inappropriate reaction to common cause variation will make matters worse. Common cause and special causes affecting processes over time have been discussed in Chaps. 2–4.

In the actual demonstration, a funnel is placed above a circular target. The objective is to drop a marble through the funnel as close to the target as possible. A pen or pencil is used to mark the spot where the marble actually hits. Usually, 20 or more drops are performed in order to establish the pattern and extent of variation about the target. The funnel represents common causes affecting a system. Despite the operator's best efforts, the marble will not land exactly on the target each time. The operator can react to this variability in one of four ways:

1. Do not move the funnel.
2. Measure the distance the hit is from the target and move the funnel an equal distance, but in the opposite direction (error relative to the previous position).
3. Measure the distance the hit is from the target and move the funnel this distance in the opposite direction, starting at the target (error relative to the target).
4. Move the funnel to be exactly over the location of the last hit.

Use Python to compare these four strategies using simulation data.

Exercise 7.3 Design a 50 runs experimental array for running the piston simulator using different options available in the `mistat` package:

- Latin hypercube (simple): *mistat.design.doe.lhs*
- Latin hypercube (space filling): *mistat.design.doe.space_filling_lhs*
- Random k-means cluster: *mistat.design.doe.random_k_means*
- Maximin reconstruction: *mistat.design.doe.maximin*
- Halton sequence-based: *mistat.design.doe.halton*
- Uniform random matrix: *mistat.design.doe.uniform_random*

Compare the results.

Exercise 7.4 Fit a Gaussian process model to data generated by the six designs listed in Exercise 7.3 and compare the MSE of the model fits.

Exercise 7.5 Using a uniform random design, generate a stochastic emulator for the piston simulator in order to get 0.02 s cycle time with minimal variability.

Exercise 7.6 Using a Latin hypercube design, generate a stochastic emulator for the piston simulator in order to achieve 0.02 s cycle time with minimal variability. Compare your results to what you got in Exercise 7.5.

Chapter 8
Cybermanufacturing and Digital Twins

Preview Cybermanufacturing is a name given to smart manufacturing systems which are part of the fourth industrial revolution. These systems combine sensor technologies with flexible manufacturing and advanced analytics. In this chapter we introduce the main elements of cybermanufacturing as background and context to modern industrial analytics. Digital twins are related to cybermanufacturing but carry a wider scope. The idea is to provide a digital platform that parallels physical assets. This has implications, for example, in healthcare, where MRI imaging is interpreted on the spot with artificial intelligence models trained on millions of images (https://www.aidoc.com/). Other application domains of digital twins include agriculture, smart cities, transportation, autonomous vehicles, added manufacturing, and 3D printing, etc. The chapter covers the topics of computer complexity, computational pipelines, and reproducibility of analytic findings. It presents an integration of models for enhanced information quality, the Bayesian flow analysis, and the Open ML community where datasets and data flows are uploaded in the spirit of open data. An additional topic covered in the chapter covers customer survey models used in modern companies to map their improvement journey.

8.1 Introduction to Cybermanufacturing

In Chap. 1, we present the evolution of industry, from the first to the fourth industrial revolution—Industry 4.0. In this chapter, we focus on cybermanufacturing, the most representative realization of the fourth industrial revolution. We emphasize the analytic aspects of cybermanufacturing and relate them to other chapters in the book.

In the era of Industry 4.0, advanced communication, computation, and control infrastructures get integrated with sensor technology into cyber-physical systems

Supplementary Information The online version contains supplementary material available at (https://doi.org/10.1007/978-3-031-28482-3_8).

R. S. Kenett et al., *Industrial Statistics*, Statistics for Industry, Technology, and Engineering, https://doi.org/10.1007/978-3-031-28482-3_8

incorporating a network of multiple manufacturing steps. Such systems enable the transition from conventional manufacturing into cybermanufacturing. Conventional manufacturing relied on data-driven decision-making methods, such as statistical process control introduced in Chap. 2, to monitor and improve the performance of individual manufacturing systems. Cybermanufacturing, with physical equipment, sensor technologies, computer simulations, and advanced analytics, provides significantly enhanced monitoring capabilities. Moreover, digital twins, introduced in Sect. 1.4, enable high information quality monitoring, diagnostic, prognostic, and prescriptive analysis.

With modern analytic methods, cybermanufacturing enhances manufacturing efficiency, cost reduction, product quality, flexibility, and domain knowledge discovery. This applies not only to large manufacturing corporations, like Stanley Black and Decker (Cisco 2019) and Siemens (2022) but also to small and medium-sized companies (Kuo et al. 2017).

Within cybermanufacturing, computation services refer to manufacturing data automatically collected and processed in computation units such as the Cloud and Fog nodes (Chen and Jin 2021). Computation services provide real-time online computation results to meet on-demand computation requests from manufacturing processes, systems, and users. With the advancement in Internet of Things (IoT) and smart manufacturing (Yang et al. 2019), computation services minimize labor-intensive training and effectively use data analytics and machine learning methods.

In this chapter, we present modeling and analysis methods in cybermanufacturing. The next section reviews challenges in manufacturing analytics.

8.2 Cybermanufacturing Analytics

The third industrial revolution, introduced in Chap. 1, involved embedded systems such as sensors and programmable logic controllers to achieve automation in manufacturing. With the extensive use of embedded systems, the third industrial revolution significantly improved throughput, efficiency, and product quality in the manufacturing industry, while reducing reliance on manual operations. This opened the era of "smart manufacturing," which is utilizing sensor data to enable data-driven decision-making and equipment managed by numerical controllers (Kenett et al. 2018b). Cybermanufacturing is the next phase in industry, leveraging advances in manufacturing technologies, sensors, and analytics (Kenett and Redman 2019; Kang et al. 2021b). Suppose that X is a set of process variables (scalar, vector, or matrix) and Y are performance variables (scalar, vector, or matrix). Modeling consists of identifying the relationship f, such that $Y = f(X)$, or an approximation f', such that $Y = f'(X) + \varepsilon$ where ε is an error term. Modeling and analysis provide the foundation for process monitoring, root-cause diagnosis, and control.

Modeling can be based on physical principles such as thermodynamics, fluid mechanics and dynamical systems and involve deriving exact solutions for ordinary or partial differential equations (ODE/PDEs) or solving an approximation of ODE/PDEs via numerical methods such as finite element analysis. It aims at deriving the exact relationship f, or its approximation (or discretization) $\tilde{f}$, between process variables X and performance variables Y (Chinesta 2019; Dattner 2021). When there is a significant gap between the assumption of physical principles and the actual manufacturing conditions, empirical models derived from statistically designed of experiments (DOE) presented in Chaps. 5–7 are needed. First principle models and empirically derived models can be integrated in a hybrid modeling approach (von Stosch et al. 2014).

The statistical design of experiments (DOE) methodology originated in agricultural experiments (Fisher 1919). DOE methods have been widely applied in manufacturing and in computer simulations (Box et al. 2005; Santner et al. 2003; Wu and Hamada 2011; Kenett and Zacks 2021; Kenett and Vicario 2021). The design and analysis of physical experiments provides information about a manufacturing process under controllable settings. The design and analysis of digital computer experiments can seek information also when physical experiments are too costly or impossible to conduct.

After identifying a set of process variables X, the goal of DOE is to derive a good approximation of the relationship between X and performance variables Y (denoted as f') so as to minimize the discrepancy between Y and $f'(X)$. Computer model calibration is conducted so that a model is calibrated with observational process data and provides more accurate results (Kennedy and O'Hagan 2001; Kenett and Vicario 2021).

Smart manufacturing exploits advances in sensing technologies, with in situ process variables, having an impact on modeling and analysis. This enables online updates and provides improvements in real-time product quality and process efficiency (Kenett and Bortman 2021). An example is the control of machine tool positioning error using sensor data from multiple thermal sensors (Yang and Ni 2005). Another advance has been the development of soft sensors which provide online surrogates to laboratory tests (Tham et al. 1989). Soft sensors provide online information that emulates traditionally time demanding lab tests (Reis and Kenett 2018).

There are two important challenges in manufacturing analytics: (1) data integration, also called data fusion, and (2) development and deployment of analytic methods. Data fusion refers to the methods of integrating different models and data sources or different types of datasets (Jin and Deng 2015; Dalla Valle and Kenett 2018). Machine learning and data analytics refers to building a mathematical model based on data, such that the model can make predictions without being explicitly programmed to do so (see Chapter 7 and Chapter 8 in *Modern Statistics*, Kenett et al. 2022b). In particular, deep neural networks have shown superior performance in modeling complex manufacturing processes (Wang et al. 2018a). Data fusion and data analytics play crucial roles in cybermanufacturing as they provide accurate approximations of the relationship between process variable X and performance variables Y, denoted as f', by utilizing experimental and/or simulation data. In predictive analytics, models are validated by splitting the data into training and validation sets. The structure of data needs to be accounted in the cross-validation. An approach called befitting cross-validation (BCV) is proposed in Kenett et al. (2022a). In the next section we review the information quality framework in the context of cybermanufacturing.

8.3 Information Quality in Cybermanufacturing

Analytics in smart manufacturing is affected by some fundamental limitations. First, the scalability of conventional data fusion methods is limited. This is due to disconnected manufacturing systems and nonintegrated cyber resources (e.g., computation units, data storage). The reliability of external computation resources such as cloud computing is affected by network conditions and this can be problematic. Flexibility (i.e., the ability for re-configuration) of the entire system is therefore necessary for supporting Industry 4.0 operations (e.g., production plan, facility layout, etc.). This requires effective deployment of cybermanufacturing solutions such as MLOps described below.

MLOps is the process of taking an experimental Machine Learning model into a production web system. The acronym is a compound of "Machine Learning" and the continuous development practice of DevOps in the software field. Machine Learning models are tested and developed in isolated experimental systems. When an algorithm is ready to be launched, data scientists, DevOps, and Machine Learning engineers transition the algorithm to production systems. MLOps applies to the entire lifecycle—from integration with model generation (software development lifecycle, continuous integration/continuous delivery), orchestration, and deployment, to health, diagnostics, governance, and business impact metrics (Kenett and Redman 2019).

To streamline computation service in cybermanufacturing, it is necessary to identify a configuration of data analytics and/or machine learning methods providing the best computation performances. A computation pipeline consists of sequences of method applications involving data collection, data preprocessing, and data analytics methods (Chen and Jin 2018, 2021). Section 8.5 is dedicated to computational pipelines.

The literature is often discussing data quality but it is important to make the distinction between data quality and information quality. Data quality is an intrinsic feature of the collected data. Information quality is conditioned on the goals of the analysis and is affected by the analysis and management of its outcomes. Data quality concerns require preprocessing (e.g., filtering or cleaning) before data modeling and analysis which determines the generation of information quality. In that transition, many dimensions need to be considered. To evaluate data quality, several assessment frameworks have been proposed (Wang et al. 1995). To ensure information quality, a framework based on four components and eight dimensions has been proposed in Kenett and Shmueli (2016), which is denoted as InfoQ.

The framework was presented in *Modern Statistics* (Kenett et al. 2022b). Here, we consider the application of InfoQ to Industry 4.0 and cybermanufacturing as reviewed in Kenett et al. (2018b). In the InfoQ framework, information quality is defined as the utility, U, derived by applying a method of analysis, f, to a dataset, D, conditioned on the analysis goal, i.e., InfoQ$(U, f, D, g) = U(f(D|g))$.

To assess InfoQ, the following eight dimensions are considered: (1) Data Resolution, (2) Data Structure, (3) Data Integration, (4) Temporal Relevance, (5) Chronology of Data and Goal, (6) Generalizability, (7) Operationalization, and (8) Communication. Specifically, each of the eight dimensions can be quantified with respect to the components U, f, D, and g by answering a set of questions to help derive InfoQ values. A sample checklist, with such questions, is provided in Table 8.1. For more details on the calculation of InfoQ in a practical setting, the reader is referred to the literature, e.g., Reis and Kenett (2018).

The InfoQ framework provides criteria for evaluating information quality in a contextualized computation task. Figure 8.1 provides a general view of information quality dimensions in the context of a computational pipeline sketch.

Information-poor datasets lead to severe limitations in cybermanufacturing. First, machine learning methods may be affected by a low signal-to-noise ratio, which limits the effectiveness and efficiency of manufacturing modeling and analysis. Secondly, cybermanufacturing involves the collection of data from heterogeneous manufacturing systems which brings a wide variety of data types and heterogeneous data structures. This leads to unbalanced and misaligned datasets that are not easy to integrate. Lastly, in the era of Industry 4.0, a single type of data can involve multiple contextualized computation tasks. For example, the data related to equipment (e.g., equipment vibration) may be used for fault diagnosis, preventive maintenance scheduling, and quality prediction at the same time.

However, as information quality depends on the objective of a contextualized computation task, a single dataset may or may not conform to the information quality standards required in the multiple contextualized computation tasks. This makes it challenging to consistently ensure information quality.

The information quality can be used in the combination of models. Kenett and Salini (2011) propose this approach in the context of customer surveys. We expand on this example which provides an example of an analysis of ordinal data collected through a questionnaire. Section 8.3 in *Modern Statistics* (Kenett et al. 2022b) provides details on the survey. Here we focus on an information quality ensemble analysis where three models are combined for enhanced information quality.

Assume you have 4 goals in running and analyzing an annual customer satisfaction survey:

1. Decide where to launch improvement initiatives
2. Identify the drivers of overall satisfaction
3. Detect positive or negative trends
4. Set up improvement goals

Based on these goals a questionnaire is designed and distributed to company customers. To demonstrate the approach we refer to the dataset **ABC2.csv** consisting

Table 8.1 Information Quality (InfoQ) checklist

Dimension	Questions
1. Data resolution	1.1 Is the data scale used aligned with the stated goal?
	1.2 How reliable and precise are the measuring devices or data sources?
	1.3 Is the data analysis suitable for the data aggregation level?
2. Data structure	2.1 Is the type of the data used aligned with the stated goal?
	2.2 Are data integrity details (corrupted/missing values) described and handled appropriately?
	2.3 Are the analysis methods suitable for the data structure?
3. Data integration	3.1 Are the data integrated from multiple sources? If so, what is the credibility of each source?
	3.2 How is the integration done? Are there linkage issues that lead to dropping crucial information?
	3.3 Does the data integration add value in terms of the stated goal?
	3.4 Does the data integration cause any privacy or confidentiality concerns?
4. Temporal relevance	4.1 Considering the data collection, data analysis and deployment stages, is any of them time-sensitive?
	4.2 Does the time gap between data collection and analysis cause any concern?
	4.3 Is the time gap between the data collection and analysis and the intended use of the model (e.g., in terms of policy recommendations) of any concern?
5. Chronology of data and goal	5.1 If the stated goal is predictive, are all the predictor variables expected to be available at the time of prediction?
	5.2 If the stated goal is causal, do the causal variables precede the effects?
	5.3 In a causal study, are there issues of endogeneity (reverse-causation)?
6. Generalizability	6.1 Is the stated goal statistical or scientific generalizability?
	6.2 For statistical generalizability in the case of inference, does the paper answer the question "What population does the sample represent?"
	6.3 For generalizability in the case of a stated predictive goal (predicting the values of new observations; forecasting future values), are the results generalizable to the to-be-predicted data?
	6.4 Does the paper provide sufficient detail for the type of needed reproducibility and/or repeatability, and/or replicability?
7. Operationalization	7.1 Are the measured variables themselves of interest to the study goal, or their underlying construct?
	7.2 Are there justifications for the choice of variables?
	7.3 What action items can be derived from the findings?
	7.4 Is it stated who can be affected (positively or negatively) by the findings?
	7.5 Can the affected parties do something about it?
	7.6 Would you know if you achieved your post study objectives?
8. Communication	8.1 Is the exposition of the goal, data, and analysis clear?
	8.2 Is the exposition level appropriate for the audience?
	8.3 Are all statements formulated without confusion or misunderstanding?

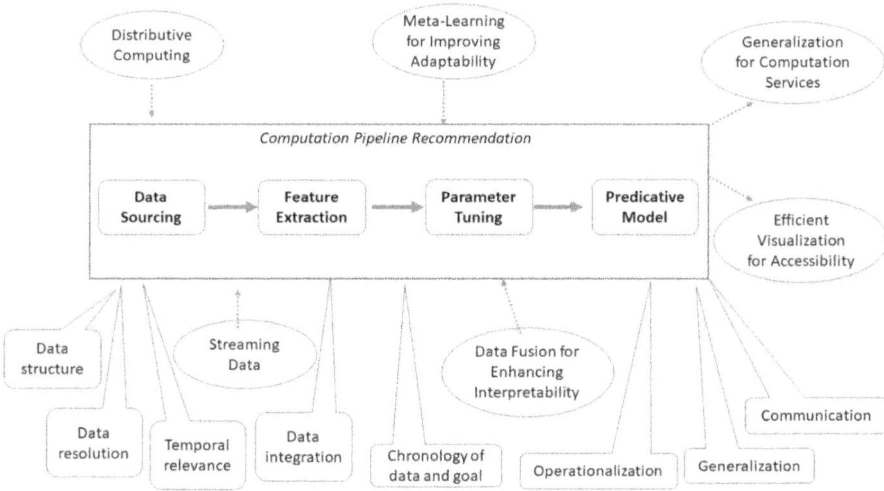

Fig. 8.1 Cybermanufacturing analytics from an information quality perspective

of survey data from an electronic product company's annual customer satisfaction survey collected from 266 companies (customers). The dataset includes, for each company, its location (country) and survey responses regarding:

- Equipment
- SalesSup (sales support)
- TechnicalSup (technical support)
- Suppliers
- AdministrativeSup (administrative support)
- TermsCondPrices (terms, conditions, and prices)
- Satisfaction: overall satisfaction
- Recommendation: recommending the product to others
- Repurchase: intent to repurchase

The response data are ordinal data ranging from 1 (very low satisfaction, very unlikely) to 5 (very high satisfaction, very likely). More information on this survey is available as Example 8.3 in *Modern Statistics* (Kenett et al. 2022b) and in Kenett and Salini (2009).

In analyzing this survey data, we use Bayesian Networks, CUB models, and control charts. These three approaches are introduced below. This is followed by a qualitative information quality assessment on four InfoQ dimensions: Data Integration, Generalizability, Operationalization, and Communication. Since we use the same data in all three models, the remaining four InfoQ dimensions are identical for all models.

An InfoQ assessment of the three models concludes this section with a discussion on how combining the three models enhances information quality. The approach can be generalized to cybermanufacturing applications where, for example, several models are combined in process control applications.

Bayesian Networks

Bayesian networks (BN) implement a graphical model structure known as a directed acyclic graph (DAG) that is popular in Statistics, Machine Learning, and Artificial Intelligence. BN are both mathematically rigorous and intuitively understandable. They enable an effective representation and computation of the joint probability distribution (JPD) over a set of random variables.

The structure of a DAG is defined by two sets: the set of nodes and the set of directed edges (arrows). The nodes represent random variables and are drawn as circles labeled by the variables' names. The edges represent direct dependencies among the variables and are represented by arrows between nodes. In particular, an edge from node X_i to node X_j represents a statistical dependence between the corresponding variables. Thus, the arrow indicates that a value taken by variable X_j depends on the value taken by variable X_i. Node X_i is then referred to as a "parent" of X_j and, similarly, X_j is referred to as the "child" of X_i. An extension of these genealogical terms is often used to define the sets of "descendants," i.e., the set of nodes from which the node can be reached on a direct path.

The structure of the acyclic graph guarantees that there is no node that can be its own ancestor or its own descendent. Such a condition is of vital importance to the factorization of the joint probability of a collection of nodes. Although the arrows represent direct causal connection between the variables, the reasoning process can operate on a BN by propagating information in any direction. A BN reflects a simple conditional independence statement, namely that each variable, given the state of its parents, is independent of its non-descendants in the graph. This property is used to reduce, sometimes significantly, the number of parameters that are required to characterize the JPD of the variables. This reduction provides an efficient way to compute the posterior probabilities given the evidence present in the data (See Chap. 10). In addition to the DAG structure, which is often considered as the "qualitative" part of the model, one needs to specify the "quantitative" parameters of the model. These parameters are described by applying the Markov property, where the conditional probability distribution at each node depends only on its parents. For discrete random variables, this conditional probability is often represented by a table, listing the local probability that a child node takes on each of the feasible values—for each combination of values of its parents. The joint distribution of a collection of variables can be determined uniquely by these local conditional probability tables.

In the context of a customer survey, a BN analysis provides a visual causality map linking the various survey variables and target variables such as overall satisfaction; recommendation and repurchasing intentions. Figures 8.2 and 8.3 represent the BN of variables representing overall satisfaction from the various questionnaire topics, the country of the respondent and responses to Overall Satisfaction, Recommendation and Repurchasing Intention. Figure 8.2 presents the DAG with the variable names as nodes; Fig. 8.3 shows the distribution of responses on a 1–5 scale. Many industrial companies are running such surveys. In case the company has a listing of its customers, the survey questionnaire is often sent to all customers. In such

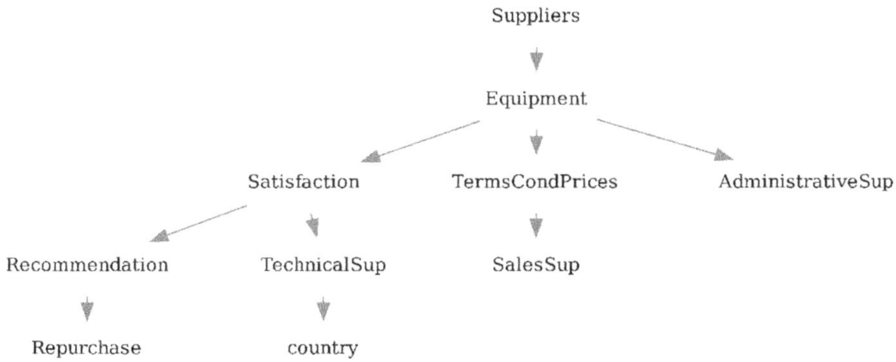

Fig. 8.2 Bayesian Network of the ABC data (with names of variables)

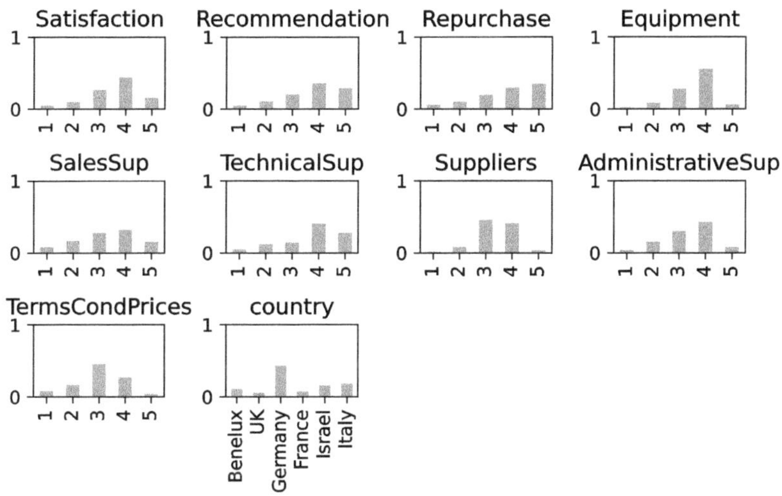

Fig. 8.3 Distribution of variables of the ABC data derived from Bayesian Network using belief propagation

cases, the nonresponse patterns need to be evaluated for possible bias. Industrial companies operating through dealers or serving unlisted customers need to check that the target frame is well covered.

By studying the BN in this case study one can see that an intervention to improve satisfaction levels from Technical Support or Equipment and Systems will increase Overall Satisfaction and eventually Recommendation and Repurchasing Intentions. As an example, consider the BN with and without conditioning on the highest recommendation level. Without conditioning, the highest level of satisfaction from Technical Support (percentage of "5") is 26%. When conditioning the network on the response "5" to recommendation, 26% increases to 37%. The implication is that if the organization increases the percentage of customers with top level satisfaction from Technical Support from 26% to 37%, recommendation levels will reach their maximum. Management can use this analysis to justify a target of 37% for the percentage of customers rating "5" their overall satisfaction from Technical Support.

We summarize now the InfoQ characteristics of a Bayesian Network analysis of the customer survey data.

A: Data Integration: Bayesian Networks are particularly effective in integrating qualitative and quantitative data.
B: Generalizability: The diagnostic and predictive capabilities of Bayesian Networks provide generalizability to population subsets. The causality relationship provides further generalizability to other contexts such as organizational processes or specific job functions.
C: Operationalization: The use of a model with conditioning capabilities provides an effective tool to set up improvement goals and diagnose pockets of dissatisfaction.
D: Communication: The visual display of a Bayesian Network makes it particularly appealing to decision makers who feel uneasy with mathematical models.

In the next section we present CUB, a sophisticated approach to analyze categorical data, such a data generated by responses on rating scales.

CUB Models

Responses to customer satisfaction surveys are governed by specific experience and psychological considerations. When faced with discrete alternatives, people make choices by pairwise comparison of the items or by sequential removals. Such choices are affected by both uncertainty in the choice and pure randomness. Modeling the distribution of responses is far more precise than considering single summary statistics. Such considerations lead to the development of the CUB (Combination of uniform and shifted binomial random variables) model, originally proposed in Piccolo (2003). The CUB model is applied to the study of sampling surveys where subjects express a definite opinion selected from an ordered list of categories with m alternatives. The model differentiates between satisfaction level from an item and randomness of the final choice. These unobservable components are defined as *feeling* and *uncertainty*, respectively.

Feeling is the result of several factors related to the respondent such as country of origin, position in the company, and years of experience. This is represented by a sum of random variables which converges to a unimodal continuous distribution. To model this, CUB models feeling by a shifted Binomial random variable, characterized by a parameter ζ and a mass b_r for response r where:

$$b_r(\zeta) = \binom{m-1}{r-1}\zeta^{m-r}(1-\zeta)^{r-1}, \qquad r = 1, 2, \ldots m.$$

Uncertainty is a result of variables such as the time to answer, the degree of personal involvement of the responder with the topic being surveyed, the availability of information, fatigue, partial understanding of the item, lack of self-confidence,

Table 8.2 CUB model estimates and their standard deviations

Topic	Estimates of π (std)	Estimates of ζ (std)
Overall satisfaction	0.875 (0.060)	0.338 (0.020)
Equipment and systems	0.999 (0.043)	0.363 (0.018)
Sales support	0.640 (0.091)	0.389 (0.028)
Technical support	0.719 (0.067)	0.235 (0.023)
Supplies and orders	1.000 (0.081)	0.404 (0.017)
Contracts and pricing	1.000 (0.082)	0.490 (0.017)

laziness, apathy, boredom, etc. A basic model for these effects is a discrete uniform random variable:

$$U_r(m) = \frac{1}{m}, \qquad r = 1, 2, \ldots m.$$

The integrated CUB discrete choice model is:

$$\Pr(R = r) = \pi b_r(\zeta) + (1 - \pi)U_r(m)., \qquad r = 1, 2, \ldots m; 0 \leq \pi \leq 1,$$

and

$$E(R) = \frac{m+1}{2} + \pi(m-1)\left(\frac{1}{2} - \zeta\right).$$

In applying the CUB model to the ABC data, Iannario and Piccolo (2011) observe that customers express a judgment with no uncertainty parameters with regard to Equipment and Systems, Supplies and Orders and Contracts and Pricing and with a limited uncertainty in the other items. They also note that satisfaction is higher for questions on Technical Support and Equipment and Systems. Thus, in this case study, customers are relatively satisfied with the equipment supplied by the ABC Company and, to a lesser extent, with Sales Support. Specifically the authors report the estimates presented in Table 8.2.

Summarizing the information quality characteristics of the CUB model provides the following remarks:

A: Data Integration: CUB models integrate the intensity of feeling toward a certain item with the response uncertainty. These two components can be also explained by using appropriate covariates.

B: Generalizability: The model is not generalizable per se. Its components offer, however, interesting cognitive and psychological interpretations.

C: Operationalization: The model is mostly focused on explaining the outcomes of a survey. Insights on uncertainty and feelings can lead to interesting diverse initiatives.

D: Communication: The model estimates can be visually presented with bar plots or otherwise.

In the next section we discuss and application to survey data using control charts introduced in Chap. 2.

Control Charts

Perceived quality, satisfaction levels, and customer complaints can be effectively controlled with control charts used in the context of statistical process control (SPC). SPC methods are introduced in Chap. 2. Control charts are generally classified into two groups. When quality characteristics are measured on a continuous scale, we have a *control chart for variables*. When the quality characteristic is classified by attributes, then *control charts for attributes* are used. In analyzing customer satisfaction survey data, we can use control charts to identify a shift from previous surveys or investigate the achievement of pre-set targets. In general, we test the hypothesis:

$$\begin{cases} H_0 : \theta = \theta_0 \\ H_1 : \theta \neq \theta_0 \end{cases}$$

where θ can be the mean, the standard error, or a proportion, depending on the particular kind and scope of the control chart (i.e., for variables or for attributes). All the above details also hold when we are interested in testing a specific shift of the parameter such as $\theta > \theta_0$ or $\theta < \theta_0$. In these cases, only one control limit, either upper control limit (UCL) or lower control limit (LCL), is reported on the control chart. Specifically, the p chart with control limits

$$\bar{p} \pm k\sqrt{\frac{\bar{p}(1-\bar{p})}{n}}$$

is used to monitor the percentage of respondents who answered "5" (Very High) to a question on overall satisfaction, where n is the number of respondents and k is a constant multiplier of the binomial standard deviation used to set up the control limits. The value $k = 2$ is often applied in applications of control charts to the analysis of customer satisfaction data.

A p chart of the percentage of respondents which rated their satisfaction level as "5" in the Equipment and Systems and the Sales Support questions is presented in Fig. 8.4. We call these percentages "TOP5". The chart shows an average TOP5 proportion for Equipment and Systems questions of 14.4%. Question 9 on "uptime" is showing up with a TOP5 proportion significantly higher than the average, indicating that "uptime" is an area that stands out as an area of excellence from the customer's point of view. The Sales Support average TOP5 proportion is 18.2% with question 14, on satisfaction from response time by sales personnel, significantly high. Because of the small number of questions, the UCL and LCL are positioned at 2 standard deviations above and below the average central line (CL).

Specifically, the questions displayed in Fig. 8.4, and, in brackets, the number of response "5" out of 262 responses, are:

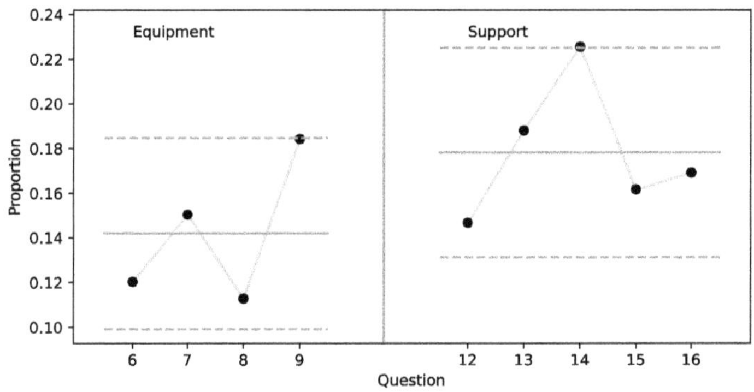

Fig. 8.4 *p* chart of proportion of "5" in questions on equipment and systems and sales support

Equipment and Systems

q6 The equipment's features and capabilities meet your needs (32).
q7 Improvements and upgrades provide value (40).
q8 Output quality meets or exceeds expectations (30).
q9 Uptime is acceptable (49).

Sales Support

q12 Verbal promises have been honored (39).
q13 Sales personnel communicate frequently enough with you (50).
q14 Sales personnel respond promptly to requests (60).
q15 Sales personnel are knowledgeable about equipment (43).
q16 Sales personnel are knowledgeable about market opportunities (45).

Summarizing the information quality of the control chart analysis of the ABC data:

A: Data Integration: Control charts can be split by covariate values. Basic univariate control charts do not provide an effective data integration approach.
B: Generalizability: The analysis provides insights relevant to the data at hand without generalizable theory.
C: Operationalization: The findings clearly distinguish significant from random effects, thereby helping decision makers to effectively focus their improvement efforts.
D: Communication: The visual display of a control chart makes it very appealing for communication and visualization of the analysis.

Based on the above subjective evaluations of Bayesian Network, CUB model, and control chart analysis of the ABC data, we list in Table 8.3, InfoQ scores of the 4 assessed dimensions. These assessment account for the 4 goals listed at the beginning of this section.

Table 8.3 InfoQ assessment of the Bayesian Network, CUB model, and control chart analysis

InfoQ dimension	Model		
	Bayesian Network	CUB model	Control chart
A. Data integration	5	4	3
B. Generalizability	3	5	2
C. Operationalization	5	3	5
D. Communication	4	3	5

As we can see none of these models provides a consistent advantage. The approach suggested here is to apply all three models and combine them in a dashboard in order to enhance information quality. This approach represents a general principle of ensemble modeling that can be easily deployed in cybermanufacturing. The next section is a review of general modeling in cybermanufacturing.

8.4 Modeling in Cybermanufacturing

Cybermanufacturing focuses on the convergence of the physical entities (e.g., manufacturing equipment) and the cyber entities (e.g., simulated equipment), such that the dynamic changes of the physical entities can be predicted and analyzed through the corresponding cyber entities (Qi and Tao 2018). Therefore, the existing efforts aimed at achieving realistic cyber entities via accurate computer simulation models and machine learning methods (Qi and Tao 2018; Schluse et al. 2018). An example, in the context of decision tree, predictive analytics is the work of Ben-Gal et al. (2014). In that paper, the authors presented the dual information distance (DID) method, which selects features by considering both immediate contributions to the classification as well as their future potential effects. Specifically, the DID method constructs classification trees by finding the shortest paths over a graph of partitions that are defined by the selected features. The authors demonstrated that the method takes into account both the orthogonality between the selected partitions as well as the reduction of uncertainty on the class partition, such that it outperforms popular classifiers in terms of average depth and classification accuracy. However, computation complexity involving computer simulations and data preprocessing/communication across distributed manufacturing system is becoming one of the most challenging issues in realizing realistic cyber entities. First, high-fidelity computer simulations, which enable accurate prediction of the behavior of physical entities via the cyber entities, are typically too time-consuming. This issue becomes more challenging when the manufacturing process involves computationally intensive multiphysics computer simulations (Dbouk 2017). For example, recent work indicates that a single run of computer simulation for the fused deposition modeling process takes more than 20 h (Li et al. 2018), which could result in a significant delay in updating the cyber entities. Secondly, as the advancement of sensing and communication systems enables the collection of enormous data from distributed manufacturing systems, machine learning methods to build the cyber entities require significantly higher computation cost and/or communication bandwidth across cybermanufacturing infrastructure.

The issue of computation complexity leads to limitations in cybermanufacturing (Singh et al. 2018; Modoni et al. 2019; Bevilacqua et al. 2020; Rasheed et al. 2020). First, computation complexity involving modeling complex behaviors of heterogeneous manufacturing systems and their interactions delays the manufacturing modeling and analysis for personalized demands, which limits the timeliness of personalization. The issue is important, since cybermanufacturing aims at efficient personalization of products by utilizing heterogeneous manufacturing systems connected. Second, computational complexity also affects the ability to generate information quality (Kenett and Shmueli 2016). Insufficient storage or computation power to handle data with adequate resolution can negatively impact the delivery of outputs from analytical work to the right persons, in the right way, at the right time, thereby reducing information quality.

Manufacturing processes involve complex physical mechanisms. Therefore, underlying engineering knowledge, such as cause-effect relationships, first principle models, and computer simulation models (e.g., finite element analysis) and design rules, may be incomplete. Here, incomplete knowledge can be due to (1) incomplete understanding of the underlying physical mechanism (e.g., first principle model, material properties), (2) incomplete information about model parameters, and (3) stochastic behavior or uncertainties associated with the system or numerical algorithms. To address the issue, computer model calibration (Kennedy and O'Hagan 2001; Higdon et al. 2008, 2013; Wong et al. 2017) has been continuously studied to compensate the incomplete knowledge with observational data, and design for variation (Reinman et al. 2012) has been studied to reduce the variation of products under the incomplete knowledge and uncertainties. However, in the era of Industry 4.0, it is becoming more challenging to address the issue for the following reasons. First, while the core of cybermanufacturing is to take advantage of multimodal manufacturing data, the data can mislead the decision-making processes if incomplete knowledge (e.g., invalid assumption in modeling a manufacturing process) involves the interpretation of the data. Second, since the existing efforts typically assume a single or only a few manufacturing systems (Feng et al. 2017), existing computer experimental design, modeling, and calibration are not easily scalable to the scenario where a lot of heterogeneous manufacturing systems connected in cybermanufacturing. In these cases, the dependability and effectiveness of cybermanufacturing may be questioned, especially in case a delicate and complex situation requires decision-making in a real-time manner (Broy et al. 2012). These issues are more common in the newly introduced additive manufacturing (Babu and Goodridge 2015; Yang et al. 2017; Dilberoglu et al. 2017; Jared et al. 2017; Li et al. 2018; Mahmoudi et al. 2018; Sabbaghi et al. 2018; Kenett et al. 2021a).

In summary, incomplete engineering knowledge leads to limitations in cybermanufacturing. First, the manufacturing design process becomes inefficient when underlying engineering knowledge is incomplete. Specifically, it has been speculated that 75% of the cost involving product development is committed early in the engineering design process when the knowledge of the product is unclear and/or incomplete (Chandrasegaran et al. 2013). Second, when the computer simulation or data-driven models for a manufacturing process are limited in scope, the models cannot provide adequate predictions for prognostics and health management in cybermanufacturing (Weiss et al. 2015). This can result in inefficient planning, maintenance, and logistics due to the inaccurate prediction of equipment status (Davis et al. 2012; Edgar and Pistikopoulos 2018).

Cybermanufacturing focuses on personalization and customized production, which will generate a wide variety of heterogeneous data (Thoben et al. 2017). In the meantime, the adequacy of a machine learning method to such heterogeneous data may be significantly different due to the underlying statistical characteristics (e.g., the distribution of data) and/or contextualized computation tasks (e.g., fault diagnosis or quality control a specific manufacturing process) (Chen and Jin 2018). Here, we call the different adequacy as the "border" of the machine learning methods. Thus, it is important to match a specific dataset/contextualized computation task with a proper machine learning method within the border to ensure the efficiency and effectiveness of manufacturing modeling and analysis.

In current practice, a typical paradigm to identify which machine learning method for use is often heuristic based on domain knowledge of a specific contextualized computation task and/or data scientist's personal experience in data analysis. Clearly, such a heuristic manner could require a large number of trial-and-errors for identifying an efficient and effective machine learning method under a given contextualized computation task. It calls for a systematic methodology to understand the border among different machine learning methods, especially in the field of manufacturing modeling and analysis.

There are several challenges in Industry 4.0 due to the lack of systematic understanding of the borders among different machine learning methods. We list some of them below. First, considering the heterogeneous manufacturing systems connected in cybermanufacturing, it will require considerable lead time for identifying a proper machine learning method for each manufacturing system and computation task. For example, for a thermal spray coating process using heterogeneous spray guns, it is reported that linear regression model worked well for one spray gun was not applicable to the other spray guns, due to the violation of the assumption of samples from the same underlying distribution (Chen and Jin 2018). Second, it is known that manufacturing processes and systems are likely to be dynamic in model relationship, due to a number of factors from raw materials, equipment status, and environment. For example, it is reported that the model parameters for crystal growth process should be adjusted based on the degradation level of the equipment (Jin et al. 2019). However, most of the machine learning methods cannot generate dynamic models. Therefore, it will be beneficial to efficiently match the optimal machine learning method with the degradation levels. Third, cybermanufacturing often requires different accuracy of machine learning methods with the consideration of computational cost and utility costs. A lack of understanding of borders among machine learning methods could increase efforts to select the methods not only be adequate but also be reliable and responsive. As shown in Kang et al. (2021a), a tradeoff between the computational cost of designs and the accuracy of surrogate models could facilitate the identification of the feasible design region, which is crucial in the timeliness of personalized product realization in Industry 4.0. Meanwhile, the time latency in machine learning training process, and the unreliable computation due to computation node failure or loss of communication to Cloud will prohibit the use of advanced, but computation intensive algorithms.

When machine learning methods are employed, different researchers or practitioners tend to choose different configurations (e.g., splitting of the samples for training and testing), even when they analyze the same dataset (Botvinik-Nezer et al. 2020). This flexibility leads to difficulties in the reproducibility analytical studies and needs to be accounted for and controlled in manufacturing modeling and analysis. However, even though there have been consistent efforts to address the issue in science (Botvinik-Nezer et al. 2020; Kenett and Rubinstein 2021), the manufacturing industry is less concerned with the issue of reproducibility of analytical studies via machine learning (Kenett 2020). In other words, companies tend to overlook the experimental works designed to improve processes and products for reproducibility using adequate statistical criteria. In the meantime, fierce competition in the era of Industry 4.0 allows only short-term opportunities to try out new products and/or new process setups, which calls for ensuring the reproducibility of analytical studies in a contextualized computation task.

A lack of reproducibility of analytical studies via machine learning leads to the following challenges in cybermanufacturing. First, in the manufacturing industry, a lack of reproducibility of machine learning methods can result in misleading decision-making, which is very costly and time-consuming. For example, it is reported that around 50% of the costs incurred in new product development tend to be spent on unnecessary design iteration (Schulze and Störmer 2012), which can be avoided by accurate and reliable predictions. Second, since cybermanufacturing involves efficient utilization of heterogeneous manufacturing systems connected to cybermanufacturing network (Lee et al. 2015; Jeschke et al. 2017; Wang et al. 2020), reproducibility should be ensured such that consistent product quality can be achieved across the cybermanufacturing network. Lastly, a lack of reproducibility of machine learning methods can result in increased product variation, which can deteriorate customer satisfaction (Luo et al. 2005; Dharmesti and Nugroho 2013). It is an important issue, since improved customer satisfaction is one of the most important goals to be achieved in the context of Industry 4.0 (Bortolini et al. 2017; de Man and Strandhagen 2017; Bär et al. 2018).

8.5 Computational Pipelines

The concept of computation pipelines for machine learning is suggested from the software engineering community to systematically organize a sequence of method options, including data collection, data preprocessing, data filtering, feature selection (optional), data fusion/machine learning methods, computation, and post-processing (Chen and Jin 2018). For example, Scikit-learn, a machine learning library for Python, applies a computation pipeline to assemble several steps that can be cross-validated together with different setting parameters (Pedregosa et al. 2011). Similarly, TensorFlow (Abadi et al. 2016) and PyTorch (Paszke et al. 2022), two widely used deep learning platforms, implement the idea of computational graph to organize computational pipelines.

In the manufacturing industry, most relevant works involving computation pipelines have focused on constructing an autonomous framework to tune a specific computation pipeline or only a limited number of method options. Examples of such works include the application of computation pipelines for preventive maintenance operation (O'Donovan et al. 2015), fault prognostics (Kozjek et al. 2017), and production planning (Wang et al. 2018b). While the aforementioned works are applicable to a specific contextualized computation task, they cannot be adequate in different tasks when modeling assumptions are violated (e.g., the underlying distribution of data is different). In other words, to ensure the effectiveness of manufacturing modeling and analysis, one should efficiently switch to a proper computation pipeline from a number of alternatives that fits well with the scenario. However, the current practice relies on trial-and-errors according to domain knowledge and experiences, which is too time-consuming to identify the optimal method options for a proper computation pipeline.

An open source tool to automate experimentation and model building is OpenML. It is available in https://www.openml.org. OpenML is a database from which entities can be downloaded and uploaded. Communication with the database goes through an open API which is a collaborative, automated machine learning environment that involves:

- Datasets automatically analyzed, annotated, and organized online
- Machine learning pipelines automatically shared from many libraries
- Extensive APIs to integrate OpenML into your own tools and scripts
- Reproducible results (e.g., models, evaluations) for easy comparison and reuse
- Collaborate in real time, right from your existing tools
- Make your work more visible, reusable, and easily citable

The OpenML platform requires you to first upload a data flow. The data flow identifies a particular machine learning algorithm from a library or framework such as Weka, mlr, or scikit-learn. It needs to contain a name, details about its version and a list of settable hyperparameters. A run is a particular flow, that is an algorithm, with a particular parameter setting, applied to a particular task.

A data preparation step is needed. This involves assessing missing data, duplicated records, missing values, outliers, typos, and many other issues that weaken the quality of the data and hinder advanced analysis. A precursor to modelling and analysis is data preparation pre-screen (Yi et al. 2019).

We follow here a classification of the status of data into quality bands proposed by Lawrence (2017); Castelijns et al. (2020) and introduced in Chapter 7 of *Modern Statistics* (Kenett et al. 2022b). The quality bands are labelled: C, B, A, AA, and AAA.

These labels represent the level of usability of datasets:

Band C (Conceive) refers to the stage that the data is still being ingested. If there is information about the dataset, it comes from the data collection phase and how the data was collected. The data has not yet been introduced to a programming environment or tool in a way that allows operations to be performed on the dataset. The possible analyses to be performed on the dataset in order to gain value from the data possibly have not been conceived yet, as this can often only be determined after inspecting the data itself.

Band B (Believe) refers to the stage in which the data is loaded into an environment that allows cleaning operations. However, the correctness of the data is not fully assessed yet, and there may be errors or deficiencies that invalidate further analysis. Therefore, analyses performed on data at this level are often more cursory and exploratory with visualization methods to ascertain the correctness of the data.

In band A (Analyze), the data is ready for deeper analysis. However, even if there are no more factual errors in the data, the quality of an analysis or machine learning model is greatly influenced by how the data is represented. For instance, operations such as feature selection and normalization can greatly increase the accuracy of machine learning models. Hence, these operations need to be performed before arriving at accurate and adequate machine learning models or analyses.

In band AA (Allow Analysis), we consider the context in which the dataset is allowed to be used. Operations in this band detect, quantify, and potentially address any legal, moral, or social issues with the dataset, since the consequences of using illegal, immoral, or biased datasets can be enormous. Hence, this band is about verifying whether analysis can be applied without (legal) penalties or negative social impact. One may argue that legal and moral implications are not part of data cleaning, but rather distinct parts of the data process. However, we argue that readiness is about learning the ins and outs of your dataset and detecting and solving any potential problems that may occur when analyzing and using a dataset.

Band AAA is reached when you determine that the dataset is clean. The data is self-contained and no further input is needed from the people that collected or created the data.

A Python application providing scores to datasets based on these bands is available in https://github.com/pywash/pywash. Figure 8.5 shows step B of the application. Once missing values are handled, Band A allows detecting outliers and scaling of features. The application is unfortunately no longer maintained and requires specific Python library versions. We provide a configuration file to setup and run the application inside a dedicated docker container on the `mistat` repository at https://github.com/gedeck/mistat.

Computation pipeline recommendation has been adopted not only to improve the quality prediction but also to improve other important sectors of Industry 4.0: informative visualization and efficient human-machine collaboration. In the following-up research of Chen and Jin (2021), they extended the concept of computation pipeline recommendation to the personalization of a visualization system, which is called Personalized Recommender System for Information visualization Methods via Extended matrix completion (PRIME). The main improvement of

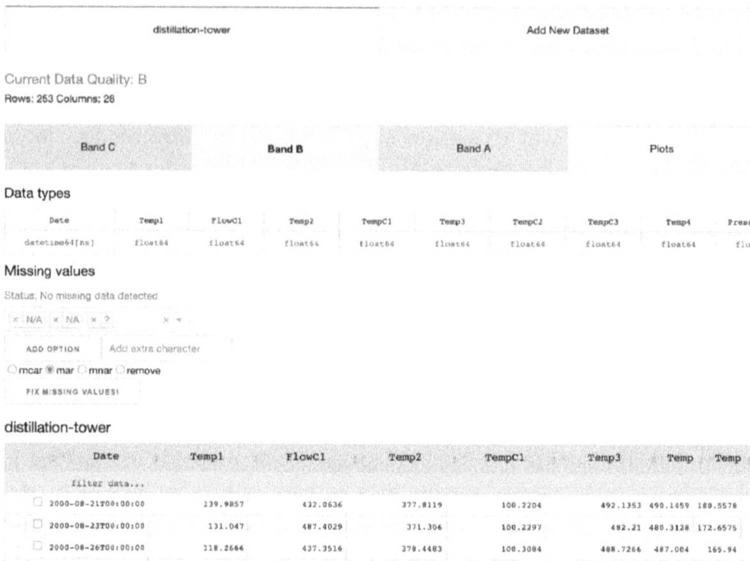

Fig. 8.5 Screenshot of PYWASH software

PRIME is incorporating wearable sensor data for pipeline recommendation. This allows pipeline recommendation to include human-computer interaction in the acquisition of insights from complex datasets. Specifically, PRIME models covariates (i.e., wearable sensor data) to predict recommendation scores (e.g., perceived complexity, mental workload, etc.). This allows users to adapt visualization specific to a contextualized computation task. In addition, PRIME can make accurate recommendations for new users or new contextualized computation tasks based on historical wearable sensor signals and recommendation scores. Chen and Jin (2021) demonstrate that PRIME achieves satisfactory recommendation accuracy for adapting visualization, even when there are limited historical datasets. This capability contributes to designing a new generation of visualization systems that adapt to users' real-time status. PRIME can support researchers in reducing the sample size requirements to quantify individual differences, and practitioners in adapting visualizations according to user states and contextualized computation tasks in a real-time manner.

The generalization and further advancement of computation pipeline recommendation provides a systematic methodology to explore various method options. Specifically, statistical computational performance can be chosen to address information quality, computation complexity, incomplete engineering knowledge, adequacy of machine learning methods, or reproducibility issues. For example, an InfoQ scores can be used to recommend a computation pipeline with acceptable information quality. To achieve this a computational pipeline recommendation needs to incorporate such issues in a quantitative manner. Reis and Kenett (2018) use this approach in a computational pipeline used in the chemical process industry.

8.6 Digital Twins

In the era of Industry 4.0, the integration of physical assets and digital assets in cybermanufacturing opens up new opportunities for enhanced productivity, higher flexibility, and reduced costs. In the previous section we introduced PRIME, a pipeline recommendation system including human-computer interaction in the acquisition of insights from complex datasets. In this section we expand on the background and content of digital twins introduced in Sect. 1.4.

A digital twin is a digital representation of a physical object or process (Kenett and Bortman 2021). The concept was initially conceived within the aerospace industry and evolved to general cyber-physical systems (Shafto et al. 2010). Modern understanding of system characteristics is influenced by the introduction of big data and the industrial internet of things (IIoT) solutions (Lee et al. 2015). The development of a digital twin implements a holistic approach to data acquisition, modelling and analysis, as multiple interconnected components are assembled to produce a decision support tool (Grieves and Vickers 2017; Grieves 2022). Simulation modelling is one of the key components of digital twins. It is used in the verification and evaluation of engineering systems and their performance and functionality (Kenett and Vicario 2021). In manufacturing, the virtual representation of production enables the acquisition of information on the behavior of the product. A product's features can be analyzed both online and off-line and their characteristics predicted prior to the end of the manufacturing process.

The digital twin provides a platform for tracking and monitoring systems and processes implementing the methods described in Chaps. 2–4. An example of such capabilities is a modern car. There are many censors in new cars that work as one turns on the engine. Signals appear as soon as something is wrong. For examples air pressure in tires, temperature of the engine, driving close to another car, etc. These indications are derived from a built-in tracking and monitoring system installed on board.

Condition-based maintenance (CBM) is also an application of digital twins. It is based on the concept that maintenance operations should be done only when necessary (see Chap. 9). The purpose of CBM is to prevent a deterioration in the effectiveness of a system which can lead to a total failure. It aims to reduce maintenance costs by optimizing planning of maintenance operations such as preventive replacement of damaged component. For an effective CBM, prediction of the remaining useful life (RUL) of components is required. Evaluation of the components' RUL requires not only diagnosis faults but also the estimation of the fault location and severity.

We proceed with an example of a rotating machine digital twin. Common health monitoring methods for rotating machines are based on signal monitoring, usually acceleration signals and recently strain sensing. These methods are developed to monitor and diagnose deterioration of critical components. Figure 8.6 is a schematic model of a typical damaged bearing.

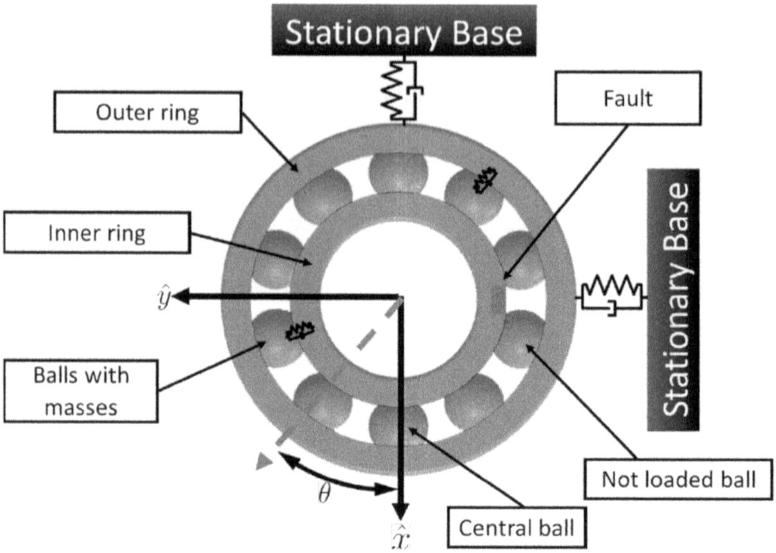

Fig. 8.6 A typical model of damaged bearing

The effect of a damage on the dynamic behavior of the system is used in order to develop an efficient tool to estimate the existence and the severity of a damage. Using a combination of experiments and simulations contributes to the understanding of how the system behaves in the presence of damage and, in addition, to study how the fault affects the vibration profile. Such models are used during the lifecycle of a machine, as part of the machine's digital twin, to diagnose the machine condition, to optimize the operation such that its key performance goals are achieved.

The key issue is to understand the physical behavior of the machine, the vibration signal of the healthy state and in the presence of a fault. A dynamic model of the system is constructed. In most cases, a closed-form solution is not possible. Hence, a numerical solution for the healthy and the damaged cases are obtained. The solution is verified and validated with experimental data. The final model results are used to develop physical understanding of the system behavior under different working conditions and manufacturing tolerances. The model results enable a better understating of the experimental data and play a major role in the development of diagnostic and prognostic algorithms, using Condition Indicators (CIs). On the other hand, the experimental results are used to validate the simulation and to establish the confidence in the model and to understand its limitations.

The rotating machine digital twin can incorporate a non-linear dynamic model of the motor behavior (Kenett and Bortman 2021). The model simulates the two gears, the stiffness of the bearings, the brake, and the torsion of the shafts, the backlash in the system, as well as the surface roughness of the gear teeth. The components included in the model are the ones affecting the system vibration signal.

The components are assumed to be rigid bodies. The surface roughness is described by a displacement-excitation function along the pressure line. The contact between the gear teeth is simulated as slices of linear springs.

A practical gear transmission contains surface imperfections that directly influence the vibration signature. The surface imperfections may restrict the ability to diagnose faults using vibration analysis. The digital twin can simulate the gear tooth surface to better understand the limits of fault detection in the presence of different levels of gear imperfections. The tooth profile deviation is defined with respect to the involute profile. The dynamic model is used to simulate the vibrations of gears with different types and sizes of faults. The model takes into consideration the irregularity of the gear teeth representing a realistic system.

For the purpose of validation, simulations are compared with data from experiments under similar conditions. After validation, the model is used to study the effect of surface quality. Low precision gear profile grade reduces the ability to detect faults. However, gears with high-quality tooth surface allow detection of smaller faults and classification of the fault size. A model estimates the distribution of results generated by profile deviations, allowing robust analysis of diagnostic capabilities. This corresponds to robustness studies presented in Chap. 6.

Another important issue in gear motors is the discontinuity contact occurs primarily from the presence of clearance between meshing teeth. The gap between the width of a tooth space and the thickness of the engaging tooth is called backlash. The main goal of this example is to develop a CI for detection backlash based on vibration signatures. Damping increase arising because of oil-film in the gap between two teeth of a meshing gear needs to be taken into account.

The effects of different backlash levels on the vibration signals indicate that acceleration increases with higher backlash level. The same trend was observed in the tangential axis. The energy level of the signal increases as function of backlash level.

A dynamic model for gear system simulations takes into consideration the clearance between the gear teeth and oil-film effects. Simulations using the model show that there is a significant impact of the backlash on the dynamic response of the gear pair. A reliable dynamic model that simulates the dynamics of gear systems is an important tool for gear diagnostics. Using this model enables identification of the influence of backlash on the vibration signal.

This brief overview of a rotating machine digital twin presents an example where monitoring, diagnostic, prognostic, and prescriptive analytics is implemented.

Example 8.1 To provide a hands on experience with a digital twin we use the piston simulator introduced in Chap. 7. Instead of actual data, we use the *PistonSimulator* to create sets of sensor data and cycle times for this example.

Monitoring During normal operations, the cycle times of the experiment are similar to what is shown in Fig. 8.7. The data were created using a simulation with all factors set to the mid points of their respective ranges. While monitoring the operation of our actual system, we observe an unusual change in cycle times; it is shown in Fig. 8.8. What could have caused this change?

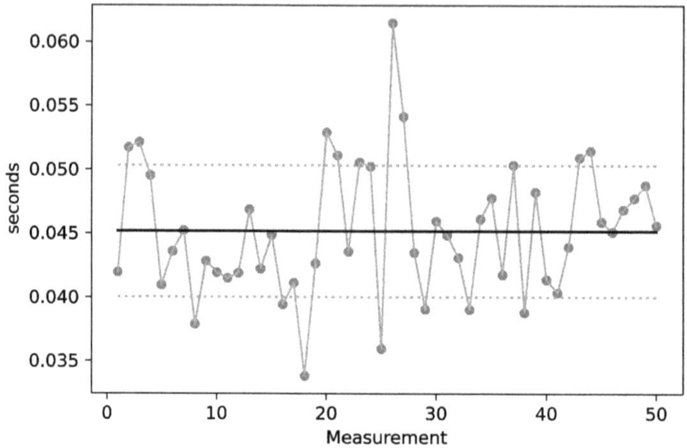

Fig. 8.7 Piston cycle time under normal operation. Horizontal lines show the mean and ± one standard deviation

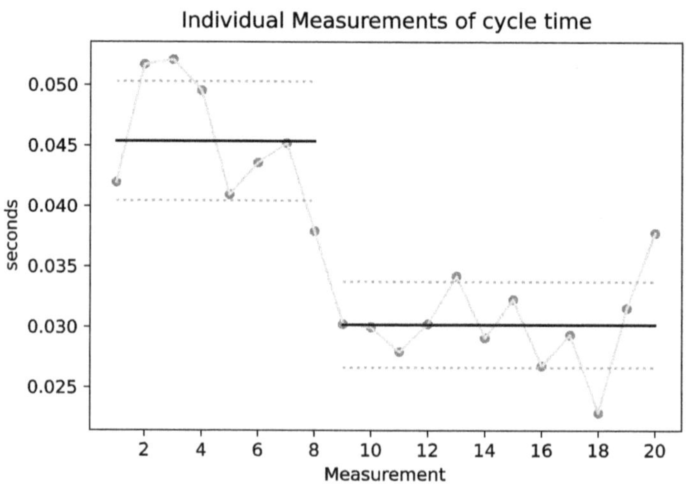

Fig. 8.8 Piston cycle time shows an unusual change

Diagnostics Figure 8.9 analyzes changes in the sensor data during the experiment. From this graph, we can assume that the noticeable changes in the initial gas volume `v0` are likely responsible for the decrease in cycle time. To confirm this hypothesis, we need some diagnostic investigation. We design an experimental setup with 1280 $(= 10 \cdot 2^7)$ runs using a Latin hypersquare design with all seven factors varied.

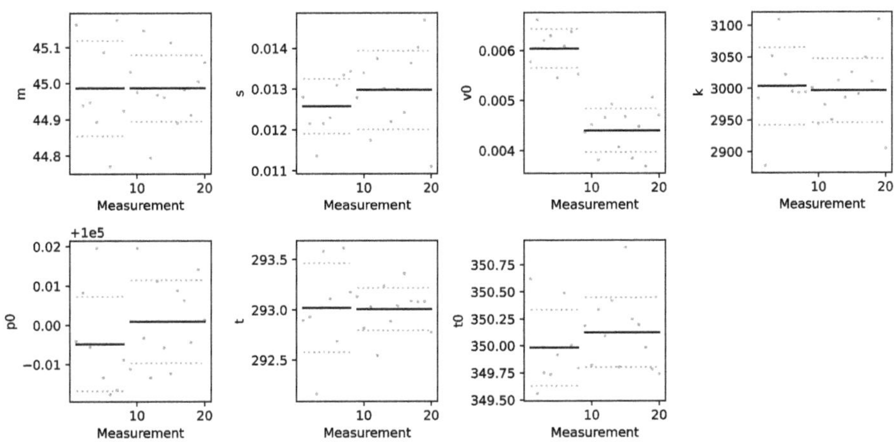

Fig. 8.9 Variation of sensor data during the unusual change in piston cycle time

```
from mistat.design import doe

Factors = {
    'm': (30, 60),
    's': (0.005, 0.02),
    'k': (1_000, 5_000),
    't': (290, 296),
    'p0': (90_000, 110_000),
    'v0': (0.002, 0.01),
    't0': (340, 360),
}
Design = doe.lhs(Factors, num_samples=1280)
Design = Design.to_dict(orient = 'list')
experiment = mistat.PistonSimulator(n_simulation=1, seed=1, **Design)
experimentData = experiment.simulate()
```

Using a neural network to analyze the 1280 experiments we can offer enhanced diagnostic and prognostic capabilities as part of a *digital twin*. Using a grid search we determine that a neural network with three layers (7, 6, 1) and six nodes in the hidden layer, adequately fits the data.[1]

```
from sklearn.neural_network import MLPRegressor
from sklearn.preprocessing import MinMaxScaler
from sklearn.pipeline import make_pipeline
from sklearn.compose import TransformedTargetRegressor

predictors = ['m', 's', 'k', 't', 'p0', 'v0', 't0']
X = experimentData[predictors]
y = experimentData['seconds']

# create a pipeline that first scales the predictors to the range 0 to 1
```

[1] The Python code for the grid search using cross validation can be found at https://gedeck.github.io/mistat-code-solutions/IndustrialStatistics. In some cases, a cross validation strategy that takes data structure into account can be more suitable; see, e.g., Kenett et al. (2022a).

```
# followed by a neural network model. The outcome variable is also
# rescaled to a range of 0 to 1. This is achieved using TransformedTargetRegressor.
model = TransformedTargetRegressor(
    regressor=make_pipeline(
        MinMaxScaler(),
        MLPRegressor(max_iter=1000, activation='tanh',
            hidden_layer_sizes=(5, ), learning_rate_init=0.01,
            early_stopping=True, random_state=0,
        )
    ),
    transformer=MinMaxScaler(),
)
_ = model.fit(X, y)
```

Applying such a model, we can determine the importance of individual factors on cycle time. We use the *permutation_importance* method to achieve this. Permutation importance measures the effect on model performance if a predictor is randomly shuffled. Besides neural network models we can use boosted trees, random forests, support vector machines or penalized regression such as lasso or elastic nets.

```
from sklearn.inspection import permutation_importance

result = permutation_importance(model, X, y, n_repeats=10, random_state=0)
result.importances_mean
result.importances_std
permImportance = pd.DataFrame({
    'predictor': predictors,
    'mean': result.importances_mean,
    'std': result.importances_std,
    'low': result.importances_mean - result.importances_std,
    'high': result.importances_mean + result.importances_std,
})
permImportance
```

	predictor	mean	std	low	high
0	m	0.005183	0.001588	0.003596	0.006771
1	s	0.956525	0.027363	0.929162	0.983888
2	k	0.042135	0.005193	0.036942	0.047329
3	t	0.001199	0.000764	0.000435	0.001963
4	p0	0.005786	0.001829	0.003957	0.007615
5	v0	0.832526	0.026581	0.805945	0.859108
6	t0	0.003173	0.001533	0.001640	0.004706

The result of this analysis (see also Fig. 8.10) shows that the piston surface area s and the initial gas volume $v0$ have the strongest influence on cycle time. All other factors have only a small influence. Looking at a contour plot confirms our analysis. Figure 8.11 shows the change of cycle time as a function of piston surface area s and the initial gas volume $v0$. The overlayed experimental sensor data from Fig. 8.8 show that the drop in cycle time can be explained by a reduction in initial gas volume $v0$.

Prognostics As $v0$ has such a strong influence, can we predict future values of $v0$? In the following Python code, an ARIMA model is fitted to the sensor data that showed the effect. The best model for several combinations of p, d, and q is determined using the AIC of the model.

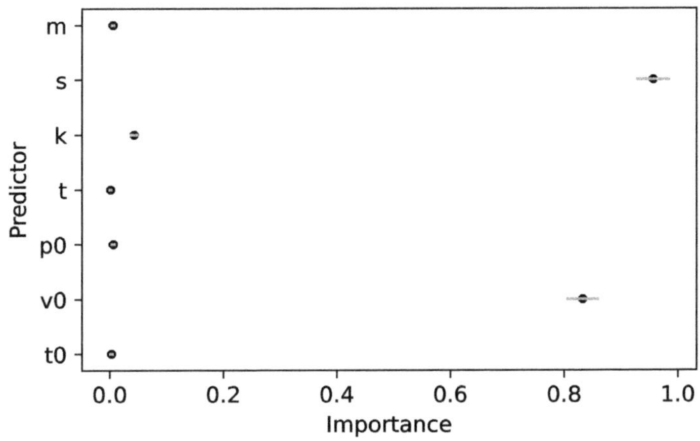

Fig. 8.10 The importance of factors on cycle time derived from the analysis of the digital twin

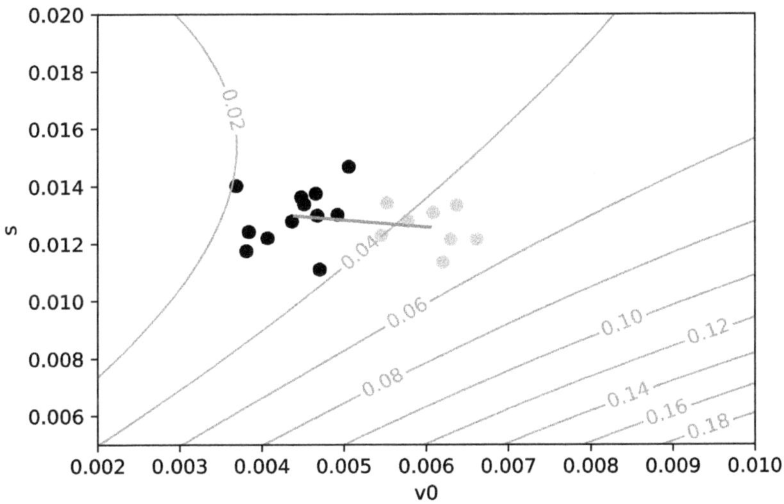

Fig. 8.11 Contour plot determined using the neural network model that shows the change in cycle time as a function of the two most important factors. All other factors were fixed at the average value of the sensor data. The grey and black dots show the experimental observations before and after the observed change from Fig. 8.8

```
import warnings
warnings.filterwarnings('ignore', category=UserWarning)
from statsmodels.tsa.api import SARIMAX

# Define the p, d and q parameters to take any value between 0 and 2
p = d = q = range(0, 3)

results = None
best = None
# generate all combinations of (p, d, q) triplets and keep the model
```

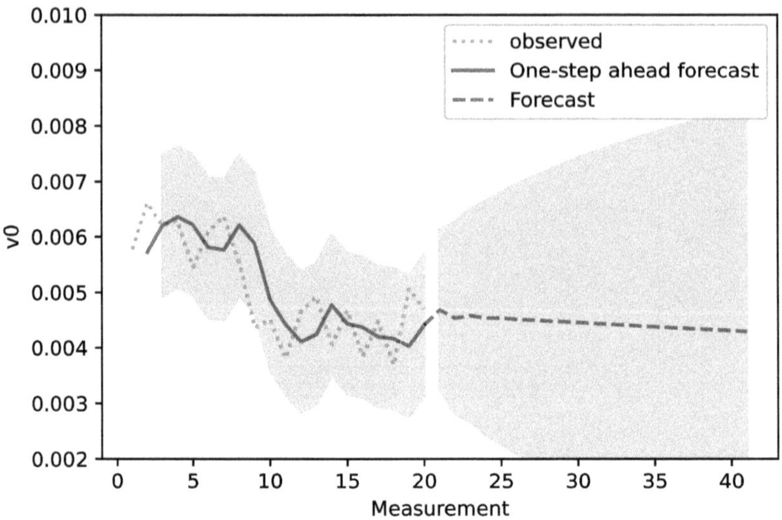

Fig. 8.12 Long term forecast of $v0$ values using an ARIMA model

```
# with the lowest AIC
for param in list(itertools.product(p, d, q)):
    mod = SARIMAX(sensorDataShort['v0'], order=param)
    temp = mod.fit(method='nm', maxiter=600, disp=False)
    if results is None or results.aic > temp.aic:
        results = temp
        best = param
print('ARIMA{} - AIC:{}'.format(best, results.aic))
```

```
ARIMA(2, 0, 0) - AIC:-226.33201069362354
```

The prediction of the best model for $v0$ and their confidence intervals are shown in Fig. 8.12. The rapid increase of the confidence interval tells us that it is not possible to forecast future values of $v0$.

Prescriptive Analytics With the *digital twin* model, we can derive an optimal combination of factors with an approach similar to the case study from Sect. 6.4. For example, as can be seen from the contour plot of Fig. 8.11, a larger surface area would move the operating space of the piston into a space where cycle time is less sensitive to changes in the initial gas volume $v0$; the response surface there is flatter. For a discussion of systematic approaches see Bates et al. (2006). ■

8.7 Chapter Highlights

The main concepts and tools introduced in this chapter include:

- Cybermanufacturing elements
- Information quality

- Modeling in cybermanufacturing
- Computational pipelines
- Digital twins
- Monitoring analytics
- Diagnostic analytics
- Prognostic analytics
- Prescriptive analytics
- Ensemble modeling
- Customer survey models
- Computer experiments

8.8 Exercises

Exercise 8.1 The PENSIM simulation software modelling penicillin production (Birol et al. 2002) is a fed-batch fermentor.[2] It simulates a fed-batch penicillin production process and includes variables such as pH, temperature, aeration rate, agitation power, feed flow rate of the substrate and a Raman probe.

The **PENSIM_100** dataset consists of 100 observations derived from the simulator. These are observational data collected under the same process set up. Variability in responses is induced by the varying process variables

A. Process set up:

1. `s0`: initial sugar concentration (15 g/L)
2. `x0`: initial biomass concentration (0.1 g/L)
3. `pH`: pH set point (5)
4. `T`: temperature set point (298 °K)
5. `air`: aeration (8.6 L/min)
6. `stirring`: agitation rate (29.9 W)
7. `time`: culture time (350 h)
8. `feed`: sugar feed rate (0.0426 L/h)

B. Process outputs:

1. `P`: Final penicillin concentration
2. `X`: Final biomass concentration

C. Process variables:

1. `Fg`: aeration rate
2. `RPM`: agitation rate
3. `Fs`: subst. feed

[2] http://www.industrialpenicillinsimulation.com.

4. `Ts`: subst. temp.
5. `S`: substrate
6. `DO`: dissolved oxygen
7. `Uvis`: viscosity
8. `CO2`: off-gas CO2
9. `Hi`: heat inflow
10. `Ti`: temperature inflow
11. `Ho`: heat outflow
12. `Fw`: water for injection

Predict the process outputs P and X from the 12 process variables using two different models. Compare and contrast the models.

Some options are multivariate least square regressions, regression trees, random forests and neural networks, Bayesian Networks (Chapters 4, 7, and 8 in *Modern Statistics*, Kenett et al. 2022b), response surfaces (Chap. 5) and Kriging (Gaussian) models (Chap. 7).

Exercise 8.2 The PENSIM simulator introduced in Exercise 8.1 has been used to design and analyze a central composite design experiment (see Sect. 5.9). The dataset is available as **PENSIM_CCD.csv**.

1. Evaluate the experimental design set up (see Sect. 5.10)
2. Fit a second order response surface model to both X and P (see Sect. 5.9)
3. Compose a qualitative description of the models

Exercise 8.3 Example 4.5 provides an example of time series tracking engine vibrations of railway vehicle suspension systems. These suspensions can be affected by wheel flats with significant impact on system performance and safety. The dataset **ORDER_PSD.csv** includes three series where time is in units of revolution order. This angular resampling transformation is eliminating the variability in revolution time. The three time series correspond to vibrations in healthy suspensions and with wheel flats of 10 mm and 20 mm. In the analysis use the log transformed data.

1. Fit an ARIMA model to the healthy suspension vibration data (see Chapter 6, *Modern Statistics*, Kenett et al. 2022b)
2. Fit the same model to the 10 mm and 20 mm wheel flat
3. Compare the model parameters

Exercise 8.4 A company operates in 8 cities. The company product is temperature sensitive and management is interested in clustering the 8 locations by temperature characteristics. Monthly average daily minimum and maximum temperatures in these 8 cities, from 2000–2012, is available as dataset **TEMP_WORLD.csv**.[3]

[3] Also available for download: https://www.stat.auckland.ac.nz/~wild/data/data_from_iNZight/TimeSeriesDatasets_130207/TempWorld1.csv.

1. Use a smoother to compare the maximum and minimum monthly average temperatures in the 8 cities.
2. Group the cities using maximum and minimum temperature patterns using hierarchical clusters.
3. Group the cities using maximum and minimum temperature patterns using K-means clusters.

Chapter 9
Reliability Analysis

Preview The previous chapter dwelled on design decisions of product and process developers that are aimed at optimizing the quality and robustness of products and processes. This chapter is looking at performance over time and discusses basic notions of repairable and non-repairable systems. Graphical and nonparametric techniques are presented together with classical parametric techniques for estimating life distributions. Special sections cover reliability demonstration procedures, sequential reliability testing, burn-in procedures, and accelerated life testing. Design and testing of reliability is a crucial activity of organizations adopting advanced quality and industrial standards discussed in Chap. 1.

Systems and products are considered to be of high quality if they conform to their design specifications and appeal to the customer. However, products can fail, due to degradation over time or due to some instantaneous shock. A system or a component of a system is said to be **reliable** if it continues to function, according to specifications, for a long time. Reliability of a product is a dynamic notion, over time. We say that a product is highly reliable if the probability that it will function properly for a specified period is close to 1. As will be defined later, the reliability function, $R(t)$, is the probability that a product will function in at least t units of time.

We distinguish between the reliability of systems which are unrepairable and that of repairable systems. A repairable system, after failure, goes through a period of repair and then returns to function normally. Highly reliable systems need less repair. Repairable systems that need less repair are more available to operate and are therefore more desirable. **Availability** of a system at time t is the probability that the system will be up and running at time t. To increase the availability of repairable systems, maintenance procedures are devised. Maintenance schedules are designed to prevent failures of a system by periodic replacement of parts, tuning, cleaning, etc. It is very important to develop maintenance procedures, based on the

Supplementary Information The online version contains supplementary material available at (https://doi.org/10.1007/978-3-031-28482-3_9).

R. S. Kenett et al., *Industrial Statistics*, Statistics for Industry, Technology, and Engineering, https://doi.org/10.1007/978-3-031-28482-3_9

reliability properties of the components of systems, which are cost effective and helpful to the availability of the systems. An alternative to scheduled maintenance is condition-based maintenance (CBM) introduced in Chaps. 1 and 8. Both scheduled maintenance and CBM require investigations of the reliability of systems and subsystems.

One of the intriguing features of failure of components and systems is their random nature. We consider the length of time that a part functions till failure as a random variable, called the **life length** of the component or the system. The distribution functions of life length variables are called **life distributions**. The role of statistical reliability theory is to develop methods of estimating the characteristics of life distributions from failure data and to design experiments called life tests. A subject connected to life testing is **accelerated life testing**. Highly reliable systems may take a long time till failure. In accelerated life tests, early failures are induced by subjecting the systems to higher than normal stress. In analyzing the results of such experiments, one has to know how to relate failure distributions under stressful conditions to those under normal operating conditions. The present chapter provides the foundations to the theoretical and practical treatment of life distributions and life testing.

The following examples illustrate the economic importance of reliability analysis in industry.

Florida Power and Light: A reduction of power plant outage rate from 14% to less than 4% generated \$300 million savings to the consumer, on an investment of \$5 million for training and consulting. Customer service interruptions dropped from 100 min per year to 42 min per year.

Tennessee Valley Authority (TVA): The Athens Utilities Board is one of 160 power distributors supplied by TVA with a service region of 100 square miles, 10,000 customers, and a peak load of 80 MW. One year's worth of trouble service data was examined in three South Athens feeders. The primary circuit failure rate was 15.3 failures/year/mile, restoring service using automatic equipment took, on the average, 3 min per switch, while manual switching requires approximately 20 min. Line repair generally takes 45 min. The average outage cost for an industrial customer in the USA is \$11.87/kWh. Without automation the yearly outage cost for a 6000 kW load per year is, on the average, \$540K. The automation required to restore service in 3 min in South Athens costs about \$35K. Automation has reduced outage costs to \$340K. These improvements in reliability of the power supply have therefore produced an average return on investment of \$9.7 for every dollar invested in automation.

AT&T: An original plan for a transatlantic telephone cable called for three spares to back up each transmitter in the 200 repeaters that would relay calls across the seabed. A detailed reliability analysis with SUPER (System Used for Prediction and Evaluation of Reliability) indicated that one spare is enough. This reduced the cost of the project by 10%—and AT&T won the job with a bid just 5% less than that of its nearest competitor.

AVX: The levels of reliability achieved by tantalum capacitors, along with their small size and high stability, are promoting their use in many applications that are electrically and environmentally more aggressive than in the past. The failure rates are 0.67 FIT (failures in 10^9 component hours) with shorts contributing approximately 67% of the total.

Siemens: Broadband transmission systems use a significant number of microwave components and these are expected to work without failure from first switch-on. The 565 Mbit coaxial repeater uses 30 diodes and transistor functions in each repeater which adds up to 7000 SP87-11 transistors along the 250 km link. The link must not fail within 15 years and redundant circuits are not possible because of the complex circuitry. Accelerated life testing demonstrated that the expected failure rate of the SP87-11 transistor is less than 1 FIT, thus meeting the 15 years requirement.

National Semiconductor: A single-bit error in microelectronic device can cause an entire system crash. In developing the BiCmos III component, one-third of the design team was assigned the job of improving the component's reliability. Accelerated life tests under high temperature and high humidity (145 °C, 85% relative humidity and under bias) proved the improved device to have a failure rate below 100 FIT. In a system using 256-kbit BiCmos III static random access memories, this translates to less than one failure in 18 years.

Lockheed: Some 60% of the cost of military aircraft now goes for its electronic systems, and many military contracts require the manufacturer to provide service at a fixed price for product defects that occur during the warranty period. Lockheed Corporation produces switching logic units used in the US Navy S-3A antisubmarine aircraft to distribute communications within and outside the aircraft. These units were high on the Pareto of component failures. They were therefore often removed for maintenance, thereby damaging the chassis. The mean time between failures for the switching logic units was approximately 100 h. Changes in the design and improved screening procedures increased the mean time between failures to 500 h. The average number of units removed each week from nine aircraft dropped from 1.8 to 0.14.

9.1 Basic Notions

9.1.1 Time Categories

The following time categories play an important role in the theory of reliability, availability, and maintainability of systems:

I. **Usage-Related Time Categories**

   (a) **Operating time** is the time interval during which the system is in actual operation.

(b) **Scheduled operating time** is the time interval during which the system is required to properly operate.
(c) **Free time** is the time interval during which the system is scheduled to be off duty.
(d) **Storage time** is the time interval during which a system is stored as a spare part.

II. **Equipment Condition Time Categories**

(a) **Up time** is the time interval during which the system is operating or ready for operation.
(b) **Down time** is the time interval out of the scheduled operating time during which the system is in state of failure (inoperable).
Down time is the sum of

(i) Administrative time
(ii) Active repair time
(iii) Logistic time (repair suspension due to lack of parts)

III. **Indices**

$$\textbf{Scheduled Operating Time} = \text{operating time } + \text{down time}$$

$$\textbf{Intrinsic Availability} = \frac{\text{operating time}}{\text{operating time} + \text{active repair time}}$$

$$\textbf{Availability} = \frac{\text{operating time}}{\text{operating time} + \text{down time}}$$

$$\textbf{Operational Readiness} = \frac{\text{Up time}}{\text{total calendar time}}.$$

Example 9.1 A machine is scheduled to operate for two shifts a day (8 h each shift), five days a week. During the last 48 weeks, the machine was "down" five times. The average down time is partitioned into

1. Average administrative time = 9 [hr]
2. Average repair time = 30 [hr]
3. Average logistic time = 7.6 [hr]

Thus, the total down time in the 48 weeks is

$$\text{down time} = 5 \times (9 + 30 + 7.6) = 233 \text{ [hr]}.$$

The total scheduled operating time is $48 \times 16 \times 5 = 3840$ [hr]. Thus, the total operating time is 3607 [hr]. The indices of availability and intrinsic availability are

$$\text{Availability} = \frac{3607}{3840} = 0.9393.$$

$$\text{Intrinsic Availability} = \frac{3607}{3607 + 150} = 0.9601.$$

Finally the operational readiness of the machine is

$$\text{Operational Readiness} = \frac{8064 - 233}{8064} = 0.9711.$$

■

9.1.2 Reliability and Related Functions

The length of life (lifetime) of a (product) system is the length of the time interval, T, from the initial activation of it till its failure. If a system is switched on and off, we consider the total active time of the system till its failure. T is a non-negative random variable. The distribution of T is called a **life distribution**. We generally assume that T is a continuous random variable, having a p.d.f. $f_T(t)$ and a c.d.f. $F_T(t)$. The **reliability function** of a (product) system is defined as

$$\begin{aligned} R(t) &= \Pr\{T \geq t\} \\ &= 1 - F_T(t), \quad t \geq 0. \end{aligned} \tag{9.1.1}$$

The expected life length of a product is called the **mean time till failure** (MTTF). This quantity is given by

$$\begin{aligned} \mu &= \int_0^\infty t f_T(t)\, \mathrm{d}t \\ &= \int_0^\infty R(t)\, \mathrm{d}t. \end{aligned} \tag{9.1.2}$$

The instantaneous **hazard function** of a product, also called the **failure rate** function, is defined as

$$h(t) = \frac{f(t)}{R(t)}, \quad t \geq 0. \tag{9.1.3}$$

Notice that $h(t)$ and $f(t)$ have the dimension of $1/T$. That is, if T is measured in hours, the dimension of $h(t)$ is [1/hr].

Notice that $h(t) = \frac{\mathrm{d}}{\mathrm{d}t} \log(-R(t))$. Accordingly,

$$R(t) = \exp\left\{-\int_0^t h(u)\, \mathrm{d}u\right\}. \tag{9.1.4}$$

The function

$$H(t) = \int_0^t h(u)\, du \tag{9.1.5}$$

is called the **cumulative hazard rate** function.

Example 9.2 In many applications of reliability theory, the exponential distribution with mean μ is used as the distribution of T. In this case,

$$f_T(t) = \frac{1}{\mu} \exp\{-t/\mu\}, \quad t \geq 0$$

and

$$R(t) = \exp\{-t/\mu\}, \quad t \geq 0.$$

In the exponential distribution model, the reliability function diminishes from 1 to 0 exponentially fast, relative to μ.

The hazard rate function of an exponential distribution is

$$h(t) = \frac{\frac{1}{\mu} \cdot \exp\{-t/\mu\}}{\exp\{-t/\mu\}} = \frac{1}{\mu}, \quad t \geq 0.$$

That is, the exponential model is valid for cases where the hazard rate function is a constant independent of time. If the MTTF is $\mu = 100$ [hr], we expect 1 failure per 100 [hr], i.e., $h(t) = \frac{1}{100}\left[\frac{1}{\text{hr}}\right]$. ■

9.2 System Reliability

In this section we show how to compute the reliability function of a system, as a function of the reliability of its components (modules). Thus, if we have a system comprised of k subsystems (components or modules), having reliability functions $R_1(t), \cdots, R_k(t)$, the reliability of the system is given by

$$R_{sys}(t) = \psi(R_1(t), \cdots, R_k(t)); \quad t \geq 0. \tag{9.2.1}$$

The function $\psi(\cdot)$ is called a **structure function**. It reflects the functional relationship between the subsystems and the system. In the present section we discuss some structure functions of simple systems. We also assume that the random variables $T_1, \cdots, T_k$, representing the life length of the subsystems, are **independent**.

Consider a system having two subsystems (modules) C_1 and C_2. We say that the subsystems are connected in series, if a failure of either one of the subsystems causes

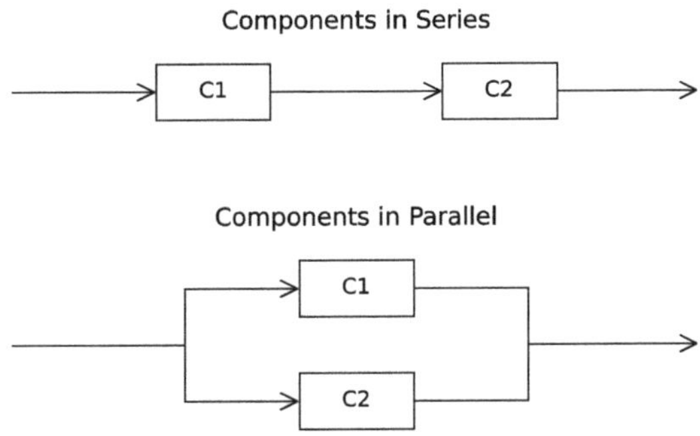

Fig. 9.1 Block diagrams for systems in series and in parallel

immediate failure of the system. We represent this series connection by a **block diagram**, as in Fig. 9.1. Let I_i $(i = 1, \cdots, k)$ be indicator variables, assuming the value 1 if the component C_i does not fail during a specified time interval $(0, t_0)$. If C_i fails during $(0, t_0)$, then $I_i = 0$. A **series structure function** of k components is

$$\psi_s(I_1, \cdots, I_k) = \prod_{i=1}^{k} I_i. \tag{9.2.2}$$

The expected value of I_i is

$$E\{I_i\} = \Pr\{I_i = 1\} = R_i(t_0). \tag{9.2.3}$$

If the system is connected in series, then, since $T_1, \ldots, T_k$ are independent,

$$\begin{aligned} R_{sys}^{(s)}(t_0) &= E\{\psi_s(I_1, \cdots, I_k)\} = \prod_{i=1}^{k} R_i(t_0) \\ &= \psi_s(R_1(t_0), \cdots, R_k(t_0)). \end{aligned} \tag{9.2.4}$$

Thus, the system reliability function for subsystems connected in series is given by $\psi_s(R_1, \cdots, R_k)$, where $R_1, \cdots, R_k$ are the reliability values of the components.

A system comprised of k subsystems is said to be **connected in parallel** if the system fails when **all** subsystems fail. In a parallel connection, it is sufficient that one of the subsystems will function for the whole system to function.

The structure function for parallel connection is

$$\psi_p(I_1, \cdots, I_k) = 1 - \prod_{i=1}^{k}(1 - I_i). \tag{9.2.5}$$

The reliability function for a system in parallel is, in the case of independence,

$$\begin{aligned} R_{sys}^{(p)}(t_0) &= E\{\psi_p(I_1, \cdots, I_k)\} \\ &= 1 - \prod_{i=1}^{k}(1 - R_i(t_0)). \end{aligned} \tag{9.2.6}$$

Example 9.3 A computer card has 200 components, which should function correctly. The reliability of each component, for a period of 200 h of operation, is $R = 0.9999$. The components are independent of one another. What is the reliability of the card, for this time period? Since all the components should function, we consider a series structure function. Thus, the system reliability for $t_0 = 200$ [hr] is

$$R_{sys}^{(s)}(t_0) = (0.9999)^{200} = 0.9802.$$

Thus, despite the fact that each component is unlikely to fail, there is a probability of 0.02 that the card will fail within 200 h. If each of the components has only a reliability of 0.99, the card reliability is

$$R_{sys}^{(s)}(t_0) = (0.99)^{200} = 0.134.$$

This shows why it is so essential in the electronic industry to demand from the vendors of the components highly reliable products.

Suppose that there is room for some redundancy on the card. It is therefore decided to use parts having reliability of $R = 0.99$ and duplicate each component in a parallel structure. The parallel structure of duplicated components is considered a module. The reliability of each module is $R_M = 1 - (1 - 0.99)^2 = 0.9999$. The reliability of the whole system is now

$$R_{sys}^{(s)} = (R_M)^{200} = 0.9802.$$

Thus, by changing the structure of the card, we achieve 0.98 reliability with 200 pairs of components, each with a reliability value of 0.99. ■

Systems may have more complicated structures. In Fig. 9.2, we see the block diagram of a system consisting of 5 components. Let $R_1, R_2, \cdots, R_5$ denote the reliability values of the 5 components $C_1, \cdots, C_5$, respectively. Let M_1 be the module consisting of components C_1 and C_2, and let M_2 be the module consisting of the other components. The reliability of M_1 for some specified time interval is

$$R_{M_1} = R_1 R_2.$$

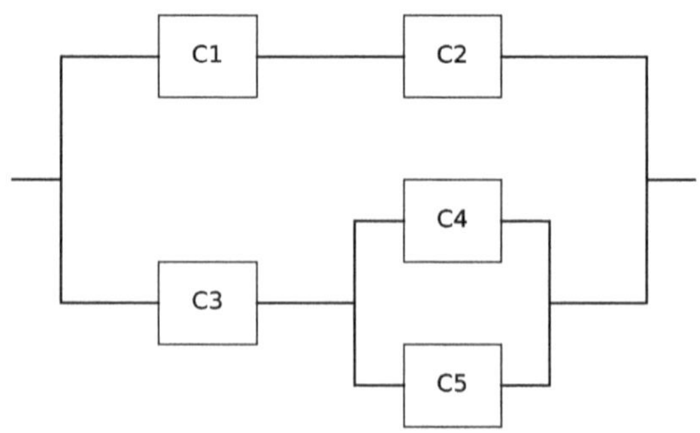

Fig. 9.2 A parallel–series structure

The reliability of M_2 is

$$\begin{aligned} R_{M_2} &= R_3(1-(1-R_4)(1-R_5)) \\ &= R_3(R_4+R_5-R_4R_5) \\ &= R_3R_4+R_3R_5-R_3R_4R_5. \end{aligned}$$

Finally, the system reliability for that block diagram is

$$\begin{aligned} R_{sys} &= 1-(1-R_{M_1})(1-R_{M_2}) \\ &= R_{M_1}+R_{M_2}-R_{M_1}R_{M_2} \\ &= R_1R_2+R_3R_4+R_3R_5-R_3R_4R_5 \\ &- R_1R_2R_3R_4-R_1R_2R_3R_5+R_1R_2R_3R_4R_5. \end{aligned}$$

Another important structure function is that of **k out of n** subsystems. In other words, if a system consists of n subsystems, it is required that **at least** k, $1 \le k < n$, subsystems will function, throughout the specified time period, in order that the system will function. Assuming independence of the lifetimes of the subsystems, we construct the reliability function of the system, by simple probabilistic considerations. For example, if we have 3 subsystems having reliability values, for the given time period, of R_1, R_2, R_3 and at least 2 out of the 3 should function, then the system reliability is

$$\begin{aligned} R_{sys}^{2(3)} &= 1-(1-R_1)(1-R_2)(1-R_3)-R_1(1-R_2)(1-R_3) \\ &- R_2(1-R_1)(1-R_3)-R_3(1-R_1)(1-R_2) \\ &= R_1R_2+R_1R_3+R_2R_3-2R_1R_2R_3. \end{aligned}$$

If all the subsystems have the same reliability value R, for a specified time period, then the reliability function of the system, in a k out of n structure, can be computed by using the binomial c.d.f. $B(j; n, R)$, i.e.,

$$R_{sys}^{k(n)} = 1 - B(k-1; n, R). \tag{9.2.7}$$

Example 9.4 A cooling system for a reactor has 3 identical cooling loops. Each cooling loop has two identical pumps connected in parallel. The cooling system requires that 2 out of the 3 cooling loops operate successfully. The reliability of a pump over the life span of the plant is $R = 0.6$. We compute the reliability of the cooling system.

First, the reliability of a cooling loop is

$$\begin{aligned} R_{cl} &= 1-(1-R)^2 = 2R-R^2 \\ &= 1.2-0.36 = 0.84. \end{aligned}$$

Finally, the system reliability is

$$R_{sys}^{2(3)} = 1 - B(1; 3, 0.84) = 0.9314.$$

This reliability can be increased by choosing pumps with higher reliability. If the pump reliability is 0.9, the loop's reliability is 0.99 and the system's reliability is 0.9997. ■

9.3 Availability of Repairable Systems

Repairable systems alternate during their functional life through cycles of up phase and down phase. During the up phase, the system functions as required, till it fails. At the moment of failure, the system enters the down phase. The system remains in this down phase until it is repaired and activated again. The length of time the system is in the up phase is called the **time till failure** (TTF). The length of time the system is in the down phase is called the **time till repair** (TTR). Both TTF and TTR are modeled as random variables, T and S, respectively. We assume here that T and S are independent. The **cycle time** is the random variable $C = T + S$.

The process in which the system goes through these cycles is called a **renewal process**. Let $C_1, C_2, C_3, \cdots$ be a sequence of cycles of a repairable system. We assume that $C_1, C_2, \cdots$ are i.i.d. random variables.

Let $F(t)$ be the c.d.f. of the TTF and $G(t)$ the c.d.f. of the TTR. Let $f(t)$ and $g(t)$ be the corresponding p.d.f. Let $K(t)$ denote the c.d.f. of C. Since T and S are independent random variables,

$$\begin{aligned} K(t) &= \Pr\{C \le t\} \\ &= \textstyle\int_0^t f(x) P\{S \le t - x\}\, dx \\ &= \textstyle\int_0^t f(x) G(t - x)\, dx. \end{aligned} \tag{9.3.1}$$

Assuming that $G(0) = 0$, differentiation of $K(t)$ yields the p.d.f. of the cycle time, $k(t)$, namely

$$k(t) = \int_0^t f(x) g(t - x)\, dx. \tag{9.3.2}$$

The operation of getting $k(t)$ from $f(t)$ and $g(t)$ is called a **convolution**.

The **Laplace transform** of an integrable function $f(t)$, on $0 < t < \infty$, is defined as

$$f^*(s) = \int_0^\infty e^{-ts} f(t)\, dt, \quad s \ge 0. \tag{9.3.3}$$

Notice that if $f(t)$ is a p.d.f. of a non-negative continuous random variable, then $f^*(s)$ is its moment generating function (m.g.f.) at $-s$. Since $C = T + S$ and T and S are independent, the m.g.f. of C is $M_C(u) = M_T(u)M_S(u)$, for all $u \leq u^*$ at which these m.g.f. exist. In particular, if $k^*(s)$ is the Laplace Transform of $k(t)$,

$$k^*(s) = f^*(s)g^*(s), \quad s \geq 0. \tag{9.3.4}$$

Example 9.5 Suppose that T is exponentially distributed like $E(\beta)$, and S is exponentially distributed like $E(\gamma)$, $0 < \beta, \gamma < \infty$, i.e.,

$$f(t) = \frac{1}{\beta} \exp\{-t/\beta\},$$

$$g(t) = \frac{1}{\gamma} \exp\{-t/\gamma\}.$$

The p.d.f. of C is

$$\begin{aligned} k(t) &= \int_0^t f(x)g(t-x)\,\mathrm{d}x \\ &= \begin{cases} \frac{1}{\beta-\gamma}(e^{-t/\beta} - e^{-t/\gamma}), & \text{if} \beta \neq \gamma \\ \frac{t}{\beta^2} e^{-t/\beta}, & \text{if } \beta = \gamma. \end{cases} \end{aligned}$$

The corresponding Laplace transforms are

$$\begin{aligned} f^*(s) &= (1 + s\beta)^{-1}, \\ g^*(s) &= (1 + s\gamma)^{-1}, \\ k^*(s) &= (1 + s\beta)^{-1}(1 + s\gamma)^{-1}. \end{aligned}$$

■

Let $N_F(t)$ denote the number of failures of a system during the time interval $(0, t]$. Let $W(t) = E\{N_F(t)\}$. Similarly, let $N_R(t)$ be the number of repairs during $(0, t]$ and $V(t) = E\{N_R(t)\}$. Obviously $N_R(t) \leq N_F(t)$ for all $0 < t < \infty$.

Let $A(t)$ denote the probability that the system is up at time t. $A(t)$ is the **availability function** of the system. In unrepairable systems, $A(t) = R(t)$.

Let us assume that $W(t)$ and $V(t)$ are differentiable, and let $w(t) = W'(t)$ and $v(t) = V'(t)$.

The **failure intensity function** of repairable systems is defined as

$$\lambda(t) = \frac{w(t)}{A(t)}, \quad t \geq 0. \tag{9.3.5}$$

Notice that if the system is unrepairable, then $W(t) = F(t)$, $w(t) = f(t)$, $A(t) = R(t)$, and $\lambda(t)$ is the hazard function $h(t)$. Let $Q(t) = 1 - A(t)$ and $v(t) = V'(t)$. The **repair intensity function** is

$$\mu(t) = \frac{v(t)}{Q(t)}, \quad t \geq 0. \tag{9.3.6}$$

The function $V(t) = E\{N_R(t)\}$ is called the **renewal function**. Notice that

$$\begin{aligned}\Pr\{N_R(t) \geq n\} &= \Pr\{C_1 + \cdots + C_n \leq t\} \\ &= K_n(t), \quad t \geq 0,\end{aligned} \tag{9.3.7}$$

where $K_n(t)$ is the c.d.f. of $C_1 + \cdots + C_n$.

Since $N_R(t)$ is a non-negative random variable, the renewal function is

$$\begin{aligned}V(t) &= \sum_{n=1}^{\infty} \Pr\{N_r(t) \geq n\} \\ &= \sum_{n=1}^{\infty} K_n(t).\end{aligned} \tag{9.3.8}$$

Example 9.6 Suppose that $TTF \sim E(\beta)$ and that the repair is instantaneous. Then, C is distributed like $E(\beta)$ and $K_n(t)$ is the c.d.f. of $G(n, \beta)$, i.e.,

$$K_n(t) = 1 - P\left(n - 1; \frac{t}{\beta}\right), \quad n = 1, 2, \cdots,$$

where $P(j; \lambda)$ is the c.d.f. of a Poisson random variable with mean λ. Thus, in the present case,

$$\begin{aligned}V(t) &= \sum_{n=1}^{\infty} \left(1 - P\left(n - 1; \frac{t}{\beta}\right)\right) \\ &= E\left\{\text{Pois}\left(\frac{t}{\beta}\right)\right\} = \frac{t}{\beta}, \quad t \geq 0.\end{aligned}$$

Here $\text{Pois}\left(\frac{t}{\beta}\right)$ designates a random variable having a Poisson distribution with mean t/β. ■

At time t, $0 < t < \infty$, there are two possible events:

E_1: The first cycle is not yet terminated.
E_2: The first cycle has terminated at some time before t.

Accordingly, $V(t)$ can be written as

$$V(t) = K(t) + \int_0^t k(x)V(t - x)\,dx. \tag{9.3.9}$$

The derivative of $V(t)$ is called the **renewal density**. Let $v(t) = V'(t)$. Since $V(0) = 0$, we obtain by differentiating this equation that

$$v(t) = k(t) + \int_0^t k(x)v(t-x)\,\mathrm{d}x. \tag{9.3.10}$$

Let $v^*(s)$ and $k^*(s)$ denote the Laplace transforms of $v(t)$ and $k(t)$, respectively. Then, from the above equation,

$$v^*(s) = k^*(s) + k^*(s)v^*(s), \tag{9.3.11}$$

or, since $k^*(s) = f^*(s)g^*(s)$,

$$v^*(s) = \frac{f^*(s)g^*(s)}{1 - f^*(s)g^*(s)}. \tag{9.3.12}$$

The renewal density $v(t)$ can be obtained by inverting $v^*(s)$.

Example 9.7 As before, suppose that the TTF is $E(\beta)$ and that the TTR is $E(\gamma)$. Let $\lambda = \frac{1}{\beta}$ and $\mu = \frac{1}{\gamma}$

$$f^*(s) = \frac{\lambda}{\lambda + s},$$

and

$$g^*(s) = \frac{\mu}{\mu + s}.$$

Then

$$\begin{aligned} v^*(s) &= \frac{\lambda\mu}{s^2 + (\lambda + \mu)s} \\ &= \frac{\lambda\mu}{\lambda + \mu}\left(\frac{1}{s} - \frac{1}{s + \lambda + \mu}\right). \end{aligned}$$

$\frac{1}{s}$ is the Laplace transform of 1, and $\frac{\lambda+\mu}{s+\lambda+\mu}$ is the Laplace transform of $E\left(\frac{1}{\lambda+\mu}\right)$. Hence

$$v(t) = \frac{\lambda\mu}{\lambda + \mu} - \frac{\lambda\mu}{\lambda + \mu}e^{-t(\lambda+\mu)}, \quad t \geq 0.$$

Integrating $v(t)$, we obtain the renewal function

$$V(t) = \frac{\lambda\mu}{\lambda + \mu}t - \frac{\lambda\mu}{(\lambda + \mu)^2}(1 - e^{-t(\lambda+\mu)}), \quad 0 \leq t < \infty.$$

In a similar fashion, we can show that

$$W(t) = \frac{\lambda\mu}{\lambda+\mu}t + \frac{\lambda^2}{(\lambda+\mu)^2}(1 - e^{-t(\lambda+\mu)}), \quad 0 \le t < \infty.$$

Since $W(t) > V(t)$ if, and only if, the last cycle is still incomplete and the system is down, the probability, $Q(t)$, that the system is down at time t is

$$\begin{aligned} Q(t) &= W(t) - V(t) \\ &= \frac{\lambda}{\lambda+\mu} - \frac{\lambda}{\lambda+\mu}e^{-t(\lambda+\mu)}, \quad t \ge 0. \end{aligned}$$

Thus, the availability function is

$$\begin{aligned} A(t) &= 1 - Q(t) \\ &= \frac{\mu}{\lambda+\mu} + \frac{\lambda}{\lambda+\mu}e^{-t(\lambda+\mu)}, \quad t \ge 0. \end{aligned}$$

Notice that the availability at large values of t is approximately

$$\lim_{t\to\infty} A(t) = \frac{\mu}{\lambda+\mu} = \frac{\beta}{\beta+\gamma}.$$

■

The availability function $A(t)$ can be determined from $R(t)$ and $v(t)$ by solving the equation

$$A(t) = R(t) + \int_0^t v(x)R(t-x)\,\mathrm{d}x. \tag{9.3.13}$$

The Laplace transform of this equation is

$$A^*(s) = \frac{R^*(s)}{1 - f^*(s)g^*(s)}, \quad 0 < s < \infty. \tag{9.3.14}$$

This theory can be useful in assessing different system structures, with respect to their availability. The following asymptotic (large t approximations) results are very useful. Let μ and σ^2 be the mean and variance of the cycle time.

(1) $$\lim_{t\to\infty} \frac{V(t)}{t} = \frac{1}{\mu} \tag{9.3.15}$$

(2) $$\lim_{t\to\infty} (V(t+a) - V(t)) = \frac{a}{\mu}, \quad a > 0 \tag{9.3.16}$$

(3) $$\lim_{t\to\infty} \left(V(t) - \frac{t}{\mu}\right) = \frac{\sigma^2}{2\mu^2} - \frac{1}{2}. \tag{9.3.17}$$

If the p.d.f. of C, $k(t)$, is continuous, then

(4) $$\lim_{t\to\infty} v(t) = \frac{1}{\mu} \tag{9.3.18}$$

(5) $$\lim_{t\to\infty} \Pr\left\{\frac{N_R(t) - t/\mu}{(\sigma^2 t/\mu^3)^{1/2}} \le z\right\} = \Phi(z) \tag{9.3.19}$$

(6) $$A_\infty = \lim_{T\to\infty} \frac{1}{T}\int_0^T A(t)\,\mathrm{d}t = \frac{E\{TTF\}}{E\{TTF\} + E\{TTR\}}. \tag{9.3.20}$$

According to (1), the expected number of renewals, $V(t)$, is approximately t/μ, for large t. According to (2), we expect approximately a/μ renewals in a time interval of length $(t, t+a)$, when t is large. The third result (3) says that t/μ is an under (over) estimate, for large t, if the squared coefficient of variation σ^2/μ^2 of the cycle time is larger (smaller) than 1. The last three properties can be interpreted in a similar fashion. We illustrate these asymptotic properties with examples.

Example 9.8 Consider a repairable system. The TTF [hr] has a gamma distribution like $G(2, 100)$. The TTR [hr] has a Weibull distribution $W(2, 2.5)$. Thus, the expected TTF is $\mu_T = 200$ [hr], and the expected TTR is $\mu_s = 2.5 \times \Gamma\left(\frac{3}{2}\right) = 1.25\sqrt{\pi} = 2.2$ [hr]. The asymptotic availability is

$$A_\infty = \frac{200}{202.2} = 0.989.$$

That is, in the long run, the proportion of total availability time is 98.9%.

The expected cycle time is $\mu_c = 222.2$ and the variance of the cycle time is

$$\begin{aligned}\sigma_c^2 &= 2 \times 100^2 + 6.25\left[\Gamma(2) - \Gamma^2\left(\frac{3}{2}\right)\right] \\ &= 20{,}000 + 1.34126 = 20{,}001.34126.\end{aligned}$$

Thus, during 2000 [hr] of scheduled operation, we expect close to $\frac{2000}{202.2} \cong 10$ renewal cycles. The probability that $N_R(2000)$ will be less than 11 is

$$\Pr\{N_R(2000) \le 11\} \cong \Phi\left(\frac{2}{1.91}\right) = \Phi(1.047) = 0.8525.$$

■

An important question is determining the probability, for large values of t, that we will find the system operating and will continue to operate without a failure for at least u additional time units. This function is called the **asymptotic operational reliability** and is given by

$$R_\infty(u) = A_\infty \cdot \frac{\int_u^\infty R(u)\,\mathrm{d}u}{\mu_T}, \quad 0 \le u, \tag{9.3.21}$$

where $R(u) = 1 - F_T(u)$.

Example 9.9 We continue discussing the case of Example 9.8. In this case,

$$\begin{aligned} F_T(u) &= \Pr\{G(2, 100) \leq u\} \\ &= \Pr\left\{G(2, 1) \leq \frac{u}{100}\right\} \\ &= 1 - P\left(1; \frac{u}{100}\right) = 1 - e^{-u/100} - \frac{u}{100} e^{-u/100}, \end{aligned}$$

and

$$R(u) = e^{-u/100} + \frac{u}{100} e^{-u/100}.$$

Furthermore, $\mu_T = 200$ and $A_\infty = 0.989$. Hence

$$\begin{aligned} R_\infty(u) &= 0.989 \cdot \frac{\int_u^\infty \left(1 + \frac{x}{100}\right) e^{-x/100}\, \mathrm{d}x}{200} \\ &= \frac{98.9}{200} \left(2 + \frac{u}{100}\right) e^{-u/100}. \end{aligned}$$

Thus, $R_\infty(0) = 0.989$, $R_\infty(100) = 0.546$, and $R_\infty(200) = 0.268$. ■

We conclude the section by introducing two Python functions from the `mistat` package, *availabilityEBD*, and *renewalEBD* which provide the bootstrap EBD of the number of renewals in a specified time interval and the EBD of the asymptotic availability index A_∞, based on observed samples of failure times and repair times. These programs provide computer-aided estimates of the renewal distribution and of the precision of A_∞. We illustrate this in the following example.

Example 9.10 Consider again the renewal process described in Example 9.8. Consider $n = 50$ observed values of i.i.d. TTF from $G(2, 100)$ and $n = 50$ observed repair times. We run *renewalEBD* with $n = 1000$ bootstrap samples to obtain an EBD of the number of renewals in 1000 [hr].

```
np.random.seed(1)
ttf = stats.gamma(2, scale=100).rvs(50)
ttr = stats.gamma(2, scale=1).rvs(50)

_ = mistat.availabilityEBD(ttf, ttr, n=1000, seed=1)
result = mistat.renewalEBD(ttf, ttr, time=1000, n=1000, seed=1)
np.quantile(result, [0.025, 0.975])
```

```
The estimated MTTF from ttf is 199.50
The estimated MTTR from ttr is 2.00
The estimated asymptotic availability is 0.9901

count    1000.000000
mean        0.989978
std         0.001434
min         0.984414
25%         0.989123
50%         0.990071
```

```
75%           0.990993
max           0.993743
Name: availability EBD, dtype: float64
The estimated MEAN NUMBER Of RENEWALS is 6.70
count      1000.000000
mean          6.698000
std           1.532039
min           3.000000
25%           6.000000
50%           7.000000
75%           8.000000
max          13.000000
Name: number of renewals EBD, dtype: float64
```

```
array([ 4., 10.])
```

The program yields that the mean number of renewals for 1000 h of operation is 6.70. This is the bootstrap estimate of $V(1000)$. The asymptotic approximation is $1000/202.2 = 4.946$. The bootstrap confidence interval for $V(1000)$ at 0.95 level of confidence is (4,9). This confidence interval covers the asymptotic approximation. Accordingly, the bootstrap estimate of 6.7 is not significantly different from the asymptotic approximation. ■

Additional topics of interest are maintenance, repairability, and availability. The objective is to increase the availability by instituting maintenance procedures and by adding standby systems and repairmen. The question is what the optimal maintenance period is and how many standby systems and repairmen to add. The interested reader is referred to Zacks (1992, Ch. 4) and Gertsbakh (1989).

In the following sections we discuss statistical problems associated with reliability assessment, when one does not know definitely the model and the values of its parameters.

9.4 Types of Observations on TTF

The analysis of data depends on the type of observations available. Dealing with TTF and TTR random variables, we wish to have observations which give us the exact length of time interval from activation (failure) of a system (component) till its failure (repair). However, one can find that proper records have not been kept, and instead one can find only the number of failures (repairs) in a given period of time. These are discrete random variables rather than the continuous ones under investigation. Another type of problem typical to reliability studies is that some observations are **censored**. For example, if it is decided to put n identical systems on test for a specified length of time t^*, we may observe only a random number, K_n, of failures in the time interval $(0, t^*]$. For the other $n - K_n$ systems which did not fail, we have only partial information, i.e., their TTF is greater than t^*. The observations on these systems are called **right censored**. In the above example n units are put on test at the same time. The censoring time t^* is a fixed time. Sometimes we have observations with **random censoring**. This is the case when we carry a study for a fixed length of time t^* [years], but the units (systems) enter the study at random times between 0 and t^*, according to some distribution.

Suppose that a unit enters the study at the random time τ, $0 < \tau < t^*$, and its TTF is T. We can observe only $W = \min(T, t^* - \tau)$. Here the censoring time is the random variable $t^* - \tau$. An example of such a situation is when we sell a product under warranty. The units of this product are sold to different customers at random times during the study period $(0, t^*)$. Products that fail are brought back for repair. If this happens during the study period, we have an uncensored observation on the TTF of that unit; otherwise the observation is censored, i.e., $W = t^* - \tau$.

The censored observations described above are time censored. Another type of censoring is **frequency censoring**. This is done when n units are put on test at the same time, but the test is terminated the instant the rth failure occurs. In this case the length of the test is the rth order statistic of failure times $T_{n,r}$ $(r = 1, \cdots, n)$. Notice that $T_{n,r} = T_{(r)}$, where $T_{(1)} < T_{(2)} < \cdots < T_{(n)}$ are the order statistics of n i.i.d. TTF's. If T is distributed exponentially, $E(\beta)$, for example, the expected length of the experiment is

$$E\{T_{n,r}\} = \beta \left(\frac{1}{n} + \frac{1}{n-1} + \cdots + \frac{1}{n-r+1} \right).$$

There may be substantial time saving if we terminate the study at the rth failure, when $r < n$. For example, in the exponential case, with $E\{T\} = \beta = 1000$ [hr] and $n = 20$,

$$E\{T_{20,20}\} = 1000 \times \left(1 + \frac{1}{2} + \frac{1}{3} + \cdots + \frac{1}{20} \right) = 3597.7 \text{ [hr]}.$$

On the other hand, for $r = 10$ we have $E\{T_{20,10}\} = 668.8$ [hr]. Thus, a frequency censored experiment with $r = 10$ and $n = 20$, $\beta = 1000$ lasts on the average only 19% of the time length of an uncensored experiment. We will see later how one can determine the optimal n and r for estimating the mean TTF (MTTF) in the exponential case.

9.5 Graphical Analysis of Life Data

In this section we discuss graphical procedures for fitting a life distribution to failure data and derive estimates of the parameters from the graphs.

Let $t_1, t_2, \cdots, t_n$ be n uncensored observation on i.i.d. random variables $T_1, \cdots, T_n$, having some life distribution $F(t)$.

The empirical c.d.f., given $t_1, \cdots, t_n$, is defined as

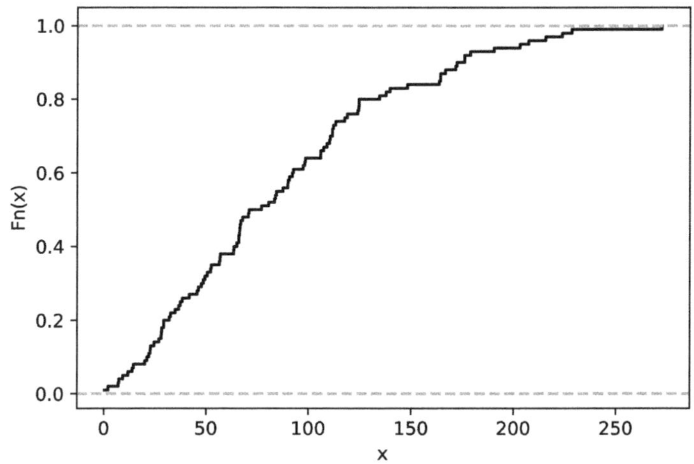

Fig. 9.3 The empirical c.d.f. of a random sample of 100 variables from $W(1.5, 100)$

$$F_n(t) = \frac{1}{n}\sum_{i=1}^{n} I\{t_i \le t\}, \tag{9.5.1}$$

where $I\{t_i \le t\}$ is the indicator variable, assuming the value 1 if $t_i \le t$ and the value 0 otherwise. A theorem in probability theory states that the empirical c.d.f. $F_n(t)$ converges to $F(t)$, as $n \to \infty$.

In Fig. 9.3 we present the empirical c.d.f. of a random sample of 100 variables having the Weibull distribution $W(1.5, 100)$. Since $F_n(t_{(i)}) = \frac{i}{n}$ for $i = 1, 2, \cdots, n$, the $\frac{i}{n}$th quantile of $F_n(t)$ is the ordered statistic $t_{(i)}$. Accordingly, if $F(t)$ has some specific distribution, the scattergram of

$$\left(F^{-1}\left(\frac{i}{n}\right), t_{(i)}\right) \quad (i = 1, \cdots, n)$$

should be around a straight line with slope 1. The plot of $t_{(i)}$ versus $F^{-1}\left(\frac{i}{n}\right)$ is called a **Q–Q Plot** (quantile versus quantile probability). The Q–Q plot is the basic graphical procedure to test whether a given sample of failure times is generated by a specific life distribution. Since $F^{-1}(1) = \infty$ for the interesting life distribution, the quantile of F is taken at $\frac{i}{n+1}$ or at some other $\frac{i+\alpha}{n+\beta}$, which give better plotting position for a specific distribution. For the normal distribution, $\frac{i-3/8}{n+1/4}$ is used.

If the distribution depends on location and scale parameters, we plot $t_{(i)}$ against the quantiles of the standard distribution. The intercept and the slope of the line fitted through the points yield estimates of these location and scale parameters. For example, suppose that $t_1, \cdots, t_n$ are values of a sample from an $N(\mu, \sigma^2)$ distribution. Thus, $t_{(i)} \approx \mu + \sigma\Phi^{-1}\left(\frac{i}{n}\right)$. Thus, if we plot $t_{(i)}$ against $\Phi^{-1}\left(\frac{i}{n}\right)$, we should have points around a straight line whose slope is an estimate of σ and intercept an estimate of μ.

We focus attention here on three families of life distributions:

1. The shifted exponential
2. The Weibull
3. The lognormal

The **shifted exponential** c.d.f. has the form

$$F(t; \mu, \beta) = \begin{cases} 1 - \exp\left\{\frac{t-\mu}{\beta}\right\}, & t \geq \mu \\ \\ 0, & t < \mu. \end{cases} \tag{9.5.2}$$

The starting point of the exponential distribution $E(\beta)$ is shifted to a point μ. Location parameters of interest in reliability studies are $\mu \geq 0$. Notice that the pth quantile, $0 < p < \infty$, of the shifted exponential is

$$t_p = \mu + \beta(-\log(1 - p)). \tag{9.5.3}$$

Accordingly, for exponential Q–Q plots, we plot $t_{(i)}$ versus $E_{i,n} = -\log\left(1 - \frac{i}{n+1}\right)$. Notice that in this plot, the intercept estimates the location parameter μ, and the slope estimates β. In the Weibull case, $W(\nu, \beta)$, the c.d.f. is

$$F(t; \nu, \beta) = 1 - \exp\left\{-\left(\frac{t}{\beta}\right)^{\nu}\right\}, \quad t \geq 0. \tag{9.5.4}$$

Thus, if t_p is the pth quantile,

$$\log t_p = \log\beta + \frac{1}{\nu}\log(-\log(1 - p)). \tag{9.5.5}$$

For this reason, we plot $\log t_{(i)}$ versus

$$W_{i,n} = \log\left(-\log\left(1 - \frac{i}{n+1}\right)\right), \quad i = 1, \cdots, n. \tag{9.5.6}$$

The slope of the straight line estimates $1/\nu$ and the intercept estimates $\log\beta$. In the lognormal case, we plot $\log t_{(i)}$ against $\Phi^{-1}\left(\frac{i-3/8}{n+1/4}\right)$.

Example 9.11 In Fig. 9.4, we present the Q–Q plot of 100 values generated at random from an exponential distribution $E(5)$. We fit a straight line through the origin to the points by the method of least squares.

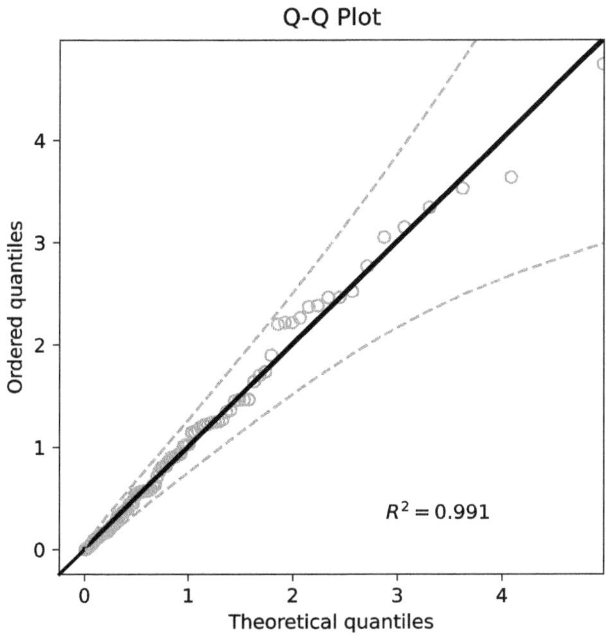

Fig. 9.4 Q–Q plot of a sample of 100 values from $E(5)$

```
np.random.seed(1)
rv = stats.expon(scale=5).rvs(100)

# Use stats.probplot to get x and Ei values
res = stats.probplot(rv, dist=stats.expon, rvalue=True)
df = pd.DataFrame({'Ei': res[0][0], 'x': res[0][1]})
model = smf.ols('x ~ Ei - 1', data=df).fit()
print(f'regression parameter beta={model.params[0]:.3f}')
print(f'estimate median = {np.log(2) * model.params[0]:.3f}')
print(f'true median = {np.median(rv):.3f}')
```

```
regression parameter beta=4.774
estimate median = 3.309
true median = 3.185
```

A linear regression routine provides the line

$$\hat{x} = 4.773 * E.$$

Accordingly, the slope of a straight line fitted to the points provides an estimate of the true mean and standard deviation, $\beta = 5$. An estimate of the median is

$$\hat{x}(0.693) = 0.693 \times 4.773 = 3.309.$$

The true median is $Me = 3.185$.

```
np.random.seed(1)
rv = stats.weibull_min(2, scale=2.5).rvs(100)

# Use stats.probplot to get x and Wi values
res = stats.probplot(rv, dist=stats.weibull_min, sparams=[1], rvalue=True)
df = pd.DataFrame({'Wi': np.log(res[0][0]), 'x': np.log(res[0][1])})
model = smf.ols('x ~ Wi', data=df).fit()
intercept, slope = model.params
print(f'intercept {intercept:.3f} / slope {slope:.3f}')
z
beta = np.exp(intercept)
nu = 1/slope
print(f'regression parameter nu={nu:.3f}')
print(f'regression parameter beta={beta:.3f}')
print(f'estimated median = {beta * np.log(2) ** (1/nu):.3f}')
print(f'estimated mean = {beta * gamma(1 + 1/nu):.3f}')
print(f'estimated std = {beta * np.sqrt(gamma(1 + 2/nu) - gamma(1+1/nu)**2):.3f}')
print(f'sample median = {np.median(rv):.3f}')
print(f'sample mean = {np.mean(rv):.3f}')
print(f'sample std = {np.std(rv):.3f}')
```

```
intercept 0.904 / slope 0.608
regression parameter nu=1.646
regression parameter beta=2.470
estimated median = 1.977
estimated mean = 2.209
estimated std = 1.378
sample median = 1.994
sample mean = 2.148
sample std = 1.146
```

In Fig. 9.5, we provide a probability plot of $n = 100$ values generated from a Weibull distribution with parameters $\nu = 2$ and $\beta = 2.5$.

Least squares fitting of a straight line to these points yields the line

$$\hat{y} = 0.904 + 0.608W.$$

Accordingly, we obtain the following estimates:

$$\begin{aligned}
\hat{\nu} &= 1/.608 = 1.646 \\
\hat{\beta} &= \exp(0.904) = 2.470 \\
\text{Median} &= \hat{\beta}(\ln 2)^{1/\hat{\nu}} = 1.977.
\end{aligned}$$

The true median is equal to $\beta(\ln 2)^{1/\nu} = 2.081$. The estimate of the mean is

$$\begin{aligned}
\hat{\mu} &= \hat{\beta}\,\Gamma\left(1 + \frac{1}{\hat{\nu}}\right) \\
&= 2.080.
\end{aligned}$$

The true mean is $\mu = \beta\,\Gamma(1.5) = 2.216$. Finally, an estimate of the standard deviation is

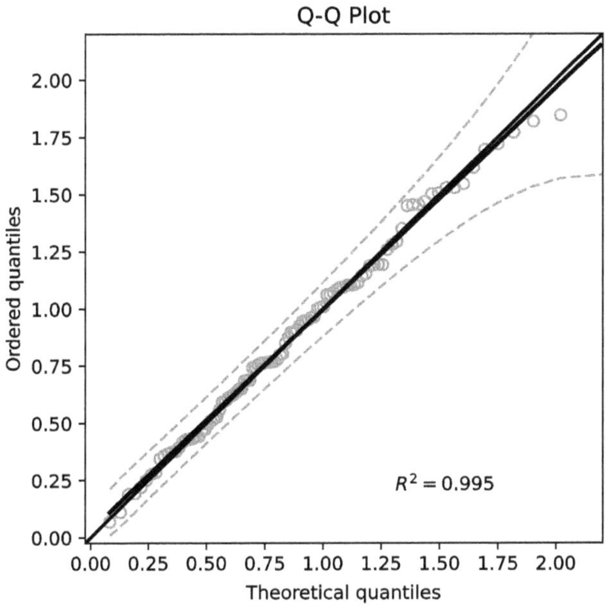

Fig. 9.5 Q–Q plot of a sample of 100 from $W(2, 2.5)$

$$\begin{aligned}\hat{\sigma} &= \hat{\beta}\left(\Gamma\left(1+\frac{2}{\hat{\nu}}\right) - \Gamma^2\left(1+\frac{1}{\hat{\nu}}\right)\right)^{1/2} \\ &= 1.054.\end{aligned}$$

The true value is $\sigma = \beta(\Gamma(2) - \Gamma^2(1.5))^{1/2} = 1.158$. ■

If observations are censored from the left or from the right, we plot the quantiles only from the uncensored part of the sample. The plotting positions take into consideration the number of censored values from the left and from the right. For example, if $n = 20$ and the 2 smallest observations are censored, the plotting positions are

i	$t_{(i)}$	$\frac{i}{n+1}$
1	—	—
2	—	—
3	$t_{(3)}$	$\frac{3}{21}$
⋮		
20	t_{20}	$\frac{20}{21}$

9.6 Nonparametric Estimation of Reliability

The nonparametric Kaplan–Meier method yields an estimate, called the **Product Limit** (**PL**) estimate of the reliability function, without an explicit reference to the life distribution. The estimator of the reliability function at time t is denoted by $\hat{R}_n(t)$, where n is the number of units put on test at time $t = 0$. If all the failure times $0 < t_1 < t_2 < \cdots < t_n < \infty$ are known, then the PL estimator is equivalent to

$$\hat{R}_n(t) = 1 - F_n(t), \tag{9.6.1}$$

where $F_n(t)$ is the empirical CDF defined earlier.

In some cases either random or non-random censoring or withdrawals occur and we do not have complete information on the exact failure times. Suppose that $0 < t_1 < t_2 < \cdots < t_k < \infty$, $k \leq n$, are the failure times and $w = n - k$ is the total number of withdrawals.

Let $I_j = (t_{j-1}, t_j)$, $j = 1, \cdots, k+1$, with $t_0 = 0$, $t_{k+1} = \infty$, be the time intervals between recorded failures. Let W_j be the number of withdrawals during the time interval I_j. The PL estimator of the reliability function is then

$$\hat{R}_n(t) = I\{t < t_1\} + \sum_{i=2}^{k+1} I\{t_{i-1} \leq t \leq t_i\} \prod_{j=1}^{i-1} \left(1 - \frac{1}{n_{j-1} - w_j/2}\right), \tag{9.6.2}$$

where $n_0 = n$, and n_l is the number of operating units just prior to the failure time t_l.

Usually, when units are tested in the laboratory under controlled conditions, there may be no withdrawals. This is not the case, however, if tests are conducted in field conditions, and units on test may be lost, withdrawn or destroyed for reasons different from the failure phenomenon under study.

Suppose now that systems are installed in the field as they are purchased (random times). We decide to make a follow-up study of the systems for a period of two years. The time till failure of systems participating in the study is recorded. We assume that each system operates continuously from the time of installment until its failure. If a system has not failed by the end of the study period, the only information available is the length of time it has been operating. This is a case of multiple censoring. At the end of the study period, we have the following observations $\{(T_i, \delta_i), i = 1, \cdots, n\}$, where n is the number of systems participating in the study, T_i is the length of operation of the ith system (TTF or time till censoring), and $\delta_i = 1$ if ith observation is not censored and $\delta_i = 0$ otherwise.

Let $T_{(1)} \leq T_{(2)} \leq \cdots \leq T_{(n)}$ be the order statistic of the operation times and let $\delta_{j_1}, \delta_{j_2}, \cdots, \delta_{j_n}$ be the δ-values corresponding to the ordered T values where j_i is the index of the ith order statistic $T_{(i)}$, i.e., $T_{(i)} = T_j$, $(i = 1, \cdots, n)$.

The PL estimator of $R(t)$ is given by

$$\hat{R}_n(t) = I\{t < T_{(1)}\} + \sum_{i=1}^{n} I\{T_{(i)} \le T_{(i+1)}\} \prod_{j=1}^{i} \left(1 - \frac{\delta_j}{n-j+1}\right). \tag{9.6.3}$$

Another situation occurs in the laboratory or in field studies when the exact failure times cannot be recorded. Let $0 < t_1 < t_2 < \cdots < t_k < \infty$ be fixed inspection times. Let w_i be the number of withdrawals and f_i the number of failures in the time interval I_i $(i = 1, \cdots, k+1)$. In this case the formula is modified to be

$$\hat{R}_n(t) = I\{t < t_1\} + \sum_{i=2}^{k+1} I\{t_i \le t < t_{i+1}\} \prod_{j=1}^{i-1} \left(1 - \frac{f_j}{n_{j-1} - \frac{w_j}{2}}\right). \tag{9.6.4}$$

This version of the estimator of $R(t)$, when the inspection times are fixed (not random failure times), is called the **actuarial estimator**.

In the following examples we illustrate these estimators of the reliability function.

Example 9.12 A machine is tested before shipping to the customer for a one week period (120 [hr]) or till failure, whichever comes first. Twenty such machines were tested consecutively. In Table 9.1, we present the ordered time till failure or time till censor (TTF/TTC) of the 20 machines, the factors $(1 - \delta_i/(n - i + 1))$, and the PL estimator $\hat{R}(t_i)$, $i = 1, \cdots, 20$. ■

9.7 Estimation of Life Characteristics

In Chapter 3 of *Modern Statistics* (Kenett et al. 2022b), we studied the estimation of parameters of distributions and of functions of these parameters. We discussed point estimators and confidence intervals. In particular, we discussed unbiased estimators, least squares estimators, maximum likelihood estimators, and Bayes estimators. All these methods of estimation can be applied in reliability studies. We discuss here maximum likelihood estimation of the parameters of common life distributions, like the exponential and the Weibull, and some nonparametric techniques, for censored and uncensored data.

9.7.1 Maximum Likelihood Estimators for Exponential TTF Distribution

We start with the case of **uncensored observations**. Thus, let $T_1, T_2, \cdots, T_n$ be i.i.d. random variables distributed with an exponential distribution, $E(\beta)$. Let

Table 9.1 Failure times [hr] and PL estimates

i	$T_{(i)}$	$\left(1-\frac{\delta_i}{n-i+1}\right)$	$\hat{R}(T_i)$
1	4.787715	0.95	0.95
2	8.378821	0.9473684	0.9
3	8.763973	0.9444444	0.85
4	13.77360	0.9411765	0.8
5	29.20548	0.9375	0.75
6	30.53487	0.9333333	0.7
7	47.96504	0.9285714	0.65
8	59.22675	0.9230769	0.6
9	60.66661	0.9166667	0.55
10	62.12246	0.9090909	0.5
11	67.06873	0.9	0.45
12	92.15673	0.8888889	0.4
13	98.09076	0.875	0.35
14	107.6014	0.8571429	0.3
15	120	1	0.3
16	120	1	0.3
17	120	1	0.3
18	120	1	0.3
19	120	1	0.3
20	120	1	0.3

$t_1, \cdots, t_n$ be their sample realization (random sample). The likelihood function of $\beta, 0 < \beta < \infty$, is

$$L(\beta; \mathbf{t}) = \frac{1}{\beta^n} \exp\left\{-\frac{1}{\beta}\sum_{i=1}^{n} t_i\right\}. \tag{9.7.1}$$

It is easy to check that the maximum likelihood estimator (MLE) of β is the sample mean

$$\hat{\beta}_n = \bar{T}_n = \frac{1}{n}\sum_{i=1}^{n} T_i. \tag{9.7.2}$$

$\bar{T}_n$ is distributed like $G\left(n, \frac{\beta}{n}\right)$. Thus, $E\{\hat{\beta}_n\} = \beta$ and $V\{\hat{\beta}_n\} = \frac{\beta^2}{n}$. From the relationship between the Gamma and the χ^2 distributions, we have that $\hat{\beta}_n \sim \frac{\beta}{2n}\chi^2[2n]$. Thus, a $(1-\alpha)$ level **confidence interval** for β, based on the MLE $\hat{\beta}_n$, is

$$\left(\frac{2n\hat{\beta}_n}{\chi^2_{1-\alpha/2}[2n]}, \frac{2n\hat{\beta}_n}{\chi^2_{\alpha/2}[2n]}\right). \tag{9.7.3}$$

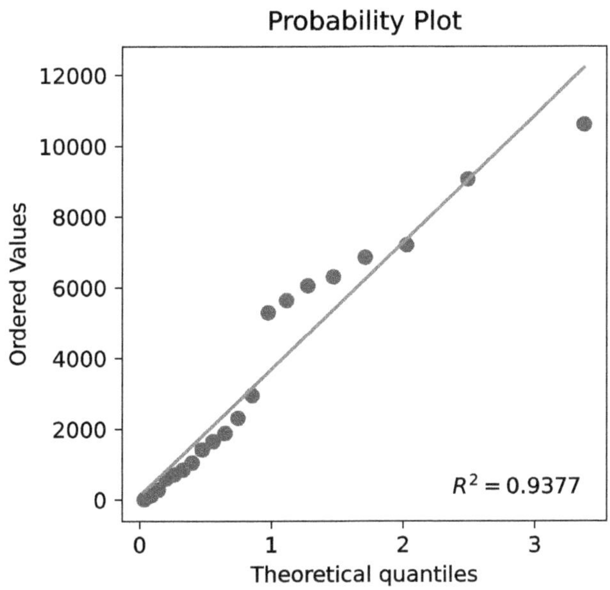

Fig. 9.6 Q–Q plot for failure times of electric generators

For large samples, we can use the normal approximation $\hat{\beta}_n \pm z_{1-\alpha/2}\frac{\hat{\beta}_n}{\sqrt{n}}$.

Example 9.13 The failure times of 20 electric generators (in [hr]) are

121.5	1425.5	2951.2	5637.9
1657.2	592.1	10609.7	9068.5
848.2	5296.6	7.5	2311.1
279.8	7201.9	6853.7	6054.3
1883.6	6303.9	1051.7	711.5

```
failtime = mistat.load_data('FAILTIME.csv')

fig, ax = plt.subplots(figsize=(4, 4))
res = stats.probplot(failtime, dist=stats.expon, plot=ax, rvalue=True)
df = pd.DataFrame({'Ei': res[0][0], 'x': res[0][1]})
model = smf.ols('x ~ Ei - 1', data=df).fit()
print(f'regression parameter beta={model.params[0]:.3f}')
```

```
regression parameter beta=3644.933
```

Exponential probability plotting (see Fig. 9.6) of these data yields a scatter around the line with a slope of 3644.93 and $R^2 = 0.94$. The exponential model fits the failure times quite well.

We can also fit an exponential model to the data using the `lifelines` package.

```
epf = lifelines.ExponentialFitter().fit(failtime)
epf.summary
beta = epf.lambda_
```

	Coef	SE(coef)	Coef lower 95%	Coef upper 95%
lambda_	3543.4	792.3	1990.4	5096.3

The *ExponentialFitter* estimates $\lambda = e^{\beta}$. It calculates the confidence interval using the normal approximation. To calculate the confidence interval using Eq. (9.7.3), use the following Python code:

```
beta = epf.lambda_
n = len(failtime)
ci_lower = 2*n*beta / stats.chi2.ppf(1-0.05/2, 2 * n)
ci_upper = 2*n*beta / stats.chi2.ppf(0.05/2, 2 * n)
ci_lower_approx = epf.summary.loc['lambda_', 'coef lower 95%']
ci_upper_approx = epf.summary.loc['lambda_', 'coef upper 95%']
```

The maximum likelihood estimator (MLE) of the mean time to failure (MTTF), β, yields $\hat{\beta}_{20} = 3543.4$ [hr]. Notice that the MLE is different, but not significantly from the above graphical estimate of β. Indeed, the standard error of $\hat{\beta}_{20}$ is S.E. $= \hat{\beta}_{20}/\sqrt{20} = 792.328$.

Confidence interval (Eq. (9.7.3)), at level of 0.95, for β is given by (2388.5, 5800.9). The normal approximation to the confidence interval is (1990.4, 5096.3). The sample size is not sufficiently large for the normal approximation to be effective. ■

When the observations are **time censored** by a fixed constant t^*, let K_n denote the number of uncensored observations. K_n is a random variable having the binomial distribution $B(n, 1 - \exp\{-t^*/\beta\})$. Let $\hat{p}_n = \frac{K_n}{n}$. $\hat{p}_n$ is a consistent estimator of $1 - \exp\{-t^*/\beta\}$. Hence, a consistent estimator of β is

$$\tilde{\beta}_n = -t^*/\log(1 - \hat{p}_n). \tag{9.7.4}$$

This estimator is not efficient, since it is not based on observed failures. Moreover, if $K_n = 0$, $\tilde{\beta}_n = 0$. Using the expansion method shown in Sect. 9.3, we obtain the asymptotic variance of $\tilde{\beta}_n$:

$$AV\{\tilde{\beta}_n\} \cong \frac{\beta^4}{nt^{*2}} \cdot \frac{1 - e^{-t^*/\beta}}{e^{-t^*/\beta}}. \tag{9.7.5}$$

The likelihood function of β in this time censoring case is

$$L(\beta; K_n, \mathbf{T}_n) = \frac{1}{\beta^{K_n}} \exp\left\{-\frac{1}{\beta}\left(\sum_{i=1}^{K_n} T_i + t^*(n - K_n)\right)\right\}. \tag{9.7.6}$$

Also here, if $K_n = 0$, the MLE of β does not exist. If $K_n \geq 1$, the MLE is

$$\hat{\beta}_n = \frac{S_{n,K_n}}{K_n}, \tag{9.7.7}$$

where $S_{n,K_n} = \sum_{i=1}^{K_n} T_i + (n - K_n)t^*$ is the **total time on test** of the n units.

The theoretical evaluation of the properties of the MLE $\hat{\beta}_n$ is complicated. We can, however, get information on its behavior by simulation.

Example 9.14 For a sample of size $n = 50$, with $\beta = 1000$ and $t^* = 2000$, we first estimate $\tilde{\beta}_n$ using the previous formula.

```
# prepare sample
np.random.seed(1)
n = 50
t_star = 2000
ft = stats.expon.rvs(scale=1000, size=n)
ft[ft>t_star] = t_star

# calculation of MLE
Kn = sum(ft < t_star)
S_nKn = sum(ft[ft<t_star]) + (n - Kn) * t_star
beta_n = S_nKn / Kn
print(f' beta_n: {beta_n:.1f}')
print(f' sd(beta_n): {beta_n / np.sqrt(n):.1f}')
```

```
beta_n: 970.1
sd(beta_n): 137.2
```

The standard deviation of $\tilde{\beta}_n$ with the above values of n, β, and t^* is 137.1.

We can also use bootstrap to estimate β. As $\Pr\{K_{50} = 0\} = \exp\{-100\} \doteq 0$, we expect that $\hat{\beta}_n$ will exist in all the simulation runs.

```
ev = ft < t_star
idx = list(range(len(ft)))
def stat_func(x):
    epf = lifelines.ExponentialFitter().fit(ft[x], ev[x])
    return epf.params_['lambda_']

ci, dist = pg.compute_bootci(idx, func=stat_func, n_boot=100, confidence=0.95,
                             method='per', seed=1, return_dist=True)
print(f' Mean: {np.mean(dist):.1f}')
print(f' Median: {np.median(dist):.1f}')
print(f' Std: {np.std(dist):.1f}')
```

```
Mean: 985.2
Median: 979.5
Std: 180.9
```

For 100 MLE's of β, obtained by this simulation, we have a mean = 985.2, a median = 979.5, and a standard deviation = 180.9. ■

Example 9.15 As an extension of Exercise 9.13, assume now that data were censored at 7000 [h].

```
# censor data  at 7000 and derive event vector
event = failtime < 7000
failtime[failtime > 7000] = 7000
```

We repeat the bootstrap analysis with the censored dataset.

```
idx = list(range(len(failtime)))
def stat_func(x):
    epf = lifelines.ExponentialFitter().fit(failtime[x], event[x])
    return epf.params_['lambda_']

ci, dist = pg.compute_bootci(idx, func=stat_func, n_boot=100, confidence=0.95,
                             method='per', seed=1, return_dist=True)
print(f' Mean: {np.mean(dist):.1f}')
print(f' 95%-CI: {ci[0]:.1f} - {ci[1]:.1f}')
```

```
Mean: 3801.4
95%-CI: 2398.8 - 5690.6
```

The actual value of $\hat{\beta}_{20}$, which is estimated from the uncensored data, is 3543.4. This is within the 95% confidence interval and close to the mean bootstrap value ■

Under **failure censoring**, the situation is simpler. Suppose that the censoring is at the rth failure. The total time on test is $S_{n,r} = \sum_{i=1}^{r} T_{(i)} + (n-r)T_{(r)}$. In this case,

$$S_{n,r} \sim \frac{\beta}{2}\chi^2[2r] \tag{9.7.8}$$

and the MLE $\hat{\beta}_{n,r} = \frac{S_{n,r}}{r}$ is an unbiased estimator of β, with variance

$$V\{\hat{\beta}_{n,r}\} = \frac{\beta^2}{r},$$

or

$$S.E.\{\hat{\beta}_{n,r}\} = \frac{\beta}{\sqrt{r}}.$$

If we wish to have a certain precision, so that S.E.$\{\hat{\beta}_{n,r}\} = \gamma\beta$, then $r = \frac{1}{\gamma^2}$. Obviously $n \geq r$.

Suppose that we pay for the test c_2 \$ per unit and c_1 \$ per time unit, for the duration of the test. Then, the total cost of the test is

$$TK_{n,r} = c_1 T_{n,r} + c_2 n. \tag{9.7.9}$$

For a given r, we choose n to minimize the expected total cost. The resulting formula is

$$n^0 \doteq \frac{r}{2}\left(1+\left(1+\frac{4c_1}{rc_2}\beta\right)^{1/2}\right). \tag{9.7.10}$$

The problem is that the optimal sample size n^0 depends on the unknown β. If one has some prior estimate of β, it could be used to determine a good starting value for n.

Example 9.16 Consider a design of a life testing experiment with frequency censoring and exponential distribution of the TTF. We require that S.E.$\{\hat{\beta}_{n,r}\} = 0.2\beta$. Accordingly, $r = \left(\frac{1}{0.2}\right)^2 = 25$. Suppose that we wish to minimize the total expected cost, at $\beta = 100$ [hr], where $c_1 = c_2 = 2$ \$. Then,

$$n^0 \doteq \frac{25}{2}\left(1+\left(1+\frac{4}{25}100\right)^{1/2}\right) = 64.$$

The expected duration of this test is

$$E\{T_{64,25}\} = 100\sum_{i=1}^{25}\frac{1}{65-i} = 49.0 \text{ [hr]}.$$

■

9.7.2 Maximum Likelihood Estimation of the Weibull Parameters

Let $t_1, \cdots, t_n$ be uncensored failure times of n random variables having a Weibull distribution $W(\nu, \beta)$. The likelihood function of (ν, β) is

$$L(\nu, \beta; \mathbf{t}) = \frac{\nu^n}{\beta^{n\nu}}\left(\prod_{i=1}^{n} t_i\right)^{\nu-1} \exp\left\{-\sum_{i=1}^{n}\left(\frac{t_i}{\beta}\right)^{\nu}\right\}, \tag{9.7.11}$$

$0 < \beta, \nu < \infty$. The MLE of ν and β are the solutions $\hat{\beta}_n$ and $\hat{\nu}_n$ of the equations

$$\hat{\beta}_n = \left(\frac{1}{n}\sum_{i=1}^{n} t_i^{\hat{\nu}_n}\right)^{1/\hat{\nu}_n}, \tag{9.7.12}$$

and

$$\hat{\nu}_n = \left[\frac{\sum_{i=1}^{n} t_i^{\hat{\nu}_n} \log t_i}{\sum_{i=1}^{n} t_i^{\hat{\nu}_n}} - \frac{1}{n} \sum_{i=1}^{n} \log(t_i) \right]^{-1}. \tag{9.7.13}$$

All logarithms are on base e (ln).

The equation for $\hat{\nu}_n$ is solved iteratively by the recursive equation

$$\hat{\nu}^{(j+1)} = \left[\frac{\sum_{i=1}^{n} t_i^{\hat{\nu}(j)} \log(t_i)}{\sum_{i=1}^{n} t_i^{\hat{\nu}(j)}} - \frac{1}{n} \sum_{i=1}^{n} \log(t_i) \right]^{-1}, \quad j = 0, 1, \cdots, \tag{9.7.14}$$

where $\hat{\nu}^{(0)} = 1$.

To illustrate, we simulated a sample of $n = 50$ failure times from $W(2.5, 10)$. In order to obtain the MLE, we have to continue the iterative process until the results converge. We show here the obtained values, as functions of the number of iterations.

# iter	$\hat{\beta}$	$\hat{\nu}$
10	11.437	2.314
20	9.959	2.367
30	9.926	2.368
40	9.925	2.368

It seems that 40 iterations yield sufficiently accurate solutions.

Confidence intervals for $\hat{\nu}_n$ and $\hat{\beta}_n$ can be determined, for large samples, by using large sample approximation formulae for the standard errors of the MLE, which are

$$SE\{\hat{\beta}_n\} \cong \frac{\hat{\beta}_n}{\sqrt{n}\,\hat{\nu}_n} \cdot 1.053 \tag{9.7.15}$$

and

$$SE\{\hat{\nu}_n\} \cong 0.780 \frac{\hat{\nu}_n}{\sqrt{n}}. \tag{9.7.16}$$

The large sample confidence limits are

$$\hat{\beta}_n \pm z_{1-\alpha/2} S.E.\{\hat{\beta}_n\}, \tag{9.7.17}$$

and

$$\hat{\nu}_n \pm z_{1-\alpha/2} S.E.\{\hat{\nu}_n\}. \tag{9.7.18}$$

In the above numerical example, the MLE $\hat{\beta}_{50} = 9.925$ and $\hat{\nu}_{50} = 2.368$. Using these values, we obtain the large sample approximate confidence intervals, with level of confidence $1-\alpha = 0.95$, to be (8.898, 11.148) for β and (1.880, 2.856) for ν.

We can derive bootstrapping confidence intervals. The bootstrap confidence limits are the $\alpha/2$th and $(1-\alpha/2)$th quantile of the simulated values which produced confidence intervals (8.378, 11.201) for β and (1.914, 3.046) for ν. The difference between these confidence intervals and the large sample approximation ones is not significant.

Maximum likelihood estimation in censored cases is more complicated and will not be discussed here. Estimates of ν and β in the censored case can be obtained from the intercept and slope of the regression line in the Q–Q plot.

Example 9.17 Using the censored data from Exercise 9.16, we estimate the $\lambda = e^{\beta}$ parameter of a fit using the Weibull distribution.

```
def stat_func(x):
    epf = lifelines.WeibullFitter().fit(failtime[x], event[x])
    return epf.params_['lambda_']
ci, dist = pg.compute_bootci(idx, func=stat_func, n_boot=100, confidence=0.95,
                             method='per', seed=1, return_dist=True)
print(f' Mean: {np.mean(dist)}')
print(f' 95%-CI: {ci[0]:.1f} - {ci[1]:.1f}')
```

```
Mean: 3695.8021438582273
95%-CI: 2188.6 - 5794.3
```

■

9.8 Reliability Demonstration

Reliability demonstration is a procedure for testing whether the reliability of a given device (system) at a certain age is sufficiently high. More precisely, a time point t_0 and a desired reliability R_0 are specified, and we wish to test whether the reliability of the device at age t_0, $R(t_0)$, satisfies the requirement that $R(t_0) \geq R_0$. If the life distribution of the device is completely known, including all parameters, there is no problem of reliability demonstration—one computes $R(t_0)$ exactly and determines whether $R(t_0) \geq R_0$. If, as is generally the case, either the life distribution or its parameters are unknown, then the problem of reliability demonstration is that of obtaining suitable data and using them to test the statistical hypothesis that $R(t_0) \geq R_0$ versus the alternative that $R(t_0) < R_0$. Thus, the theory of testing statistical hypotheses provides the tools for reliability demonstration. In the present section we review some of the basic notions of hypothesis testing as they pertain to reliability demonstration.

In the following subsections we develop several tests of interest in reliability demonstration. We remark here that procedures for obtaining confidence intervals for $R(t_0)$, which were discussed in the previous sections, can be used to test hypotheses. Specifically, the procedure involves computing the upper confidence limit of a $(1 - 2\alpha)$-level confidence interval for $R(t_0)$ and comparing it with the value R_0. If the upper confidence limit exceeds R_0, then the null hypothesis $H_0 : R(t_0) > R_0$ is accepted, otherwise it is rejected. This test will have a significance level of α.

For example, if the specification of the reliability at age $t = t_0$ is $R = 0.75$ and the confidence interval for $R(t_0)$, at level of confidence $\gamma = 0.90$, is $(0.80, 0.85)$, the hypothesis H_0 can be immediately accepted at a level of significance of $\alpha = (1-\gamma)/2 = 0.05$. There is a duality between procedures for testing hypotheses and for confidence intervals.

9.8.1 Binomial Testing

A random sample of n devices is put on life test simultaneously. Let J_n be the number of failures in the time interval $[0, t_0)$, and $K_n = n - J_n$. We have seen that $K_n \sim B(n, R(t_0))$. Thus, if H_0 is true, i.e., $R(t_0) \geq R_0$, the values of K_n will tend to be larger, in a probabilistic sense. Thus, one tests H_0 by specifying a critical value C_α and rejecting H_0 whenever $K_n \leq C_\alpha$. The critical value C_α is chosen as the largest value satisfying

$$F_B(C_\alpha; n, R_0) \leq \alpha.$$

The OC function of this test, as a function of the true reliability R, is

$$\begin{aligned} \text{OC}(R) &= \Pr\{K_n > C_\alpha \mid R(t_0) = R\} \\ &= 1 - F_B(C_\alpha; n, R). \end{aligned} \tag{9.8.1}$$

If n is large, then one can apply the normal approximation to the Binomial CDF. In these cases, we can determine C_α to be the integer most closely satisfying

$$\Phi\left(\frac{C_\alpha + 1/2 - nR_0}{(nR_0(1 - R_0))^{1/2}}\right) = \alpha. \tag{9.8.2}$$

Generally, this will be given by

$$C_\alpha = \text{integer closest to } \{nR_0 - 1/2 - z_{1-\alpha}(nR_0(1 - R_0))^{1/2}\}, \tag{9.8.3}$$

where $z_{1-\alpha} = \Phi^{-1}(1 - \alpha)$. The OC function of this test in the large sample case is approximated by

$$\text{OC}(R) \cong \Phi\left(\frac{nR - C_\alpha - 1/2}{(nR(1 - R))^{1/2}}\right). \tag{9.8.4}$$

The normal approximation is quite accurate whenever $n > 9/(R(1-R))$.

If in addition to specifying α we specify that the test has Type II error probability β, when $R(t_0) = R_1$, then the normal approximation provides us with a formula for the necessary sample size:

$$n \doteq \frac{(z_{1-\alpha}\sigma_0 + z_{1-\beta}\sigma_1)^2}{(R_1 - R_0)^2}, \tag{9.8.5}$$

where $\sigma_i^2 = R_i(1 - R_i)$, $i = 0, 1$.

Example 9.18 Suppose that we wish to test at significance level $\alpha = 0.05$ the null hypothesis that the reliability at age 1000 [hr] of a particular system is at least 85%. If the reliability is 80% or less, we want to limit the probability of accepting the null hypothesis to $\beta = 0.10$. Our test is to be based on K_n, the number of systems, out of a random sample of n, surviving at least 1000 h of operation. Setting $R_0 = 0.85$ and $R_1 = 0.80$, we have $\sigma_0 = 0.357$, $\sigma_1 = 0.4$, $z_{0.95} = 1.645$, $z_{0.90} = 1.282$. Substituting above, we obtain that the necessary sample size is $n = 483$. The critical value is $C_{0.05} = 397$.

We see that in binomial testing one may need very large samples to satisfy the specifications of the test. If in the above problem we reduce the sample size to $n = 100$, then $C_{0.05} = 79$. However, now the probability of accepting the null hypothesis when $R = 0.80$ is $\text{OC}(0.8) = \Phi(0.125) = 0.55$, which is considerably higher than the corresponding probability of 0.10 under $n = 483$. ■

9.8.2 Exponential Distributions

Suppose that we know that the life distribution is exponential $E(\beta)$, but β is unknown. The hypotheses

$$H_0 : R(t_0) \geq R_0$$

versus

$$H_1 : R(t_0) < R_0$$

can be rephrased in terms of the unknown parameter, β, as

$$H_0 : \beta \geq \beta_0$$

versus

$$H_1 : \beta < \beta_0,$$

where $\beta_0 = -t_0/\ln R_0$. Let $t_1, \cdots, t_n$ be the values of a (complete) random sample of size n. Let $\bar{t}_n = \frac{1}{n}\sum_{i=1}^{n} t_i$. The hypothesis H_0 is rejected if $\bar{t}_n < C_\alpha$, where

$$C_\alpha = \frac{\beta_0}{2n}\chi^2_\alpha[2n]. \tag{9.8.6}$$

The OC function of this test, as a function of β, is

$$\begin{aligned}\mathrm{OC}(\beta) &= \Pr\{\bar{t}_n > C_\alpha \mid \beta\} \\ &= \Pr\{\chi^2[2n] > \tfrac{\beta_0}{\beta}\chi^2_\alpha[2n]\}.\end{aligned} \tag{9.8.7}$$

If we require that at $\beta = \beta_1$ the OC function of the test will assume the value γ, then the sample size n should satisfy

$$\frac{\beta_0}{\beta_1}\chi^2_\alpha[2n] \geq \chi^2_{1-\gamma}[2n].$$

The quantiles of $\chi^2[2n]$, for $n \geq 15$, can be approximated by the formula

$$\chi^2_p[2n] \cong \frac{1}{2}(\sqrt{4n} + z_p)^2. \tag{9.8.8}$$

Substituting this approximation and solving for n, we obtain the approximation

$$n \cong \frac{1}{4}\frac{(z_{1-\gamma} + z_{1-\alpha}\sqrt{\zeta})^2}{(\sqrt{\zeta} - 1)^2}, \tag{9.8.9}$$

where $\zeta = \beta_0/\beta_1$.

Example 9.19 Suppose that in Example 9.18, we know that the system lifetimes are exponentially distributed. It is interesting to examine how many systems would have to be tested in order to achieve the same error probabilities as before, if our decision were now based on $\bar{t}_n$.

Since $\beta = -t/\ln R(t)$, the value of the parameter β under $R(t_0) = R(1000) = 0.85$ is $\beta_0 = -1000/\ln(0.85) = 6153$ [hr], while its value under $R(t_0) = 0.80$ is $\beta_1 = -1000/\ln(0.80) = 4481$ [hr]. Substituting these values into (9.3.5), along with $\alpha = 0.05$ and $\gamma = 0.10$ (γ was denoted by β in Example 9.18), we obtain the necessary sample size $n \cong 87$.

Thus we see that the additional knowledge that the lifetime distribution is exponential, along with the use of complete lifetime data on the sample, allows us to achieve a greater than fivefold increase in efficiency in terms of the sample size necessary to achieve the desired error probabilities. ■

We remark that if the sample is censored at the rth failure, then all the formulae developed above apply after replacing n by r and $\bar{t}_n$ by $\hat{\beta}_{n,r} = T_{n,r}/r$.

Example 9.20 Suppose that the reliability at age $t = 250$ [hr] should be at least $R_0 = 0.85$. Let $R_1 = 0.75$. The corresponding values of β_0 and β_1 are 1538 [hr] and 869 [hr], respectively. Suppose that the sample is censored at the $r = 25$th failure. Let $\hat{\beta}_{n,r} = T_{n,r}/25$ be the MLE of β. H_0 is rejected, with level of significance $\alpha = 0.05$ if

$$\hat{\beta}_{n,r} \leq \frac{1538}{50} \chi^2_{0.05}[50] = 1069 \text{ [hr]}.$$

The Type II error probability of this test, at $\beta = 869$, is

$$\begin{aligned} \text{OC}(869) &= \Pr\{\chi^2[50] > \frac{1538}{869} \chi^2_{0.05}[50]\} \\ &= \Pr\{\chi^2[50] > 61.5\} \\ &\doteq 1 - \Phi\left(\frac{61.5 - 50}{\sqrt{100}}\right) \\ &= 0.125. \end{aligned}$$

■

Sometimes in reliability demonstration an overriding concern is keeping the number of items tested to a minimum, subject to whatever accuracy requirements are imposed. This could be the case, for example, when testing very complex and expensive systems. In such cases, it may be worthwhile applying a sequential testing procedure, where items are tested one at a time in sequence until the procedure indicates that testing can stop and a decision be made. Such an approach would also be appropriate when testing prototypes of some new design, which are being produced one at a time at a relatively slow rate.

In Chap. 3 we have introduced the Wald SPRT for testing hypotheses with binomial data. Here we reformulate this test for reliability testing.

9.8.2.1 The SPRT for Binomial Data

Without any assumptions about the lifetime distribution of a device, we can test hypotheses concerning $R(t_0)$ by simply observing whether or not a device survives to age t_0. Letting K_n represent the number of devices among n randomly selected ones surviving to age t_0, we have $K_n \sim B(n, R(t_0))$. The likelihood ratio is given by

$$\lambda_n = \left(\frac{1 - R_1}{1 - R_0}\right)^n \left(\frac{R_1(1 - R_0)}{R_0(1 - R_1)}\right)^{K_n}. \tag{9.8.10}$$

Thus,

$$\ln \lambda_n = n \ln \left(\frac{1 - R_1}{1 - R_0} \right) - K_n \ln \left(\frac{R_0(1 - R_1)}{R_1(1 - R_0)} \right).$$

It follows that the SPRT can be expressed in terms of K_n as follows:

$$\begin{aligned} &\text{Continue sampling if } -h_1 + sn < K_n < h_2 + sn, \\ &\text{Accept } H_0 \text{ if } K_n \geq h_2 + sn, \\ &\text{Reject } H_0 \text{ if } K_n \leq -h_1 + sn, \end{aligned}$$

where

$$\begin{cases} s = \ln\left(\frac{1-R_1}{1-R_0}\right) \Big/ \ln\left(\frac{R_0(1-R_1)}{R_1(1-R_0)}\right), \\ h_1 = \ln\left(\frac{1-\gamma}{\alpha}\right) \Big/ \ln\left(\frac{R_0(1-R_1)}{R_1(1-R_0)}\right), \\ h_2 = \ln\left(\frac{1-\alpha}{\gamma}\right) \Big/ \ln\left(\frac{R_0(1-R_1)}{R_1(1-R_0)}\right). \end{cases} \tag{9.8.11}$$

α and γ are the prescribed probabilities of Type I and Type II errors. Note that if we plot K_n vs. n, the accept and reject boundaries are parallel straight lines with common slope s and intercepts h_2 and $-h_1$, respectively.

The OC function of this test is expressible (approximately) in terms of an implicit parameter ψ. Letting

$$R^{(\psi)} = \begin{cases} \dfrac{1-\left(\frac{1-R_1}{1-R_0}\right)^{\psi}}{\left(\frac{R_1}{R_0}\right)^{\psi}-\left(\frac{1-R_1}{1-R_0}\right)^{\psi}}, & \psi \neq 0 \\ s, & \psi = 0, \end{cases} \tag{9.8.12}$$

we have that the OC function at $R(t_0) = R^{(\psi)}$ is given by

$$\text{OC}(R^{(\psi)}) \approx \begin{cases} \dfrac{\left(\frac{1-\gamma}{\alpha}\right)^{\psi}-1}{\left(\frac{1-\gamma}{\alpha}\right)^{\psi}-\left(\frac{\gamma}{1-\alpha}\right)^{\psi}}, & \psi \neq 0 \\ \dfrac{\ln\left(\frac{1-\gamma}{\alpha}\right)}{\ln\left(\frac{(1-\alpha)(1-\gamma)}{\alpha\gamma}\right)}, & \psi = 0. \end{cases} \tag{9.8.13}$$

It is easily verified that for $\psi = 1$, $R^{(\psi)}$ equals R_0 and $\mathrm{OC}(R^{(\psi)})$ equals $1 - \alpha$, while for $\psi = -1$, $R^{(\psi)}$ equals R_1 and $\mathrm{OC}(R^{(\psi)})$ equals γ.

The expected sample size, or **average sample number** (ASN), as a function of $R^{(\psi)}$, is given by

$$\mathrm{ASN}(R^{(\psi)}) \approx \begin{cases} \dfrac{\ln \frac{1-\gamma}{\alpha} - \mathrm{OC}(R^{(\psi)}) \ln\left(\frac{(1-\alpha)(1-\gamma)}{\alpha\gamma}\right)}{\ln \frac{1-R_1}{1-R_0} - R^{(\psi)} \ln\left(\frac{R_0(1-R_1)}{R_1(1-R_0)}\right)}, & \psi \neq 0 \\ \\ \dfrac{h_1 h_2}{s(1-s)}, & \psi = 0. \end{cases} \tag{9.8.14}$$

The ASN function will typically have a maximum at some value of R between R_0 and R_1 and decrease as R moves away from the point of maximum in either direction.

Example 9.21 Consider Example 9.19, where we had $t = 1000$ [hr], $R_0 = 0.85$, $R_1 = 0.80$, $\alpha = 0.05$, $\gamma = 0.10$. Suppose now that systems are tested sequentially, and we apply the SPRT based on the number of systems still functioning at 1000 [hr]. The parameters of the boundary lines are $s = 0.826$, $h_1 = 8.30$, and $h_2 = 6.46$.

The OC and ASN functions of the test are given in Table 9.2, for selected values of ψ.

Compare the values in the ASN column to the sample size required for the corresponding fixed-sample test, $n = 483$. It is clear that the SPRT effects a considerable saving in sample size, particularly when $R(t_0)$ is less than R_1 or greater than R_0. Note also that the maximum ASN value occurs when $R(t_0)$ is near s. ■

9.8.2.2 The SPRT for Exponential Lifetimes

When the lifetime distribution is known to be exponential, we have seen the increase in efficiency gained by measuring the actual failure times of the parts being tested. By using a sequential procedure based on these failure times, further gains in efficiency can be achieved.

Expressing the hypotheses in terms of the parameter β of the lifetime distribution $E(\beta)$, we wish to test $H_0 : \beta \geq \beta_0$ vs. $H_1 : \beta < \beta_0$, with significance level α and Type II error probability γ, when $\beta = \beta_1$, where $\beta_1 < \beta_0$. Letting $\mathbf{t}_n = (t_1, \cdots, t_n)$ be the times till failure of the first n parts tested, the likelihood ratio statistic is given by

$$\lambda_n(\mathbf{t}_n) = \left(\frac{\beta_0}{\beta_1}\right)^n \exp\left(-\left(\frac{1}{\beta_1} - \frac{1}{\beta_0}\right)\sum_{i=1}^{n} t_i\right). \tag{9.8.15}$$

Table 9.2 OC and ASN values for the SPRT

ψ	$R^{(\psi)}$	$\text{OC}(R^{(\psi)})$	$\text{ASN}(R^{(\psi)})$
−2.0	0.7724	0.0110	152.0
−1.8	0.7780	0.0173	167.9
−1.6	0.7836	0.0270	186.7
−1.4	0.7891	0.0421	208.6
−1.2	0.7946	0.0651	234.1
−1.0	0.8000	0.1000	263.0
−0.8	0.8053	0.1512	294.2
−0.6	0.8106	0.2235	325.5
−0.4	0.8158	0.3193	352.7
−0.2	0.8209	0.4357	370.2
0.0	0.8259	0.5621	373.1
0.2	0.8309	0.6834	360.2
0.4	0.8358	0.7858	334.8
0.6	0.8406	0.8629	302.6
0.8	0.8453	0.9159	269.1
1.0	0.8500	0.9500	238.0
1.2	0.8546	0.9709	210.8
1.4	0.8590	0.9833	187.8
1.6	0.8634	0.9905	168.6
1.8	0.8678	0.9946	152.7
2.0	0.8720	0.9969	139.4

Thus,

$$\ln \lambda_n(\mathbf{t}_n) = n \ln(\beta_0/\beta_1) - \left(\frac{1}{\beta_1} - \frac{1}{\beta_0}\right) \sum_{i=1}^{n} t_i.$$

The SPRT rules are accordingly

$$\text{Continue sampling if } -h_1 + sn < \sum_{i=1}^{n} t_i < h_2 + sn,$$

$$\text{Accept } H_0 \text{ if } \sum_{i=1}^{n} t_i \geq h_2 + sn,$$

$$\text{Reject } H_0 \text{ if } \sum_{i=1}^{n} t_i \leq -h_1 + sn,$$

where

$$\begin{aligned} s &= \ln(\beta_0/\beta_1) \Big/ \left(\tfrac{1}{\beta_1} - \tfrac{1}{\beta_0}\right), \\ h_1 &= \ln((1-\gamma)/\alpha) \Big/ \left(\tfrac{1}{\beta_1} - \tfrac{1}{\beta_0}\right), \\ h_2 &= \ln((1-\alpha)/\gamma) \Big/ \left(\tfrac{1}{\beta_1} - \tfrac{1}{\beta_0}\right). \end{aligned} \tag{9.8.16}$$

Thus, if we plot $\sum_{i=1}^{n} t_i$ vs. n, the accept and reject boundaries are again parallel straight lines.

As before, let ψ be an implicit parameter, and define

$$\beta^{(\psi)} = \begin{cases} \dfrac{(\beta_0/\beta_1)^{\psi}-1}{\psi\left(\frac{1}{\beta_1}-\frac{1}{\beta_0}\right)}, & \psi \neq 0 \\ \dfrac{\ln(\beta_0/\beta_1)}{\frac{1}{\beta_1}-\frac{1}{\beta_0}}, & \psi = 0. \end{cases} \tag{9.8.17}$$

Then the OC and ASN functions are approximately given by

$$\mathrm{OC}(\beta^{(\psi)}) \approx \begin{cases} \dfrac{((1-\gamma)/\alpha)^{\psi}-1}{((1-\gamma)/\alpha)^{\psi}-(\gamma/(1-\alpha))^{\psi}}, & \psi \neq 0 \\ \dfrac{\ln((1-\gamma)/\alpha)}{\ln((1-\alpha)(1-\gamma)/\alpha\gamma)}, & \psi = 0 \end{cases} \tag{9.8.18}$$

and

$$\mathrm{ASN}(\beta^{(\psi)}) \approx \begin{cases} \dfrac{\ln((1-\gamma)/\alpha)-\mathrm{OC}(\beta^{(\psi)})\ln((1-\alpha)(1-\gamma)/\alpha\gamma)}{\ln(\beta_0/\beta_1)-\beta^{(\psi)}\left(\frac{1}{\beta_1}-\frac{1}{\beta_0}\right)}, & \psi \neq 0 \\ \dfrac{h_1 h_2}{s^2}, & \psi = 0. \end{cases} \tag{9.8.19}$$

Note that when $\psi = 1$, $\beta^{(\psi)}$ equals β_0, while when $\psi = -1$, $\beta^{(\psi)}$ equals β_1.

Example 9.22 Continuing Example 9.19, recall we had $\alpha = 0.05$, $\gamma = 0.10$, $\beta_0 = 6153$, $\beta_1 = 4481$. The parameters of the boundaries of the SPRT are $s = 5229$, $h_1 = 47662$, $h_2 = 37124$. The OC and ASN functions, for selected values of ψ, are given in Table 9.3.

In Example 9.19, we saw that the fixed-sample test with the same α and γ requires a sample size of $n = 87$. Thus, in the exponential case as well, we see that the SPRT can result in substantial savings in sample size. ■

It is impractical to perform a sequential test, like the one described in the above example by running one system, waiting till it fails, renewing it and running it again and again until a decision can be made. In the above example, if the MTTF of the system is close to the value of $\beta_0 = 6153$ [hr], it takes on the average about 256 days

Table 9.3 OC and ASN values for the SPRT

ψ	$\beta^{(\psi)}$	OC($\beta^{(\psi)}$)	ASN($\beta^{(\psi)}$)
−2.0	3872	0.0110	34.3
−1.8	3984	0.0173	37.1
−1.6	4101	0.0270	40.2
−1.4	4223	0.0421	43.8
−1.2	4349	0.0651	47.9
−1.0	4481	0.1000	52.4
−0.8	4618	0.1512	57.1
−0.6	4762	0.2235	61.4
−0.4	4911	0.3193	64.7
−0.2	5067	0.4357	66.1
0.0	5229	0.5621	64.7
0.2	5398	0.6834	60.7
0.4	5575	0.7858	54.8
0.6	5759	0.8629	48.1
0.8	5952	0.9159	41.5
1.0	6153	0.9500	35.6
1.2	6363	0.9709	30.6
1.4	6582	0.9833	26.4
1.6	6811	0.9905	22.9
1.8	7051	0.9946	20.1
2.0	7301	0.9969	17.8

between failures, and on the average about 36 failures till decision is reached. This trial may take over 25 years. There are three ways to overcome this problem. The first is to put on test several systems simultaneously. Thus, if in the trial described in the above example 25 systems are tested simultaneously, the expected duration of the test will be reduced to one year. Another way is to consider a test based on a continuous time process, not on discrete samples of failure times. The third possibility of reducing the expected test duration is to perform **accelerated life testing**. In the following sections we discuss these alternatives.

9.8.2.3 The SPRT for Poisson Processes

Suppose that we put n systems on test starting at $t = 0$. Suppose also that any system which fails is instantaneously renewed, and at the renewal time it is as good as new. In addition we assume that the life characteristics of the systems are identical, the TTF of each system is **exponential** (with the same β), and failures of different systems are **independent** of each other.

Under these assumptions, the number of failures in each system, in the time interval $(0, t]$, is a Poisson random variable with mean λt, where $\lambda = 1/\beta$.

Let $X_n(t)$ be the total number of failures among all the n systems during the time interval $(0, t]$. $X_n(t) \sim \text{Pos}(n\lambda t)$, and the collection $\{X_n(t);\ 0 < t < \infty\}$ is called a **Poisson process**. We add the initial condition that $X_n(0) = 0$.

The random function $X_n(t), 0 < t < \infty$, is a non-decreasing step function which jumps one unit at each random failure time of the system. The random functions $X_n(t)$ satisfy:

(i) $X_n(t), \sim \text{Pos}(n\lambda t)$, all $0 < t < \infty$.
(ii) For any $t_1 < t_2$, $X_n(t_2) - X_n(t_1)$ is independent of $X_n(t_1)$.
(iii) For any $t_1, t_2, 0 < t_1 < t_2 < \infty$, $X_n(t_2) - X_n(t_1) \sim \text{Pos}(n\lambda(t_2 - t_1))$.

We develop now the SPRT based on the random functions $X_n(t)$.

The hypotheses $H_0 : \beta \geq \beta_0$ versus $H_1 : \beta \leq \beta_1$, for $0 < \beta_1 < \beta_0 < \infty$, are translated to the hypotheses $H_0 : \lambda \leq \lambda_0$ versus $H_1 : \lambda \geq \lambda_1$ where $\lambda = 1/\beta$. The likelihood ratio at time t is

$$\Lambda(t; X_n(t)) = \left(\frac{\lambda_1}{\lambda_0}\right)^{X_n(t)} \exp\{-nt(\lambda_1 - \lambda_0)\}. \tag{9.8.20}$$

The test continues as long as the random graph of $(T_n(t), X_n(t))$ is between the two linear boundaries

$$b_U(t) = h_2 + sT_n(t), \quad 0 \leq t < \infty$$

and

$$b_L(t) = -h_1 + sT_n(t), \quad 0 \leq t < \infty,$$

where $T_n(t) = nt$ is the total time on test at t,

$$h_1 = \frac{\ln\left(\frac{1-\alpha}{\gamma}\right)}{\ln\left(\frac{\lambda_1}{\lambda_0}\right)},$$

$$h_2 = \frac{\ln\left(\frac{1-\gamma}{\alpha}\right)}{\ln\left(\frac{\lambda_1}{\lambda_0}\right)}, \tag{9.8.21}$$

and

$$s = \frac{\lambda_1 - \lambda_0}{\ln\left(\frac{\lambda_1}{\lambda_0}\right)}.$$

The instant $X_n(t)$ jumps above $b_U(t)$, the test terminates, and H_0 is rejected; on the other hand, the instant $X_n(t) = b_L(t)$ the test terminates and H_0 is accepted.

Acceptance of H_0 entails that the reliability meets the specified requirement. Rejection of H_0 may lead to additional engineering modification to improve the reliability of the system.

The OC function of this sequential test is the same as that in the exponential case. Let τ denote the random time of termination. It can be shown that $\Pr_\lambda\{\tau < \infty\} = 1$ for all $0 < \lambda < \infty$. The expected deviation of the test is given approximately by

$$E_\lambda\{\tau\} = \frac{1}{\lambda n} E_\lambda\{X_n(\tau)\}, \tag{9.8.22}$$

where

$$E_\lambda\{X_n(\tau)\} \cong \begin{cases} \frac{h_2 - \mathrm{OC}(\lambda)(h_1+h_2)}{1-s/\lambda}, & \text{if } \lambda \neq s \\ h_1 h_2, & \text{if } \lambda = s. \end{cases} \tag{9.8.23}$$

It should be noticed that the last formula yields the same values as the formula in the exponential case for $\lambda = 1/\beta^{(\psi)}$. The SPRT of the previous section can terminate only after a failure, while the SPRT based on $X_n(t)$ may terminate while crossing the lower boundary $b_L(t)$, before a failure occurs.

The minimal time required to accept H_0 is $\tau_0 = h_1/ns$. In the case of Example 9.21, with $n = 20$, $\tau_0 = 9.11536/(20 \times 0.0001912) = 2383.2$ [hr], that is, over 99 days of testing without any failure. The SPRT may be, in addition, frequency censored by fixing a value x^* so that as soon as $X_n(t) \geq x^*$ the test terminates and H_0 is rejected. In Example 9.21 we see that the expected number of failures at termination may be as large as 66. We can censor the test at $x^* = 50$. This will reduce the expected duration of the test but will increase the probability of a Type I error, α. Special programs are available for computing the operating characteristics of such censored tests, but these are beyond the scope of the present text.

9.9 Accelerated Life Testing

It is often impractical to test highly reliable systems, or components, under normal operating conditions because no failures may be observed during long periods of time. In accelerated life testing, the systems are subjected to higher than normal stress conditions in order to generate failures. The question is how to relate failure distributions, under higher than normal stress conditions, to those under normal conditions?

Accelerated life testing is used by engineers in testing materials like food and drugs, lubricants, concrete and cement, building materials, and nuclear reactor materials. The stress conditions are generally, mechanical load, vibrations, high temperatures, high humidity, high contamination, etc. Accelerated testing is used for semiconductors including transistors, electronic devices such as diodes, random access memories, plastic encapsulants, etc. The reader is referred to Nelson (2004) for a survey of methods and applications. The statistical methodology of accelerated life testing is similar to the methods described earlier in this chapter, including graphical analysis and maximum likelihood estimation. The reader is referred to Meeker et al. (2021), Nelson (2004) and Mann et al. (1974), for details. We describe below some of the models used to relate failures under various stress conditions.

9.9.1 *The Arrhenius Temperature Model*

This model is widely used when the product failure time is sensitive to high temperature. Applications include electrical insulations and dielectric (see Goba 1969), solid state and semiconductors (Peck et al. 1994), battery cells, lubricants and greases, plastics, and incandescent light filaments.

The **Arrhenius law** states that the rate of simple chemical reaction depends on temperature as follows:

$$\lambda = A\exp\{-E/(kT)\}, \tag{9.9.1}$$

where E is the activation energy (in electron volts, k is the Boltzmann constant, 8.6171×10^{-5} electron volts per °C, T is the absolute Kelvin temperature (273.16+ °C), and A is a product parameter, which depends on the test conditions and failure characteristics. In applying the Arrhenius model to failure times distribution, we find the Weibull–Arrhenius life distribution, in which the scale parameter β of the Weibull distribution is related to temperature, T, according to the function

$$\beta(T) = \lambda\exp\left\{A + \frac{B}{T}\right\}, \quad B > 0, \tag{9.9.2}$$

where λ, A, and B are fitted empirically to the data.

9.9.2 *Other Models*

Another model is called the **lognormal Arrhenius** model, in which the log failure time is normally distributed with mean $A + B/T$ and variance σ^2. According to this model, the expected failure time is $\exp\{A + B/T + \sigma^2/2\}$. Another model prevalent in the literature relates the expected failure time to a stress level V according to the **inverse power model**

$$MTTF(V) = \frac{C}{V^p}, \quad C > 0. \tag{9.9.3}$$

The statistical data analysis methodology is to fit an appropriate model to the data, usually by maximum likelihood estimation, and then predict the MTTF of the system under normal conditions or some reliability or availability function. Tolerance intervals, for the predicted value, should be determined.

9.10 Burn-In Procedures

Many products show a relatively high frequency of early failures. For example, if a product has an exponential distribution of the TTF with MTTF of $\beta = 10{,}000$ [hr], we do not expect more than 2% of the product to fail within the first 200 [hr]. Nevertheless, many products designed for high value of MTTF show a higher than expected number of early failures. This phenomenon led to the theory that the hazard rate function of products is typically a U-shaped function. In its early life, the product is within a phase with monotone decreasing hazard rate. This phase is called the "infant mortality" phase. After this phase, the product enters a phase of "maturity" in which the hazard rate function is almost constant. Burn-in procedures are designed to screen (burn) the weak products within the plant, by setting the product to operate for several days, in order to give the product a chance to fail in the plant and not in the field, where the loss due to failure is high.

How long should a burn-in procedure last? Jensen and Petersen (1991) discuss this and other issues in designing burn-in procedures. We present here some basic ideas.

Burn-in procedures discussed by Jensen and Petersen are based on a model of a mixed life distribution. For example, suppose that experience shows that the life distribution of a product is Weibull, $W(\nu, \beta_1)$. A small proportion of units manufactured may have generally short life, due to various reasons, which is given by another Weibull distribution, say $W(\nu, \beta_0)$, with $\beta_0 < \beta_1$. Thus, the life distribution of a randomly chosen product has a distribution which is a mixture of $W(\nu, \beta_0)$ and $W(\nu, \beta_1)$, i.e.,

$$F(t) = 1 - \left[p \exp\left\{-\left(\frac{t}{\beta_0}\right)^{\nu}\right\} + (1-p)\exp\left\{-\left(\frac{t}{\beta_1}\right)^{\nu}\right\}\right], \tag{9.10.1}$$

for $t > 0$. The objective of the burn-in is to let units having the $W(\nu, \beta_0)$ distribution an opportunity to fail in the plant. The units that do not fail during the burn-in have, for their remaining life, a life distribution closer to the desired $W(\nu, \beta_1)$.

Suppose that a burn-in continues for t^* time units. The conditional distribution of the time till failure T, given that $\{T > t^*\}$, is

$$F^*(t) = \frac{\int_{t^*}^{t} f(u)\,\mathrm{d}u}{1 - F(t^*)}, \qquad t \geq t^*. \tag{9.10.2}$$

The c.d.f. $F^*(t)$, of units surviving the burn-in, starts at t^*, i.e., $F^*(t^*) = 0$ and has MTTF

$$\beta^* = t^* + \int_{t^*}^{\infty} (1 - F^*(t))\,\mathrm{d}t. \tag{9.10.3}$$

We illustrate this in the following example on mixtures of exponential life times.

Example 9.23 Suppose that a product is designed to have an exponential life distribution, with mean of $\beta = 10{,}000$ [hr]. A proportion $p = 0.05$ of the products comes out of the production process with a short MTTF of $\gamma = 100$ [hr]. Suppose that all products go through a burn-in for $t^* = 200$ [hr].

The c.d.f. of the TTF of units which did not fail during the burn-in is

$$\begin{aligned} F^*(t) &= 1 - \frac{0.05\exp\{-\frac{t}{100}\} + 0.95\exp\{-\frac{t}{10{,}000}\}}{0.05\exp\{-\frac{200}{100}\} + 0.95\exp\{-\frac{200}{10{,}000}\}} \\ &= 1 - \frac{1}{0.93796}\left[0.05\exp\left\{-\frac{t}{100}\right\} + 0.95\exp\left\{-\frac{t}{10,000}\right\}\right] \end{aligned}$$

for $t \geq 200$. The mean time till failure, for units surviving the burn-in, is thus

$$\begin{aligned} \beta^* &= 200 + \frac{1}{0.93796}\int_{200}^{\infty}\left(0.05\exp\left\{-\frac{t}{100}\right\} + 0.95\exp\left\{-\frac{t}{10,000}\right\}\right)\mathrm{d}t \\ &= 200 + \frac{5}{0.93796}\exp\left\{-\frac{200}{100}\right\} + \frac{9500}{0.93796}\exp\left\{-\frac{200}{10,000}\right\} \\ &= 10{,}128.53 \text{ [hr]}. \end{aligned}$$

A unit surviving 200 h of burn-in is expected to operate an additional 9928.53 h in the field. The expected life of these units without the burn-in is $0.05 \times 200 + 0.95 \times 10{,}000 = 9510$ [hr]. The burn-in of 200 h in the plant is expected to increase the mean life of the product in the field by 418 h. Whether this increase in the MTTF justifies the burn-in depends on the relative cost of burn-in in the plant to the cost of failures in the field. The proportion p of "short life" units plays also an important role. If this proportion is $p = 0.1$ rather than 0.05, the burn-in increases the MTTF in the field from 9020 h to 9848.95 h. One can easily verify that for $p = 0.2$, if the income for an hour of operation of one unit in the field is $C_p = 5\$$ and the cost of the burn-in per unit is 0.15$ per hour, then the length of burn-in which maximizes the expected profit is about 700 h. ■

9.11 Chapter Highlights

The main concepts and definitions introduced in this chapter include:

- Life distributions
- Accelerated life testing
- Availability
- Time categories
- Up time
- Down time
- Intrinsic availability
- Operational readiness
- Mean time to Failure (MTTF)
- Reliability function
- Failure rate
- Structure function
- Time till failure (TTF)
- Time till repair (TTR)
- Cycle time
- Renewal function
- Censored data
- Product limit (PL) estimator
- Average sample number (ASN)
- Sequential probability ratio test (SPRT)
- Burn-in procedure

9.12 Exercises

Exercise 9.1 During 600 h of manufacturing time, a machine was up 510 h. It had 100 failures which required a total of 11 h of repair time. What is the MTTF of this machine? What is its mean time till repair, MTTR? What is the intrinsic availability?

Exercise 9.2 The frequency distribution of the lifetime in a random sample of $n = 2000$ solar cells, under accelerated life testing is the following:

$t[10^3[\text{hr}]$	0–1	1–2	2–3	3–4	4–5	5–
Prof. freq.	0.15	0.25	0.25	0.10	0.10	0.15

The relationship of the scale parameters of the life distributions, between normal and accelerated conditions, is 10:1.

(i) Estimate the reliability of the solar cells at age $t = 4.0$ [yr].
(ii) What proportion of solar cells are expected to survive 40,000 [hr] among those which survived 20,000 [hr]?

Exercise 9.3 The CDF of the lifetime [months] of an equipment is

$$F(t) = \begin{cases} t^4/20736, & 0 \le t < 12 \\ \\ 1, & 12 \le t. \end{cases}$$

(i) What is the failure rate function of this equipment?
(ii) What is the MTTF?
(iii) What is the reliability of the equipment at 4 months?

Exercise 9.4 The reliability of a system is

$$R(t) = \exp\{-2t - 3t^2\}, \quad 0 \le t < \infty.$$

(i) What is the failure rate of this system at age $t = 3$?
(ii) Given that the system reached the age of $t = 3$, what is its reliability for two additional time units?

Exercise 9.5 An aircraft has four engines but can land using only two engines.

(i) Assuming that the reliability of each engine, for the duration of a mission, is $R = 0.95$, and that engine failures are independent, compute the mission reliability of the aircraft.
(ii) What is the mission reliability of the aircraft if at least one functioning engine must be on each wing?

Exercise 9.6

(i) Draw a block diagram of a system having the structure function

$$R_{\text{sys}} = \psi_s(\psi_p(\psi_{M_1}, \psi_{M_2}), R_6), \quad \psi_{M_1} = \psi_p(R_1, R_2 R_3), \quad \psi_{M_2} = \psi_2(R_4, R_5)$$

(ii) Determine R_{sys} if all the components act independently and have the same reliability $R = 0.8$.

Exercise 9.7 Consider a system of n components in a series structure. Let $R_1, \cdots, R_n$ be the reliabilities of the components. Show that

$$R_{\text{sys}} \ge 1 - \sum_{i=1}^{n}(1 - R_i).$$

Exercise 9.8 A 4 out of 8 system has identical components whose life lengths T [weeks] are independent and identically distributed like a Weibull $W\left(\frac{1}{2}, 100\right)$. What is the reliability of the system at $t_0 = 5$ weeks?

Exercise 9.9 A system consists of a main unit and two standby units. The lifetimes of these units are exponential with mean $\beta = 100$ [hr]. The standby units undergo no failure while idle. Switching will take place when required. What is the MTTF of the system? What is the reliability function of this system?

Exercise 9.10 Suppose that the TTF in a renewal cycle has a $W(\alpha, \beta)$ distribution and that the TTR has a lognormal distribution $\text{LN}(\mu, \sigma)$. Assume further that TTF and TTR are independent. What are the mean and standard deviation of a renewal cycle.

Exercise 9.11 Suppose that a renewal cycle has the normal distribution $N(100, 10)$. Determine the p.d.f. of $N_R(200)$.

Exercise 9.12 Let the renewal cycle C be distributed like $N(100, 10)$. Approximate $V(1000)$.

Exercise 9.13 Derive the renewal density $v(t)$ for a renewal process with $C \sim N(100, 10)$.

Exercise 9.14 Two identical components are connected in parallel. The system is not repaired until both components fail. Assuming that the TTF of each component is exponentially distributed, $E(\beta)$, and the total repair time is $G(2, \gamma)$, derive the Laplace transform of the availability function $A(t)$ of the system.

Exercise 9.15 Simulate a sample of 100 TTF of a system comprised of two components connected in parallel, where the life distribution of each component (in hours) is $E(100)$. Similarly, simulate a sample of 100 repair times (in hours), having a $G(2, 1)$ distribution. Estimate the expected value and variance of the number of renewals in 2000 [hr].

Exercise 9.16 In a given life test, $n = 15$ units are placed to operate independently. The time till failure of each unit has an exponential distribution with mean 2000 [hr]. The life test terminates immediately after the 10th failure. How long is the test expected to last?

Exercise 9.17 If n units are put on test and their TTF are exponentially distributed with mean β, the time elapsed between the rth and $(r + 1)$th failure, i.e., $\Delta_{n,r} = T_{n,r+1} - T_{n,r}$, is exponentially distributed with mean $\beta/(n - r)$, $r = 0, 1, \cdots, n-1$. Also, $\Delta_{n,0}, \Delta_{n,2}, \cdots, \Delta_{n,n-1}$ are independent. What is the variance of $T_{n,r}$? Use this result to compute the variance of the test length in the previous exercise.

Exercise 9.18 Consider again the previous exercise. How would you estimate unbiasedly the scale parameter β if the r failure times $T_{n,1}, T_{n,2}, \cdots, T_{n,r}$ are given? What is the variance of this unbiased estimator?

Exercise 9.19 Simulate a random sample of 100 failure times, following the Weibull distribution $W(2.5, 10)$. Draw a Weibull Probability plot of the data. Estimate the parameters of the distribution from the parameters of the linear regression fitted to the Q–Q plot.

Exercise 9.20 The following is a random sample of the compressive strength of 20 concrete cubes [kg/cm^2]:

94.9, 106.9, 229.7, 275.7, 144.5, 112.8, 159.3, 153.1, 270.6, 322.0,

216.4, 544.6, 266.2, 263.6, 138.5, 79.0, 114.6, 66.1, 131.2, 91.1

Make a lognormal Q–Q plot of these data and estimate the mean and standard deviation of this distribution.

Exercise 9.21 The following data represent the time till first failure [days] of electrical equipment. The data were censored after 400 days.

$$13,\ 157,\ 172,\ 176,\ 249,\ 303,\ 350,\ 400^+,\ 400^+.$$

(Censored values appear as x^+.) Make a Weibull Q–Q plot of these data and estimate the median of the distribution.

Exercise 9.22 Make a PL (Kaplan–Meier) estimate of the reliability function of an electronic device, based on 50 failure times in dataset **ELECFAIL.csv**.

Exercise 9.23 Assuming that the failure times in dataset **ELECFAIL.csv** come from an exponential distribution $E(\beta)$, compute the MLE of β and of $R(50; \beta) = \exp\{-50/\beta\}$. [The MLE of a function of a parameter is obtained by substituting the MLE of the parameter in the function.] Determine confidence intervals for β and for $R(50; \beta)$ at level of confidence 0.95.

Exercise 9.24 The following are values of 20 random variables having an exponential distribution $E(\beta)$. The values are censored at $t^* = 200$.

96.88, 154.24, 67.44, 191.72, 173.36, 200, 140.81, 200, 154.71, 120.73,

24.29, 10.95, 2.36, 186.93, 57.61, 99.13, 32.74, 200, 39.77, 39.52.

Determine the MLE of β. Use β equal to the MLE, to estimate the standard deviation of the MLE and to obtain confidence interval for β, at level $1 - \alpha = 0.95$. [This simulation is called an empirical Bootstrap.]

Exercise 9.25 Determine n^0 and r for a frequency censoring test for the exponential distribution, where the cost of a unit is 10 times bigger than the cost per time unit of testing. We wish that S.E.$\{\hat{\beta}_n\} = 0.1\beta$, and the expected cost should be minimized at $\beta = 100$ [hr]. What is the expected cost of this test, at $\beta = 100$, when $c_1 = \$1$ [hr].

Exercise 9.26 Dataset **WEIBUL.csv** contains the values of a random sample of size $n = 50$ from a Weibull distribution.

(i) Obtain MLE of the scale and shape parameters β and ν.
(ii) Use the MLE estimates

of β and ν, to obtain parametric bootstrap EBD of the distribution of $\hat{\beta}$, $\hat{\nu}$, with $M = 500$ runs. Estimate from this distribution the standard deviations of $\hat{\beta}$ and $\hat{\nu}$. Compare these estimates to the large sample approximations.

Exercise 9.27 In binomial life testing by a fixed size sample, how large should the sample be in order to discriminate between $R_0 = 0.99$ and $R_1 = 0.90$, with $\alpha = \beta = 0.01$? [α and β denote the probabilities of error of Type I and II.]

Exercise 9.28 Design the Wald SPRT for binomial life testing, in order to discriminate between $R_0 = 0.99$ and $R_1 = 0.90$, with $\alpha = \beta = 0.01$. What is the expected sample size, ASN, if $R = 0.9$?

Exercise 9.29 Design a Wald SPRT for exponential life distribution, to discriminate between $R_0 = 0.99$ and $R_1 = 0.90$, with $\alpha = \beta = 0.01$. What is the expected sample size, ASN, when $R = 0.90$?

Exercise 9.30 $n = 20$ computer monitors are put on accelerated life testing. The test is an SPRT for Poisson processes, based on the assumption that the TTF of a monitor, in those conditions, is exponentially distributed. The monitors are considered to be satisfactory if their MTBF is $\beta \geq 2000$ [hr] and considered to be unsatisfactory if $\beta \leq 1500$ [hr]. What is the expected length of the test if $\beta = 2000$ [hr].

Exercise 9.31 A product has an exponential life time with MTTF $\beta = 1,000$ [hr]. 1% of the products come out of production with MTTF of $\gamma = 500$ [hr]. A burn-in of $t^* = 300$ [hr] takes place. What is the expected life of units surviving the burn-in? Is such a long burn-in justified?

Chapter 10
Bayesian Reliability Estimation and Prediction

Preview It is often the case that information is available on the parameters of the life distributions from prior experiments or prior analysis of failure data. The Bayesian approach provides the methodology for formal incorporation of prior information with current data. This chapter presents reliability estimation and prediction from a Bayesian perspective. It introduces the reader to prior and posterior distributions used in Bayesian λ reliability inference, discusses loss functions and Bayesian estimators and nonparametric distribution-free Bayes estimators of reliability. A section is dedicated to Bayesian credibility and prediction intervals. A final section covers empirical Bayes methods.

10.1 Prior and Posterior Distributions

Let $X_1, \cdots, X_n$ be a random sample from a distribution with a p.d.f. $f(x; \boldsymbol{\theta})$, where $\boldsymbol{\theta} = (\theta_1, \cdots, \theta_k)$ is a vector of k parameters, belonging to a parameter space Θ. So far we assumed that the $\boldsymbol{\theta}$ is an unknown constant. In the Bayesian framework, $\boldsymbol{\theta}$ is considered a random vector with specified distribution. The distribution of $\boldsymbol{\theta}$ is called a **prior distribution**. The problem of which prior distribution to adopt for the Bayesian model is challenging, since the values of $\boldsymbol{\theta}$ are not directly observable. The discussion of this problem is beyond the scope of the book.

Let $h(\theta_1, \cdots, \theta_k)$ denote the joint p.d.f. of $(\theta_1, \cdots, \theta_k)$, corresponding to the prior distribution. This p.d.f. is called the **prior p.d.f.** of $\boldsymbol{\theta}$. The joint p.d.f. of X and $\boldsymbol{\theta}$ is

$$g(x, \boldsymbol{\theta}) = f(x; \boldsymbol{\theta})h(\boldsymbol{\theta}). \tag{10.1.1}$$

The marginal p.d.f. of X, which is called the **predictive p.d.f.**, is

$$f^*(x) = \int \underset{\Theta}{\cdots} \int f(x; \boldsymbol{\theta})h(\boldsymbol{\theta})\, \mathrm{d}\theta_1 \cdots \mathrm{d}\theta_k. \tag{10.1.2}$$

Supplementary Information The online version contains supplementary material available at (https://doi.org/10.1007/978-3-031-28482-3_10).

R. S. Kenett et al., *Industrial Statistics*, Statistics for Industry, Technology, and Engineering, https://doi.org/10.1007/978-3-031-28482-3_10

Furthermore, the conditional p.d.f. of $\boldsymbol{\theta}$ given $X = x$ is

$$h(\boldsymbol{\theta} \mid x) = g(x, \boldsymbol{\theta})/f^*(x). \tag{10.1.3}$$

This conditional p.d.f. is called the **posterior p.d.f.** of $\boldsymbol{\theta}$, given x. Thus, starting with a prior p.d.f., $h(\boldsymbol{\theta})$, we convert it, after observing the value of x, to the posterior p.d.f. of $\boldsymbol{\theta}$ given x.

If $x_1, \cdots, x_n$ is a random sample from a distribution with a p.d.f. $f(x; \boldsymbol{\theta})$ then the posterior p.d.f. of $\boldsymbol{\theta}$, corresponding to the prior p.d.f. $h(\boldsymbol{\theta})$, is

$$h(\boldsymbol{\theta} \mid \mathbf{x}) = \frac{\prod_{i=1}^{n} f(x_i; \boldsymbol{\theta}) h(\boldsymbol{\theta})}{\int \underset{\Theta}{\cdots} \int \prod_{i=1}^{n} f(x_i; \theta) h(\boldsymbol{\theta})\, \mathrm{d}\theta_1 \cdots \mathrm{d}\theta_k}. \tag{10.1.4}$$

For a given sample, $\mathbf{x}$, the posterior p.d.f. $h(\boldsymbol{\theta} \mid \mathbf{x})$ used in most types of Bayesian inference.

Example 10.1 **Binomial Distributions** $X \sim B(n; \theta)$, $0 < \theta < 1$.
The p.d.f. of X is

$$f(x; \theta) = \binom{n}{x} \theta^x (1-\theta)^{n-x}, \quad x = 0, \cdots, n.$$

Suppose that θ has a prior Beta distribution, with p.d.f.

$$h(\theta; \nu_1, \nu_2) = \frac{1}{B(\nu_1, \nu_2)} \theta^{\nu_1 - 1} (1-\theta)^{\nu_2 - 1}, \tag{10.1.5}$$

$0 < \theta < 1, 0 < \nu_1, \nu_2 < \infty$, where $B(a, b)$ is the **complete beta function**

$$\begin{aligned} B(a, b) &= \int_0^1 x^{a-1} (1-x)^{b-1}\, \mathrm{d}x \\ &= \frac{\Gamma(a)\Gamma(b)}{\Gamma(a+b)}. \end{aligned}$$

The posterior p.d.f. of θ, given $X = x$, is

$$h(\theta \mid x) = \frac{1}{B(\nu_1 + X, \nu_2 + n - X)} \theta^{\nu_1 + x - 1} (1-\theta)^{\nu_2 + n - x - 1}, \quad 0 < \theta < 1. \tag{10.1.6}$$

Notice that the posterior p.d.f. is also that of a Beta distribution, with parameters $\nu_1 + x$ and $\nu_2 + n - x$. The expected value of the posterior distribution of θ, given $X = x$, is

$$\begin{aligned} E\{\theta \mid x\} &= \frac{1}{B(\nu_1 + x, \nu_2 + n - x)} \int_0^1 \theta^{\nu_1 + x} (1-\theta)^{\nu_2 + n - x - 1}\, \mathrm{d}\theta \\ &= \frac{B(\nu_1 + x + 1, \nu_2 + n - x)}{B(\nu_1 + x, \nu_2 + n - x)} = \frac{\nu_1 + x}{\nu_1 + \nu_2 + n}. \end{aligned} \tag{10.1.7}$$

The function *updateBetaMixture*, available in the `mistat` package computes the posterior distribution for a mixture of betas prior distribution with proportion p. The inputs to this function are a mixture of beta distributions `betaMixture` and `data`, a list of the number of successes and number of failures in the sample. The mixture is characterized by the beta distributions and their mixing probabilities.

The example below consists of 12 Binomial trials. The Beta prior first parameter can be interpreted as the number of successes in 12 trials. The output of the function is an updated definition of the mixture—`probabilities` are the posterior mixing probabilities, and `distributions` the updated posterior beta densities.

In the example below, the prior distribution of the binomial parameter, θ, is split evenly between two Beta distributions, with expected values, 0.5 and 0.88, respectively. The Binomial experiment produced 10 successes in 12 trials, an estimated probability of success of 0.83, much closer to the second beta.

```
from mistat import bayes

betaMixture = bayes.Mixture(
    probabilities=[0.5, 0.5],
    distributions=[bayes.BetaDistribution(a=1, b=1),
                   bayes.BetaDistribution(a=15, b=2)])
data = [10, 2]
result = bayes.updateBetaMixture(betaMixture, data)
thetas = [round(d.theta(), 2) for d in result.distributions]

print(f'A posteriori: {result.probabilities}')
print(f'Updated beta distributions:\n{result.distributions}')
print(f'Update theta values:\n{thetas}')
```

```
A posteriori: [0.28455284552845506, 0.7154471544715449]
Updated beta distributions:
[BetaDistribution(a=11, b=3), BetaDistribution(a=25, b=4)]
Update theta values:
[0.79, 0.86]
```

A posteriori, the mix of beta distributions is 0.28 and 0.72, respectively, strongly favoring the second beta distribution. The expected values of the posterior beta distributions are 0.79 and 0.86, clearly more in line with the observed data. ■

Example 10.2 **Poisson Distributions** $X \sim P(\lambda), 0 < \lambda < \infty$.
The p.d.f. of X is

$$f(x; \lambda) = e^{-\lambda} \frac{\lambda^x}{x!}, \quad x = 0, 1, \cdots .$$

Suppose that the prior distribution of λ is the gamma distribution, $G(\nu, \tau)$. The prior p.d.f. is thus

$$h(\lambda; \nu, \tau) = \frac{1}{\tau^\nu \Gamma(\nu)} \lambda^{\nu-1} e^{-\lambda/\tau}. \tag{10.1.8}$$

The posterior p.d.f. of λ, given $X = x$, is

$$h(\lambda \mid x) = \frac{\lambda^{\nu+x-1}}{\left(\frac{\tau}{1+\tau}\right)^{\nu+x} \Gamma(\nu + x)} e^{-\lambda(1+\tau)/\tau}. \tag{10.1.9}$$

That is, the posterior distribution of λ, given $X = x$, is $G(\nu+x, \frac{\tau}{1+\tau})$. The posterior expectation of λ, given $X = x$, is $(\nu + x)\tau/(1 + \tau)$.

The function *updateGammaMixture* in the `mistat` package, computes the posterior distribution of λ. The inputs to this function are similar to the inputs to the function *updateBetaMixture* described above.

```
mixture = bayes.Mixture(
    probabilities=[0.5, 0.5],
    distributions=[
        bayes.GammaDistribution(shape=1, rate=1),
        bayes.GammaDistribution(shape=15, rate=2),
    ]
)
data = {'y': [5], 't': [1]}
result = bayes.updateGammaMixture(mixture, data)

print(f'A posteriori: {result.probabilities}')
print(f'Updated beta distributions:\n{result.distributions}')
```

```
A posteriori: [0.1250977996957064, 0.8749022003042937]
Updated beta distributions:
[GammaDistribution(shape=6, rate=2), GammaDistribution(shape=20,
rate=3)]
```

■

Example 10.3 **Exponential Distributions** $X \sim E(\beta)$.
The p.d.f. of X is

$$f(x; \beta) = \frac{1}{\beta} e^{-x/\beta}.$$

Let β have an inverse-gamma prior distribution, IG(ν, τ). That is, $\frac{1}{\beta} \sim G(\nu, \tau)$. The prior p.d.f. is

$$h(\beta; \nu, \tau) = \frac{1}{\tau^{\nu}\Gamma(\nu)\beta^{\nu+1}} e^{-1/\beta\tau}. \tag{10.1.10}$$

Then, the posterior p.d.f. of β, given $X = x$, is

$$h(\beta \mid x) = \frac{(1 + x\tau)^{\nu+1}}{\tau^{\nu+1}\Gamma(\nu + 1)\beta^{\nu+2}} e^{-(x+1/\tau)/\beta}. \tag{10.1.11}$$

That is, the posterior distribution of β, given $X = x$, is IG$(\nu + 1, \frac{\tau}{1+x\tau})$. The posterior expectation of β, given $X = x$, is $(x + 1/\tau)/(\nu + 1)$. ■

The likelihood function $L(\boldsymbol{\theta}; \mathbf{x})$ is a function over a parameter space Θ. In the definition of the posterior p.d.f. of $\boldsymbol{\theta}$, given $\mathbf{x}$, we see that any factor of $L(\boldsymbol{\theta}; \mathbf{x})$ which does not depend on $\boldsymbol{\theta}$ is irrelevant. For example, the binomial p.d.f., under θ, is

$$f(x;\theta) = \binom{n}{x}\theta^x(1-\theta)^{n-x}, \quad x = 0, 1, \cdots, n,$$

$0 < \theta < 1$. The factor $\binom{n}{x}$ can be omitted from the likelihood function in Bayesian calculations. The factor of the likelihood which depends on θ is called the **kernel** of the likelihood. In the above binomial example, $\theta^x(1-\theta)^{n-x}$ is the kernel of the binomial likelihood. If the prior p.d.f. of θ, $h(\theta)$, is of the same functional form (up to a proportionality factor which does not depend on θ) as that of the likelihood kernel, we call that prior p.d.f. a **conjugate** one. As shown in Examples 10.1 to 10.3, the beta prior distributions are conjugate to the binomial model, the gamma prior distributions are conjugate to the Poisson model and the inverse-gamma priors are conjugate to the exponential model.

If a conjugate prior distribution is applied, the posterior distribution belongs to the conjugate family.

One of the fundamental problems in Bayesian analysis is that of the choice of a prior distribution of θ. From a Bayesian point of view, the prior distribution should reflect the prior knowledge of the analyst on the parameter of interest. It is often difficult to express the prior belief about the value of $\boldsymbol{\theta}$ in a p.d.f. form. We find that analysts apply, whenever possible, conjugate priors whose means and standard deviations may reflect the prior beliefs. Another common approach is to use a "diffused," "vague" or Jeffrey's prior, which is proportional to $|I(\theta)|^{1/2}$, where $I(\theta)$ is the Fisher information function (matrix). For further reading on this subject the reader is referred to Box and Tiao (1992), Good (2003) and Press (1989).

10.2 Loss Functions and Bayes Estimators

In order to define Bayes estimators we must first specify a **loss function**, $L(\hat{\boldsymbol{\theta}}, \boldsymbol{\theta})$, which represents the cost involved in using the estimate $\hat{\boldsymbol{\theta}}$ when the true value is $\boldsymbol{\theta}$. Often this loss is taken to be a function of the distance between the estimate and the true value, i.e., $|\hat{\boldsymbol{\theta}} - \boldsymbol{\theta}|$. In such cases, the loss function is written as

$$L(\hat{\boldsymbol{\theta}}, \boldsymbol{\theta}) = W(|\hat{\boldsymbol{\theta}} - \boldsymbol{\theta}|).$$

Examples of such loss functions are

$$\text{Squared-error loss:} \quad W(|\hat{\boldsymbol{\theta}} - \boldsymbol{\theta}|) = (\hat{\boldsymbol{\theta}} - \boldsymbol{\theta})^2,$$

$$\text{Absolute error loss:} \quad W(|\hat{\boldsymbol{\theta}} - \boldsymbol{\theta}|) = |\hat{\boldsymbol{\theta}} - \boldsymbol{\theta}|.$$

The loss function does not have to be symmetric. For example, we may consider the function

$$L(\hat{\theta}, \theta) = \begin{cases} \alpha(\theta - \hat{\theta}), & \text{if } \hat{\theta} \le \theta \\ \beta(\hat{\theta} - \theta), & \text{if } \hat{\theta} > \theta \end{cases},$$

where α and β are some positive constants.

The **Bayes estimator** of $\boldsymbol{\theta}$, with respect to a loss function $L(\hat{\boldsymbol{\theta}}, \boldsymbol{\theta})$, is defined as the value of $\hat{\boldsymbol{\theta}}$ which minimizes the **posterior risk**, given x, where the posterior risk is the expected loss with respect to the posterior distribution. For example, suppose that the p.d.f. of X depends on several parameters $\theta_1, \cdots, \theta_k$, but we wish to derive a Bayes estimator of θ_1 with respect to the squared-error loss function. We consider the marginal posterior p.d.f. of θ_1, given **x**, $h(\theta_1 \mid x)$. The posterior risk is

$$R(\hat{\theta}_1, \mathbf{x}) = \int (\hat{\theta}_1 - \theta_1)^2 h(\theta_1 \mid \mathbf{x}) \, d\theta_1.$$

It is easily shown that the value of $\hat{\theta}_1$ which minimizes the posterior risk $R(\hat{\theta}_1, \mathbf{x})$ is the **posterior expectation** of θ_1:

$$E\{\theta_1 \mid \mathbf{x}\} = \int \theta_1 h(\theta_1 \mid \mathbf{x}) \, d\theta_1.$$

If the loss function is $L(\hat{\theta}_1, \hat{\theta}) = |\hat{\theta}_1 - \theta_1|$, the Bayes estimator of θ_1 is the **median** of the posterior distribution of θ_1 given **x**.

10.2.1 Distribution-Free Bayes Estimator of Reliability

Let J_n denote the number of failures in a random sample of size n, during the period $[0, t)$. The reliability of the device on test at age t is $R(t) = 1 - F(t)$, where $F(t)$ is the CDF of the life distribution. Let $K_n = n - J_n$. The distribution of K_n is the binomial $B(n, R(t))$. Suppose that the prior distribution of $R(t)$ is uniform on $(0, 1)$. This prior distribution reflects our initial state of ignorance concerning the actual value of $R(t)$.

The uniform distribution is a special case of the Beta distribution with $\nu_1 = 1$ and $\nu_2 = 1$. Hence, according to Example 10.1, the posterior distribution of $R(t)$, given K_n, is a Beta distribution with parameters $\nu_1 = K_n + 1$ and $\nu_2 = 1 + n - K_n$. Hence, the Bayes estimator of $R(t)$, with respect to the squared-error loss function, is

$$\begin{aligned} \hat{R}(t; K_n) &= E\{R(t) \mid K_n\} \\ &= \frac{K_n + 1}{n + 2}. \end{aligned} \tag{10.2.1}$$

If the sample size is $n = 50$, and $K_{50} = 27$, the Bayes estimator of $R(t)$ is $\hat{R}(t;27) = 28/52 = 0.538$. Notice that the MLE of $R(t)$ is $\hat{R}_{50} = 27/50 = 0.540$. The sample size is sufficiently large for the MLE and the Bayes estimator to be numerically close. If the loss function is $|\hat{R} - R|$, the Bayes estimator of R is the median of the posterior distribution of $R(t)$ given K_n, i.e., the median of the beta distribution with parameters $\nu_1 = K_n + 1$ and $\nu_2 = n - K_n + 1$.

Generally, if ν_1 and ν_2 are integers then the median of the beta distribution is

$$\text{Me} = \frac{\nu_1 F_{0.5}[2\nu_1, 2\nu_2]}{\nu_2 + \nu_1 F_{0.5}[2\nu_1, 2\nu_2]}, \tag{10.2.2}$$

where $F_{0.5}[j_1, j_2]$ is the median of the $F[j_1, j_2]$ distribution. Substituting $\nu_1 = K_n + 1$ and $\nu_2 = n - K_n + 1$ in (10.2.2), we obtain that the Bayes estimator of $R(t)$ with respect to the absolute error loss is

$$\hat{R}(t) = \frac{(K_n + 1)F_{0.5}[2K_n + 2, 2n + 2 - 2K_n]}{n + 1 - K_n + (K_n + 1)F_{0.5}[2K_n + 2, 2n + 2 - 2K_n]}. \tag{10.2.3}$$

Numerically, for $n = 50$, $K_n = 27$, $F_{0.5}[56, 48] = 1.002$, and $\hat{R}(t) = 0.539$. The two Bayes estimates are very close.

10.2.2 Bayes Estimator of Reliability for Exponential Life Distributions

Consider a Type II censored sample of size n from an exponential distribution, $E(\beta)$, with censoring at the r-th failure. Let $t_{(1)} \leq t_{(2)} \leq \cdots \leq t_{(r)}$ be the ordered failure times. For squared-error loss, the Bayes estimator of $R(t) = e^{-t/\beta}$ is given by

$$\begin{aligned} \hat{R}(t) &= E\{R(t) \mid t_{(1)}, \cdots, t_{(r)}\} \\ &= E\{e^{-t/\beta} \mid t_{(1)}, \cdots, t_{(r)}\}. \end{aligned} \tag{10.2.4}$$

This conditional expectation can be computed by integrating $e^{-t/\beta}$ with respect to the posterior distribution of β, given $t_{(1)}, \cdots, t_{(r)}$.

Suppose that the prior distribution of β is IG(ν, τ). One can easily verify that the posterior distribution of β given $t_{(1)}, \cdots, t_{(r)}$ is the inverted-gamma IG$(\nu + r, \frac{\tau}{1+T_{n,r}\tau})$ where $T_{n,r} = \sum_{i=1}^{r} t_{(i)} + (n - r)t_{(r)}$. Hence, the Bayes estimator of $R(t) = \exp(-t/\beta)$ is, for squared-error loss,

$$
\begin{aligned}
\hat{R}(t) &= \frac{(1+T_{n,r}\tau)^{r+\nu}}{\tau^{r+\nu}\Gamma(r+\nu)} \int_0^\infty \frac{1}{\beta^{r+\nu+1}} \exp\left(-\frac{1}{\beta}\left(T_{n,r}+\frac{1}{\tau}+t\right)\right) \mathrm{d}\beta \\
&= \left(\frac{1+T_{n,r}\tau}{1+(T_{n,r}+t)\tau}\right)^{r+\nu}.
\end{aligned}
\tag{10.2.5}
$$

Note that the estimator only depends on n through $T_{n,r}$.

In the following table we provide a few values of the Bayes estimator $\hat{R}(t)$ for selected values of t, when $\nu = 3$, $r = 23$, $T_{n,r} = 2242$ and $\tau = 10^{-2}$, along with the corresponding MLE, which is

$$
\text{MLE} = e^{-t/\hat{\beta}_{n,r}} = e^{-rt/T_{n,r}}.
$$

t	50	100	150	200
$\hat{R}(t)$	0.577	0.337	0.199	0.119
MLE	0.599	0.359	0.215	0.129

If we have a series structure of k modules, and the TTF of each module is exponentially distributed, then formula (10.2.5) is extended to

$$
\hat{R}_{sys}(t) = \prod_{i=1}^{k} \left(1 - \frac{t\tau_i}{1+T_{n,r_i}^{(i)}\tau_i + t\tau_i}\right)^{\gamma_i+\nu_i}, \tag{10.2.6}
$$

where $T_{n,r_i}^{(i)}$ is the total time on test statistic for the i-th module, r_i is the censoring frequency of the observations on the i-th module, τ_i and ν_i are the prior parameters for the i-th module. As in (10.2.5), (10.2.6) is the Bayes estimator for the squared-error loss, under the assumption that the MTTFs of the various modules are priorly independent. In a similar manner one can write a formula for the Bayes estimator of the reliability of a system having a parallel structure.

10.3 Bayesian Credibility and Prediction Intervals

Bayesian credibility intervals at level γ are intervals $C_\gamma(\mathbf{x})$ in the parameter space Θ, for which the posterior probability that $\boldsymbol{\theta} \in C_\gamma(\mathbf{x})$ is at least γ, i.e.,

$$
\Pr\{\theta \in C_\gamma(\mathbf{x}) \mid \mathbf{x}\} \geq \gamma. \tag{10.3.1}
$$

$\Pr\{E \mid \mathbf{x}\}$ denotes the posterior probability of the event E, given $\mathbf{x}$. The Bayesian credibility interval for θ, given $\mathbf{x}$, has an entirely different interpretation than that of the confidence intervals discussed in the previous sections. While the confidence level of the classical confidence interval is based on the sample-to-sample variability of the interval, for fixed θ, the credibility level of the Bayesian credibility interval is based on the presumed variability of θ, for a fixed sample.

10.3.1 Distribution-Free Reliability Estimation

In Sect. 10.2.1 we develop the Bayes estimator, with respect to squared-error loss, of the reliability at age t, $R(t)$, when the data available are the number of sample units which survive at age t, namely K_n. We have seen that the posterior distribution of $R(t)$, given K_n, for a uniform prior is the Beta distribution with $\nu_1 = K_n + 1$ and $\nu_2 = n - K_n + 1$. The Bayesian credibility interval at level γ is the interval whose limits are the ϵ_1- and ϵ_2-quantiles of the posterior distribution, where $\epsilon_1 = (1-\gamma)/2$, $\epsilon_2 = (1+\gamma)/2$. These limits can be determined with aid of R, getting the quantile of the F-distribution, according to the formulae

$$\text{Lower limit} = \frac{(K_n + 1)}{(K_n + 1) + (n - K_n + 1)F_{\epsilon_2}[2n + 2 - 2K_n, 2K_n + 2]} \tag{10.3.2}$$

and

$$\text{Upper limit} = \frac{(K_n + 1)F_{\epsilon_2}[2K_n + 2, 2n + 2 - 2K_n]}{(n - K_n + 1) + (K_n + 1)F_{\epsilon_2}[2K_n + 2, 2n + 2 - 2K_n]}. \tag{10.3.3}$$

In Sect. 10.2.1 we considered the case of $n = 50$ and $K_n = 27$. For $\gamma = 0.95$ we need

$$F_{0.975}[48, 56] = 1.725$$

and

$$F_{0.975}[56, 48] = 1.746.$$

Thus, the Bayesian credibility limits obtained for $R(t)$ are 0.403 and 0.671. Recall the Bayes estimator was 0.538.

10.3.2 Exponential Reliability Estimation

In Sect. 10.2.2 we develop a formula for the Bayes estimator of the reliability function $R(t) = \exp(-t/\beta)$ for Type II censored data. We saw that if the prior on β is $\text{IG}(\nu, \tau)$ then the posterior distribution of β, given the data, is $\text{IG}(\nu + r, \tau/(1 + \tau T_{n,r})$. Thus, γ level Bayes credibility limits for β are given by $\beta_{L,\gamma}$ (lower limit) and $B_{U,\gamma}$ (upper limit), where

$$\beta_{L,\gamma} = \frac{T_{n,r} + 1/\tau}{G_{\epsilon_2}(\nu + r, 1)} \tag{10.3.4}$$

and

$$\beta_{U,\gamma} = \frac{T_{n,r} + 1/\tau}{G_{\epsilon_1}(\nu + r, 1)}. \tag{10.3.5}$$

Moreover, if ν is an integer then we can replace $G_p(\nu + r, 1)$ by $\frac{1}{2}\chi^2_p[2\nu + 2r]$. Finally, since $R(t) = \exp(-t/\beta)$ is an increasing function of β, the γ-level Bayes credibility limits for $R(t)$ are

$$R_{L,\gamma}(t) = \exp(-t/\beta_{L,\gamma}) \tag{10.3.6}$$

and

$$R_{U,\gamma}(t) = \exp(-t/\beta_{U,\gamma}). \tag{10.3.7}$$

If we consider the values $\nu = 3$, $r = 23$, $T_{n,r} = 2242$, and $\tau = 10^{-2}$ we need for $\gamma = 0.95$, $\chi^2_{0.025}[52] = 33.53$ and $\chi^2_{0.975}[52] = 73.31$. Thus,

$$\beta_{L,0.95} = 63.91 \quad \text{and} \quad \beta_{U,0.95} = 139.73.$$

The corresponding Bayesian credibility limits for $R(t)$, at $t = 50$, are $R_{L,0.95}(50) = 0.457$ and $R_{U,0.95}(50) = 0.699$.

10.3.3 Prediction Intervals

In Sect. 10.3.2 we introduce the notion of prediction intervals of level γ. This notion can be adapted to the Bayesian framework in the following manner.

Let $\mathbf{X}$ be a sample from a distribution governed by a parameter θ; we assume that θ has a prior distribution. Let $h(\theta \mid \mathbf{x})$ denote the posterior p.d.f. of θ, given $\mathbf{X} = \mathbf{x}$. $\mathbf{x}$ represents the values of a random sample already observed. We are interested in predicting the value of some statistic $T(\mathbf{Y})$ based on a future sample $\mathbf{Y}$ from the same distribution. Let $g(t;\theta)$ denote the p.d.f. of $T(\mathbf{Y})$ under θ. Then the **predictive distribution** of $T(\mathbf{Y})$, given $\mathbf{x}$, is

$$g^*(t \mid \mathbf{x}) = \int_\Theta g(t;\theta)h(\theta \mid \mathbf{x})\,d\theta. \tag{10.3.8}$$

A **Bayesian prediction interval** of level γ for $T(Y)$, given $\mathbf{x}$, is an interval $(T_L(\mathbf{x}), T_U(\mathbf{x}))$ which contains a proportion γ of the predictive distribution, i.e., satisfying

$$\int_{T_L(\mathbf{x})}^{T_U(\mathbf{x})} g^*(t \mid \mathbf{x})\,dt = \gamma. \tag{10.3.9}$$

Generally, the limits are chosen so that the tail areas are each $(1-\gamma/2)$. We illustrate the derivation of a Bayesian prediction interval in the following example.

Example 10.4 Consider a device with an exponential lifetime distribution $E(\beta)$. We test a random sample of n of these, stopping at the r-th failure. Suppose the prior distribution of β is IG(ν,τ). Then, as seen in Sect. 10.2.2, the posterior distribution of β given the ordered failure times $t_{(1)},\cdots,t_{(r)}$ is IG$(\nu+r, \frac{\tau}{1+T_{n,r}\tau})$, where $T_{n,r} = \sum_{i=1}^{r} t_{(i)} + (n-r)t_{(r)}$.

Suppose we have an additional s such devices, to be used one at a time in some system, replacing each one immediately upon failure by another. We are interested in a prediction interval of level γ for T, the time until all s devices have been used up. Letting $\mathbf{Y} = (Y_1,\cdots,Y_s)$ be the lifetimes of the devices, we have $T(\mathbf{Y}) = \sum_{i=1}^{s} Y_i$. Thus, $T(\mathbf{y})$ has a $G(s,\beta)$ distribution. Substituting in (10.3.8), it is easily shown that the predictive p.d.f. of $T(\mathbf{Y})$, given $t_{(1)},\cdots,t_{(r)}$, is

$$g^*(t \mid t_{(1)},\cdots,t_{(r)}) = \left(B(s,\nu+r)(T_{n,r}+1/\tau)\right)^{-1} \cdot \left(\frac{\tau}{t+T_{n,r}+1/\tau}\right)^{s-1}\left(\frac{T_{n,r}+1/\tau}{t+T_{n,r}+1/\tau}\right)^{r+\nu+1}. \tag{10.3.10}$$

Making the transformation

$$U = (T_{n,r}+1/\tau)/(T(\mathbf{Y})+T_{n,r}+1/\tau)$$

one can show that the predictive distribution of U given $t_{(1)},\cdots,t_{(r)}$ is the Beta$(r+\nu,s)$ distribution. If we let $\text{Be}_{\epsilon_1}(r+\nu,s)$ and $\text{Be}_{\epsilon_2}(r+\nu,s)$ be the ϵ_1—and ϵ_2-quantiles of Beta $(r+\nu,s)$, where $\epsilon_1 = (1-\gamma)/2$ and $\epsilon_2 = (1+\gamma)/2$, then the lower and upper Bayesian prediction limits for $T(\mathbf{Y})$ are

$$T_L = \left(T_{n,r}+\frac{1}{\tau}\right)\left(\frac{1}{\text{Be}_{\epsilon_2}(\nu+r,s)}-1\right) \tag{10.3.11}$$

and

$$T_U = \left(T_{n,r} + \frac{1}{\tau}\right)\left(\frac{1}{\mathrm{Be}_{\epsilon_1}(\nu + r, s)} - 1\right). \qquad (10.3.12)$$

If ν is an integer, the prediction limits can be expressed as

$$T_L = \left(T_{n,r} + \frac{1}{\tau}\right)\frac{s}{\nu + r}F_{\epsilon_1}[2s, 2\nu + 2r] \qquad (10.3.13)$$

and

$$T_U = \left(T_{n,r} + \frac{1}{\tau}\right)\frac{s}{\nu + r}F_{\epsilon_2}[2s, 2\nu + 2r].$$

Formulae (10.3.12) and (10.3.13) are applied in the following example:

Twenty computer monitors are put on test starting at time $t_0 = 0$. The test is terminated at the sixth failure ($r = 6$). The total time on test was $T_{20,6} = 75{,}805.6$ [hr]. We wish to predict the time till failure [hr] of monitors which are shipped to customers. Assuming that TTF $\sim E(\beta)$ and ascribing β a prior IG$(5, 10^{-3})$ distribution, we compute the prediction limits T_L and T_U for $s = 1$, at level $\gamma = 0.95$.

In this case $2\nu + 2r = 22$ and $F_{0.025}[2, 22] = 1/F_{0.975}[22, 2] = 1/39.45 = 0.0253$. Moreover, $F_{0.975}[2, 22] = 4.38$. Thus,

$$T_L = 76805.6\frac{1}{11} \times 0.0253 = 176.7 \text{ [hr]}$$

and

$$T_U = 76805.6\frac{1}{11} \times 4.38 = 30,582.6 \text{ [hr]}.$$

We have high confidence that a monitor in the field will not fail before 175 h of operation. ■

10.3.4 Applications with Python: Lifelines and pymc

In Sect. 9.7.2 we discussed the maximum likelihood estimation of the scale parameter β and the shape parameter ν of the Weibull life distribution. We saw that the estimation of the scale parameter, when the shape parameter is known, is straight forward and simple. On the other hand, when the shape parameter is unknown, the estimation requires an iterative solution which converges to the correct estimates. The analysis there was done for uncensored data. In reliability life testing we often encounter right censored data, when at termination of the study some systems have not failed. With censored data, the likelihood function has to be modified, and the maximum likelihood estimation is more complicated.

In this section we show how to use Python, in order to derive an analysis of right censored data. We apply methods described in Chaps. 9 and 10 to the dataset **SYSTEMFAILURE.csv**. The dataset **SYSTEMFAILURE.csv** consists of 208 observations on systems operating at 90 geographically dispersed sites. Twelve systems are newly installed and are labeled as "Young." All the other systems are labeled "Mature." Out of the 208 observations, 68 (33%) report time stamps of a failure (uncensored). The other observations are censored, as indicated by the value 1 in the censor variable column. We are interested in the estimated failure rate at 3,000,000 time units of operation.

A measure of time, the time stamp, is recorded for each observation in the data. This variable is presented in operational units (activity time), at time of observation. The bigger the time, the longer the system performed. The observations with a value 0 of the censor variable, represent length of operation till failure of the systems.

Before we build models, we preprocess the data. To avoid numerical problems due to the large values of the time unit, we divide the time stamp by 1,000,000.

```
systemFailure = mistat.load_data('SYSTEMFAILURE')
systemFailure['Time stamp'] = systemFailure['Time stamp'] / 1_000_000
systemFailure['Young'] = [0 if v == 'Mature' else 1
                          for v in systemFailure['System Maturity']]
systemFailure = systemFailure[['Time stamp', 'Censor', 'Young']]
systemFailure.head()
```

	Time stamp	Censor	Young
0	1.574153	1	0
1	2.261043	0	0
2	1.726097	1	0
3	1.178089	1	0
4	1.354856	1	0

As a first analysis we fit a parametric Weibull model using `lifelines`.

```
kmf = lifelines.WeibullFitter()
kmf.fit(systemFailure['Time stamp'], event_observed=systemFailure['Censor']==0)
print(f'Scale: {kmf.lambda_:.3f}')
print(f'Shape: {kmf.rho_:.4f}')
```

```
Scale: 4.351
Shape: 0.7226
```

The estimated Weibull scale and shape parameters are 4.351 and 0.723, respectively. Note that notation in the `lifelines` package are `lambda_` for the scale β and `rho_` for the shape ν parameters of the Weibull distribution $W(\nu, \beta)$.

In Fig. 10.1 we see the estimated failure rate together with its confidence region. The profile shows an estimate of the probability that a system fails before the designated 3,000,000 time units. At this designated time, the estimated probability is P = 53.4%. This estimator has a 95% confidence interval of (44.1%–63.2%).

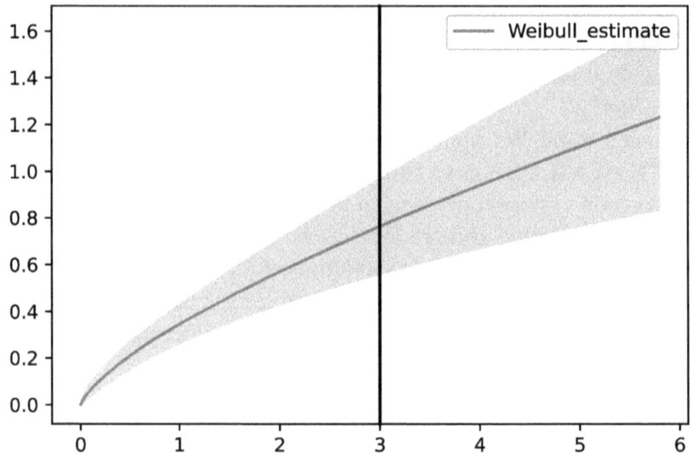

Fig. 10.1 Distribution profile of parametric Weibull model fitted to system failure data

```
failureRate = 1 - kmf.predict(3_000_000 / 1_000_000)
ciCumDensity = kmf.confidence_interval_cumulative_density_
fr_low, fr_high = ciCumDensity[ciCumDensity.index > 3].iloc[0,]

print('Parameteric model:')
print(f'Mean of failure rates at 3,000,000: {failureRate:.3f}')
print(f'95%-confidence interval at 3,000,000: [{fr_low:.3f}, {fr_high:.3f}]')
```

```
Parameteric model:
Mean of failure rates at 3,000,000: 0.534
95%-confidence interval at 3,000,000: [0.441, 0.632]
```

An alternative to the parameteric fit, is to use Bayesian inference. The pymc package is a Python package that uses advanced Markov chain Monte Carlo (MCMC) algorithms for Bayesian statistical modeling and probabilistic machine learning.

We describe the likelihood for the observed data using a Weibull distribution $W(\nu, \beta)$. The Weibull distribution is implemented in pymc using *pm.Weibull* (the argument `alpha` represents the shape parameter ν and `beta` the scale β). To include the censored data, we require the logarithm of the Weibull survival function defined as:

$$W_{\text{survival}}(t; \nu, \beta) = e^{-\left(\frac{t}{\beta}\right)^{\nu}}.$$

```
def weibull_log_sf(y, nu, beta):
    return - T.exp(nu * T.log(y / beta))
```

Using this function, the pymc model is defined as:

```
# extract observed and censored observations a numpy arrays
censored = systemFailure['Censor'].values == 1
y_observed = systemFailure['Time stamp'][~censored].values
y_censored = systemFailure['Time stamp'][censored].values

with pm.Model() as weibull_model_uninformative:
    beta = pm.Uniform('beta', lower=0.5, upper=10) # scale
    nu = pm.Uniform('nu', lower=0.5, upper=1.1) # shape

    y_obs = pm.Weibull('y_obs', alpha=nu, beta=beta, observed=y_observed)
    y_cens = pm.Potential('y_cens', weibull_log_sf(y_censored, nu, beta))
```

The model first defines the prior distributions for the `beta` and `nu` parameters of the Weibull distribution. This is then associated with the observed failures. The likelihood of the uncensored data is combined with the likelihood, the logarithm of the survival function, of the censored failure information.

The `pymc` package uses Hamiltonian Monte Carlo with a no U-turn sampler (NUTS) to explore the (β, ν) parameter space with respect to the likelihood information. For details see Salvatier et al. (2016). The model is trained using the *sample* function.

```
with weibull_model_uninformative:
    trace_uninformative = pm.sample(1000, random_seed=123, progressbar=False,
                                    return_inferencedata=True)
```

```
Auto-assigning NUTS sampler...
Initializing NUTS using jitter+adapt_diag...
Multiprocess sampling (4 chains in 4 jobs)
NUTS: [beta, nu]
Sampling 4 chains for 1_000 tune and 1_000 draw iterations (4_000 +
4_000 draws total) took 3 seconds.
```

```
with weibull_model_uninformative:
    az.plot_trace(trace_uninformative)
plt.tight_layout()
```

There are a number of diagnostic plots used to analyze the model training. The trace plot shows the resulting posterior distribution and the change of the parameters β and ν in the chains. The trace plot in Fig. 10.2 shows no unusual behavior.

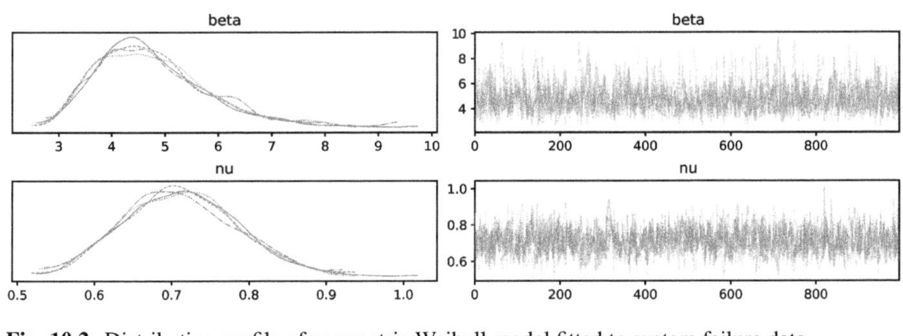

Fig. 10.2 Distribution profile of parametric Weibull model fitted to system failure data

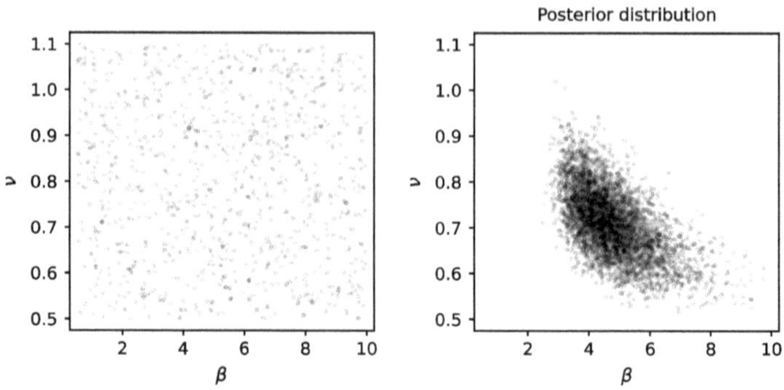

Fig. 10.3 Parameter values sampled from prior and posterior distribution of a Weibull model fitted to system failure data using uninformative priors

It is also interesting to compare the prior and posterior distributions of the model parameters. Figure 10.3 shows that the uniform prior distribution is uninformative and not biased toward the actual values. If domain knowledge is available, the uninformative priors can be replaced with biased, informative priors. The following model replaces the uniform distribution with gamma distributions centered around the area of high probability of the parameters.

```
with pm.Model() as weibull_model_informative:
    beta = pm.Gamma('beta', alpha=4.5 * 7, beta=7) # scale
    nu = pm.Gamma('nu', alpha=0.7 * 100, beta=100) #shape

    y_obs = pm.Weibull('y_obs', alpha=nu, beta=beta, observed=y_observed)
    y_cens = pm.Potential('y_cens', weibull_log_sf(y_censored, nu, beta))

    trace_informative = pm.sample(1000, random_seed=123, progressbar=False,
                                  return_inferencedata=True)
```

```
Auto-assigning NUTS sampler...
Initializing NUTS using jitter+adapt_diag...
Multiprocess sampling (4 chains in 4 jobs)
NUTS: [beta, nu]
Sampling 4 chains for 1_000 tune and 1_000 draw iterations (4_000 +
4_000 draws total) took 2 seconds.
```

Figure 10.4 shows that using informative priors leads to a more thorough sampling of the area of higher likelihood, leading to a tighter distribution of the parameter values. In both cases, the resulting

We can now use the Bayesian model to derive estimates for the probability of system failure at 3,000,000 time units. In order to make our analysis more concise we first define two utility functions. The function *sampleFailureRates* uses the model and the training trace to sample pairs of ν and β parameters from the posterior distribution. The values are used with the *weibull_min* distribution from `scipy` to derive failure rate curves for time points in the range 0 to 10.

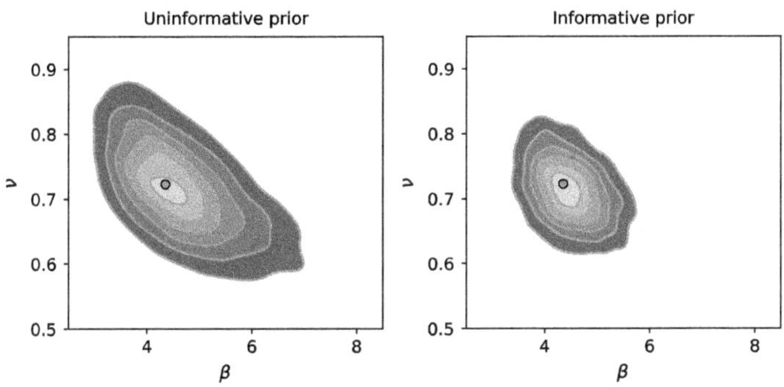

Fig. 10.4 Distribution of sampled parameter values using models defined with uninformative and informative priors

```
def sampleFailureRates(model, model_trace, nu_var='nu', beta_var='beta'):
    t_plot = np.linspace(0, 10, 101)
    t_plot[0] = 0.00001
    with model:
        pp_trace = pm.sample_posterior_predictive(model_trace,
            var_names=[nu_var, beta_var], progressbar=False, random_seed=123)
    sampled = az.extract_dataset(pp_trace.posterior_predictive)
    curves = [stats.weibull_min.cdf(t_plot, nu, scale=beta)
              for beta, nu in zip(sampled[beta_var], sampled[nu_var])]
    curves = np.array(curves)
    return {'time': t_plot, 'failure_rates': curves,
            'mean_failure_rate': np.mean(curves, axis=0)}
```

Using the ensemble of failure rate curves, we derive the mean and 95%-highest posterior density (HPD) interval at a given time using the function *estimatedFailureRate*.

```
def estimatedFailureRate(failureRates, at_time=3.0):
    idx = np.argmax(failureRates['time'] >= at_time)
    curves = failureRates['failure_rates']
    failure_rate = np.mean(curves, axis=0)[idx]
    print(f'Mean of failure rates at 3,000,000: {failure_rate:.3f}')
    hdi_95 = az.hdi(np.array(curves), hdi_prob=0.95)[idx, :]
    print(f'95%-HPD at 3,000,000: {hdi_95.round(3)}')
    return failure_rate
```

We now apply these utility functions to our two models.

```
sampledCurves = sampleFailureRates(weibull_model_uninformative,
                                   trace_uninformative)
_ = estimatedFailureRate(sampledCurves)


sampledCurvesInformative = sampleFailureRates(weibull_model_informative,
                                              trace_informative)
_ = estimatedFailureRate(sampledCurvesInformative)
```

```
Sampling: [beta, nu]
Sampling: [beta, nu]
Mean of failure rates at 3,000,000: 0.530
95%-HPD at 3,000,000: [0.247 0.907]
Mean of failure rates at 3,000,000: 0.534
95%-HPD at 3,000,000: [0.446 0.625]
```

Table 10.1 Estimated failure rates and 95%-HPD at 3,000,000 time units

Model	Failure rate	95%-CI or 95%-HPD
Parametric estimate	53.4%	[44.1%–63.2%]
Uninformative priors	52.0%	[42.2%–61.4%]
Informative priors	53.1%	[46.8%–59.0%]

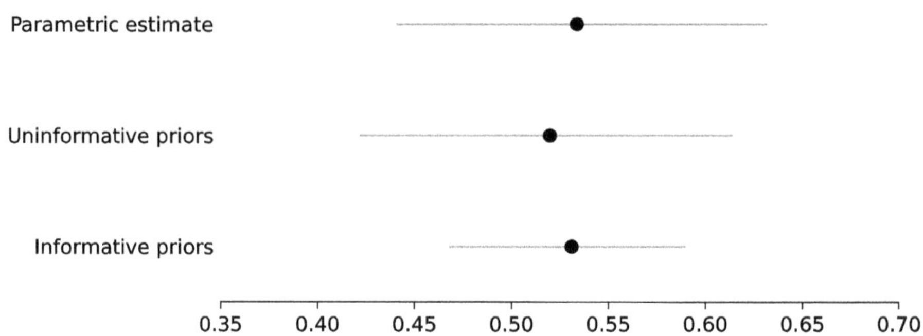

The results are summarized in Table 10.1. We can see that the mean failure rate estimates of all three models are comparable. The uniform prior is reflecting the lack of prior information. It reduced the point estimate. The informative prior is a more pointed prior and this produced a predictive value equal to the parametric point estimate with a shorter HPD than the corresponding confidence interval. Note that the interpretation of the HPD is probabilistic, making assertions on the posterior failure rate probabilities while the confidence interval refers to a statement on the long-term coverage of the intervals constructed by this method.

To conclude Chaps. 9 and 10 on reliability, we refer again to **SYSTEMFAILURE.csv** and assess the impact on reliability of the maturity level of the system. As mentioned, we have 12 systems labeled as "Young," are they behaving differently?

We extend the model with the vague, uninformative priors to estimate the parameters for both mature and young systems at the same time. The trace of the sampling process is shown in Fig. 10.5.

```
# split the events both by their censored and young status
censored = systemFailure['Censor'].values == 1
young = systemFailure['Young'].values == 1

y_observed = systemFailure['Time stamp'][~censored & ~young].values
y_censored = systemFailure['Time stamp'][censored & ~young].values
y_observed_young = systemFailure['Time stamp'][~censored & young].values
y_censored_young = systemFailure['Time stamp'][censored & young].values

with pm.Model() as weibull_model_maturity:
    beta = pm.Uniform('beta', lower=0.5, upper=10) # scale
    nu = pm.Uniform('nu', lower=0.5, upper=1.1) # shape
    beta_young = pm.Uniform('beta_young', lower=0, upper=10) # scale
    nu_young = pm.Uniform('nu_young', lower=0, upper=1.1) # shape

    y_obs = pm.Weibull('y_obs', alpha=nu, beta=beta, observed=y_observed)
    y_cens = pm.Potential('y_cens', weibull_log_sf(y_censored, nu, beta))
    y_obs_young = pm.Weibull('y_obs_young', alpha=nu_young, beta=beta_young,
            observed=y_observed_young)
    y_cens_young = pm.Potential('y_cens_young', weibull_log_sf(y_censored_young,
                                                    nu_young, beta_young))

    trace_maturity = pm.sample(2000, tune=3500, random_seed=123,
          progressbar=False, return_inferencedata=True)
```

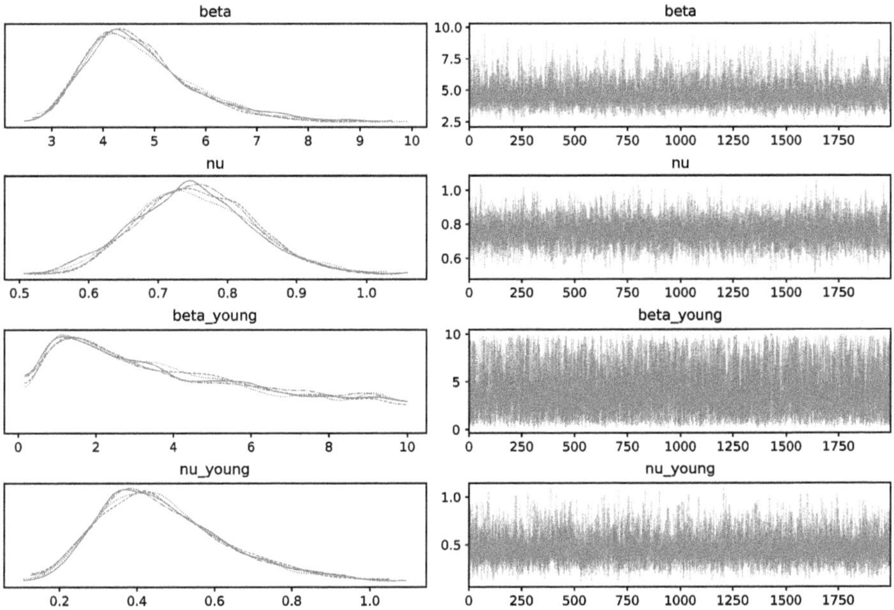

Fig. 10.5 Trace of sampling of Weibull model fitted to system failure data separating between young and mature systems. Observed events are overlaid in circles (mature) and squares (young)

```
Auto-assigning NUTS sampler...
Initializing NUTS using jitter+adapt_diag...
Multiprocess sampling (4 chains in 4 jobs)
NUTS: [beta, nu, beta_young, nu_young]
Sampling 4 chains for 3_500 tune and 2_000 draw iterations (14_000 +
8_000 draws total) took 11 seconds.
```

We see a difference between the mature and young systems. The estimated failure rates and their 95% HPD intervals are shown in Fig. 10.6. As expected, mature systems have lower failure rates. This is often experienced in new product introduction with early deployment problems affecting the young systems. The failure rates at 3,000,000 time units are:

	Failure rate	95%-HPD
Mature systems	51.8%	[42.3%–61.4%]
Young system	64.7%	[43.0%–94.6%]

The uncertainty is very wide for the young systems, due to the small number of data points.

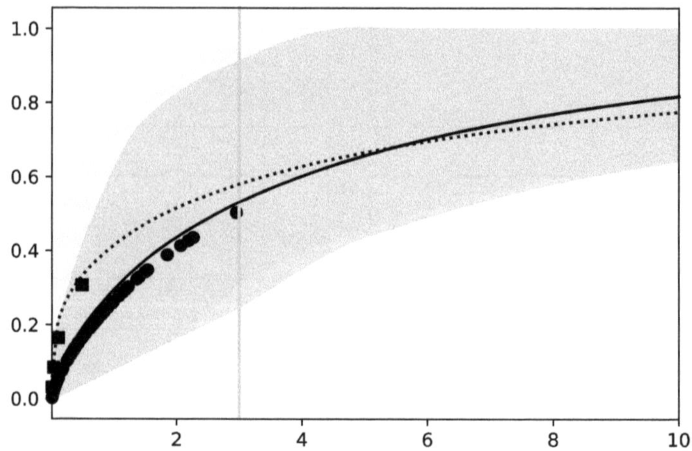

Fig. 10.6 Bayesian estimated failure rates 95% HPD intervals for mature (dark grey, solid line) and young (light grey, dotted line) systems

10.4 Credibility Intervals for the Asymptotic Availability of Repairable Systems: The Exponential Case

Consider a repairable system. We take observations on n consecutive renewal cycles. It is assumed that in each renewal cycle, TTF $\sim E(\beta)$ and TTR $\sim E(\gamma)$. Let $t_1, \cdots, t_n$ be the values of TTF in the n cycles and $s_1, \cdots, s_n$ be the values of TTR. One can readily verify that the likelihood function of β depends on the statistic $U = \sum_{i=1}^{n} t_i$ and that of γ depends on $V = \sum_{i=1}^{n} s_i$. U and V are called the **likelihood** (or **minimal sufficient**) **statistics**. Let $\lambda = 1/\beta$ and $\mu = 1/\gamma$. The asymptotic availability is $A_\infty = \mu/(\mu + \lambda)$.

In the Bayesian framework we assume that λ and μ are priorly independent, having prior gamma distributions $G(\nu, \tau)$ and $G(\omega, \zeta)$, respectively. One can verify that the posterior distributions of λ and μ, given U and V, are $G(n + \nu, U + \tau)$ and $G(n + \omega, V + \zeta)$, respectively. Moreover, λ and μ are posteriorly independent. Routine calculations yield that

$$\frac{\frac{1-A_\infty}{A_\infty}(U + \tau)}{\frac{1-A_\infty}{A_\infty}(U + \tau) + (V + \zeta)} \sim \text{Beta}(n + \nu, n + \omega),$$

where $\text{Beta}(p, q)$ denotes a random variable having a Beta distribution, with parameters p and q, $0 < p, q < \infty$. Let $\epsilon_1 = (1 - \gamma)/2$ and $\epsilon_2 = (1 + \gamma)/2$. We obtain that the lower and upper limits of the γ-level credibility interval for A_∞ are A_{∞,ϵ_1} and A_{∞,ϵ_2} where

$$A_{\infty,\epsilon_1} = \left[1 + \frac{V+\zeta}{U+\tau} \cdot \frac{\mathrm{Be}_{\epsilon_2}(n+\nu, n+\omega)}{\mathrm{Be}_{\epsilon_1}(n+\omega, n+\nu)}\right]^{-1} \tag{10.4.1}$$

and

$$A_{\infty,\epsilon_2} = \left[1 + \frac{V+\zeta}{U+\tau} \cdot \frac{\mathrm{Be}_{\epsilon_1}(n+\nu, n+\omega)}{\mathrm{Be}_{\epsilon_2}(n+\omega, n+\nu)}\right]^{-1}, \tag{10.4.2}$$

where $\mathrm{Beta}_\epsilon(p, q)$ is the ϵ-th quantile of Beta(p, q). Moreover, the quantiles of the Beta distribution are related to those of the F-distribution according to the following formulae:

$$\mathrm{Be}_{\epsilon_2}(a_1, a_2) = \frac{\frac{a_1}{a_2} F_{\epsilon_2}[a_1, a_2]}{1 + \frac{a_1}{a_2} F_{\epsilon_2}[a_1, a_2]} \tag{10.4.3}$$

and

$$\mathrm{Be}_{\epsilon_1}(a_1, a_2) = \frac{1}{1 + \frac{a_2}{a_1} F_{\epsilon_2}[a_2, a_1]}. \tag{10.4.4}$$

We illustrate these results in the following example.

Example 10.5 Observations were taken on $n = 72$ renewal cycles of an insertion machine. It is assumed that TTF $\sim E(\beta)$ and TTR $\sim E(\gamma)$ in each cycle. The observations gave the values $U = 496.9$ [min] and $V = 126.3$ [min]. According to these values, the MLE of A_∞ is $\hat{A}_\infty = 496.9/(496.9 + 126.3) = 0.797$. Assume the gamma prior distributions for λ and μ, with $\nu = 2$, $\tau = 0.001$, $\omega = 2$ and $\zeta = 0.005$. We obtain from (10.4.3) and (10.4.4) for $\gamma = 0.95$,

$$\mathrm{Be}_{0.025}(74, 74) = 0.4198, \quad \mathrm{Be}_{0.975}(74, 74) = 0.5802.$$

Finally, the credibility limits obtained from (10.4.1) and (10.4.2) are $A_{\infty,0.025} = 0.740$, and $A_{\infty,0.975} = 0.845$. To conclude this example we remark that the Bayes estimator of A_∞, for the absolute deviation loss function, is the median of the posterior distribution of A_∞, given (U, V), namely $A_{\infty,0.5}$.

In the present example $n + \nu = n + \omega = 74$. The Beta(74, 74) distribution is symmetric. Hence $\mathrm{Be}_{0.5}(74, 74) = 0.5$. To obtain the $A_{\infty,0.5}$ we solve the equation

$$\frac{\frac{1-A_{\infty,0.5}}{A_{\infty,0.5}}(U+\tau)}{\frac{1-A_{\infty,0.5}}{A_{\infty,0.5}}(U+\tau) + (V+\zeta)} = \mathrm{Be}_{0.5}(n+\nu, n+\omega).$$

In the present case we get

$$A_{\infty,0.5} = \left(1 + \frac{V+\zeta}{U+\tau}\right)^{-1} = \frac{1}{1+\frac{126.305}{496.901}} = 0.797.$$

This is equal to the value of the MLE. ■

10.5 Empirical Bayes Method

Empirical Bayes estimation is designed to utilize the information in large samples to estimate the Bayes estimator, without specifying the prior distribution. We introduce the idea in relation to estimating the parameter, λ, of a Poisson distribution.

Suppose that we have a sequence of independent trials, in each trial a value of λ (failure rate) is chosen from some prior distribution $H(\lambda)$, and then a value of X is chosen from the Poisson distribution $\mathcal{P}(\lambda)$. If this is repeated n times we have n pairs $(\lambda_1, x_1), \cdots, (\lambda_n, x_n)$. The statistician, however, can observe only the values $x_1, x_2, \cdots, x_n$. Let $f_n(i)$, $i = 0, 1, 2, \cdots$, be the empirical p.d.f. of the observed variable X, i.e., $f_n(i) = \frac{1}{n}\sum_{j=1}^{n} I\{x_j = i\}$.

A new trial is to be performed. Let Y be the observed variable in the new trial. It is assumed that Y has a Poisson distribution with mean λ which will be randomly chosen from the prior distribution $H(\lambda)$. The statistician has to estimate the new value of λ from the observed value y of Y. Suppose that the loss function for erroneous estimation is the squared-error loss, $(\hat{\lambda} - \lambda)^2$. The Bayes estimator, if $H(\lambda)$ is known, is

$$E_H\{\lambda \mid y\} = \frac{\int_0^\infty \lambda^{y+1} e^{-\lambda} h(\lambda)\, \mathrm{d}\lambda}{\int_0^\infty \lambda^y e^{-\lambda} h(\lambda)\, \mathrm{d}\lambda}, \tag{10.5.1}$$

where $h(\lambda)$ is the prior p.d.f. of λ.

The predictive p.d.f. of Y, under H, is

$$f_H(y) = \frac{1}{y!}\int_0^\infty \lambda^y e^{-\lambda} h(\lambda)\, \mathrm{d}\lambda. \tag{10.5.2}$$

The Bayes estimator of λ (10.5.1) can be written in the form

$$E_H\{\lambda \mid y\} = (y+1)\frac{f_H(y+1)}{f_H(y)}, \quad y = 0, 1, \cdots. \tag{10.5.3}$$

The empirical p.d.f. $f_n(y)$ converges (by the Strong Law of Large Numbers) in a probabilistic sense, as $n \to \infty$, to $f_H(y)$. Accordingly, replacing $f_H(y)$ in (10.5.3) with $f_n(y)$ we obtain an estimator of $E_H\{\lambda \mid y\}$ based on the past n trials. This estimator is called an **empirical Bayes estimator** (EBE) of λ:

Table 10.2 Empirical distribution of number of soldering defects (per 100,000 points)

x	0	1	2	3	4	5	6	7	8	9
$f(x)$	4	21	29	32	19	14	13	5	8	5
x	10	11	12	13	14	15	16	17	18	19
$f(x)$	9	1	2	4	4	1	4	2	1	1
x	20	21	22	23	24	25	26	Total		
$f(x)$	1	1	1	2	1	2	1	188		

$$\hat{\lambda}_n(y) = (y+1)\frac{f_n(y+1)}{f_n(y)}, \quad y = 0, 1, \cdots. \tag{10.5.4}$$

In the following example we illustrate this estimation method.

Example 10.6 $n = 188$ batches of circuit boards were inspected for soldering defects. Each board has typically several hundred soldering points, and each batch contained several hundred boards. It is assumed that the number of soldering defects, X (per 10^5 points), has a Poisson distribution. In Table 10.2 we present the frequency distribution of X among the 188 observed batches.

Accordingly, if in a new batch the number of defects (per 10^5 points) is $y = 8$, the EBE of λ is $\hat{\lambda}_{188}(8) = 9 \times \frac{5}{8} = 5.625$ (per 10^5), or 56.25 (per 10^6 points), i.e., 56.25 PPM. After observing $y_{189} = 8$ we can increase $f_{188}(8)$ by 1, i.e., $f_{189}(8) = f_{188}(8) + 1$, and observe the next batch. ■

The above method of deriving an EBE can be employed for any p.d.f. $f(x;\theta)$ of a discrete distribution, such that

$$\frac{f(x+1;\theta)}{f(x;\theta)} = a(x) + b(x)\theta.$$

In such a case, the EBE of θ is

$$\hat{\theta}_n(x) = \frac{f_n(x+1)}{f_n(x)b(x)} - \frac{a(x)}{b(x)}. \tag{10.5.5}$$

Generally, however, it is difficult to obtain an estimator which converges, as n increases, to the value of the Bayes estimator. A **parametric** EB procedure is one in which, as part of the model, we assume that the prior distribution belongs to a parametric family, but the parameter of the prior distribution is consistently estimated from the past data. For example, if the model assumes that the observed TTF is $E(\beta)$ and that $\beta \sim \mathrm{IG}(\nu, \tau)$, instead of specifying the values of ν and τ, we use the past data to estimate. We may obtain an estimator of $E\{\theta \mid T, \nu, \tau)$ which converges in a probabilistic sense, as n increases, to the Bayes estimator. An example of such a parametric EBE is given below.

Example 10.7 Suppose that $T \sim E(\beta)$ and β has a prior $\mathrm{IG}(\nu, \tau)$. The Bayes estimator of the reliability function is given by (10.2.5).

Let $t_1, t_2, \cdots, t_n$ be past independent observations on T.

The expected value of T under the predictive p.d.f. is

$$E_{\tau,\nu}\{T\} = \frac{1}{\tau(\nu-1)}, \tag{10.5.6}$$

provided $\nu > 1$. The second moment of T is

$$E_{\tau,\nu}\{T^2\} = \frac{2}{\tau^2(\nu-1)(\nu-2)}, \tag{10.5.7}$$

provided $\nu > 2$.

Let $M_{1,n} = \frac{1}{n}\sum_{i=1}^{n} t_i$ and $M_{2,n} = \frac{1}{n}\sum_{i=1}^{n} t_i^2$. $M_{1,n}$ and $M_{2,n}$ converge in a probabilistic sense to $E_{\tau,\nu}\{T\}$ and $E_{\tau,\nu}\{T^2\}$, respectively. We estimate τ and ν by the **method of moment equations**, by solving

$$M_{1,n} = \frac{1}{\hat{\tau}(\hat{\nu}-1)} \tag{10.5.8}$$

and

$$M_{2,n} = \frac{2}{\hat{\tau}^2(\hat{\nu}-1)(\hat{\nu}-2)}. \tag{10.5.9}$$

Let $D_n^2 = M_{2,n} - M_{1,n}^2$ be the sample variance. Simple algebraic manipulations yield the estimators

$$\hat{\tau}_n = \frac{(D_n^2 - M_{1,n}^2)}{[M_{1,n}(D_n^2 + M_{1,n}^2)]}, \tag{10.5.10}$$

$$\hat{\nu}_n = \frac{2D_n^2}{D_n^2 - M_{1,n}^2}, \tag{10.5.11}$$

provided $D_n^2 > M_{1,n}^2$. It can be shown that for large values of n, $D_n^2 > M_{1,n}^2$ with high probability.

Substituting the empirical estimates $\hat{\tau}_n$ and $\hat{\nu}_n$ in (10.2.5) we obtain a parametric EBE of the reliability function. ■

For additional results on the EBE of reliability functions, see Martz and Waller (1982) and Tsokos and Shimi (1977).

10.6 Chapter Highlights

The main concepts and definitions introduced in this chapter include:

- Prior distribution
- Predictive distribution

- Posterior distribution
- Beta function
- Conjugate distributions
- Bayes estimator
- Posterior risk
- Posterior expectation
- Distribution-free estimators
- Credibility intervals
- Minimal sufficient statistics
- Empirical Bayes method

10.7 Exercises

Exercise 10.1 Suppose that the TTF of a system is a random variable having exponential distribution, $E(\beta)$. Suppose also that the prior distribution of $\lambda = 1/\beta$ is $G(2.25, 0.01)$.

(i) What is the posterior distribution of λ, given $T = 150$ [hr]?
(ii) What is the Bayes estimator of β, for the squared-error loss?
(iii) What is the posterior SD of β?

Exercise 10.2 Let $J(t)$ denote the number of failures of a device in the time interval $(0, t]$. After each failure the device is instantaneously renewed. Let $J(t)$ have a Poisson distribution with mean λt. Suppose that λ has a gamma prior distribution, with parameters $\nu = 2$ and $\tau = 0.05$.

(i) What is the predictive distribution of $J(t)$?
(ii) Given that $J(t)/t = 10$, how many failures are expected in the next time unit?
(iii) What is the Bayes estimator of λ, for the squared-error loss?
(iv) What is the posterior SD of λ?

Exercise 10.3 The proportion of defectives, θ, in a production process has a uniform prior distribution on (0, 1). A random sample of $n = 10$ items from this process yields $K_{10} = 3$ defectives.

(i) What is the posterior distribution of θ?
(ii) What is the Bayes estimator of θ for the absolute error loss?

Exercise 10.4 Let $X \sim \mathcal{P}(\lambda)$ and suppose that λ has the Jeffrey improper prior $h(\lambda) = \frac{1}{\sqrt{\lambda}}$. Find the Bayes estimator for squared-error loss and its posterior SD.

Exercise 10.5 Apply formula (10.2.3) to determine the Bayes estimator of the reliability when $n = 50$ and $K_{50} = 49$.

Exercise 10.6 A system has three modules, M_1, M_2, M_3. M_1 and M_2 are connected in series and these two are connected in parallel to M_3, i.e.,

$$R_{sys} = \psi_p(R_3, \psi_s(R_1, R_2)) = R_3 + R_1R_2 - R_1R_2R_3,$$

where R_i is the reliability of module M_i. The TTFs of the three modules are independent random variables having exponential distributions with prior $\text{IG}(\nu_i, \tau_i)$ distributions of their MTTF. Moreover, $\nu_1 = 2.5$, $\nu_2 = 2.75$, $\nu_3 = 3$, $\tau_1 = \tau_2 = \tau_3 = 1/1000$. In separate independent trials of the TTF of each module we obtained the statistics $T_n^{(1)} = 4565$ [hr], $T_n^{(2)} = 5720$ [hr] and $T_n^{(3)} = 7505$ [hr], where in all three experiments $n = r = 10$. Determine the Bayes estimator of R_{sys}, for the squared-error loss.

Exercise 10.7 $n = 30$ computer monitors were put on test at a temperature of 100°F and relative humidity of 90% for 240 [hr]. The number of monitors which survived this test is $K_{30} = 28$. Determine the Bayes credibility interval for $R(240)$, at level $\gamma = 0.95$, with respect to a uniform prior on $(0, 1)$.

Exercise 10.8 Determine a $\gamma = .95$ level credibility interval for $R(t)$ at $t = 25$ [hr] when TTF $\sim E(\beta)$, $\beta \sim \text{IG}(3, 0.01)$, $r = 27$, $T_{n,r} = 3500$ [hr].

Exercise 10.9 Under the conditions of Exercise 10.8 determine a Bayes prediction interval for the total life of $s = 2$ devices.

Exercise 10.10 A repairable system has exponential TTF and exponential TTR, which are independent of each other. $n = 100$ renewal cycles were observed. The total times till failure were 10,050 [hr] and the total repair times were 500 [min]. Assuming gamma prior distributions for λ and μ with $\nu = \omega = 4$ and $\tau = 0.0004$ [hr], $\zeta = 0.01$ [min], find a $\gamma = 0.95$ level credibility interval for A_∞.

Exercise 10.11 In reference to Example 10.6, suppose that the data of Table 10.2 were obtained for a Poisson random variable where $\lambda_1, \cdots, \lambda_{188}$ have a gamma (ν, τ) prior distribution.

(i) What is the predictive distribution of the number of defects per batch?
(ii) Find the formulae for the first two moments of the predictive distribution.
(iii) Find, from the empirical frequency distribution of Table 10.2, the first two sample moments.
(iv) Use the method of moment equations to estimate the prior parameters ν and τ.
(v) What is the Bayes estimator of λ if $X_{189} = 8$?

Chapter 11
Sampling Plans for Batch and Sequential Inspection

Preview Traditional supervision consists of keeping close control of operations and progress, the focus of attention being the product or process outputs. A direct implication of this approach is to guarantee product quality through inspection and screening. The chapter discusses sampling techniques and measures of inspection effectiveness. Performance characteristics of sampling plans are discussed and guidelines for choosing economic sampling plans are presented. The basic theory of single-stage acceptance sampling plans for attributes is first presented including the concepts of Acceptable Quality Level and Limiting Quality Level. Formulas for determining sample size, acceptance levels, and operating characteristic functions are provided. Moving on from single-stage sampling, the chapter covers double sampling and sequential sampling using Wald's sequential probability ratio test. One section deals with acceptance sampling for variable data. Other topics covered include computations of Average Sample Numbers and Average Total Inspection for rectifying inspection plans. Modern Skip-Lot sampling procedures are introduced and compared to the standard application of sampling plans where every lot is inspected. The Deming "all or nothing" inspection criterion is presented and the connection between sampling inspection and statistical process control is made. Special sections are dedicated to sequential methods of software applications such as one- and two-arm bandit models used in A/B testing and software reliability models used in determining release readiness of software versions. Throughout the chapter we show Python code which is used to perform various calculations and generate appropriate tables and graphs.

Supplementary Information The online version contains supplementary material available at (https://doi.org/10.1007/978-3-031-28482-3_11).

R. S. Kenett et al., *Industrial Statistics*, Statistics for Industry, Technology, and Engineering, https://doi.org/10.1007/978-3-031-28482-3_11

11.1 General Discussion

Sampling plans for product inspection are quality assurance schemes, designed to test whether the quality level of a product conforms with the required standards. These methods of quality inspection are especially important when products are received from suppliers or vendors on whom we have no other assessment of the quality level of their production processes. Generally, if a supplier has established procedures of statistical process control which assure the required quality standards are met (see Chaps. 2, 3, and 4), then sampling inspection of his shipments may not be necessary. However periodic auditing of the quality level of certified suppliers might be prudent to ensure that these do not drop below the acceptable standards. Quality auditing or inspection by sampling techniques can also be applied within the plant, at various stages of the production process, e.g., when lots are transferred from one department to another. Another area of application relates to software applications where alternative versions are tested by splitting real-time traffic (A/B testing) or test results are tracked to determine shipping readiness (software reliability).

In this chapter we discuss various sampling and testing procedures, designed to maintain quality standards. In particular, single, double, and sequential sampling plans for attributes and single sampling plans for continuous measurements are studied. We discuss also testing via tolerance limits, sequential bandit problems, and software reliability models. The chapter describes some of the established standards, and in particular the Skip Lot procedure, which appears in modern standards.

We introduce a range of concepts and tools associated with sampling inspection schemes. The methods presented below can be implemented in Python and we provide implementations in the `mistat` package. Modern nomenclature has evolved. A product unit which did not meet the quality specifications or requirements was called **defective**. This term has been changed to **nonconforming**. Thus, in early standards, like MIL-STD 105E, we find the term "defective items" and "number of defects." In modern standards like ANSI/ASQC Z1.4 and the international standard ISO 2859, the term used is nonconforming. We use the two terms interchangeably. Similarly, the acronyms LTPD and LQL, which will be explained later, will also be used interchangeably.

A **lot** is a collection of N elements which are subject to quality inspection. Accordingly, a lot is a finite real population of products. **Acceptance** of a lot is a quality approval, providing the "green light" for subsequent use of the elements of the lot. Generally, we refer to lots of raw material, of semi-finished or finished products, etc., which are purchased from vendors or produced by subcontractors. Before acceptance, a lot is typically subjected to quality inspection unless the vendor has been certified and its products are delivered directly, without inspection, to the production line. The purchase contracts typically specify the acceptable quality level and the method of inspection.

In general, it is expected that a lot contains no more than a certain percentage of nonconforming (defective) items, where the test conditions that classify an item as defective are usually well specified. One should decide if a lot has to be subjected to a complete inspection, item by item, or whether it is sufficient to determine acceptance using a sample from the lot. If we decide to inspect a sample, we must determine how large it is and what is the criterion for accepting or rejecting the lot. Furthermore, the performance characteristics of the procedures in use should be understood.

The **proportion of nonconforming items** in a lot is the ratio $p = M/N$, where M is the number of defective items in the whole lot and N is the size of the lot. If we choose to accept only lots with zero defectives, we have to inspect each lot completely, item by item. This approach is called 100% inspection. This is the case, for example, when the items of the lots are used in a critical or very expensive system. A communication satellite is an example of such a system. In such cases, the cost of inspection is negligible compared to the cost of failure. On the other hand, there are many situations in which complete inspection is impossible (e.g., destructive testing) or impractical (because of the large expense involved). In this situation, the two parties involved, the customer and its supplier, specify an **acceptable quality level** (AQL) and a **limiting quality level** (LQL). When the proportion of defectives, p, in the lot is not larger than the AQL, the lot is considered good and should be accepted with high probability. If, on the other hand, the proportion of defectives in the lot is greater than the LQL, the lot should be rejected with high probability. If p is between the AQL and the LQL, then either acceptance or rejection of the lot can happen with various probability levels.

How should the parties specify the AQL and LQL levels? Usually, the AQL is determined by the quality requirements of the customer who is going to use the product. The producer of the product, which is the supplier, tries generally to demonstrate to the customer that his production processes maintain a capability level in accordance with the customer's or consumer's requirements. Both the AQL and LQL are specified in terms of proportions p_0 and p_t of nonconforming in the process.

The risk of rejecting a good lot, i.e., a lot with $p \leq \text{AQL}$, is called the **producer's risk**, while the risk of accepting a bad lot, i.e., a lot for which $p \geq \text{LQL}$, is called the **consumer's risk**. Thus, the problem of designing an acceptance sampling plan is that of choosing:

1. The method of sampling
2. The sample size
3. The acceptance criteria for testing the hypothesis

$$H_0 : p \leq \text{AQL},$$

against the alternative

$$H_1 : p \geq \text{LQL},$$

so that the probability of rejecting a good lot will not exceed a value α (the level of significance) and the probability of accepting a bad lot will not exceed β. In this context, α and β are called the **producer's risk** and the **consumer's risk**, respectively.

11.2 Single-Stage Sampling Plans for Attributes

A single-stage sampling plan for an attribute is an acceptance/rejection procedure for a lot of size N, according to which a random sample of size n is drawn from the lot, without replacement. Let M be the number of defective items (elements) in the lot, and let X be the number of defective items in the sample. Obviously, X is a random variable whose range is $\{0, 1, 2, \cdots, n^*\}$, where $n^* = \min(n, M)$. The distribution function of X is the hypergeometric distribution $H(N, M, n)$, (see Section 2.3.2, *Modern Statistics*, Kenett et al. 2022b) with the probability distribution function (p.d.f.)

$$h(x; N, M, n) = \frac{\binom{M}{x}\binom{N-M}{n-x}}{\binom{N}{n}}, \quad x = 0, \cdots, n^* \tag{11.2.1}$$

and the cumulative distribution function (c.d.f.)

$$H(x; N, M, n) = \sum_{j=0}^{x} h(j; N, M, n). \tag{11.2.2}$$

In Python, you can use the *hypergeom* distribution of the `scipy.stats` package. The relevant methods are *hypergeom.pmf(x, N, n, M)* for p.d.f. and *hypergeom.cdf(x, N, n, M)* for the c.d.f. Note that in comparison to our nomenclature the order for N, M, and n the `scipy` functions is different.

Suppose we consider a lot of $N = 100$ items to be acceptable if it has no more than $M = 5$ nonconforming items and non-acceptable if it has more than $M = 10$ nonconforming items. For a sample of size $n = 10$, we derive the hypergeometric distribution $H(100, 5, 10)$ and $H(100, 10, 10)$. From Table 11.1, we see that, if such

Table 11.1 The p.d.f. and c.d.f. of $H(100, 5, 10)$ and $H(100, 10, 10)$

j	$h(j; 100, 5, 10)$	$H(j; 100, 5, 10)$
0	0.5838	0.5838
1	0.3394	0.9231
2	0.0702	0.9934
3	0.0064	0.9997
4	0.0003	1.0000

j	$h(j; 100, 10, 10)$	$H(j; 100, 10, 10)$
0	0.3305	0.3305
1	0.4080	0.7385
2	0.2015	0.9400
3	0.0518	0.9918
4	0.0076	0.9993
5	0.0006	1.0000

a lot is accepted whenever $X = 0$, the consumer's risk of accepting a lot which should be rejected is

$$\beta = H(0; 100, 10, 10) = 0.3305.$$

The producer's risk of rejecting an acceptable lot is

$$\alpha = 1 - H(0; 100, 5, 10) = 0.4162.$$

As before, let p_0 denote the AQL and p_t the LQL. Obviously, $0 < p_0 < p_t < 1$. Suppose that the decision is to accept a lot whenever the number of nonconforming X is not greater than c, i.e., $X \leq c$. c is called the **acceptance number**. For specified values of p_0, p_t, α, and β, we can determine n and c so that

$$\Pr\{X \leq c \mid p_0\} \geq 1 - \alpha \tag{11.2.3}$$

and

$$\Pr\{X \leq c \mid p_t\} \leq \beta. \tag{11.2.4}$$

Notice that n and c should satisfy the inequalities

$$H(c; N, M_0, n) \geq 1 - \alpha \tag{11.2.5}$$

$$H(c; N, M_t, n) \leq \beta, \tag{11.2.6}$$

where $M_0 = [Np_0]$ and $M_t = [Np_t]$ and $[a]$ is the integer part of a. In Table 11.2, a few numerical results show how n and c depend on p_0 and p_t, when the lot is of size $n = 100$ and $\alpha = \beta = 0.05$. To achieve this in Python, we use the *findPlan* function from the `mistat` package.

```
from mistat.acceptanceSampling import findPlan
findPlan(PRP=[0.01, 0.95], CRP=[0.08, 0.05], oc_type='hypergeom', N=100)
```

```
Plan(n=46, c=1, r=2)
```

We see that, even if the requirements are not very stringent, for example, when $p_0 = 0.01$ and $p_t = 0.05$, the required sample size is $n = 65$. If in such a sample there is more than 1 defective item, then the entire lot is rejected. Similarly, if $p_0 = 0.03$ and $p_t = 0.05$, then the required sample size is $n = 92$, which is almost the entire lot. On the other hand, if $p_0 = 0.01$ and p_t is greater than .20, we need no more than 20 items in the sample. If we relax the requirement concerning α and β and allow higher producer's and consumer's risks (`PRP` and `CRP`), the required sample size will be smaller, as shown in Table 11.3.

An important characterization of an acceptance sampling plan is given by its **operating characteristic** (OC) function. This function, denoted by OC(p), yields

Table 11.2 Sample size, n, and critical level, c, for single-stage acceptance sampling with $N = 100$ and $\alpha = \beta = 0.05$

p_0	p_t	n	c	r	p_0	p_t	n	c	r
0.01	0.05	65	1	2	0.03	0.05	92	3	4
0.01	0.08	46	1	2	0.03	0.08	71	3	4
0.01	0.11	36	1	2	0.03	0.11	56	3	4
0.01	0.14	29	1	2	0.03	0.14	37	2	3
0.01	0.17	24	1	2	0.03	0.17	31	2	3
0.01	0.20	20	1	2	0.03	0.20	27	2	3
0.01	0.23	18	1	2	0.03	0.23	24	2	3
0.01	0.26	16	1	2	0.03	0.26	21	2	3
0.01	0.29	14	1	2	0.03	0.29	19	2	3
0.01	0.32	13	1	2	0.03	0.32	13	1	2

Table 11.3 Sample size, n, and critical level, c, for single-stage acceptance sampling, $N = 100$, $\alpha = 0.10$, and $\beta = 0.20$

p_0	p_t	n	c	r	p_0	p_t	n	c	r
0.01	0.05	49	1	2	0.03	0.05	83	3	4
0.01	0.08	33	1	2	0.03	0.08	46	2	3
0.01	0.11	25	1	2	0.03	0.11	35	2	3
0.01	0.14	20	1	2	0.03	0.14	28	2	3
0.01	0.17	9	0	1	0.03	0.17	16	1	2
0.01	0.20	7	0	1	0.03	0.20	14	1	2
0.01	0.23	6	0	1	0.03	0.23	12	1	2
0.01	0.26	6	0	1	0.03	0.26	11	1	2
0.01	0.29	5	0	1	0.03	0.29	10	1	2
0.01	0.32	5	0	1	0.03	0.32	9	1	2

the probability of accepting a lot having proportion p of defective items. If we let $M_p = [Np]$, then we can calculate the OC function by

$$\mathrm{OC}(p) = H(c; N, M_p, n). \tag{11.2.7}$$

We can calculate and visualize the operating characteristics curve using the function *OperatingCharacteristics2c* from the `mistat` package as follows:

```
from mistat.acceptanceSampling import OperatingCharacteristics2c

X = OperatingCharacteristics2c(50, 1, oc_type='hypergeom', N=100,
                               pd=np.linspace(0, 0.15, 300))
df = pd.DataFrame({'p': X.pd, 'OC(p)': X.paccept})
ax = df.plot(x='p', y='OC(p)', legend=False, linestyle=':', color='grey')
ax.set_ylabel('OC(p)')

X = OperatingCharacteristics2c(50, 1, oc_type='hypergeom', N=100,
                               pd=[i / 100 for i in range(16)])
df = pd.DataFrame({'p': X.pd, 'OC(p)': X.paccept})
ax = df.plot.scatter(x='p', y='OC(p)', legend=False, ax=ax, color='black')
plt.show()
```

Table 11.4 The OC function of a single-stage acceptance sampling plan, $N = 100$, $n = 50$, and $c = 1$

p	OC(p)	p	OC(p)
0.00	1.000000	0.08	0.029723
0.01	1.000000	0.09	0.015429
0.02	0.752525	0.10	0.007830
0.03	0.500000	0.11	0.003890
0.04	0.308654	0.12	0.001894
0.05	0.181089	0.13	0.000904
0.06	0.102201	0.14	0.000423
0.07	0.055875	0.15	0.000194

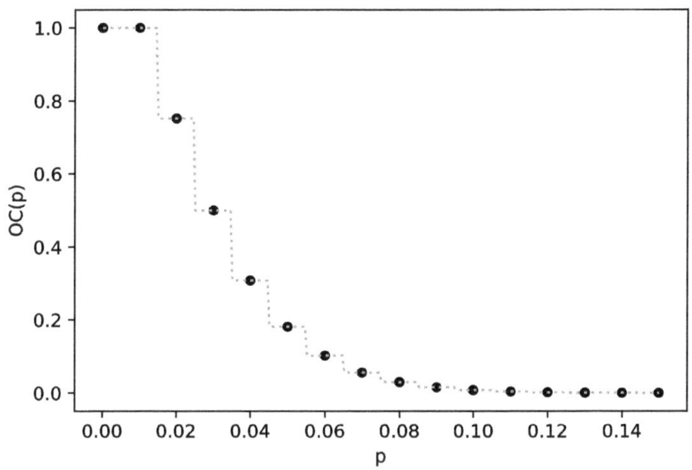

Fig. 11.1 Operating characteristics curve for a single-stage acceptance sampling plan, $N = 100$, $n = 50$, and $c = 1$

In Table 11.4, we present a few values of the OC function for single-stage acceptance sampling, for lot size $N = 100$, sample size $n = 50$, and acceptance number $c = 1$. In Fig. 11.1, we present the graph of the OC function, corresponding to Table 11.4.

11.3 Approximate Determination of the Sampling Plan

If the sample size, n, is not too small, the c.d.f. of the hypergeometric distribution can be approximated by the normal distribution. More specifically, for large values of n, we have the following approximation:

$$H(a; N, M, n) \doteq \Phi\left(\frac{a + 0.5 - nP}{\left(nPQ\left(1 - \frac{n}{N}\right)\right)^{1/2}}\right), \tag{11.3.1}$$

where $P = M/N$ and $Q = 1 - P$.

Table 11.5 Hypergeometric c.d.f.'s and their normal approximations

	H(j;100,30,20)		H(j;100,50,20)		H(j;100,80,20)	
a	Hypergeometric	Normal	Hypergeometric	Normal	Hypergeometric	Normal
0	0.0003	0.0013	0.0000	0.0000	0.0000	0.0000
1	0.0039	0.0070	0.0000	0.0000	0.0000	0.0000
2	0.0227	0.0281	0.0000	0.0001	0.0000	0.0000
3	0.0824	0.0863	0.0004	0.0006	0.0000	0.0000
4	0.2092	0.2066	0.0025	0.0030	0.0000	0.0000
5	0.4010	0.3925	0.0114	0.0122	0.0000	0.0000
6	0.6151	0.6075	0.0392	0.0401	0.0000	0.0000
7	0.7954	0.7934	0.1054	0.1056	0.0000	0.0000
8	0.9115	0.9137	0.2270	0.2266	0.0000	0.0000
9	0.9693	0.9719	0.4016	0.4013	0.0001	0.0000
10	0.9915	0.9930	0.5984	0.5987	0.0006	0.0003
11	0.9982	0.9987	0.7730	0.7734	0.0039	0.0025
12	0.9997	0.9998	0.8946	0.8944	0.0181	0.0144
13	1.0000	1.0000	0.9608	0.9599	0.0637	0.0591
14			0.9886	0.9878	0.1727	0.1743
15			0.9975	0.9970	0.3647	0.3773
16			0.9996	0.9994	0.6084	0.6227
17			1.0000	0.9999	0.8242	0.8257
18					0.9502	0.9409
19					0.9934	0.9856

The first question to ask is how large should n be? The answer to this question depends on how close we wish the approximation to be. Generally, if $0.2 < P < 0.8$, $n = 20$ is large enough to yield a good approximation, as illustrated in Table 11.5.

If $P < 0.2$ or $P > 0.8$, we usually need larger sample sizes to attain good approximation. We show now how the constants (n, c) can be determined. The two requirements to satisfy are $\text{OC}(p_0) = 1 - \alpha$ and $\text{OC}(p_t) = \beta$. These requirements are expressed approximately by the following two equations:

$$\begin{aligned} c + \frac{1}{2} - np_0 &= z_{1-\alpha}\left(np_0q_0\left(1 - \frac{n}{N}\right)\right)^{1/2} \\ c + \frac{1}{2} - np_t &= -z_{1-\beta}\left(np_tq_t\left(1 - \frac{n}{N}\right)\right)^{1/2}. \end{aligned} \tag{11.3.2}$$

Approximate solutions to n and c, n^*, and c^* respectively, are

$$n^* \cong \frac{n_0}{1 + n_0/N}, \tag{11.3.3}$$

Table 11.6 Exact and approximate single-stage sampling plans for $\alpha = \beta = 0.05$, $N = 500$, 1000, 2000, $p_0 = 0.01$, and $p_t = 0.03, 0.05$

		$p_0 = 0.01, p_t = 0.03$				$p_0 = 0.01, p_t = 0.05$			
N	Method	n	c	$\hat{\alpha}$	$\hat{\beta}$	n	c	$\hat{\alpha}$	$\hat{\beta}$
500	Exact	254	4	0.033	0.050	139	3	0.023	0.050
	Approx.	248	4	0.029	0.060	127	2	0.107	0.026
1000	Exact	355	6	0.028	0.050	146	3	0.045	0.049
	Approx.	330	5	0.072	0.036	146	3	0.045	0.049
2000	Exact	414	7	0.038	0.049	176	4	0.026	0.050
	Approx.	396	6	0.082	0.032	157	3	0.066	0.037

where

$$n_0 = \frac{(z_{1-\alpha}\sqrt{p_0 q_0} + z_{1-\beta}\sqrt{p_t q_t})^2}{(p_t - p_0)^2}, \tag{11.3.4}$$

and

$$c^* \cong n^* p_0 - \frac{1}{2} + z_{1-\alpha}\sqrt{n^* p_0 q_0 (1 - n^*/N)}. \tag{11.3.5}$$

In Table 11.6, we present several single-stage sampling plans (n, c) and their approximations (n^*, c^*). We provide also the corresponding attained risk levels $\hat{\alpha}$ and $\hat{\beta}$. We see that the approximation provided for n and c yields risk levels which are generally close to the nominal ones.

```
from mistat.acceptanceSampling import findPlanApprox

def attainedRiskLevels(plan, p0, pt):
  hat_alpha = 1 - stats.hypergeom(N, int(p0 * N), plan.n).cdf(plan.c)
  hat_beta = stats.hypergeom(N, int(pt * N), plan.n).cdf(plan.c)
  return np.array([hat_alpha, hat_beta])

print('Exact results (p0=0.01, pt=0.03)')
for N in (500, 1000, 2000):
    plan = findPlan(PRP=[0.01, 0.95], CRP=[0.03, 0.05], oc_type='hypergeom', N=N)
    print(N, plan, attainedRiskLevels(plan, 0.01, 0.03).round(3))


print('Approximate results (p0=0.01, pt=0.03)')
for N in (500, 1000, 2000):
    plan = findPlanApprox(PRP=[0.01, 0.95], CRP=[0.03, 0.05], N=N)
    print(N, plan, attainedRiskLevels(plan, 0.01, 0.03).round(3))

print('Exact results (p0=0.01, pt=0.05)')
for N in (500, 1000, 2000):
    plan = findPlan(PRP=[0.01, 0.95], CRP=[0.05, 0.05], oc_type='hypergeom', N=N)
    print(N, plan, attainedRiskLevels(plan, 0.01, 0.05).round(3))

print('Approximate results (p0=0.01, pt=0.05)')
for N in (500, 1000, 2000):
    plan = findPlanApprox(PRP=[0.01, 0.95], CRP=[0.05, 0.05], N=N)
    print(N, plan, attainedRiskLevels(plan, 0.01, 0.05).round(3))
```

```
Exact results (p0=0.01, pt=0.03)
500 Plan(n=254, c=4, r=5) [0.033 0.05 ]
1000 Plan(n=355, c=6, r=7) [0.028 0.05 ]
2000 Plan(n=414, c=7, r=8) [0.038 0.049]
Approximate results (p0=0.01, pt=0.03)
500 Plan(n=248, c=4, r=5) [0.029 0.06 ]
1000 Plan(n=330, c=5, r=6) [0.072 0.036]
2000 Plan(n=396, c=6, r=7) [0.082 0.032]
Exact results (p0=0.01, pt=0.05)
500 Plan(n=139, c=3, r=4) [0.023 0.05 ]
1000 Plan(n=146, c=3, r=4) [0.045 0.049]
2000 Plan(n=176, c=4, r=5) [0.026 0.05 ]
Approximate results (p0=0.01, pt=0.05)
500 Plan(n=127, c=2, r=3) [0.107 0.026]
1000 Plan(n=146, c=3, r=4) [0.045 0.049]
2000 Plan(n=157, c=3, r=4) [0.066 0.037]
```

11.4 Double Sampling Plans for Attributes

A double sampling plan for attributes is a two-stage procedure. In the first stage, a random sample of size n_1 is drawn, without replacement, from the lot. Let X_1 denote the number of defective items in this first stage sample. Then the rules for the second stage are the following: if $X_1 \leq c_1$, sampling terminates and the lot is accepted; if $X_1 \geq c_2$, sampling terminates and the lot is rejected; and if X_1 is between c_1 and c_2, a second stage random sample, of size n_2, is drawn, without replacement, from the remaining items in the lot. Let X_2 be the number of defective items in this second stage sample. Then, if $X_1 + X_2 \leq c_3$, the lot is accepted, and if $X_1 + X_2 > c_3$, the lot is rejected.

Generally, if there are very few (or very many) defective items in the lot, the decision to accept or reject the lot can be reached after the first stage of sampling. Since the first stage samples are smaller than those needed in a single-stage sampling , a considerable saving in inspection cost may be attained.

In this type of sampling plan, there are five parameters to select, namely, n_1, n_2, c_1, c_2, and c_3. Variations in the values of these parameters affect the operating characteristics of the procedure, as well as the expected number of observations required (i.e., the total sample size). Theoretically, we could determine the optimal values of these five parameters by imposing five independent requirements on the OC function and the function of expected total sample size, called the **Average Sample Number** or **ASN function**, at various values of p. However, to simplify this procedure, it is common practice to set $n_2 = 2n_1$ and $c_2 = c_3 = 3c_1$. This reduces the problem to that of selecting just n_1 and c_1. Every such selection will specify a particular double sampling plan. For example, if the lot consists of $N = 150$ items and we choose a plan with $n_1 = 20$, $n_2 = 40$, $c_1 = 2$, and $c_2 = c_3 = 6$, we will achieve certain properties. On the other hand, if we set $n_1 = 20$, $n_2 = 40$, $c_1 = 1$, and $c_2 = c_3 = 3$, the plan will have different properties.

The formula of the OC function associated with a double sampling plan $(n_1, n_2, c_1, c_2, c_3)$ is

$$\text{OC}(p) = H(c_1; N, M_p, n_1) + \sum_{j=c_1+1}^{c_2-1} h(j; N, M_p, n_1) H(c_3 - j; N - n_1, M_p - j, n_2), \tag{11.4.1}$$

where $M_p = [Np]$. Obviously, we must have $c_2 \geq c_1 + 2$, for otherwise the plan is a single-stage plan. The probability $\Pi(p)$ of stopping after the first stage of sampling is

$$\begin{aligned}\Pi(p) &= H(c_1; N, M_p, n_1) + 1 - H(c_2 - 1; N, M_p, n_1) \\ &= 1 - [H(c_2 - 1; N, M_p, n_1) - H(c_1; N, M_p, n_1)].\end{aligned} \tag{11.4.2}$$

The expected total sample size, ASN, is given by the formula

$$\begin{aligned}\text{ASN}(p) &= n_1 \Pi(p) + (n_1 + n_2)(1 - \Pi(p)) \\ &= n_1 + n_2[H(c_2 - 1; N, M_p, n_1) - H(c_1; N, M_p, n_1)].\end{aligned} \tag{11.4.3}$$

In Table 11.7, we present the OC function and the ASN function for the double sampling plan (20, 40, 2, 6, 6,), for a lot of size $N = 150$.

We see from Table 11.7 that the double sampling plan illustrated here is not stringent. The probability of accepting a lot with 10% defectives is 0.80 and the probability of accepting a lot with 15% defectives is 0.40. If we consider the plan (20, 40, 1, 3, 3), a more stringent procedure is obtained, as shown in Table 11.8 and Fig. 11.2. The probability of accepting a lot having 10% defectives has dropped to 0.32 and that of accepting a lot with 15% defectives has dropped to 0.15. Table 11.8 shows that the ASN is 23.1 when $p = 0.025$ (most of the time the sampling is terminated after the first stage), and the ASN is 29.1 when $p = 0.15$. The maximum ASN occurs around $p = 0.10$.

Table 11.7 The OC and ASN of a double sampling plan (20,40,2,6,6), $N = 150$

p	OC(p)	ASN(p)	p	OC(p)	ASN(p)
0.000	1.0000	20.0	0.275	0.0477	38.9
0.025	1.0000	20.3	0.300	0.0268	35.2
0.050	0.9969	22.9	0.325	0.0145	31.6
0.075	0.9577	26.6	0.350	0.0075	28.4
0.100	0.8011	32.6	0.375	0.0044	26.4
0.125	0.5871	38.3	0.400	0.0021	24.3
0.150	0.4000	42.7	0.425	0.0009	22.7
0.175	0.2930	44.6	0.450	0.0004	21.6
0.200	0.1891	45.3	0.475	0.0002	21.1
0.225	0.1184	44.1	0.500	0.0001	20.6
0.250	0.0715	41.4			

Table 11.8 The OC and ASN for the double sampling plan (20,40,1,3,3), $N = 150$

p	OC(p)	ASN(p)	p	OC(p)	ASN(p)
0.000	1.0000	20.0	0.275	0.0100	21.5
0.025	0.9851	23.1	0.300	0.0050	20.9
0.050	0.7969	28.6	0.325	0.0024	20.5
0.075	0.6018	31.2	0.350	0.0011	20.3
0.100	0.3881	32.2	0.375	0.0006	20.2
0.125	0.2422	31.2	0.400	0.0003	20.1
0.150	0.1468	29.1	0.425	0.0001	20.0
0.175	0.0987	27.3	0.450	0.0000	20.0
0.200	0.0563	25.2	0.475	0.0000	20.0
0.225	0.0310	23.5	0.500	0.0000	20.0
0.250	0.0165	22.2			

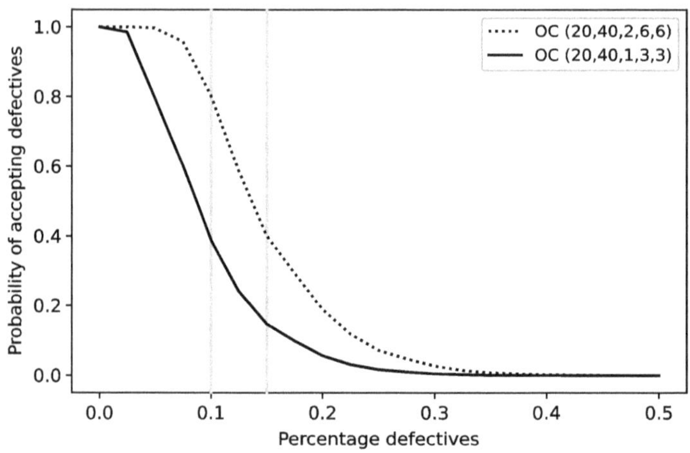

Fig. 11.2 Comparison of double sampling plans (20,40,2,6,6) and (20,40,1,3,3), $N = 150$

To determine an acceptable double sampling plan for attributes, suppose, for example, that the population size is $N = 1000$. Define AQL $= 0.01$ and LQL $= 0.03$. If $n_1 = 200$, $n_2 = 400$, $c_1 = 3$, $c_2 = 9$, and $c_3 = 9$, then OC(0.01) $= 0.957$ and OC(0.03) $= 0.151$. Thus, $\alpha = 0.011$ and $\beta = 0.119$. The double sampling plan with $n_1 = 120$, $n_2 = 240$, $c_1 = 0$, and $c_2 = c_3 = 7$ yields $\alpha = 0.044$ and $\beta = 0.084$. For the last plan, the expected sample sizes are ASN(0.01) $= 288$ and ASN(0.03) $= 336$. These expected sample sizes are smaller than the required sample size of $n = 355$ in a single-stage plan. Moreover, with high probability, if $p \leq p_0$ or $p \geq p_t$, the sampling will terminate after the first stage with only $n_1 = 120$ observations. This is a factor of threefold decrease in the sample size, over the single sampling plan. There are other double sampling plans which can do even better.

If the lot is very large and we use large samples in stage one and stage two, the formulae for the OC and ASN function can be approximated by

$$\mathrm{OC}(p) \cong \Phi\left(\frac{c_1 + 1/2 - n_1 p}{(n_1 pq(1 - n_1/N))^{1/2}}\right)$$
$$+ \sum_{j=c_1+1}^{c_2-1} \left[\Phi\left(\frac{j + 1/2 - n_1 p}{(n_1 pq(1 - n_1/N))^{1/2}}\right) - \Phi\left(\frac{j - 1/2 - n_1 p}{(n_1 pq(1 - n_1/N))^{1/2}}\right)\right]$$
$$\cdot \Phi\left(\frac{c_3 - j + 1/2 - n_2 p}{\left(n_2 pq\left(1 - \frac{n_2}{Nn_1}\right)\right)^{1/2}}\right), \qquad (11.4.4)$$

and

$$\mathrm{ASN}(p) = n_1 + n_2 \left[\Phi\left(\frac{c_2 - 1/2 - n_1 p}{n_1 pq(1 - n_1/N))^{1/2}}\right)\right.$$
$$\left. - \Phi\left(\frac{c_1 + 1/2 - n_1 p}{(n_1 pq(1 - n_1/N))^{1/2}}\right)\right]. \qquad (11.4.5)$$

In Table 11.9, we present the OC and the ASN functions for double sampling from a population of size $N = 1000$, when the parameters of the plan are $(100, 200, 3, 6, 6,)$. The exact values thus obtained are compared to the values obtained from the large sample approximation formulae. In the next section the idea of double sampling is generalized in an attempt to reach acceptance decisions quicker and therefore at reduced costs.

Table 11.9 The exact and approximate OC and ASN functions for the double sampling plan (100,200,3,6,6), $N = 1000$

	OC(p)		ASN(p)	
p	Exact	Approx.	Exact	Approx.
0.01	0.998	0.999	102.4	100.8
0.02	0.897	0.896	124.1	125.0
0.03	0.658	0.640	156.4	163.5
0.04	0.421	0.401	175.6	179.2
0.05	0.243	0.236	174.7	172.3
0.06	0.130	0.134	160.6	155.7
0.07	0.064	0.074	142.7	138.7
0.08	0.030	0.040	127.1	125.1
0.09	0.014	0.021	115.8	115.5

11.5 Sequential Sampling and A/B Testing

The A/B testing is a common practice these days of testing which treatment or action, A or B, is preferred by a customer. Two alternative actions are presented before a customer, who should choose one of the two in order to maximize the expected reward. The reward is not certain in any case, and the probability of reward is unknown. This problem is similar to the classical "Two-Armed Bandit" problem. A gambler is standing in front of a slot machine and has the opportunity to try his luck in N trials. If he pulls the left hand, the probability of reward is p_1, and the probability of reward on the right hand is p_2. If the probabilities of success are known, the gambler will always pull the hand having the largest probability. What should be his strategy when the probabilities are unknown?

Much research was done on this problem in the 70s and the 80s. The reader is referred to the books of Gittins et al. (2011) and Berry and Fristedt (1985). In this section we start with the One-Armed Bandit (OAB) for Bernoulli trials and then discuss the Two-Armed Bandit (TAB) problem.

11.5.1 The One-Armed Bernoulli Bandits

The one-armed Bernoulli bandit is a simpler case, where the probability of success in arm A is known, λ say. The probability p of success in arm B is unknown. It is clear that in this case we have to start with a sequence of trials on arm B (the learning phase) and move to arm A as soon as we are convinced that $p < \lambda$. The trials are Bernoulli trials, which means all trials on arm A or arm B are independent. The results of each trial are binary ($J = 1$ for success and $J = 0$ for failure). The probabilities of success in all trials at the same arm are equal.

Suppose that n trials have been performed on arm B. Let $X_n = \sum_{j=1}^{n} J_j$. The distribution of X_n is binomial, $B(n, p)$.

I. The Bayesian Strategy

In a Bayesian framework, we start with a uniform prior distribution for p. The posterior distribution of p, given (n, X_n), is $B(X_n + 1, n + 1 - X_n)$, i.e.,

$$P\{p \leq \xi | n, X_n\} = \frac{1}{B(X_n + 1, n + 1 - X_n)} \int_0^{\xi} u^{X_n} (1 - u)^{n - X_n} \, du, \quad 0 < \xi < 1. \tag{11.5.1}$$

The function $B(a, b) = \Gamma(a)\Gamma(b)/\Gamma(a+b)$ is called the complete beta function. The right-hand side of (11.5.1) is called the incomplete beta function ratio and is denoted as $I_x(a, b)$. The predictive distribution of J_{n+1}, given X_n, is

$$P\{J_{n+1} = 1 | X_n\} = \frac{X_n + 1}{n + 2}.$$

The posterior probability that $\{p < \lambda\}$ is the λ-quantile of the above beta distribution, which is the incomplete beta function ratio $I_\lambda(X_n + 1, n + 1 - X_n)$.

A relatively simple Bayesian stopping rule for arm B is the first n greater than or equal to an initial sample size k, at which the posterior probability is greater than some specified value γ, i.e.,

$$M_\gamma = \min\{n \geq k : I_\lambda(X_n + 1, n + 1 - X_n) \geq \gamma\}. \tag{11.5.2}$$

That is, at the first time on arm B in which (11.5.2) is satisfied, one moves to arm A and stays there for the rest of the $N - n$ trials.

Example 11.1 In the present example, we simulate a Bayesian OAB Bernoulli process, in which $\lambda = 0.5$ and $N = 50$. If we choose to play all the N trials on arm A, our expected reward is $N\lambda = 25$ (reward units). On the other hand, in the OAB, we start with an initial sample of size $k = 10$ on arm B. We also wish to switch from arm B to arm A with confidence probability $\gamma = 0.95$. We illustrate the random process with two cases:

Case (i) $p = 0.6$: This probability for arm B of $p = 0.6$ is unknown. We make first k trials on arm B and get at random k results according to binomial $B(10, 0.6)$. Using `scipy`, the 0.1-quantile of the binomial $B(10, 0.6)$ is

```
print(f'0.1-quantile B(10,0.6):  {stats.binom(10, 0.6).ppf(0.1)}')
```

```
0.1-quantile B(10,0.6):  4.0
```

In 90% of the cases, we get 4 or more wins. Assume that we get 4 wins. The posterior distribution is in this case $B(4 + 1, 10 + 1 - 4) = B(5, 7)$. Using this posterior, the probability that nothing has changed is

```
print(f'B(5,7)-cdf :  {stats.beta(5, 7).cdf(0.5)}')
```

```
B(5,7)-cdf :  0.7255859375
```

Thus we expect that in 90% of the possible results we stay in the $k + 1$ trial at arm B. Notice that even if we have another loss, $X_{11} = 4$, we have $B(4+1, 11+1-4) = B(5, 8)$ and therefore

```
print(f'B(5,8)-cdf :  {stats.beta(5, 8).cdf(0.5)}')
```

```
B(5,8)-cdf :  0.80615234375
```

and we stay with arm B. Thus, with high probability, we will stay with arm B all the 50 trials, with an expected reward of $50 \times 0.6 = 30$.

Case (ii) $p = 0.3$: We might get at random 2 wins.

```
np.random.seed(5)
print(f'{stats.binom(10, 0.3).rvs(1)} wins')
```

```
[2] wins
```

Table 11.10 Simulation estimates of the expected stopping time and the associated reward, for $N = 50$, $\lambda = 0.5$, $k = 10$, $\gamma = 0.95$, and number of runs $N_s = 1000$

p	$E\{M_\gamma\}$	std$\{M_\gamma\}$	$E\{\text{Reward}\}$	std{Reward}
0.40	31.631	16.938	21.950	2.016
0.45	39.078	15.676	23.352	2.882
0.50	44.359	12.756	25.360	3.395
0.55	46.846	9.910	27.637	3.738
0.60	49.013	5.791	30.404	3.665
0.70	49.882	2.152	35.753	3.251

In this case, $B(2 + 1, 10 + 1 - 2) = B(3, 9)$ and therefore,

```
print(f'B(3,9)-cdf :  {stats.beta(3, 9).cdf(0.5)}')
```

```
B(3,9)-cdf :  0.96728515625
```

We move immediately to arm A, with the expected reward of $2 + 40 \times 0.5 = 22$.

In the following table we present the results of 1000 simulation runs.

```
np.random.seed(1)

N=50; lambda_=0.5; k0=10; gamma=0.95; Ns=1000

results = []
for p in (0.4, 0.45, 0.5, 0.55, 0.6, 0.7):
  r = acceptanceSampling.simulateOAB(N, p, lambda_, k0, gamma, Ns)
  results.append({
      'p': p,
      'Mgamma_mean': r.mgamma.mean,
      'Mgamma_std': r.mgamma.std,
      'Reward_mean': r.reward.mean,
      'Reward_std': r.reward.std,
  })
```

In each run we recorded the mean value of the stopping time M_γ, its standard deviation, and the mean value of the expected reward and its standard deviation. The computations were done with the program *acceptanceSampling.simulateOAB* and are summarized in Table 11.10.

We see in Table 11.10 that, according to the present strategy, the cost of ignorance about p (loss of reward) is pronounced only if $p < 0.5$. For example, if we knew that $p = 0.4$, we would have started with arm A, with an expected reward of 25 rather than 21.950. The loss in expected reward when $p = 0.45$ is not significant. The expected reward when $p \geq 0.5$ is not significantly different from what we could achieve if we knew p. ■

II. The Bayesian Optimal Strategy for Bernoulli Trials

As in the previous strategy, we assume that the prior distribution of p is uniform on (0,1). The optimal strategy is determined by **Dynamic Programming**. The principle of Dynamic Programming is to optimize the future possible trials, irrespective of what has been done in the past. We consider here as before a truncated game, in which only N trials are allowed. Thus we start with the last trial and proceed inductively backward.

(i) Suppose we have already done $N-1$ trials. The expected reward for the Nth trial is

$$R_N(X_{N-1}) = I\{\text{if arm A is chosen}\}$$
$$= \lambda + I\{\text{if arm B is chosen}\}\frac{X_{N-1}+1}{N+1}. \tag{11.5.3}$$

Thus, the maximal predictive expected reward for the last trial is

$$\rho^{(0)}(X_{N-1}) = \max\left\{\lambda, \frac{X_{N-1}+1}{N+1}\right\} \tag{11.5.4}$$
$$= \lambda I\{X_{N-1} < \lambda(N+1)-1\}$$
$$+ \frac{X_{N-1}+1}{N+1} I\{X_{N-1} \geq \lambda(N+1)-1\}. \tag{11.5.5}$$

(ii) After $N-2$ trials, if we are at arm A, we stay there, but if we are at arm B our predictive reward is

$$R_{N-1}(X_{N-2}) = 2\lambda I\{\text{if we are at arm A}\} + \frac{X_{N-2}+1}{N}$$
$$+ E\{\rho^{(0)}(X_{N-2}+J_{N-1})|X_{N-2}\} I\{\text{if we chose arm B}\}. \tag{11.5.6}$$

The maximal predictive expected reward is

$$\rho^{(1)}(X_{N-2}) = \max\left\{2\lambda, \frac{X_{N-2}+1}{N}\rho^{(0)}(X_{N-2}+1)\right.$$
$$\left. + \frac{N-1-X_{N-1}}{N}\rho^{(0)}(X_{N-2}) + \frac{X_{N-2}+1}{N}\right\}. \tag{11.5.7}$$

(iii) By backward induction, we define for all $1 \leq n \leq N-2$

$$\rho^{(n)}(X_{N-n-1}) = \max\left\{(n+1)\lambda, \frac{X_{N-n-1}+1}{N-n+1}\rho^{(n-1)}(X_{N-n-1}+1)\right.$$
$$\left. + \frac{N-n-X_{N-n-1}}{N-n+1}\rho^{(n-1)}(X_{N-n-1}) + \frac{X_{N-n-1}+1}{N-n+1}\right\} \tag{11.5.8}$$

and

$$\rho^{(N-2)}(X_1) = \max\left\{(N-1)\lambda, \frac{X_1+1}{3}\rho^{(N-2)}(X_1+1)\right.$$

Table 11.11 Values of $\rho^{(n)}(X_{N-n-1})$, for $N = 10, n = 0, \ldots, 9$

n	0	1	2	3	4	5	6	7	8	9	10
0	0.500	0.500	0.500	0.500	0.500	0.545	0.636	0.727	0.818	0.909	1.000
1	1.000	1.000	1.000	1.000	1.023	1.200	1.400	1.600	1.800	2.000	
2	1.500	1.500	1.500	1.500	1.677	2.000	2.333	2.667	3.000		
3	2.000	2.000	2.000	2.088	2.504	3.000	3.500	4.000			
4	2.500	2.500	2.500	2.897	3.573	4.286	5.000				
5	3.000	3.000	3.199	4.014	5.000	6.000					
6	3.500	3.500	4.288	5.603	7.000						
7	4.000	4.394	6.024	8.000							
8	4.500	6.147	9.000								
9	5.824	10.000									

$$+\frac{2-X_1}{3}\rho^{(N-2)}(X_1)+\frac{X_1+1}{3}\Bigg\}. \tag{11.5.9}$$

Finally, since the procedure starts at arm B and $P\{X_1 = 0\} = P\{X_1 = 1\} = 1/2$, we get that the maximal expected reward is

$$\rho^{(N-1)} = \frac{\rho^{(N-2)}(0) + \rho^{(N-2)}(1)}{2}.$$

Example 11.2 In the following example we illustrate the values of $\rho^{(n)}(X_{N-n-1})$, for given (N, λ), where n designates the number of available future trials. These values are computed with the function *optimalOAB* from the `mistat` package.

Since the table is too big, we illustrate these for $N = 10$. We get the values shown in Table 11.11.

```
from mistat.acceptanceSampling import optimalOAB
result = optimalOAB(10, 0.5)
print(f'Case (10, 0.5): {result.max_reward:.3f}')
print(f'Case (50, 0.5): {optimalOAB(50, 0.5).max_reward:.3f}')
```

```
Case (10, 0.5): 7.912
Case (50, 0.5): 40.175
```

Accordingly, the maximal predictive reward in following this strategy is $(5.824+10.000)/2 = 7.912$. For each n, we stay in arm A as long as the maximal reward is $(n + 1) \times 0.5$. Since the table is quite big, the function *optimalOAB* returns the maximal predictive reward in addition to the table. To compare this with the case of Table 11.10, *optimalOAB* yields for N=50 and $\lambda = 0.5$ the maximal reward of 40.175. ■

11.5.2 Two-Armed Bernoulli Bandits

The two-armed bandit (TAB) is the case when the probabilities of reward at the two arms are unknown. We consider here the truncated game, in which N trials are allowed at both arms. The sufficient statistics after n trials are $(N^{(1)}(n), X_{N^{(1)}}, N^{(2)}(n), Y_{N^{(2)}})$, where $N^{(1)}(n)$ and $N^{(2)}(n)$ are the number of trials on arm A and arm B for the first n trials, respectively. $X_{N^{(1)}}$ and $Y_{N^{(2)}}$ are the number of successes at arms A and B. The optimal strategy is much more complicated than in the OAB case. If the two arms act independently, the situation is less complicated. The rewards from the two arms are cumulative. In principle one could find an optimal strategy by dynamic programming. It is however much more complicated than in the OAB case. Gittins and Jones (1974) proved that one can compute an index for each arm separately and apply in the next trial the arm having the maximal index value. We provide here a strategy which yields very good results for a large total number of trials N. This strategy starts with k trials on any arm, say arm A. If all the k trials yield k successes, i.e., $X_k = k$, we continue all the rest $N - k$ trials on arm A. If the first $m = \lfloor k/2 \rfloor$ trials are all failures, i.e., $X_m = 0$, we immediately switch to arm B. We then compute the posterior estimator of the probability of success in arm A, p_A, and use it in the dynamic programming for one arm known probability (function *optimalOAB*) starting at arm B.

```
optimalOAB(45, 0.143).max_reward
```

```
33.870065529505496
```

Example 11.3 Consider the case of TAB with $N = 50$ and $k = 10$. If $X_5 = 0$, we switch to arm B. According to the $beta(1, 1)$ prior for p_A, the Bayesian estimator is $\hat{p}_A = 1/7 = 0.143$ with predictive expected reward of optimalOAB(45, 0.143) = 33.87. On the other hand, if $X_{10} = 10$, we stay at arm A till the end, with expected reward of $10 + 40 \times (11/12) = 46.67$. In Table 11.12, we present all the other possibilities. ■

There is ample literature on the armed-bandits problem, for example, see Chapter 8 of Zacks (2009).

Table 11.12 Expected reward when $N = 50$ and $k = 10$

X_{10}	$E\{\text{Reward}\}$
1	31.150
2	32.413
3	33.819
4	35.380
5	37.093
6	38.970
7	41.033
8	43.249
9	45.667

11.6 Acceptance Sampling Plans for Variables

It is sometimes possible to determine whether an item is defective or not by performing a measurement on the item which provides a value of a continuous random variable X and comparing it to specification limits. For example, in Chapter 1 of *Modern Statistics* (Kenett et al. 2022b), we discussed measuring the strength of yarn. In this case a piece of yarn is deemed defective if its strength X is less than ξ, where ξ is the required minimum strength, i.e., its lower specification limit. The proportion of defective yarn pieces in the population (or very large lot) is the probability that $X \leq \xi$.

Suppose now that X has a normal distribution with mean μ and variance σ^2. (If the distribution is not normal, we can often reduce it to a normal one by a proper transformation.) Accordingly, the proportion of defectives in the population is

$$p = \Phi\left(\frac{\xi - \mu}{\sigma}\right). \tag{11.6.1}$$

We have to decide whether $p \leq p_0$ (= AQL) or $p \geq p_t$ (= LQL), in order to accept or reject the lot.

Let x_p represent the pth quantile of a normal distribution with mean μ and standard deviation σ. Then

$$x_p = \mu + z_p\sigma. \tag{11.6.2}$$

If it were the case that $x_{p_0} \geq \xi$, we should accept the lot since the proportion of defectives is less than p_0. Since we do not know μ and σ, we must make our decision on the basis of estimates from a sample of n measurements. We decide to reject the lot if

$$\bar{X} - kS < \xi$$

and **accept** the lot if

$$\bar{X} - kS \geq \xi.$$

Here, $\bar{X}$ and S are the usual sample mean and standard deviation, respectively. The factor k is chosen so that the producer's risk (the risk of rejecting a good lot) does not exceed α. The values of the factor k are given approximately by the formula

$$k \doteq t_{1-\alpha, p_0, n},$$

where

$$t_{1-a,b,n} = \frac{z_{1-b}}{1 - z_{1-a}^2/2n} + \frac{z_{1-a}\left(1 + \frac{z_b^2}{2} - \frac{z_{1-a}^2}{2n}\right)^{1/2}}{\sqrt{n}\left(1 - \frac{z_{1-a}^2}{2n}\right)}. \tag{11.6.3}$$

The OC function of such a test is given approximately (for large samples) by

$$\mathrm{OC}(p) \approx 1 - \Phi\left(\frac{(z_p + k)/\sqrt{n}}{(1 + k^2/2)^{1/2}}\right), \tag{11.6.4}$$

where $k = t_{1-\alpha,p,n}$. We can thus determine n and k so that

$$\mathrm{OC}(p_0) = 1 - \alpha$$

and

$$\mathrm{OC}(p_t) = \beta.$$

These two conditions yield the equations

$$(z_{p_t} + k)\sqrt{n} = z_{1-\beta}(1 + k^2/2)^{1/2}$$

and (11.6.5)

$$(z_{p_0} + k)\sqrt{n} = z_{\alpha}(1 + k^2/2)^{1/2}.$$

The solution for n and k yields

$$n = \frac{(z_{1-\alpha} + z_{1-\beta})^2(1 + k^2/2)}{(z_{p_t} - z_{p_0})^2}, \tag{11.6.6}$$

and

$$k = (z_{p_t} z_{\alpha} + z_{p_0} z_{\beta})/(z_{1-\alpha} + z_{1-\beta}). \tag{11.6.7}$$

In other words, if the sample size n is given by the above formula, we can replace $t_{1-\alpha,p,n}$ by the simpler term k and accept the lot if

$$\bar{X} - kS \geq \xi.$$

The statistic $\bar{X} - kS$ is called a **lower tolerance limit**.

Example 11.4 Consider the example of testing the compressive strength of concrete cubes presented in Chapter 1 in *Modern Statistics* (Kenett et al. 2022b). It is required that the compressive strength be larger than 240 [kg/cm^2]. We found that $Y = \ln X$ had an approximately normal distribution. Suppose that it is required to decide whether to accept or reject this lot with the following specifications: $p_0 = 0.01$, $p_t = 0.05$, and $\alpha = \beta = 0.05$. According to the normal distribution,

$$z_{p_0} = -2.326, \quad z_{p_t} = -1.645$$

and

$$z_{1-\alpha} = z_{1-\beta} = 1.645.$$

Thus, according to the above formulas, we find $k = 1.9855$ and $n = 70$. Hence, with a sample size of 70, we can accept the lot if $\bar{Y} - 1.9855S \geq \xi$, where $\xi = \ln(240) = 5.48$. ■

The sample size required in this single-stage sampling plan for variables is substantially smaller than the one we determined for the single-stage sampling plan for attributes (which was $n = 176$). However, the sampling plan for attributes is free of any assumption about the distribution of X, while in the above example we had to assume that $Y = \ln X$ is normally distributed. Thus, there is a certain trade-off between the two approaches. In particular, if our assumptions concerning the distribution of X are erroneous, we may not have the desired producer's and consumer's risks.

The above procedure of acceptance sampling for variables can be generalized to **upper and lower tolerance limits**, double sampling, and sequential sampling. The interested reader can find more information on the subject in (Duncan 1986, Ch. 12–15). Berry and Fristedt (1985) applied tolerance limits for the appraisal of ceramic substrates in the multivariate case.

11.7 Rectifying Inspection of Lots

Rectifying inspection plans are those plans which call for a complete inspection of a **rejected lot** for the purpose of replacing the defectives by non-defective items. (Lots that are accepted are not subjected to rectification.) We shall assume that the tests are non-destructive, that all the defective items in the sample are replaced by good ones, and that the sample is replaced in the lot.

If a lot contains N items and has a proportion p of defectives before the inspection, the proportion of defectives in the lot after inspection is

$$p' = \begin{cases} 0, & \text{if lot is rejected,} \\ \\ p(N - X)/N, & \text{if lot is accepted,} \end{cases} \tag{11.7.1}$$

where X is the number of defectives in the sample. If the probability of accepting a lot by a given sampling plan is $\text{OC}(p)$, then the expected proportion of outgoing defectives is when sampling is single stage by attribute,

$$E\{p'\} = p\,\text{OC}(p)\left(1 - \frac{n}{N}R_s^*\right), \tag{11.7.2}$$

Table 11.13 AOQ values for rectifying plan $N = 1000$, $n = 250$, and $c = 5$

p	OC(p)	R_s^*	AOQ
0.005	1.000	1.0000	0.004
0.010	0.981	0.9710	0.007
0.015	0.853	0.8730	0.010
0.020	0.618	0.7568	0.010
0.025	0.376	0.6546	0.008
0.030	0.199	0.5715	0.005
0.035	0.094	0.5053	0.003

where

$$R_s^* = \frac{H(c-1; N-1, [Np]-1, n-1)}{H(c; N, [Np], n)}. \tag{11.7.3}$$

If n/N is small, then

$$E\{p'\} \cong p\mathrm{OC}(p). \tag{11.7.4}$$

The expected value of p' is called the **Average Outgoing Quality** and is denoted by AOQ.

The formula for R_s^* depends on the method of sampling inspection. If the inspection is by double sampling, the formula is considerably more complicated.

In Table 11.13, we present the AOQ values corresponding to a rectifying plan, when $N = 1000$, $n = 250$, and $c = 5$.

The AOQL (Average Outgoing Quality Limit) of a rectifying plan is defined as the maximal value of AOQ. Thus the AOQL corresponding to the plan of Table 11.13 is approximately 0.01. The AOQ given is presented graphically in Fig. 11.3.

We also characterize a rectifying plan by the **average total inspection** (ATI) associated with a given value of p. If a lot is accepted, only n items (the sample size) have been inspected, while if it is rejected, the number of items inspected is N. Thus,

$$\begin{aligned} \mathrm{ATI}(p) &= n\mathrm{OC}(p) + N(1 - \mathrm{OC}(p)) \\ &= n + (N - n)(1 - \mathrm{OC}(p)). \end{aligned} \tag{11.7.5}$$

This function is increasing from n (when $p = 0$) to N (when $p = 1$).

In our example, the lot contains $N = 1000$ items and the sample size is $n = 250$. The graph of the ATI function is presented in Fig. 11.4.

Dodge and Romig (1998) published tables for the design of single and double sampling plans for attributes, for which the AOQL is specified and the ATI is minimized at a specified value of p. In the following table, we provide a few values of n and c for such a single sampling plan, for which the AOQL = 0.01 (Table 11.14).

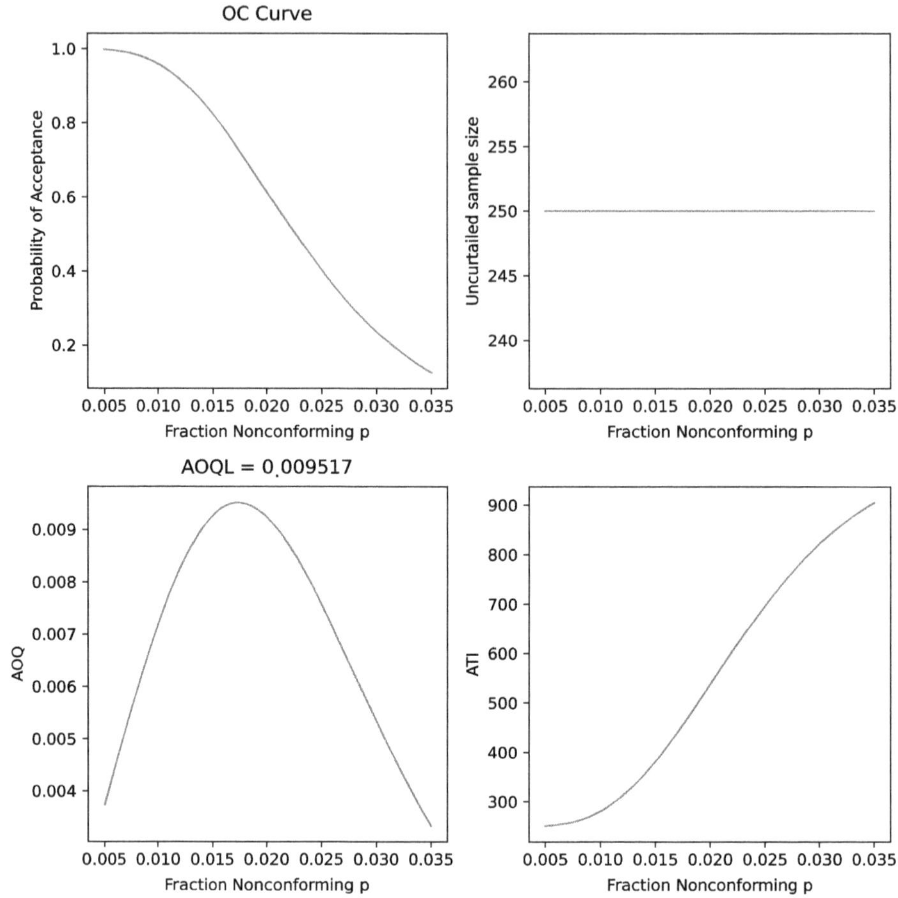

Fig. 11.3 AOQ curve for single sampling plan with $N = 1000$, $n = 250$, and $c = 5$

According to this table, for a lot of size 2000, to guarantee an AOQL of 1% and minimal ATI at $p = 0.01$, one needs a sample of size $n = 180$, with $c = 3$. For another method of determining n and c, see (Duncan 1986, Ch. 16).

Rectifying sampling plans with less than 100% inspection of rejected lots have been developed and are available in the literature.

11.8 National and International Standards

During World War II, the US Army developed standards for sampling acceptance schemes by attributes. Army Ordinance tables were prepared in 1942 and the Navy issued its own tables in 1945. Joint Army and Navy standards were issued in 1949.

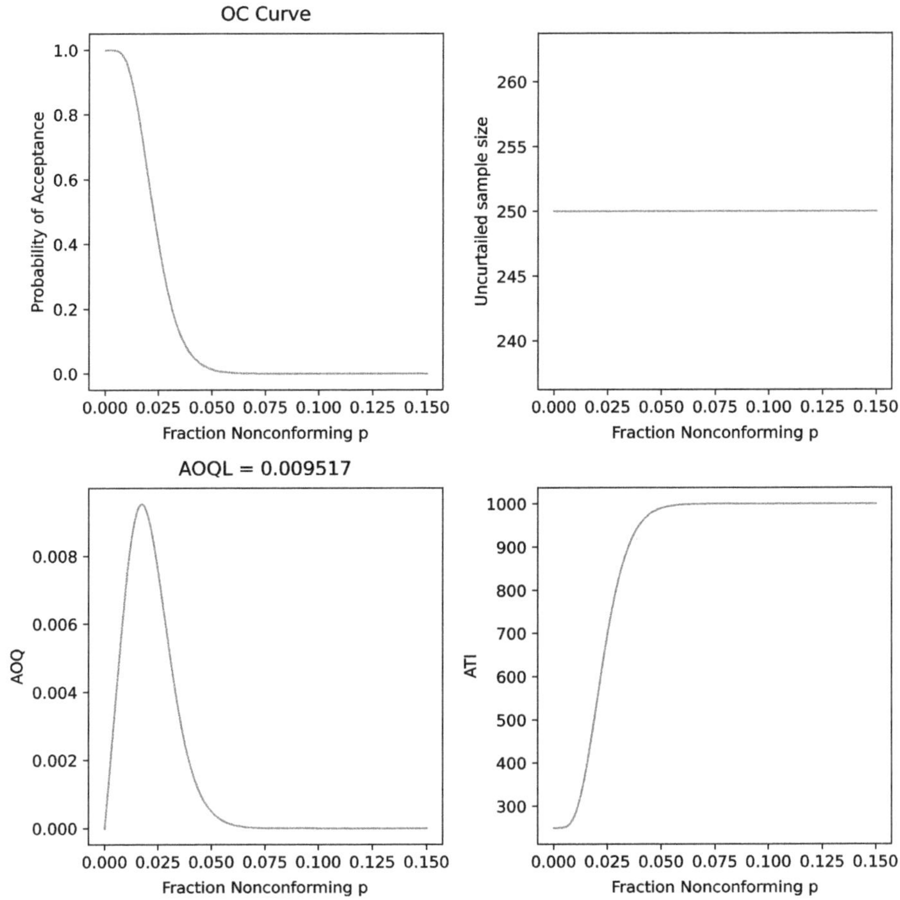

Fig. 11.4 ATI curve for single sampling plan with $N = 1000$, $n = 250$, and $c = 5$

These standards were superseded in 1950 by the common standards, named MIL-STD-105A. The MIL-STD-105D was issued by the US Government in 1963 and slightly revised as MIL-STD-105E in 1989. These standards, however, are gradually being phased out by the Department of Defense. The American National Standards Institute (ANSI) adopted the military standards with some minor modifications, as ANSI Z1.4 standards. These were adopted in 1974 by the International Organization for Standardization as ISO 2859. In 1981, ANSI Z1.4 was adopted by the American Society for Quality Control with some additions, and the standards issued were named ANSI/ASQC Z1.4.

The military standards were designed to inspect incoming lots from a variety of suppliers. The requirement from all suppliers is to satisfy specified quality levels for the products. These quality levels are indexed by the **AQL**. It is expected that a supplier sends in continuously series of lots (shipments). All these lots are subjected

Table 11.14 Selected values of (n, c) for a single sampling plan with AOQL $= 0.01$ and ATI minimum at p

p	0.004–0.006		0.006–0.008		0.008–0.01	
N	n	c	n	c	n	c
101–200	32	0	32	0	32	0
201–300	33	0	33	0	65	1
501–600	75	1	75	1	75	1
1001–2000	130	2	130	2	180	3

to quality inspection. At the beginning an AQL value is specified for the product. The type of sampling plan is decided (single, double, sequential, etc.). For a given lot size and type of sampling, the parameters of the sampling procedure are determined. For example, if the sampling is single stage by attribute, the parameters (n, c) are read from the tables. The special feature of the MIL-STD-105E is that lots can be subjected to **normal**, **tightened**, or **reduced** inspection. Inspection starts at a normal level. If two out of five consecutive lots have been rejected, a switch to tightened inspection level takes place. Normal inspection is reinstituted if five consecutive lots have been accepted. If ten consecutive lots remain under tightened inspection, an action may take place to discontinue the contract with the supplier. On the other hand, if the last ten lots have all been accepted at a normal inspection level and the total number of defective units found in the samples from these ten lots is less than a specified value, then a switch from normal to reduced inspection level can take place.

We do not reproduce here the MIL-STD-105 tables. The reader can find detailed explanation and examples in (Duncan 1986, Ch. 10). We conclude with the following example.

Example 11.5 Suppose that for a given product AQL $= 0.01$ (1%). The size of the lots is $N = 1000$. The military standard specifies that a single-stage sampling for attributes, under normal inspection, has the parameters $n = 80$ and $c = 2$. Using Python, we get the following QC values for this plan:

```
plan = acceptanceSampling.SSPlanBinomial(1000, 80, 2,
                                          p=(0.01, 0.02, 0.03, 0.04, 0.05))
```

p	0.01	0.02	0.03	0.04	0.05
OC(p)	0.953	0.784	0.568	0.375	0.231

Thus, if the proportion of nonconforming, p, of the supplier is less than AQL, the probability of accepting a lot is larger than 0.953. A supplier that continues to ship lots with $p = 0.01$ has a probability of $(0.953)^{10} = 0.621$ that all the 10 lots will be accepted, and the inspection level will be switched to a reduced one. Under the reduced level, the sample size from the lot is reduced to $n = 32$. The corresponding acceptance number is $c = 1$. Thus, despite the fact that the level of quality of the supplier remains good, there is a probability of $0.38 = 1 - 0.953^{10}$ that there will be no switch to reduced inspection level after the tenth lot. On the other hand, the probability that there will be no switch to tightened level of inspection before the sixth lot is inspected is 0.9859. This is the probability that after each inspection the next lot will continue to be inspected under normal level. If there is no deterioration in the quality level of the supplier and $p = 0.03$, the probability that the inspection level will be switched to "tightened" after five inspections is 0.722. ■

11.9 Skip-Lot Sampling Plans for Attributes

We have seen in the previous section that according to the MIL-STD-105E, if a supplier keeps shipping high-quality lots, then after a while his lots are subjected to inspection under reduced level. All lots are inspected under a reduced level inspection scheme, as long as their quality level remains high. The **Skip-Lot Sampling Plans** (SLSP), which was proposed by Liebesman and Saperstein (1983), introduces a new element of savings if lots continue to have very low proportions of nonconforming items. As we will see below, instead of just reduced level of inspection of high-quality lots, the SLSP plans do not necessarily inspect such lots. If the lots coming in from a given supplier qualify for skipping, then they are inspected only with probability 0.5. This probability is later reduced to 0.33 and to 0.2, if the inspected lots continue to be almost free of nonconforming items. Thus, suppliers that continue to manufacture their product, with proportion of defectives p, considerably smaller than the specified AQL stand a good chance to have only a small fraction of their lots inspected. The SLSP which will be specified below was adopted as the ISO2859/3 standard in 1986.

11.9.1 The ISO 2859 Skip-Lot Sampling Procedures

Am SLSP has to address three main issues:

1. What are the conditions for beginning or reinstating the Skip-Lot (SL) state?
2. What is the fraction of lots to be skipped?
3. Under what conditions should one stop skipping lots, on a temporary or permanent basis?

The fraction of lots to be skipped is the probability that a given lot will not be inspected. If this probability for example is 0.8, we generate a random number, U, with uniform distribution on (0, 1). If $U < 0.8$, inspection is skipped; otherwise the lot is inspected.

We define three states:

State 1. Every lot is inspected.
State 2. Some lots are skipped and not inspected.

State 3. All lots are inspected, pending a decision of disqualification (back to state 1) or resumption of SL (back to state 2).

Lot by lot inspection is performed during state 3, but the requirements to requalify for Skip-Lot inspection are less stringent than the initial qualification requirements.

Switching rules apply to 4 transitions between states: Qualification (State 1 to State 2), Interruption (State 2 to State 3), Resumption (State 3 to State 2), and Disqualification (State 3 to State 1).

The switching rules for the SLSP procedure are listed below.

Skip-Lot Switching Rules

We specify here the rules appropriate for single sampling by attributes. Other rules are available for other sampling schemes.

(A) **Qualification**. (State 1 → State 2).

1. Ten consecutive lots are accepted.
2. The total number of defective items in the samples from the ten lots is smaller than critical level given in Table 11.15.
3. The number of defective items in each one of the last two lots is smaller than the values specified in Table 11.16.
4. Supplier has a stable manufacturing organization, continuous production and other traits which qualify him to be high quality stable manufacturer.

(B) **Interruption**. (State 2 → State 3)

1. An inspected lot has in the sample more defectives than specified in Table 11.16.

(C) **Resumption**. (State 3 → State 2)

1. Four consecutive lots are accepted.
2. The last two lots satisfy the requirements of Table 11.16.

(D) **Disqualifications**. (State 3 → State 1)

1. Two lots are rejected within ten consecutively inspected lots or
2. Violation of the supplier qualification criteria (item A4 above)

We have seen in the previous section that, under normal inspection, MIL-STD-105E specifies that, for AQL $= 0.01$ and lots of size $N = 1,000$, random samples of size $n = 80$ should be drawn. The critical level was $c = 2$. If 10 lots have been accepted consecutively, the total number of observed defectives is $S_{10} \leq 20$. The total sample size is 800, and according to Table 11.15, S_{10} should not exceed 3 to qualify for a switch to State 2. Moreover, according to Table 11.16, the last two samples should each have less than 1 defective item. Thus, the probability to qualify for State 2, on the basis of the last 10 samples, when $p = \text{AQL} = 0.01$ is

Table 11.15 Minimum cumulative sample size in ten lots for skip-lot qualifications

Cumulative no. of defectives	AQL (%)						
	0.65	1.0	1.5	2.5	4.0	6.5	10.0
0	400	260	174	104	65	40	26
1	654	425	284	170	107	65	43
2	883	574	383	230	144	88	57
3	1098	714	476	286	179	110	71
4	1306	849	566	340	212	131	85
5	1508	980	653	392	245	151	98
6	1706	1109	739	444	277	171	111
7	1902	1236	824	494	309	190	124
8	2094	1361	907	544	340	209	136
9	2285	1485	990	594	371	229	149
10	2474	1608	1072	643	402	247	161
11	2660	1729	1153	692	432	266	173
12	2846	1850	1233	740	463	285	185
13	3031	1970	1313	788	493	303	197
14	3214	2089	1393	836	522	321	209
15	3397	2208	1472	883	552	340	221
16	3578	2326	1550	930	582	358	233
17	3758	2443	1629	977	611	376	244
18	3938	2560	1707	1024	640	394	256
19	4117	2676	1784	1070	669	412	268
20	4297	2793	1862	1117	698	430	279

Table 11.16 Individual lot acceptance numbers for skip-lot qualification

	AQL(%)						
Sample size	0.65	1.0	1.5	2.5	4.0	6.5	10.0
2	–	–	–	–	–	0	0
3	–	–	–	–	0	0	0
5	–	–	–	0	0	0	1
8	–	–	0	0	0	1	1
13	–	0	0	0	1	1	2
20	0	0	0	1	1	2	3
32	0	0	1	1	2	3	5
50	0	1	1	2	3	5	7
80	1	1	2	3	5	7	11
125	1	2	3	4	7	11	16
200	2	3	4	7	11	17	25
315	3	4	7	11	16	25	38
500	5	7	10	16	25	39	58
800	7	11	16	25	38	60	91
1250	11	16	23	38	58	92	138
2000	17	25	36	58	91	144	217

$$QP = b^2(0; 80, 0.01)B(3; 640, 0.01)$$
$$= (0.4475)^2 \times 0.1177 = 0.0236.$$

Thus, if the fraction defective level is exactly at the AQL value, the probability for qualification is only 0.02. On the other hand, if the supplier maintains the production at fraction defective of $p = 0.001$, then the qualification probability is

$$QP = b^2(0; 80, 0.001)B(3; 640, 0.001)$$
$$= (0.9231)^2 \times 0.9958 = 0.849.$$

Thus, a supplier who maintains a level of $p = 0.001$, when the AQL $= 0.01$, will probably be qualified after the first ten inspections and will switch to State 2 of skipping lots. Eventually only 20% of his lots will be inspected, under this SLSP standard, with high savings to both producer and consumer. This illustrates the importance of maintaining high-quality production processes. In Chaps. 2 and 3, we discussed how to statistically control the production processes, to maintain stable processes of high quality. Generally, for the SLSP to be effective, the fraction defective level of the supplier should be smaller than half of the AQL. For p level close to the AQL, the SLSP and the MIL-STD 105E are very similar in performance characteristics.

11.10 The Deming Inspection Criterion

Deming (1982) has derived a formula to express the expected cost to the firm caused by sampling of lots of incoming material. The importance of the Deming inspection criterion formula is that it provides an economic perspective on the alternatives of management by inspection or management by process control and process improvement (see Sect. 1.2). In some cases, investing in inspection equipment that provides high throughput sorting capabilities is more economical than investing in process control methods and technology (Chaps. 2–4). The drawback of inspection is that it is focused on product characteristics and not on production processes affecting product characteristics. The knowledge required in implementing inspection-based systems is minimal compared to process control which combines technological and operator dimensions. More knowledge is an industry 4.0 requirement so that decisions to remain at the level of screening and sorting induce limiting industrial capabilities (see Chap. 8). Decisions on investments in process control can be justified with Deming's formula we develop next. Let us define

N = the number of items in a lot
k_1 = the cost of inspecting one item at the beginning of the process
q = the probability of a conforming item

p = the probability of a nonconforming item
Q = $\mathrm{OC}(p) =$ probability of accepting a lot
k_2 = the cost to the firm when one nonconforming item is moved downstream to a customer or to the next stage of the production process
p'' = the probability of nonconforming items being in an accepted lot
n = the sample size inspected from a lot of size N

Thus, the total expected cost per lot is

$$EC = \frac{Nk_1}{q}\left[1 + Qq\left(\frac{k_2}{k_1}p'' - 1\right)\left(1 - \frac{n}{N}\right)\right]. \qquad (11.10.1)$$

If $(k_2/k_1)p'' > 1$, then any sampling plan increases the cost to the firm and $n = N$ (100% inspection) becomes the least costly alternative.

If $(k_2/k_1)p'' < 1$, then the value $n = 0$ yields the minimum value of EC so that no inspection is the alternative of choice.

Now p'' can be only somewhat smaller than p. For example, if $N = 50$, $n = 10$, $c = 0$, and $p = 0.04$, then $p'' = 0.0345$. Substituting p for p'' gives us the following rule:

If $(k_2/k_1)p > 1$, inspect every item in the lot

If $(k_2/k_1)p < 1$, accept the lot without inspection.

The Deming assumption is that the process is under control and that p is known. Sampling plans such as MIL-STD-105D do not make such assumptions and, in fact, are designed for catching shifts in process levels.

To keep the process under control, Deming suggests the use of control charts and Statistical Process Control (SPC) procedures which are discussed in Chaps. 2 and 3.

The assumption that a process is under control means that the firm has absorbed the cost of SPC as internal overhead or as a piece-cost. Deming's assertion then is that assuming up front the cost of SPC implementation is cheaper, in the long run, than doing business in a regime where a process may go out of control undetected until its output undergoes acceptance sampling.

11.11 Published Tables for Acceptance Sampling

In this section we list some information on published tables and schemes for sampling inspection by attribute and by variables. The material given here follows Chapters 24–25 of Juran (1979). We shall not provide an explanation here concerning the usage of these tables. The interested practitioner can use the instructions attached to the tables and/or read more about the tables in (Juran 1979, Ch. 24–25) or in Duncan (1986).

I. Sampling by Attributes

1. **MIL-STD-105E**

   Type of sampling: Single, double, and multiple
   Type of application: General
   Key features: Maintains average quality at a specified level; aims to minimize rejection of good lots; and provides single sampling plans for specified AQL and producer's risk.
   Reference: MIL-STD-105E, Sampling Procedures and Tables for Inspection by Attributes, Government Printing Office, Washington, D.C.

2. **Dodge-Romig**

   Type of sampling: Single and double. *Type of application:* Where 100% rectifying of lots is applicable. *Key features:* One type of plan uses a consumer's risk of $\beta = 0.10$. Another type limits the AOQL. Protection is provided with minimum inspection per lot. *Reference:* Dodge and Romig (1998)

3. **H107**

   Type of sampling: Continuous single stage
   Type of application: When production is continuous and inspection is non-destructive.
   Key features: Plans are indexed by AQL, which generally start with 100% inspection until some consecutive number of units free of defects are found. Then inspection continues on a sampling basis until a specified number of defectives are found.
   Reference: H-107, Single-Level Continuous Sampling Procedures and Tables for Inspection by Attribute, Government Printing Office, Washington, D.C.

II. Sampling by Variables

1. **MIL-STD-414**

   Assumed distribution: Normal
   Criteria specified: AQL
   Features: Lot evaluation by AQL. It includes tightened and reduced inspection.
   Reference: Sampling Procedures and Tables for Inspection by Variables for Percent Defectives, MIL-STD-414, Government Printing Office, Washington, D.C.

2. **H-108**

   Assumed distribution: Exponential
   Criteria specified: Mean Life (MTBF)
   Features: Life testing for reliability specifications
   Reference: H-108, Sampling Procedures and Tables for Life and Reliability Testing (Based on Exponential Distribution), US Department of Defense, Quality Control and Reliability Handbook, Government Printing Office, Washington, D.C.

11.12 Sequential Reliability Testing

Sequential methods in reliability testing have been in use from the pioneering work of Dvoretzky et al. (1953), Epstein and Sobel (1955), and Kiefer and Wolfowitz (1956). Sequential life testing and sampling acceptance for the exponential distribution had been codified in the Military Standards 781C document. Later, in the 60s and 70s, many papers appeared on survival analysis and among them also studies on sequential methods. Some of these are Epstein (1960), Basu (1971), Mukhopadhyay (1974), and Bryant and Schmee (1979), among others. In this section we review these methods in an introductory approach. A comprehensive summary of these methods is given in the article of Basu (1991).

Let T denote the cumulative operating time till failure (TTF) of a system. The distribution of T is the "life distribution" and there are several life distribution models including the Exponential, Shifted-Exponential, Erlang, Weibull, and Extreme-Value distribution (see Sect. 9.7).

Consider, for example, the sequential analysis of the reliability of a system with an Exponential life distribution, with mean time between failures (MTBF) $= \theta$. The cumulative distribution function $F_T(t; \theta) = 1 - \exp(t/\theta)$, and the reliability function $R(t) = \exp(t/\theta)$. Estimation of $R(t_0)$ at a specified time t_0 is based on consecutive sequence of continuous failure times observations.

A particularly interesting question is establishing when, during testing, the MTBF is shown to be bigger than a prespecified value θ_o. Testing hypotheses about the MTBF is based on the Wald SPRT. Such testing can be evaluated with an operating characteristic curve that plots the probability of acceptance as a function of θ_o. The evaluation of the operating characteristics of sequential methods can be done via Wald's approximations, asymptotic analysis, or numerical techniques. The difficulty is in identifying the exact distributions of stopping times, i.e., the time instance when the MTBF is declared to be bigger than θ_o. Algorithms for the numerical determination of the operating characteristics of sequential procedures were developed by Aroian and Robison (1969), Aroian (1976), Zacks (1980, 1992, 1997), and others. In this section we focus on the application of sequential reliability testing to system and software testing.

The definition of system and software reliability is the probability of execution without failure for some specified interval, called the mission time (Kenett 2007). This definition is compatible with that used for hardware reliability, though the failure mechanisms in software components may differ significantly. System and software reliability is applicable both as a tool complementing development testing, in which faults are found and removed, and for certification testing, when a system or software product is either accepted or rejected as meeting its quality requirements. When software is in operation, failure rates can be computed by computing number of failures, say, per hours of operation. The predicted failure rate corresponding to the steady state behavior of the software is usually a key indicator of great interest. The predicted failure rate may be regarded as high when compared to other systems. We should keep in mind, however, that the specific weight of the failures indicating severity of impact is not accounted for within the failure category being tracked. In the bug tracking data base, all failures within one category are equal. Actual interpretation of the predicted failure rates, accounting for operational profile and specific failure impact, is therefore quite complex. Predicted failure rates should therefore be considered in management decisions at an aggregated level. For instance, the decision to promote software from system test status to acceptance test status can be based on a comparison of predicted failure rates to actual, as illustrated below.

Reliability specifications should be verified with a specified level of confidence. Interpreting failure data is also used to determine if a system can be moved from development to beta testing with selected customers and then from beta testing to official shipping. Both applications to development testing and certification testing rely on mathematical models for tracking and predicting software reliability. Many system and software reliability models have been suggested. Moreover lessons learned from object oriented development are used to better design Web Services and Service Oriented Architecture systems for both better reliability and usability (Bai and Kenett 2009). In this section we review the classical reliability models that apply to software and overall system reliability.

The Jelinski–Moranda model (Jelinski and Moranda 1972) is the first published Markov model, which has profound influences on software reliability modeling thereafter. The main assumptions of this model are:

(a) The number of initial faults is an unknown but fixed constant.
(b) A detected fault is removed immediately and no new faults are introduced.
(c) Times between failures are independent, exponentially distributed random quantities.
(d) Each remaining software fault contributes the same amount to the software failure intensity.

Denote by N_0 the number of initial faults in the software before the testing starts, then the initial failure intensity is $N_0\phi$, where ϕ is a constant of proportionality denoting the failure intensity contributed by each fault. Denote by T_i, $i = 1, 2, \ldots, N_0$, the time between $(i-1)$th and ith failures, then T_i's are independent, exponentially distributed random variables with parameter

$$\lambda_i = \phi\left[N_0 - (i-1)\right], \qquad i = 1, 2, \ldots, N_0.$$

Many modified versions of the Jelinski–Moranda model have been studied in the literature. Schick and Wolverton (1978) proposed a model assuming that times between failures are not exponential but follow Rayleigh distribution. Shanthikumar (1981) generalized the Jelinski–Moranda model by using general time-dependent transition probability function. Xie (1991) developed a general decreasing failure intensity model allowing for the possibility of different fault sizes. Whittaker et al. (2000) considered a model that allows use of prior testing data to cover the real-world scenario in which the release build is constructed only after a succession of repairs to buggy pre-release builds. Boland and Singh (2003) consider a birth-process approach to a related software reliability model and Lipow considers data aggregated over various time intervals (Lipow 1978). The Lipow model assumes that:

(a) The rate of error detection is proportional to the current error content of a program.
(b) All errors are equally likely to occur and are independent of one another.
(c) Each error is of the same order of severity as any other error.
(d) The error rate remains constant over the testing interval.
(e) The software is operated in a similar manner as the anticipated operational usage
(f) During a testing interval i, f_i errors are discovered, but only n_i errors are corrected in the time frame.

When software is in operation, failure rates can be computed by computing number of failures, say, per hours of operation. The predicted failure rate corresponding to the steady state behavior of the software is usually a key indicator of great interest. The predicted failure rate may be regarded as high when compared to other systems. We should keep in mind, however, that the specific weight of the failures indicating severity of impact is not accounted for within the failure category being tracked. In the bug tracking data base, all failures within one category are equal. Actual micro-interpretation of the predicted failure rates, accounting for operational profile and specific failure impact, is therefore quite complex. Predicted failure rates should therefore be considered in management decisions at a macro, aggregated level. For instance, the decision to promote software from system test status to acceptance test status can be based on a comparison of predicted failure rates to actual, as illustrated below. Since the error rate remains constant during each of the M testing periods (assumption (d)), the failure rate during the ith testing period is

$$Z(t) = \phi\,[N - F_i], \qquad t_{i-1} \le t \le t_i,$$

where ϕ is the proportionality constant, N is again the total number of errors initially present in the program, $F_{i-1} = \sum_{j=1}^{i-1} n_j$ is the total number of errors corrected up through the $(i-1)$-th testing intervals, and t_i is the time measured in either CPU or wall clock time at the end of the ith testing interval, $x_i = t_i - t_{i-1}$. The t_i's are fixed and thus are not fixed as in the Jelinski–Moranda model. Taking the number of failures, f_i, in the ith interval to be a Poisson random variable with mean $Z(t_i)x_i$, the likelihood is

$$L(f_1, \ldots, f_M) = \prod_{i=1}^{M} \frac{(\phi[N - F_{i-1}]x_i)^{f_i} \exp\left(-\phi[N - F_{i-1}]x_i\right)}{f_i!}.$$

Taking the partial derivatives of $L(f)$ with respect to ϕ and N and setting the resulting equations to zero, we derive the following equations satisfied by the maximum likelihood estimators $\hat{\phi}$ and $\hat{N}$ of ϕ and N:

$$\hat{\phi} = \frac{F_M/A}{\hat{N} + 1 - B/A} \quad \text{and} \quad \frac{F_M}{\hat{N} + 1 - B/A} = \sum_{i=1}^{M} \frac{f_i}{\hat{N} - F_{i-1}},$$

where

$$F_M = \sum_{i=1}^{M} f_i, \quad \text{the total number of errors found in the } M \text{ periods of testing,}$$

$$B = \sum_{i=1}^{M} (F_{i-1} + 1)x_i, \quad \text{and}$$

$$A = \sum_{i=1}^{M} x_i, \quad \text{the total length of the testing period.}$$

From these estimates, the maximum likelihood estimate of the mean time until the next failure (MTTF) given the information accumulated in the M testing periods is equal to $\frac{1}{\hat{\phi}(\hat{N} - F_M)}$.

The Jelinski–Moranda model and the various extensions to this model are classified as time domain models. They rely on a physical modeling of the appearance and fixing of software failures. The different sets of assumptions are translated into differences in mathematical formulations.

For non-independent data, a non-homogeneous Poisson process (NHPP) can be assumed. Denote by $N(t)$ the number of observed failures until time t, and the main assumptions of this type of models are:

(a) $N(0) = 0$.
(b) $\{N(t), t \geq o\}$ has independent increments.
(c) At time t, $N(t)$ follows a Poisson distribution with parameter $m(t)$, i.e.,

$$P\{N(t) = n\} = \frac{(m(t))^n}{n!} \exp(-m(t)), \qquad n = 0, 1, 2, \cdots,$$

where $m(t)$ is called the mean value function of the NHPP, which describes the expected cumulative number of experienced failures in time interval $(0, t]$.

The failure intensity function, $\lambda(t)$, is defined as

$$\lambda(t) \equiv \lim_{\Delta t \to 0} \frac{P\{N(t + \Delta t) - N(t) > 0\}}{\Delta t} = \frac{dm(t)}{dt}, \qquad t \geq 0$$

Generally, by using a different mean value function of $m(t)$, we get different NHPP models (Fig. 11.5).

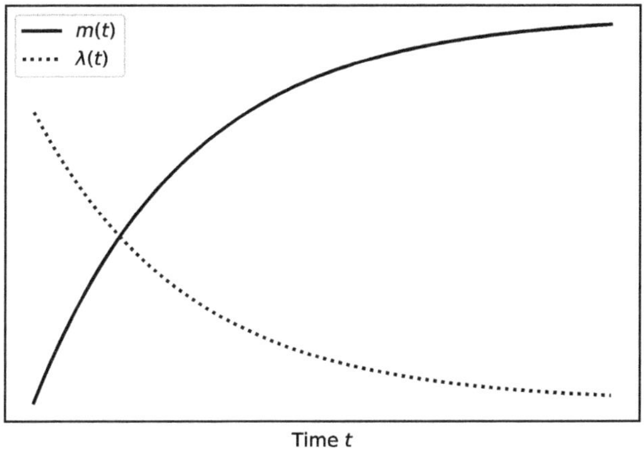

Fig. 11.5 An example of failure intensity function $\lambda(t)$ and mean value function $m(t)$

An NHPP model was proposed by Goel and Okumoto (1979) and many other NHPP models are modification or generalization of this model. The mean value function of the Goel–Okumoto model is

$$m(t) = a\left[1 - \exp(-bt)\right], \quad a > 0,\ b > 0,$$

where a is the expected number of faults to be eventually detected and b is the failure occurrence rate per fault. The failure intensity function of the Goel–Okumoto model is

$$\lambda(t) = ab\exp(-bt).$$

Musa and Okumoto (1984) developed a logarithmic Poisson execution time model. The mean value function is

$$m(t) = \frac{1}{\varphi}\ln\left(\lambda_0\varphi t + 1\right), \quad \varphi > 0,\ \lambda_0 > 0,$$

where λ_0 is the initial failure intensity and φ is the failure intensity decay parameter. Since this model allows an infinite number of failures to be observed, it is also called an infinite failure model.

It is sometimes observed that the curve of the cumulative number of faults is S-shaped. Several different S-shaped NHPP models have been proposed in the existing literature. Among them, the most interesting ones are the delayed S-shaped NHPP model (Yamada et al. 1984) and the inflected S-shaped NHPP model (Ohba 1984). The mean value function of the delayed S-shaped NHPP model is

$$m(t) = a\left[1 - (1 + bt)\exp(-bt)\right], \quad a > 0,\ b > 0$$

and the mean value function of the inflected S-shaped NHPP model is

$$m(t) = \frac{a\left[1 - \exp(-bt)\right]}{1 + c\exp(-bt)}, \quad a > 0,\ b > 0,\ c > 0.$$

An interesting model called log-power model was proposed in Xie and Zhao (1993). It has the mean value function

$$m(t) = a\left[\ln(1+t)\right]^b, \quad a > 0,\ b > 0.$$

This model is a modification of the traditional Duane model for general repairable system. A useful property is that if we take the logarithmic on both sides of the mean value function, we have

$$\ln m(t) = \ln a + b \ln\ln(1+t).$$

Hence a graphical procedure is established. If we plot the observed cumulative number of failures versus $(t+1)$, the plot should tend to be on a straight line on a log–log scale. This can be used to easily estimate the model parameters and, more importantly, to validate the model.

Example 11.6 The dataset **FAILURE_J3** contains the cumulative number of failures on a software project over a period of 41 weeks. The shape of the curve suggests that the Goel–Okumoto or the S-shaped Yamada model should provide good fits. We first define the two functions using Python.

```
def GoelOkumoto(t, a, b):
    return a * (1 - np.exp(-b * t))

def Yamada(t, a, b):
    return a * (1 - (1+b*t)*np.exp(-b*t))
```

The `scipy` function *curve_fit* allows to fit the function to the data.

```
def optimizeModelFit(model, data):
    fit = optimize.curve_fit(model, data['T'], data['CFC'])
    popt = fit[0]
    # add the fit to the dataset
    data[model.__name__] = [model(t, *popt) for t in data['T']]
    return popt

data = mistat.load_data('FAILURE_J3')
goFit = optimizeModelFit(GoelOkumoto, data)
ohbaFit = optimizeModelFit(Yamada, data)
```

Figure 11.6 shows the resulting fit curves. The S-shaped Yamada model leads to a better fit and describes the data better. ■

Bayesian assumptions in an NHPP model have been proposed by Littlewood and Verrall (1973). This Bayesian software reliability model assumes that times between

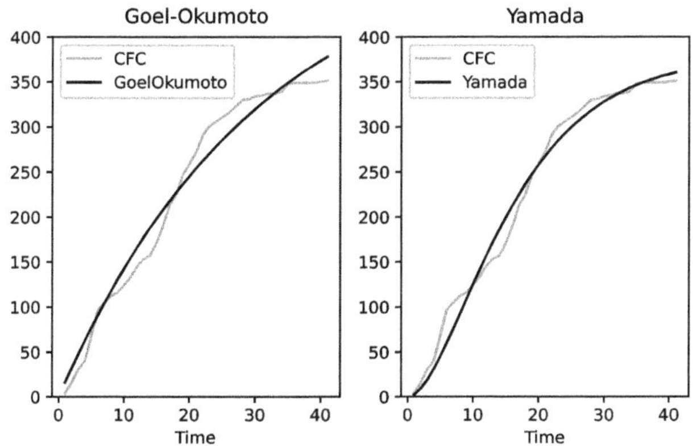

Fig. 11.6 Goel–Okumoto and Yamada models fitted to cumulative failure count data **FAILURE_J3**

failures are exponentially distributed with a parameter that is treated as a random variable with a Gamma prior distribution.

In system and software reliability model, parameters have to be estimated with historical data and maximum likelihood estimation (MLE) is a commonly adopted method for parameter estimation.

Failure data is of two different types, i.e., numbers of failures or failure times. For the first case, denote by n_i the number of failures observed in time interval $(s_{i-1}, s_i]$, where $0 \equiv s_0 < s_1 \ldots s_k$ and s_i $(i > 0)$ is the prescribed time point in the software testing process, and then the likelihood function for an NHPP model with mean value function $m(t)$ is

$$L(n_1, n_2, \ldots, n_k) = \prod_{i=1}^{k} \frac{[m(s_i) - m(s_{i-1})]^{n_i} \exp\{-[m(s_i) - m(s_{i-1})]\}}{n_i!}.$$

The parameters in $m(t)$ can be estimated by maximizing the likelihood function given above. Usually, numerical procedures have to be used.

For the second case, denote by T_i, $i = 1, 2, \ldots, k$, the observed k failure times in a software testing process, and then the likelihood function is

$$L(T_1, T_2, \ldots, T_k) = \exp[-m(T_k)] \prod_{i=1}^{k} \lambda(T_i).$$

In order to find asymptotic confidence intervals for the k model parameters, the derivation of the Fisher information matrix is needed, which is given by

$$I(\theta_1, \ldots, \theta_k) \equiv \begin{bmatrix} -E\left[\frac{\partial^2 \ln L}{\partial \theta_1^2}\right] & -E\left[\frac{\partial^2 \ln L}{\partial \theta_2 \partial \theta_1}\right] & \cdots & -E\left[\frac{\partial^2 \ln L}{\partial \theta_k \partial \theta_1}\right] \\ -E\left[\frac{\partial^2 \ln L}{\partial \theta_1 \partial \theta_2}\right] & -E\left[\frac{\partial^2 \ln L}{\partial \theta_2^2}\right] & \cdots & -E\left[\frac{\partial^2 \ln L}{\partial \theta_k \partial \theta_2}\right] \\ \vdots & \vdots & & \vdots \\ -E\left[\frac{\partial^2 \ln L}{\partial \theta_1 \partial \theta_k}\right] & -E\left[\frac{\partial^2 \ln L}{\partial \theta_2 \partial \theta_k}\right] & \cdots & -E\left[\frac{\partial^2 \ln L}{\partial \theta_k^2}\right] \end{bmatrix}.$$

From the asymptotic theory of MLE, when n approaches to infinity, $\left[\hat{\theta}_1, \ldots, \hat{\theta}_k\right]$ converges in distribution to k-variate normal distribution with mean $[\theta_1, \ldots, \theta_k]$ and covariance matrix I^{-1}. That is, the asymptotic covariance matrix of the MLEs is

$$V_e \equiv \begin{bmatrix} \text{Var}(\hat{\theta}_1) & \text{Cov}(\hat{\theta}_1, \hat{\theta}_2) & \cdots & \text{Cov}(\hat{\theta}_1, \hat{\theta}_k) \\ \text{Cov}(\hat{\theta}_2, \hat{\theta}_1) & \text{Var}(\hat{\theta}_2) & \cdots & \text{Cov}(\hat{\theta}_2, \hat{\theta}_k) \\ \vdots & \vdots & & \vdots \\ \text{Cov}(\hat{\theta}_k, \hat{\theta}_1) & \text{Cov}(\hat{\theta}_k, \hat{\theta}_2) & \cdots & \text{Var}(\hat{\theta}_k) \end{bmatrix} = I^{-1}.$$

Therefore, the asymptotic $100(1-\alpha)\%$ confidence interval for $\hat{\theta}_i$ is

$$\left(\hat{\theta}_i - z_{\alpha/2}\sqrt{\text{Var}(\hat{\theta}_i)}, \quad \hat{\theta}_i + z_{\alpha/2}\sqrt{\text{Var}(\hat{\theta}_i)}\right), \quad i = 1, \ldots, k,$$

where $z_{\alpha/2}$ is the $1-\alpha/2$ percentile of the standard normal distribution and the quantity $\text{Var}(\hat{\theta}_i)$ can be obtained from the covariance matrix given above.

Since the true values of $\hat{\theta}_i$'s are unknown, the observed information matrix is often used

$$\hat{I}(\hat{\theta}_1, \ldots, \hat{\theta}_k) \equiv \begin{bmatrix} -\frac{\partial^2 \ln L}{\partial \theta_1^2} & -\frac{\partial^2 \ln L}{\partial \theta_2 \partial \theta_1} & \cdots & -\frac{\partial^2 \ln L}{\partial \theta_k \partial \theta_1} \\ -\frac{\partial^2 \ln L}{\partial \theta_1 \partial \theta_2} & -\frac{\partial^2 \ln L}{\partial \theta_2^2} & \cdots & -\frac{\partial^2 \ln L}{\partial \theta_k \partial \theta_2} \\ \vdots & \vdots & & \vdots \\ -\frac{\partial^2 \ln L}{\partial \theta_1 \partial \theta_k} & -\frac{\partial^2 \ln L}{\partial \theta_2 \partial \theta_k} & \cdots & -\frac{\partial^2 \ln L}{\partial \theta_k^2} \end{bmatrix}_{\substack{\theta_1 = \hat{\theta}_1 \\ \cdots \\ \theta_k = \hat{\theta}_k}},$$

and the confidence interval for $\hat{\theta}_i$ can be calculated.

If $\Phi \equiv g(\theta_1, \ldots, \theta_k)$, where $g(\cdot)$ is a continuous function, then as n converges to infinity, $\hat{\Phi}$ converges in distribution to normal distribution with mean Φ and variance

$$\text{Var}(\hat{\Phi}) = \sum_{i=1}^{k} \sum_{j=1}^{k} \frac{\partial g}{\partial \theta_i} \cdot \frac{\partial g}{\partial \theta_j} \cdot v_{ij},$$

where v_{ij} is the element of the ith row and jth column of the matrix above. The asymptotic $100(1-\alpha)\%$ confidence interval for $\hat{\Phi}$ is

$$\left(\hat{\Phi} - z_{\alpha/2}\sqrt{\text{Var}(\hat{\Phi})}, \quad \hat{\Phi} + z_{\alpha/2}\sqrt{\text{Var}(\hat{\Phi})}\right).$$

The above result can be used to obtain the confidence interval for some useful quantities such as failure intensity or reliability.

Example 11.7 Assume that there are two model parameters, a and b, which is quite common in most of the software reliability models, and the Fisher information matrix is given by

$$I(\theta_1, \ldots, \theta_k) \equiv \begin{bmatrix} -E\left[\frac{\partial^2 \ln L}{\partial a^2}\right] & -E\left[\frac{\partial^2 \ln L}{\partial a \partial b}\right] \\ -E\left[\frac{\partial^2 \ln L}{\partial a \partial b}\right] & -E\left[\frac{\partial^2 \ln L}{\partial b^2}\right] \end{bmatrix}.$$

The asymptotic covariance matrix of the MLEs is the inverse of this matrix:

$$V_e = I^{-1} = \begin{bmatrix} \text{Var}(\hat{a}) & \text{Cov}(\hat{a}, \hat{b}) \\ \text{Cov}(\hat{a}, \hat{b}) & \text{Var}(\hat{b}) \end{bmatrix}.$$

For illustrative purposes, we take the data cited in Table 1 in Zhang and Pham (1998). The observed information matrix is

$$\hat{I} \equiv \begin{bmatrix} -\frac{\partial^2 \ln L}{\partial a^2} & -\frac{\partial^2 \ln L}{\partial a \partial b} \\ -\frac{\partial^2 \ln L}{\partial a \partial b} & -\frac{\partial^2 \ln L}{\partial b^2} \end{bmatrix}_{\substack{a=\hat{a} \\ b=\hat{b}}} = \begin{bmatrix} 0.0067 & 1.1095 \\ 1.1095 & 4801.2 \end{bmatrix}.$$

We can then obtain the asymptotic variance and covariance of the MLE as follows:

$$\text{Var}(\hat{a}) = 154.85, \qquad \text{Var}(\hat{b}) = 2.17 \times 10^{-4},$$
$$\text{Cov}(\hat{a}, \hat{b}) = -0.0358.$$

The 95% confidence intervals on parameters a and b are $(117.93, 166.71)$ and $(0.0957, 0.1535)$, respectively. Plugging these numbers in

$$m(t) = a\left[\ln(1+t)\right]^b, \quad a > 0, \; b > 0.$$

gives us a range of estimates of the software reliability growth performance. With such models, we can determine if and when the system is ready for deployment in the market. ■

In general, a software development process consists of the following four major phases: specification, design, coding, and testing. The testing phase is the most costly and time-consuming one. It is thus very much important for the management to spend the limited testing-resource efficiently. For the optimal testing-resource allocation problem, the following assumptions are made:

(a) A software system is composed of n independent modules which are developed and tested independently during the unit testing phase.
(b) In the unit testing phase, each software module is subject to failures at random times caused by faults remaining in the software module.
(c) The failure observation process of software module i is modeled by an NHPP with mean value function $m_i(t)$ or failure intensity function $\lambda_i(t) \equiv \frac{dm_i(t)}{dt}$.

A total amount of testing time T is available for the whole software system that consists of a few modules. Testing time should be allocated to each software module in such a way that the reliability of the system after unit testing phase will be maximized.

Finally, Kenett and Pollak (1986, 1996) propose the application of the Shiryaev–Roberts sequential change control procedure to determine if a system or software under test has reached a required level of reliability. This approach does not require a specific model, such as those listed above, and has been therefore labeled "semi parametric." The Shiryaev–Roberts procedure is based on a statistic that is a sum of likelihood ratios. If there is no change, it is assumed that the observations follow a known distribution whose density is denoted as $f_{\nu=\infty}$, and if there is a change at time $\nu = k$, then the density of the observations is denoted as $f_{\nu=k}$. Denoting the likelihood ratio of the observations $X_1, X_2, \ldots, X_n$ when $\nu = k$ by

$$\Lambda_{n,k} = \frac{f_{\nu=k}(X_1, X_2, \ldots, X_n)}{f_{\nu=\infty}(X_1, X_2, \ldots, X_n)}$$

where the observations may be dependent, the Shiryaev-Roberts surveillance statistic is

$$R_n = \sum_{k=1}^{n} \Lambda_{n,k}.$$

The scheme calls for releasing the system for distribution at

$$N_A = \min\{n \mid R_n \geq A\},$$

where A is chosen so that the average number of observations until false alarm (premature release) is equal to (or larger than) a prespecified constant B. Under fairly general conditions, there exists a constant $c > 1$ such that

$$\lim_{A\to\infty} E_{\nu=\infty}(N_A/A) = c,$$

where $E()$ stands for the expected value so that setting $A = B/c$ yields a scheme that approximately has B as its average number of observations until a possible premature release of the software.

If $f_\theta(x)$ represents an exponential distribution with parameter θ, where $\theta = w_0$ is a prespecified level of failure rate where the system is deemed unreliable if its failure rate exceeds it, and $\theta = w_1$ is an acceptable failure rate ($w_1 < w_0$), then

$$R_n = \sum_{k=1}^{n} \Lambda_{n,k} = \sum_{k=1}^{n} \left(\frac{w_1}{w_0}\right)^{n-k+1} \exp\left((w_0 - w_1)\sum_{i=k}^{n} X_i\right).$$

In this case, the computation is recursive and

$$R_{n+1} = \left(\frac{w_1}{w_0}\right) \exp\left((w_0 - w_1)X_{n+1}\right)(1 + R_n).$$

Tracking R_n, and comparing it to A, provides an easily implemented procedure for determining when a system or software version is ready for release.

In this section we reviewed a range of models used in sequential reliability testing. The inputs to these models consist of data on time of failure or a number of failures. Sequential and sampling based methods are used to monitor product and process quality. Designed experiments are used to design and improve products and processes. The book covers traditional and modern methods used to achieve enhanced monitoring, optimized designs, and reliable systems and products. Python is used throughout so that the reader can try the methods described within, reproduce the examples, and assess the learning with exercises that are accompanied by solutions.

11.13 Chapter Highlights

The main concepts and definitions introduced in this chapter include:

- Lot
- Acceptable quality level
- Limiting quality level
- Producer's risk
- Consumer's risk
- Single-stage sampling
- Acceptance number
- Operating characteristic
- Double sampling plan
- ASN—function
- Sequential sampling
- Sequential probability ratio test (SPRT)

- Rectifying inspection
- Average outgoing quality (AOQ)
- Average total inspection (ATI)
- Tightened, normal or reduced inspection levels
- Skip-lot sampling plans
- Sequential reliability testing
- One arm bandit (OAT)
- Two-arm bandit (TAB)
- A/B testing
- Software reliability testing

11.14 Exercises

Exercise 11.1 Determine single sampling plans for attributes, when the lot is $N = 2500$, $\alpha = \beta = 0.01$, and

(i) $AQL = 0.005$, $LQL = 0.01$
(ii) $AQL = 0.01$, $LQL = 0.03$
(iii) $AQL = 0.01$, $LQL = 0.05$

Exercise 11.2 Investigate how the lot size, N, influences the single sampling plans for attributes, when $\alpha = \beta = 0.05$, $AQL = 0.01$, $LQL = 0.03$, by computing the plans for $N = 100$, $N = 500$, $N = 1,000$, $N = 2,000$.

Exercise 11.3 Compute the $OC(p)$ function for the sampling plan computed in Exercise 11.1(iii). What is the probability of accepting a lot having 2.5% of nonconforming items?

Exercise 11.4 Compute the large sample approximation to a single sample plan for attributes (n^*, c^*), with $\alpha = \beta = 0.05$ and $AQL = 0.025$, $LQL = 0.06$. Compare these to the exact results. The lot size is $N = 2,000$.

Exercise 11.5 Repeat the previous Exercise with $N = 3000$, $\alpha = \beta = 0.10$, $AQL = 0.01$, and $LQL = 0.06$.

Exercise 11.6 Obtain the OC and ASN functions of the double sampling plan, with $n_1 = 200$, $n_2 = 2n_1$, $c_1 = 5$, and $c_2 = c_3 = 15$, when $N = 2,000$.

(i) What are the attained α and β when $AQL = 0.015$ and $LQL = 0.05$?
(ii) What is the ASN when $p = AQL$?
(iii) What is a single sampling plan having the same α and β? How many observations we expect to save if $p = AQL$? Notice that if $p = LQL$, the present double sampling plan is less efficient than the corresponding single sampling plan.

Exercise 11.7 Compute the OC and ASN values for a double sampling plan with $n_1 = 150$, $n_2 = 200$, $c_1 = 5$, and $c_2 = c_3 = 10$, when $N = 2,000$. Notice how high β is when $LQL = 0.05$. The present plan is reasonable if $LQL = 0.06$. Compare this plan to a single sampling one for $\alpha = 0.02$, $\beta = 0.10$, $AQL = 0.02$, and $LQL = 0.06$.

Exercise 11.8 Determine a sequential plan for the case of AQL $= 0.02$, LQL $= 0.06$, and $\alpha = \beta = 0.05$. Compute the OC and ASN functions of this plan. What are the ASN values when $p =$ AQL, $p =$ LQL, and $p = 0.035$?

Exercise 11.9 Compare the single sampling plan and the sequential one when AQL $= 0.01$, LQL $= 0.05$, $\alpha = \beta = 0.01$, and $N = 10,000$. What are the expected savings in sampling cost if each observation costs \$1, and $p =$ AQL?

Exercise 11.10 Use the `mistat` function *simulateOAB* to simulate the expected rewards, for $p = 0.4(0.05)0.8$, when $N = 75$, $\lambda = 0.6$, $k = 15$, $\gamma = 0.95$, and $Ns = 1000$.

Exercise 11.11 Use the `mistat` function *optimalOAB* to predict the expected reward under the optimal strategy, when $N = 75$, $\lambda = 0.6$.

Exercise 11.12 Consider the two-armed bandit (TAB) with $N = 40$ and $K = 10$. Make a table of all the possible predicted rewards.

Exercise 11.13 Determine n and k for a continuous variable size sampling plan, when $(p_0) = AQL = 0.01$ and $(p_t) = LQL = 0.05$, $\alpha = \beta = 0.05$.

Exercise 11.14 Consider dataset **ALMPIN.csv**. An aluminum pin is considered as defective if its cap diameter is smaller than 14.9 [mm]. For the parameters $p_0 = 0.01$ and $\alpha = 0.05$, compute k and decide whether to accept or reject the lot, on the basis of the sample of $n = 70$ pins. What is the probability of accepting a lot with proportion of defectives of $p = 0.03$?

Exercise 11.15 Determine the sample size and k for a single sampling plan by a normal variable, with the parameters $AQL = 0.02$, $LQL = 0.04$, and $\alpha = \beta = 0.10$.

Exercise 11.16 A single sampling plan for attributes, from a lot of size $N = 500$, is given by $n = 139$ and $c = 3$. Each lot that is not accepted is rectified. Compute the AOQ, when $p = 0.01$, $p = 0.02$, $p = 0.03$, and $p = 0.05$. What are the corresponding ATI values?

Exercise 11.17 A single sampling plan, under normal inspection, has probability $\alpha = 0.05$ of rejection, when $p = AQL$. What is the probability, when $p = AQL$ in 5 consecutive lots, that there will be a switch to tightened inspection? What is the probability of switching to a tightened inspection if p increases so that $OC(p) = 0.7$?

Exercise 11.18 Compute the probability for qualifying for State 2, in a Skip-Lot sampling plan, when $n = 100$, $c = 1$. What is the upper bound on S_{10}, in order to qualify for State 2, when $AQL = 0.01$? Compute the probability QP for State 2 qualification.

Exercise 11.19 The **FAILURE_J2** dataset contains the cumulative failure counts of a software project collected over a period of 181 weeks. Fit the following models to the data and visualize the results:

- Goel–Okumoto $f(t) = a[1 - \exp(-bt)]$
- Musa–Okumoto $f(t) = \frac{1}{\varphi} \log(\lambda_0 \varphi t + 1)$
- S-shaped Yamada $f(t) = a(1 - (1 + bt) \exp(-bt))$
- Inflected S-shaped Ohba $f(t) = \frac{a(1-\exp(-bt))}{1+c\exp(-bt)}$

Which model describes the data best?

Exercise 11.20 Continuing with Exercise 11.19, simulate cases where you only have data for the first 25, 50, 75, 100, or 125 weeks and fit Goel–Okumoto and inflected S-shaped models to these subsets.

Discuss the results with respect to using the models to extrapolate the expected failure count to predict the expected failure count into the future.

Exercise 11.21 The dataset **FAILURE_DS2** contains cumulative failure counts of a software project collected over a period of 18 weeks. Fit an inflected S-shaped models to these data.

You will see that the large initial number of failures leads to an insufficient fit of the data. Create a second fit where the initial number of failures is ignored and discuss the results.

Appendix A
Introduction to Python

There are many excellent books and online resources that can introduce you to Python. Python itself comes with an excellent tutorial that you can find at https://docs.python.org/3/tutorial/. Instead of duplicating here what has been improved over many years, we suggest the reader to follow the Python tutorial. In particular, we recommend reading the following chapters in the tutorial:

- An Informal Introduction to Python
- More Control Flow Tools
- Data Structures

In the following, we will point out a selection of more specialized topics that we use in the code examples throughout the book.

A.1 List, Set, and Dictionary Comprehensions

Many data handling tasks require the creation of lists or dictionaries. We can use a `for` loop in this case:

```
the_list = []
for i in range(10):
  the_list.append(2 * i)
the_list
```

```
[0, 2, 4, 6, 8, 10, 12, 14, 16, 18]
```

Instead of using the `for` loop, Python has a more concise way of achieving the same outcome using what is called a list comprehension:

R. S. Kenett et al., *Industrial Statistics*, Statistics for Industry, Technology, and Engineering, https://doi.org/10.1007/978-3-031-28482-3

```
the_list = [2 * i for i in range(10)]
the_list
```

```
[0, 2, 4, 6, 8, 10, 12, 14, 16, 18]
```

List comprehensions can also be used if the addition to the list is conditional. In the following example, we create a list of numbers divisible by 3.

```
the_list = []
for i in range(20):
  if i % 3 == 0:
    the_list.append(i)

the_list = [i for i in range(20) if i % 3 == 0]
the_list
```

```
[0, 3, 6, 9, 12, 15, 18]
```

The list comprehension is easier to read.

A similar construct can also be used to create sets:

```
letters = ['a', 'y', 'x', 'a', 'y', 'z']
unique_letters = {c for c in letters}
unique_letters
```

```
{'a', 'x', 'y', 'z'}
```

The set comprehension uses curly brackets instead of the square brackets in list comprehensions.

Dictionary comprehensions create dictionaries. The following example creates a dictionary that maps a number to its square. We show first the implementation using a `for` loop and then the dictionary comprehension:

```
squares = {}
for i in range(10):
  squares[i] = i * i

squares = {i: i * i for i in range(10)}
squares
```

```
{0: 0, 1: 1, 2: 4, 3: 9, 4: 16, 5: 25, 6: 36, 7: 49, 8: 64, 9: 81}
```

A.2 Scientific Computing Using `numpy` and `scipy`

The Python packages `numpy` and `scipy` provide fast data structures and algorithms for scientific computing. They are very popular and form the foundation on which many other data science packages in Python are built on.

For example, `numpy` implements multidimensional arrays and operations for their manipulation. Here is an example:

```
import numpy as np

data = np.array([[1, 2, 3], [4, 5, 6]])
print(data)
print('Shape:', data.shape)

print('Total sum:', data.sum())
print('Column sum:', data.sum(axis=0))
print('Row sum:', data.sum(axis=1))
```

```
[[1 2 3]
 [4 5 6]]
Shape: (2, 3)
Total sum: 21
Column sum: [5 7 9]
Row sum: [ 6 15]
```

The function *np.array* creates the numpy array using a Python list of lists. Using the *sum* method of the numpy array, we can calculate the sum of all array elements. If we want to know the column or row sums, we can use the same method with the `axis` keyword argument.

The `scipy` package is used in this book for a variety of tasks. Many of our applications make use of the numerous probability distributions in the `scipy.stats` module. The implementations allow to generate random numbers for a distribution and give access to its probability density function (p.d.f.), the cumulative distribution function (c.d.f.), and its inverse. For example:

```
from scipy import stats
# define normal distribution with mean 27 and standard deviation 5
normal_distribution = stats.norm(loc=27, scale=5)

# generate 5 random variables
print(normal_distribution.rvs(size=5))

# calculate 5th-percentile
print(f'5th-percentile: {normal_distribution.ppf(0.05):.2f}')
```

```
[25.74640076 26.26699152 25.4434667  26.80802939 21.18634297]
5th-percentile: 18.78
```

Both packages provide a large amount of functionality, which we cannot cover here. We highly recommend studying their documentation in detail.

A.3 Pandas Data Frames

Most of the datasets used in this book are either in list form or tabular. The `pandas` package (https://pandas.pydata.org/) implements these data structures. The `mistat` package returns the data as either pandas DataFrame or Series objects.

```
import mistat

almpin = mistat.load_data('ALMPIN')
print('ALMPIN', type(almpin))

steelrod = mistat.load_data('STEELROD')
print('STEELROD', type(steelrod))
```

```
ALMPIN <class 'pandas.core.frame.DataFrame'>
STEELROD <class 'pandas.core.series.Series'>
```

The DataFrame and Series objects offer additional functionality to use them in an efficient and fast manner. As an example, here is the calculation of the column means:

```
almpin.mean()
```

```
diam1        9.992857
diam2        9.987286
diam3        9.983571
capDiam     14.984571
lenNocp     49.907857
lenWcp      60.027857
dtype: float64
```

The `describe` method returns basic statistics for each column in a DataFrame.

```
almpin.describe().round(3)
```

```
        diam1   diam2   diam3  capDiam  lenNocp  lenWcp
count  70.000  70.000  70.000   70.000   70.000  70.000
mean    9.993   9.987   9.984   14.985   49.908  60.028
std     0.016   0.018   0.017    0.019    0.044   0.048
min     9.900   9.890   9.910   14.880   49.810  59.910
25%     9.990   9.982   9.980   14.980   49.890  60.000
50%    10.000   9.990   9.990   14.990   49.910  60.020
75%    10.000  10.000   9.990   14.990   49.928  60.050
max    10.010  10.010  10.010   15.010   50.070  60.150
```

As the `pandas` package is used frequently in many machine learning packages, we recommend that you make yourself familiar with it by reading the documentation.

A.4 Data Visualization Using `pandas` and `matplotlib`

Packages like `pandas` or `seaborn` support a variety of visualizations that are often sufficient for exploratory data analysis. However there may be cases where you want to customize the graph further to highlight aspects of your analysis. As these packages often use the `matplotlib` package (https://matplotlib.org/) as their foundation, we can achieve this customization using basic `matplotlib` commands.

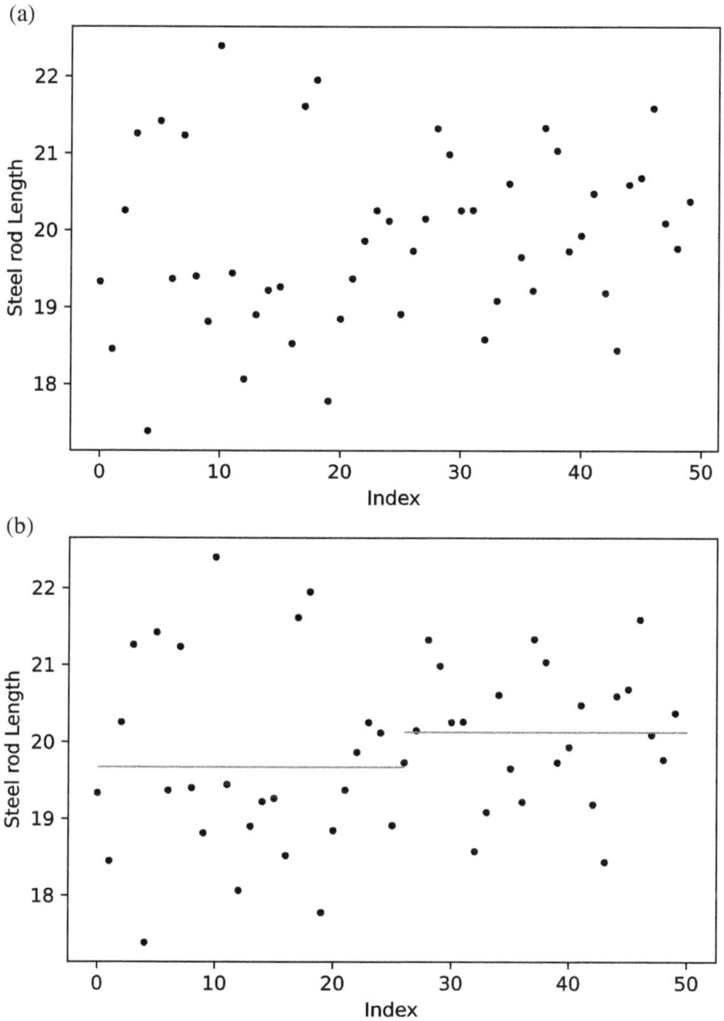

Fig. A.1 Data visualization using pandas and customization. (**a**) Default graph created using pandas. (**b**) Customization of (b) using `matplotlib` commands

This is demonstrated in Fig. A.1. Here, we use the `matplotlib` axis object that is returned from the `pandas` plot function to add additional lines to the graph.

Each figure in this book was created using Python. The source code can be found in the accompanying repository at https://github.com/gedeck/mistat-code-solutions and in the `mistat` package maintained at https://github.com/gedeck/mistat.

Appendix B
List of Python Packages

`arviz`:
Exploratory analysis of Bayesian models
https://pypi.org/project/arviz/
https://github.com/arviz-devs/arviz

`dtreeviz`:
A Python 3 library for sci-kit learn, XGBoost, LightGBM, and Spark decision tree visualization
https://pypi.org/project/dtreeviz/
https://github.com/parrt/dtreeviz

`lifelines`:
Survival analysis in Python, including Kaplan Meier, Nelson Aalen, and regression https://pypi.org/project/lifelines/
https://lifelines.readthedocs.io/
https://github.com/CamDavidsonPilon/lifelines

`matplotlib`:
Python plotting package
https://pypi.org/project/matplotlib/
https://matplotlib.org/

`mistat`:
Modern Statistics/Industrial Statistics: A Computer Based Approach with Python
https://pypi.org/project/mistat/

`numpy`:
NumPy is the fundamental package for array computing with Python
https://pypi.org/project/numpy/
https://numpy.org/

`pandas`:
Powerful data structures for data analysis, time series, and statistics
https://pypi.org/project/pandas/
https://pandas.pydata.org/

R. S. Kenett et al., *Industrial Statistics*, Statistics for Industry, Technology, and Engineering, https://doi.org/10.1007/978-3-031-28482-3

`pingouin`
Pingouin: statistical package for Python
https://pypi.org/project/pingouin/
https://pingouin-stats.org/
`pwlf`
pwlf: fit piecewise linear functions to data
https://pypi.org/project/pwlf/
https://github.com/cjekel/piecewise_linear_fit_py
`pyDOE2`:
A Python 3 library for sci-kit learn, XGBoost, LightGBM, and Spark decision tree visualization
https://pypi.org/project/pyDOE2/
https://github.com/clicumu/pyDOE2
`pyKriging`:
A Kriging Toolbox for Python
https://pypi.org/project/pyKriging/
https://github.com/clicumu/pyKriging
`pymc3`:
Probabilistic Programming in Python: Bayesian Modeling and Probabilistic Machine Learning with Theano
https://pypi.org/project/pymc3/ https://github.com/pymc-devs/pymc
`scikit-learn` (sklearn):
A set of python modules for machine learning and data mining
https://pypi.org/project/scikit-learn/
https://scikit-learn.org/
`scipy`:
SciPy: Scientific Library for Python
https://pypi.org/project/scipy/
https://www.scipy.org/
`seaborn`:
seaborn: statistical data visualization
https://pypi.org/project/seaborn/
https://seaborn.pydata.org/
`statsmodels`:
Statistical computations and models for Python
https://pypi.org/project/statsmodels/
https://www.statsmodels.org/
`theano-pymc`:
Optimizing compiler for evaluating mathematical expressions on CPUs and GPUs
https://pypi.org/project/Theano-PyMC/ http://deeplearning.net/software/theano/

Appendix C
Code Repository and Solution Manual

The source code for code examples and all figures in this book both are available from the GitHub repository https://github.com/gedeck/mistat-code-solutions or from https://gedeck.github.io/mistat-code-solutions/.

The repository also contains solutions for the exercises.

R. S. Kenett et al., *Industrial Statistics*, Statistics for Industry, Technology, and Engineering, https://doi.org/10.1007/978-3-031-28482-3

Bibliography

Abadi M, Barham P, Chen J, Chen Z, Davis A, Dean J, Devin M, Ghemawat S, Irving G, Isard M, Kudlur M, Levenberg J, Monga R, Moore S, Murray DG, Steiner B, Tucker P, Vasudevan V, Warden P, Wicke M, Yu Y, Zheng X (2016) TensorFlow: a system for large-scale machine learning. In: 12th USENIX symposium on operating systems design and implementation (OSDI 16), pp 265–283

Abadie A, Diamond A, Hainmueller J (2015) Comparative politics and the synthetic control method. Am J Polit Sci 59(2):495–510. https://doi.org/10.1111/ajps.12116

ANSI (2010) ANSI/ISA-95.00.01 enterprise-control system integration – part 1: models and terminology. Technical report. American National Standards Institute, Washington

Aoki M (1989) Optimization of stochastic systems, 2nd edn. Topics in Discrete-time dynamics. Academic Press, Boston

Aroian LA (1976) Applications of the direct method in sequential analysis. Technometrics 18(3):301–306. https://doi.org/10.2307/1268739

Aroian LA, Robison DE (1969) Direct methods for exact truncated sequential tests of the mean of a normal distribution. Technometrics 11(4):661–675. https://doi.org/10.1080/00401706.1969.10490729

Babu SS, Goodridge R (2015) Additive manufacturing. Mat Sci Technol 31(8):881–883. https://doi.org/10.1179/0267083615Z.000000000929

Bai X, Kenett RS (2009) Risk-based adaptive group testing of semantic web services. In: 2009 33rd annual IEEE international computer software and applications conference, vol 2, pp 485–490. https://doi.org/10.1109/COMPSAC.2009.180

Bal M, Hashemipour M (2009) Virtual factory approach for implementation of holonic control in industrial applications: a case study in die-casting industry. Robot Comput Integr Manuf 25(3):570–581. https://doi.org/10.1016/j.rcim.2008.03.020

Bär K, Herbert-Hansen ZNL, Khalid W (2018) Considering industry 4.0 aspects in the supply chain for an SME. Prod Eng 12(6):747–758. https://doi.org/10.1007/s11740-018-0851-y

Barnard GA (1959) Control charts and stochastic processes. J R Stat Soc Ser B 21(2):239–271

Basu AP (1971) On a sequential rule for estimating the location parameter of an exponential distribution. Nav Res Logist Q 18(3):329–337. https://doi.org/10.1002/nav.3800180305

Basu AP (1991) Sequential methods. In: Ghosh BK, Sen PK (eds) Handbook of sequential analysis. CRC Press, Boca Raton, pp 581–592

Bates RA, Kenett RS, Steinberg DM, Wynn HP (2006) Achieving robust design from computer simulations. Qual Technol Quantit Manag 3(2):161–177. https://doi.org/10.1080/16843703.2006.11673107

R. S. Kenett et al., *Industrial Statistics*, Statistics for Industry, Technology, and Engineering, https://doi.org/10.1007/978-3-031-28482-3

Ben-Gal I, Dana A, Shkolnik N, Singer G (2014) Efficient construction of decision trees by the dual information distance method. Qual Technol Quantit Manag 11(1):133–147. https://doi.org/10.1080/16843703.2014.11673330

Ben-Michael E, Feller A, Rothstein J (2021a) The augmented synthetic control method. J Am Stat Assoc 116(536):1789–1803. https://doi.org/10.1080/01621459.2021.1929245

Ben-Michael E, Feller A, Rothstein J (2021b) Synthetic controls with staggered adoption. J R Stat Soc Ser B (Stat Methodol). https://doi.org/10.1111/rssb.12448

Berry DA, Fristedt B (1985) Bandit problems: sequential allocation of experiments. Monographs on statistics and applied probability. Springer Netherlands, Berlin. https://doi.org/10.1007/978-94-015-3711-7

Bevilacqua M, Bottani E, Ciarapica FE, Costantino F, Di Donato L, Ferraro A, Mazzuto G, Monteriù A, Nardini G, Ortenzi M, Paroncini M, Pirozzi M, Prist M, Quatrini E, Tronci M, Vignali G (2020) Digital twin reference model development to prevent operators' risk in process plants. Sustainability 12(3):1088. https://doi.org/10.3390/su12031088

Birol G, Ündey C, Çinar A (2002) A modular simulation package for fed-batch fermentation: penicillin production. Comput Chem Eng 26(11):1553–1565. https://doi.org/10.1016/S0098-1354(02)00127-8

Boland P, Singh H (2003) A birth-process approach to Moranda's geometric software-reliability model. IEEE Trans Reliab 52(2):168–174. https://doi.org/10.1109/TR.2003.813166

Bortolini M, Ferrari E, Gamberi M, Pilati F, Faccio M (2017) Assembly system design in the Industry 4.0 era: a general framework. IFAC-PapersOnLine 50(1):5700–5705. https://doi.org/10.1016/j.ifacol.2017.08.1121

Botvinik-Nezer R, Holzmeister F, Camerer CF, Dreber A, Huber J, Johannesson M, Kirchler M, Iwanir R, Mumford JA, Adcock RA, Avesani P, Baczkowski BM, Bajracharya A, Bakst L, Ball S, Barilari M, Bault N, Beaton D, Beitner J, Benoit RG, Berkers RMWJ, Bhanji JP, Biswal BB, Bobadilla-Suarez S, Bortolini T, Bottenhorn KL, Bowring A, Braem S, Brooks HR, Brudner EG, Calderon CB, Camilleri JA, Castrellon JJ, Cecchetti L, Cieslik EC, Cole ZJ, Collignon O, Cox RW, Cunningham WA, Czoschke S, Dadi K, Davis CP, Luca AD, Delgado MR, Demetriou L, Dennison JB, Di X, Dickie EW, Dobryakova E, Donnat CL, Dukart J, Duncan NW, Durnez J, Eed A, Eickhoff SB, Erhart A, Fontanesi L, Fricke GM, Fu S, Galván A, Gau R, Genon S, Glatard T, Glerean E, Goeman JJ, Golowin SAE, González-García C, Gorgolewski KJ, Grady CL, Green MA, Guassi Moreira JF, Guest O, Hakimi S, Hamilton JP, Hancock R, Handjaras G, Harry BB, Hawco C, Herholz P, Herman G, Heunis S, Hoffstaedter F, Hogeveen J, Holmes S, Hu CP, Huettel SA, Hughes ME, Iacovella V, Iordan AD, Isager PM, Isik AI, Jahn A, Johnson MR, Johnstone T, Joseph MJE, Juliano AC, Kable JW, Kassinopoulos M, Koba C, Kong XZ, Koscik TR, Kucukboyaci NE, Kuhl BA, Kupek S, Laird AR, Lamm C, Langner R, Lauharatanahirun N, Lee H, Lee S, Leemans A, Leo A, Lesage E, Li F, Li MYC, Lim PC, Lintz EN, Liphardt SW, Losecaat Vermeer AB, Love BC, Mack ML, Malpica N, Marins T, Maumet C, McDonald K, McGuire JT, Melero H, Méndez Leal AS, Meyer B, Meyer KN, Mihai G, Mitsis GD, Moll J, Nielson DM, Nilsonne G, Notter MP, Olivetti E, Onicas AI, Papale P, Patil KR, Peelle JE, Pérez A, Pischedda D, Poline JB, Prystauka Y, Ray S, Reuter-Lorenz PA, Reynolds RC, Ricciardi E, Rieck JR, Rodriguez-Thompson AM, Romyn A, Salo T, Samanez-Larkin GR, Sanz-Morales E, Schlichting ML, Schultz DH, Shen Q, Sheridan MA, Silvers JA, Skagerlund K, Smith A, Smith DV, Sokol-Hessner P, Steinkamp SR, Tashjian SM, Thirion B, Thorp JN, Tinghög G, Tisdall L, Tompson SH, Toro-Serey C, Torre Tresols JJ, Tozzi L, Truong V, Turella L, van 't Veer AE, Verguts T, Vettel JM, Vijayarajah S, Vo K, Wall MB, Weeda WD, Weis S, White DJ, Wisniewski D, Xifra-Porxas A, Yearling EA, Yoon S, Yuan R, Yuen KSL, Zhang L, Zhang X, Zosky JE, Nichols TE, Poldrack RA, Schonberg T (2020) Variability in the analysis of a single neuroimaging dataset by many teams. Nature 582(7810):84–88. https://doi.org/10.1038/s41586-020-2314-9

Box G, Kramer T (1992) Statistical process monitoring and feedback adjustment: a discussion. Technometrics 34(3):251–267. https://doi.org/10.2307/1270028

Box GEP, Tiao GC (1992) Bayesian inference in statistical analysis, 1st edn. Wiley-Interscience, New York

Box G, Bisgaard S, Fung C (1988) An explanation and critique of Taguchi's contributions to quality engineering. Qual Reliab Eng Int 4(2):123–131. https://doi.org/10.1002/qre.4680040207

Box GEP, Hunter JS, Hunter WG (2005) Statistics for experimenters: design, innovation, and discovery, 2nd edn. Wiley, Hoboken

Box GEP, Jenkins GM, Reinsel GC, Ljung GM (2015) Time series analysis: forecasting and control, 5th edn. Wiley, New York

Broy M, Cengarle MV, Geisberger E (2012) Cyber-physical systems: imminent challenges. In: Proceedings of the 17th monterey conference on large-scale complex IT systems: development, operation and management. Springer, Berlin, pp 1–28. https://doi.org/10.1007/978-3-642-34059-8_1

Bryant CM, Schmee J (1979) Confidence limits on MTBF for sequential test plans of MIL-STD 781. Technometrics 21(1):33–42. https://doi.org/10.1080/00401706.1979.10489720

Castelijns LA, Maas Y, Vanschoren J (2020) The ABC of data: a classifying framework for data readiness. In: Cellier P, Driessens K (eds) Machine learning and knowledge discovery in databases. Communications in computer and information science. Springer International Publishing, Cham, pp 3–16. https://doi.org/10.1007/978-3-030-43823-4_1

Chandler AD Jr (1993) The visible hand: the managerial revolution in American Business, unknown edn. Belknap Press: An Imprint of Harvard University Press, Cambridge

Chandrasegaran SK, Ramani K, Sriram RD, Horváth I, Bernard A, Harik RF, Gao W (2013) The evolution, challenges, and future of knowledge representation in product design systems. Comput Aided Des 45(2):204–228. https://doi.org/10.1016/j.cad.2012.08.006

Chen H (1994) A multivariate process capability index over a rectangular solid tolerance zone. Stat Sin 4(2):749–758

Chen X, Jin R (2018) Data fusion pipelines for autonomous smart manufacturing. In: 2018 IEEE 14th international conference on automation science and engineering (CASE), pp 1203–1208. https://doi.org/10.1109/COASE.2018.8560567

Chen X, Jin R (2021) AdaPipe: a recommender system for adaptive computation pipelines in cyber-manufacturing computation services. IEEE Trans Industr Inform 17(9):6221–6229. https://doi.org/10.1109/TII.2020.3035524

Chinesta F (2019) Hybrid twins: the new data-driven and physics-based alliance. In: Kongoli F, Aifantis E, Chan A, Gawin D, Khalil N, Laloui L, Pastor M, Pesavento F, Sanavia L (eds) 2019 – sustainable industrial processing summit SIPS2019 volume 7: Schrefler Intl. Symp./geomechanics and applications for sustainable development, vol 7. Flogen Star Outreach, Montreal, pp 185–186

Choi S, Kim BH, Do Noh S (2015) A diagnosis and evaluation method for strategic planning and systematic design of a virtual factory in smart manufacturing systems. Int J Precis Eng Manuf 16(6):1107–1115. https://doi.org/10.1007/s12541-015-0143-9

Cisco (2019) Leading tools manufacturer transforms operations with IoT. Technical report. Cisco

Dalla Valle L, Kenett RS (2018) Social media big data integration: a new approach based on calibration. Expert Syst Appl 111:76–90. https://doi.org/10.1016/j.eswa.2017.12.044

Dattner I (2021) Differential equations in data analysis. WIREs Comput Stat 13(6):e1534. https://doi.org/10.1002/wics.1534

Davidyan G, Bortman J, Kenett RS (2021) Towards the development of an operational digital twin of a railway system. In: 9th PHM conference, Tel Aviv

Davis S (1997) Future perfect: tenth anniversary edition, updated edn. Basic Books, Reading

Davis J, Edgar T, Porter J, Bernaden J, Sarli M (2012) Smart manufacturing, manufacturing intelligence and demand-dynamic performance. Comput Chem Eng 47:145–156. https://doi.org/10.1016/j.compchemeng.2012.06.037

Dbouk T (2017) A review about the engineering design of optimal heat transfer systems using topology optimization. Appl Therm Eng 112:841–854. https://doi.org/10.1016/j.applthermaleng.2016.10.134

Debevec M, Simic M, Herakovic N (2014) Virtual factory as an advanced approach for production process optimization. Int J Simul Model 13:66–78. https://doi.org/10.2507/IJSIMM13(1)6.260

Dehnad K (ed) (1989) Quality control, robust design, and the Taguchi Method. Springer US, Boston. https://doi.org/10.1007/978-1-4684-1472-1_1

de Man JC, Strandhagen JO (2017) An industry 4.0 research agenda for sustainable business models. Procedia CIRP 63:721–726. https://doi.org/10.1016/j.procir.2017.03.315

Deming WE (1967) In memoriam: Walter A. Shewhart, 1891–1967. Am Stat 21(2):39–40. https://doi.org/10.1080/00031305.1967.10481808

Deming WE (1982) Quality productivity and competitive position, 1st edn. Massachusetts Inst Technology, Cambridge

Deming WE (1991) Out of the crisis. The MIT Press, Boston

Derringer G, Suich R (1980) Simultaneous optimization of several response variables. J Qual Technol 12(4):214–219. https://doi.org/10.1080/00224065.1980.11980968

Dharmesti MDD, Nugroho SS (2013) The Antecedents of online customer satisfaction and customer loyalty. J Bus Retail Manag Res 7(2)

Dilberoglu UM, Gharehpapagh B, Yaman U, Dolen M (2017) The role of additive manufacturing in the era of industry 4.0. Procedia Manuf 11:545–554. https://doi.org/10.1016/j.promfg.2017.07.148

Dodge HF, Romig HG (1998) Sampling inspection tables: single and double sampling, 2nd edn. Wiley, Hoboken

Draper NR, Smith H (1998) Applied regression analysis, 3rd edn. Wiley, New York

Duncan AJ (1956) The economic design of X charts used to maintain current control of a process. J Am Stat Assoc 51(274):228–242. https://doi.org/10.1080/01621459.1956.10501322

Duncan AJ (1971) The economic design of $\bar{X}$-charts when there is a multiplicity of assignable causes. J Am Stat Assoc 66(333):107–121. https://doi.org/10.1080/01621459.1971.10482230

Duncan AJ (1978) The economic design of p-charts to maintain current control of o process: some numerical results. Technometrics 20(3):235–243. https://doi.org/10.1080/00401706.1978.10489667

Duncan AJ (1986) Quality control and industrial statistics. Irwin, Homewood

Dvoretzky A, Kiefer J, Wolfowitz J (1953) Sequential decision problems for processes with continuous time parameter. Testing hypotheses. Ann Math Stat 24(2):254–264. https://doi.org/10.1214/aoms/1177729031

Edgar TF, Pistikopoulos EN (2018) Smart manufacturing and energy systems. Comput Chem Eng 114:130–144. https://doi.org/10.1016/j.compchemeng.2017.10.027

Epstein B (1960) Statistical life test acceptance procedures. Technometrics 2(4):435–446. https://doi.org/10.1080/00401706.1960.10489910

Epstein B, Sobel M (1955) Sequential life tests in the exponential case. Ann Math Stat 26(1):82–93. https://doi.org/10.1214/aoms/1177728595

Faltin FW, Kenett RS, Ruggeri F (eds) (2012) Statistical methods in healthcare. Wiley, New York

Feng W, Wang C, Shen ZJM (2017) Process flexibility design in heterogeneous and unbalanced networks: a stochastic programming approach. IISE Trans 49(8):781–799. https://doi.org/10.1080/24725854.2017.1299953

Figini S, Kenett RS, Salini S (2010) Optimal scaling for risk assessment: merging of operational and financial data. Qual Reliab Eng Int 26(8):887–897. https://doi.org/10.1002/qre.1158

Fisher RA (1919) XV.—The correlation between relatives on the supposition of Mendelian inheritance. Earth Environ Sci Trans R Soc Edinb 52(2):399–433

Fisher RA (1935) The design of experiments. Oliver and Boyd, Ltd., Edinburgh

Fox B (1988) Duracell loses prestige defence contract. New Scientist 119:39

Fuchs C, Kenett RS (1987) Multivariate tolerance regions and F-tests. J Qual Technol 19(3):122–131. https://doi.org/10.1080/00224065.1987.11979053

Gandin L (1963) Objective analysis of meteorological fields: GIMIZ, Gidrometeorologicheskoe Izdatelstvo, Leningrad 1963: Transl. from the Russian. Israel program for scientific translations, GIMIZ, Gidrometeorologicheskoe Izdatelstvo, Leningrad

Gertsbakh IB (1989) Statistical reliability theory. Marcel Dekker, New York

Ghosh S (1990) Statistical design and analysis of industrial experiments. Marcel Dekker, New York

Gibra IN (1971) Economically optimal determination of the parameters of $\bar{X}$-control chart. Manag Sci 17(9):635–646. https://doi.org/10.1287/mnsc.17.9.635
Gittins JC, Jones DM (1974) A dynamic allocation index for the sequential design of experiments. In: Gani JM, Sarkadi K, Vincze I (eds) Progress in statistics, vol 1. North-Holland Pub. Co., Amsterdam, pp 241–266
Gittins J, Glazebrook K, Weber R (2011) Multi-armed bandit allocation indices, 2nd edn. Wiley, New York
Goba FA (1969) Bibliography on thermal aging of electrical insulation. IEEE Trans Electr Insul EI-4(2):31–58. https://doi.org/10.1109/TEI.1969.299070
Godfrey AB (1986) Report: the history and evolution of quality in AT&T. AT&T Tech J 65(2):9–20. https://doi.org/10.1002/j.1538-7305.1986.tb00289.x
Godfrey AB, Kenett RS (2007) Joseph M. Juran, a perspective on past contributions and future impact. Qual Reliab Eng Int 23(6):653–663. https://doi.org/10.1002/qre.861
Goel AL, Okumoto K (1979) Time-dependent error-detection rate model for software reliability and other performance measures. IEEE Trans Reliab R-28(3):206–211. https://doi.org/10.1109/TR.1979.5220566
Good IJ (2003) The estimation of probabilities: an essay on modern Bayesian methods, 1st edn. The MIT Press, Cambridge
Goos (2011) Optimal design of experiments: a case study approach, 1st edn. Wiley, Hoboken
Grieves M (2022) Intelligent digital twins and the development and management of complex systems. https://digitaltwin1.org/articles/2-8/v1
Grieves M, Vickers J (2017) Digital twin: mitigating unpredictable, undesirable emergent behavior in complex systems. In: Kahlen FJ, Flumerfelt S, Alves A (eds) Transdisciplinary perspectives on complex systems: new findings and approaches. Springer International Publishing, Cham, pp 85–113. https://doi.org/10.1007/978-3-319-38756-7_4
Gruber A, Yanovski S, Ben Gal I (2021) Condition-based maintenance via a targeted Bayesian Network Meta-Model. In: Kenett RS, Swarz RS, Zonnenshain A (eds) Systems engineering in the fourth industrial revolution big data. Novel Technologies, and Modern Systems Engineering, Wiley, Hoboken
Haridy S, Wu Z, Castagliola P (2011) Univariate and multivariate approaches for evaluating the capability of dynamic-behavior processes (case study). Stat Methodol 8(2):185–203. https://doi.org/10.1016/j.stamet.2010.09.003
Hermann M, Pentek T, Otto B (2015) Design principles for industrie 4.0 scenarios: a literature review. Working Paper No. 01/2015. Technische Universität Dortmund, Dortmund. https://doi.org/10.13140/RG.2.2.29269.22248
Higdon D, Gattiker J, Williams B, Rightley M (2008) Computer model calibration using high-dimensional output. J Am Stat Assoc 103(482):570–583
Higdon D, Gattiker J, Lawrence E, Pratola M, Jackson C, Tobis M, Habib S, Heitmann K, Price S (2013) Computer model calibration using the ensemble Kalman filter. Technometrics 55(4):488–500
Hints R, Vanca M, Terkaj W, Marra ED (2011) A virtual factory tool to enhance the integrated design of production systems. In: Proceedings of the DET2011 7th international conference on digital enterprise technology, Athens, pp 28–30
Hoadley B (1981) The quality measurement plan (QMP). Bell Syst Tech J 60(2):215–273. https://doi.org/10.1002/j.1538-7305.1981.tb00239.x
Huang D, Allen TT (2005) Design and analysis of variable fidelity experimentation applied to engine valve heat treatment process design. J R Stat Soc Ser C Appl Stat 54(2):443–463. https://doi.org/10.1111/j.1467-9876.2005.00493.x
Iannario M, Piccolo D (2011) CUB models: statistical methods and empirical evidence. In: Modern analysis of customer surveys. John Wiley & Sons, Ltd., Hoboken, chap 13, pp 231–258. https://doi.org/10.1002/9781119961154.ch13
IMT S (2013) Are virtual factories the future of manufacturing? Technical report.
Ishikawa K (1986) Guide to quality control, revised, subsequent edn. Asian Productivity Organization, White Plains

Jain S, Shao G (2014) Virtual factory revisited for manufacturing data analytics. In: Proceedings of the 2014 winter simulation conference, WSC '14. IEEE Press, Savannah, pp 887–898

Jalili M, Bashiri M, Amiri A (2012) A new multivariate process capability index under both unilateral and bilateral quality characteristics. Qual Reliab Eng Int 28(8):925–941. https://doi.org/10.1002/qre.1284

Jared BH, Aguilo MA, Beghini LL, Boyce BL, Clark BW, Cook A, Kaehr BJ, Robbins J (2017) Additive manufacturing: toward holistic design. Scr Mater 135:141–147. https://doi.org/10.1016/j.scriptamat.2017.02.029

Jelinski Z, Moranda P (1972) Software reliability research. In: Freiberger W (ed) Statistical computer performance evaluation. Academic Press, Cambridge, pp 465–484. https://doi.org/10.1016/B978-0-12-266950-7.50028-1

Jensen F, Petersen NE (1991) Burn-in: an engineering approach to the design and analysis of burn-in procedures, 1st edn. Wiley, Chichester

Jeschke S, Brecher C, Meisen T, Özdemir D, Eschert T (2017) Industrial internet of things and cyber manufacturing systems. In: Jeschke S, Brecher C, Song H, Rawat DB (eds) Industrial internet of things: cybermanufacturing systems. Springer series in wireless technology. Springer International Publishing, Cham, pp 3–19. https://doi.org/10.1007/978-3-319-42559-7_1

Jin R, Deng X (2015) Ensemble modeling for data fusion in manufacturing process scale-up. IIE Trans 47(3):203–214. https://doi.org/10.1080/0740817X.2014.916580

Jin R, Deng X, Chen X, Zhu L, Zhang J (2019) Dynamic quality-process model in consideration of equipment degradation. J Qual Technol 51(3):217–229. https://doi.org/10.1080/00224065.2018.1541379

John S (1963) A tolerance region for multivariate normal distributions. Sankhya; Series A 25:363–368

John PWM (1990) Statistical methods in engineering and quality assurance, 1st edn. Wiley-Interscience, New York

Juran JM (1979) Quality control handbook. Mcgraw-Hill, New York

Juran JM (1986) The quality trilogy: a universal approach to managing for quality. In: 40th annual quality congress – American Society for quality control, ASQC transactions of: 19–21 May 1986, Anaheim, California, 1st edn. American Society for Quality Control, Inc., Milwaukee

Juran JM (ed) (1995) A history of managing for quality, 1st edn. Asq Pr, Milwaukee

Kackar RN (1985) Off-line quality control, parameter design, and the Taguchi Method. J Qual Technol 17(4):176–188. https://doi.org/10.1080/00224065.1985.11978964

Kang S, Deng X, Jin R (2021a) A cost-efficient data-driven approach to design space exploration for personalized geometric design in additive manufacturing. J Comput Inf Sci Eng 21(6). https://doi.org/10.1115/1.4050984

Kang S, Jin R, Deng X, Kenett RS (2021b) Challenges of modeling and analysis in cybermanufacturing: a review from a machine learning and computation perspective. J Intell Manuf https://doi.org/10.1007/s10845-021-01817-9

Kelly T, Kenett RS, Newton E, Roodman G, Wowk A (1991) Total quality management also applies to a school of management. In: Proceedings of the 9th IMPRO conference, Atlanta

Kenett RS (1991) Two methods for comparing Pareto charts. J Qual Technol 23(1):27–31. https://doi.org/10.1080/00224065.1991.11979280

Kenett RS (2007) Software failure data analysis. In: Ruggeri F, Kenett RS, Faltin FW (eds) Encyclopedia of statistics in quality and reliability. Wiley, Hoboken

Kenett RS (2008) From data to information to knowledge. Six Sigma Forum Magazine, pp 32–33

Kenett RS (2019) Applications of Bayesian networks. Trans Mach Learn Data Mining 12(2):33–54

Kenett RS (2020) Reviewing of applied research with an industry 4.0 perspective. SSRN scholarly paper ID 3591808. Social Science Research Network, Rochester. https://doi.org/10.2139/ssrn.3591808

Kenett RS, Bortman J (2021) The digital twin in industry 4.0: a wide-angle perspective. Qual Reliab Eng Int 38(3):1357–1366. https://doi.org/10.1002/qre.2948

Kenett RS, Coleman S (2021) Data and the fourth industrial revolution. Significance 18(3):8–9. https://doi.org/10.1111/1740-9713.01523
Kenett RS, Kenett DA (2008) Quality by design applications in biosimilar pharmaceutical products. Accred Qual Assur 13(12):681–690. https://doi.org/10.1007/s00769-008-0459-6
Kenett RS, Pollak M (1986) A semi-parametric approach to testing for reliability growth, with application to software systems. IEEE Trans Reliab 35(3):304–311. https://doi.org/10.1109/TR.1986.4335439
Kenett RS, Pollak M (1996) Data-analytic aspects of the Shiryayev-Roberts control chart: surveillance of a non-homogeneous Poisson process. J Appl Stat 23(1):125–138. https://doi.org/10.1080/02664769624413
Kenett RS, Raanan Y (eds) (2010) Operational risk management: a practical approach to intelligent data analysis, 1st edn. Wiley, Chichester
Kenett RS, Redman TC (2019) The real work of data science: turning data into information, better decisions, and stronger organizations, 1st edn. Wiley, Hoboken
Kenett RS, Rubinstein A (2021) Generalizing research findings for enhanced reproducibility: an approach based on verbal alternative representations. Scientometrics 126(5):4137–4151. https://doi.org/10.1007/s11192-021-03914-1
Kenett RS, Salini S (2009) New frontiers: Bayesian networks give insight into survey-data analysis. Qual Prog 42:30–36
Kenett RS, Salini S (2011) Modern analysis of customer satisfaction surveys: comparison of models and integrated analysis. Appl Stoch Model Bus Ind 27(5):465–475. https://doi.org/10.1002/asmb.927
Kenett RS, Shmueli G (2014) On information quality. J R Stat Soc A Stat Soc 177(1):3–38. https://doi.org/10.1111/rssa.12007
Kenett RS, Shmueli G (2016) Information quality: the potential of data and analytics to generate knowledge, 1st edn. Wiley, Chichester
Kenett RS, Vicario G (2021) Challenges and opportunities in simulations and computer experiments in industrial statistics: an industry 4.0 perspective. Adv Theory Simul 4(2):2000254. https://doi.org/10.1002/adts.202000254
Kenett RS, Vogel B (1991) Going beyond main-effect plots. Qual Prog 24(2):71–73
Kenett RS, Zacks S (2021) Modern industrial statistics: with applications in R, MINITAB, and JMP, 3rd edn. Wiley, Hoboken
Kenett RS, Ruggeri F, Faltin FW (eds) (2018a) Analytic methods in systems and software testing. Wiley, Hoboken
Kenett RS, Zonnenshain A, Fortuna G (2018b) A road map for applied data sciences supporting sustainability in advanced manufacturing: the information quality dimensions. Procedia Manuf 21:141–148. https://doi.org/10.1016/j.promfg.2018.02.104
Kenett RS, Swarz RS, Zonnenshain A (eds) (2021a) Systems engineering in the fourth industrial revolution: big data, Novel Technologies, and Modern Systems Engineering, 1st edn. Wiley, Hoboken
Kenett RS, Yahav I, Zonnenshain A (2021b) Analytics as an enabler of advanced manufacturing. In: Kenett RS, Swarz RS, Zonnenshain A (eds) Systems engineering in the fourth industrial revolution big data, Novel Technologies, and Modern Systems Engineering. Wiley, Hoboken
Kenett RS, Gotwalt C, Freeman L, Deng X (2022a) Self-supervised cross validation using data generation structure. Appl Stoch Model Bus Ind. https://doi.org/10.1002/asmb.2701
Kenett RS, Zacks S, Gedeck P (2022b) Modern statistics: a computer-based approach with python, 1st edn. Springer, Birkhäuser
Kennedy MC, O'Hagan A (2001) Bayesian calibration of computer models. J R Stat Soc Ser B (Stat Methodol) 63(3):425–464. https://doi.org/10.1111/1467-9868.00294
Kiefer J (1959) Optimum experimental designs. J R Stat Soc Ser B (Methodol) 21(2):272–319
Kiefer J, Wolfowitz J (1956) Sequential tests of hypotheses about the mean occurrence time of a continuous parameter Poisson process. Naval Res Logist Q 3(3):205–219. https://doi.org/10.1002/nav.3800030308
Kotz S, Johnson NL (1993) Process capability indices, 1st edn. Chapman and Hall/CRC, London

Kozjek D, Vrabič R, Kralj D, Butala P (2017) A data-driven holistic approach to fault prognostics in a cyclic manufacturing process. Procedia CIRP 63:664–669. https://doi.org/10.1016/j.procir.2017.03.109

Kuo CJ, Ting KC, Chen YC, Yang DL, Chen HM (2017) Automatic machine status prediction in the era of industry 4.0. J Syst Archit EUROMICRO J 81(C):44–53. https://doi.org/10.1016/j.sysarc.2017.10.007

Lawrence ND (2017) Data readiness levels. arXiv:170502245 [cs] 1705.02245

Lee J, Bagheri B, Kao HA (2015) A cyber-physical systems architecture for industry 4.0-based manufacturing systems. Manuf Lett 3:18–23. https://doi.org/10.1016/j.mfglet.2014.12.001

Li J, Jin R, Yu HZ (2018) Integration of physically-based and data-driven approaches for thermal field prediction in additive manufacturing. Mat Des 139:473–485. https://doi.org/10.1016/j.matdes.2017.11.028

Liebesman BS, Saperstein B (1983) A proposed attribute skip-lot sampling program. J Qual Technol 15(3):130–140. https://doi.org/10.1080/00224065.1983.11978860

Lin KM, Kacker RN (2012) Optimizing the wave soldering process. In: Dehnad K (ed) Quality control, robust design, and the Taguchi Method, 1989th edn., Wadsworth BrooksCole, Pacific Grove, pp 143–157

Lipow M (1978) Models for software reliability. In: Proceedings of the winter meetings of the aerospace division of the American Society for Mechanical Engineers, vol 78-WA/Aero-18, pp 1–11

Littlewood B, Verrall JL (1973) A Bayesian reliability growth model for computer software. J R Stat Soc Ser C Appl Stat 22(3):332–346. https://doi.org/10.2307/2346781

Lucas JM (1982) Combined Shewhart-CUSUM quality control schemes. J Qual Technol 14(2):51–59. https://doi.org/10.1080/00224065.1982.11978790

Lucas JM, Crosier RB (1982) Fast initial response for CUSUM quality-control schemes: give your CUSUM a head start. Technometrics 24(3):199–205. https://doi.org/10.1080/00401706.1982.10487759

Luo L, Kannan PK, Besharati B, Azarm S (2005) Design of robust new products under variability: marketing meets design*. J Prod Innov Manag 22(2):177–192. https://doi.org/10.1111/j.0737-6782.2005.00113.x

Mahmoudi M, Tapia G, Karayagiz K, Franco B, Ma J, Arroyave R, Karaman I, Elwany A (2018) Multivariate calibration and experimental validation of a 3D finite element thermal model for laser powder bed fusion metal additive manufacturing. Integ Mat Manuf Innov 7(3):116–135. https://doi.org/10.1007/s40192-018-0113-z

Mann NR, Schafer RE, Singpurwalla ND (1974) Methods for statistical analysis of reliability and life data, 1st edn. Wiley, New York

Martz HF, Waller RA (1982) Bayesian reliability analysis, 1st edn. Wiley, New York

Matheron G (1963) Principles of geostatistics. Econ Geol 58(8):1246–1266. https://doi.org/10.2113/gsecongeo.58.8.1246

Meeker WQ, Escobar LA, Pascual FG (2021) Statistical methods for reliability data, 2nd edn. Wiley, Hoboken

Modoni GE, Caldarola EG, Sacco M, Terkaj W (2019) Synchronizing physical and digital factory: benefits and technical challenges. Procedia CIRP 79:472–477. https://doi.org/10.1016/j.procir.2019.02.125

Mukhopadhyay N (1974) Sequential estimation of location parameter in exponential distributions. Calcutta Statist Assoc Bull 23(1-4):85–96. https://doi.org/10.1177/0008068319740105

Musa JD, Okumoto K (1984) A logarithmic Poisson execution time model for software reliability measurement. In: Proceedings of the 7th international conference on software engineering, ICSE '84. IEEE Press, Orlando, pp 230–238

Nasr M (2007) Quality by design (QbD) – a modern system approach to pharmaceutical development and manufacturing – FDA perspective. In: FDA quality initiatives workshop, Maryland

Nelson WB (2004) Accelerated testing: statistical models, test plans, and data analyses, paperback edn. Wiley-Interscience, Hoboken

Nguyen NK, Pham TD (2016) Small mixed-level screening designs with orthogonal quadratic effects. J Qual Technol 48(4):405–414. https://doi.org/10.1080/00224065.2016.11918176

O'Donovan P, Leahy K, Bruton K, O'Sullivan DTJ (2015) An industrial big data pipeline for data-driven analytics maintenance applications in large-scale smart manufacturing facilities. J Big Data 2(1):25. https://doi.org/10.1186/s40537-015-0034-z

Ohba M (1984) Software reliability analysis models. IBM J Res Dev 28(4):428–443. https://doi.org/10.1147/rd.284.0428

Oikawa T, Oka T (1987) New techniques for approximating the stress in pad-type nozzles attached to a spherical shell. Trans Am Soc Mechan Eng 109:188–192

Olavsrud T (2017) 15 data and analytics trends that will dominate 2017. https://www.cio.com/article/3166060/15-data-and-analytics-trends-that-will-dominate-2017.html

Page ES (1954) Continuous inspection schemes. Biometrika 41(1–2):100–115. https://doi.org/10.1093/biomet/41.1-2.100

Page ES (1962) A modified control chart with warning lines. Biometrika 49(1–2):171–176. https://doi.org/10.1093/biomet/49.1-2.171

Pao TW, Phadke MS, Sherrerd CS (1985) Computer response time optimization using orthogonal array experiments. In: IEEE international communication conference, Chicago, pp 890–895

Paszke A, Gross S, Chintala S, Chanan G (2022) PyTorch: tensors and dynamic neural networks in Python with strong GPU acceleration. PyTorch

Peck DS, Trapp OD, Components Technology Institute (1994) Accelerated testing handbook, 5th edn. Components Technology Institute, Huntsville

Pedregosa F, Varoquaux G, Gramfort A, Michel V, Thirion B, Grisel O, Blondel M, Prettenhofer P, Weiss R, Dubourg V, Vanderplas J, Passos A, Cournapeau D, Brucher M, Perrot M, Duchesnay E (2011) Scikit-learn: machine learning in Python. J Mach Learn Res 12:2825–2830

Phadke MS (1989) Quality engineering using robust design, illustrated edn. Prentice Hall, Englewood Cliffs

Phadke MS, Kackar RN, Speeney DV, Grieco MJ (1983) Off-line quality control in integrated circuit fabrication using experimental design. Bell Syst Tech J 62(5):1273–1309. https://doi.org/10.1002/j.1538-7305.1983.tb02298.x

Piccolo D (2003) On the moments of a mixture of uniform and shifted binomial random variables. Quaderni di Statistica 5:85–104

Press SJ (1989) Bayesian statistics: principles, models, and applications, 1st edn. Wiley, New York

Qi Q, Tao F (2018) Digital twin and big data towards smart manufacturing and industry 4.0: 360 degree comparison. IEEE Access 6:3585–3593. https://doi.org/10.1109/ACCESS.2018.2793265

Quinlan J (1985) Product improvement by application of Taguchi Methods. In: Third supplier symposium on Taguchi Methods. American Supplier Institute, Inc, Dearborn

Rasheed A, San O, Kvamsdal T (2020) Digital twin: values, challenges and enablers from a modeling perspective. IEEE Access 8:21980–22012. https://doi.org/10.1109/ACCESS.2020.2970143

Rathore AS, Mhatre R (eds) (2009) Quality by design for biopharmaceuticals: principles and case studies, 1st edn. Wiley-Interscience, Hoboken

Reinman G, Ayer T, Davan T, Devore M, Finley S, Glanovsky J, Gray L, Hall B, Jones CC, Learned A, Mesaros E, Morris R, Pinero S, Russo R, Stearns E, Teicholz M, Teslik-Welz W, Yudichak D (2012) Design for variation. Qual Eng 24(2):317–345. https://doi.org/10.1080/08982112.2012.651973

Reis MS, Kenett RS (2018) Assessing the value of information of data-centric activities in the chemical processing industry 4.0. AIChE J 64(11):3868–3881. https://doi.org/10.1002/aic.16203

Romano D, Vicario G (2002) Reliable estimation in computer experiments on finite-element codes. Qual Eng 14(2):195–204. https://doi.org/10.1081/QEN-100108676

Sabbaghi A, Huang Q, Dasgupta T (2018) Bayesian model building from small samples of disparate data for capturing in-plane deviation in additive manufacturing. Technometrics 60(4):532–544. https://doi.org/10.1080/00401706.2017.1391715

Sacks J, Welch WJ, Mitchell TJ, Wynn HP (1989) Design and analysis of computer experiments. Stat Sci 4(4):409–423. https://doi.org/10.1214/ss/1177012413

Salvatier J, Wiecki TV, Fonnesbeck C (2016) Probabilistic programming in Python using PyMC3. PeerJ Comput Sci 2:e55. https://doi.org/10.7717/peerj-cs.55

Santner TJ, Williams BJ, Notz WI (2003) The design and analysis of computer experiments. Springer series in statistics. Springer, New York. https://doi.org/10.1007/978-1-4757-3799-8

Schick G, Wolverton R (1978) An analysis of competing software reliability models. IEEE Trans Softw Eng SE-4(2):104–120. https://doi.org/10.1109/TSE.1978.231481

Schluse M, Priggemeyer M, Atorf L, Rossmann J (2018) Experimentable digital twins—streamlining simulation-based systems engineering for industry 4.0. IEEE Trans Ind Inf 14(4):1722–1731. https://doi.org/10.1109/TII.2018.2804917

Schulze A, Störmer T (2012) Lean product development – enabling management factors for waste elimination. Int J Technol Manag 57(1/2/3):71–91. https://doi.org/10.1504/IJTM.2012.043952

Shafto M, Conroy M, Doyle R, Glaessgen E, Kemp C, LaMoigne J, Wang L (2010) DRAFT modeling, simulation, information technology & processing roadmap – technology area 11. Technical report. National Aeronautics and Space Administration

Shanthikumar JG (1981) A general software reliability model for performance prediction. Microelectron Reliab 21(5):671–682. https://doi.org/10.1016/0026-2714(81)90059-7

Shewhart WA (1926) Quality control charts. Bell Syst Tech J 5(4):593–603. https://doi.org/10.1002/j.1538-7305.1926.tb00125.x

Siemens (2022) Transforming manufacturing—the future happens now. https://new.siemens.com/us/en/company/topic-areas/transforming-manufacturing.html

Singh S, Shehab E, Higgins N, Fowler K, Tomiyama T, Fowler C (2018) Challenges of digital twin in high value manufacturing: SAE 2018 4th aerospace systems and technology conference, ASTC 2018. SAE technical papers 2018 November. https://doi.org/10.4271/2018-01-1928

SUPAC (1997) SUPAC-SS: nonsterile semisolid dosage forms; Scale-up and post-approval changes: chemistry, manufacturing and controls; In vitro release testing and in vivo bioequivalence documentation. Guidance for industry, Center for Drug Evaluation and Research (CDER)

Taguchi G (1987) Systems of experimental design, vols 1–2. UNIPUB/Kraus International Publications, New York

Taguchi G, Konishi S (1987) Taguchi methods orthogonal arrays and linear graphs: tools for quality engineering. Amer Supplier Inst, Dearborn

Tang B, Deng LY (1999) Minimum G2-aberration for nonregular fractional factorial designs. Ann Stat 27(6):1914–1926

Terkaj W, Tolio T, Urgo M (2015) A virtual factory approach for in situ simulation to support production and maintenance planning. CIRP Ann Manuf Technol 64:451–454. https://doi.org/10.1016/j.cirp.2015.04.121

Tham MT, Morris AJ, Montague GA (1989) Soft-sensing: a solution to the problem of measurement delays. Chem Eng Res Des 67:547–554

Thoben KD, Wiesner S, Wuest T (2017) "Industrie 4.0" and smart manufacturing – a review of research issues and application examples. Int J Automat Technol 11(1):4–16. https://doi.org/10.20965/ijat.2017.p0004

Tolio T, Sacco M, Terkaj W, Urgo M (2013) Virtual factory: an integrated framework for manufacturing systems design and analysis. Procedia CIRP 7:25–30. https://doi.org/10.1016/j.procir.2013.05.005

Tsokos CP, Shimi IN (eds) (1977) The theory and applications of reliability with emphasis on Bayesian and nonparametric methods. Academic Press, New York

Tsong Y, Hammerstrom T, Sathe P, Shah VP (1996) Statistical assessment of mean differences between two dissolution data sets. Drug Inform J 30(4):1105–1112. https://doi.org/10.1177/009286159603000427

Volvo Group Global (2017) Virtual twin plant shorten lead times. https://www.volvogroup.com/en/news-and-media/news/2017/mar/virtual-twin-plant-shorten-lead-times.html von Stosch M, Oliveira R, Peres J, Feyo de Azevedo S (2014) Hybrid semi-parametric modeling in process systems engineering: past, present and future. Comput Chem Eng 60:86–101. https://doi.org/10.1016/j.compchemeng.2013.08.008

Wang RY, Storey VC, Firth CP (1995) A framework for analysis of data quality research. IEEE Trans Knowl Data Eng 7(4):623–640. https://doi.org/10.1109/69.404034

Wang J, Ma Y, Zhang L, Gao RX, Wu D (2018a) Deep learning for smart manufacturing: methods and applications. J Manuf Syst 48:144–156. https://doi.org/10.1016/j.jmsy.2018.01.003

Wang J, Yang J, Zhang J, Wang X, Zhang WC (2018b) Big data driven cycle time parallel prediction for production planning in wafer manufacturing. Enterp Inf Syst 12(6):714–732. https://doi.org/10.1080/17517575.2018.1450998

Wang J, Xu C, Zhang J, Bao J, Zhong R (2020) A collaborative architecture of the industrial internet platform for manufacturing systems. Robot Comput Integ Manuf 61:101854. https://doi.org/10.1016/j.rcim.2019.101854

Weindling JI (1967) Statistical properties of a general class of control charts treated as a Markov process. PhD thesis. Columbia University, New York

Weindling JI, Littauer SB, Oliveira JTD (1970) Mean action time of the $\bar{X}$ control chart with warning limits. J Qual Technol 2(2):79–85. https://doi.org/10.1080/00224065.1970.11980418

Weiss BA, Vogl G, Helu M, Qiao G, Pellegrino J, Justiniano M, Raghunathan A (2015) Measurement science for prognostics and health management for smart manufacturing systems: key findings from a roadmapping workshop. In: Proceedings of the annual conference of the prognostics and health management society prognostics and health management society conference 6:046

Whittaker JA, Rekab K, Thomason MG (2000) A Markov chain model for predicting the reliability of multi-build software. Inform Softw Technol 42(12):889–894. https://doi.org/10.1016/S0950-5849(00)00122-1

Wong RKW, Storlie CB, Lee TCM (2017) A frequentist approach to computer model calibration. J R Stat Soc Ser B (Stat Methodol) 79(2):635–648

Wu CFJ, Hamada MS (2011) Experiments: planning, analysis, and optimization. John Wiley & Sons, Hoboken

Wynn HP (1972) Results in the theory and construction of D-optimum experimental designs. J R Stat Soc Ser B (Methodol) 34(2):133–147

Xie M (1991) Software reliability modelling. World Scientific, Singapore

Xie M, Zhao M (1993) On some reliability growth models with simple graphical interpretations. Microelectron Reliab 33(2):149–167. https://doi.org/10.1016/0026-2714(93)90477-G

Yamada S, Ohba M, Osaki S (1984) S-shaped software reliability growth models and their applications. IEEE Trans Reliab R-33(4):289–292. https://doi.org/10.1109/TR.1984.5221826

Yang H, Ni J (2005) Dynamic neural network modeling for nonlinear, nonstationary machine tool thermally induced error. Int J Mach Tools Manuf 45(4–5):455-465. https://doi.org/10.1016/j.ijmachtools.2004.09.004

Yang Z, Eddy D, Krishnamurty S, Grosse I, Denno P, Lu Y, Witherell P (2017) Investigating grey-box modeling for predictive analytics in smart manufacturing. In: ASME 2017 international design engineering technical conferences and computers and information in engineering conference. American Society of Mechanical Engineers Digital Collection. https://doi.org/10.1115/DETC2017-67794

Yang H, Kumara S, Bukkapatnam ST, Tsung F (2019) The internet of things for smart manufacturing: a review. IISE Trans 51(11):1190–1216. https://doi.org/10.1080/24725854.2018.1555383

Yashchin E (1985) On a unified approach to the analysis of two-sided cumulative sum control schemes with headstarts. Adv Appl Probab 17(3):562–593. https://doi.org/10.2307/1427120

Yashchin E (1991) Some aspects of the theory of statistical control schemes. IBM J Res Develop 31:199–205. https://doi.org/10.1147/RD.312.0199

Yi G, Herdsman C, Morris J (2019) A MATLAB toolbox for data pre-processing and multivariate statistical process control. Chemom Intell Lab Syst 194:103863. https://doi.org/10.1016/j.chemolab.2019.103863

Zacks S (1973) Sequential design for a fixed width interval estimation of the common mean of two normal distributions. I. The case of one variance known. J Am Stat Assoc 68(342):422–427. https://doi.org/10.2307/2284090

Zacks S (1980) Numerical determination of the distributions of stopping variables associated with sequential procedures for detecting epochs of shift in distributions of discrete random variables numerical determination of the distributions of stopping variables associated with sequential procedures. Commun Stat Simul Comput 9(1):1–18. https://doi.org/10.1080/03610918008812134

Zacks S (1992) Introduction to reliability analysis: probability models and statistical methods. Springer texts in statistics. Springer, New York. https://doi.org/10.1007/978-1-4612-2854-7

Zacks S (1997) Distributions of first exit times for Poisson Processes with lower and upper linear boundaries. In: Johnson NL, Balakrishnan N (eds) Advances in the theory and practice of statistics: a volume in honor of Samuel Kotz, 1st edn. Wiley-Interscience, New York

Zacks S (2009) Stage-wise adaptive designs, 1st edn. Wiley, Hoboken

Zahran A, Anderson-Cook CM, Myers RH (2003) Fraction of design space to assess prediction capability of response surface designs. J Qual Technol 35(4):377–386

Zhang X, Pham H (1998) A software cost model with error removal times and risk costs. Int J Syst Sci 29(4):435–442. https://doi.org/10.1080/00207729808929534

Index

R. S. Kenett et al., *Industrial Statistics*, Statistics for Industry, Technology, and Engineering, https://doi.org/10.1007/978-3-031-28482-3

Q

R

T

U

V

W

X

GPSR Compliance
The European Union's (EU) General Product Safety Regulation (GPSR) is a set of rules that requires consumer products to be safe and our obligations to ensure this.

If you have any concerns about our products, you can contact us on

ProductSafety@springernature.com

In case Publisher is established outside the EU, the EU authorized representative is:

Springer Nature Customer Service Center GmbH
Europaplatz 3
69115 Heidelberg, Germany

www.ingramcontent.com/pod-product-compliance
Ingram Content Group UK Ltd.
Pitfield, Milton Keynes, MK11 3LW, UK
UKHW021256031026
15588UKWH00001B/489
9783031284830